ASPA CLASSICS

Conceived of and sponsored by the American Society for Public Administration (ASPA), the ASPA Classic Series publishes volumes on topics that have been, and continue to be, central to the contemporary development of the field. The ASPA Classics are intended for classroom use, library adoptions, and general reference. Drawing from the *Public Administration Review (PAR)* and other ASPA-related journals, each volume in the series is edited by a scholar who is charged with presenting a thorough and balanced perspective on an enduring issue.

Each volume is devoted to a topic of continuing and crosscutting concern to the administration of virtually all public sector programs. Public servants carry out their responsibilities in a complex, multidimensional environment, and each collection will address a necessary dimension of their performance. ASPA Classics volumes bring together the dialogue on a particular topic over several decades and in a range of journals.

The volume editors are to be commended for volunteering to take on such substantial projects and for bringing together unique collections of articles that might not otherwise be readily available to scholars and students.

ASPA CLASSICS

Public Budgeting
Policy, Process, and Politics

An ASPA Classics Volume

Edited by
Irene S. Rubin

M.E.Sharpe
Armonk, New York
London, England

Library of Congress Cataloging-in-Publication Data

Public budgeting : policy, process, and politics / edited by Irene S. Rubin.
    p. cm. — (ASPA classics)
  Includes bibliographical references and index.
  ISBN 978-0-7656-1690-6 (cloth : alk. paper) — ISBN 978-07656-1691-3 (pbk. : alk. paper)
  1. Finance, Public. 2. Budget. I. Rubin, Irene.

HJ141.P785 2008
352.4'8—dc22   2007036474

Printed in the United States of America

The paper used in this publication meets the minimum requirements of
American National Standard for Information Sciences
Permanence of Paper for Printed Library Materials,
ANSI Z 39.48-1984.

                                   ∞

BM (c)   10   9   8   7   6   5   4   3   2   1
BM (p)   10   9   8   7   6   5   4   3   2   1

CONTENTS

INTRODUCTION

This book is not a selection of budget classics, those often reprinted essays that frame the way budget scholars look at their field. Nor is it an attempt to chronicle the intellectual history of public budgeting. Rather, it is a selection from ASPA-affiliated journals of articles that address the most important theoretical and practical problems underlying public budgeting.

The choice of problems and the selection of essays are framed by several editorial assumptions.

The field of public budgeting is dynamic. Not only does the literature change as theory develops and evidence accumulates, but the phenomenon that we watch and analyze also changes. These essays try to capture that sense of dynamism, of ideas reacting against ideas, of evidence modifying theory, and theory shaping inquiry. In keeping with the assumption that the field is open to a wide range of opinion, many of the parts contain different points of view on the same subject.

Public budgeting is different from private sector and individual budgeting, and worthy of separate inquiry and its own theory. Private sector organizations budget behind closed doors, rebudget as often as they wish, their budgets do not have to last a year or more, and projections can be revised at will. Individuals don't have to deal with elaborate budgeting rules and layers of constraints on how much they can earn, what they can spend money on, or what services they must provide at what level of quality. And individuals do not have to worry about what other people would like to spend money on and negotiate agreements with them before any money can be spent.

Public budgeting is different in a democracy than in an authoritarian state. Public budgeting as it occurs in the United States is embedded in its history and institutions and is understandable only in that context. A society is more or less democratic depending on the transparency and accountability of the budget process, the responsiveness of government to public priorities, and the amount of participation of citizens in the budget process.

Budget process and format make a difference. It matters, for example, whether the president has a line-item veto, what the role of citizen interest groups is in setting the performance standards for programs, and whether budget presentations adhere to a standard set of definitions. It matters whether citizens have the option of initiating rules concerning budgeting and taxation, to overrule public administrators if government gets too far out of line. And it matters whether legislators receive budget proposals in time to read and think about them before voting on them. Procedures for putting together the budget influence not only the level of participation of various actors, but also make some outcomes easier to achieve, and foster more or less transparency in budget presentations.

Budgeting is guided in practice not only by laws and rules, but also by norms. Norms are principles or guidelines that are widely shared. Those norms can be difficult to see because they are taken for granted, but may become visible when they are violated. One of the most important norms of budgeting in general is *balance.* One of the main norms of governmental budgeting in particular is *fiscal conservatism,* being more careful with the public's money than one would be with one's own. There are specific norms that inform budgeting in a democracy, the collective purpose of which is to maintain public trust. These norms include spending earmarked revenue for its agreed upon purposes, following the budget that is derived in public and not changing it substantively later when the public is not present, and making financial transactions transparent. The latter involves leaving a paper trail so others can follow financial transactions and using a consistent set of definitions so that comparisons over time make sense.

SCOPE OF THE BOOK

This book includes journal articles published by ASPA or its parts primarily over the last 25 years. Most of the major themes that appear in the literature appear in ASPA-affiliated journals sooner or later. Restricting the book to articles from ASPA-affiliated journals is thus not a major problem. Restricting the book to the last 25 years requires more explanation. There are several reasons for that limited time focus. So much has happened in public budgeting over the last 25 years, that the literature has bloomed, and very little of it has yet been sifted or organized. Major intellectual developments, shifting budget contexts, and changes in budgeting processes have not yet been collated.

Over the last 25 years, the field has experienced a shift from incrementalism (which argues that nothing much changes in budgeting from year to year, that policy decisions are removed from the budget process, and that agency requests drive the budget process) toward more complex views of decision making that integrate top down and bottom up decisions and that include economic and policy analysis. At the same time, federal and state budgets have shifted away from annually funded bureaus toward entitlement programs that span many years and provide monetary benefits to those who meet program requirements. Also over this period, we have witnessed the growth and gradual curtailment of huge deficits and their current reemergence at the national level, major shifts in intergovernmental relations, changes in budget formats, and the growth and development of legislative budget staff and a more equal relationship between the executive and legislative branches. The journal *Public Budgeting and Finance* began in 1981, covering these major issues.

Another reason for concentrating on the last 25 years is that recent articles often recapitulate prior history and debate, giving the context over time, where earlier pieces cannot foresee the issues that occurred later. These recent pieces often provide references to the earlier literature, so that readers who want to follow a long-term thread can do so using this book as a starting place.

ORGANIZATION OF THE BOOK

This book begins with descriptions of what public budgeting is, where it came from, what it is for, moves on to the relationship between budget process and outcomes, and from there to the constraints on budgeting, the legal context in which it operates, and adaptations to those constraints, such as contracting out. It concludes with the ethics and norms that underlie budgeting in a democracy. Several selections point out that these norms are not always observed, implicitly raising the question of why they are sometimes ignored. The book thus ends on a question, rather than an answer, which suits the topic of ethics and the open-ended invitation to research and debate that this book represents.

The parts are meant to be cumulative, in that each part frames and explains the parts that come later. Part 2 on budgeting in a democracy helps to introduce the part on the roles of budget actors, explaining how citizens exercise direct democracy to limit taxation and how courts intervene in budgets to maintain citizen rights. Part 3 on roles in turn helps explain the part on constraints on budgeting. Those constraints can be so extensive and so rigid that they make budget allocation and service delivery more difficult, tempting public officials to evade the norms of balance, transparency, and accountability in order to meet programmatic and political demands. Thus, Part 5 on constraints provides a backdrop for the part on rules and ethics.

To illustrate one set of connections between the parts, the Orange County financial crisis described in Part 7 was a direct consequence of the Proposition 13 tax limitation in California described in Part 4. Tax limitations are an example of direct democracy, introduced in Part 2 and further described in Part 3. Because county officials in Orange County, California, wrestling with the impacts of Proposition 13, wanted a source of revenue other than taxation, they asked no questions about excessive interest returns on investments. The norm of fiscal conservativism was thus violated. The risky investments collapsed, resulting in the loss of millions of dollars. The reader thus travels from democratic structures and processes (citizen initiatives) to excessive budget constraints (Proposition 13), to efforts to get around those constraints resulting in violation of budgeting norms and ethics (the Orange County budgetary meltdown).

Similarly, readers can begin with a description of the roles of different budget actors, move on to the theory of incrementalism, which assumes that departments and agencies drive the budget from the bottom up, and then to critiques of incrementalism. Later parts discuss entitlements, which push up spending and successive budget processes intended to foster balance, which left little room for departmental or agency requests to drive the budget at the national level. In the final part, the norms of balance are discussed, so the reader can understand the intense pressure to rebalance the budget, and why and how the departments' role in budgeting was curtailed. Thoughtful readers will find many other connections between the selections and between the parts.

Public Budgeting

PART 1

WHAT IS A PUBLIC BUDGET? ORIGINS AND PURPOSES

The first essay describes what public budgeting is and how it differs from individual and family budgeting; the second describes the origins of public budgeting in the United States. The next two pieces deal with what budgeting is designed to do, and how it accomplishes those goals. Together, the pieces in this part introduce several themes that are echoed throughout the book. The first is that government budgeting is necessarily and appropriately different from private sector budgeting; the second is that waves of budget reform are aimed at adapting public budgeting to the problems of the day, such as departmental overspending, mobilizing resources to solve societal problems such as health care, or cutting back spending to reduce taxes and the scope of government. Budgeting changes because the problems budgets confront change.

Most people approach public budgeting from the nearest thing that they know, either business budgeting or family budgeting. Joseph White's essay contends that both comparisons are flawed. White argues that economic theories based on modeling individuals' behavior miss their mark because they pay inadequate attention to the actual structure of budgeting, which provides any number of constraints. Far from being the expansionary enterprise envisioned by those describing "the budget maximizing bureaucrat," in the United States, budgeting is a process marked by competition among committees and branches of government and limited by revenue ceilings and spending caps. Budgeting implies both the articulation of demands and needs and prioritizing those demands and needs to keep totals in some kind of discipline.

The second selection, "Who Invented Public Budgeting in the United States?," tracks the origin of modern governmental budgeting to the early 1900s. This essay argues that business did not develop budgeting but rather that government, borrowing from the social services, came up with a model that was later imposed on businesses. This history was obscured by reformers who were funded by the business community and sought its approval by touting the excellence of business. The essay reinforces the idea that business and government are different, and that the level of accountability required from government is much higher. Using the budget and accounting data to achieve public accountability was a major concern of early budget reformers.

The third essay introduces the idea that budgeting and its key functions change over time, depending on which problems are dominant at the moment. Allen Schick argues that budgets differentially emphasize spending controls, management improvements, or planning, while still performing all three functions. He describes a succession of reforms, from line-item budgets geared to spending controls, to program budgeting that facilitates productivity and management improvement, to complex integrated planning and management documents advocated by PPBS, planning program budgeting systems. Each reform addressed the dominant problems of the era.

3

CHAPTER 1

MAKING "COMMON SENSE" OF FEDERAL BUDGETING

JOSEPH WHITE

Budgeting is a ubiquitous, frequently controversial, and almost always dissatisfying aspect of government. Because it influences so many decisions and provokes so much debate, budgeting attracts study from a wide variety of perspectives, ranging from welfare economics to public choice, public administration, political science, and political anthropology.

Federal budgeting has been especially controversial over the past two decades of partisan war over the unbalanced budget. These battles have provoked a great deal of explanation (Drew, 1996; Gilmour, 1990; Haas, 1990; Hager and Pianin, 1997; Makin and Ornstein, 1994; Maraniss and Weisskopf, 1996; Penner and Abramson, 1988; Schick, 1990; Steuerle, 1991; White and Wildavsky, 1991; Woodward 1994). As a participant in the explanatory effort, I have been struck by the extent to which public debate and attitudes seem to proceed not from the insights of academic fields but from a different set of perspectives.

The distinction is most evident in attitudes towards budget balance. Although there are macroeconomic arguments for balancing the federal budget, the discipline of economics provides no basis for saying that the different between balance and, say, a deficit of one half of one percent of the gross domestic product is very significant. Yet "balance" per se has great political meaning. James D. Savage (1988) has described the roots of the balanced budget ideal in American politics. His argument about the political values and interests the ideal has served can explain who chooses to manipulate the appeal, but it cannot fully explain the attraction of the balanced budget ideal for apolitical, inattentive citizens.

Instead, budget balance and other values tend to be based on simple principles, such as, "I have to balance my budget so the government should, too." This is a commonsense understanding: it operates by considering government budgeting as if it were something closer to everyday experience for most people (thus, common and sensible).

Unfortunately, application of what passes for commonsense about federal budgeting almost inevitably leads to disappointment. Governments do not budget the way citizens think individuals or families or business firms do or should.

From *Public Administration Review,* vol. 58, no. 2 (March/April 1998), 101–108. Copyright © 1998 by American Society for Public Administration. Reprinted with permission.

Ironically, only part of the misunderstanding is because government is different; the rest is because the standards applied to government budgeting are not followed in everyday life, either.

This essay will highlight some points about budgeting, especially federal budgeting, that are revealed by making the comparison with financial planning for individuals or households carefully, rather than casually. Both causal explanations and normative conclusions follow from the analysis. My goals are to show that federal budgeting is less alien than it may often seem, to offer a new perspective on some common arguments in academic as well as citizen discourse, and to provide an example that may be used for further discussion of both budgeting and other subjects in public administration.

The first section compares budgeting for an individual (or any unit with only one relevant decision maker) and a representative government.[1] One theme involves how individuals' interests aggregate into collective decisions. The common argument that intense minorities force excessive spending by demanding it at the expense of inattentive majorities is basically wrong. But a less common argument about the natural inconsistency of collective as opposed to individual choice provides a basic explanation of the difficulty of deficit reduction. A second theme involves whether standards based on the experience of individuals either make sense for government or can convince individuals to support government action. I will show why the common argument that people must sacrifice for deficit reduction for "our grandchildren" should not be expected to convince rational individuals to pay. And, what should be obvious but is usually ignored, deficit reduction is almost inevitably unequal, rather than the "equal sacrifice" demanded by political rhetoric.

The second section then emphasizes the human relations aspects of budgeting, comparing budgeting for households (especially families) and for governments. This comparison shows how common critiques of budgeting depend on particular assumptions about the nature of the community, rather than on obvious standards of rationality and fairness. For instance, the virtue of budget balance itself, as a form of responsibility, must be balanced against the virtue of keeping promises within a community.

GOVERNMENT VERSUS INDIVIDUAL BUDGETING

"Other Peoples' Money"

Begin with the commonly made contrast between government and individual decision making. In private life individuals who consider spending also bear the costs. In government, those who campaign for spending of some sort bear very little of the cost. Thus government supposedly spends too much because of demands to spend "other peoples' money." In the words of a former economics professor at Texas A&M:

> the average spending bill we voted on in the last Congress cost about $50 million. The average beneficiary got between $500 and $700. There are 100 million taxpayers, so the average taxpayer paid 50 cents. You don't need a lot of economics to understand that somebody getting $700 is willing to do a lot more than somebody who is paying 50 cents. So every time you vote on every issue, all the people who want the program are looking over your right shoulder and nobody's looking over your left shoulder (Gramm, 1982, 37).

Nothing could be more commonsensical. This critique recurs in other forms with other protagonists. Thus William Niskanen (1971) emphasizes the incentives of "budget-maximizing bureaucrats" who get benefits (agency budgets) without having to worry about costs at all. Rational choice political theorists, such as Ken Shepsle and Barry Weingast (1984), or Emerson Niou and Peter Ordeshook (1985), emphasize the legislative side of the story.

The analogy is correct as far as it goes: the participants identified do have different incentives in competing for government budgets than the incentives individuals have in spending their own money. The analogy does not explain growing federal spending because it ignores the actual decision-making processes and the presence of other constraints.

Thus Senator Gramm is describing authorizations bills, which do not in fact spend the money. Programs compete with each other in appropriations bills that average $40 billion apiece, not $50 million. The appropriations committees are working to fit their bills into totals defined (formally or informally) outside the committees. Once the total came from the president's budget, after 1974 it came from the Congressional Budget Resolution, and since 1990 it has come from multi-year caps, or annual totals, negotiated in various budget summit agreements. But the process since the 1920s has been organized to keep spending within some total (White, 1995).

More powerful legislators may gain electoral advantage from using their power to direct disproportionate shares of federal projects back home. But such power shapes shares, not totals. The programs being described by Senator Gramm, by Shepsle and Weingast, and by other analysts as subject to the intense interest/small costs phenomenon would be distributive, discretionary spending programs. As Charles L. Schultze (1984), John Ellwood (1984), and many others have shown, such programs have long been a shrinking share of the economy, dwarfed as sources of budget growth by the major entitlement programs, such as Social Security and Medicare, which have strong support from majorities of voters.

Niskanen's description of bureaucratic influence exaggerates or misstates both bureaucrats' interests and their power. His hypothesis was carefully assessed in a volume edited by Andre Blais and Stephane Dion (1991), which shows that many of Niskanen's underlying assumptions are highly questionable. Niskanen never specified which officials should be the agents of the theory. A theory that relies on bureaucrats' information advantages should emphasize top civil servants. Yet many of them do not display the hypothesized values, in part because their economic interest in larger budgets is ambiguous in a civil service system that does not automatically turn larger budgets into higher salaries. Public-sector unionism may provide a force for higher spending, but that has little to do with higher civil servants and "bureaucratic" power per se, and should be important only where the members are a big enough interest group to have serious power (e.g. teachers and police in cities, not the employees of the Food and Drug Administration in federal budgeting). The direct power of bureaucrats of other sorts relative to other contestants in the battle to shape federal budget totals does not seem great. All other things being equal, people in agencies surely want higher budgets and ask for them. But all sorts of people in politics want things they don't get. Niskanen's errors in stating his protagonists' interests and power leave only a cliché behind.

In common applications, the "other peoples' money" argument seeks explanation from analogy alone without sufficient attention to how government itself works. Many other factors, such as alternative sources of constraint, counter the logic that Senator Gramm and so many others emphasize.

That the most common comparison between individual and government decision making does not explain spending totals or imbalance, however, only shows that the comparison is poorly made, not that it could not be useful. Consider an alternative version.

Aggregating Individual Preferences into Collective Preference

Both the public as revealed by polls and elites as revealed by the tone and content of news reports have long supported a balanced budget—in principle. Majority coalitions endorsing any particular method to balance the budget have been much rarer. After 17 years of budget balance wars, Congress and the president enacted legislation in 1997 that promises a balanced federal budget by 2002, 33 years since the last one in 1969. That was possible mainly because good economic news allowed a much smaller package of deficit reductions than had been achieved in previous efforts (especially efforts in 1990 and 1993).

Plain old ignorance is one reason that support for budget balance is not accompanied by support for the practical means to achieve it. Many voters believe the federal government spends much more of its budget on unpopular programs like welfare and foreign aid than it does. Individuals should know more (on average) about their own budgets. But what about the elites that supposedly know better? Are they simply constrained by the public's ignorance?

As Kenneth Arrow (1951) argued long ago, consistent personal preferences can aggregate into inconsistent social preferences. In the budgeting case, if each citizen can think of the spending that he or she would cut to balance the budget, and the distribution of preferences about cuts is wide enough, it is possible for individuals to know they would balance the budget, and for the large majorities to oppose any particular measure.

Imagine that ten people contribute $9,000 each to a community with $100,000 in expenses, leaving a deficit of $10,000. The expenses are divided into ten activities, costing $10,000 each. Each person supports nine of the activities, and each opposes a different one. Each contributor has a consistent position about how to balance the budget (cut the program he or she dislikes) but 90 percent of the group would oppose cutting any specific program. Nobody would see a need to raise taxes, since each individual's spending preferences would fit available revenue. Everybody would oppose an across-the-board cut of $1,000 from each program because each would see such a cut as eliminating $9,000 in the wrong places in order to cut $1,000 in the right place. Everybody in the community wants a balanced budget, and knows it is possible, but it would not occur.

The numbers are different in federal budgeting, but the basic principle is the same. Informed liberal Democrats could sincerely endorse a balanced budget if it were achieved with defense cuts and higher taxes. Conservative Republicans would cut lots of programs for liberal constituencies. Rural legislators would cut urban programs, and vice versa. Investment bankers and the editors of the *Washington Post* would slash entitlements for the (affluent?) elderly. As a result, over the nearly two decades of effort to balance the budget almost everyone could view the failure to do so as unnecessary, while large majorities opposed any particular plan. That helps to explain not only the difficulty of balancing the budget, but one of the most peculiar aspects of the budget debate—the fact that compromise on achieving this goal, unlike many others, has been widely viewed as illegitimate. Since everybody knew it "could" be done, failure to do so seemed unnecessary.

Setting an overall budget constraint impedes aggressive minorities from exploiting majorities. It does not provide a way to assemble majorities to cut existing programs. So the "commonsense" understanding of the difference between individual and collective decision making is less instructive than the version based on Arrow's (1951) insights.

Budget Balance and Saving for Individuals and Governments

The practical difficulty of budget balance is only one issue; its desirability is another. The error in the commonsense statement "I have to balance my budget so the government should balance its own" is clear enough. In everyday life the poor may have to balance their budgets because they cannot get credit, but the rest of us often borrow. When our debt service burden becomes a smaller share of our income, we often go out and borrow more, such as to buy a larger house or nicer car.

That said, we should take a closer look at the analogy. Given that borrowing is common, why do individuals claim they have to balance their budgets?

One answer might be that individuals (or firms) can borrow as long as it increases their assets. Thus borrowing for a house is different from some government spending. That interpretation is used to justify capital budgeting for governments. It should not be as convincing as capital budgeting advocates would like, because the government receives a much smaller share of the economic benefits of its investment than any private investor would (the government receives only its tax share of the economy). But it surely doesn't support the balanced budget norm.

Business firms basically attend to their debt burden, rather than saying debt per se is bad. Given stable interest rates, individuals and firms can run a deficit—that is, increase their debt—in a year by the same proportion as their income rises, without having to pay a larger share of income as interest. So why would individuals have to balance? One answer might be, that they have to balance over a lifetime, even if they do not balance in a given year. People, unlike business firms, expect to die. If you are going to die, you cannot pay interest forever.

A cynic would say that if you are going to die you have no need to worry about the people who will not get paid afterwards. A better reason for balance is that individuals expect to retire. Retirement matters because most people expect that their income will fall dramatically when they retire. Debt service would suddenly become a much larger part of income, and possibly insupportable. They need to reduce or eliminate their debt before retiring.

The federal government, however, will neither retire nor die.[2] Given current debt levels, the federal government could run deficits of just below two percent of gross domestic product forever, other things not much worse than equal, without increasing the cost of servicing the debt as a share of the economy. As an organization, its financial health would be stable or improving.

There is a weak analogy between certain activities of the federal government and personal retirement, and campaigners for a balanced budget strive mightily to alert the public to this condition. In the future, a growing proportion of Americans will be retired so the costs of spending for pensions and health care will be more of a burden. As a long-term concern, that is in no way comparable to the entire country retiring and living off investments.[3] Still, it provides a good reason to be cautious about debt burdens.

Political rhetoric goes too far, however, when caution about future debt is transmuted into a conventional wisdom that the federal government must balance its budget so the nation can save for America's future. Many eminent economists maintain that the best way to pay for future social insurance costs is to produce a larger economy through greater national savings, which the government can create by manipulating government savings. This argument is turned into shorthand demands for "saving for America's future" or that America "grow up before it grows old" (Reischauer, 1997; Rauch, 1997; Seidman, 1990; Peterson, 1996). The logic, then, is that the government can budget and save for the future like an individual can. We must balance the budget or run a surplus "for our grandchildren." This ubiquitous analogy fails as both economics and politics. Increasing government savings has virtues, but not to the extent the analogy suggests.

Government cannot save for the nation in the same way that individuals save and invest for themselves for three reasons. First, an increase in government savings (lower deficits) can have the effect of reducing private savings, for some of the victims of benefit cuts or tax increases will reduce their personal savings to maintain some of their threatened consumption (CBO, 1997, 63). Thus an increase in government savings does not produce an equal increase in national savings. No such translation problem applies to personal savings. Second, as an increase in savings brings about an increase in investment, the larger capital stock that results means that there is more depreciation. At some point higher savings only replace the higher level of depreciation, and there is no further increment to productivity (CBO, 1993, 74–75). The same effect occurs when any business firm invests in real capital goods, but it does not occur when individuals invest in market instruments. Third, much of the increase in domestic savings that would result from an increase in government savings would not go to new investment. It would go to displace foreign ownership of investment goods. Such displacement is good because it means that Americans earn profits instead of foreigners earning them, but not as good as new investment because it does not increase productivity and therefore does not add to the gross domestic product (GDP) (CBO, 1993, 75).

For such reasons, the Congressional Budget Office in 1993 projected that "private investment might increase by about 30 percent of the decline in government borrowing" from a deficit reduction package (CBO, 1993, 76). Government "saving" does not equal national investment in the same way that individual saving equals individual investment.

Many economists who campaign for reducing the deficit or creating a surplus recognize some or all of these factors yet they cite a common rule of thumb: an increase in national savings of 1 percent of GDP will over a few decades yield a permanent increase in the size of the economy of the same size. Therefore, these economists even propose a budget surplus to raise savings (Aaron and Bosworth, 1997; Schultze, 1997). Yet the question of costs and benefits might give budget balancers pause. The prospect of the economy being 1 percent larger in 20 years might not justify abolishing the Navy, or federal Medicaid support, or some similarly large amount of federal activity. If deficit reduction is an investment, the return may legitimately be criticized as too low. The analogy should be followed all the way through.

Moreover, why would people agree to sacrifice their own consumption to reduce the deficit in order to help their grandchildren instead of just saving more for them personally? A woman can save more herself and put it in an account for her grandchildren, or she can let the government reduce her consumption by taxing or cutting spending and hope her grandchildren are the ones who actually benefit. Under what theory would one expect voters to let the government take their money and hope instead of increasing their own investments and being (relatively) sure?

No theory of individual self-interest would suggest such an outcome. The "savings" argument therefore implies that one should care more about the collective than about oneself and one's family. That is rarely made explicit, because it would be unlikely to work—especially since, even then, the virtue of deficit reduction would depend on what public goods are sacrificed.

If the logic of aggregating preferences suggests that appeals to interest in higher savings should fail, however, then how does deficit reduction occur at all? It occurs because of the most basic difference between deciding for collectives and deciding for individuals. An individual cannot exploit himself, but one part of the nation can exploit another. Majorities may take from minorities. If a majority takes "savings" mostly from a minority, then both the limited return and its uncertainty will matter less to the winners, for they have not given up as much consumption to begin with.

Unequal Sacrifice in Deficit Reduction

Any distributional analysis of deficit reduction packages will be controversial. Spending is compared to baselines whose underlying implications may themselves be disputed. For example, if spending on Medicare is lower than projected, is that a "cut" or not? The incidence of spending in many programs is difficult to define. For example, is spending on urban mass transit assistance targeted more to low-wage workers who use the system or to higher-wage unionized bus drivers? In many cases spending cuts are designed to obscure incidence. This is especially clear in the case of the most significant budget reduction innovation of the 1990s, long-term caps on discretionary appropriations.

Nevertheless, I doubt any analyst would maintain that any of the deficit-reduction packages since 1981 have met a standard of "sharing the pain" remotely equally. In the 1981 Omnibus Budget Reconciliation Act, about half of the total savings came from programs for the poor or working poor, the unemployed, and cities. Many other voters, of course, received major benefits from tax cuts or increases in defense spending.[4] In the 1982 Tax Equity and Fiscal Responsibility Act, about half of the deficit reduction came from business taxes, medical providers, dairy farmers, and civil service retirees. Cuts to business seemed justified even to many Republicans since they only repealed part of the massive benefits enacted the year before (White and Wildavsky, 1991, 249–58; *Congressional Quarterly,* 1985, 30; *National Journal,* 1982). The tax provisions of the Deficit Reduction Act of 1984 were a remarkably and intentionally obscure set of revenue raisers. Its priorities resembled those of the 1982 act, though on a substantially smaller scale (*Congressional Quarterly Almanac,* 1985).

The original package negotiated by Richard Darman (director of the Office of Management and Budget) with the Democratic congressional leadership in 1990 was an exception that proved the rule, being fairly balanced and therefore defeated by majorities of both parties on the House floor (White and Wildavsky, 1991). In the version that was passed, the major targets were the military, higher-income groups, and medical providers—hardly equal sacrifice. Thus, the revenue provisions lowered taxes for the lowest quintile while raising them most for the highest income groups.[5] If we allocate the unspecified savings in discretionary programs for fiscal years 1994 and 1995 evenly between defense and domestic spending, defense accounts for more than 70 percent of the five-year total.[6] With the Congress and the presidency then (barely) controlled by one party, the 1993 Omnibus Reconciliation Act favored Democratic priorities at least as clearly. Although savings in discretionary spending were expected to be much less targeted on the military, the Medicare savings were even more tilted towards providers, taxes were a larger part of the package, and approximately two-thirds of the revenue increases targeted wealthier Americans.[7]

The Republicans in 1995 tested the rule again and proved it again. Although they clearly favored Republican over Democratic priorities, the specific increases in the Part B premium and the potential impact of the bill's large Medicare and Medicaid cuts in programs for the elderly and disabled made it easy for President Clinton to rally majority public support for his veto.

The budget deficit reduction agreement of 1997 returns to the logic of targeting a minority. The Medicare cuts mainly target providers (at least in the five-year horizon that the agreement emphasizes). The discretionary spending cuts are obscure, and the president has claimed that the most popular priorities will be protected. Many voters can even expect tax cuts.

If the goal is deficit reduction, *inequality of sacrifice is not the problem but the solution.* Whether that is the same as "inequity" is a matter of values: if the people paying "deserve" to pay, then one may say the result is fair. But inequality is what we should expect from the difference between individual and collective decision making: *what for an individual is setting priorities, in a government becomes winners taking from losers.*

In the absence of a massive collective spirit, or perhaps very well-developed processes of corporatist consensus-building, the ability of a representative government to reduce a deficit depends on the extent to which majorities are willing and able to take from minorities. That is difficult but possible within the political system that James Madison and other founders designed to inhibit what Madison called the tyranny of the majority. Yet one aspect of the Madisonian design makes deficit reduction more likely than it otherwise would be—frequent elections. Frequent elections mean that the governing coalition can change often. Then a new majority may exploit a different minority. If different groups pay at different times, the total budget cuts and tax increases may be larger and more equal than in any single package. It is much easier to imagine the provisions of the 1993 and 1997 packages passing separately than as a single bill. Government may impose more pain if the governing coalition changes frequently.

GOVERNMENT AS A HOUSEHOLD, NOT AN INDIVIDUAL

We have considered whether the logic of savings and debt that applies to individuals applies to governments as well. The collective nature of government has another dimension: relationships among citizens. Relationships among citizens are a crucial aspect of government budgeting, because the budget is the set of terms by which people live together in the policy. It states who contributes what, and who receives what.

Commitments and Promises in Government Budgeting

Individuals budget so as to avoid discovering later that they cannot consume something that they want a lot, because earlier they consumed something that (in retrospect) they do not want as much. Individuals, however, can also change their consumption preferences when faced with unexpected constraint. I might plan to buy a new car, discover I have less money than I thought, and decide I don't really want it enough to borrow.

Imagine instead, that a high school student's parents promise to buy her a car, if she gets all As in her junior year. She gets all As, but her mother does not get an anticipated raise. The facts that they promised their daughter a benefit, she met the standard, and refusing would send a bad message about how much she can rely on the family all provide strong arguments for borrowing rather than breaking the promise.

Governments also make commitments, and the moral force of those commitments conflicts with the norm of budget balance. Such arguments are especially common in objections to changing the rules for retirement programs on workers who are close to the retirement age, but they can be made in many other contexts. *Government budgets are not plans to enforce personal responsibility but sets of promises that define the terms under which citizens live together—who contributes and who receives what.* Breaking budget promises therefore involves more difficult steps—the losers might be able to fight—and more questionable choices—to have losers. This concern for relationship among citizens explains the cause for "shared sacrifice," which unfortunately conflicts with the realities of self-interested coalition building.

Power Structures and Power Stakes

In any government other than an absolute dictatorship, numerous participants disagree about policy and contend for power. Within the federal process the most basic purpose of budgeting, as far as Congress is concerned, is to exercise legislative control over the executive establishment. Arguably, that is the most basic purpose according to the Constitution as well: its authors viewed legislative control of the purse as fundamental to representative government (Savage, 1988). The implications of such power stakes for the structure and content of federal budgeting are numerous and deep. Here, however, we are considering only how to understand those power concerns. Are they somehow illegitimate or strange?

No. Similar power stakes exist within any household. Whenever people must act together, there will be questions of fairness applied to both contributions and benefits. Conflict then will involve not only individual cases, but the implications of cases for the relationships among participants. In any group, not just the federal government, questions of status and power are posed by resource allocations.

Rationality about power stakes helps explain why one tactic for balancing the budget does little good. We can call this the "break the problem into sequential pieces" approach. The Gramm-Rudman-Hollings law, for example, was presented as a way to make balancing the budget more manageable by dividing the task into five successive steps, of $36 billion each, instead of a single $180 billion leap (White and Wildavsky, 1991). Economically, such an approach makes sense because a more gradual transition reduces the shock to the economy. Politically, it did not work at all. Any group that did not fight very hard against being targeted for a cut in the first round would have thereby acknowledged its subordination and set itself up for attack in successive rounds, too. No group would trust other groups to take the hit in the next round just because it had already paid. So opposition to deficit cuts in the first year remained daunting. The ubiquity of power and status stakes means that norms and procedures that do not lead to efficiency, such as incrementalism and fair shares, nevertheless may make the collective more effective by reducing conflict.

Representation and the Pork Barrel

To say that behaviors in government budgeting are analogous to how people act in more familiar parts of life should not foreclose efforts at reform. It might, however, moderate expectations.

One last application of our analogies may raise some questions about the definitions of sin and virtue in budgeting. In a family we take for granted that some members contribute more than others. Indeed, they contribute according to their means. We also expect that different members of the family receive different benefits: one child is in art school and the other goes to camp; Johnny takes skating lessons and Jacki takes tennis; Dad goes bowling and Mom to the ball games. Family budgets thus are filled with special interest spending that benefits only minorities. Logically, what each part gets is no other part's business, so long as the recipient is satisfied and the distribution meets some standard of fairness. Why, then, is federal budgeting not considered in the same way?

Why are pork and logrolling so widely considered illegitimate? If a group of minorities get together to agree on benefits, why is that considered to be at the expense of the whole? How is it different from different members of the family having different activities?

On the right of the political spectrum, the answer may be that many Americans see government as an alien force and view helping others as a personal choice, not a collective one. To them, government does not represent a community of affection and obligation remotely similar to a family. They might accept government action for classic collective goods such as national security, but the narrower the benefits, the more corrupt and illegitimate government action will seem. Then objection to deficits and pork is as much an argument about the nature of the community (or lack thereof) as a position on fiscal policy.

Many on the left may see the government as the decision-making process for a community in which citizens should care about and take care of each other. But they can believe some parts of the community are getting too much. Liberals think the military big brother is the favorite child. Tom Foley, who was majority whip when Gramm-Rudman was passed, said at the time that it was "about taking the only child of the president's official family that he really loves, holding it in a dark basement, and sending him its ear!"

The family is probably too strong a standard of community for most polities. After all, in families we might expect the strong (parents) to sacrifice for the weak (kids) in a way that only the most left-wing citizens would support.[8] One may also argue that the decision-making process in government is more open to capture by the self-interested "children," because government does not have a strong (paternal? maternal?) central authority to guarantee pursuit of the overall good. Yet such arguments still direct attention to beliefs about the nature of the community. The interests of a community and its parts are not inherently opposed; serving different individual concerns may be one of the purposes of a group. So criticism of special interest spending may hide a judgment about the community and how it should be organized.

CONCLUSION

This essay has used analogies to individuals and households to illuminate how federal budgeting works. The results range from analysis of why tactics such as the savings and do-it-in pieces arguments fail, to highlighting the assumptions about community behind rhetoric about the pork-barrel. I have emphasized especially the differences between individual and collective decision making.

I do not mean to suggest that comparing government activities to those of individuals or households is the best form of analysis. I do suggest that people do it all the time, consciously or not, and that students of public administration might find ideas for their analysis and language for their explanations by improving on everyday discourse and by considering analogies between their work and everyday discourse more carefully. Politics and public administration tend to be disrespected because the public (and "experts") do not understand why politics deviates from ideals, especially when those ideals are not based on the realities of governance in the first place. I hope to have shown the value of investigating commonsense about budgeting. Perhaps others can do the same for the other aspects of government.

ACKNOWLEDGMENTS

The author would like to thank Jim Pfiffner, Irene Rubin, and anonymous reviewers for their contributions to improving this manuscript as well as the Brookings Institution and Twentieth Century Fund for support of related work. None of these individuals, institutions, or their officers are responsible for the author's errors.

NOTES

1. In principle, a truly patriarchal family or an absolute dictatorship, would budget more like an individual. In practice I suggest that there is an element of attention to other peoples' preferences and of concern for perceived commitments that sets more constraints on decision makers in even the most patriarchal family or dictatorial state, compared to individual decisions.

2. Or rather, if the government is going to disappear, the federal deficit is probably not what we should be worrying about.

3. For instance, greater costs for programs for the elderly are likely to be accompanied by low costs for the programs (such as education). Demographic effects that raise spending in some areas can lower it in others. Also, the economic burdens and benefits for workers associated with an aging society are much more complex than a pure budgetary perspective suggest; see Cutler et al. 1990.

4. The figure is based on summing fiscal year 1982 cuts in budget authority for unemployment compensation, trade adjustment assistance, food stamps, Supplemental Security Income, Medicaid, housing programs, nutrition assistance, Aid to Families with Dependent Children, low-income energy assistance, elementary education assistance, Comprehensive Employment Training Act programs, and various local services bloc grants, and adding half of the savings from cuts to the Urban Mass Transportation Administration, the Community Development Block Grant program, and the Urban Development Action Grant program, as reported in Ellwood (1982) Table 1.13, and comparing that total to gross budget authority savings. As a share of net savings, which would include the increases to defense and other favored accounts, the figure would be higher.

5. Calculations produced by the majority staff of the House Ways and Means Committee in a memo dated October 26, 1990.

6. Figures are from Hoagland (1990). Hoagland was then director of the minority staff of the Senate

Budget Committee. One could instead refer to U.S. House of Representatives (1990), but the story would be much the same The major difference is in how the earned income tax credit is classified.

7. See *Congressional Quarterly Almanac,* 1993, 133, for a summary table, and 124–139 for details. I am including two tax increases that were not in the summary table, the reduced deduction for club dues and a reduction in the compensation that can be counted for qualified retirement plans.

8. An anonymous reviewer deserves credit for this point.

REFERENCES

Aaron, Henry J., and Barry P. Bosworth (1997). "Preparing for the Baby Boomers' Retirement." In Robert D. Reischauer, ed., *Setting National Priorities: Budget Choices for the Next Century.* Washington, DC: The Brookings Institution, 263–301.

Arrow, Kenneth J. (1951). *Social Choice and Individual Values.* New York: John Wiley.

Blais, Andre, and Stephane Dion, eds. (1991). The *Budget-Maximizing Bureaucrat: Appraisals and Evidence.* Pittsburgh: University of Pittsburgh Press.

Congressional Quarterly Almanac (1983). Vol. XXXVIII, 1982.

———— (1985). Vol. XL, 1984.

———— (1994). Vol. XLX, 1993.

Cutler, David M., James M. Poterba, Louise M. Sheiner, and Lawrence H. Summers, 1990. "An Aging Society: Opportunity or Challenge?" *Brookings Papers on Economic Activity.* 1: 1–73.

Drew. Elizabeth (1996). *Showdown: The Struggle Between the Gingrich Congress and the Clinton White House.* New York: Simon & Schuster.

Ellwood, John W. (1982). "The Size and Distribution of Budget Reductions." In John W. Ellwood, ed., *Reductions in U.S. Domestic Spending.* New Brunswick, NJ: Transaction Books, 33–70.

———— (1984). "Comment." In Gregory B. Mills and John L. Palmer, eds., *Federal Budget Policy in the 1980s.* Washington, DC: The Urban Institute, 368–78.

Gilmour, John B. (1990). *Reconcilable Differences?: Congress the Budget Process, and the Deficit.* Berkeley: University of California Press.

Gramm, Phil (1982). *The Role of Government in a Free Society.* Dallas: The Fischer Institute.

Haas, Lawrence J. (1990). *Running on Empty: Bush Congress, and the Politics of a Bankrupt Government.* New York: Business One Irwin.

Hager, George, and Eric Pianin (1997). *Mirage: Why Neither Democrats Nor Republicans Can Balance the Budget, End the Deficit, and Satisfy the Public.* New York: Times Books.

Hoagland, G. William (1990). "The Omnibus Budget Reconciliation Act of 1990 and U.S. Budget Outlook." Paper presented at the American Enterprise Institute-Japan Economic Foundation Working Group Meeting. Kyoto, Japan, November 19–20.

Makin, John H., and Norman J. Ornstein (1994). *Debt and Taxes: How America Got Into Its Budget Mess and What to Do About It.* Washington, DC: American Enterprise Institute.

Maraniss, David, and Michael Weisskopf (1996). *Tell Newt to Shut Up!* New York: Simon & Schuster.

National Journal (1982). "Congress' Deficit Cuts: Sizable, But So Are the Remaining Deficits." 21 August 1982, 1451, 1477–78.

Niou, Emerson S., Peter C. Ordeshook (1985). "Universalism in Congress." *American Journal of Political Science.* 29 May, 246–58.

Niskanen, William A. (1971). *Bureaucracy and Representative Government.* Chicago: Aldine Atherton.

Penner, Rudolph G., and Alan J. Abramson (1988). *Broken Purse Strings: Congressional Budgeting, 1974–88.* Washington, DC: The Urban Institute.

Peterson, Peter G. (1996). *Will America Grow Up Before It Grows Old? How the Coming Social Security Crisis Threatens You, Your Family, and Your Country.* New York: Random House.

Rauch, Jonathan (1997). "Ducking the Challenge." *National Journal* 8 February, 260–66.

Reischauer, Robert D., ed. (1997). *Setting National Priorities: Budget Choices for the Next Century.* Washington, DC: The Brookings Institution.

Savage, James D. (1988). *Balanced Budgets and American Politics.* Ithaca, NY: Cornell University Press.

Schick, Allen (1990). *The Capacity to Budget.* Washington, DC: The Urban Institute.

Schultze, Charles L. (1984). "Comment." In Gregory B. Mills and John L. Palmer, eds., *Federal Budget Policy in the 1980s.* Washington, DC: The Urban Institute, 379–84.

———— (1997). "Is Faster Growth the Cure for Budget Deficits?" In Robert D. Reischauer, ed., *Setting*

National Priorities: Budget Choices for the Next Century. Washington, DC: The Brookings Institution, 35–74.

Seidman, Laurence S. (1990). *Saving for America's Future: Parables and Policies.* Armonk, NY: M.E. Sharpe, Inc.,

Shepsle, Kenneth A., and Barry R. Weingast (1984). "Legislative Politics and Budget Outcomes." In Gregory B. Mills and John L. Palmer, eds., *Federal Budget Policy in the 1980s.* Washington, DC: The Urban Institute, 343–67.

Steuerle, C. Eugene (1991). *The Tax Decade: How Taxes Came to Dominate the Public Agenda.* Washington, DC: The Urban Institute.

U.S. Congressional Budget Office (1993). *The Economic and Budget Outlook, Fiscal Years 1994–1998.* Washington, DC: Government Printing Office.

———(1997). *The Economic and Budget Outlook: Fiscal Years 1998–2007.* Washington, DC: Government Printing Office.

U.S. House Committee on the Budget. Fiscal Year 1991 Budget Agreement Summary Materials. Report prepared by the majority staff.

White, Joseph (1995). "Appropriations." In Donald C. Bacon, Roger H. Davidson, and Morton Keller, eds. *The Encyclopedia of the U.S. Congress,* Vol 1. New York: Simon & Schuster, 69–73.

White, Joseph, and Aaron Wildavsky (1991). *The Deficit and the Public Interest: The Search for Responsible Budgeting in the 1980s.* Berkeley and New York: University of California Press and The Russell Sage Foundation.

Woodward, Bob (1994). *The Agenda: Inside the Clinton White House.* New York: Simon & Schuster.

CHAPTER 2

WHO INVENTED BUDGETING IN THE UNITED STATES?

IRENE S. RUBIN

It has often been argued that the business community was the origin and model of improved public financial practices in the United States, including budgeting, in the early 20th century. This point of view is not the only one in the literature, but it has been around for a long time. Early budget reformers often attributed their proposals to businessmen. Henry Bruere, one of the directors of the New York Bureau of Municipal Research, attributed some of the bureau's budget innovations to railroad financier E. H. Harriman; Frederick Cleveland, one of the most important founders and promoters of executive budgeting in the United States, claimed the methods of accounting he wanted to introduce to the public sector were already established in the management of private corporations (Cleveland, 1980).

The adoption of the city manager form of government, promoted by businessmen, often involved the advocacy and adoption of business techniques, furthering the impression that business practices were superior to those in the public sector. For example, a description of Dayton, Ohio, before and after the adoption of the city manager system includes the following:

> The finance department revised traditional city purchasing and accounting practices to conform with private business practices. Purchasing was centralized and specs drawn up for all purchases. Prior to 1914, the accounting system was a check on cash receipts and disbursements only, there were no cost records for city repairs and construction work. There was no way to assure that people receiving city pay were actually doing city work. All city workers received their pay in cash, there was no definite city payroll, and property records did not exist. A central account office was created, accounting was made accrual based, with the ability to monitor appropriations, accounts receivable and accounts payable (Sealander, 1988, pp. 119–120).

Such descriptions strongly suggested that improved business practices predated improved public financial practices and constituted a model for government.

Groups of businessmen have frequently pressed government to adopt business efficiency in government (Shuman, 1992, p. 31). The first director of the Bureau of the Budget, Charles G. Dawes, was one of a number of businessmen trying to set up business practices in government in 1921; part of the thrust of that effort was to import business accounting and especially balance sheets to government. Dawes advocated accrual budgeting as a way of making reporting uniform throughout the federal government and between government and business. Business used balance sheets and accruals of assets and liabilities, so government should too. Dawes stated his opinion forcefully:

> Every habit, every custom, personal or administrative, which has arisen out of a decentralized status quo of the present 43 departments and independent establishments of government . . . which militated against the recognition in governmental business of those principles of business organization incident to successful private administration, we have fought from the beginning and succeeded, in my judgment, in largely eliminating (Dawes, 1923, p. 229).

The clear assumption was the superiority of business methods. More recent innovations such as zero-based budgeting were invented for business and then touted for the public sector. Similar origins can be cited for management-by-objectives, which some governments integrated into budget formats or the budget process.

The argument that business financial practices were better earlier and provided a model for government is especially important today, because the superiority of business is again being touted, and used as a reason for contracting out and for reducing the scope of government services. What if it turned out on examination, that the source of government financial improvements was not business, but government officials and university professors?

In fact, government officials and academics did play a larger role in introducing public budgeting and accounting in the United States than did business. Businessmen pressed for reform, but the proposals for change were usually generated by reformers in government, universities, and social service agencies. The role of business techniques as a model has been greatly exaggerated. The history of early public budgeting in the United States suggests that the public should have more confidence in the public sector's capacity for experimentation, evaluation, and reform. This early budget history also suggests that the public should be skeptical and demand evidence for continuing claims about the superiority of business management.

The evidence that government officials and university professors played a major role introducing public budgeting and financial management reform is of three types.

First, the quality of financial management in the private sector in the early 20th century was generally poor. Moreover, many of the much-touted improvements in business accounting were invented by public officials in an effort to facilitate regulation of railroads and utilities. Those improvements were later held up to government officials in an effort to pressure them to adopt the new techniques.

Second, much of the development of the reform agenda in budgeting came from the experience of practitioners, who were experimenting and sharing innovations, and academics who were examining the experience of public organizations around the world and helping to formulate reform proposals. Many of the reformers went back and forth between government and universities.

Third, the development of budget reform proposals by government officials preceded in the main the development of bureaus of municipal research. The research bureaus, whose functions included surveys of existing administrative practices and recommendations for reform, were dominated by business people. The bureaus' professional staff, in efforts to keep themselves funded, generally deferred to business ideologies and preferences. Business was widely respected after the Progressive era, and the research bureaus could not go against the dominant belief in the excellence of business over government without losing their reason for existing as well as their funding sources. It was primarily the staff of these bureaus who wrote the history of efforts to reform budgeting. They carried their particular bias into historical narratives later treated as neutral.[1]

BUSINESS MANAGEMENT WAS POOR

Improvements in accounting generally preceded improvements in budget process. Reformers felt that improved management could not take place unless the quality of financial information fed to reformed administrators improved. Moreover, better financial reporting provided the possibility of greater public accountability. Better accounting was associated with better budgeting, and many of the reformers who worked in accounting made recommendations for budgetary improvements after improvements in accounting were in place.

The quality of business accounting was generally considered poor before the beginning of public budgeting, even in the railroads, which were considered the precursors of modern corporate management. The poor recordkeeping of the railroads was of particular public concern because the railroads were large, borrowed heavily from citizens and governments, and were often subsidized by governments. When they went under, they took a heavy toll on public finance. The railroads were also important to commerce; their ability to set rates threatened large segments of the population, setting in motion early efforts to regulate them. These regulatory efforts confronted poor and highly disparate bookkeeping, making it difficult if not impossible to see what the rates should be, and whether the companies were making profits or losses.

Frederick Cleveland was a long-time student of railroad finances. He argued that railroad accounting was poor and in some cases corrupt. He saw the independent auditor as the necessary protector of the railroad investor, to make corporate information public (Cleveland, 1905). In *Railroad Finances* (co-authored with Fred Powell), published in 1912, he summarized some of the poor practices that characterized railroad management until the early 1900s. He noted, for example, that some unscrupulous railroad managers overstated net profits by underfunding purchases of capital stock and charging some equipment purchases to capital that should have been charged to operating expenses. He reported that this practice was brought to an end in 1906 by the Hepburn act, in which the Interstate Commerce Commission (ICC) promulgated uniform accounting principles for the railroads. The railroads were required to set up formal depreciation accounts for all equipment (pp. 91–92). Cleveland and Powell also noted that the railroads generally did not provide informative reports (p. 213):

> . . . in most railroad financial statements, there has been no attempt to distinguish capital resources from current resources, and there has been no regard for the truth even in the statement of the amounts and sources of capital actually obtained by the corporation. . . . In many instances, shareholders are as uninformed after reading a published balance sheet as if none had been rendered. Dividends have been declared out of capital; corporate estates have been wasted; railroads have been reduced to bankruptcy by their officers without any suggestion either in accounts or reports as to the facts. And while this was being done, shareholder and creditors have been led to believe that the corporation was in a sound financial condition. Corporate estates have been managed for the benefit of trustees; published statements have been used for the manipulation of the stock market and the enhancement of private fortunes through stock deals; in fact, the whole purpose of one transportation enterprise after another

has been subverted to the private interests of those who were in possession and who alone knew the facts. Even directors have been so ignorant of the true state of affairs that the officers have been permitted to act in open defiance of public law and business morality for years without even arousing a suspicion (pp. 120–121).

Railroads were considered to be among the largest, most complex, and most sophisticated of private corporations. Cleveland's description of railroad finances, however, did not make them sound as if they had much to offer government in the way of a model. On the contrary, according to Cleveland, federal regulations helped eliminate some of the worst railroad abuses.

One of the major stimuli for the improvement of accounting and reporting in railroads was the creation of the federal Interstate Commerce Commission (ICC) in 1887. This agency represented the then new Progressive era image of activist government as a potential counterweight to business. The new agency was in the position of regulating the rates of the railroads, but found that it could not judge the profits of the companies, and began to develop better accounting tools in consultation with the railroads. Having designed such improved accounting and imposed it on businesses, government officials were pressured to make similar improvements in their own operations.

One of the leading reformers in accounting at this time was Henry Carter Adams. After a stint as an academic, he served as chief statistician of the ICC from 1887 to 1911 (Rosenberry, 1948). His first report was on railway statistics. He argued with state regulators on the need for uniformity and helped persuade the railroads to go along by asking them for suggestions on forms for collecting standardized information (Rosenberry, 1948, p. 37). In 1906, Adams secured the adoption by Congress of an amendment to the act to regulate commerce that required railway companies to make uniform reports in accordance with regulations set by the commission, with heavy penalties for failure to comply. Once the enabling legislation was in place, Adams found he could not recruit trained staff, so he started his own course in railway administration at the University of Michigan in 1910. The accounting system that Adams set up was later extended to other utilities and other jurisdictions (Rosenberry, 1948, p. 39). The ICC was credited with helping modernize all corporate accounting because of its emphasis on debt and stock as claims on total assets, and its emphasis on income measurement (Dusenbury, 1985, p. 5).

Once the ICC set up accounting systems and imposed them on private sector organizations, the federal government was pressured to adopt analogous measures for itself. Frederick Cleveland, an accountant, a professor, a director of the New York Bureau of Municipal Research, and then Director of Taft's Economy and Efficiency Commission, argued in 1912 that if the government could impose major accounting changes on business, it better impose similar changes on itself. He called for an educational campaign that would make it dangerous for anyone to "stand in the way of the demand for the same kind of a reorganization and reformation of methods in the Government as has been demanded for life insurance, banking, and railroad companies." He further argued,

The Government is spending $1,500,000 each year regulating the business methods of railroads in the interest of the public; it is spending about $200,000 each year in supervision of national banking; it is spending over $200,000 each year regulating interstate corporations, through the Bureau of Corporations, besides carrying on prosecutions at very high cost through the Department of Justice. What the Government does with $1,000,000,000 of revenues raised each year; how it conducts its own business, what is the element of waste and inefficiency in carrying on activities that reach the home and vital interests of every citizen, is of vastly greater importance to the average man than is the manner in which a railroad company keeps its accounts (Goodnow, c. 1912, quoting from Cleveland, p. 15).

W.F. Willoughby, another key budget reformer, was a former government official, first a statistician for the Department of Labor, and later a treasurer and budget reformer in Puerto Rico. He was also a member of Taft's Efficiency and Economy Commission. After the commission was dissolved, he became director of the Institute for Government Research, which was later incorporated into The Brookings Institution. The early mission of that institute was to lobby for the adoption of federal budget reforms. Like Cleveland, Willoughby argued that if the federal government was going to regulate business procedures, it had better put it own house in order.

> It is inconsistent to the last degree that governments should insist that corporations controlled by them should have systems of accounting and reporting corresponding to the most approved principles of modern accountancy while not providing for equally efficient systems for the management of their own financial affairs. The demand for improved methods of public administration has thus inevitably centered primarily upon the demand for improved methods of financial administration and, in order that this may be secured, upon the specific demand for the adoption of a budgetary system as the central feature of such improved system (Willoughby, 1918, pp. 4–5).

Both Cleveland and Willoughby referred to the role that the federal government played in introducing high standards of accounting and reporting to private sector organizations. It was not the details of these private sector accounting systems that these reformers advocated, it was the improvement of financial management. If the government could force improved financial management on business, then it could put its own house in order.

GOVERNMENT EXPERIMENTATION AND MONITORING AS THE SOURCE OF REFORM PROPOSALS

Federal regulation of private industry was one source of inspiration for reform in financial management practices; another source was innovation in cities. These innovations include accounting and budgeting reforms designed by public officials. Major reforms of the accounting system in Chicago from 1901 to 1903 highlight a process in which reform-minded administrators exchanged ideas with each other and gave advice to private sector accountants trying to devise improved financial management systems for public sector organizations.

In 1903, Frederick Cleveland made a report on the Chicago reform to the National Municipal League in his capacity as the league's secretary of the Committee on Uniform Municipal Accounts. A group of businessmen in the Merchants Club requested an accountancy study; the study justified a major overhaul of the accounting system. The businessmen wanted improved public management, but nothing in the overhaul plan suggested that Chicago should use business accounting methods. On the contrary, an accounting system was invented for Chicago, after consultation between the accounting firm of Haskins and Sells and the Committee on Uniform Accounts of the National Municipal League. At it was being applied, the accountants had to deal with ordinances, local traditions, and statutes, matters not relevant to business accounting. The accounting forms Chicago adopted were not identical with those recommended by the National Municipal League but were compatible with them.

Cleveland described in his report where the ideas for the National Municipal League Committee on Uniform Accounts came from. The schedules of the committee were drawn from the accounting experience of members, beginning with small places like Brookline, Massachusetts, extending to other cities, until 1902, when the state of Ohio mandated accounting reforms for all cities in the state. The committee's recommended pattern of accounts came from the experience of cities as public officials invented, shared, modified, and implemented new techniques (Cleveland, 1980, originally published 1903, p. 232).

The National Municipal League, in consultation with LeGrand Powers of the Bureau of the Census, tried to standardize accounting categories for cities; cities that were modernizing their accounting systems tried to conform to these standardized accounts. LeGrand Powers urged accountants to design accounting systems for cities with due consideration for their administrative problems and the legal duties of city officials. He argued that accountants should not impose business accounting on cities (Powers, 1906). When Minneapolis modernized its accounting in 1904, it set up an accounting system specifically adapted to its complex charter, and with council approval, adopted the standard accounting categories set up by Powers in the Census Bureau. The system Minneapolis adopted did not come from business, but, as in Chicago, was invented for it (Wilmot, 1906).

The National Municipal League was a result of maturing reform movements in many cities across the country. When the league drew up and recommended a model city charter, its provisions had been tried out in individual cities across the land (Glaab and Brown, 1983, p. 198). Academics observed and summarized the experiences of different cities and described foreign practices to local officials. W. F. Willoughby noted that the National Municipal League recommended an executive budget as early as 1899.

> This fundamental feature [that electing good men was not enough] was appreciated by municipal reformers prior to the establishment of bureaus of municipal research. Thus the National Municipal League as early as 1899 included in its draft of a model municipal corporation act a section providing that "It shall be the duty of the Mayor from time to time to make such recommendations to the Council as he may deem to be for the welfare of the city and on the—day of—in each year to submit to the Council the annual budget of current expenses of the city, any item in which may be reduced or omitted by the Council; but the Council shall not increase any item in nor the total of said budget" (Willoughby, 1918, pp. 6–7).

By the end of the 1800s, many city councils had been stripped of the power to appropriate money outside of budgets that were submitted by mayors, comptrollers, or other specifically designated agencies. Cities adopted budget reforms first and set a pattern for later adoptions by state and national government.

THE DISTORTIONS OF THE RESEARCH BUREAUS

Budget reforms were initially designed by government officials and academic reformers and spread by them and others. Later, additional reforms were invented by staff members of municipal research bureaus, the first and most famous of which was the New York Bureau of Municipal Research. Regardless of whether the reform was invented by themselves or by government officials, research bureau staff, in an effort to sell the reforms, often claimed they were based on the excellence of business practices.

Luther Gulick, who was both a participant and an observer in the reform process, disputed the claim of business origins of the reforms introduced by research bureaus:

> the kind of budget methods developed by the Bureau were not used in business either. In order to awaken public support, the municipal researchers at times catered to popular semantics that would

help sell ideas; since the business model was popular, the Bureau often cited the "principles of business administration" as its model. In point of fact, the business schools which sprang up in later years often got their ideas from the New York bureau (Dahlberg, 1966, p. 172).

It was not simply a matter that business ideas were popular, however; it was business leaders who funded most research bureaus, and who influenced what the bureaus would work on. In the light of the dependence of bureau staff on business funding and the willingness of business con-tributors to insist that the bureaus conform to their ideas, the tendency of staff members to defer to business excellence regardless of their knowledge of the public origins of budget reforms is understandable.

Henry Bruere, of the New York Bureau of Municipal Research, gave an example from the early days of the bureau that illustrates both the nature of business influence on bureaus in setting agendas, and the way that influence reinforced the idea that business was the source of government innovation in financial management. He described the wealthy backers of the bureau, including E. H. Harriman, the railroad magnate. He mentioned that Harriman was particularly interested in the idea of giving to the government what he had strongly advocated and fostered in the Union Pacific and other railroads, "namely of getting a solid basis in accountancy for management. His ideas were expressed in those days very largely in emphasizing the importance of knowing what it cost per ton mile to handle freight and to have cost accounting in railroad management which was more or less of a novelty. So we took up that idea" (Bruere, 1949, p. 36). The year was 1906, just as Henry Carter Adams succeeded in getting Congress to mandate railroad conformity to ICC accounting standards.

Bruere's description sounds contradictory to the account of railroad finances given by Cleve-land several years later. Harriman did use data on average cost per ton mile in his railroad work (Mitchell, 1907), and his railroads were distinctive in terms of the extent to which he invested in their improvements and equipment. He is known, however, primarily as a financier who used one company to buy equity in other companies, and bought up other railroads in an attempt to control as much of the traffic as possible. In doing that, he watered stock and shifted expenditures from operating to capital and capital to operating. In 1906, he was investigated by the ICC for precisely such matters; although he was not found guilty of wrongdoing, his financial practices were widely aired (Kennan, 1969). One analyst described the financial reports of the Union Pacific as the best available but noted some weaknesses in them. For example, the average cost per car per annum reported in the Union Pacific's annual reports was not borne out in the computations, and expenses for new heavier engines were attributed to maintenance costs rather than capital (Mitchell, 1907, p. 244). In this area, Harriman's accounting hardly provided a model for government.

Moreover, cost accounting for railroads had long been advocated but had not been widely adopted, except for crude measures of cost per ton mile which were mandated by the ICC. James Lyne, editor of *Railway Age,* wrote in 1961 that the industry had operated for a century with little knowledge of the costs of specific operations (Poole, 1961, p. *viii*). Ernest Poole, a former employee of the Southern Pacific Railroad argued that because railroads had monopolies, they charged as much as they could get and still make a profit. If all the railroad rates times the amount of traffic at each rate generated more revenue than costs, the railroad was a success; if not, it was time to seek a rate increase (Poole, 1961, p. 1.). This practice had led to the development of consider-able sophistication in marginal costing; the railroad companies had to know the cost of hauling additional loads of lumber, and the actual additional costs of hauling finished products west and raw materials east. The results of this pricing structure appeared highly unfair to shippers, such as higher rates for short hauls than long ones, and cheaper prices for products that had alternative ways to get to market and more expensive prices for products with no alternatives. Government regulation put an end to this practice, and reduced the railroads' capacity to produce such accounting data (Dusenbury, 1985). Because the result of marginal pricing was so apparently inequitable, it did not set a pattern for government to use.

William Allen, another director of the New York bureau, brought budget ideas with him from the welfare agency he had worked for before he came to the New York bureau, the Association for Improving the Condition of the Poor (AICP). Frank Tucker, the general agent of the AICP, established a pattern of budgeting in 1897 that Allen was very familiar with. Tucker's system included handling outgoing and incoming funds through one desk and one ledger, and creating breakdowns of the budget showing exactly how each department used its share of the budget (Allen, 1908, p. 156). Receipts were all deposited in a single fund, the general fund, and transferred out to other specialized funds as appropriate and documented. All departmental requests had to go through the finance department, where they were compared with each other and pared back, if necessary to achieve balance (Allen, 1908, p. 159). After Tucker's system was in place, the AICP used and extended the accounting system to evaluate and modify new procedures for visiting the poor and dispensing welfare (Allen, 1908, pp. 160–161.). Allen was more concerned with measuring outcomes than cost per unit; he saw the accounting system as a way of evaluating procedures and programs for efficiency and effectiveness.

The contribution to public budgeting of the New York Bureau of Municipal Research and other later research bureaus has become part of the standard history of public budgeting in the United States, but the roles of Frank Tucker of the AICP, LeGrand Powers of the Census Bureau, and Henry Carter Adams of the ICC have been minimized or ignored. One result has been an exaggeration of the role of business in providing an example to government.

Bureaus of municipal research were not supported by the broad public, although in some cities they were supported by the city government; they were supported by a small number of wealthy business people (Gill, 1944, pp. 134–146). In order to gain funding, the bureaus often had to modify their missions from the more progressive agenda of their enthusiastic origins to tax limitations with antigovernment overtones. The original mission was public money well spent, not the reduction of the scope of government, but appeals to tax reduction were more productive of funding and attracted a membership that was basically antigovernment (Gill, 1944).

The bureaus were encouraged by their patrons to examine the misdeeds of the political machines, but not of big business. When William H. Allen of the New York Bureau of Municipal Research challenged the Rockefellers, at first through their education foundation that he thought was making mistakes and was poorly run, and later through criticism of a city land deal for the Rockefellers, the Rockefellers saw to it first that Allen lost the support of other wealthy supporters of the bureau, and second, that he was fired. They also severely limited the scope of possible research that the bureau could do in New York City, and although Allen protested, the bureau's board accepted the constraints (Allen, 1950, p. 244).

It is not surprising in this context that the staff of research bureaus gave deference in their publications to the wonders of business efficiency, regardless of the accuracy of the claim. As Dwight Waldo commented,

> It must be recognized of course, that in some measure apparent acceptance of business, use of business analogy and dollar-and-cents arguments, must be attributed to strategic or tactical considerations.
>
> Administrative study was dependent, directly or indirectly, upon business support; and generally no plan for administrative reform could hope for a trial without the approval of the business community (Waldo, 1948, p. 44).

The business orientation of the research bureaus had a great impact on the interpretation given to early budget history because it was often the bureau staffers who told the story of how public budgeting was adopted in the United States. Their interpretation was further strengthened by the tendency of later scholars to trace back intellectual history from key events. The budget reforms of 1921 were preceded by the work of the Taft Commission. The Taft Commission was headed by Frederick Cleveland, who had formerly headed the New York Bureau of Municipal Research. Thus the work of the New York bureau in introducing budgeting to New York City in 1907 is sometimes taken as the origin of the executive budget (although it was not an executive budget). There is no direct connection back from the 1921 act to the National Municipal League,[2] so the model charter of the National Municipal League in 1899, which advocated an executive budget and was formed on the basis of government officials' experience, has been downplayed or ignored.

CONCLUSIONS

Public administration practitioners and academic researchers and advisers often initiated budget and accounting reforms, or borrowed them with modification from other governments. Sometimes they introduced those reforms to and forced them on business. Reformers came together in professional associations to share innovations and to study examples of good government. Business played little role in providing examples for government to follow, although business leaders called for reform and often funded its study and implementation. Business-supported research bureaus had a disproportionate effect on how the story of budget reform was told; that story telling overemphasized the importance of business as a model of good management.

These conclusions have several implications for the present. Cooperation between government officials and academics was smooth and useful; this level of cooperation does not always occur in our times. It is good to look back on an example of what we can accomplish together. Second, in a time of loss of public confidence in government, it is important to remember that creative and significant reforms emanated from public officials and academic public administrators. It is also important to understand how the myth of business superiority in management was promulgated and came to be so widely accepted. A richer and more balanced historical narrative may help restore the confidence of the public in the public service and the confidence of the public service in itself after years of abuse from the media, citizens, and elected officials.

NOTES

An earlier version of this article was presented at the American Political Science Association Meetings, Chicago, Illinois, September 3, 1992.

1. The bureau researchers boasted of their neutrality as they documented the reforms they helped implement. Chester Rightor, Don Sowers, and Walter Matscheck (1919), all former employees of the Dayton Bureau of Municipal Research, wrote a book evaluating the city manager form of government in Dayton, which the bureau had helped to introduce. In their preface, they argue "An analysis of the situation will disclose the fact that former staff members of the Dayton Bureau of Municipal Research are perhaps the logical persons to write such a book since there can be assumed thereby a certainty of disinterestedness. . . . It is a function of Bureaus of Governmental Research, and the profession of Bureau men, to make unbiased, scientific studies of governmental affairs" (p. ix).

2. There was, however, an indirect connection from the Taft Economy and Efficiency Commission and the National Municipal League model charter. Frank Goodnow served on both and may well have carried the recommendations of the Municipal League to Washington when he participated in the Taft Commission. However, evidence linking Goodnow to support of the stripping of budget power from the legislature is meagre. He seems to have advocated executive presentation of the budget proposal but also advocated real responsibility for the legislature in reviewing and approving or disapproving it so that it would reflect public wishes (Goodnow, 1900, pp. 74–88).

REFERENCES

Allen, William H., 1908. *Efficient Democracy* New York: Dodd, Mead.

———. 1950. *Reminiscences.* Microfiches, Oral History Collection, Housed at Columbia University.

Bruere, Henry, 1949. *Reminiscences.* Microfiches, Oral History Collection, Housed at Columbia University.

Cleveland, Frederick, 1980, originally published by Longmans Green, 1909. "Chicago's Accounting Reform." Paper Presented the Ninth Annual Conference of the National Municipal League, Detroit, Michigan, April 23, 1903. In *Chapters on Municipal Administration and Accounting,* 219–243. New York: Arno Reprint.

Cleveland, Frederick A., 1905. "Advantages of an Independent Railway Audit to the Investor." *Journal of Accountancy,* vol. 1, pp. 386–395.

Cleveland, Frederick A., and Fred Wilbur Powell. 1912. Railroad Finance. New York: D. Appleton and Company.

Dahlberg, Jane S., 1966. *The New York Bureau of Municipal Research: Pioneer in Government Administration.* New York: New York University.

Dawes, Charles G., 1923. *The First Year of the Budget of the United States.* New York: Harper and Brothers Publishers.

Dusenbury, Richard., 1985. "The Effect of ICC Regulation on the Accounting Practices of Railroads Since 1887." Working Paper 62, The Academy of Accounting Historians. offset.

Gill, Norman. 1944. *Municipal Research Bureaus: A Study of the Nation's Leading Citizen Supported Agencies.* Washington, DC: American Council on Public Affairs.

Glaab, Charles N. and Theodore A. Brown, 1983. *A History of Urban America,* 3rd Ed., New York: MacMillan.

Goodnow, Frank J., 1900. "The Place of the Council and of the Mayor in the Organization of Municipal Government—The Necessity of Distinguishing Legislation from Administration." In the National Municipal League, *A Municipal Program,* New York: MacMillan, pp. 74–88.

Goodnow, Frank J. C., 1912. "What the President's Promise of a Budget Means." Typed Speech or Press Release, in the Manuscript Collection, Eisenhower Library, Johns Hopkins University.

Kennan, George, 1969, originally published 1922. *E. H. Harriman: A Biography.* Freeport, NY: Books for Libraries Press.

Mitchell, Thomas Warner, 1907. "An Evaluation of the Annual Reports of the Union Pacific." *Journal of Accountancy,* vol. 3 (January) pp. 238–248.

Poole, Ernest C., 1962. *Costs—A Tool for Railway Management.* New York: Simmons-Boardman.

Powers, Le Grand, 1906. "Letter to the Editors" *Journal of Accountancy,* vol. 2 (June), 160.

Rightor, Chester E., Don Sowers, and Walter Matschek, 1919. *City Manager in Dayton. Four Years of Commission Manager Government, 1914–1917; and Comparisons with Four Preceding Years under the Mayor Council Plan, 1910–1913.* New York: MacMillan.

Rosenberry, Marvin, 1948. "Henry Carter Adams." In Earl D. and Vander Velde Lewis G. Babst, eds., *Michigan and the Cleveland Era: Sketches of University of Michigan Staff Members and Alumni Who Served the Cleveland Administrations 1885–1889 and 1893–1897.* Ann Arbor, MI: University of Michigan Press.

Sealander, Judith, 1988. *Grand Plans: Business Progressivism and Social Change in Ohio's Miami Valley, 1890–1929.* Lexington, Ky.: University of Kentucky Press, pp. 119–120.

Shuman, Howard E., 1992. *Politics and the Budget: The Struggle Between the President and Congress,* 3d ed. Englewood Cliffs, NJ: Prentice Hall.

Waldo, Dwight, 1948. *The Administrative State: A Study of the Political Theory of American Public Administration.* New York: Ronald Press.

Willoughby, William F., 1918. The Movement for Budgetary Reform in the States. Brookings reprint series. New York: D. Appleton and Co.

Wilmot, H. W., 1906. "Municipal Accounting Reform." *Journal of Accountancy* vol. 2 (May), pp. 97–108.

CHAPTER 3

THE ROAD TO PPB
The Stages of Budget Reform

ALLEN SCHICK

Among the new men in the nascent PPB staffs and the fellow travellers who have joined the bandwagon, the mood is of "a revolutionary development in the history of government management." There is excited talk about the differences between what has been and what will be; of the benefits that will accrue from an explicit and "hard" appraisal of objectives and alternatives; of the merits of multiyear budget forecasts and plans; of the great divergence between the skills and role of the analyst and the job of the examiner; of the realignments in government structure that might result from changes in the budget process.

This is not the only version, however. The closer one gets to the nerve centers of budget life—the Divisions in the Bureau of the Budget and the budget offices in the departments and agencies—the more one is likely to hear that "there's nothing very new in PPB; it's hardly different from what we've been doing until now." Some old-timers interpret PPB as a revival of the performance budgeting venture of the early 1950's. Others belittle the claim that—before PPB—decisions on how much to spend for personnel or supplies were made without real consideration of the purposes for which these inputs were to be invested. They point to previous changes that have been in line with PPB, albeit without PPB's distinctive package of techniques and nomenclature. Such things as the waning role of the "green sheets" in the central budget process, the redesign of the appropriation structure and the development of activity classifications, refinements in work measurement, productivity analysis, and other types of output measurement, and the utilization of the Spring Preview for a broad look at programs and major issues.

Between the uncertain protests of the traditional budgeteer and the uncertain expectations of the *avant garde,* there is a third version. The PPB system that is being developed portends a radical change in the central function of budgeting, but it is anchored to half a century of tradition and evolution. The budget system of the future will be a product of past and emerging developments; that is, it will embrace both the budgetary functions introduced during earlier stages of reform as well as the planning function which is highlighted by PPB. PPB is the first budget system *designed* to accommodate the multiple functions of budgeting.

From *Public Administration Review,* vol. 26, no. 6 (November/December 1966), 243–258. Copyright © 1966 by American Society for Public Administration. Reprinted with permission.

THE FUNCTIONS OF BUDGETING

Budgeting always has been conceived as a process for systematically relating the expenditure of funds to the accomplishment of planned objectives. In this important sense, there is a bit of PPB in every budget system. Even in the initial stirrings of budget reform more than 50 years ago, there were cogent statements on the need for a budget system to plan the objectives and activities of government and to furnish reliable data on what was to be accomplished with public funds. In 1907, for example, the New York Bureau of Municipal Research published a sample "program memorandum" that contained some 125 pages of functional accounts and data for the New York City Health Department.[1]

However, this orientation was not *explicitly* reflected in the budget systems—national, state, or local—that were introduced during the first decades of this century, nor is it *explicitly* reflected in the budget systems that exist today. The plain fact is that planning is not the only function that must be served by a budget system. The *management* of ongoing activities and the *control* of spending are two functions which, in the past, have been given priority over the planning function. Robert Anthony identifies three distinct administrative processes, strategic planning, management control, and operational control.

> **Strategic planning** is the process of deciding on objectives of the organization, on changes in these objectives, on the resources used to attain these objectives, and on the policies that are to govern the acquisition, use, and disposition of these resources.

> **Management control** is the process by which managers assure that resources are obtained and used effectively and efficiently in the accomplishment of the organization's objectives.

> **Operational control** is the process of assuring that specific tasks are carried out effectively and efficiently.[2]

Every budget system, even rudimentary ones, comprises planning, management, and control processes. Operationally, these processes often are indivisible, but for analytic purposes they are distinguished here. In the context of budgeting, *planning* involves the determination of objectives, the evaluation of alternative courses of action, and the authorization of select programs. Planning is linked most closely to budget preparation, but it would be a mistake to disregard the management and control elements in budget preparation or the possibilities for planning during other phases of the budget year. Clearly, one of the major aims of PPB is to convert the annual routine of preparing a budget into a conscious appraisal and formulation of future goals and policies. Management involves the programming of approved goals into specific projects and activities, the design of organizational units to carry out approved programs, and the staffing of these units and the procurement of necessary resources. The management process is spread over the entire budget cycle; ideally, it is the link between goals made and activities undertaken. *Control* refers to the process of binding operating officials to the policies and plans set by their superiors. Control is predominant during the execution and audit stages, although the form of budget estimates and appropriations often is determined by control considerations. The assorted controls and reporting procedures that are associated with budget execution—position controls, restrictions on transfers, requisition procedures, and travel regulations, to mention the more prominent ones—have the purpose of securing compliance with policies made by central authorities.

Very rarely are planning, management, and control given equal attention in the operation of budget systems. As a practical matter, planning, management, and control have tended to be competing processes in budgeting with no neat division of functions among the various participants. Because time is scarce, central authorities must be selective in the things they do. Although this scarcity counsels the devolution of control responsibilities to operating levels, the lack of reliable and relied-on internal control systems has loaded central authorities with control functions at the expense of the planning function. Moreover, these processes often require different skills and generate different ways of handling the budget mission, so that one type of perspective tends to predominate over the others. Thus, in the staffing of the budget offices, there has been a shift from accountants to administrators as budgeting has moved from a control to a management posture. The initial experience with PPB suggests that the next transition might be from administrators to economists as budgeting takes on more of the planning function.

Most important, perhaps, are the differential informational requirements of planning, control, and management processes. Informational needs differ in terms of time spans, levels of aggregation, linkages with organizational and operating units, and input-output foci. The apparent solution is to design a system that serves the multiple needs of budgeting. Historically, however, there has been a strong tendency to homogenize informational structures and to rely on a single classification scheme to serve all budgetary purposes. For the most part, the informational system has been structured to meet the purposes of control. As a result, the type of multiple-purpose budget system envisioned by PPB has been avoided.

An examination of budget systems should reveal whether greater emphasis is placed *at the central levels* on planning, management, or control. A *planning orientation* focuses on the broadest range of issues: What are the long-range goals and policies of the government and how are these related to particular expenditure choices? What criteria should be used in appraising the requests of the agencies? Which programs should be initiated or terminated, and which expanded or curtailed? A *management orientation* deals with less fundamental issues: What is the best way to organize for the accomplishment of a prescribed task? Which of several staffing alternatives achieves the most effective relationship between the central and field offices? Of the various grants and projects proposed, which should be approved? A *control orientation* deals with a relatively narrow range of concerns: How can agencies be held to the expenditure ceilings established by the legislature and chief executive? What reporting procedures should be used to enforce propriety in expenditures? What limits should be placed on agency spending for personnel and equipment?

It should be clear that every budget system contains planning, management, and control features. A control orientation means the subordination, not the absence, of planning and management functions. In the matter of orientations, we are dealing with relative emphases, not with pure dichotomies. The germane issue is the balance among these vital functions at the central level. Viewed centrally, what weight does each have in the design and operation of the budget system?

THE STAGES OF BUDGET REFORM

The framework outlined above suggests a useful approach to the study of budget reform. Every reform alters the planning-management-control balance, sometimes inadvertently, usually deliberately. Accordingly, it is possible to identify three successive stages of reform. In the first stage, dating roughly from 1920 to 1935, the dominant emphasis was on developing an adequate system of expenditure control. Although planning and management considerations were not altogether absent (and indeed occupied a prominent role in the debates leading to the Budget and Accounting Act of 1921), they were pushed to the side by what was regarded as the first priority, a reliable system of expenditure accounts. The second stage came into the open during the New Deal and reached its zenith more than a decade later in the movement for performance budgeting. The management orientation, paramount during this period, made its mark in the reform of the appropriation structure, development of management improvement and work measurement programs, and the focusing of budget preparation on the work and activities of the agencies The third stage, the full emergence of which must await the institutionalization of PPB, can be traced to earlier efforts to link planning and budgeting as well as to the analytic criteria of welfare economics, but its recent development is a product of modern informational and decisional technologies such as those pioneered in the Department of Defense.

PPB is predicated on the primacy of the planning function; yet it strives for a multipurpose budget system that gives adequate and necessary attention to the control and management areas. Even in embryonic stage, PPB envisions the development of crosswalk grids for the conversion of data from a planning to a management and control framework, and back again. PPB treats the three basic functions as compatible and complementary elements of a budget system, though not as coequal aspects of central budgeting. In ideal form, PPB would centralize the planning function and delegate *primary* managerial and control responsibilities to the supervisory and operating levels respectively.

In the modern genesis of budgeting, efforts to improve planning, management, and control made common cause under the popular banner of the executive-budget concept. In the goals and lexicon of the first reformers, budgeting meant executive budgeting. The two were inseparable. There was virtually no dissent from Cleveland's dictum that "to be a budget it must be prepared and submitted by a responsible executive . . ."[3] Whether from the standpoint of planning, management or control, the executive was deemed in the best position to prepare and execute the budget. As Cleveland argued in 1915, only the executive "could think in terms of the institution as a whole," and, therefore, he "is the only one who can be made responsible for leadership."[4]

The executive budget idea also took root in the administrative integration movement, and here was allied with such reforms as functional consolidation of agencies, elimination of independent boards and commissions, the short ballot, and strengthening the chief executive's appointive and removal powers. The chief executive often was likened to the general manager of a corporation, the Budget Bureau serving as his general staff.

Finally, the executive budget was intended to strengthen honesty and efficiency by restricting the discretion of administrators in this role. It was associated with such innovations as centralized purchasing and competitive bidding, civil service reform, uniform accounting procedures, and expenditure audits.

THE CONTROL ORIENTATION

In the drive for executive budgeting, the various goals converged. There was a radical parting of the ways, however, in the conversion of the budget idea into an operational reality. Hard choices had to be made in the design of expenditure accounts and in the orientation of the budget office. On both counts, the control orientation was predominant.

In varying degrees of itemization, the expenditure classifications established during the first wave of reform were based on objects-of-expenditure, with detailed tabulations of the myriad items required to operate an administrative unit—personnel, fuel, rent, office supplies, and other inputs. On these "line-itemizations" were built technical routines for the compilation and review of estimates and the disbursement of funds. The leaders in the movement for executive budgeting, however, envisioned a system of functional classifications focusing on the work to be accomplished. They regarded objects-of-expenditure as subsidiary data to be included for informational purposes. Their preference for functional accounts derived from their conception of the budget as a planning instrument, their disdain for objects from the contemporary division between politics and administration.[5] The Taft Commission vigorously opposed object-of-expenditure appropriations and recommended that expenditures be classified by class of work, organizational unit, character of expense, and method of financing. In its model budget, the Commission included several functional classifications.[6]

In the establishment of a budget system for New York City by the Bureau of Municipal Research, there was an historic confrontation between diverse conceptions of budgeting.

In evolving suitable techniques, the Bureau soon faced a conflict between functional and object budgeting. Unlike almost all other budget systems which began on a control footing with object classifications, the Bureau turned to control (and the itemization of objects) only after trial-and-error experimentation with program methods.

When confronted with an urgent need for effective control over administration, the Bureau was compelled to conclude that this need was more critical than the need for a planning-functional emphasis. "Budget reform," Charles Beard once wrote, "bears the imprint of the age in which it originated."[7] In an age when personnel and purchasing controls were unreliable, the first consideration was how to prevent administrative improprieties.

> In the opinion of those who were in charge of the development of a budget procedure, the most important service to be rendered was the establishing of central controls so that responsibility could be located and enforced through elected executives. . . . The view was, therefore, accepted, that questions of administration and niceties of adjustment must be left in abeyance until central control has been effectively established and the basis has been laid for careful scrutiny of departmental contracts and purchases as well as departmental work.[8]

Functional accounts had been designed to facilitate rational program decisions, not to deter officials from misfeasance. "The classification by 'functions' affords no protection; it only operates as a restriction on the use which may be made of the services."[9] The detailed itemization of objects was regarded as desirable not only "because it provides for the utilization of all the machinery of control which has been provided, but it also admits to a much higher degree of perfection than it has at present attained."[10]

With the introduction of object accounts, New York City had a three-fold classification of expenditures: (1) by organizational units; (2) by functions; and (3) by objects. In a sense, the Bureau of Municipal Research was striving to develop a budget system that would serve the multiple purposes of budgeting simultaneously. To the Bureau, the inclusion of more varied and detailed data in the budget was a salutory trend; all purposes would be served and the public would have a more complete picture of government spending. Thus the Bureau "urged from the beginning a classification of costs in as many different ways as there are stories to be told."[11] But the Bureau did not anticipate the practical difficulties which would ensue from the multiple classification scheme. In the 1913 appropriations act

> there were 3992 distinct items of appropriation. . . . Each constituted a distinct appropriation, besides which there was a further itemization of positions and salaries of personnel that multiplied this number several times, each of which operated as limitations on administrative discretion.[12]

This predicament confronted the Bureau with a direct choice between the itemization of objects and a functional classification. As a solution, the Bureau recommended retention of object accounts and the total "defunctionalization" of the budget; in other words, it gave priority to the objects and the control orientation they manifested. Once installed, object controls rapidly gained stature as an indispensable deterrent to administrative misbehavior. Amelioration of the adverse effects of multiple classifications was to be accomplished in a different manner, one which would strengthen the planning and management processes. The Bureau postulated a fundamental distinction between the purposes of budgets and appropriations and between the types of classification suitable for each.

> . . . an act of appropriation has a single purpose—that of putting a limitation on the amount of obligations which may be incurred and the amount of vouchers which may be drawn to pay for personal services, supplies, etc. The only significant classification of appropriation items, therefore, is according to persons to whom drawing accounts are given and the classes of things to be bought.[13]

Appropriations, in sum, were to be used as statutory controls on spending. In its "Next Steps" proposals, the Bureau recommended that appropriations retain "exactly the same itemization so far as specifications of positions and compensations are concerned and, therefore, the same protection."[14]

Budgets, on the other hand, were regarded as instruments of planning and publicity. They should include "all the details of the work plans and specifications of cost of work."[15] In addition to the regular object and organization classifications, the budget would report the "total cost incurred, classified by *functions*—for determining questions of policy having to do with service rendered as well as to be rendered, and laying a foundation for appraisal of results."[16] The Bureau also recommended a new instrument, a *work program,* which would furnish "a detailed schedule or analysis of each function, activity, or process within each organization unit. This analysis would give the total cost and the unit cost wherever standards were established."[17]

Truly a far-sighted conception of budgeting! There would be three documents for the three basic functions of budgeting. Although the Bureau did not use the analytic framework suggested above, it seems that the appropriations were intended for control purposes, the budget for planning purposes, and the work program for management purposes. Each of the three documents would have its specialized information scheme, but jointly they would comprise a multipurpose budget system not very different from PPB, even though the language of crosswalking or systems analysis was not used.

Yet the plan failed, for in the end the Bureau was left with object accounts pegged to a control orientation. The Bureau's distinction between budgets and appropriations was not well understood, and the work-program idea was rejected by New York City on the ground that adequate accounting backup was lacking. The Bureau had failed to recognize that the conceptual distinction between budgets and appropriations tends to break down under the stress of informational demands. If the legislature appropriates by objects, the budget very likely will be classified by objects. Conversely, if there are no functional accounts, the prospects for including such data in the budget are diminished substantially. As has almost always been the case, the budget came to mirror the appropriations act; in each, objects were paramount. It remains to be seen whether PPB will be able to break this interlocking informational pattern.

By the early 1920's the basic functions of planning and management were over-looked by those who carried the gospel of budget reform across the nation. First generation budget workers concentrated on perfecting and spreading the widely approved object-of-expenditure approach, and budget writers settled into a nearly complete preoccupation with forms and with factual descriptions of actual and recommended procedures. Although ideas about the use of the budget for planning and management purposes were retained in Buck's catalogs of "approved" practices,[18] they did not have sufficient priority to challenge tradition.

From the start, Federal budgeting was placed on a control, object-of-expenditure footing, the full flavor of which can be perceived in reading Charles G. Dawes' documentary on *The First Year of the Budget of The United States*. According to Dawes,

> the Bureau of the Budget is concerned only with the humbler and routine business of Government. Unlike cabinet officers, it is concerned with no question of policy, save that of economy and efficiency.[19]

This distinction fitted neatly with object classifications that provided a firm accounting base for the routine conduct of government business, but no information on policy implications of public expenditures. Furthermore, in its first decade, the Bureau's tiny staff (40 or fewer) had to coordinate a multitude of well-advertised economy drives which shaped the job of the examiner as being that of reviewing itemized estimates to pare them down. Although Section 209 of the Budget and Accounting Act had authorized the Bureau to study and recommend improvements in the organization and administrative practices of Federal agencies, the Bureau was overwhelmingly preoccupied with the business of control.

THE MANAGEMENT ORIENTATION

Although no single action represents the shift from a control to a management orientation, the turning point in this evolution probably came with the New Deal's broadening perspective of government responsibilities.

During the 1920's and 1930's, occasional voices urged a return to the conceptions of budgeting advocated by the early reformers. In a notable 1924 article, Lent D. Upson argued vigorously that "budget procedure had stopped halfway in its development," and he proposed six modifications in the form of the budget, the net effect being a shift in emphasis from accounting control to functional accounting.[20] A similar position was taken a decade later by Wylie Kilpatrick who insisted that "the one fundamental basis of expenditure is functional, an accounting of payments for the services performed by government."[21]

Meanwhile, gradual changes were preparing the way for a reorientation of budgeting to a management mission. Many of the administrative abuses that had given rise to object controls were curbed by statutes and regulations and by a general upgrading of the public service. Reliable accounting systems were installed and personnel and purchasing reforms introduced, thereby freeing budgeting from some of its watchdog chores. The rapid growth of government activities and expenditures made it more difficult and costly for central officials to keep track of the myriad objects in the budget. With expansion, the bits and pieces into which the objects were itemized became less and less significant, while the aggregate of activities performed became more significant. With expansion, there was heightened need for central management of the incohesive sprawl of administrative agencies.

The climb in activities and expenditures also signaled radical changes in the role of the budget system. As long as government was considered a "necessary evil," and there was little recognition of the social value of public expenditures, the main function of budgeting was to keep spending in check. Because the outputs were deemed to be of limited and fixed value, it made sense to use the budget for central control over inputs. However, as the work and accomplishments of public agencies came to be regarded as benefits, the task of budgeting was redefined as the effective marshalling of fiscal and organizational resources for the attainment of benefits. This new posture focused attention on the problems of managing large programs and organizations, and on the opportunities for using the budget to extend executive hegemony over the dispersed administrative structure.

All these factors converged in the New Deal years. Federal expenditures rose rapidly from $4.2 billion in 1932 to $10 billion in 1940. Keynesian economics (the full budgetary implications of which are emerging only now in PPB) stressed the relationship between public spending and the condition of the economy. The President's Committee on Administrative Management (1937) castigated the routinized, control-minded approach of the Bureau of the Budget and urged that budgeting be used to coordinate Federal activities under presidential leadership. With its transfer in 1939 from the Treasury to the newly-created Executive Office of the President, the Bureau was on its way to becoming the leading management arm of the Federal Government. The Bureau's own staff was increased ten-fold; it developed the administrative management and statistical coordination functions that it still possesses; and it installed apportionment procedures for budget execution. More and more, the Bureau was staffed from the ranks of public administration rather than from accounting, and it was during the Directorship of Harold D. Smith (1939–46) that the Bureau substantially embraced the management orientation.[22] Executive Order 8248 placed the President's imprimatur on the management philosophy. It directed the Bureau

> to keep the President informed of the progress of activities by agencies of the Government with respect to work proposed, work actually initiated, and work completed, together with the relative timing of work between the several agencies of the Government; all to the end that the work programs of the several agencies of the executive branch of the Government may be coordinated and that the monies appropriated by the Congress may be expended in the most economical manner possible to prevent overlapping and duplication of effort.

Accompanying the growing management use of the budget process for the appraisal and improvement of administrative performance and the scientific management movement with its historical linkage to public administration were far more relevant applications of managerial cost accounting to governmental operations. Government agencies sought to devise performance standards and the rudimentary techniques of work measurement were introduced in several agencies including the Forest Service, the Census Bureau, and the Bureau of Reclamation.[23] Various professional associations developed grading systems to assess administrative performance as well as the need for public services. These crude and unscientific methods were the forerunners of more sophisticated and objective techniques. At the apogee of these efforts, Clarence Ridley and Herbert Simon published *Measuring Municipal Activities: A Survey of Suggested Criteria for Appraising Administration,* in which they identified five kinds of measurement—(1) needs, (2) results, (3) costs, (4) effort, and (5) performance—and surveyed the obstacles to the measurement of needs and results. The latter three categories they combined into a measure of administrative efficiency. This study provides an excellent inventory of the state of the technology prior to the breakthrough made by cost-benefit and systems analysis.

At the close of World War II, the management orientation was entrenched in all but one aspect of Federal budgeting—the classification of expenditures. Except for isolated cases (such as TVA's activity accounts and the project structure in the Department of Agriculture), the traditional object accounts were retained though the control function had receded in importance. In 1949 the Hoover Commission called for alterations in budget classifications consonant with the management orientation. It recommended "that the whole budgetary concept of the Federal Government should be refashioned by the adoption of a budget based upon functions, activities, and projects."[24] To create a sense of novelty, the Commission gave a new label—performance budgeting—to what had long been known as functional or activity budgeting. Because its task force had used still another term—program budgeting—there were two new terms to denote the budget innovations of that period. Among writers there was no uniformity in usage, some preferring the "program budgeting" label, others "performance budgeting," to describe the same things. The level of confusion has been increased recently by the association of the term "program budgeting" (also the title of the Rand publication edited by David Novick) with the PPB movement.

Although a variety of factors and expectations influenced the Hoover Commission, and the Commission's proposals have been interpreted in many ways, including some that closely approximate the PPB concept, for purposes of clarity, and in accord with the control-management-planning framework, performance budgeting *as it was generally understood and applied* must be distinguished from the emergent PPB idea. The term "performance budgeting" is hereafter used in reference to reforms set in motion by the Hoover Commission and the term "program budgeting" is used in conjunction with PPB.

Performance budgeting is management oriented; its principal thrust is to help administrators to assess the work-efficiency of operating units by (1) casting budget categories in functional terms, and (2) providing work-cost measurements to facilitate the efficient performance of prescribed activities. Generally, its method is particularistic, the reduction of work-cost data into discrete, measurable units. Program budgeting (PPB) is planning-oriented; its main goal is to rationalize policy making by providing (1) data on the costs and benefits of alternative ways of attaining proposed public objectives, and (2) output measurements to facilitate the effective attainment of chosen objectives. As a policy device, program budgeting departs from simple engineering models of efficiency in which the objective is fixed and the quantity of inputs and outputs is adjusted to an optimal relationship. In PPB, the objective itself is variable; analysis may lead to a new statement of objectives. In order to enable budget makers to evaluate the costs and benefits of alternative expenditure options, program budgeting focuses on expenditure aggregates; the details come into play only as they contribute to an analysis of the total (the system) or of marginal trade-offs among competing proposals. Thus, in this macroanalytic approach, the accent is on comprehensiveness and on grouping data into categories that allow comparisons among alternative expenditure mixes.

Performance budgeting derived its ethos and much of its technique from cost accounting and scientific management; program budgeting has drawn its core ideas from economics and systems analysis. In the performance budgeting literature, budgeting is described as a "tool of management" and the budget as a "work program." In PPB, budgeting is an allocative process among competing claims, and the budget is a statement of policy. Chronologically, there was a gap of several years between the bloom of performance budgeting and the first articulated conceptions of program budgeting. In the aftermath of the first Hoover report, and especially during the early 1950's, there was a plethora of writings on the administrative advantages of the performance budget. Substantial interest in program budgeting did not emerge until the mid-1950's when a number of economists (including Smithies, Novick, and McKean) began to urge reform of the Federal budget system. What the economists had in mind was not the same thing as the Hoover Commission.

In line with its management perspective, the Commission averred that "the all-important thing in budgeting is the work or service to be accomplished, and what that work or service will cost."[25] Mosher followed this view closely in writing that "the central idea of the performance budget . . . is that the budget process be focused upon programs and functions—that is, accomplishments to be achieved, work to be done."[26] But from the planning perspective, the all-important thing surely is not the work or service to be accomplished but the objectives or purposes to be fulfilled by the investment of public funds. Whereas in performance budgeting, work and activities are treated virtually as ends in themselves, in program budgeting work and services are regarded as intermediate aspects, the process of converting resources into outputs. Thus, in a 1954 Rand paper, Novick defined a program as "the sum of the steps or interdependent activities which enter into the attainment of a specified objective. The program, therefore, is the end objective and is developed or budgeted in terms of all the elements necessary to its execution."[27] Novick goes on to add, "this is not the sense in which the government budget now uses the term."

Because the evaluation of performance and the evaluation of program are distinct budget functions, they call for different methods of classification which serves as an intermediate layer between objects and organizations. The activities relate to the functions and work of a distinct operating unit; hence their classification ordinarily conforms to organizational lines. This is the type of classification most useful for an administrator who has to schedule the procurement and utilization of resources for the production of goods and services. Activity classifications gather under a single rubric all the expenditure data needed by a manager to run his unit. The evaluation of programs, however, requires an end-product classification that is oriented to the mission and purposes of government. This type of classification may not be very useful for the manager, but it is of great value to the budget maker who has to decide how to allocate scarce funds among competing claims. Some of the difference between end-product and activity classifications can be gleaned by comparing the Coast Guard's existing activity schedule with the proposed program structure on the last page of Bulletin 66–3. The activity structure which was developed under the aegis of performance budgeting is geared to the operating responsibilities of the Coast Guard: Vessel Operations, Aviation Operations, Repair and Supply Facilities, and others. The proposed program structure is hinged to the large purposes sought through Coast Guard operations: Search and Rescue, Aids to Navigation, Law Enforcement, and so on.

It would be a mistake to assume that performance techniques presuppose program budgeting or that it is not possible to collect performance data without program classifications. Nevertheless, the view has gained hold that a program budget is "a transitional type of budget between the orthodox (traditional) character and object budget on the one hand and performance budget on the other."[28] Kammerer and Shadoan stress a similar connection. The former writes that "a *performance* budget carries the program budget one step further: into *unit costs*."[29] Shadoan "envisions 'performance budgeting' as an extension of . . . the program budget concept to which the element of unit work measurement has been added."[30] These writers ignore the divergent functions served by performance and program budgets. It is possible to devise and apply performance techniques without relating them to, or having the use of, larger program aggregates. A cost accountant or work measurement specialist can measure the cost or effort required to perform a repetitive task without probing into the purpose of the work or its relationship to the mission of the organization. Work measurement—"a method of establishing an equitable relationship between the volume of work performed and manpower utilized"—[31] is only distantly and indirectly related to the process of determining governmental policy at the higher levels. Program classifications are vitally linked to the making and implementation of policy through the allocation of public resources. As a general rule, performance budgeting is concerned with the *process of work* (what methods should be used) while program budgeting is concerned with the *purpose of work* (what activities should be authorized).

Perhaps the most reliable way to describe this difference is to show what was tried and accomplished under performance budgeting. First of all, performance budgeting led to the introduction of activity classifications, the management-orientation of which has already been discussed. Second, narrative descriptions of program and performance were added to the budget document. These statements give the budget-reader a general picture of the work that will be done by the organizational unit requesting funds. But unlike the analytic documents currently being developed under PPB, the narratives have a descriptive and justificatory function; they do not provide an objective basis for evaluating the cost-utility of an expenditure. Indeed, there hardly is any evidence that the narratives have been used for decision making; rather they seem best suited for giving the uninformed outsider some glimpses of what is going on inside.

Third, performance budgeting spawned a multitude of work-cost measurement explorations. Most used, but least useful, were the detailed workload statistics assembled by administrators to justify their requests for additional funds. On a higher level of sophistication were attempts to apply the techniques of scientific management and cost accounting to the development of work and productivity standards. In these efforts, the Bureau of the Budget had a long involvement, beginning with the issuance of the trilogy of work measurement handbooks in 1950 and reaching its highest development in the productivity-measurement studies that were published in 1964. All these applications were at a level of detail useful for managers with operating or supervisory responsibilities, but of scant usefulness for top-level officials who have to determine organizational objectives and goals. Does it really help top officials if they know that it cost $0.07 to wash a pound of laundry or that the average postal employee processes 289 items of mail per hour? These are the main fruits of performance measurements, and they have an importance place in the management of an organization. They are of great value to the operating official who has the limited function of getting a job done, but they would put a crushing burden on the policy maker whose function is to map the future course of action.

Finally, the management viewpoint led to significant departures from PPB's principle that the expenditure accounts should show total systems cost. The 1949 National Security Act (possibly the first concrete result of the Hoover report) directed the segregation of capital and operating costs in the defense budget. New York State's performance–budgeting experiment for TB hospitals separated expenditures into cost centers (a concept derived from managerial cost accounting) and within each center into fixed and variable costs. In most manpower and work measurements, labor has been isolated from other inputs. Most important, in many states and localities (and implicitly in Federal budgeting) the cost of continuing existing programs has been separated from the cost of new or expanded programs. This separation is useful for managers who build up a budget in terms of increments and decrements from the base, but it is a violation of program budgeting's working assumption that all claims must be pitted against one another in the competition for funds. Likewise, the forms of separation previously mentioned make sense from the standpoint of the manager, but impair the planner's capability to compare expenditure alternatives.

THE PLANNING ORIENTATION

The foregoing has revealed some of the factors leading to the emergence of the planning orientation. Three important developments influenced the evolution from a management to a planning orientation.

1. Economic analysis—macro and micro—has had an increasing part in the shaping of fiscal and budgetary policy.
2. The development of new informational and decisional technologies has enlarged the applicability of objective analysis to policy making. And,
3. There has been a gradual convergence of planning and budgetary processes.

Keynesian economics with its macroanalytic focus on the impact of governmental action on the private sector had its genesis in the underemployment economy of the Great Depression. In calling attention to the opportunities for attaining full employment by means of fiscal policy, the Keynesians set into motion a major restatement of the central budget function. From the utilization of fiscal policy to achieve economic objectives, it was but a few steps to the utilization of the budget process to achieve fiscal objectives. Nevertheless, between the emergence and the victory of the new economics, there was a lapse of a full generation, a delay due primarily to the entrenched balanced-budget ideology. But the full realization of the budget's economic potential was stymied on the revenue side by static tax policies and on the expenditure side by status spending policies.

If the recent tax policy of the Federal Government is evidence that the new economics has come of age, it also offers evidence of the long-standing failure of public officials to use the taxing power as a variable constraint on the economy. Previously, during normal times, the tax structure was accepted as given, and the task of fiscal analysis was to forecast future tax yields so as to ascertain how much would be available for expenditure. The new approach treats taxes as variable, to be altered periodically in accord with national policy and economic conditions. Changes in tax rates are not to be determined (as they still are in virtually all States and localities) by how much is needed to cover expenditures but by the projected impact of alternative tax structures on the economy.

It is more than coincidental that the advent of PPB has followed on the heels of the explicit utilization of tax policy to guide the economy. In macroeconomics, taxes and expenditures are mirror images of one another; a tax cut and an expenditure increase have comparable impacts. Hence, the hinging of tax policy to economic considerations inevitably led to the similar treatment of expenditures. But there were (and remain) a number of obstacles to the utilization of the budget as a fiscal tool. For one thing, the conversion of the budget process to an economic orientation probably was slowed by the Full Employment Act of 1946 which established the Council of Economic Advisers and transferred the Budget Bureau's fiscal analysis function to the Council. The institutional separation between the CEA and the BOB and between fiscal policy and budget making was not compensated by cooperative work relationships. Economic analysis had only a slight impact on expenditure policy. It offered a few guidelines (for example, that spending should be increased during recessions) and a few ideas (such as a shelf of public works projects), but it did not feed into the regular channels of budgeting. The business of preparing the budget was foremost a matter of responding to agency spending pressures, not of responding to economic conditions.

Moreover, expenditures (like taxes) have been treated virtually as givens, to be determined by the unconstrained claims of the spending units. In the absence of central policy instructions, the agencies have been allowed to vent their demands without prior restraints by central authorities and without an operational set of planning guidelines. By the time the Bureau gets into the act, it is faced with the overriding task of bringing estimates into line with projected resources. In other words, the Bureau has had a budget-cutting function, to reduce claims to an acceptable level. The President's role has been similarly restricted. He is the *gatekeeper* of Federal budgeting. He directs the pace of spending increases by deciding which of the various expansions proposed by the agencies shall be included in the budget. But, as the gatekeeper, the President rarely has been able to look back at the items that have previously passed through the gate; his attention is riveted to those programs that are departures from the established base. In their limited roles, neither the Bureau nor the President has been able to inject fiscal and policy objectives into the forefront of budget preparation.

It will not be easy to wean budgeting from its utilization as an administrative procedure for financing ongoing programs to a decisional process for determining the range and direction of public objectives and the government's involvement in the economy. In the transition to a planning emphasis, an important step was the 1963 hearings of the Joint Economic Committee on *The Federal Budget as an Economic Document.* These hearings and the pursuant report of the JEC explored the latent policy opportunities in budget making. Another development was the expanded time horizons manifested by the multiyear expenditure projections introduced in the early 1960's. Something of a breakthrough was achieved via the revelation that the existing tax structure would yield cumulatively larger increments of uncommitted funds—estimated as much as $50 billion by 1970—which could be applied to a number of alternative uses. How much of the funds should be "returned" to the private sector through tax reductions and how much through expenditure increases? How much should go to the States and localities under a broadened system of Federal grants? How much should be allocated to the rebuilding of cities, to the improvement of education, or to the eradication of racial injustices. The traditional budget system lacked the analytic tools to cope with these questions, though decisions ultimately would be made one way or another. The expansion of the time horizon from the single year to a multiyear frame enhances the opportunity for planning and analysis to have an impact on future expenditure decisions. With a one-year perspective, almost all options have been foreclosed by previous commitments; analysis is effective only for the increments provided by self-generating revenue increases or to the extent that it is feasible to convert funds from one use to another. With a longer time span, however, many more options are open, and economic analysis can have a prominent part in determining which course of action to pursue.

So much for the macroeconomic trends in budget reform. On the microeconomic side, PPB traces its lineage to the attempts of welfare economists to construct a science of finance predicted on the principle of marginal utility. Such a science, it was hoped, would furnish objective criteria for determining the optimal allocation of public funds among competing uses. By appraising the marginal costs and benefits of alternatives (poor relief versus battleships in Pigou's classic example), it would be possible to determine which combination of expenditures afforded maximum utility. The quest for a welfare function provided the conceptual underpinning for a 1940 article on "The Lack of a Budgetary Theory" in which V. O. Key noted the absence of a theory which would determine whether "to allocate x dollars to activity A instead of activity B."[32] In terms of its direct contribution to budgetary practice, welfare economics has been a failure. It has not been possible to distill the conflicts and complexities of political life into a welfare criterion or homogeneous distribution formula. But stripped of its normative and formal overtones, its principles have been applied to budgeting by economists such as Arthur Smithies. Smithies has formulated a budget rule that "expenditure proposals should be considered in the light of the objectives they are intended to further, and in general final expenditure decisions should not be made until all claims on the budget can be considered."[33] PPB is the application of this rule to budget practice. By structuring expenditures so as to juxtapose substitutive elements within program categories, and by analyzing the costs and benefits of the various substitutes, PPB has opened the door to the use of marginal analysis in budgeting.

Actually, the door was opened somewhat by the development of new decisional and informational technologies, the second item on the list of influences in the evolution of the planning orientation. Without the availability of the decisional-informational capability provided by cost-benefit and systems analysis, it is doubtful that PPB would be part of the budgetary apparatus today. The new technologies make it possible to cope with the enormous informational and analytic burdens imposed by PPB. As aids to calculation, they furnish a methodology for the analysis of alternatives, thereby expanding the range of decision-making in budgeting.

Operations research, the oldest of these technologies, grew out of complex World War II conditions that required the optimal coordination of manpower, material, and equipment to achieve defense objectives. Operations research is most applicable to those repetitive operations where the opportunity for qualification is highest. Another technology, cost-benefit analysis, was intensively adapted during the 1950's to large-scale water resource investments, and subsequently to many other governmental functions. Systems analysis is the most global of these technologies. It involves the skillful analysis of the major factors that go into the attainment of an interconnected set of objectives. Systems analysis has been applied in DOD to the choice of weapons systems, the location of military bases, and the determination of sealift-airlift requirements. Although the extension of these technologies across-the-board to government was urged repeatedly by members of the Rand Corporation during the 1950's, it was DOD's experience that set the stage for the current ferment. It cannot be doubted that the coming of PPB has been pushed ahead several years or more by the "success story" in DOD.

The third stream of influence in the transformation of the budget function has been a closing of the gap between planning and budgeting. Institutionally and operationally, planning and budgeting have run along separate tracks. The national government has been reluctant to embrace central planning of any sort because of identification with socialist management of the economy. The closest thing we have had to a central planning agency was the National Resources Planning Board in the 1939–1943 period. Currently, the National Security Council and the Council of Economic Advisors have planning responsibilities in the defense and fiscal areas. As far as the Bureau of the Budget is concerned, it has eschewed the planning function in favor of control and management. It many States and localities, planning and budgeting are handled by separate organizational units: in the States, because limitations on debt financing have encouraged the separation of the capital and operating budgets; in the cities, because the professional autonomy and land-use preoccupations of the planners have set them apart from the budgeters.

In all governments, the appropriations cycle, rather than the anticipation of future objectives, tends to dictate the pace and posture of budgeting. Into the repetitive, one-year span of the budget is wedged all financial decisions, including those that have multiyear implications. As a result, planning, if it is done at all, "occurs independently of budgeting and with little relation to it."[34] Budgeting and planning, moreover, invite disparate perspectives: the one is conservative and negativistic; the other, innovative and expansionist. As Mosher has noted, "budgeting and planning are apposite, if not opposite. In extreme form, the one means saving; the other, spending."[35]

Nevertheless, there has been some *rapprochement* of planning and budgeting. One factor is the long lead-time in the development and procurement of hardware and capital investments. The multiyear projections inaugurated several years ago were a partial response to this problem. Another factor has been the diversity of government agencies involved in related functions. This has given rise to various *ad hoc* coordinating devices, but it also has pointed to the need for permanent machinery to integrate dispersed activities. Still another factor has been the sheer growth of Federal activities and expenditures and the need for a rational system of allocation. The operational code of planners contains three tenets relevant to these budgetary needs: (1) planning is future-oriented; it connects present decisions to the attainment of a desired future state of affairs; (2) planning, ideally, encompasses all resources involved in the attainment of future objectives. It strives for comprehensiveness. The *master plan* is the one that brings within its scope all relevant factors; (3) planning is means-ends oriented. The allocation of resources is strictly dictated by the ends that are to be accomplished. All this is to say that planning is an economizing process, though planners are more oriented to the future than economists. It is not surprising that planners have found the traditional budget system deficient,[36] nor is it surprising that the major reforms entailed by PPB emphasize the planning function.

Having outlined the several trends in the emerging transition to a planning orientation, it remains to mention several qualifications. First, the planning emphasis is not predominant in Federal budgeting at this time. Although PPB asserts the paramountcy of planning, PPB itself is not yet a truly operational part of the budget machinery. We are now at the dawn of a new era in budgeting; high noon is still a long way off. Second, this transition has not been preceded by a reorientation of the Bureau of the Budget. Unlike the earlier change-over from control to management in which the alteration of budgetary techniques *followed* the revision of the Bureau's role, the conversion from management to planning is taking a different course—first, the installation of new techniques; afterwards, a reformulation of the Bureau's mission. Whether this sequence will hinder reform efforts is a matter that cannot be predicted, but it should be noted that in the present instance the Bureau cannot convert to a new mission by bringing in a wholly new staff, as was the case in the late 1930's and early 1940's.

WHAT DIFFERENCE DOES IT MAKE?

The starting point for the author was distinguishing the old from the new in budgeting. The interpretation has been framed in analytic terms, and budgeting has been viewed historically in three stages corresponding to the three basic functions of budgeting. In this analysis, an attempt has been made to identify the difference between the existing and the emerging as a difference between management and planning orientations.

In an operational sense, however, what difference does it make whether the central budget process is oriented toward planning rather than management? Does the change merely mean a new way of making decisions, or does it mean different decisions as well? These are not easy equations to answer, particularly since the budget system of the future will be a compound of all three functions. The case for PPB rests on the assumption that the form in which information is classified and used governs the actions of budget makers, and, conversely, that alterations in form will produce desired changes in behavior. Take away the assumption that behavior follows form, and the movement for PPB is reduced to a trivial manipulation of techniques—form for form's sake without any significant bearing on the conduct of budgetary affairs.

Yet this assumed connection between roles and information is a relatively uncharted facet of the PPB literature. The behavioral side of the equation has been neglected. PPB implies that each participant will behave as a sort of Budgetary Man, a counterpart of the classical Economic Man and Simon's Administrative Man.[37] Budgetary Man, whatever his station or role in the budget process, is assumed to be guided by an unwavering commitment to the rule of efficiency; in every instance he chooses that alternative that optimizes the allocation of public resources.

PPB probably takes an overly mechanistic view of the impact of form on behavior and underestimates the strategic and volitional aspects of budget making. In the political arena, data are used to influence the "who gets what" in budgets and appropriations. If information influences behavior, the reverse also is true. Indeed, data are more tractable than roles; participants are more likely to seek and use data which suit their preferences than to alter their behavior automatically in response to formal changes.

All this constrains, rather than negates, the impact of budget form. The advocates of PPB, probably in awareness of the above limitations, have imported into budgeting men with professional commitments to the types of analysis and norms required by the new techniques, men with a background in economics and systems analysis, rather than with general administrative training.

PPB aspires to create a different environment for choice. Traditionally, budgeting has defined its mission in terms of identifying the existing base and proposed departures from it—"This is where we are; where do we from here?" PPB defines its mission in terms of budgetary objectives and purposes—"Where do we want to go? What do we do to get there?" The environment of choice under traditional circumstances is *incremental;* in PPB it is *teletic.* Presumably, these different processes will lead to different budgetary outcomes.

A budgeting process which accepts the base and examines only the increments will produce decisions to transfer the present into the future with a few small variations. The curve of government activities will be continuous, with few zigzags or breaks. A budget-making process which begins with objectives will require the base to compete on an equal footing with new proposals. The decisions will be more radical than those made under incremental conditions. This does not mean that each year's budget will lack continuity with the past. There are sunk costs that have to be reckoned, and the benefits of radical changes will have to outweigh the costs of terminating prior commitments. Furthermore, the extended time span of PPB will mean that big investment decisions will be made for a number of years, with each year being a partial installment of the plan. Most important, the political manifestations of sunk costs—vested interests—will bias decisions away from radical departures. The conservatism of the political system, therefore, will tend to minimize the decisional differences between traditional and PPB approaches. However, the very availability of analytic data will cause a shift in the balance of economic and political forces that go into the making of a budget.

Teletic and incremental conditions of choice lead to still another distinction. In budgeting, which is committed to the established base, the flow of budgetary decisions is upward and aggregative. Traditionally, the first step in budgeting, in anticipation of the call for estimates, is for each department to issue its own call to prepare and to submit a set of estimates. This call reaches to the lowest level capable of assembling its own estimates. Lowest level estimates form the building blocks for the next level where they are aggregated and reviewed and transmitted upward until the highest level is reached and the totality constitutes a department-wide budget. Since budgeting is tied to a base, the building-up-from-below approach is sensible; each building block estimates the cost of what it is already doing plus the cost of the increments it wants. (The building blocks, then, are decisional elements, not simply informational elements as is often assumed.)

PPB reverses the informational and decisional flow. Before the call for estimates is issued, top policy has to be made, and this policy constrains the estimates prepared below. For each lower level, the relevant policy instructions are issued by the superior level prior to the preparation of estimates. Accordingly, the critical decisional process—that of deciding on purposes and plans—has a downward and disaggregative flow.

If the making of policy is to be antecedent to the costing of estimates, there will have to be a shift in the distribution of budget responsibilities. The main energies of the Bureau of the Budget are now devoted to budget preparation; under PPB these energies will be centered on what we may term *prepreparation*—the stage of budget making that deals with policy and is prior to the preparation of the budget. One of the steps marking the advent of the planning orientation was the inauguration of the Spring Preview several years ago for the purposes of affording an advance look at departmental programs.

If budget-making is to be oriented to the planning function, there probably will be a centralization of policy-making, both within and among departments. The DOD experience offers some precedent for predicting that greater budgetary authority will be vested in department heads than heretofore, but there is no firm basis for predicting the degree of centralization that may derive from the relatedness of objectives pursued by many departments. It is possible that the mantle of central budgetary policy will be assumed by the Bureau; indeed, this is the expectation in many

Table 3.1

Some Basic Differences Between Budget Orientations

Characteristics	Control	Management	Planning
Personnel Skill	Accounting	Administration	Economics
Information Focus	Objects	Activities	Purposes
Key Budget Stage (central)	Execution	Preparation	Pre-preparation
Breadth of Measurement	Discrete	Discrete/activities	Comprehensive
Role of Budget Agency	Fiduciary	Efficiency	Policy
Decisional-Flow	Upward-aggregative	Upward-aggregative	Downward-disaggregative
Type of Choice	Incremental	Incremental	Teletic
Control Responsibility	Central	Operating	Operating
Management Responsibility	Dispersed	Central	Supervisory
Planning Responsibility	Dispersed	Dispersed	Central
Budget-Appropriations Classifications	Same	Same	Different
Appropriations-Organizational Link	Direct	Direct	Crosswalk

agencies. On the other hand, the Bureau gives little indication at this time that it is willing or prepared to take this comprehensive role.

CONCLUSION

The various differences between the budgetary orientations are charted in the table presented here (Table 3.1). All the differences may be summed up in the statement that the ethos of budgeting will shift from justification to analysis. To far greater extent than heretofore, budget decisions will be influenced by explicit statements of objectives and by a formal weighting of the costs and benefits of alternatives.

NOTES

The author is indebted to Henry S. Rowen and Paul Feldman of the Bureau of the Budget and to the many Federal officials who guided him during a summer's sojourn along the road to PPB.

1. New York Bureau of Municipal Research, *Making a Municipal Budget* (New York: 1907), pp. 9–10.

2. Robert N. Anthony, *Planning and Control Systems: A Framework for Analysis* (Boston: 1965), pp. 16–18.

3. Frederick A. Cleveland, "Evolution of the Budget Idea in the United States," *Annals of the American Academy of Political and Social Science*, LXII (1915), 16.

4. Ibid., p. 17.

5. See Frank J. Goodnow, "The Limit of Budgetary Control" *Proceedings of the American Political Science Association* (Baltimore: 1913), p. 72; also William F. Willoughby, "Allotment of Funds by Executive Officials, An Essential Feature of Any Correct Budgetary System," ibid., pp. 78–87.

6. U.S., President's Commission on Economy and Efficiency, *The Need for a National Budget* (Washington: 1912), pp. 210–213.

7. Charles A. Beard, "Prefatory Note," ibid., p. vii.

8. New York Bureau of Municipal Research, "Some Results and Limitations of Central Financial Control in New York City," *Municipal Research*, LXXXI (1917), 10.

9. "Next Steps . . . ," op. cit., p. 39.

10. "Next Steps . . . ," op. cit., p. 67.

11. "Some Results and Limitations . . . ," op. cit., p. 9.

12. "Next Steps . . . ," op. cit., p. 35.

13. Ibid. p. 7.

14. "Next Steps . . . ," p. 39.

15. "Some Results and Limitations . . . ," op. cit., p. 7.

16. Ibid., p. 9.

17. "Next Steps . . . ," op cit., p. 30.

18. See A. E. Buck, *Public Budgeting* (New York: 1929), pp. 181–88.

19. Charles G. Dawes, *The First Year of the Budget of the United States* (New York: 1923), preface, p. ii.

20. Lent D. Upson, "Half-time Budget Methods," *The Annals of the American Academy of Political and Social Science*, CXIII (1924), 72.

21. Wylie Kilpatrick, "Classification and Measurement of Public Expenditure," *The Annals of the American Academy of Political and Social Science,* CXXXIII (1936), 20.

22. See Harold D. Smith, *The Management of Your Government* (New York: 1945).

23. Public Administration Service, *The Work Unit in Federal Administration* (Chicago: 1937).

24. U.S. Commission on Organization of the Executive Branch of the Government, *Budgeting and Accounting* (Washington: 1949), 8.

25. Ibid.

26. Frederick C. Mosher, *Program Budgeting: Theory and Practice* (Chicago: 1954), p. 79.

27. David Novick, *Which Program Do We Mean in "Program Budgeting?"* (Santa Monica: 1954), p. 17.

28. Lennox L. Moak and Kathryn W. Killian, *A Manual of Techniques for the Preparation, Consideration, Adoption, and Administration of Operating Budgets* (Chicago: 1963), p. 11.

29. Gladys M. Kammerer, *Program Budgeting: An Aid to Understanding* (Gainesville: 1959), p. 6.

30. Arlene Theuer Shadoan, *Preparation, Review, and Execution of the State Operating Budget* (Lexington: 1963), p. 13.

31. U.S. Bureau of the Budget, *A Work Measurement System* (Washington: 1950), p. 2.

32. V. O. Key, "The Lack of a Budgetary Theory," *The American Political Science Review*, XXXIV (1940), 1138.

33. Arthur Smithies, *The Budgetary Process in the United States* (New York: 1955), p. 16.

34. Mosher, op. cit. , p. 47–48.

35. ibid. , p. 48.

36. See Edward C. Banfield, "Congress and the Budget: A Planner's Criticism," *The American Political Science Review*, XLIII (1949), 1217–1227.

37. Herbert A. Simon, *Administrative Behavior* (New York: 1957).

PART 2

BUDGETING IN A DEMOCRACY; INSTITUTIONAL ARRANGEMENTS

How does budgeting in democracy differ from budgeting in nondemocratic states? How does constitutionalism frame public budgeting? How does the separation of and balance of powers between the executive and legislative branches that characterizes democracy in the United States influence or structure budgeting?

The first two pieces outline the executive budget reforms in the United States, which grant primary power to formulate the budget proposal to the president at the national level, or the governor or mayor at the state and local levels. Executive budget reforms at the state and local level preceded those at the national level. The cities began to use executive budgeting at the end of the 1800s. The idea picked up support at the federal level beginning around 1910, and eventuated in the 1921 Budget and Accounting Act. Over the years, evidence accumulated that the executive budget model didn't deliver all that it promised. The reform, while widely implemented, remained controversial—was too much power over the budget given to the executive? Not enough?

In the first two selections, Naomi Caiden outlines the history of the executive budget in the United States at the federal level, and Bernard Pitsvada boldly questions whether the executive budget reforms have worked, and whether it might be better to return to a more legislatively centered budget process. Pitsvada's arguments are debated by other budget scholars, whose comments are also included here.

In the states, especially, executive power to propose the budget was enhanced by the ability to veto particular items in the appropriations, a power the president of the United States coveted, and got, briefly, before it was declared unconstitutional. Veto power has been controversial in the states, based as it is on the assumption that executives will always be more responsible than legislatures and will veto pork projects legislators wish to fund. (Contrary to this theory, in Illinois in recent years the governor has enhanced the legislature's ability to spend on pork projects, and refused to take legislators' pet projects out of the budget even when the state faced severe revenue shortfalls.) Glenn Abney and Thomas Lauth document the use and abuse of veto power in the states and the gradual rebalancing of powers between the executive and legislative branches.

In the last selection in this part, Krishna Tummala and Marilyn Wessel describe what is called direct democracy, and its implications for budgeting. In direct democracy, citizens take matters in their own hands, making their own policy decisions by popular election, issue by issue, rather than allowing the normal legislative process to operate. These efforts occur when citizens are fed up with the results of the ordinary representative government, especially if some politician can see gain in leading such a popular movement. On the one hand, these direct actions can be a serious corrective for a government run amok, but on the other, they tend to oversimplify complex decisions, constraining government with overly harsh and inflexible rules. Many of those who have written about direct democracy in budgeting are critical of it, but there should be no question of its importance. Proposition 13 in California, a property tax limitation which is discussed in later parts, is an example of direct democracy.

CHAPTER 4

PARADOX, AMBIGUITY, AND ENIGMA
The Strange Case of the Executive Budget and the United States Constitution

NAOMI CAIDEN

What has become of the executive budget? Drawn from European experience, it was a popular proposal at all levels of government in the United States at the beginning of the century, a keystone in a Progressive agenda of reform. Adopted at the federal level in 1921, it stood for 50 years or more as a dominant institution in national economic and fiscal policy making. But in the mid-1980s, the federal budget process is widely perceived as in a state of crisis, and the meaning and significance of the executive budget are open to question.

Current confusions may often be traced to past misunderstandings and unfounded expectations. The place of the executive budget in the United States constitutional context has never really been clear, and the institution as adopted and developed differed from the initial proposal. The original concept espoused by budget reformers implied an executive budget monopoly, justified by a doctrine of administrative neutrality, at odds both with contemporary practice and the separation of powers. In this sense the executive budget was a paradox. The Budget and Accounting Act of 1921 modified this concept by retaining legislative initiative in appropriations and stressing the executive budget as a means of gaining executive responsibility and strengthening legislative budgetary control. Later the justification of policy-making capacity was added to that of administrative efficiency. In this sense, the executive budget was an integral part of the separation of powers, reflecting constitutional ambiguities regarding the place and limits of executive power, though these were overshadowed by acceptance of executive leadership.

Presently, neither original nor later meaning appears accurate. Assertions of executive budget monopoly on grounds of administrative neutrality seem inapposite, but expectations of executive prerogative from the original concept linger. Responsibility, the foundation of the modified executive budget, also seems to have evaporated: the executive budget is now simply a bargaining counter in a complex game in which the legislature often takes the initiative and the executive adopts a reactive stance. The result is the opposite of intention. Orderly processes break down or are bypassed; budget figures are open to a variety of interpretations; and budget outcomes appear to be beyond control of either branch of government. The executive budget still exists in form, but its significance as an institution has become an enigma.

From *Public Administration Review,* vol. 47, no. 1 (January/February 1987), 84–92. Copyright © 1987 by American Society for Public Administration. Reprinted with permission.

THE EXECUTIVE BUDGET AS PARADOX

Nothing is said about the executive budget in the Constitution. In an understandable reaction to colonial experience, Congress was given the power to raise revenue and enact appropriations [Article I, Section 7 (1); Section 8 (1); Section 9 (7)]. But constitutional vagueness on the meaning of executive power [Article I, Section I (1)] extended to the question of financial management. The Constitution required that "a regular Statement and Account of the Receipts and Expenditures of all public Money shall be published from time to time" [Article I Section 9 (7)], but as Frederick Mosher has pointed out, "the Constitution was silent on who should initiate financial plans and proposals, who should manage the finances, who should keep the accounts, and who should audit transactions."[1]

The vagueness is not really surprising, since at the time public budgets in the sense we know them today did not exist, and a model of responsible constitutional government had not yet emerged. *The Federalist Papers* shed little light on the issue. Madison's distaste for factions extended to any faction in control of a legislative majority and ruled out an executive dependent on the legislature.[2] His advocacy of shared and overlapping powers made no mention of budgetary control. In contrast, Hamilton believed that most government was limited to executive details "and falls peculiarly within the province of the executive department," including "the preparatory plans of finance, the application and disbursement of the public moneys in conformity to the general appropriations of the legislature."[3]

The initial legislation establishing the Treasury, however, made no mention of the President, required Senate confirmation for the appointment of the Secretary to the Treasury, and gave the Secretary the responsibility of submitting estimates directly to Congress. In Mosher's words, "Insofar as there was a budget at all, it was a congressional budget."[4]

One hundred years later, Woodrow Wilson criticized financial administration, contending that it had developed without real acknowledgement from one of balanced powers to congressional supremacy, resulting in a divorce between the formal and the living constitutions. Congress had entered more and more into the details of administration until the secretaries of departments were the real executives responsible only to the powerful committees of Congress to the point where "the Committees are the ministers and the titular ministers only confidential clerks."[5] The charges against Congress were many. It had no direct contact with finances and no grasp of details; each committee went its own way; financial policy was unstable and strayed from the paths of wisdom and providence; the major concern was commercial policy protecting manufacturing interests, not regular financial administration. The President was head of the administration but did not have control.

The "vast alteration in the conditions of government" and constraints in revenue necessitated, in Wilson's view, quite a different kind of financial administration, centered "in the hands of a few highly-trained and skillful men acting subject to a very strict responsibility."[6] Congress needed to have "the estimates translated and expanded in condensed statements by skilled officials who have made it their business . . . to know thoroughly what they are talking about."[7] Revenues and expenditures should be treated as "initially adjustable parts of a single, uniform, self-consistent system. They can be so treated only when they are under the management of a single body; only when all financial arrangements are based upon schemes prepared by a few men of trained minds and accordant principles, who can act with easy agreement and with perfect confidence in each other."[8]

How much of all this rhetoric was an accurate portrayal or a caricature either in Wilson's time or subsequently is unclear. Aaron Wildavsky has pointed out that as far as can be ascertained, nineteenth century appropriations appeared to be more or less stable, and despite lack of a central budget there was a powerful though informal ability to coordinate expenditure and revenue.[9] Through its committees Congress did control the budget and consistently pressed for economy.[10] Its appropriations decisions were guided by the Book of Estimates (the combined estimates of departments) and other executive proposals.[11]

But by the beginning of the twentieth century arguments for an executive budget were gaining force as part of a Progressive agenda of governmental reform. Issues of conservation of natural resources, railroad regulation, revision of banking and currency laws, and tariff reform appeared to demand national solutions for which, it was believed, the federal government as currently organized was ill-prepared.[12] In the reformers' diffuse program for change, the exercise of governmental power was a key element.[13] It followed that government had to be made efficient, in the sense of optimal use of resources to achieve social good.[14] Administration should be expert, scientific, and neutral, the domain of trained professionals. It was a separate function, quite distinct from politics.

The reformers drew on their successful reforms in municipal government where the executive assumed primary responsibility for city business. They were also influenced by the example of rising business firms whose increased scale and complexity had brought about a managerial revolution. Administrative modernization required executive management, so that lines of authority flowed smoothly from central authority according to a hierarchical model of bureaucracy.

Finally, the reformers looked to the practices of foreign governments where centralized budgets had become ubiquitous. Rene Stourm's authoritative text, *The Budget,* extolled executive monopoly over the budget function.[15] Admiringly United States reformers compared the British Cabinet system in which a unified executive dominated Parliament and commanded administration, including the budget, with the dispersal of power in their own government where lines of communication ran from departments directly to the powerful committees of Congress. In the view of a leading reformer, Frederick Cleveland, modern society required executive government, which in the United States meant that administration should be headed by a popularly-elected, effective President.[16]

The executive budget idea was most clearly spelled out by William Willoughby in *The Problem of a National Budget:* Willoughby saw the budget as essential for efficient and economical administration of public affairs, and he saw the President as responsible for government. The budget should be formulated by the executive alone, and only the executive should propose expenditures because "accountability can be enforced and efficiency secured only when responsibility is definitely located in a single authority."[17] The executive was superior to the legislature in budgetary matters because "The executive alone is in a position to determine in detail the administrative needs of the governed and intelligently to formulate an annual work program."[18]

It followed that the chief executive must be recognized as the head of the administration, which should be organized as an integrated hierarchy. Heads of departments should not be allowed to bring financial proposals before the legislature. Whereas contemporary theory cast the chief executive in the negative role of reviewing and reducing estimates as submitted by the spending departments, his role should now be affirmative: "a positive, constructive work program emanating from a responsible administrator in chief."[19]

Willoughby believed that "the legislature should be largely if not wholly excluded from the direct determination of the appropriation of funds."[20] Ideally the legislature's role should be only to discuss and criticize the budget, acting as a strong moral check on the executive. But realizing that total legislative exclusion was impractical, Willoughby wished to restrict legislative determination to "such large questions of appropriation only as can in any sense be regarded as legislative" allowing considerable administrative discretion through lump sum appropriations and transfers.[21]

How did all this relate to the Constitution and, in particular, the separation of powers? The problem of constitutional allocation of responsibility for administration, and whether the President should be regarded as chief administrator, has been much debated between those who see executive power as a highly limited grant from Congress, and those who believe the Founders sought an effective administration. In general the reformers were hostile to the separation of powers.[22] Cleveland went so far as to assert that the Constitution erred and that it must give way to modern exigencies.[23] Willoughby, less extreme, thought that power over administration was clearly allocated to Congress, but modern administration required that it be delegated to the President. But there was no need to reform the Constitution, as the reformers proposed "mere administrative changes, rationalized by principles of efficiency and the value of good order."[24] The constitutional question was effectively bypassed through "a narrow and apolitical administrative solution."[25]

From a constitutional perspective, the paradox of the executive budget lay in the juxtaposition of a virtual executive monopoly of power over the budget with the separation of powers. In the British system, executive command over policy and administration was justified by Cabinet collective responsibility to the House of Commons: a government that failed to gain enough votes to pass its budget, an avowedly political program, might be forced to resign. In the United States, the separation of executive and legislature precluded such a check on the proposed wide powers of the executive: an executive could continue in office without the confidence of the legislature, even if it could not obtain passage of its budget. The proposal for an executive budget might thus be seen as a grab for power, concealed in the language of administrative neutrality. But this paradox was averted, though it remained a possibility, since the executive budget was not adopted in its pure form.

THE AMBIGUITY OF THE EXECUTIVE BUDGET

The eventual enactment of the executive budget by Congress in the 1921 Budget and Accounting Act represented a triumph of persuasion by the reformers. Their victory may be attributed to a general acceptance of the virtues of management related to perceived administrative and budgetary defects, of a plausible division of labor between President and Congress, and of the idea of responsibility. In addition, the form of the executive budget in the Act departed somewhat from the original model. As time passed, the executive budget came to fit in well with an expanded concept of presidential power, and its ambiguities were temporarily overshadowed.

The progenitor of the Budget Act was the 1912 Report of the President's Commission on Economy and Efficiency.[26] Although rejected by Congress at the time, it set out the premises and arguments for legislative action following World War I. The Report drew heavily on the efficiency movement with its emphasis on management and technical proficiency. Federal government operations had been the subject of concern since the 1880s, and persistent deficits in the early years of the twentieth century had focused attention on its financial management. The thrust of the Report was that managerial expertise and leadership would enhance congressional budgetary control. No other mechanism could produce efficient management which required government to choose priorities in the face of limited resources, to balance expenditures against revenues, and to coordinate estimates. The information provided to Congress fell well short of the constitutional requirement of "a regular statement and account of receipts and disbursements." Estimates of appropriations, receipts, and expenditures prepared and submitted by the Secretary to the Treasury provided inadequate data for considering policy questions, used inconsistent classifications and lacked coordination.[27]

To reform the situation the Report envisaged a division of labor between Congress and the

President in which the former retained ultimate power over appropriations and the President took on the role of general manager, proposing and implementing the decisions of Congress, in line with the classic policy-administration dichotomy. The key change would be in the nature of the budget. Up to this point, the Report explained, "the budget has been primarily an affair of the Congress rather than the President . . . the Book of Estimates our nearest approach to a budget, is rather a more or less well-digested mass of information submitted by agents of the Legislature to the Legislature for the consideration of legislative committees to enable the Legislature both to originate and to determine the policy which is to be carried out by the Executive during the coming budgetary period." The Commission proposed a complete reversal of this procedure through the establishment of a budget: "a proposal to be prepared by the administration and submitted to the legislature." The executive branch would submit "a statement to the Legislature which would be its account of stewardship as well as its proposals for the future."[28] The budget would be "an instrument of *legislative control* over the administration." The act of appropriation would also enable the executive or its agents to exercise *administrative control* over the government's liabilities and expenditures.[29]

In short, the budget was to be an instrument for responsibility in government. The annual program would be prepared by the administration and submitted to the legislature. The administration would be responsible for proposals submitted, and Congress would be responsible for considering and acting on each proposal made.[30] To ensure efficiency and economy it was essential that executive responsibility be established for "the manner in which business is transacted in each of the departments and establishments."[31] Thus there should be central control over appointments, accounting, and reporting. Estimates of expenditure would be submitted to the President, who as head of the administration would present them as a definite administrative program.[32]

The Commission presented the executive budget not as a paradox in the separation of powers, but "an effective means whereby these constitutional principles may be maintained with integrity. . . ."[33] The legislature, whose role was consideration of questions of policy, would gain by receiving expert advice, enabling review of efficiency and economy based on facts, and by the assumption of responsibility by the executive for its proposals. The executive would gain through "his ability to bring together the facts and opinions necessary to the clear formulation of proposals for which he is willing actively to work as the responsible officer." The people would gain because "they are taken into the confidence of their official agents. . . . Therein" concluded the Commission, "lie the practical use and purpose of the mission, lie the practical use and purpose of the budget."[34]

All these arguments left plenty of room for ambiguity. For example, the Commission got into quite a tangle about whether the President had to spend money appropriated by Congress that had *not* been included in the executive budget, or whether appropriations were in fact mandatory or allowed him discretion to decide whether they should be spent. There was doubt about the position of the President as chief executive. At one point the Report referred to him as "part of the legislature" and later as prime minister, but more frequently he was regarded as "representative of the people at large,"[35] "the one officer of Government who represents the people as a whole,"[36] a concept far more than simply head of administration and one with possible plebiscitary overtones.

But such complexities aside, the Report, which also discussed comparative budget practices, was a remarkable document which paved the way for the modified executive budget adopted in 1921. At about the same time a single Appropriations Committee was established in both House and Senate. A Bureau of the Budget, under the control of the chief executive, was created to coordinate the estimates. Departments had to present estimates to Congress through the President's budget. A General Accounting Office was instituted to handle the audit function. But Congress retained the right to act as it wished on the President's budget, although the reformers would have preferred an end to its power to make spending proposals.[37]

The Budget and Accounting Act divided power between the President and Congress without deciding who should prevail. It also left open the question of presidential power over the executive branch. A "public administration" view, in Louis Fisher's words, saw the President as in complete charge of a hierarchy.[38] Congress, according to this model, could only consent and grant, while the executive had the function of planning expenditures. But it appears that the framers of the Act held an opposing view: Congress created the departments, and they were its agents. According to Hugh Heclo, "Presidential capacities to coordinate the activities of the executive branch were created and countenanced because they met the needs of Congress, particularly the newly created appropriations process."[39] The Act recognized a relationship between finance and management and gave both executive and legislature some jurisdiction over each.

Despite the ambiguities of the Act, there was little problem in practice in the early years. The prevailing emphasis on economy in government meant an essentially negative role for the presidential budgetary function. The coordinative powers of the Bureau of the Budget (originally developed on the initiative of Congress) were directed to cutting back present outlays and avoiding new commitments.[40] But the process was ill-adapted to substantive policy development,[41] and as the presidency moved to a positive role during the New Deal, moves were made to institutionalize and legitimize presidential power over the budget.

The Brownlow Committee, established during Franklin Roosevelt's second term in office, was the first of a number of official committees and commissions concerned with management of the executive budget. It saw the preparation and execution of the budget as essentially executive tasks, and the budget as a primary instrument for management in the executive branch. The purpose of a budget system was to provide in financial terms for planning, information, and control and to establish an integrated financial program in harmony with long-range and general economic policies. While the legislature should control general policy, the executive should be in charge of the details of administration. Executive control over the budget should be institutionalized in the Bureau of the Budget which would act as a general staff, the "right arm of the President for the central fiscal management of the vast administrative machine."[42] This theme was echoed in the two Hoover Commissions, internal self-study reports of the Bureau of the Budget, two unpublished reports on government organization during the Johnson Administration, and the Advisory Council on Executive Organization in 1969. The Bureau of the Budget gained important legislative and clearance functions. The logic of Keynesian control of the economy, the "permanent emergency" in foreign affairs and the role of the presidency in spearheading social programs, seemed to place the budget process as a major tool of executive policy making.[43] The justification of policy-making capacity was thus added to that of administrative efficiency. The executive budget reflected an alliance between the values of neutral competence and executive leadership.[44]

THE ENIGMA OF THE EXECUTIVE BUDGET

The executive budget was accepted into the United States constitutional order during the first part of the twentieth century partly because it fitted well with an emphasis on presidential leadership and power and partly because of basic agreements between the executive and legislative branches that prevented raising the questions left unanswered by the 1921 Budget Act. But the presidency of Richard Nixon brought the issues of the President's relationship with the administration and with Congress to the forefront of public concern and sharply revealed the ambiguities of the executive budget.

Nixon, it seems, took the "public administration" view of the executive budget at face value. He sought to reorganize the executive branch as the domain of the managerial presidency.[45] He also sought to achieve his policy agenda through an administrative strategy. The budget became a crucial battleground between Congress and President and the understandings upon which the executive budget had been based broke down. Quite apart from his power to initiate a budget, the President did have extensive administrative powers over expenditures, including lump sum appropriations contingency funds, reprogramming, transfers between accounts, timing of obligations, and impoundments.[46] As long as these were used with restraint, with at least the tacit consent of Congress and not to implement independent policies, they were tolerated as necessary discretion on the part of the executive branch. But with the polarization of issues between a Republican President and a Democratic Congress, the politics of accommodation were disrupted. Both Congress and President grasped for spending control, Congress by requiring certain agencies to submit their requests directly to it at the same time as to the Office of Management and Budget,[47] Nixon through unacceptable policy impoundment of funds. The President's assertion of power, bypassing the normal budget process to achieve his objectives, underlined the fragility of the 1921 compromise. In Allen Schick's words, impoundment as unilateral action "offered no clear-cut procedure for resolving budgetary impasses between the two branches."[48] On the contrary, it "invited stalemate and protracted conflict," which were only resolved by the forced resignation of the President, regulation by Congress of future impoundments, and the establishment of a congressional budget process that provided Congress with institutional capacity that could potentially rival that of the presidency.[49]

There was no intrinsic reason why the strengthening of the congressional budget process should threaten the executive budget as set out in the 1921 Act. The 1974 Act provided Congress with the opportunity to vote upon significant budget totals—total budget authority, total outlays, surplus of deficit, and functional allocations—and to use these as framework for the detailed appropriations decisions. Institutional reforms therefore established Budget Committees in each House and set up a timetable which "sandwiched" the budget process between first and second concurrent resolutions of Congress, the former proposing targets and the latter confirming ceilings. In order to bring appropriations totals in line with those of a preferred second resolution, a reconciliation process would enable Congress to instruct its authorizing and appropriations committees to meet stipulated expenditure goals. The Act established a Congressional Budget Office to provide analytical capacity, and to defeat the specific and contingent problems which had sparked reform, Congress took action to regulate impoundments.

The President's budget retained its function as a proposal upon which Congress would take action, and for the first six years there was little problem. Emphasis on both sides was primarily on economic stimulus and reduction of unemployment and later on expenditure restraint. Figures for budget authority and outlays in the first and second resolutions diverged from those of the President's budgets, but not in a consistent fashion, although Congress typically set defense targets lower and human resource targets higher.[50] Whereas congressional spending targets were set well above presidential requests under Ford, spending levels in the Carter Administration and congressional budgets were almost indistinguishable.[51]

But there were already signs that the executive budget as a guiding and controlling force was no longer living up to expectations. Even in the 1960s, budget routines were acting as a constraint as order and regularity began to disappear from the political agenda and presidents "were forced to frequently adjust their spending and revenue targets in order to accommodate last-minute policy decisions and changing economic conditions." Both Kennedy and Johnson had developed their legislative programs independent of the budget process, and the legislative agenda and budget preparation had drifted apart. As presidents matured in office their interest in the budget tended to wane, and its routine turned into a grind, "a constraint on their ability to act and as an obstacle to achieving their objectives."[52]

By the late 1970s budgetary control, whether by executive or legislature, had become a serious problem. The dominance of indexed entitlements, debt interest and other multiyear commitments made federal expenditures rigid in nature and difficult to change in the short term. Because such a large part of expenditures was determined by the levels of key economic indicators—unemployment, inflation, economic growth, interest rates—budget outcomes were also hard to predict in conditions of economic volatility. As budget constraints had tightened, a growing area of "overspill" had emerged, hidden spending beyond the confines of the regular budget consisting of the spending of off-budget agencies, loans and loan guarantees, and a wide variety of tax expenditures of concessions. The budget seemed to be carried along by events more than it shaped them, when in 1980 a president was elected with a definite promise to change direction.

The so-called Reagan revolution might be regarded as a test case for the executive budget as the new President's agenda was to use the federal budget as a major tool for implementation of a program that included reductions in taxation, reversal of priorities between domestic and defense spending, and a general decrease in the level of federal spending. The success or failure of this revolution is still being debated, but the attempt once more brought to the difficulties of the executive budget.[53]

It all started out brightly enough along classical lines: a presidential program spelled out for deliberation in a detailed document. True, the budget represented a political program rather than the administrative justification of the original concept, but this use of the executive budget had long been legitimized. It was also possible to justify the use of an additional source of power, the integrating device of reconciliation as used with the Congressional first budget resolution.[54] This *congressional* procedure (initially used under Carter) enabled the vexing questions of legislative entitlements to be dealt with within the budget framework and budget cuts to be presented and voted upon as a single package. It was used by the *Administration* to achieve unprecedented cuts in federal domestic expenditures, with of course the consent of Congress. But from this point, the executive budget began to unravel.

The first problem undoubtedly lay in the old question of separation of powers. Congress had to be reckoned with, and once again a Republican President faced a Democratic House of Representatives. While the Administration was able to garner sufficient political support to gain passage of the reconciliation bill, the way the procedure was employed was seen by many as a manifestation of executive power overstepping the conventional boundaries of the executive role. Over one hundred pages of changes in authorizations and appropriations including legislative amendments were hurriedly pushed through Congress with virtually no debate on substance. Though reconciliation continued to be employed in subsequent years, it was no longer acceptable as a major device for shaping the budget.

The executive budget also lost credibility as a responsible document because of the quality of its figures. National budgets of the late twentieth century stand and fall on their assumptions and projections of how specific measures will affect revenues and outlays in the short and long term. Where these assumptions are wrong, as they undoubtedly were in 1981, or worse still, are cynically used for political purposes, as the Director of the Office of Management and Budget (OMB) at the time has admitted, a budget will have a fictional quality, and those who took figures on trust once, will be unlikely to do so again.[55]

Once the damage was done, and a structural deficit beyond easy political repair had opened up, the ambiguities of the executive budget were fully revealed. The two potential dangers inherent in the concept—deadlock between the two branches and executive irresponsibility—began to characterize the budget process which became increasingly unpredictable from year to year as procedures broke down and trust eroded. It would be impossible to recount the complexities of the budget battle in these few pages, but it does appear that the executive budget no longer fulfills its expected role.

First, budgeting has become continuous, since it has become virtually impossible to resolve all the disputes in the course of a single budget cycle. Continuing resolutions have more often than not replaced appropriations. Budget initiatives take place throughout the year, and the regularity that used to characterize the cyclical budget process has been lost.

Secondly, while the budget remains important, many significant development take place outside it. The most notable events have been reforms in social security financing and impending tax reform, both of which took place independent of the budget process. The periodic raising of the debt ceiling has become a routine occasion for gaining of political advantage. The executive has also had more frequent resort to deferrals of funds.[56]

Third, in the prevailing complexity, it has been very unclear what budget figures really do mean.[57] Outlay figures and revenue estimates upon which deficit projections depend are particularly hazy, sensitive to economic miscalculation and political manipulation. Estimates of savings, especially where projected many years ahead, are confusing and misleading. There are also highly complex forms of expenditure used by agencies that are virtually incomprehensible to the lay person.

Fourth, for several years the President's budget has been pronounced "dead on arrival," and Congress has put together its own starting position for budgetary debate. Far from being the initiator and driving force in the budgetary process, the executive budget has been a tentative "opening shot." While reiterating a firm belief in a balanced budget, the President's budget has consistently proposed ever higher deficits. After presentation of his budget, the President has simply reacted to congressional proposals, set out positions from which he would refuse to retreat, and intervened vigorously in negotiations where the political issue was important to him.

Finally, from a general sense of frustration and with the support of the executive branch, Congress passed the Gramm-Rudman-Hollings Act, which attempted to take budgetary decisions out of the hands of both legislature and executive. If a budget could not be agreed upon in which deficit reductions would reach a specified target each year, there would be automatic sequestrations from appropriations across the board in all programs not exempt from the Act.[58] The calculations and implementation of these provisions would lie neither with legislature nor executive, but with the General Accounting Office. Speculation as to the exact reasons why participants chose to pass or accept this legislation, its technical constitutionality, or its ultimate consequences lie beyond the scope of this article. But it is a sad commentary on the fate of the executive budget.

CONCLUSION

One of the most striking characteristics of rapid change in human affairs is the concomitant development of language. Not only are new terms created to describe new phenomena, but existing words may also change in meaning. For some, this deviation from exact form represents linguistic deterioration, inadmissible imprecision, and plain wrong use of words. Others accept expansion and modification of language as positive developments, evidence of flexible adaptation and enhancement of conceptual capacity

Political institutions are subject to similar considerations. According to one view, institutions, processes, and procedures *shape* politics and determine political outcomes. Institutions are relevant and their definition, design, and integrity are crucial. From another point of view, institutions *re-*

flect politics and develop and respond to the demands of political participants at any given time. They have little validity of their own and constitute a mere starting point in the political battle. In particular, the United States Constitution has left open political outcomes without prejudicing them by stipulating rigid institutional relationships.

The enigma of the executive budget lies in the argument between these two perspectives. According to the first, the substantive intent of the institution provides the source of criteria for judgment. There are number of criteria. If the budget is seen as an entirely executive prerogative, because it is a purely managerial category, then there has never been a federal executive budget as this concept was never accepted. At the other extreme, it would also be misleading to think of the executive budget as simply a proposal put together by the executive for the disposal of Congress, since the President had sole power to present estimates, to veto appropriations, and to implement the budget. The executive budget has not been treated as a self-contained document, but has always involved relationships with Congress and with the administration. Its utility has been justified not only in terms of management, but with the erosion of the policy-administration dichotomy, with policy as well. As an institution it carried within it the potential for breakdown through the possibilities of deadlock (where the legislature rejects a presidential program but the President continues his term in office) and executive irresponsibility (where an executive thwarted by Congress uses whatever means are available at his disposal). Both these possibilities spell institutional breakdown, since the minimum condition for the executive budget—responsibility in budgeting—no longer fulfills expectations.

From the second perspective, the concept of the executive budget looks quite different. The executive budget has little meaning beyond its form, a document produced by the executive as advice to Congress, drawing upon the resources of the executive branch. It shares the ambiguities of the United States system of government, where the executive-legislature relationship has been deliberately left fluid. The notion of the executive budget may be traced back to the Constitution, and its emergence was evolutionary in nature without a sharp break in practice (irrespective of reform rhetoric). It has since developed because it has been perceived as useful. If there is any breakdown, it is a political breakdown to be mended by political means. The executive budget remains available to be employed as and when participants feel it would serve their purposes.

Both perspectives have validity. Institutions are important: they structure the rules and conventions by which the political game is played. They do develop, and their purposes and effects change over time. The executive budget is an elusive concept, and short of radical constitutional reform, it is likely to remain so. But it should be noted that where words get left behind the reality they seek to describe, where meanings are confused or distorted, and where they arouse expectations that are no longer fulfilled, the purposes of language are defeated, form and substance diverge, and judgment is clouded.

NOTES

Appreciation is expressed to Jesse Burkhead (Syracuse University), Louis Fisher (Congressional Research Service), Fred Riggs (University of Hawaii), Allen Schick (University of Maryland), and Aaron Wildavsky (University of California, Berkeley) for criticisms and suggestions. The work is, however, the sole responsibility of the author.

1. Frederick C. Mosher, *A Tale of Two Agencies: A Comparative Analysis of the General Accounting Office and the Office of Management and Budget* (Baton Rouge: Louisiana State University Press, 1984), p.14.

2. *The Federalist Papers* (New York: Mentor New American Library, 1961), p. 308.

3. *Ibid.*, pp. 435–6.

4. Mosher, *op, cit.*, p. 16.

5. Woodrow Wilson, *Congressional Government: A Study in American Politics* (New York: Houghton Mifflin, 1925), p. 180.

6. *Ibid.*, p. 135.

7. *Ibid.*, p. 148.

8. *Ibid.*, p. 181.

9. Carolyn Webber and Aaron Wildavsky, *A History of Taxation and Expenditure in the Western World* (New York: Simon and Schuster, 1986), p. 369.

10. *Ibid.,* p. 405.

11. Personal letter from Allen Schick.

12. H. Landon Warner, ed., *Reforming American Life in the Progressive Era* (New York: Pitman, 1971), p. 10.

13. *Ibid.,* p. 4.

14. Peri E. Arnold, *Making the Managerial Presidency: Comprehensive Reorganization Planning 1905–1980 (*Princeton: Princeton University Press, 1986), p. 20.

15. Rene Stourm, *The Budget* (New York: Appleton, 1917).

16. Arnold, *op. cit.,* p. 15.

17. William F. Willoughby, *The Problem of a National Budget* (New York: Appleton, 1918), p. 29.

18. *Ibid.,* p. 30.

19. *Ibid.,* p. 32.

20. *Ibid.,* p. 39.

21. *Ibid.,* pp. 145–6.

22. Dwight Waldo, *The Administrative State* (New York: Ronald Press, 1948), p. 105.

23. Webber and Wildavsky, *op. cit.,* p. 403.

24. *Idem.;* Arnold, *op. cit.,* p. 403.

25. *Ibid.,* p. 14.

26. Report of the President's Commission on Economy and Efficiency (Taft Commission), *The Need for a National Budget* (Washington; United States House of Representatives, Document No. 854, June 27, 1912).

27. *Ibid.,* p. 27.

28. *Ibid.,* p. 10.

29. *Ibid.,* p. 11.

30. *Ibid.,* p. 141.

31. *Ibid.,* p. 143.

32. *Ibid.,* p. 145

33. *Ibid.,* p. 136.

34. *Ibid.,* p. 139.

35. *Ibid.,* p. 141.

36. *Ibid.,* p. 145.

37. Willoughby, *op. cit.,* pp. 145–6.

38. Louis Fisher, "Congress and the President in the Administrative Process: The Uneasy Alliance," in Hugh Heclo and Lester M. Salamon, eds., *The Illusion of Presidential Government* (Boulder: Westview Press, 1981), pp. 23–4.

39. Hugh Heclo, "Introduction: The Presidential Illusion," in Heclo and Salamon, *op. cit.,* p. 6; Richard Neustadt, "Presidency and Legislation: the Growth of Central Clearance," *American Political Science Review,* vol. 48 (September 1954), p. 643.

40. Neustadt, 1954, *op. cit.,* pp. 644–646.

41. *Ibid.,* p. 647.

42. "Report of the President's Committee on Administrative Management," *Public Budgeting and Finance,*vol. 1 (Spring 1981), p. 85.

43. There is a huge literature on the growth in power and prestige of the President. An excellent summary may be found in William Andrews, "The Presidency, Congress and Constitutional Theory," in Aaron Wildavsky, ed., *Perspectives on the Presidency* (Boston: Little Brown, 1975), pp. 24–25.

44. See Herbert Kaufman, "Emerging Conflicts in the Doctrines of Public Administration," *American Political Science Review,* vol. 50 (December 1956), pp. 1057–1073. See also Herbert Kaufman, "End of An Alliance: Public Administration in the 1980s," John Gaus Lecture delivered at the Annual Meeting of the American Political Science Association, Washington, DC, August 29, 1986, in which he argued that the fundamental inconsistency between neutral competence and executive leadership is now being revealed.

45. See Richard Nathan, *The Administrative Presidency* (New York: John Wiley, 1983).

46. Louis Fisher *Presidential Spending Power* (Princeton: Princeton University Press, 1975).

47. Allen Schick, *Congress and Money* (Washington: Urban Institute, 1980), p. 22.

48. *Ibid.,* p. 48.

49. See *ibid.;* for a brief account see Naomi Caiden, "The Politics of Subtraction" in Allen Schick, ed., *Congress and the Making of Economic Policy* (Washington: American Enterprise Institute, 1984), pp. 100–130.

50. Louis Fisher, "Ten Years of the Budget Act: Still Searching for Controls," *Public Budgeting and Finance,* vol. 5 (Autumn 1985), pp. 4–6 See also Allen Schick, ed., *Crisis in the Budget Process: Exercising Political Choice* (Washington: American Enterprise Institute, 1986), pp. 20–21

51. Dennis L. Ippolito, "Reform, Congress and the President," in W. Thomas Wander, F. Ted Hebert, and Gary W. Copeland, eds., *Congressional Budgeting; Politics, Process and Power* (Baltimore: Johns Hopkins, 1984), pp. 134–5.

52. Allen Schick, "The Problem of Presidential Budgeting," in Heclo and Salamon, *op. cit.,* pp. 92–3.

53. Much of the section that follows draws heavily on Joseph White, "What Budgeting Cannot Do: Lessons of Reagan's and Other Years." Paper presented at the Annual Meeting of the American Political Science Association, Washington, DC, August 28–31, 1986.

54. See Allen Schick, *Reconciliation and the Congressional Budget Process* (Washington: American Enterprise Institute, 1981).

55. See David Stockman, *The Triumph of Politics* (New York: Harper and Row, 1986).

56. *Washington Post* (March 3 1986); p. A 10; *Los Angeles Times* (March 12 1986), Part 1, p. 11.

57. See Mark S. Kamlet, David C. Mowery, and Tsai-Tsu Su, "Who Do You Trust: An Analysis of Executive and Congressional Economic Forecasts"; John Ellwood, "Budget Authority vs. Outlays as Measures of Budget Policy." Papers presented at the Annual Meeting of the American Political Science Association, Washington, August 28–31, 1986.

58. See Charles W. Washington "The President's Budget for Fiscal Year 1987," *Public Budgeting and Finance,* vol. 6 (Summer 1986), pp. 3–26.

CHAPTER 5

THE EXECUTIVE BUDGET
An Idea Whose Time Has Passed

BERNARD T. PITSVADA

In recent years the most pervasive criticism of Congress from all parts of the political spectrum has been its perceived failure "to control spending." Periodically, presidents at odds with Congress over national priorities have also leveled this charge. However, the executive branch rarely enters into debates over which branch of government really speaks for the "people," that is, should legitimately set priorities. Instead, the attacks concentrate on how Congress does business. Criticism focuses on process rather than outcomes.

For example, the presidential budget message accompanying the Fiscal Year (FY) 1987 budget submission to Congress, stated, "The Congressional budget process is foundering; last year it fell apart time and time again. The budget resolution and appropriation bills were months late in passing. . . ."[1] To correct this problem, as though it were the heart of the differences between the president and Congress, President Reagan suggested several procedural reforms—the balanced budget Constitutional amendment, the line-item veto, and Presidential signature (approval) of congressional budget resolutions. Thus repairing the "process" fixed the "problem."

The FY 1988 budget message continued the debate. The current budget process has failed to provide a disciplined and responsible mechanism for consideration of the Federal budget. Budget procedures are cumbersome, complex, and convoluted. They permit and encourage a process that results in evasion of our duty to the American people. . . ." After a brief summary of his objections, Reagan concluded "The words alone are obscure and confusing; the process behind it is chaotic. The process must be streamlined and made more accountable."[2]

The "congressional budget process," the subject of so much criticism, is the set of procedures and actions initiated by the Budget and Impoundment Control Act of 1974 as amended by the Balanced Budget and Emergency Deficit Control Act of 1985 (otherwise known as Gramm-Rudman-Hollings). Currently these laws provide for Congress to pass, on a predetermined schedule, a budget resolution which sets targets and binding limits on federal spending by nineteen broad functional categories such as Income Security, Transportation, Agriculture and National Defense. This process did not replace previous procedures but simply added to them. Congress must still pass authorizing legislation and thirteen appropriation acts to

From *Public Budgeting and Finance,* vol. 8, no. 1 (Spring 1988), 85–94, and replies by Naomi Caiden, 95–99, Louis Fisher, 100–103, and Lance LeLoup, 104–107. Copyright © 1988 by Public Financial Publications, Inc. Reprinted with permission.

implement the budget resolutions (unless Congress resorts to an omnibus appropriation as it did in 1986).

The current budget process is complex and cumbersome. Critics point out that the budget has become so consuming that there is time for little else on the congressional agenda. Despite all this effort Congress has been able to pass all the appropriation acts before the beginning of the fiscal year only once since the 1974 Act has been in place—and that law moved the beginning of the fiscal year from July 1 to October 1. Late appropriations and thus continuing resolutions have become the norm and not the exception.

It has also been charged that the congressional budget process has heightened conflict, both with the executive and within Congress itself. Debates and votes on the total size of the budget with its resulting deficits are more difficult politically than the piecemeal enactment of various parts of the budget as was the rule before the act was passed.

The "budget problem" is thus traced to complexity and conflict, allegedly a direct result of the congressional budget process. The solution usually offered is to amend the Congressional Budget Act. But conflict preceded the act as well as followed it and may be held to stem from difficulties in adapting to resource constraints prevalent in many Western industrialized countries, rather than specific procedures. Complexity may equally derive from political circumstances, a reaction to polarization and refusals to compromise. Overall, it is possible that current budgetary difficulties may rest in some other part of the process.

THE FEDERAL EXECUTIVE BUDGET

It may be somewhat eccentric to suggest that perhaps it is not the congressional budget process that is at fault but rather that venerable tribute to orthodox public administration theory—the Budget and Accounting Act of 1921 that is the heart of the budgetary process problem. The 1921 act mandated the submission of an executive budget to Congress fifteen days after Congress convened each year. Gramm-Rudman-Hollings moved this submission date to the first Monday after January 3 regardless of when Congress convenes. An executive budget is a document estimating receipts and outlays submitted by the chief executive to the legislature covering all components of the executive branch. The proposal requests appropriations, indicates the executive's programs and priorities and acts as an executive management tool for execution and accountability. At the federal level the chief executive, the president, with the assistance of the Office of Management and Budget and the multitude of federal agencies, submits a consolidated unified budget request to Congress in a single, prescribed format.

While contemporary public administrators viewed the executive budget as a means of improving economy, efficiency and accountability by consolidating power and responsibility under the president, Congress originally hoped to use the new budget document and the process used to prepare it to reduce spending and make government more businesslike in its operations. The debates before passage of the 1921 act abound with observations such as those by Senator Swanson (D., Va):

> I believe it will coordinate the various departments of the Government and make them more economical and effective and save much duplication in work and much waste and extravagence of expenditure.[3]

and Senator Edge (R., N.J.):

> . . . it will have a wonderful moral effect on the present state of mind of all the American people if we do adopt the budget plan of administering the Government, and through that action they

recognize that their Congress is preparing to transform the Government of their country, their Government, into something resembling a business organization, with its consequent saving.[4]

The few voices that questioned such optimism were quickly quieted and the bill was enacted into law giving the president the major responsibility for budget preparation of a consolidated document on the grounds that "He is the only officer of the administrative branch who is interested in the Government as a whole rather than in one particular part. He is the only administrative officer who is elected by the people and thus can be held politically responsible for his actions."[5]

In reading the select committee report that recommended the 1921 law with 65 years of hindsight it is significant to note (1) in that era of limited government, Congress viewed the individual cabinet and bureau officers rather than Congress itself as the president's opposition regarding what should be included in the budget and (2) the extent to which Congress convinced itself that the power to prepare the executive budget did not enhance executive power at the expense of legislative power.[6] Time has demonstrated the extent of these two congressional miscalculations as agreement between the president and Congress on budgetary content has not always been present and executive power has grown in budgetary matters largely at the expense of Congress.

Assigning responsibility to the president to submit a comprehensive budget plan for the entire executive branch which Congress would debate and then enact resulted in delegating to the president the establishment of a baseline from which decisions were to be made. The assumption that the presidentially-prepared executive budget would be an adequate point of departure against which to base the congressional review of the budget has proved a workable premise for most of the period since 1921.[7] This has been the case because budgets were largely "controllable" and presidents and Congresses have generally seen eye to eye through hot wars, cold wars, limited wars, recessions and prosperity on the size and general direction of annual budgets. The disagreements on details were worked out through a series of incremental changes as described by Wildavsky and Fenno in their pioneer works.[8] "Incrementalism" was the general rule of the day. However, there have been two periods when differences over budget priorities between the president and Congress were major issues and resulted in public battles.

During the early to mid 1970's when Republican President Nixon lacked the votes in either house of the Democratically controlled Congress to impose his priorities on the budget, he resorted to the practice of impounding funds, i.e., declining to spend appropriated funds on the grounds of "fighting inflation" or "controlling spending." The fact that these attempts were focused on programs that President Nixon opposed was not lost on his critics. After resorting to case-by-case law suits by individual members of Congress to force the spending of impounded funds, Congress as a whole resorted to a more permanent solution. It passed a law, the Budget and Impoundment Control Act of 1974, to clarify the conditions under which presidents could delay or refuse to spend appropriated funds. Mr. Nixon's departure from the presidency shortly thereafter put the final touch to this budgetary battle. In this case amending procedures had a positive effect in defusing conflict.

The second major set of budgetary battles between the two branches began in 1981 with the election of Ronald Reagan to the presidency. Except for the successful resort to the device of reconciliation in that first year, budgetary impasse has been the name of the game despite the fact that the Senate was controlled by the president's party between 1981 and 1986. At the base of the current budgetary confrontation is the persistent congressional reaction to the president's budget submissions as being unrealistic and unpassable documents. The current jargon is that the budget is "dead on arrival" or even "dead before arrival" on Capitol Hill. This implies that the budget document is simply the first proposal on the table and that serious negotiations and major compromise must follow. The president for his part usually refuses to negotiate a compromise at first, and holds to his position that the submitted executive budget truly reflects "his" position. When compromise is reached it comes after long delays and bitter negotiations. The authors of the 1921 law have had their way in the name of strengthening the chief executive and executive accountability. But a question may be raised as to who is really "responsible" for a budget that is perceived to be unrealistic in the light of current political realities by those called upon to enact it? Is this what the framers of the 1921 law had in mind? I doubt it.

WHY IT DOESN'T WORK

One major reason for these apparent differing perceptions regarding its utility is that the executive budget today is a far different document than it was a half century ago. The composition of the budget has changed drastically since 1921. Most of the current budget is locked in by previous decisions. Debt servicing and rising levels of entitlements are not susceptible to short-run changes through the appropriations process (approximately 60 percent of outlays in FY 1986 were in this category). They are indeed "uncontrollable" in the short run, therefore, not susceptible to change from year to year. In addition, budgetary programs are intertwined with the overall performance of the economy. This necessitates preparing assumptions regarding economic growth, inflation, unemployment and interest rates upon which to base budgetary estimates. Outcomes in the economy however, are not under government control and these have a direct affect on government outlays. As a result outlays often differ significantly from what was proposed in the budget and thereby reduce the utility and credibility of the budget submission. Regardless of agreement or disagreement the executive budget today offers less discretion and less opportunity for control by the executive that it did in previous years. Defense now remains the only major area of budgetary discretion.

What appears to be in order is a budget document prepared by a process that more closely reflects the political and economic realities of the day. It would also help the budget to be enacted if it did not embody every political issue of the day. This tends to cause the process to break down simply because of overload. One possibility out of the current impasse is to formulate a budget that reflects a legislative-executive consensus before the budget is prepared and submitted. Such a budget would represent a significant departure from the executive budget we now have. The executive budget concept is so widely accepted in public administration as the conventional tool for budgetary submission that to question it appears out of the question. It is used throughout all levels of government in this country, including most large cities and virtually all states—but there are exceptions.

Throughout most of our history we have looked at the several states as a logical testing place for innovation and reform. States tried new devices for governing, and it they worked the case could be made for adoption by other states or the federal government. In this sense states have been viewed as laboratories for testing new ideas about governing or as one recent source labeled them as " . . . experimental stations for social policy. . . ."[9] This is true regarding procedural changes as well as substantive policy measures. As a case in point the executive budget concept itself was a successfully tried at the state and local level before federal adoption of the idea in 1921. For a variety of reasons we have tended to neglect this source of innovation in recent years. Perhaps it would be worthwhile to examine how the states prepare their budgets to ascertain if there is something that works at that level which might be applicable to the federal level. Because a process or procedure is perceived "to work" at one level of government does not mean that it will necessarily be applicable to another level or in another setting. Nevertheless, despite differences in size, outlook and history, simply to ignore what the states are doing represents a degree of intellectual arrogance that we can ill afford.

The major fundamental differences in state budgeting when compared with federal budgetary practices have been discussed in the relevant literature. This list ordinarily includes capital budgeting, biennial budgets, line-item vetoes, balanced operating budgets, laws mandating budgetary equilibrium or growth limitations, differing fiscal years and restrictions on legislative changes to executive budgets. Of all these procedures biennial budgeting appears the most likely change that will be adopted at the federal level. In fact the Department of Defense submitted a biennial budget in FY 88–89. Beyond this usual litany, two states have what appear to be significantly different approaches to budget preparation—in effect departures from the traditional idea of an executive budget.[10]

ALTERNATIVE STATE MODELS

The two states that depart the most from the executive budget concept are South Carolina and Mississippi—both states with relatively "weak" governors (structurally, not personally). In the 1940s, V.O. Key quoting state politicians referred to South Carolina government as "legislative government."[11] These states' budget practices demonstrate rather ingenious methods to defuse budgetary conflict before it begins.

South Carolina has a State Budget and Control Board (BCB) which is composed of individuals from the executive and legislative branches. The board consists of the governor as chairman and four other members, who are also elected officials. They are the state treasurer, the comptroller general, the chairman of the Senate Finance Committee and the chairman of the House Ways and Means Committee. The board also has an independent staff.

The BCB staff assists in the development of revenue estimates for the state thereby setting the parameters for the budget. Since the South Carolina constitution precludes deficit spending these estimates become a critical part of budget preparation. The BCB staff also provides guidelines for agency budget preparation including monetary ceilings. The agencies prepare the budget requests and submit them to the BCB and after the BCB deliberates and makes its decisions, the budgets are returned to agencies by the BCB staff for preparation of a line-item detail budget. The line-item budget is incorporated into a General Appropriation Bill to be reviewed by the legislature and passed. After this sequence of events the budget is reviewed by the legislature (first the House and then the Senate), enacted and signed by the governor into law. The governor does have an "item veto" which enables him to exercise a degree of final flexibility over the appropriations.

The South Carolina Supreme Court upheld the constitutionality of the BCB in 1977 (*State, ex rel. McLeod v. Edwards,* 269 S.C. 75 at 84).[12] Since the BCB includes two key members of the legislative branch, the legislature is likely to approve the budget. In addition, the high degree of legislative involvement in the administration of state programs which is typical in South Carolina is further increased by BCB direct participation in the earliest stages of budget development.

The state of Mississippi has another unique system. In Mississippi there is a Joint Legislative Budget Committee whose membership consists of the president pro tem of the state senate, the lieutenant governor, chairman of the Senate Appropriations Committee, one member of the Senate designated by the lieutenant governor, chairman of the House Ways and Means Committee, chairman of the House Appropriations Committee, the Speaker of the House and two additional House members appointed by the Speaker. Governed by this committee is a Legislative Budget Office (LBO) which is mandated to prepare a balanced budget every year. The LBO requires all state agencies to file budget requests in a form and level of detail mandated by the LBO. The LBO then can reduce or eliminate any item requests. The office is authorized to conduct hearings in order to determine valid agency requirements. Notice of such proposed hearings is given to the governor's budget officer who may attend to look out for the governor's interest. Since 1984 the governor has the legal responsibility to submit a balanced budget to the LBO. Any recommendations from the governor that would unbalance the budget must include recommended revenue sources.

Obviously what works in South Carolina and Mississippi will not necessarily work anywhere else. After all 48 states do use a system closer to the executive budget. Overall, it is very unlikely that either the South Carolina or Mississippi approach to budget preparation would ever be adopted *in toto* at the federal level. They are detailed here only to demonstrate the imaginative type of approach that is used and works elsewhere. The moral of the story is simply that government does not collapse where chief executives share budget preparation responsibilities with the legislature.

While the details and specifics of these two states differ, the basic idea underlying such techniques for preparing the state budget are the same. They are attempts to overcome the built-in problems inherent in the separation of powers. In effect they represent a melding of the budgetary powers of the legislature and executive in an attempt to improve performance. The literature of political science reform is filled with ideas about how to overcome deadlocks in policy that appear to result from the separation of powers. The usual preferred solutions would take our federal system several steps closer to parliamentary government. However, such changes would require amending the Constitution. For this very reason the proposals rarely are taken seriously.

In discussing state governments the most recent *Book of the States* observes, "Considerable executive-legislative stress still exists in the budget process and in determining the role each branch should play in the development and implementation of the budget."[13] The same holds true at the federal level to the detriment of our ability to govern ourselves. Gramm-Rudman can only be understood in this context. According to David Stockman, one of the chief actors in the budget breakdowns of the 1980s, Gramm-Rudman was a "two-by-four" approach Congress used to send the president a message about the budgetary imbalance (spending vs revenues) after they were unable to communicate in a more reasonable manner.[14] Budgeting by two-by-four is a questionable way to do business. It certainly does not represent the separation of powers in the best light.

PROPOSAL: THE FEDERAL JOINT BUDGETARY COUNCIL

What is worth thinking about is to consider some version of the South Carolina-Mississippi concept of a joint legislative-executive council to decide what should be included in the annual federal budget submission. For example, I propose a council consisting of representatives of the president, secretary of Treasury, Speaker of the House, president pro tem of the Senate and comptroller general be established as a starting point. OMB and the Congressional Budget Office could act as honest brokers to develop common economic assumptions, perform the necessary calculation and project appropriate estimates of budgetary proposals in support of the Joint Budgetary Council. The basic objective of this council, or any similarly composed group, would be to develop a budget proposal that was "alive on arrival" on Capitol Hill and could be used as a recognized baseline against which Congress could make incremental adjustments. To facilitate agreement, the council would have to adopt certain limiting ground rules regarding the extent to which new program initiatives or program terminations could be included in the annual budget submission. Fisher aptly points out that today "There is chronic confusion about which budget is the budget: the president's, the first budget resolution, the second budget resolution, the second budget resolution revised or a succession of reestimates, updates, and revised baselines."[15] Fine tuning of existing policies from an agreed upon baseline is probably all the budget cycle can realistically accommodate on an annual basis within legislatively mandated time tables and fiscal year constraints.

Congress as an entity of 535 individuals cannot build a budget from the ground. It needs a viable starting place for its review and neither the budget resolutions nor executive budget has been a definitive enough starting place in recent years. Incrementalism as a decision-making tool has both its critics and advocates. Nevertheless, the extent to which the basic economic assumptions and programs are agreed upon, the more readily can incremental adjustments be reached. In reality since so much of the budget is "uncontrollable" and related to price level adjustments, we have a variation of this at present.[16] Why not recognize and build on it? Under a Joint Budgetary Council approach the debate over whether something is included in the budget would precede budget submission. This should help eliminate the inclusion of "pie in the sky" proposals such as to eliminate the Departments of Energy and Education from the budget submissions. Legislation for such change should of necessity be considered separately and in its own schedule and not clutter up the budget timetable.

Whether or not we have a Department of Energy is a policy question more than it is a budgetary question, although it certainly has budgetary aspects. When we try to saddle the budget with all the controversial issues on the political agenda we overload the budgetary system and increase the likelihood of missed deadlines and continuing resolutions. In summary, major changes to programs should be submitted by the administration to be considered as normal aspects of the legislative process. The impact of such proposals would not be included in the budget submission. The budget submission should be limited to incremental adjustments to all ongoing program within certain parameters (say ±5 percent or ±10 percent) agreed upon by a joint legislative executive council. For those programs such as debt payments, unemployment compensation and social security payments, the joint OMB/CBO projections determine the budgeted amount. If the council could agree on larger changes to specific programs there would be nothing to preclude it in exceptional cases.

As a residual benefit of such a procedure, a joint legislative-executive budget should eliminate the necessity that Congress pass any budget resolutions to establish the parameters of a "congressional budget." The budget when submitted could move directly to the authorization/appropriation process. This act alone should free numerous legislative hours currently diverted to wrangling with the president over budget priorities. In addition the budget could probably be submitted to Congress two or three months later than is now required. This later submission date should enhance the accuracy of budgetary projections because of closer proximity to the beginning of the budgetary fiscal year.

This approach if implemented by law certainly would not cause any great additional difficulty if the legislative and executive branches were controlled by the same political party. Similar practice already occurs informally when both branches are in agreement. In cases where the two branches are not in agreement as they have not been since 1981, the question can be asked, "Could this way of doing business be any worse than what we now have?" Something needs to be done to restore amity and stability to the budget process because similar budgetary problems are likely to continue for the remainder of the century. The public's confidence needs to be restored. Closing down the government for eight hours does little in this direction. Political battles are part of a healthy, democratic system but political posturing should not bring the workings government to a halt.

The issue might be raised as to whether or not such a joint legislative-executive council would run afoul of the separation of powers on Constitutional grounds. The answer is probably not although predicting Supreme Court decisions is a risky business especially when the Court tends to see the separation of powers as a rather mechanical process as described in the *Chadha* decision. As a country, we operated from 1787 to 1921 with an informal system that developed the so-called Book of Estimates based upon unwritten agreements and understandings between cabinet and bureau level officials and congressional committee chairman. While few would advocate a return to this type of freelance, undisciplined approach the overriding principle remains—members of the executive branch and members of the legislative branch can work together to determine the direction of budget policy.

CONCLUSION

There is not necessarily superior wisdom, a higher sense of purpose nor greater concern with execution of the laws in the executive branch than in the legislative branch or vice versa. As Fisher has stated, "The record is inescapable: long before the New Deal period or even the Budget and Accounting Act of 1921, Congress decided that fiscal accountability and control could not be safeguarded by vesting those powers solely in the President and his assistants."[17] Some authors find the recent trend toward reducing the "integrity and responsibility" of the executive budget as properly disturbing.[18] Equally disturbing however is persistent budgetary impasse that portends possible long-run economic disaster for the country. Recent congressional hearings on reform of the budget process continue to focus on proposals such as multi-year budgeting, consolidating the authorizing and appropriating functions, better economic assumptions and projections and a modified line-item veto authority.[19] The question remains as to whether this type of minor adjustment is enough.

The bottom line to this entire matter is that the executive budget no longer provides the advantages that its sponsors assumed in 1921. In fact it offers several disadvantages its sponsors never dreamed. Presidents and Congresses often have differing views on national needs as embodied in budgetary programs and priorities. Both views are legitimate and must be resolved through the political process where political power counts more than questions of administrative efficiency. New procedures and processes are needed and these can be achieved simply by amending the Budget and Accounting Act of 1921 to call for a joint legislative-executive council budget to replace the executive budget. The executive budget was not found inscribed in stone on some sacred mountain and discovered by Warren G. Harding of all people. It is time to rethink the concept and seriously consider alternatives such as the one offered in this paper.

NOTES

I would like to extend my thanks to Mr. William T. Putnam, former Executive Director of the State of South Carolina Budget & Control Board, who acquainted me with how that body operates and for having read an early version of this manuscript. The viewpoints and opinions expressed in this paper are mine and do not reflect the position of my employer.

1. *Budget of the United States, Fiscal Year 1987,* p. M-9.

2. *Budget of the United States, Fiscal Year 1988,* pp. M-12, M-13.

3. *U.S. Congressional Record,* 66th Congress, 2d Sess., (1920), Vol. 59, Part 6, 6280.

4. Ibid, 6350.

5. U.S. Congress, House of Representatives, Select Committee of the Budget, *National Budget System* (Washington: Government Printing Office, 1921) p. 5, 67th Congress, 1st Sess., Report No. 14, 5.

6. Ibid, 4–7.

7. A highly perceptive article by Naomi Caiden, "Paradox, Ambiguity, and Enigma: The Strange Case of the Executive Budget and the United States Constitution," *Public Administration Review,* 47 (Jan./Feb. 1987): 84–92, traces the evolution of the executive budget in this role and the reasons why it no longer fulfills its original purpose.

8. Aaron Wildavsky, *The Politics of the Budgetary Process* (Boston: Little, Brown and Company, 1964), and Richard Fenno, *The Power of the Purse* (Boston: Little, Brown and Company, 1966).

9. Robert B. Albretton and Ellen M. Dran, "Balanced Budgets and State Surpluses: The Politics of

Budgeting in Illinois," *Public Administration Review*, 47 (Mar./Apr. 1987): 143.

10. *The Book of the States 1986–87 edition*, (Lexington, Kentucky: The Council of State Governments, 1986), 220–1. The chart dealing with State Budgetary practices indicates three states have budget making authority rest with other than the governor. Mississippi, South Carolina and Texas are the three states (pp. 220–1). However, in Texas the agency responsible for preparing the budget document is the Director of Management and Budget in the governor's office. In the other two states budget making authority and budget preparation exist outside the Governor's office (pp. 223–4).

11. V.O. Key, Jr., *Southern Politics* (New York: Vintage Books, 1949), 150.

12. Luther F. Carter and David S. Mann, eds. *Government in the Palmetto State* (Columbia, S.C., University of South Carolina Bureau of Governmental Research and Service, 1983). 142–6.

13. *The Book of the States*, 29.

14. David A. Stockman, *The Triumph of Politics* (New York: Avon Books, 1987), 457.

15. Louis Fisher, "Ten Years of the Budget Act: Still Searching for Controls," *Public Budgeting & Finance*, 5 (Autumn, 1985): 26.

16. Bernard T. Pitsvada and Frank D. Draper, "Making Sense of the Federal Budget the Old Fashioned Way—Incrementally," *Public Administration Review*, 44, (Sep. / Oct. 1984): 401–406.

17. Louis Fisher, "The Administrative World of *Chadha* and *Bowsher*," *Public Administration Review*, 47 (May/June 1987): 215.

18. Louis Fisher, *Constitutional Conflicts between Congress and the President:* (Princeton: Princeton University Press, 1985). 7.

19. U.S., Congress, House of Representatives, Committee on Government Operations, Subcommittee on Legislation and National Security, *Reform of the Federal Budget process,* (Washington: Government Printing Office, 1987) 100th Congress, 1st Sess.

COMMENTS

NAOMI CAIDEN

Is the executive budget an idea whose time has passed? If so, what could replace it? Bernard Pitsvada presents a diagnosis and a proposal. The validity of his proposal would depend on the accuracy of his diagnosis of the problem and the extent to which the proposal remedies it. Briefly his argument runs like this.

The problem is the budgetary process of the United States government. It is complex and time consuming. It is conflict ridden and presently at an impasse that may last beyond the turn of the century. It is uncontrollable. To account for this state of affairs, Pitsvada turns to the executive budget whose assumptions, he contends, are no longer valid, if they ever were. The Budget and Accounting Act of 1921 assumed legislative-executive harmony, the ability of the executive to achieve efficiency and economy along business lines, and the executive budget as a primary means of gaining budgetary responsibility. Instead, in the context of the separation of powers, the budget process is vulnerable to breakdown arising out of executive-legislative conflict. Because of changes in budget composition, budgetary outcomes depend more on economic assumptions than an executive talent (let alone monopoly) for efficiency. And the current system actually encourages evasion rather than enforcement of budgetary responsibility. Pitsvada therefore suggests bringing executive and legislature together to settle the budgetary framework in advance, thus stabilizing key economic assumptions and budget parameters, and reducing the political overload on the budget.

Proposals for change almost inevitably stimulate objections. There is always someone who says it can't be done, it's naive and simplistic, or it will bring horrendous consequences. For a start, the transferability of institutions and processes from one context to another is fraught with difficulties. There are important differences between the budgetary climates of states like Mississippi and South Carolina, on the one hand, and that of the federal government on the other. To the extent that successful transplantation requires similarity of conditions in original and new settings, the proposal is probably doomed. The fact that these states are somewhat exceptional perhaps also contributes to the marginality of their modes of operation. However, Gramm-Rudman demonstrates that less likely things have come to pass, so ideas should not be condemned out of hand for their origins!

A more telling objection lies in the separation of powers. The narrow constitutional issue (which would be up to the courts to decide) is of less significance than questions of function and power. For example, it has been asserted that Congress and the presidency are different in nature. The former fulfills a primarily representative function: it is an institution in which power is dispersed. The executive, on the other hand, concentrates power in a hierarchical organization. Some have contended that this distinction implies that the executive alone is appropriate for budget making and that the legislature should not imitate it either in process or intent. A budget is by definition an "executive" budget.

More troubling is the question of power. The essence of the separation of powers doctrine is that one branch of government checks the other, preventing monopoly of power by either. Since Congress and the president share a number of functions, one implication of the separation of powers is an adversary system of government. The 1921 act both blurred and emphasized this characteristic. It blurred potential interbranch conflict by assuming that there was a neutral apolitical executive budgetary role. Later developments that elevated the budget to a key policymaking instrument emphasized the potential for conflict between president and Congress should there be serious policy differences between them. For the executive budget notwithstanding, the Constitution gave Congress the power of the purse.

Whatever the defects of the separation of powers as a system of government, there appears to be no general mandate for replacing it with a parliamentary-cabinet system, where the executive is drawn from and responsible to the legislature. Discussions of budget reform have to take respective executive and legislative autonomy as given. The Pitsvada proposal, by taking key budgetary decisions out of the realm of either president or Congress, potentially changes the balance of power between them. In particular, it would seem that Congress might lose considerable power over the budget, since it would be required to defer to a joint legislative-executive council whose membership did not necessarily represent its view or structure. The views of House or Senate, let alone party interests, are not easily represented by a single representative of each. Alternatively it might be held that the president might lose power because he would be outvoted on the council, three to two, by the representatives of Congress. In any case, it seems that the adversary system of checks and balances would be undercut by creation of a body in a position to dictate policy to both branches of government, in probable contravention of constitutional intent.

Successful solutions require accurate diagnoses. Even if (and it would be a big "if") the constitutional and balance of powers objections could be overcome, there would still be the question of whether the problem of the United States budget could be cured through reforms of procedures. Do the roots of current budget difficulties—intractable deficits, prolonged deadlocks, unfinished business, and irrelevant budgets—lie in processes or politics? In proposing a process solution, it would seem initially that Pitsvada believes that the procedures are at fault and that their reform would resolve the problems. Processes structure behavior, establish decision rules, and at least to some degree influence outcomes. They provide opportunities and impose constraints.

PROCESS OR POLITICS

But Pitsvada himself expresses doubts about whether the problem is really one of process. The budgetary difficulties of the United States are paralleled by those in many other Western industrialized countries and stem from slowing economic growth, built-in budgetary inflexibility, and political dissension. The real issues—who pays and who gets, public versus private goods and services, the direction of the economy—cannot be solved through simple reform of processes. These issues involve not only political preferences and deeply held values, in addition to purely cynical political games played for political advantage, but also an economic and social reality, whose dynamics are but poorly understood.

Pitsvada's solution to the political problem of the budget is, essentially, to eliminate it. He calls for "[a] budget that can be enacted because it does not embody every political issue of the day and does not break down simply because of political overload." Remind you of something? Yes, this is the once-upon-a-time conflict-limiting process graphically described by Allen Schick at the beginning of *Congress and Money*. "Despite the potential for open and protracted strife," he told us, "the federal budget is decided each year. . . . Among the factors working to limit conflict are the budget's one-year-at-a-time approach, concentrating on the increment rather than on the total budget, avoiding explicit determination of budget priorities, and tolerating second-best—or worse—outcomes. The budget ordinarily is peacefully negotiated because the price of extended disagreement is unacceptably high to the major participants. . . . Budget makers are schooled in the necessities of accommodation."[1]

But the limits of "prudent dispute" analyzed by Schick have long ago disappeared. Debates include long-term implications of decisions and the shape of the budget as a whole. Budget cutting requires discussions of base as well as (or instead of) increment. Budget priorities are on the table, and the opportunity cost of extended disagreement is less than the political costs of unacceptable agreement. The budget process, for better or worse, has ceased to be a contained stable affair, ruled by mutual agreements that avoid the necessity even to mention basic issues. It is now an open process, and a primary focus for achievement of political goals that previously did not even exist on the national political agenda. Can we put the genie back in the bottle and depoliticize the budget? Is it possible, in the current political climate, to find sufficient agreement on basic questions to relegate budget decisions once more to the margin?

Can process legislate consensus and responsibility? Pitsvada finds the essence of "the budgetary process problem" in the false assumption of the framers of the 1921 act that the executive would, by definition, act responsibly in formulating the executive budget. The executive budget would act as a valid point of departure for Congress in passing the appropriations acts. Accordingly the budgetary problem appears to lie in the disappearance of the executive budget as an acceptable point of departure, and the marked tendency of the whole process to deadlock where one party, viz the executive, takes an obdurate stand.

The possibility of deadlock is intrinsic in the separation of powers in which one branch of government is deliberately set in a position to check the other. It is also a characteristic of what has been at least up to now a policy-neutral budgetary process that does not dictate outcomes. Both Congress and president are essentially free from process constraints in setting whatever budget policies they like in accordance with their political agendas. (Gramm-Rudman has somewhat departed from that tradition in setting definite substantive limits to executive and legislative actions.) Responsibility, viability and acceptability have been a function of politics not process. Thus, the opening up of a large structural deficit and the persistent inability to deal with it may be related to executive-legislative deadlock and executive irresponsibility, but they are also related to deeper political trends including what appears to have been a general preference on the part of the electorate for borrowing instead of taxation.

FACING REALITIES

Beyond questions of executive-legislative conflict lies the real world of the budget. The deficit itself highlights the inflexibility of the federal budget and the difficulties in influencing its direction. The major part of the budget is composed of four big ticket items: social security and other pensions, health related expenditures, defense, and interest on the national debt. The focused nature of expenditures is illustrated by the phenomenon that, in spite of the lengthy complex budget process, the real decision making appears to take place through negotiations on relatively few, though irreconcilable, issues after the final deadline. Unless agreement is made to influence these major categories, little can be done from the aspect of expenditures to meet the deficit or control fiscal policy. In the absence of willingness or ability to cut these items significantly, it will be necessary to find revenues to finance them. The crisis brought about by past policies now requires addressing basic issues of allocation and distribution: entitlements, subsides, loans and loan guarantees, the share of national wealth devoted to defense, the current and future costs of debt, and acceptable and stable sources of revenue. A period of megadeficits, doubling of the national debt. and increasing complexity of processes has generated an agenda for a virtual reconstitution of public finance. The annual budget, as Schick suggests, is probably not the most appropriate instrument for this kind of task.

Meanwhile, recent budgets have had a poor record. The changes in budget composition have contributed to budgetary sensitivity. Budget outcomes depend less on planned amounts than on the behavior of the economy. For several years, actual deficits have exceeded planned deficits by large amounts.[2] The accuracy of budget assumptions has become crucial, but even relatively small misestimates of economic growth, unemployment, inflation or interest rates may have large effects on revenues and expenditures. The sound and fury of the budget debates exist for nothing if the predictive capacity of the budget is so poor as to be irrelevant.

A third problem that has so far occasioned little debate is the size of unexpended balances. There are now over a trillion dollars, approximately equal to a single year's budget, that have accumulated from past appropriations. If trust funds, guarantee and insurance programs, long-term housing programs and certain Treasury reserves are deducted, this would still leave nearly $400 billion in civil balances and about $200 billion in defense balances. These balances, particularly those for defense, have grown sharply during the 1980s and raise significant problems for budget control now and in the future.[3]

The question may therefore be not whether there is still an executive budget, but whether there is really a budget at all, at least in the terms we know it. A budget may be through of as a set of rules for resolving conflicts within a given time frame. But the formal rules are fragile: they depend upon willingness to abide by them, mutual understanding of acceptable limits, and an appreciation of reality beyond political rhetoric, manipulation and posturing. Where these qualities are not available, budget processes break down. Budget rules enable; they do not compel in the absence of willingness to uphold them. Perhaps this is why in recent years procedural reforms have added complexity to the budget process, without augmenting its strength.

NOTES

1. Allen Schick, *Congress and Money: Budgeting, Spending and Taxing* (Washington, D.C.: Urban Institute, 1980), 19.

2. Lance LeLoup, Barbara Luck Graham and Stacey Barwick, "Deficit Politics and Constitutional Government: The Impact of Gramm-Rudman-Hollings," *Public Budgeting & Finance* 7 (Spring 1987): 85.

3. See United States General Accounting Office, "Budget Issues: Governmentwide Analysis of the Growth in Unexpended Balances," Briefing Report to the Chairman, Task Force on the Budget Process, Committee on the Budget, U.S. House of Representatives, GAO/AFMD—86–24BR (Washington. D.C.: GAO, Jan. 1986).

COMMENTS

Louis Fisher

In a budget era dominated by high-tech, computerization, and convoluted procedures, Bernard Pitsvada focuses on fundamental principles. Rather than dwell on the endless complexities of the congressional budget process, he takes us back to the objectives of the Budget and Accounting Act of 1921. He reminds us that the purpose of that statute was to fix responsibility on the president for the submission of agency estimates. Through this concentration of power it was hoped that budgeting would become more economical, efficient, and accountable. From one of the congressional reports leading to this landmark legislation he identifies the reason for delegating power to the president: "He is the only officer of the administrative branch who is interested in the Government as a whole rather in one particular part. He is the only administrative officer who is elected by the people and thus can be held politically responsible for his actions."

With the exception of two periods that Mr. Pitsvada identifies, the principles of the 1921 statute were effective in extracting the best from both branches. The president would be responsible for submitting a unified budget and taking responsibility for the aggregates: spending, revenues, and the deficit or surplus. Congress generally stayed within those aggregates but had full freedom to alter the president's priorities, moving funds from one area to another. Both branches accomplished what they were institutionally designed to do. As Pitsvada notes: "The assumption that the presidentially prepared executive budget would be an adequate point of departure against which to base the congressional review of the budget has proved a workable premise for most of the period since 1921."

The two exceptions were the impoundment battles during the Nixon administration and the budgetary deadlock during the Reagan years. In recent years, it has been characteristic of Congress to treat Reagan's budgets as "unrealistic and unpassable." Why is the President's budget no longer "an adequate point of departure?" Why are we unable to fix responsibility on the president? If the president refuses to submit a responsible budget, can Congress—given its institutional capabilities—take up the slack? Pitsvada compares this state of affairs with the intentions of the 1921 act: "a question may be raised as to who is really 'responsible' for a budget that is perceived to be unrealistic in the light of current political realities by those called upon to enact it? Is this what the framers of the 1921 law had in mind? I doubt it." I agree.

THE 1980s BUDGET PROCESS

The difference between the budgets of the 1920s and the 1980s, Pitsvada says, is partly explained by the composition of the budget. Because of interest on the debt and entitlement spending, current budgets are more "uncontrollable." The executive budget "today offers less discretion and less opportunity for control by the executive than it did in previous years. Defense now remains the only major area of budgetary discretion."

This point is well taken, but it does not adequately explain the difference between the 1920s and the 1980s. President Reagan, in 1981, made one of the most radical shifts we have ever had in budgeting: sharp increases in defense spending, modest reductions in domestic programs, deep cuts in taxes, and an astounding increase in deficits. I would argue that the congressional budget process since 1974 allows for more drastic changes than the "disjoined, fragmented, and splintered" process it replaced. Under the right circumstances, which is what we had in 1981, the national budget can undergo sweeping changes.

Consider what was done in 1981. Reagan carried 44 states in the 1980 elections, winning 489 out of 538 electoral votes. The strength of his coattails allowed the Republicans to control the Senate for the first time in 28 years and pick up 33 seats in the House of Representatives. With Republicans committed to strict party loyalty in the Senate, and a Reagan majority stitched together in the House by combining Republicans with conservative Democrats, Reagan was poised to revolutionize the budget. His tactical decision to concentrate on budget priorities, combined with his communication skills and dramatic recovery from the assassination attempt on March 30, produced stunning victories with the budget resolution, tax cut, and reconciliation bill.

These were sizeable benefits, but Reagan's victory depended on something else. Under the previous congressional budget system, where he would have had to compromise with all the competing committee systems—authorization, appropriations, and tax—it is unlikely that the administration's program would have survived. Rudolph Penner, CBO director, asked in 1985: "Would the dramatic actions of 1981 have been possible without the process? It is a question that no one will ever be able to answer with certainty. I believe, however, that it would have been difficult to achieve these results using the old, muddled way of formulating budgets." Penner concluded that Reagan would have had a tougher time getting his budget through the decentralized committee structure that existed before 1974. Allen Schick has made the same point, noting that Congress is at an advantage when it forces the president to seek accommodations through a fragmented legislative process.

The incremental quality of congressional budgeting prior to 1974 acted as a brake on radical changes. In contrast, the centralized system of the Budget Act of 1974 played into Reagan's hands. If the administration could gain control of the budget resolution, which it did, it could dictate basic policies on taxation and spending. In his book, *The Triumph of Politics,* David Stockman explains how the administration exploited the centralized congressional budget process. The constitutional prerogatives of Congress "Would have to be, in effect, suspended. Enacting the Reagan Administration's economic program meant rubber stamp approval, nothing less. The world's so-called greatest deliberative body would have to be reduced to the status of a ministerial arm of the White House."

The results of 1981 suggest that the concept of an executive budget had reached its zenith. This is an illusion. As Pitsvada correctly notes, the executive budget has been in decline for years, especially the notion of having the president submit a budget for which he would be responsible, a budget carefully combed and scrutinized by experts in the executive branch. The process of 1981 made a mockery of the latter goal. Stockman admitted, in his book, that the administration was flying blind with its supply-side theory: "a plan for radical and abrupt changes required deep comprehension—and we had none of it."

A FAILURE OF RESPONSIBILITY

Even worse, the idea of the president taking responsibility for the budget he submits has almost totally disappeared. The record since 1981 is one of Reagan submitting a budget and quickly distancing himself from it, almost before it has reached Capitol Hill. No president can take responsibility, in any real sense, for budgets that project deficits in the $200 billion range for years in a row, and yet that is what Reagan did. I know of no administration in which there has been such a total absence of responsibility and accountability at the presidential level.

How did this happen? I think part of the answer lies in the congressional budget process adopted in 1974. In reasserting its power of the purse, Congress inadvertently undermined the president's accountability. Congress assumed responsibility for more than it could discharge. During floor debate in 1983, House Majority Leader Jim Wright made this remarkable rebuttal of those who claimed that an amendment to a pending appropriations bill was "over budget." He denied that the bill was over the budget: "the amounts proposed in this amendment are well within the budgeted figures. The amounts that we have agreed to and discussed are not in excess of the congressional budget resolution. That, of course, is the budget. Now they may be in excess of certain amounts requested by the president in his budget request of last January. But that, of course, is not the budget. Congress makes the budget; the president does not."

From 1921 to 1974 the question "Is this above budget or below budget?" had meaning. There was only one budget: the president's. The budget reform of 1974 spawned many budgets: the president's, the first budget resolution, the second budget resolution, the second budget resolution revised (passed the following spring), and a seemingly endless array of other budgets to keep current with changing baselines, reestimates, and updates. The phrases "above budget" and "below budget" have lose their meaning.

The resulting confusion has produced substantial cost to democratic government. Voters can no longer fix responsibility. Members claim that amendments "are well within the budgeted figures," neglecting to say which budget is referred to. Instead of staying within the president's aggregates, members can vote generous ceilings in a budget resolution and then announce to their constituents that they have "stayed within the budget." The White House can play this game also. In 1985, President Reagan indicated that he "would accept appropriations bills, even if above my budget, that were within the limits set by Congress' own budget resolution."

Budget reformers in 1974 believed that requiring Congress to vote on a single budget resolution, rather than a multitude of appropriations, authorization, and tax bills, would force members to behave more responsibly. They would have to vote on totals, not parts. The fragmented congressional budget process was condemned in favor of centralized, systematic, and coherent legislative action. Reformers praised such words as "coordination" and "unified budget process." If the president had a centralized process, Congress would have one too.

There is great danger when one branch tries to imitate another. The president is head of an executive branch fortified by a central budget office. There is no head in Congress and no comparable powers for CBO. Congress is inherently decentralized and no amount of procedural innovations can change that basic character. The overall effect of the Budget Act of 1974 had been to undermine the president's budget as a responsible target for aggregates. Reagan essentially says to Congress: "Here is a budget $200 billion in debt. You figure it out." Congress accepts the challenge but lacks the institutional ability to deliver. We've reached the point where the stock market has to fall 500 points in a day before leaders from the two branches will sit down and talk.

Pitsvada challenges us to think about fundamentals. This is not the time to add on additional procedures and techniques, ranging from item-veto authority to capital budgeting to biennial budgeting to whatever. The process we have is flawed in its essentials. The voters cannot hold either branch accountable. The president points to Congress, but an inherently decentralized legislative branch cannot be held accountable like a single president. The authors of the 1921 act knew that. We need to restore a budget process that takes advantage of the institutional strengths of both branches. As a single executive officer assisted by a central budget bureau, the president is ideally positioned to take responsibility for aggregates. Congress is institutionally capable of staying within the president's aggregates but changing his priorities.

The present system plays on institutional weaknesses. By looking to Congress for comprehensive action, we unwittingly sapped the unity and leadership that must come from the president. By creating a system of many budgets, we opened the door to escapism, confusion, and unaccountability. How to recreate in the budget process a clear sense of institutional responsibility and capability is a central issue for the coming decade. A good place to start is to reexamine the congressional budget process of 1974, making whatever changes are necessary to restore presidential accountability for aggregates. What is the purpose of passing budget resolutions? What are their costs in terms of exhausting time and creating confusion? How many Gramm-Rudmans do we have to pass before concluding that the 1974 experiment was a failure?

COMMENTS

LANCE T. LELOUP

Through the budget turmoil of the 1980s, many aspects of the federal budget process have been attacked. The executive budget itself, however, has been a sacred cow for nearly seventy years. If anything, critics of the budget mess have advocated strengthening the president and his executive budget. Frustrated with the budget stalemate of recent years, Bernard Pitsvada is ready to send that sacred cow to the slaughter house. His specific remedies to the problems fall short, however, because they fail to confront the underlying causes of budget stalemate in the 1980s. He has performed an important service, however, since his provocative proposals provide an opportunity to examine the basis of budget deadlock, consider major budget developments, and think about meaningful ways to improve the budget process in the United States.

Like many other observers, Pitsvada has grown weary of the budgetary gridlock that has pervaded the decade. Late night sessions in the wee hours of the fiscal new year, endless continuing resolutions, debt ceilings used as a loaded gun to force a political agenda, are all behind his frustration with recent budget battles. Yet unlike most critics, Pitsvada does not point an accusing finger at Congress and its unstable budget procedures. Quite unconventionally, he blames the executive budget process and goes so far as to suggest that the executive budget is an anachronism today. In diagnosing the cause of budgetary distress, however, Pitsvada's analysis is as fundamentally flawed as those who lay the blame exclusively on Congress. Procedural chaos and instability is a symptom, not a cause. The roots of budgetary stalemate are threefold: (1) the transformation of the budget over the past two decades, (2) the profound ideological cleavages which have polarized executive and legislative branches, and (3) the underlying structure of American political institutions.

The transformation of the budget has forced a painful and only partially complete revolution in how budgets are made: from a microlevel budget process to one where macrolevel concerns dominate. These new demands of budgeting confront the 200-year-old constitutional structure of separated but shared powers which is so often characterized by governability problems and stalemate. Fundamental conflicts arise from ideological divergence over the role and scope of government, appropriate levels of taxation, and relative defense and domestic spending priorities. While procedural problems in both branches may have exacerbated conflict, they have not created it. As a result, neither an overhaul of the congressional budget process nor the scrapping of the concept of the executive budget will eliminate conflict or produce the rational consensus-building model that Pitsvada envisions.

THE STRUCTURAL TRANSFORMATION OF THE BUDGET MAKES INCREMENTALISM IRRELEVANT

Pitsvada acknowledges some of the changes in federal budgeting such as the growth of uncontrollable spending, but largely misses the significance of their impact. He insists on clinging to the outmoded and theoretically unproductive concepts of incrementalism in analyzing the budget. In this essay and in a 1984 article in *Public Administration Review,* he proves beyond a doubt that, for some, all budgets are by definition "incremental" since they change little from year to year. Meaningful prescriptions for reform depend on recognizing and understanding the profound changes in the budget in the past two decades.

Macrobudgeting (high-level decisions on spending, revenue and deficit aggregates and relative budget shares, often made from the top-down) has become increasingly prevalent in both the executive and legislative branches. Microbudgeting (intermediate level decisions on agencies, programs, and line-items, usually made from the bottom-up) remains a critical if less compelling part of the budget process. With the exception of a few diehard incrementalists, political science theorists now generally recognize the critical importance of macrolevel decisions in explaining the politics and outcomes of budgeting. Important developments, including the expansion of entitlements, tax expenditures, off-budget activities, the growing importance of projections and estimates, and the increased vulnerability of budget totals to the performance of the economy, are well documented in the literature.

Prior to 1974, the president was the only budgetary participant involved in macrobudgeting, even though the executive budget process remained primarily bottom-up. Congress moved towards macrobudgeting with the adoption of the Budget and Impoundment Control Act of 1974. Top-down macrobudgeting was emphasized in the early years of the Reagan administration under Budget Director David Stockman. Many have argued that top-down macrobudgeting in the executive branch failed; it made haphazard cuts in domestic programs, gave the Pentagon a blank check, and produced record deficits. Yet recent history should make it clear that the solution in this brave new budgetary world is not to abandon the executive budget. Quite the contrary, it is apparent that the macrobudgeting capabilities of both legislative and executive branches need to be strengthened. Given this background, what can one conclude about Pitsvada's specific proposals?

TIMING AND UNCERTAINTY PRECLUDE EARLY AGREEMENT

Pitsvada notes that in recent years, President Reagan's budgets have been "dead on arrival." That is true, but perhaps the model for the executive budget process in the 1980s should be 1981, not the deadlock of subsequent years. For once the deficits were created and the lines were drawn on both sides, stalemate ensued. Would the proposal that the U.S. eliminate the executive budget and replace it with a legislative-executive council have changed the situation then or now? No.

One reason surrounds changes in timing resulting from growing uncertainty over the numbers. As uncertainty in making budget estimates and projections has increased and as the budget has become more vulnerable to changes in the economy, decisions on key budget aggregates have been made later and later. Gramm-Rudman institutionalized the rationality of delay despite advancing the official deadlines in the congressional budget timetable. It makes little sense for Congress to make tough choices until the final numbers are arrived at in August. Recognizing the continuing conflict in priorities that has helped cause budget stalemate, how could congressional and White House negotiators possibly arrive at a meaningful consensus at this early stage?

Disagreements over taxes, spending cuts, and deficits have been so pervasive that only the onset of an imminent budget crisis and threat of government shutdown have spurred compromise. It took a stock market crash to finally get the president to the deficit bargaining table. Even then, it took negotiators over five weeks (and only hours before Gramm-Rudman cuts took effect) to arrive at the outline of a package. It seems ludicrous to imagine that negotiators could resolve those differences as much as a year, let alone months, before they are forced to.

STATE-NATIONAL BUDGET INCOMPARABILITY

The American states have often been a source of policy innovation and experimentation that later affects national policy. Current welfare reform proposals are a recent example of this. But in terms of the budget, Pitsvada's proposals also founder because of fundamental differences between budgeting at the state and national levels. And the differences have increased since 1921. The use of the federal budget as a tool of fiscal policy in the 1930s created a permanent gulf between state and national budgets. While zero-base budgeting was first introduced at the state level, it appears to have had relatively little impact at either level of government. Today, with the greater demands of macrobudgeting and managing the aggregates, the experiences of Mississippi and South Carolina are even less relevant to national budgeting than they would have been twenty years ago.

The portion of the federal budget relevant to what Pitsvada calls "orthodox public administration theory" is now but a small portion of federal outlays. What most people think of as government agencies and their programs—nondefense discretionary spending—constitute well under 20 percent of outlays. The rest of the expenditure side consists of interest, entitlements, and defense, all of which are dealt with in fundamentally different ways. Priorities can and do clash in the states. But outlays for education, highways, health—like nondefense discretionary spending—are substantially different than the majority of federal outlays today.

The existence of huge federal deficits make budgets at the state and national level barely comparable. Even though most states with balanced budget requirements deficit spend through bond issues and other forms of borrowing, the scope of the deficit problem makes decisions making at the two levels light years apart. Federal budgeters try to manage revenue and outlay aggregates in an attempt to reduce structural deficits. This is more difficult, and hence more contentious, than the problem in states of estimating revenues and making microlevel adjustments in state appropriations.

LOOKING FOR MEANINGFUL REFORMS

Pitsvada has made an honest attempt to propose a solution to a problem that has troubled many people in recent years. I share his concern with the budget deadlock that threatens the credibility of both Congress and the president as well as the health of the world economy. Yet as social scientists, we must be hardheaded about causes and effects so we can distinguish between meaningful reforms and naive panaceas.

Pitsvada concludes by noting that "the executive budget no longer provides the advantages that its sponsors assumed in 1921." That is indeed true because, as we have seen, the nature of the budget and the budget process has changed. Warren Harding would not recognize the budget today. The motivations for the executive budget in 1921, such as fiscal accountability and integrity, are now largely beside the point. Interest payments, defense, entitlements, and deficits have made such concerns seem antiquated, having driven them out along with more recent anachronisms such as PPB and ZBB. But it simply does not follow that the executive budget should be abandoned. Because budgeting has become more of a macrolevel process, the executive budget process is more critical now than ever. It needs to be adapted, not discarded.

We cannot simply convene a joint legislative-executive council and wish away fundamental conflicts and institutional deadlock. If solutions are to be found, they must attack the basis of budgetary stalemate in the first place. Strengthening macro budgeters—budget committees, congressional party leaders, OMB, and the president—is important but can only be part of the answer. The answer is not the line-item veto, the balanced budget amendment or other proposals to strengthen the presidency at the expense of Congress. Reform of the executive budget process should focus on institutionalizing top-down budgeting but so it can be applied more selectively than the heavy-handed, indiscriminate process utilized by Stockman in 1981–82. Reform in the Congress should continue to strengthen the budget process. Despite all the criticism, Gramm-Rudman and its revision adopted in 1987, strengthen macrobudgeters in Congress and weakens the appropriations committees.

The short-term solution to budget stalemate may be political; electing a president and Congress of the same party. Divided party control of Congress and the presidency is an open invitation to fiscal irresponsibility. Budget deficits have topped 3 percent of GNP almost exclusively under conditions of divided government. The long-term solution may be more structural; making more radical reforms in the Constitution, Congress, the presidency, parties and elections. Short of that, and faced with divided government and clashing partisan priorities, it may continue to take financial panic or economic crisis to break the budget impasse.

CHAPTER 6

THE END OF EXECUTIVE DOMINANCE IN STATE APPROPRIATIONS

GLENN ABNEY AND THOMAS P. LAUTH

By the middle of the 20th century, governors dominated the state budgeting process (Anton, 1966, 34–35; Howard, 1973, 318; Sharkansky, 1968, 1231; Rosenthal, 1981, 299–300). Starting with a constitutional amendment in Maryland in 1916 (Willoughby, 1918), the introduction of the executive budget in the states gave governors the capacity to direct and control state financial matters (Schick, 1971, 18). By the decades of the 1950s and 1960s, most states had adopted the executive budget, giving governors a decided advantage in the appropriation process. Governors became the dynamic factor in state political systems while legislatures were inefficient and parochial (Moe, 1988, 18). The legislative dominance of the appropriations process in place in the 19th century had clearly come to an end. Our contention is that as the 20th century ends so has gubernatorial dominance of the state appropriations process. This article examines this decline, the reasons for it, and the consequences of it.

Beginning in the 1970s, state legislatures underwent a resurgence as they became more professional (Moe, 1988, 12). In a survey of state legislative and executive budget officials in 1982, Abney and Lauth (1987) found that gubernatorial dominance in the appropriations process was not as pronounced as might be expected. In that study, 52 of the officials surveyed reported the governor to be more influential compared to 38 who cited the legislature as more influential. In 14 states both legislative and executive officials identified the governor as more influential compared to nine states in which both officials said the legislature was more influential. In noting the surprising influence of the legislature, they cited the observation of Rosenthal (1981, 206) that legislatures came to the budgetary process far better prepared than in earlier years.

Based on the results of a survey of state executive and legislative officials conducted in 1994, we find that this trend has continued and that gubernatorial dominance appears to be over. Altogether, in 1994 we received responses from 99 of the 100 chief executive and legislative budget officials; only the chief executive official in Massachusetts declined to participate. Of our 99 respondents, 36 indicated that the governor is more influential in the appropriations process, 32 cited the legislature as more influential, and 31 stated that they are about equal. Surprisingly, executive officials were not particularly more likely to perceive the governor as more influential than were legislative

Table 6.1

Perceptions of Relative Gubernatorial Influence by Type of Budget Official

Relative Influence	Executive Officers	Legislative Officers	All Officers
	(N = 49)	(N = 50)	(N = 99)
Governor is more influential	19	17	36
Influence is equal	15	16	31
Legislature is more influential	15	17	32

The respondents were asked the following question: In comparing the influence of the governor and the legislature, who has the greater influence? (A) The governor has greater influence; (B) the influence of each is about the same; or (C) the legislature has greater influence.

Table 6.2

Perceptions of Relative Influence in State Appropriations by State

Perceptions of Both Respondents by State

Both cited governor	Lean to governor	Divided to legislature	Lean to legislature	Both cited legislature
HI	AR	IA	CT	AL
IN	CA	MI	ID	AK
KY	DE	MN	ME	AZ
LA	GA	NH	MT	CO
MD	IL	ND	NE	FL
NJ	KS	OH	NM	MA
PA	MO	WA	NC	MS
TN	NV	WV	OR	OK
VT	NY		SC	TX
WI	RI		UT	
	SD			
	VA		WY	

The perceptions of the two respondents from each state were averaged. Massachusetts had only one respondent. Where a state is designated as leaning to the governor or legislature, one respondent cited the influence of the two as equal, and the other respondent cited the governor or legislature as more influential.

respondents (see Table 6.1). The similarity of the perceptions in regard to relative gubernatorial influence supports our conclusion that the dominance of the governor in the appropriations process documented at mid-century has ended.

As seen in Table 6.2, combining the perceptions of the two respondents from each state gives further evidence of this parity. When we averaged the observations of both officials from the same state, the two officials in 22 states either leaned toward the governor or both cited the governor as more influential. Officials in 20 states either leaned toward the legislature or both cited the legislature as more influential. Of the 21 states where both officials agreed as to relative ranking, in 10 states the respondents said the governor was dominant, and in 9 states both respondents cited the legislature as being dominant.

These changes in relative influence have not gone unnoticed. In his *Governors and Legislatures,* Rosenthal (1990, 201) described the changes in the competition between the two branches as follows:

What is new about the institutional bases of conflict is the sense of independence and the assertiveness of legislatures nowadays, and the defensive posture assumed by governors. Legislatures are breaching the invisible boundary between the two branches; governors are doing their utmost to draw the constitutional line and repel such incursions. The National Governors Association notes that its members have been expressing strong concern about the intrusion of the legislature into executive activities.

REASONS FOR THE DECLINE

We believe that the end of gubernatorial dominance in the state appropriations process has resulted from at least four factors. All of the factors relate to a reduction in the advantage given to governors by the executive budget. First, legislative reforms have resulted in governors' losing the ability to control the appropriations agenda—an advantage that the executive budget had given them. Second, the item veto has not generally given governors the ability to protect the executive budget from legislative encroachment. Third, the rise of greater party division between the branches in state government has increased legislative resistance to gubernatorial leadership. Fourth, states have generally not adopted reforms guaranteeing the significance and independence of the executive budget.

We lack longitudinal data to document the decline in gubernatorial influence or to relate the decline to the above factors. We can show that relative gubernatorial influence is related to the above factors. Also, we know that these factors have either changed during this period or have not developed in a manner so as to protect gubernatorial advantage.

Proposition 1. Governors have lost the ability to control the appropriations agenda.

Beginning in 1916, executive budget reform swept the nation. By the 1950s, most of the states had an executive budget in place. This power to assemble and propose an executive budget gave governors a distinct advantage over the legislature, especially in regard to information and ability to define the legislative agenda. The importance of the executive budget in maintaining gubernatorial influence continues. When our respondents were asked to indicate the factors affecting gubernatorial influence, 84 of the 99 budget officials cited the executive budget as an important factor; half cited it as the most important factor.

The executive budget gave governors an informational advantage. In the last 40 years, however, the increased capabilities of the legislative branch have offset that advantage (Balutis and Butler, 1975; Rosenthal, 1990, 140). Only 11 legislatures had a budgetary staff in 1955 (Council of State Governments, 1956). Today, all of the state legislatures have budgetary staff. This change has undermined gubernatorial domination of information.

The roles of the governor as chief executive officer and in many respects as chief budget officer may always place legislatures at a disadvantage in information. Yet, in 29 of the 50 states legislative budget officials indicated that legislatures had independence in information from the governor; 47 of the 99 respondents indicated such independence. Specifically, the respondents agreed with a statement characterizing the appropriation process in the legislature in the following manner: "The legislature is largely independent of the governor in regard to budgetary information."

This legislative capability has undermined the informational advantage of the governor and is probably a factor in the declining influence of governors. Our data indicate that those respondents citing legislative independence were more likely to perceive legislative bodies as more influential.

Of the 47 respondents citing legislative independence in information, 19 (41 percent) said the legislature is more influential compared to a similar response by 13 of the 52 respondents (25 percent) not reporting such independence. When given a list of factors affecting gubernatorial influence in the appropriations process, only 30 percent of the respondents cited gubernatorial superiority in information as a factor. Of the respondents citing such superiority as a factor, 63 percent indicated the governor to be more influential compared to 25 percent of the other respondents. Informational superiority matters, but the bias is much less in favor of governors now than at mid-century.

Proposition 2. The failure of the item veto to protect the executive budget from legislative control has exacerbated the governor's difficulty in the appropriations process.

Contemporary proponents of the item veto cite its ability to reduce governmental deficits and curtail pork barrel spending. However, the creators of this reform intended to use it to strengthen the executive's budgetary role in dealing with the legislature (Wells, 1928). Framers of the constitution for the Confederate States of America wanted to institute aspects of the parliamentary system and yet maintain the separation of powers. In particular, they wanted to enhance the role of the executive in the appropriations process by giving the president the power to put together an executive budget and an item veto to defend the budget. The framers believed that the ordinary executive veto had become a useless instrument for appropriations bills because such legislation contained a number of subjects that made it difficult to use the general veto. Allowing the president to delete particular items would guarantee the president's role in the appropriations process.

Although the Confederacy did not last long enough to test the effectiveness of the item veto in promoting executive influence in the appropriations process, the experience of the states raises questions about the underlying assumptions of the framers of its constitution. In many states, the item veto has not protected the executive budget, even though many practitioners of state government have often praised its effectiveness. When we asked our respondents whether the item veto was an important instrument aiding the influence of the governor in the appropriations process, 58 of the 99 agreed that it was. Furthermore, surveys of governors support these observations (Moore 1992; Abney and Lauth, 1994). However, the significance of the item veto in affecting gubernatorial influence appears small. Only 19 of the 58 budget officials who said that the item veto is an important factor in affecting gubernatorial influence in the appropriations process also said that the governor is more influential while 13 of the 58 said that the legislature is more influential. When we compare respondents from the 42 states that have the line-item veto with those from states that lack it, the former do not perceive the governor as more influential as would be predicted.[1] Of the 83 respondents from the item-veto states, 28 (34 percent) ranked the governor as more influential in the appropriations process as compared to 6 of the 14 respondents from the other states (43 percent). The presence of the item veto is not positively related to perception of gubernatorial influence.

The limitations of the item veto are evident. By using lump-sum appropriations in spending bills rather than detailed itemizations, legislative bodies tend to nullify the effectiveness of the item veto.[2] Only 31 of the 83 respondents from states with the item veto indicated that detailed itemization is used in appropriations bills. In most states with the item veto, governors are unable to reduce appropriations; they must veto the whole item. If the item includes money for matters of concern to the governor, the value of the veto is diminished.

In interpreting the meaning of item-veto power, courts have constricted it (Briffault, 1993). Despite efforts by a number of governors to use the item veto to reduce appropriations, in only

12 states with the item veto have courts approved the power of reduction. When we asked our respondents from executive budget agencies if the governors needed the ability to reduce items of appropriations, 32 of the 41 from states with an item veto responded positively. Given the presence of lump-sum appropriations and the absence of the reduction power, the item veto is not a corrective to the failure of the ordinary executive veto envisioned by reformers.

Respondents from states where governors have the reduction power are clearly more likely to perceive the governor as more influential than the legislature. Fourteen of the 23 respondents (61 percent) from states having governors with the reduction power regarded the governor as more influential compared to 14 of the 60 respondents (23 percent) from other item veto states. Arguably, without the reduction power in 12 states, our results would reflect greater legislative influence than gubernatorial.

A second factor that has restricted the effectiveness of the item veto is the use of narrative in appropriations bills for the purpose of placing conditions on how funds should be spent. In many of the states with the item veto, the governor may not separately veto the narrative while sustaining the monetary item.[3] In these states, the courts have viewed a veto of narrative without a veto of the item of appropriation as an affirmative act of legislation rather than the negative act of a veto. That is, in deleting such narrative, the governor is changing the content of legislation rather than nullifying legislation.

In those states where governors may delete conditions, provisos, or substantive legislation, gubernatorial influence benefits. For respondents from states that have the item veto but lack the reduction power, gubernatorial authority to delete any narrative is related positively to perceptions of gubernatorial influence; 15 percent of the respondents with governors lacking the narrative deletion authority cited the governor as more influential (N = 34), while 35 percent with governors having the deletion authority reported the governor as more influential (N = 26).

Having the authority to delete narrative may not solve the governor's problem. We asked our respondents how the legislature communicated its intent about spending. While narrative in appropriations bills was the most common method, 47 percent cited committee or conference reports, and 42 percent cited personal communications from legislative leaders and staff. Both of these methods are "veto proof."

In conclusion, the item veto may have a significant impact on the relative influence of governors, but not in the manner normally expected. The item veto has largely failed to protect the governor's executive budget. However, where the reduction and deletion power exists, the item veto correlates positively with gubernatorial influence.

Proposition 3. Increasing partisanship in state government has undermined gubernatorial influence in the appropriations process.

In the last four decades party competition in the states has increased. In 1953, the governor and both houses of the legislature were of the same party in 38 of the 46 states with partisan legislatures. By 1993, the number of such states had declined to 19 of 49 states, excluding Nebraska. In 1953, partisan control of the legislature was divided in three states. By 1993, the number of states with divided party control had increased to 18. Rosenthal (1990, 55) explains the reasons:

> This [increase] is attributable in part to candidate-centered campaigns for state legislatures and the increasing incidence of split-ticket voting. It is also attributable to the growth of the Republican Party in the South and the victories of its gubernatorial candidates in a number of southern states and to gains made by Democrats in formerly Republican states, like Vermont and Indiana, in the North.

Table 6.3

Gubernatorial Influence by Partisan Division within Government

	Partisan Division		
Relative Influence	Same political party controls both leg. and gov.'s office	Divided control of legislature	Different political parties control each branch
Governor is more influential	17	12	5
Equal influence	10	10	8
Legislature is more influential	10	5	15

This table does not include respondents indicating a nonpartisan legislature or those who indicated that the partisan arrangement changed within the last two years. The chi square probability is less than .05.

Rosenthal (1990, 56) also notes that the governor is more affected than the legislature by partisan division. Specifically, he says, "Legislatures are more likely to make life difficult for opposition-party governors than the reverse." This seems particularly true in regard to the executive budget as partisan division can lead to increased attacks upon it. Forty-eight percent of the respondents from states where the governor is of one party and both houses of the legislature are of another reported that "executive budget recommendations for expenditure increases above the base budget are significantly changed by the legislature" (N = 25). Forty-three percent of the respondents from states with divided control in the legislature reported these types of changes (N = 21). On the other hand, only 27 percent of the respondents from one-party states indicated such changes in the executive budget (N = 34).

Partisan division is related to decreased gubernatorial influence in the appropriations process. As indicated in Table 6.3, gubernatorial influence is much greater in one-party states than in states where one party controls both houses of the legislature and the other party controls the governorship. However, gubernatorial influence is not particularly stronger in states where the legislature is divided than in one-party states. Increasing partisanship in state legislatures has probably undermined gubernatorial leadership where it has led to a legislature with both houses dominated by the party in opposition to the governor's party.

Proposition 4. Since the executive budget, states have generally not adopted reforms to enhance gubernatorial influence; where adopted, reforms have enhanced gubernatorial influence.

In defending the executive budget, governors have two basic problems. The first is preventing the legislature from expanding the revenue estimate and thereby risking deficits. The second problem is defending recommendations for individual programs or items. In both areas, legislative bodies make changes. Forty-seven percent of the respondents reported that the legislative appropriations are usually higher than those proposed by the governor while 10 percent said they are usually lower. Thirty-three percent of the respondents reported that the legislature usually makes "significant changes" in the executive budget.

One reform designed to give governors the ability to constrain the legislature's appetite for spending is to assign to the governor primary authority for setting the revenue estimate. The revenue estimate is the primary authority of the governor in 25 states, of the legislature in five

Table 6.4

Gubernatorial Influence by Power to Define Revenue Estimate

	Revenue Estimate		
Relative Influence	Governor sets	Consensus between governor & legislature	Legislature sets
Governor is more influential	25	10	1
Influence is about equal	14	12	5
Legislature is more influential	14	14	4

Classifications are based on data from the Council of State Governments (1994). Respondents from Texas are not included here because an independent source sets the estimate.

states, of a consensus mechanism in 19 states, and of an independent source in one state (Council of State Governments, 1994, 322). As seen in Table 6.4, of our respondents from states where the primary responsibility is that of the governor, 25 of 53 (47 percent) reported that the governor is more influential. Only one of the 10 respondents from state where the primary responsibility of the revenue estimate belongs to the legislature indicated that the governor is more influential. Of most importance to governors is the exclusive authority to define the revenue estimate.

In one state, Maryland, the legislature cannot increase gubernatorial recommendations within the executive budget. This power significantly limits the legislature's capability to change the governor's budget. Though the legislature can pass individual bills enhancing particular items after the budget bill is passed, these single-subject bills are subject to gubernatorial veto. Both legislative and executive respondents from Maryland cited this reform as the most important factor explaining gubernatorial influence in the appropriations process. Both respondents also ranked the governor as more influential than the legislature. This reform is not new, and it remains confined to one state.

Gubernatorial authority to set the revenue estimate restricts the legislature's ability to increase the items of the executive budget. Another reform, impoundment, allows the governor to negate the legislature's changes after it has acted and after the governor has signed the bill. Any increases beyond those recommended in the executive budget presumably become strong candidates for gubernatorial impoundment. Such impoundment by President Nixon led Congress to prohibit impoundments without its approval. The legality and use of impoundment varies. Twenty-six of the 99 respondents said that it was constitutional in their states or had been given to the governor by statute. Impoundment powers are usually confined to such situations where revenue shortfalls develop during a fiscal year.

Altogether, 51 of our 99 respondents indicated that governors bad in fact used impoundment to deal with revenue shortfalls. From the perspective of gubernatorial influence, a far more important form of the power of impoundment is to allow the governor to use it for policy reasons. Only four of the respondents indicated that the governor had used impoundment to promote a policy agenda. Of these, three indicated that the governor was more influential than the legislature and the other respondent said that the two branches were equal in influence. The constitution and statutes of the state of Hawaii grant the governor considerable flexibility in regard to the use of impoundment. Apparently, this power significantly affects gubernatorial influence in that state.

Other factors besides those cited above surely affect gubernatorial influence. However, the point of this article is not to explain gubernatorial influence in the appropriations process, but to identify reforms and changes in state government that may have contributed to the decline in gubernatorial dominance.

CONSEQUENCES OF THE DECLINE

If we are correct that gubernatorial influence has declined, what results might we expect in terms of gubernatorial-legislative interaction and in terms of the direction of policy? An underlying assumption of proponents of the need for a strong executive in the appropriations process is that legislative bodies tend to be spendthrifts. Our respondents tend to confirm this assumption. Forty-seven percent of the respondents characterized legislative budgets as higher than executive budgets. Only 10 percent characterized legislative appropriations as lower. Based on this finding and the assumption cited above, it is reasonable to presume that state appropriations are being spent less carefully than at any time since the beginning of the century.

It is not correct, however, to conclude that legislatures are leading states into a new era of waste and corruption. The legislatures most likely to engage in spendthrift policies are found in states where the governor dominates the appropriations process. Of the respondents perceiving the legislature as more influential, 18 of 32 (56 percent) reported the legislature to "be much concerned about efficiency in government." In comparison, only 11 of 36 respondents (31 percent) perceiving the governor as more influential reported that the legislature was concerned about efficiency. The legislatures in states with gubernatorial domination are also more likely to pass budgets in excess of the executive budget. Fifty-eight percent of the respondents who said that the governor is more influential also reported that legislative appropriations are higher than gubernatorial recommendations. Thirty-eight percent of the respondents who ranked the legislature as more influential made that characterization. As might be expected, legislative respondents were much less likely than executive officials to perceive legislative bodies as spendthrift. However, executive respondents reflected the tendency of legislative influence to discourage spendthrift behavior.

The effects of the decline in gubernatorial influence may vary with the cause of the decline. If the decline results from partisan considerations, then the governor's budget may receive little deference. Respondents from states with divided party control reported a slightly greater tendency to make significant changes in the governor's budget than did respondents from one-party states.

If the decline results because the legislature becomes more informed, then the result will likely be more fiscal responsibility on the part of the legislature. Our data indicate that respondents reporting superior gubernatorial information were less likely than other respondents to say that the legislature is concerned about efficiency in government. Ten of the 30 respondents claiming gubernatorial superiority in information reported that "the legislature is much concerned about efficiency in government compared to a similar report by 37 of the other 69 respondents (54 percent). Furthermore, respondents reporting gubernatorial superiority in information were more likely to report that the legislature usually increases the governor's budgetary recommendation.

The increase in legislative influence has probably also changed gubernatorial-legislative interactions. Legislative influence puts governors on the defensive. Forty-seven percent of the respondents who claimed that the legislature is more influential said that the legislature makes significant changes in executive recommendations (N = 32); only 22 percent of the 36 respondents citing the governor as more influential made this characterization.

In the states dominated by legislatures, governors must rely on personal skills to defend their budgets because they lack the formal powers or the partisan allies to succeed. Twenty-three of the 32 respondents (72 percent) citing legislative dominance said that the governor's personal skills were important to gubernatorial influence in the appropriations process while only 14 of the 36 respondents (39 percent) citing gubernatorial influence said personal skills of the governors were important. Personal skills are needed most when all else fails. If we are correct that governors are losing their domination of the appropriations process, then governors will need to be more personally involved in legislative deliberations.

CONCLUSION

Although there are negative consequences associated with the decline of gubernatorial dominance of the appropriations process, there are benefits associated with increased legislative influence. In times past, executive reform was needed to end legislative corruption. Today, based on the respondents' perceptions of legislative interest in efficiency, the most responsible legislative bodies seem to be those with the most influence in the appropriations process. Often, legislative influence leads to responsibility and not to corruption. Influential legislatures tend to be the most independent in terms of information, and they are also the most likely to stress efficiency as a factor in resource allocation.

The present condition of relative parity between governors and legislatures may not continue. Tenure limits on legislators may undermine legislative expertise and shift influence in the appropriations process. On the other hand, increasing professionalism and/or partisanship in state legislatures may further undermine the influence of governors.

The achievement of parity does not mean that reformers should abandon the search for institutional devices to enable the chief executive to prepare and defend a budget. For example, when governors possess the special form of the item veto permitting them to reduce as well as delete appropriation items, then they have an effective device to defend their budgets without undermining the legislature's role in making changes in the executive budget.

Despite our emphasis in this article on relative influence, we do not believe executive-legislative influence to be a zero-sum game. Although legislatures may gain influence from greater information, the growth of professionalism in the legislature may aid the governor in achieving such budgetary goals as balance and efficiency in state fiscal matters. Indeed, rational decision making in the state appropriations process is most likely where both branches are institutionally strong (Abney and Lauth, 1987).

NOTES

1. The number of states that have the item veto is usually listed as 43. We excluded Maryland from this list, but we did not include it among the states that do not have the item veto. The Maryland constitution allows the use of the item veto against supplementary bills passed after the budget bill. In effect, the governor does not need the item veto because the legislature cannot raise items beyond gubernatorial recommendations in the budget bill. The governor may use the regular veto against supplementary bills, which are single subject in nature.

2. Detailed itemization increases a governor's opportunity to use the item veto, but it reduces the discretionary powers of administrators. Not surprisingly, the legislative use of detailed itemization is positively related to the relative influence of legislatures. For example, of those respondents reporting detailed itemization, 50 percent reported the legislature as more influential compared to a similar ranking by 34 percent of the other respondents.

3. See, for example, *State ex rel Sego v. Kirkpatrick* 86 N.M. 359 (1974); *Welden v. Ray* 229 N. W. 2d 706 (Iowa 1975); and *Henry v. Edwards* 346 So. 2d 153 (LA 1977).

REFERENCES

Abney, Glenn, and Thomas P. Lauth (1987). "Perceptions of the Impact of Governors and Legislatures in the Appropriations Process." *Western Political Quarterly* 40: 335–342.
——— (1985). *The Politics of State and City Administration.* Albany: State University of New York Press.

———— (1993). "Determinants of State Agency Success." *Public Budgeting and Financial Management* 5: 37–65.

———— (1994). "Governors and the Item Veto." Paper delivered at the annual meeting of the Southern Political Science Association.

Anton, Thomas J. (1966). *The Politics of State Expenditures in Illinois.* Urbana: University of Illinois Press.

Balutis, Alan, and Daron K. Butler (1975). *The Political Purse-Strings.* New York: Sage.

Briffault, Richard C. (1993). "The Item Veto in the States." *Temple Law Review* 66: 1171–1206.

Council of State Governments (1956). *Book of the States, 1956–57.* Chicago: Council of State Governments.

———— (1994). *Book of the States, 1994–1995.* Lexington, KY: Council of State Governments.

Howard, S. Kenneth (1973). *Changing State Budgeting.* Lexington, KY: Council of State Governments.

Moe, Ronald C. (1988). "Prospects for the Item Veto at the Federal Level: Lessons from the States." Washington DC: National Academy of Public Administration.

Moore, Stephen (1992). "How Governors Think Congress Should Reform the Budget: Results of a Survey of U.S. Governors and Former Governors." *Policy Analysis.* Washington DC: Cato Institute.

Rosenthal, Alan. (1981). *Legislative Life.* New York: Harper and Row.

———— (1990). *Governors and Legislatures.* Washington DC: Congressional Quarterly.

Schick, Allen (1971). *Budget Innovation in the States.* Washington DC: Brookings Institution.

Sharkansky, Ira (1968). "Agency Requests, Gubernatorial Support and Budget Success in State Legislatures," *American Political Science Review* 62: 1220–1231.

Wells, Roger (1928). "The Line Item Veto and State Budget Reform." *American Political Science Review* 18: 782–791.

Willoughby, Will Franklin (1918). *The Movement of Budgetary Reform in the States.* New York: D. Appleton.

CHAPTER 7

BUDGETING BY THE BALLOT
Initiatives in the State of Montana

KRISHNA K. TUMMALA AND MARILYN F. WESSEL

Citizen participation in the decision-making process and government's responsiveness to people's needs constitute the core of the democratic ethic.[1] Three institutional arrangements are devised to make democracy more democratic: initiatives, referenda, and recall. This article deals specifically with the initiative process in the State of Montana. While citizen participation could be an end in itself, it is viewed here as a means to achieve specific ends.[2] Three different initiatives are studied using four criteria to determine the efficacy of the process.

BACKGROUND

Direct democracy is an important part of the frontier tradition strongly rooted in Populism. Late 19th century dissatisfaction with unresponsive and often corrupt state and local governments led to the search for more direct forms of participation that could complement and/or bypass elected representatives.[3] In fact, citizen access to the initiative was high on the reform agenda that swept across America in the progressive era. South Dakota in 1898 became the first state to adopt a system of direct legislation through the ballot box.[4] And by November 1906, with support from labor and progressive leaders, the Populists in Montana were successful in obtaining a constitutional amendment which guaranteed citizen access to the lawmaking process.[5] To date, 24 states have provided similar opportunity for their populations.[6]

In 1972, when Montana adopted a new constitution, it opted for a document that opened up the initiative process by making it easier for citizen groups to place issues on the election ballot. Specifically, the new constitution reduced the signature requirements from eight percent of the qualified electors to five percent. In addition, Article III changed the signature distribution requirements from two-fifths of the counties to one-third of the legislative districts. The new constitution also allowed citizens to use the initiative for constitutional revision. Amendments could be placed on the ballot by obtaining signatures from ten percent of the qualified electors in two-fifths of the state's legislative districts.[7]

Despite the trend toward opening up the initiative process during the Constitutional Convention,

Article III, Section IV, plainly states that "the people may enact laws by initiative on all matters except for the appropriations of money and local or special laws."[8] It was believed that the appropriations process should be reserved for the elected representatives. Implicit in that decision was the feeling that fiscal matters are too complex to be left to citizen lawmakers.[9]

Despite the appropriations restrictions, the Montana electorate found many opportunities to take advantage of its new-found access to direct democratic participation. In the years prior to the 1972 constitutional ratification, there were 64 initiatives and referenda on the ballot for an average of nearly two issues per general election. Between 1972 and 1980 there were 25 issues put before the people for an average of about six per election.[10] Undoubtedly the simplified constitutional procedure contributed to that increased usage, but there may have been a more universal reason as well. Citizens who believed that they were overwhelmed by expanding government in the 1970s often searched for ways to re-establish their control over state and local structures.[11] A natural outgrowth of that search was manifested in the rise of public interest groups that used the initiative frequently during Montana's brief encounter with a relatively liberal political movement during the late 1960s and early 1970s. Ballot issues which established the coal severance tax trust fund and, for all practical purposes, banned nuclear plant siting are two examples of this.

By mid-decade, however, the Montana ballot had begun to provide an avenue of redress for citizen groups more worried about financial resources than about natural resources. That concern was expressed in a series of ballot issues dealing with state fiscal policy, including backdoor approaches aimed at altering the appropriations process. Three issues examined in this article illustrate the point.

1. The state-funded Homestead Tax Relief Act of 1976 requested that the legislature appropriate funds to pay taxes on the first $5,000 of the appraised value of each owner-occupied home in the state. In other words, the initiative provided a property tax break for Montana citizens. The people were asked to vote for or against "reduction of owners' property tax liabilities on owner-occupied residential property." The issue qualified for the ballot and was approved by the voters.

2. A constitutional initiative the same year to limit state spending also qualified. The proposed amendment stated that appropriations could not "exceed the sum of $375 million for any biannum [sic]" commencing prior to July 1, 1983," and added that the legislature provide for a 15 percent annual phase-out of federal funds such that no federal monies could be accepted after July 1, 1984.[12] This was not adopted.

3. In 1980 a group used the initiative process to institute a tax indexing system for Montana income tax payers. The initiative proposed that tax brackets, exemptions, standard deductions, and minimum filing requirements be adjusted each year to prevent tax increases. The initiative, which easily qualified and just as easily got voter approval, asked people to vote for or against adjusting income tax structures to prevent tax increases due solely to inflation.[13]

This marks an increased level of citizen participation in the state's fiscal policy-making arena, a domain which is typically reserved for public managers and elected officials. Popular through the process is, as Peter May and Arnold Meltsner point out, such massive citizen intervention into the fiscal side of state government calls for more than a business-as-usual response on the part of public servants.[14] For the most part, Montana's public managers have remained silent, while the state's representative body has been vocally opposed to the perceived encroachment on its function. During the 1981 legislative session, several bills were introduced to alter the requirements for initiatives, thus making the process less accessible. One of the most controversial called for doubling the required number of signatures needed to qualify an issue for the ballot. But public enthusiasm in behalf of the initiative proved so great that attempts to enact major restrictions have so far not succeeded. Initiatives are here to stay.

Given the popularity of the process, public managers, fearful of being characterized as anti-democratic, have been reluctant to discuss some of the dysfunctions that arise from the use of the initiative, especially in the fiscal policy area. Nonetheless, there are dysfunctions. To investigate these, the following questions are studied pertaining to the above-cited initiatives:

- Are backdoor appropriations decisions being made through the use of the ballot, despite the clear constitutional admonition to the contrary?
- Is relatively neutral information on these issues easily available to voters so that they can make valid judgments?
- Does the process lead to uncertainties in budget making due to the structural need to finalize revenue estimates months before the voters have ruled on fiscal ballot issues?
- Could the initiative process be politicized by candidates who foresee personal election victories tied to initiative campaigns?

THE CONSTITUTIONAL DYSFUNCTION

Despite the restraints built into the Montana Constitution to reserve the appropriations process for representative government, citizens now are taking an activist role in fiscal decision making. State Senator Dorothy Eck, who was vice president of the 1972 Constitutional Convention, acknowledged that recent ballot issues have had the effect of backdoor appropriations. That is, they have left the elective body with little choice but to spend money in the manner written into the initiative.[15] Her observation was particularly true with the passage of the 1976 Homestead Property Tax Relief Act.

Entitled, "An Act to Provide Property Tax Relief for Owner-Occupied Home-steads" (Initiative 72), the proposal's backers easily gathered the 16,000 signatures necessary to qualify for the ballot. However, because of the constitutional ban on citizen appropriations, they could not bind the legislature to approve money for property tax relief. Therefore, the initiative backers had to find a way to insure the appropriation without saying as much. Thus, the initiative states that "to the extent funds are provided by the legislature," property tax relief would be forthcoming.[16] This was buttressed by a strong media campaign telling people that the state surplus should be appropriated to cover the rebates and that the recipients could expect about $100 each.

In actuality, the legislature had little choice but to appropriate the desired money for tax relief, especially after the initiative passed by an overwhelming margin of 204,000 to 83,000.[17] The only real issue in the 1979 legislative session was one of how much money to rebate. After a series of compromises, the legislature agreed to appropriate $30 million of the state's $50 million surplus for the tax relief. That represented approximately $65 per rebate.[18] In later years a variety of payback schemes were tried, but the legislature continued to appropriate money through 1980 for property tax relief based on the success of I-72.

By the beginning of the new decade the momentum for fiscal reform had switched from property tax relief to income tax relief and another major fiscal initiative was in the making—Tax Indexing (I-86). This required that income taxes be indexed to the annual inflation rate as determined by the Consumer Price Index. A relatively new concept in the United States, indexing was in force in five states when it was introduced into Montana. An indexing bill did pass in the waning days of the 1979 legislative session, but the governor, citing revenue uncertainties, vetoed it. The veto galvanized the backers of tax indexing. Calling themselves the Montana Tax Reduction Movement, they secured the necessary 16,000 signatures to qualify the indexing initiative for the 1980 ballot. Tax indexing passed by a two-to-one margin. As with property tax relief, there were a few attempts during the 1981 legislative session to amend I-86 to cut its fiscal impact. John Clark, deputy director of the Department of Revenue, testified that the CPI overstated inflation. Indexing, he said, would better be based on the GNP price deflator. Neither the taxation committee nor the legislature agreed.[19]

Indexing differed from the homestead property tax relief initiative in several important ways. Not only was it a more complex piece of legislation, but it also had varied effects on individual taxpayers depending upon their tax rates and the rate of inflation. In the case of property tax relief, the initiative effected the return of about $30 million in general fund money to the taxpayers. With indexing, the effect was to adjust the tax tables so that about $35 million in taxes would be left uncollected.[20] Although the methods differed, the net effect on appropriations was the same. The successful use of the initiative removed a large increment of revenue from the appropriations control traditionally exercised by the legislature.

Although the spending ceiling (Constitutional Initiative 7) did not pass, its intent was also to remove large amounts of money from appropriations control. It was to have imposed a spending ceiling of $375 million and required a phase-out of federal funds.

Despite the limitations that the three fiscal policy initiatives imposed on the state appropriations process, the legislature still retained the power to change or alter any initiative deemed unwise. In fact, initiatives are carefully designed to avoid an overt infringement on the prerogative. There is little evidence, however, that elected officials will make substantive alterations in fiscal initiatives, especially those with clear voter approval. Few politicians are brave enough to accept the charge that they voted against the popular will regardless of their concerns about long-range fiscal impacts.

When the delegates to the Constitutional Convention voted to continue appropriations restrictions over a decade ago, they aimed to protect the legislative process and preclude a route by which special interest groups might secure an appropriation for a project or program of limited scope. What has happened in the intervening years is that the largest of all special interest groups—the taxpayers—has begun appropriating a substantial annual sum for themselves via the ballot. That their act represents voter frustration with the legislature's own fiscal decisions is unquestionable. That it may also be subverting constitutional intent and shifting the balance of power from a rational to a relatively nonrational arena is also a distinct possibility.

One measure of rationality is the opportunity that decision makers may have to assess complete and objective information in an attempt to choose among fiscal alternatives. Now that citizens are far more involved in that process than ever before, the lack of such information for general consumption leads to the second dysfunction in the initiative process.

THE PUBLIC INFORMATION GAP

The three issues chosen here were designed to make important decisions on long-term fiscal policy. In 1976 just over 300,000 Montanans voted on property tax relief. Nearly two-thirds of them favored the measure. In that same election, two-thirds voted against the spending ceiling. About 330,000 voted on the tax-indexing initiative issue and again more than two-thirds voted in the affirmative.[21]

As there were neither interviews nor follow-up surveys immediately after the two general elections, there are no objective data to suggest what the voters thought they were achieving by their votes on new fiscal policies in Montana. It is, however, possible to draw some conclusions from the analysis of the information available to the acquisitive voter at the time of the 1976 and 1980 elections. In brief, such an analysis suggests that while voters were being asked to make decisions as complex as any faced by their elected legislators, they had much less information than any legislator would have had in similar circumstances. And what small amount of information was available was principally limited to the political rhetoric generated by opposing sides. That, of course, is not unusual in any election year, but it becomes particularly difficult when the rhetoric amounts to a confusing and disparate series of numerical projections.

Information from several sources was made available to the electorate, such as paid advertisements, news stories, editorials, and the voter information pamphlets distributed by the secretary of state during the two elections. Data from these were surveyed and classified into four categories: (1) information that relied on quotes and/or reports from opponents or proponents of the ballot issues; (2) information which mentioned long-range cost/benefit relationships to government services, taxpayers, or the budget process; (3) information containing analysis or conclusions separate from that generated by the opposing sides; and (4) paid political advertisements.

The content analysis centered on the coverage provided by the *Great Falls Tribune* (a daily newspaper) and the voter information pamphlets that the secretary of state must issue prior to every general election. The *Tribune* was selected because it maintains its own state bureau and because it is generally considered to be among the best sources of statewide news in Montana. It is also true, however, that most Montana newspapers share the same wire service and therefore much of their coverage takes on a homogeneous quality. The voter information pamphlets were included because they are the only pieces of information that almost certainly get into the home of every registered voter. No attempt was made in this space to analyze the broadcast media. In any case, the wire services make available to most broadcast outlets the same information that appears in the newspapers, though probably in an altered form. This analysis thus assumed that readers of the *Tribune* received as much or more information on initiatives as any group of voters in the state.

During the months preceding the 1976 election, the newspaper carried only eight stories on the property tax relief initiative. Six of those stories concentrated on quotations from proponents. Parts of the six made some mention of the fiscal impacts, usually in terms of funding relief from the state's $50 million surplus. The paper ran two advertisements paid for by the proponents which characterized the initiative with the slogan: "Voting Yourself $100 in Property Tax Relief is as easy as Flipping a Switch."[22]

The stories were generally given good placement on appropriate pages; that is, none appeared to be placed where it would not be found by the reader of state political news. One story entitled "Property Tax Redress: Reduction or Shuffle?" was identified as part of an analytical series on the ballot issues. The report, however, did little more than quote proponent/opponent positions as they appeared in the voter information pamphlet.[23] The paper's own editorial asserted that "the act really encourages more political rhetoric rather than serious efforts to establish a realistic and fair tax program for our state needs."[24]

Citizens who wished to know about the issue's long-range impacts, the advisability of transferring surpluses into short-term tax relief, the problems with administering the program, or the trade-offs between funding tax relief and some other state needs were left without answers. The issue was in effect reduced to a simple voter choice for or against $100 in tax relief. As John LeFaver, who was the legislative fiscal analyst (LFA) at the time, commented: "Clearly if you ask people if they want property tax relief or not, you know where the check is going to fall."[25]

As required by law, the voter information pamphlet mailed to each registered voter in late October presented a neutral stance on all ballot issues. Each side was given a controlled amount of space and the presentation was such that none could claim the advantage of headlines or placement. But the information was prepared by the proponents as well as opponents. In short, the material in the pamphlets did not differ significantly from the press releases already issued and covered in the media. People still had no way of evaluating the numbers placed before them.

The information carried in the media on the spending ceiling initiative was sparse. There were only four stories. Two of them quoted the opposing sides, and two had some independent commentary. There were no advertisements and the voter information pamphlet carried only the opposition data with the disclaimer that the proponents had failed to submit any written statement.

The controversy as well as the coverage was much greater during the 1980 campaign over tax indexing. Unlike Homestead, which had promised appropriation of the surplus to cover tax rebates, indexing proposed not to collect the taxes in the first place.

During the months preceding the election there were 24 stories on tax indexing. The majority—20 in all—quoted the proponents or the opponents. In fact, many of the 20 were devoted to charges and counter charges about who was telling the truth as the political battle unfolded. Of the total of 24 stories, only eight mentioned any projected fiscal impacts, usually in terms of the amount of revenue the state would lose or the amount the taxpayers might expect to save. The estimates on revenue losses provided the greatest source of confusion as they seesawed from $13 million to $90 million per year. Estimates even varied among the groups working for and against the measure. The content analysis also revealed that statements on revenue impacts were obscured by using different numerical bases. For example, in one story the state revenue losses were pegged at $24 million, while in another they were characterized as a percentage (.36 percent) of the budget.[26]

Of the 24 stories , only four showed any independent analysis. Three of those were in editorial comments. One wire story used information on indexing taken from a report on the subject prepared by the Advisory Commission on Intergovernmental Relations. (Although it was not specific to Montana, ACIR largely favored indexing.[27])

As with the coverage of property tax relief, stories on indexing received good placement and the newspaper clearly aimed toward a balance. Absent, however, was any information on the assumptions which generated the various projections on tax savings or revenue losses, the long-term impact of the new policy, or the trade-offs between tax savings and other state priorities. There was also no discussion on the effects of indexing on property tax relief. Would indexing reduce the revenue available and thus kill the property tax relief voters had approved four years earlier? Or did voters think they might retain both? The issues were never addressed.

Given the dearth of analytical or nonpartisan information on tax indexing and property tax relief in the media, it would be simple to berate the lack of journalistic depth in a relatively rural state and let the issue rest. But the problem goes deeper. A recent analysis in the *Columbia Journalism Review* decried the state of economics reporting throughout the United States and suggested that in most instances stories on fiscal issues were merely a matter of soliciting opinions, or as the writer put it, "he said, she said journalism."[28] From the Montana perspective, the problems revolved around the general lack of information on fiscal issues from any source in state government or even the private sector. In that regard, the persistent news reporter is not much better off than the persistent voter.

Independent information complex fiscal policy issues like indexing, property tax relief, and the spending ceiling was and is hard to find. As Revenue Deputy Director Clark pointed out, policy analysis, particularly on the fiscal side, is directed by the assumptions from which the expert begins. During the 1980 campaign, the Republicans were routinely criticized for suggesting that tax indexing would only set back revenue projections by $13 million, while Clark's own department, which was part of a Democratic administration, was equally criticized for suggesting that the revenue bite could go as high as $90 million. In retrospect, Clark insisted that neither party was wrong in the classic sense of making mathematical errors or purposefully plugging in bogus figures.

"If you are a true believer," Clark said, "then you are conditioned by a set of assumptions."[29] And it is within the parameters of those assumptions that politicians have their impact on policy analysis. Those who wish to see a fiscal policy issue succeed begin their analysis with a set of "best case" assumptions, while the other side starts from the "worst case." The assumptions rapidly become the base for complex calculations which produce a variety of projections and estimates. The media outlets, unable to produce their own sets of check calculations, will opt for balance by resorting to "he said, she said" journalism. For their part, the voters must take their chances.

There are times when state government may supply the neutral stance needed to analyze ballot issues, but as fiscal initiatives become more and more politicized, state government workers often find themselves on one or the other side of the issue by virtue of their party affiliation. Three of the fiscal experts who served as resources for this research agreed that it is difficult for anyone to find a neutral information base from which to generate analysis on fiscal initiatives. "There are darn few places where perception is not shaded by personal prejudice," Clark said. "I think through our research division (Department of Revenue), we used to try to give neutral data as best we could unless we were told to give something that was a little bit less than neutral. There are few places where you can pick up something from the objective observer who said, 'I don't care how this comes out.' "[30]

The state's director of the Office of Budget and Program Planning (OBPP), David Lewis, agrees that neutrality is hard to achieve, and he believes that the widely varying estimates on fiscal impacts will continue as part of the political campaign. "They [the impact figures] are all based on the answer you want. None of these answers is really wrong," Lewis said. He did note, however, that in the future the public would be better served if the assumptions which undergird analysis were more specifically stated.[31]

Lewis' predecessor, George Bousilman, is less optimistic. He does not believe that neutral data on fiscal issues exist; nor did they ever in the past. "It might be that groups like the League of Women Voters have had some unvarnished information available to the public, but I don't know that they have the capability to come up with all the information [on fiscal impacts]; so I suppose the answer is no."[32]

It could be then that the search for value-free data on fiscal policy proposals is fruitless. Perhaps it is not even the right line of investigation. It may be far more appropriate to inquire if people are likely to use such data or act any differently if they do use it. Lewis jointed the other fiscal experts in expressing grave doubts:

> No, I think that a very, very small percentage of people would read it or pay any attention to it. They're going to get it in their heads through billboards, the TV advertisements, those little 15-second dudes that say "vote for Proposition 13 and we'll cut your property taxes." That's it. Analysis, no matter how well presented, is just not going to be something that the general public is going to be able to handle.[33]

During the most recent legislative session, state legislators did take a small step toward public recognition of the fiscal importance of initiatives when they adopted Senate Bill 72. It required that fiscal notes be attached to all initiatives prior to the beginning of petition drives; but it also specified that the notes are not to exceed 50 words—approximately the length of a 30-second television commercial. While there are some initiatives with negligible fiscal impacts which may well be explained in a sentence or two, it is difficult to imagine that the impacts of all future proposals may be adequately reduced to 50 words.[34]

Beyond the coverage in the media and the requirements of SB 72, the only other sources of information on fiscal initiatives may arise from reports prepared by the LFA, the Department of Revenue, and the OBPP. For the most part, these reports are compiled to satisfy legislative and executive information requests and are not generally available to the public; nor do they receive much press coverage.

Thus, the voters go to the polls with sparse knowledge of the important fiscal issues which will be laid before them. As the votes are being cast, uneasy fiscal experts in the statehouse await the outcome in the hope that the success or failure of major fiscal initiatives will not seriously jeopardize the biennial budget. The issue of budget preparation and the effect of initiatives with a substantial revenue impact creates the third dysfunction in the process of direct democracy.

THE BUDGETARY DYSFUNCTION

The problem in regard to the budget process is principally one of timing. Fiscal planners begin work on the budget in January of each even-numbered year, a full 12 months before the biennial meeting of the state legislature. The OBPP initiates the process with a series of planning and review sessions that may require several months. The object is to consider new program requests and alternatives. At the same time, officials in the Department of Revenue will begin to accumulate the data necessary to do the revenue projections for the biennium. It is a slow, painstaking process designed to inject as much rationality as possible into the document.

Although the expenditure side of the budget is exceedingly important, revenue projections are perhaps the most controversial in the preparation stages. There are, of course, certain givens in the revenue estimation procedure just as there are uncertainties, but the experts do their best to mitigate the problems. For example, fiscal planners will not finalize their revenue projections until September when they have the first payments on the coal and oil severance taxes. That level is an important variable in Montana revenue projections. Unfortunately, planners cannot wait until after the November election to include the exact nature of the revenue impacts generated by ballot issues. By the time that decision is made, the budget must be very nearly complete. Thus, fiscal managers often find themselves in the position of gambling on the election outcomes. In other words, they formulate a budget based on their best guess of which initiatives will succeed and what their aggregate fiscal impacts will be.

If the planners peg the impacts correctly and, more importantly, if they do a good job of second-guessing the electorate, the budget will not be greatly affected by the election outcome. If they miss, more than a year's work will be scrubbed in favor of a last-minute, across-the-board cut required to meet the voter mandate. Needless to say, computer technology makes it possible to re-run the budget with required adjustments in revenues and expenditures, but there is not time after the first week in November to institute the selective review and adjustment processes that may be desirable after experiencing a major decrease in revenue projections.[35]

The state's former OBPP director, Bousilman, recalled that his office prepared several scenarios in an attempt to cover all contingencies. "In 1978, there were several initiatives on the ballot with major impacts and we had to have a number of variable plans depending on whether initiative A, B, or C passed or failed or some combination of the three." The strategy was one of assumptions and educated guessing.[36]

The property tax relief initiative provides a good example. Since I-72 required that the state spend money in order to reimburse the counties for property tax reductions, an estimate for those expenses had to be worked into the budget on a contingency basis. The initiative was a controversial one and its impacts were difficult to measure. Legislative Fiscal Analyst LaFaver, who did not like the way the issue was written, characterized the dilemma thus: "It was clear to the technicians there were a lot of problems with the initiative—mechanical, not philosophical; you just couldn't read the thing and tell how the flow of work going to go."[37]

The uncertainties that the decision makers had in estimating the impacts on revenue were several. Despite the fact that campaigners had talked of providing $100 in tax relief for each property owner, no one really knew exactly what the legislature would finally appropriate. Moreover, the cost projections for the plan were based on the 1970 census data, and it was also necessary to estimate how many property owners would make the required application for relief. As the final budget document was readied for the legislature, the governor and the LFA were still at odds over the cost of the property tax relief package.

During that same budget year, planners were also faced with estimating the costs of the constitutional initiative for a spending ceiling. The magnitude of the potential impacts bewildered the experts. The issue, which called for a $375 million spending ceiling and a phase-out of federal funds, qualified for the ballot at a time when Montana was not only a net importer of federal money, but the state was also appropriating about $1.1 billion for the biennium.[38] The effect on the budget would have been so catastrophic that planners did not even bother to estimate the impact; instead they simply gambled that it wouldn't pass. Lafaver called the constitutional initiative crazy. "You're just way beyond looking at technical points and calculations . . . I don't know what role a fiscal staff can really play."[39] Only David Lewis, who was then an analyst in the OBPP, thought the spending ceiling might pass, but he admitted that he had no idea how his office would have adjusted the budget to reflect the initiative's success. In the end, the measure did fail, largely because its backers appeared to abandon the cause as election time neared and there was no solid partisan support to take up the slack. Still, the fiscal planners cast an uneasy eye on the 30,000 Montanans who had signed initiative petitions and the 86,000 citizens who had voted for the plan.

Four years later fiscal experts began the budget year with yet another initiative on the horizon that promised a substantial impact on revenue projections. The tax indexing measure seemed assured of enough signers to qualify, and most of the experts thought its passage a safe bet. The LFA's staff, as well as the OBPP and the Department of Revenue, prepared estimates on the initiative's revenue impacts. All three estimates varied, largely because of underlying assumptions. Not only was this initiative highly politicized, but its impacts were also affected by the projection of inflation rates, estimated tax receipts, and forecasts of economic activity. Despite the differences in impact estimates, most state fiscal experts thought the initiative would pass and they pegged the revenue decrease at about $35 million for budget purposes.

Despite some differences in viewpoint, the state's fiscal planners share a growing uneasiness over the use of the initiative to make fiscal policy. Although the budget has proved remarkably resilient in absorbing revenue impacts, none of the experts feels comfortable with basing an important element of the budget planning process on what amounts to second-guessing the electorate. The concern is best expressed by Lafaver:

> The more initiatives that get put on the ballot, the more chance we are going to have of passing some things that are totally haywire. . . . Now maybe we should trust the people, but I'm just not totally comfortable with it.[40]

Bousilman agreed.

I think the initiative process has been abused in this state. I don't think decisions such as income tax indexation, which is really a technical kind of issue, belong in an arena where 200,000 people—if that's the correct number—are going to be deciding an issue. I think they belong in the legislature and I think they belong in the hands of the people who are elected.[41]

He expressed the same concern even with property tax relief. Clark sounded a similar note.

I'm going to sound like a real medievalist, I suppose. [The] legislature is bad enough on these fiscal things. They act with insufficient understanding of what's going on. When you go around with some half-baked, written piece of tax law and get some signatures on it and put it on the ballot and run a nice campaign and get it in, I really don't have a very good feeling for that sort of thing, I guess. . . . [42]

Only Lewis seemed willing to accept fiscal initiatives at face value. But even he held the belief that voters will opt for their own interests regardless of the problems that may arise.

If you believe in democracy, you have to believe that it (the initiative) is a proper process. I think that people are so unhappy with the way government has worked that they don't really believe that the legislature, certainly not the Congress, reflects what they want. They want lower taxes. They want less government and if they have to do it by initiative, then that is what has to be done. . . . People vote for less taxes, period.[43]

Lewis' views are rooted in the Populist belief that people should be able to use the political process to bypass elected representatives, regardless of the budgetary dysfunctions. In recent years, however, the initiative process has also emerged as an important part of political campaign strategy. While there are no figures specific to Montana which correlate winning candidates with their sponsorship of initiatives, this altered use of the ballot may lead to the fourth dysfunction.

THE INITIATIVE AS A POLITICAL TOOL

The intent of the initiative process was to allow citizen groups who shared a common concern to take that issue to the people exclusive of an elected body. That route is still being used. But citizen groups have been joined in the last decade by political candidates who organize their own initiative campaigns and make them an important part of their political strategy. Not only does a candidate's sponsorship of an initiative provide extra visibility, but it also provides an aura of accomplishment. A person who has been successful in getting an initiative on the ballot is seen as an achiever.

Montana's immediate past governor, Thomas Judge, demonstrated that well in his 1976 re-election campaign. Rebuffed by the legislature on the issue of property tax relief, Judge formed his Montanans for Property Tax Relief group. Using campaign organizations already in place, in addition to the Democratic party structures, he obtained the signatures necessary to get the issue on the ballot. The governor also used the initiative effectively in his campaign advertisements and speeches.

William C. Barlet, who wrote critically about using the initiative to make fiscal policy in 1978, was equally critical of the governor for politicizing the initiative process. He maintained that the 1976 campaign tipped the balance of power between the executive and the legislature in favor of the former.

> Through the initiative process the governor can, in effect, sidestep the legislature first by
> selling a proposal to the electorate. The political pressures upon a legislature to comply with
> the electorate's message embodied in an initiative are a compelling force.

Barlet worried that future governors might follow and continue to mount initiative campaigns as
part of their election plans.[44]

As it turned out, the governor had no monopoly on using the initiative to gain a favorable balance of power. Four years later, after a gubernatorial veto of the tax indexing bill, a member of the
Montana legislature, Kenneth Nordvedt, demonstrated forcefully that he could just as effectively
use the initiative not only to sidestep the veto, but to aid in his own re-election and that of many
other Republicans.

However, as with any political strategy, the plan can fail and a candidate may be tied to an
initiative that cannot win popular support. The 1976 constitutional initiative on a spending ceiling
may have proved a millstone around the neck of any candidate who supported it. On the other
hand, a strong political push from a popular candidate might have meant the difference between
winning and losing the issue.

Candidates who perceive that a good initiative is important to winning find that while an initiative
campaign does require substantial work, most of the effort dovetails nicely with political strategies.
Even the requirement for signed petitions is little deterrent. Candidates who do not have enough
volunteers to collect signatures have learned that they can substitute money for organization by paying
workers based on the number of signatures obtained. Such expenditures are quite legitimate.

The challenge to the candidates and their strategists then is to come up with an initiative that
will have voter appeal. It goes without saying that an initiative which promises some manner of
voter rebate or direct savings can be expected to have the most *prima facie* appeal. At that point,
the initiative ceases to stem from an expression of popular concern, but comes instead from a
campaign strategy session which concentrates on what can be marketed and sold. That is not necessarily bad, but it does cast the process in a light different from that of its origins. It is a bit like
the shopper who is unaware of personal need for an item until a well-placed advertising campaign
delivers the proper message.

The potential dysfunction arises then not so much from the politicization of the initiative as
from the arbitrary shift of motivation from citizen groups of campaign strategists and market
researchers. LaFaver expressed the concern of many public servants when he suggested that the
combination of the initiative and the ambitious candidate may be the future's package deal. "I
mean it's a political fact of life," Lafaver said. "You don't run for office unless you run with a sexy
initiative. I'll bet we see it from now on."[45]

CONCLUSION

While initiatives are an important part of the democratic process, this analysis does throw a cloud
of suspicion. The dysfunctionalities in this process, not to mention the legal question of violating
the constitutional restriction that initiatives ought not to be used for purposes of appropriations,
provide occasion to pause and ponder. While it may sound maudlin to defend initiatives regardless
of the consequences, it would be equally foolish to dismiss them in favor of informed and rational
decisions to be made by the elite—the elected representatives and bureaucrats.

In his 1978 analysis of the problems surrounding the property tax relief initiative, an apparently discouraged Barlet concluded that, at least in the realm of fiscal policy, initiatives should
not be used. He wrote:

While the initiative process has long been represented as a bulwark of democracy, the complexities of contemporary state government operation have raised legitimate doubt as to the suitability of the initiative as a means to make state fiscal decisions. The issues involved not merely a governor's opportunity to increase leverage within the state organization, but more fundamentally it is a question of direct citizen involvement in specific policy choices affecting the fiscal operation of the state. The story of the Homestead Relief Act suggests that in the complexities of contemporary state government budgetary processes the initiative process is a sacred cow that deserves to be laid to rest [*sic*].[46]

While these concerns are legitimate and quite a few might subscribe to this viewpoint, Barlet's solution is no solution at all. From a political perspective, it is unlikely that Montanans or, for that matter, citizens of any other state would relinquish their right to direct democracy. And to argue that they should is anti-democratic. Thus, the real focus ought to be on how to inject some rationality into the initiatives and use them effectively and efficiently.

Administrative dysfunctions can be dealt with by the introduction of some procedural changes. As illustrated, fiscal initiatives create problems within the budgetary timetable because the November ballot does not permit enough time to adjust the budgetary decisions to voter verdicts on initiatives. This could be overcome by simply delaying the effective date of initiatives until the second year of the biennium. Yet another solution is to put issues with substantive budgetary impact on the primary ballot in June rather than the November ballot. Thus, at least some lead time is obtained.

The information dissemination process itself could be improved, and herein the public managers have an important role. Privy as they are to critical information regarding the probable fiscal impacts of an initiative, they could be made to be more responsive to the information demands. For example, the head of OBPP is required under law to prepare a 50-word fiscal note for each initiative petition. One would expect that such a note is of necessity a product of serious research and a distillation of a much longer report. It may be made mandatory that such a longer report also be made available to the public on request. A brief notation on the initiative petition drawing attention to the existence of such a report might direct the interested signatories and voters to the OBPP. Whether such information would indeed be sought and used are separate questions, and ought not to preempt the supply of information.

Over the last dozen or so years Montana has set up the OBPP and LFA to provide independent and objective data to the executive and legislature, respectively. In 1981 the legislature appropriated over $2 million for the biennial personnel and operations expenses of these two agencies. It is perhaps then not unreasonable to suggest that some more state dollars be spend to ensure a better informed electorate. Undoubtedly, any such attempts demand a careful study of the complex mass communication issues of information design, dissemination, and audience motivation. Fortunately, Montana did have some experience in this regard. In 1972 the state collaborated with the university system and a number of private organizations to distribute information and encourage debate on the new constitution.

Since then, the state has funded a Citizens' Advocate—a kind of public ombudsman—to help in the information flow process. Montana also has an educational telecommunications system (METS) which will provide interactive audio capabilities between a central location and 30 learning sites around the state. Library networks and various service and educational organizations can be another means for getting initiative data disseminated. Media people who act as gatekeepers in any information flow directed toward the electorate also need more neutral data on the fiscal impacts of ballot issues in order to do a critical job of reporting. Some of this information may be supplied by public managers, but media people, too, ought to accept certain responsibilities for seeking out these data.

There may well be other ways of going about this process and improving it. But all those efforts should be undertaken in a context which recognizes the realities of the initiative process as distinguished from strategies which ignore the initiatives or attempt to diminish their significance in an effective democracy.

NOTES

1. Wrote Emmette S. Redford: "The ultimate test of public policy must be the political test, that is, the will of the people affected by the policy, and, second, this will must be reflected in the processes that accord with the participative tenet of democratic morality." See his *Democracy in the Administrative State* (New York: Oxford University Press, 1969), p. 32. However, there are others, such as Woodrow Wilson, who expressed the view that the tools of direct democracy were akin to the guns that the old settler kept behind the door. They were there just in case, but the threat of their use as much as anything would help keep government responsive. See James Grady, "Popular Control: Initiative, Recall and Referendum," *Montana Constitutional Convention Studies,* No. 11, (1972), p. 5.

2. For such a distinction and the issues in measurement, see Judy B. Rosener, "Citizen Participation: Can We Measure Its Effectiveness?" *Public Administration Review,* Vol. 38, No. 5 (September/October 1979), pp. 547–563.

3. Jerry McCaffery and John Bowman, "Participatory Democracy and the Effects of Proposition 13," *Public Administration Review,* Vol. 38, No. 6 (November/December 1978), pp. 530–538.

4. Grady, op cit., p. 5.

5. Michael Malone and Richard Roeder, *Montana: A History of Two Centuries* (Seattle: University of Washington Press, 1976), pp. 196–197.

6. The states which currently provide for the initiative are: Alaska, Arizona, Arkansas, California, Colorado, Delaware, Florida, Idaho. Illinois, Maine, Massachusetts, Michigan, Missouri, Montana, Nebraska, Nevada, North Dakota, Ohio, Oklahoma, Oregon, South Dakota, Utah, Washington, and Wyoming. See *The Book of States* (Lexington, Ky: Council of State Governments, 1980–81), p. 26.

7. *Proposed 1972 Constitution of the State of Montana,* Constitutional Convention, March 22, 1972, p. 28.

8. Ibid. (emphasis supplied). There are nine other states which restrict the use of the initiative in the appropriations process. They are: Alaska, Maine, Massachusetts, Maryland, Missouri, Nevada, Ohio, Washington, Wyoming. See the *Hearings Before the Subcommittee on the Constitution of the Committee on the Judiciary,* U.S. Senate, 95th Congress, 1st Sess., SJF 67 (Washington, D.C.: U.S. Government Printing Office, 1978), pp. 286—352.

9. In fact, the occasional papers from the 1972 Constitutional Convention quote warnings from Charles Adrian, a political scientist who argued that voters should not be asked to rule, but merely to choose who would rule. To ask more, as the initiative process does, ascribes a degree of rationality to the voter that is unlikely to be present, especially when dealing with highly complex issues. See Grady, op. cit., p. 7.

10. Jim Waltermeyer, "Initiatives and Referendum Issues Since the Adoption of the Constitutional Amendment Article V, Section 1," mimeo, from the Montana Secretary of State, 1981.

11. David C. Korten, "The Management of Social Transformation," *Public Administration Review,* Vol. 41, No. 6 (November/December 1981), p. 610.

12. Frank Murray, "Voter Information for Proposed Constitutional Amendments, Referendums, Initiatives," State of Montana, November 2, 1976, pp. 20–25 and 5–9.

13. Ibid., pp. 17–23.

14. Peter May and Arnold Meltsner, "Limited Actions, Distressing Consequences: A Selected View of the California Experience," *Public Administration Review,* Vol. 41, Special Issue (January 1981), pp. 172—174.

15. Interview with Montana State Senator Dorothy Eck, December 1981.

16. William C. Barlet, "The Homestead Property Tax Relief Act," *Montana Public Affairs Report,* July 1978, pp. 1–5.

17. Waltermeyer, op. cit.

18. Barlet, op. cit.

19. Interview with John Clark, October 23, 1981.

20. Interview with David Lewis, director, Montana Office of Budget and Program planning, October 23, 1981.

21. Waltermeyer, op. cit.

22. "Voting Yourself $100 in Property Tax Relief Is As Easy as Flipping a Switch," *Great Falls Tribune,* October 25, 1976, p. 5.

23. "Property Tax Relief: Reduction or Shuffle," *Great Falls Tribune,* October 9, 1976, p. 7.

24. "Property Tax Initiative," *Great Falls Tribune,* October 29, 1976, p. 6.

25. Interview with John LaFaver, currently director, Montana Social and Rehabilitation Services, April 1981.

26. "Montanans Too Heavily Taxed, Says Williams," *Great Falls Tribune,* October 12, 1980, p. 8-A, and "Erred About 1–86," *Great Falls Tribune,* July 30, 1980, p. 5.

27. "The Inflation Tax" (Washington, D.C.: Advisory Council on Intergovernmental Relations, M117, January 1980), *passim.*

28. Chris Welles, "Scooped by Stockman," *Columbia Journalism Review,* Vol. XX, No. 5 (January/February 1982), pp. 21–23.

29. Interview with Clark, op. cit.

30. Ibid.

31. Interview with Lewis, op. cit.

32. Interview with Bousilman, October 23, 1981.

33. Interview with Lewis, op. cit.

34. Montana 47th Legislature, February 1980.

35. Interviews with Bousilman and Lewis, op. cit.

36. Interview with Bousilman, op. cit.

37. Interview with Lafaver, op. cit.

38. Murray, op. cit.

39. Interview with Lafaver, op. cit.

40. Ibid.

41. Interview with Bousilman, op. cit.

42. Interview with Clark, op. cit.

43. Interview with Lewis, op. cit.

44. Barlet, op. cit., p. 7.

45. Interview with Lafaver, op. cit.

46. Barlet, op. cit., p. 7.

PART 3

THE ROLES OF THE KEY BUDGET ACTORS AND DECISION MAKING

On the executive side, the chief executive normally delegates substantial budgeting authority to his or her central budget office, so that budget negotiations may go on between agencies and the budget office. On the legislative side, a variety of committees may deal with issues of budget and taxation. At the national and state levels, these committees normally have their own staff and may have a legislative budget office to advise them. At the local level, while the council may have a finance committee to oversee the budget, there are seldom staff who specialize in budgets. This part focuses particularly on the budget offices, their staff, and executive branch agencies, but it also includes one occasional budget actor, the courts. Legislative committees that deal with budgeting have been extensively studied, the results reported in scholarly books rather than recent journal articles, and so they are omitted here, but not for lack of importance.

Under executive budgeting, the chief executive normally delegates most of the work of preparing the budget to a budget office in the executive branch. This office gives guidance to the departments and agencies for the preparation of their budget requests, prepares a calendar for when various documents are due, evaluates the proposals, gives the agencies decisions on their requests, and then assembles those requests that have been approved into an executive budget proposal. The budget office helps the agencies translate major policy advice from the chief executive into their budget requests. It sometimes solicits spending proposals or changes in policy, while at other times it discourages or rejects such proposals. The budget office may have other roles from time to time. One of the key issues in budgeting has been what the role of this executive budget office should be, whether the requests of the agencies should be carefully sifted and cut back by the budget office, whether the budget office should set limits in advance on budget totals from the agencies, but allow them to put whatever they need most into those requests, or whether the agencies should be able to routinely make end runs around the budget office. Where the budget office strictly enforces the chief executive's policy directives and dictates budget numbers to the agencies allowing few appeals, budgeting is said to be top down; where the agencies get to set their own ceilings on requests and put their own policy preferences in their budget proposal, to be reviewed by the legislative branch, budgeting is said to be more bottom up. The actual role of budget offices has moved between these extremes at different times, in different administrations.

Frederick Mosher and Max O. Stephenson describe the role of the Office of Management and Budget, in the Executive Office of the President, during the early Reagan administration. This was a time of change for the president's budget office, involving a role shift toward more top down budgeting and more emphasis on policy, and less on examining proposals coming up from the agencies. Kurt Thurmaier and James Gosling discuss some of the same issues at the state level. They look at the degree to which budget offices at the state level are oriented to policy issues and analysis as opposed to more routine collection and examination of budget requests, examining changes over time.

Jeffrey Straussman looks at a different institutional actor, the courts, and the circumstances under which they play a role in budgeting. Straussman argues in this piece that while the courts can impose expenditures on government units by enforcing rights of citizens, and can rule some tax exactions illegal, reducing governmental discretion over budget issues, agency officials can use the courts strategically as a kind of back door into spending levels they prefer.

Herbert Persil's essay and Julie Dolan's empirical research describe the role of the agency budget director and agency bureaucrats. Persil argues that despite all the changes in budgeting from the 1980s and 1990s, agency budget directors are still important, even if they have shifted from playing a more expansive policy role to one of helping to figure out tradeoffs and negotiating the intricacies of budget laws to help protect programs during periods of cutbacks. Dolan explores the role of agency bureaucrats and finds no evidence that they always try to maximize their budget.

The next set of articles deals with the model of "incrementalism," a theory that dominated much of the budgeting literature for decades. Incrementalism means that agencies drive the budget process with their requests, and they always ask for more than they have. Incrementalism argues that budgets are "bottom up." Legislators, who would otherwise be overwhelmed with detail, examine only this year's request where it differs from prior years' budgets, that is, they only look at the increment or increase over last year. In its full blown version, incrementalist theory argues that because of a desire to keep the level of conflict down and because agencies each represent interests that remain relatively constant, each will get roughly the share of any new money that they already have. There are few or no tradeoffs in this model and little or no prioritization. This theory was eventually modified to recognize that when there was a major shift in the governing party or ideology, priorities suddenly changed considerably. Some programs got much more money than they had been getting, while others were terminated or reduced in funding. The result was long periods of stability punctuated occasionally by a big policy change. Top down policy making thus played only an occasional role.

Charles Coe and Deborah Weisel describe the strategies of police departments in obtaining their budgets, which fits the incrementalist model of agency-driven budgeting. They talk about what kind of strategies work for the police. Irene Rubin outlines some of the intellectual problems with incrementalism as advocated by its progenitor, Aaron Wildavsky. Katherine G. Willoughby and Mary A. Finn outline the variety of decision-making strategies used by executive and legislative budget office staffers. They argue that incrementalist examination of budget requests is only one of several strategies used to analyze budget requests, and is used in only a minority of cases. More important are policy issues and economic or efficiency considerations. The authors, referring to earlier research they did on this subject, conclude "These findings buttress modern notions that incrementalism is an inadequate explanation of public budgeting behavior."

Chapter 8

THE OFFICE OF MANAGEMENT AND BUDGET IN A CHANGING SCENE

Frederick C. Mosher and Max O. Stephenson, Jr.

AUTHOR'S NOTE

It is too early to provide a definitive view and appraisal of the Office of Management and Budget in the Reagan presidency. The discussion that follows is based partly on current and recent articles and a few recent monographs and books, many of which are credited in footnotes. In additon we have relied upon a considerable number of interviews with current participants and alumni of OMB as well as with some observers from outside. It would be impracticable to list those who helped us, but we are grateful to all of them. The substance of this article was completed in mid-July 1982.

INTRODUCTION

By almost any standard of evaluation, President Reagan arrived in Washington in January 1981 as both standard bearer and purveyor of a relatively consistent and straightforward set of political and social beliefs. More precisely, Reagan entered the White House widely regarded as the chief spokesperson for a conservative philosophy of government. The former California governor based his successful presidential campaign and, indeed, his political career upon a set of political and social tenets that comprehends:

1. A radical reappraisal and fundamental restructuring of the role of the central government in our federal system with an eye to paring its size, authority, and relative influence *vis-à-vis* the private sector and state and local governments.
2. A laissez faire approach to federal social and economic policy.
3. A balanced budget.
4. Activist national interest-based foreign and defense policies underpinned by a military force equal or superior to that of the Soviet Union.

5. A doctrine that American public policy—at the federal level at any rate—more faithfully reflect the nation's "traditional moral values."[1]

During the presidential campaign of 1980, he endorsed a sixth tenet: supply side economics—the encouragement of private sector investment by tax reduction.

The Reagan administration has actively pursued these broad aims by means of specific policy proposals—the principal vehicle for which has been the federal budget. Like most of his predecessors, the newly inaugurated president undertook immediate changes in the upcoming budget for fiscal 1982 which included commitments forward to 1985. His suggested changes were clearly rooted in his overarching philosophy of governance. For example, in keeping with his expressed belief that "All of us need to be reminded that the federal government did not create the states; the states created the federal government," the new president proposed dramatic cuts each year in federal domestic outlays and consolidation of many categorical grants to state and local governments into a relatively small number of block grants in functional fields.[2] He later appended a controversial proposal to exchange grant programs between the states and the federal government. The president's extensive efforts to reduce central government spending across the board also presuppose a shift of many functions and programs to the states.

The Reagan philosophy was consonant with and helped foment popular discontent with the taxation and service labels provided by federal, state, and local governments. The Proposition 13 initiative in California and similar efforts in other states, the pervasive unhappiness with the federal grant-in-aid system, and a feeling, widespread in some sectors of society, that deregulation is necessary if the private sector is to thrive—all combined to provide public support for the president's objectives.

Obviously, a principal tool of the president in giving effect to his program has been the Office of Management and Budget (OMB). This article will undertake to respond to two interrelated questions: how has the Reagan program affected the institution and the performance of the OMB? And, what will be the likely impact of the effort upon OMB in the future? These questions suggest the possibility of four different responses, and variants of all four have been encountered. The first is the OMB and the budget process will never be the same. A second is that this administration represents and probably will continue to represent but one step in a long and consistent evolutionary progression that began many years ago. A third alternative response is that while there have been significant changes, they are transitory; things will return to "normal" (variously defined) before or soon after the end of the current presidential term. And finally there is the argument that, despite all the flag-waving and rhetoric, the office and the process have not really changed; beneath the turbulent surface the institutional currents continue to flow in the same directions and with the same force as heretofore.

There is probably truth in all these responses. One's judgment depends upon the distance (or depth) of one's perception and upon which aspects of the agency and the process one is focusing. The observer must also bear in mind that the target is moving, and the platform from which he or she is looking is also moving. And they would be moving whether or not Mr. Reagan were president. While most of what is seen appears to be in movement, there may be underlying forces that are, in effect, constants—where any change would be a basic change in direction or velocity. Therefore, in order to assess the impact of the Reagan presidency upon the OMB and its associated budgetary process, it is essential to give at least cursory treatment to what went on before 1981 to ascertain the directions in which OMB was then moving.

THE BACKGROUND OF OMB

When Ronald Reagan became president, the organization now known as OMB was nearing its 60th birthday. It was created, as was the General Accounting Office, by the Budget and Accounting Act of 1921, itself the product of an economy-oriented reform wave which had been building for many years but which burst in Washington following the first World War. Its original title, the Bureau of the Budget (BoB), was then accurately descriptive. The budget was perceived as an indispensable instrument for reducing and keeping down expenditures, taxes, and debt. Economy became the objective, the basic ethos of the leaders and staff of the Bureau, and remained so for its first 18 years. Beginning in 1938 and 1939, its responsibilities and its staff were greatly enlarged to comprehend organization and management, planning, policy development and negotiation, fiscal policy, statistical coordination, and other activities. The concept behind these changes was that the Bureau should become a general staff agency for the president. In many ways it did; to this day some think that World War II and the years immediately preceding and following it were the most glorious in the Bureau's history. In the succeeding years, however, some of these activities died or moved; some new ones were added; the relative emphases on others fluctuated; field offices established during the war were dismantled. At the end of all of this, and despite some fluctuating up and down, the agency was not much larger when Reagan arrived than it had been in the 1940s, even though the scope and financial dimensions of the federal government had mushroomed.

In 1981 the budget process remained the central engine and disciplinarian of OMB, and the original motif, economy, has never been neglected. OMB continues, as it always has, to issue the guidelines, receive and review the agencies' estimates, change them or recommend changes to the president, and superintend the execution of the budget. Budget activities consume the working time of about 65 percent of OMB's Staff. Other office functions inherited by the Reagan administration included:

- Study, coordination, and recommendation on organization and management problems, particularly of an interagency or intergovernmental nature (after about three decades of fluctuating emphasis, these activities had been considerably stimulated and expanded during the Carter term but with only moderate success).
- Review and coordination of executive branch legislative proposals, testimony and comments on legislation under consideration, enacted laws, executive orders, and proclamations (some of these activities had begun almost at the outset in 1921 and have been carried on ever since).
- Review and negotiation of proposed federal regulations and regulatory changes (an activity begun under President Nixon and expanded in each succeeding administration).
- Review and coordination of forms and other kinds of papers proposed by the agencies in an effort to minimize paper work requirements on the public (an activity begun in 1942 and carried on ever since).
- Leadership and coordination in the field of statistical standards throughout the government (an activity carried on most of the time since the 1930s).
- Leadership in coordination, standardization, and improvement of management practices, particularly in financial areas (an activity carried on with varying degrees of energy and enthusiasm since the late 1930s).
- The improvement and direction of procurement policies, regulations, procedures, and reforms (the Federal Procurement Policy Act of 1974 mandated that this function be carried out by a semi-autonomous office within the OMB; this function will not be discussed in this article).

The potential range and dimensions of these activities in a government as large and diverse as ours are virtually unlimited. That their performance is even possible is a consequence partly of the development of counterpart budget and management staffs in the operating departments and agencies and their subordinate bureaus and regional offices. It is doubtful that more than a tiny fraction of one percent of the federal personnel who are working on the budget and on the other activities listed above are employed by OMB. The pyramid of federal budget and management work of which the OMB provides the organizational pinnacle is a very broad one indeed. The mass and the pressure of the work that comes its way has forced upon OMB the necessity of being selective and of relying upon others for the positive development of plans, programs, and changes and the follow-through on most of them. OMB has been more characteristically the reviewer, examiner, critic, and counter-puncher than the initiator and entrepreneur. There have been exception: in its first months, the Bureau led the government as the apostle of economy; in the years encompassing World War II from 1939 to about 1950 it was a principal leader in the planning and revamping of the major civilian organizations and programs. In the 1960s it contributed to President Johnson's Great Society, and in the late '60s it played the major role in refashioning intergovernmental relations. It provided the leadership in much of President Carter's not totally successful efforts to reorganize the executive branch. BoB or OMB was also called upon to encourage and monitor the various waves of budgetary reform—the performance budget, planning-programming-budgeting systems (PPBS), management by objectives (MBO), zero-base budgeting (ZBB). But the initiatives and the models came from outside.[3]

The role and influence of OMB as the primary staff agency of the president have been modified since World War II by a succession of developments: the establishment of the Council of Economic Advisers and other professional units in the Executive Office of the President; the creation of the Office of Personnel Management and its new-found aggressiveness in the field of management; and most of all, the growth of the non-career presidential staff, particularly the Domestic Council and its successors, which assumed leadership on substantive matters of policy and program. Further, with the resurgence of Congress in the 1970s, OMB's primacy in the field of budgeting as a whole had to be shared with the Congressional budget committees and Budget Office, and with the growing involvement of such agencies as the General Accounting Office and Congressional Research Service in budgetary and policy analyses.

Perhaps as a by-product of many of the developments discussed above, BoB-OMB has become increasingly dominated by short-term, non-career personnel. This phenomenon, usually referred to as politicization, has been growing over approximately the last 15 years. The first "principle" embodied in Circular #1 of the Budget Bureau's first director, Charles G. Dawes, was that it "must be impartial, impersonal, and nonpolitical."[4] In fact, the BoB-OMB was justly famous for its political neutrality for most of its first 50 years. Almost none of its staff, not even its directors, were politicians in the usual sense, and while the directors and their immediate assistants normally changed with new administrations, the vast majority of other officers and employees, even including many of the deputy directors, were drawn from the career civil service. A few non-career persons were authorized during the 1950s and 1960s, usually in staff positions. But early in the 1970s a group of non-career positions of associate directors was created to superintend the budget work of the estimates (then and now called program) divisions. Since that time, there have been one or more layers of non-career appointees between the director and the professional career staff. Very few of the non-career appointees have been patronage appointees in the traditional sense; most have had education and some experience considered relevant for their jobs. The rationale has been to assure responsiveness and loyalty to the president and his policies and programs. The political cast of OMB was made even more pronounced after Congress, exasperated by what many of its members considered the arrogance of the president and his budget director in financial matters, required by law (P.L. 93–250, March 2, 1974) that the appointments of both the director and his deputy be subject to confirmation by the Senate. OMB became in effect a policy arm of the president on substantive matters. Most of the OMB directors and deputies in the 1970s were qualified administrators of the president's party, but not partisan leaders. With the possible exception of Bert Lance, who served as director for only eight months, none was a leader or spokesman for his political party.

STOCKMAN, OMB, AND THE BUDGETARY PROCESS

One must preface observations about budgeting by calling attention to the differences between the first and second presidential years and their relation to the budget cycle. The presidential year, of course, runs from January to January; the fiscal, or budget, year from October to October. The budget which applies to the fiscal year beginning in October after the presidential inauguration is in fact prepared by the outgoing president. But it has become customary for a new president to recommend revisions which can be nearly equivalent to a new budget during his first spring in office. Such changes are normal. At about the same time—a few weeks after inauguration—the new administration begins work on the budget for the second year, which will be submitted to Congress the following January. Thus, the bulk of the congressional work on the first fiscal year budget and the executive branch work on he second fiscal year budget are performed during the first presidential year, while the congressional work on the second fiscal year budget occurs during the second presidential year.

Some of the differences between the presidential years are built-in and expectable. New presidents normally enjoy a honeymoon at the beginning, with high popular approval and a willingness on the part of both administration and congressional officials to follow his leadership. In the case of President Reagan, this advantage was enhanced by his personal style, his speaking ability, and his attractiveness through the media, especially television. It was further brightened by an assassin's tragic attempt upon his life and the confidence, courage, and cheer with which he responded and recovered. During his first year, Reagan rode the high crest of a very tall wave. A second expectable attribute of a new administration is less favorable: most new presidents come to Washington with abilities and staffs far better equipped to run a political campaign than to govern a nation. They arrive adorned with campaign promises but with little knowledge and the machinery to translate those pledges into deeds.

This problem was alleviated for the Reagan administration by two factors. The first was its firm ideological understanding or what it wanted to do: a perspective shared by the president's immediate followers and later by other top appointees in the administration. Second was the president's early choice of and reliance upon a very few persons in key positions who both agreed with his objectives and knew the ins and outs of congressional and bureaucratic politics in Washington. For purposes of this article and indeed of the Reagan administration, the most significant of these was David Stockman, Reagan's Director of OMB and one of his first designees, who knew from education, experience, and exhaustive study the budget process and procedures of Congress.[5]

The congressional handling of the budget during the second year of a new administration is typically very different. Promises and expectations have not been completely fulfilled. The novelty and glamour have worn off, the problems of actual governance abound, and critics have become more articulate and more confident. The Reagan administration has experienced its own version of this "second year slump" with the result that, in keeping with the historic pattern, the budget process in the first and second years of the administration have been very different from each other and, to a lesser degree, different from their predecessors. The changes in the domestic budget for the first fiscal year (1982) were dramatic and may be longest remembered. But Congress in the second year has so far been reverting in the direction of "normality" and even beyond it in some ways. The analyses that follow should be considered in this dual context.

The Executive Branch

The first Reagan year witnessed the striking and sudden emergence of OMB to the posture of principal executive leader, short of the president himself, in policy making and politics. This was made possible, perhaps inevitable, by the convergence of a number of factors. One was the president's determination that economic recovery be number one on the administration's agenda and his faith that this goal could be achieved largely by tax reduction and sharp cuts in nondefense expenditures. The principal machinery for the purpose, of course, included the budget, and the only agency equipped with the requisite scope, power, and knowledge was OMB. A second factor was the new director, Stockman himself. Never before had a budget director undertaken to testify and negotiate on the particulars of authorizing bills as did Stockman in the summer of 1981. The president and his immediate assistants contributed persuasion and not a little political arm-twisting, but the subsequent congressional results were largely a product of the efforts of Stockman and other political and career staff of OMB. Despite many changes, the final congressional determinations were basically consistent with the president's proposals.

In many ways, the budget-cutting orientation demanded by the Reagan-Stockman program came naturally to the career examiners of OMB who had long defined their own roles as bulwarks against large agency and departmental spending requests. The initial Reagan call for deep spending cuts must have fallen on a good many receptive ears. On the other hand, some felt that the decisions were made by the political officers on high without much if any participation in the decision process by career professionals. Their information, data, and analyses were instead used to provide support for decisions already made in which they had not taken effective part. There was very little input from the affected executive agencies, in part because there was insufficient time to consider agency reactions before submission of budget revisions in early February. In addition, whether or not by design, at the time the Reagan revisions for both fiscal 1982 and 1983 were developed, most affected departments and agencies were not yet staffed with the intermediate-level political appointees who ordinarily serve as the communications-decision-making links between agency heads and their cadres of professional civil servants. These appointees, especially those in assistant secretary and bureau chief positions, could normally have been expected to solicit the views of their respective career staffs as to the likely outcomes of proposed budgetary changes. Since this process obviously could not occur systematically, the Stockman-OMB budget proposals were reviewed, when they were reviewed at all, by department heads whose political views mirrored the president's and who were as yet unfamiliar with the detailed rationale for the programs under their direction.

Little wonder, under these conditions, that only three weeks after his inauguration, president Reagan was able to announce a revised budget for fiscal 1982 reflecting cuts of some $41 billion from the Carter proposals. Budget choices were most securely anchored in the president's own beliefs about what the federal government should and should not do. The guidelines were firm and exacting and the time available for consideration of alternative courses of action was extremely limited. There was probably more than usual concern within OMB about political acceptability, less about program consequences.

The proposed budget cuts for both fiscal 1982 and 1983, along with the tax cuts and revisions, were, in fact, the administration's domestic policies. They involved: severe reductions in many programs (food stamps, research and development in many fields, a large number of educational grants, a wide variety of health and welfare programs, and many others); elimination or phasing out of many other programs (public service employment, legal services, community services, and others); and delegation of some, with reduced financial support, to state governments in block grants. Further, Stockman was named the president's principal spokesman for his "New Federalism" proposals whereby complete responsibility for certain federal grant programs would be transferred to the states and the central government would assume complete responsibility for certain others.

Contrary to the dictum of General Dawes 60 years earlier, the director of OMB suddenly became the principal political strategist and public advocate of the president's program in domestic affairs; a role without precedent in the history of the agency.[7] And yet, the overwhelming concern with economy and budget cuts has returned OMB to an institutional focus reminiscent of the role played by its historical parent during the Harding, Coolidge, and Hoover administrations.

On two elements of the president's program—defense expenditures and tax cuts—Stockman's role was less dominant than on domestic expenditures. Tax reductions were treated as an integral part of the overall budget program, and OMB participated in their development and the argument for them. But later on, as impending deficits cast a dark shadow on the program as a whole, Stockman's efforts to build up revenues were apparently ineffective. Likewise, he was denied his wish to examine carefully and reduce expenditures for defense. Reagan insisted on sticking to his original game plan until Republican leaders in Congress made it clear that they would not accept these positions.

On the procedural side, OMB quietly abandoned its requirements for zero-based budgeting (ZBB) in its budget circular (A-11) in the spring of 1981. It appears, however, that some of the elements of that initiative of the Carter administration, such as the use of program priorities, have been retained.

The Legislative Branch

The two major elements of the Reagan economic program during 1981 were the Economic Recovery Tax and Omnibus Reconciliation Acts. Both were passed by Congress substantially as proposed. Both were widely considered outstanding political achievements and victories for the president. The OMB and its director were involved in efforts to secure passage of both measures, but most deeply engaged in shaping, negotiating, and even drafting the legislation which authorized the expenditure reductions. Indeed, the performance of Stockman and his associates at OMB in 1981 has no precedent in American history.

The strategy employed for this purpose hinged upon use of the first concurrent resolution and reconciliation provisions of the Congressional Budget and Impoundment Control Act of 1974.[8] The Budget Act called upon Congress to establish two spending "ceilings" by concurrent resolution. The first was to occur by May 15 of each budget year and would serve as a "target" as authorizing committees began their legislative work. The second and binding resolution was to be adopted by September 15, only two weeks before the start of the fiscal year. This was too late to permit effective use of the process.

Reconciliation as authorized was envisioned as a process which would require committees to bring their proposed spending levels in line with the ceilings established in the second resolution. Committees whose proposed expenditures exceeded that amount were "instructed" to reduce or "reconcile" their totals with the mandated levels. The necessary changes are then compiled into a single measure by the budget committees to be taken to the floor for consideration.

The strategy itself grew directly out of previous trial attempts to use the reconciliation procedure within Congress and was the joint product of Stockman and the Republican leadership. Two years earlier the Senate Budget Committee had sought, for the first time, to secure legislative savings via the reconciliation process during consideration of the second budget resolution for fiscal 1980. That effort, however, was hotly contested in conference by the then chairman of the House Budget Committee, Robert Giaimo, who opposed reconciliation on the grounds that adjournment was near and Congress could ill afford to devote itself to experiments with a "complex controversial and potentially cumbersome" procedure.[9] The subsequent failure of congressional authorizing committees to realize the savings (indeed their public disregard of specific committee requests in some cases) requested by the two budget committees for fiscal 1980 convinced their members that reconciliation, to be successful, must occur at the beginning of the congressional budget process. This conviction and a Carter administration desire to reduce the fiscal 1981 budget converged and resulted in an intense eight days of bargaining in March 1980, during which the administration and the budget committees agreed to use a little-known "elastic" phrase of the Act which authorized the budget committees to require "any other procedure which is considered appropriate to carry out the purposes of this Act" to justify applying reconciliation procedures to the first concurrent resolution.[10] Some authorizing committees affected by the resulting reconciliation instruction sought to reduce their spending not alone by reducing entitlements as formally specified in the Act, but also by effecting reductions in authorizations for discretionary spending. The Senate Budget Committee, in particular, ever alert to stretch the reach of the congressional budget process, seized upon this action to contend that all authorizations are properly the province of reconciliation. The House committee, however, refused to go along with this view in 1980. Stockman and the Republican leadership used this Senate committee understanding as precedent and extended it on a vast scale to Reagan's suggested cuts including: the wholesale elimination of provisions of existing law and programs, the adoption of spending limits for out-years, and enactment of substantive changes in statutes governing grants-in-aid. The resultant Reconciliation Act affected over 250 domestic programs, ran to 576 pages, cut more than $35 billion from Carter's 1982 federal spending proposals, and included references to myriad legislation which it modified or superseded.

Not only did Stockman strongly support this strategy, but the OMB director went much further, personally assuming leadership responsibility for shepherding the president's reconciliation proposal through Congress. Stockman and his non-career associates were omnipresent figures testifying before countless committees and subcommittees on the Reagan proposals and in the many committee and subcommittee meetings and negotiation sessions leading to passage of the Reconciliation Act. In addition, many of the career budget examiners worked closely with congressional staff in negotiating and drafting the huge Omnibus Reconciliation Act.

It is ironic that little-known provisions of an act explicitly designed to enhance the power of the Congress were instead used to augment that of the chief executive. Stockman in particular placed his own formidable talents and the immense analytic capability and detailed knowledge represented in OMB's staff at the call of this paradoxical method of achieving the president's political aims.

The peculiarly intense bargaining and extremely compact time frame in which Reagan gained his legislative victory largely excluded interest group representatives from the decision process, while vastly increasing the number and variety of communications and contacts between OMB staff at all levels and members of Congress and their respective personal and committee staffs. The first consequence suggests the temporary breakdown of a host of so-called issue networks of long-standing importance to domestic policy making. The heightened level of contact by OMB and Congress suggests a deepening OMB advocacy role with respect to political interbranch issues and conflicts. The advocacy posture may itself signal a decline in the traditional OMB concern to present the most technically accurate analysis possible. At the least, OMB evinced a new outcome-oriented stance as Stockman completely immersed himself and his institution in the task of achieving a legislature victory for the president.

The 1981 experience suggests additional observations. Reconciliation increases the uncertainty of congressional budgetary outcomes, as already "set" authorization and appropriation levels are changed markedly, quickly, and with little opportunity for study and negotiation.[11] This many also presage a decline in the relative importance of OMB-agency negotiations and decisions on the executive budget. The rapidity of the process also results in less concerted congressional attention to many decisions enacted through reconciliation both on the floor and in committee.

For both the executive and congressional sides of the budgetary process for most of Reagan's first year, Stockman and his OMB were "the biggest boys on the block," overshadowing the domestic policy machinery in the White House as well as most of the operating agencies in the executive branch. But this eminence receded as the second year began and progressed. Other issues vied with the economic for popular and presidential attention—defense, foreign affairs, social matters. Indeed, President Reagan released his proposed fiscal 1983 budget in January 1982 to a chorus of congressional skepticism engendered by suspicion of its underlying economic assumptions, concern over its projected deficit, and a pervasive sense that the spending cuts it contained were simply too deep in light of the previous year's reductions. To these concerns were added Stockman's damaging remarks in a widely read *Atlantic Monthly* article and an economy which had stubbornly refused to show signs of the president's oft-promised turnaround.[12] In early 1982 it became clear on Capitol Hill that the Reagan budget proposals would not even be considered, much less accepted, by either House without very substantial revisions. In effect, Congress tossed aside the president's budget proposal for fiscal 1983. Budget leaders in both parties developed their own spending proposals, and the Senate Finance Committee wrote a bill designed to radically increase tax revenues. Forced to abandon his own proposals, the president endorsed the Republican congressional alternatives. OMB has continued to provide data and analyses to the congressional committees concerned, but the principal negotiator on behalf of the president is James A. Baker, III, White House Chief of Staff, not David Stockman.

NON-BUDGETARY ACTIVITIES

For some years it has been customary within OMB to refer generically to most of the functions not directly related to the budget process as "the management side." This has had the doubly unfortunate effect of accentuating the difference within the OMB between budget and management, and of grouping together a number of activities only remotely related to management as it is usually defined. These have included, for example, forms control, regulation, statistical coordination, and others. There has been a certain consistency in the way in which these activities have been treated in the Reagan administration. Extraordinary vigor has been applied to reducing or eliminating those federal activities considered onerous to the general public or, more specifically, regulations and other requirements imposed upon private business and state and local governments. Management has come to mean the elimination of "fraud, waste, and abuse" (terms which have become roughly synonymous), thus the reduction of federal costs; and the transfer of programs and the costs thereof to the states. All of these activities are essentially negative so far as the federal government is concerned, and they are thus entirely consonant with the thrust of the Reagan budgetary aims in domestic affairs.

Management

Since the Bureau of the Budget was made part of the Executive Office of the President in 1939, the definition, the nature, and the extent of its management responsibilities have been in flux and a subject of sometimes heated debate. The earliest effort had to do with general organizational and procedural problems at the presidential level: reorganizations; assisting individual agencies—new ones, old ones, dying ones—in their tribulations; handling governmentwide reorganizations and procedures; helping outside study commissions (the Hoover Commission, the Heineman Commission, the Ash Council, and others); and providing leadership to the improvement of management on a governmentwide basis. Emphasis on this kind of activity declined after the 1940s. In the late 1960s a new surge of activity was directed to intergovernmental relations and coordination of the field activities of the various agencies. President Carter, pursuant to his own campaign promises, defined management very largely as reorganization, and established a new position of executive associate director of OMB for reorganization and management. At one time well over 100 OMB professionals were assigned to the task of reorganizing the federal government.

In contrast, President Reagan has not emphasized reorganization, beyond seeking to abolish the two new cabinet departments (Education and Energy) which Carter established. In keeping with his own campaign rhetoric, which promised substantial saving in expenditures through the elimination of "fraud, waste, and abuse," OMB's management staff has concentrated on standardizing, economizing, and enforcing common procedures in government travel, cash management, debt collection, and like matters. The president set up, early in his administration, a President's Council on Integrity and Efficiency, chaired by the deputy director of OMB and consisting mainly of the inspectors general of the various departments and agencies, but also including the deputy attorney general, the assistant director of investigations of the FBI, and the director of the Office of Personnel Management. The council, which is centrally staffed by OMB's management group, has concentrated on locating fraud and waste, on bringing offenders to justice, and on improving preventive procedures and controls. Other parts of the staff are engaged in efforts to decentralizing to the states, through block grants and other devices, federal activities and control over intergovernmental relations. These include severe modifications or abolition of the mechanisms set up more than a decade earlier to provide for better-coordinated planning and execution among federal agencies and with state and local governments (notably in Budget Circular A-95). A small group continues its work on improving financial management, but what remained of the old divisions of organization and personnel management was abolished in 1982, the surviving functions transferred to the program divisions. The current status of managerial and organizational activities in OMB is a source of deep disappointment to many old-timers of the Bureau of the Budget, as well as others who would revive those responsibilities as they were once defined.[13]

In some respects, the most aggressive management improvement effort of the Reagan administration was its establishment in the spring of 1982 of a Private Sector Survey on Cost Control in the Federal Government. It consists of a large number of chief executive officers of major private organizations organized in some 35 different task forces to investigate and make recommendations on improving federal management systems. They were financed and staffed by their companies and were expected to produce reports during the fall of 1982. OMB's management office is providing liaison with the group on behalf of the federal government.

The Control of Regulations

As indicated earlier, Ronald Reagan became chief executive convinced that the federal regulatory role had grown too large. In this, he was pursuing an objective which had been embraced by his three predecessors in the Oval Office. It is to the Nixon years that one must look for the first major institutional involvement of OMB in regulatory matters. Each president since has, however unevenly, expanded both the scope of rules review and the OMB role in that process. The initial effort arose from Nixon White House concern over the rules jurisdiction granted the new Environmental Protection Agency. EPA was required to give other affected agencies an opportunity to comment on its proposed rules, review and respond to those comments, and then submit the entire record of the exchange to OMB for review. Both Presidents Ford and Carter built upon this Nixon initiative, expanding OMB review jurisdiction to other executive agencies and informally to some of the independent commissions, requiring review of major rules and mandating cost-benefit analyses of proposed major rules.

President Carter was a vigorous advocate of passage of the Paperwork Reduction Act of 1980, one of whose provisions established an Office of Information and Regulatory Affairs within OMB with authority to "review any proposed rule which contains a collection of information requirement."[14] And it was to this OMB office and rules review function that President Reagan elected to graft an expanded regulatory review effort.

The dimensions of that rules review program were outlined in Executive Order 12291 of February 17, 1981, less than a month after Reagan entered office and more than a month prior to the formal statutory creation of OMB's Office of Information and Regulatory Affairs. The order specifically defined "major rule," required regulatory impact analyses for such rules, and detailed the information each such analysis was to contain. The order also created the President's Task Force on Regulatory Relief to be chaired by the vice-president and staffed by the OMB Office of Information and Regulatory Affairs, forbade issuance of proposed regulations unless their potential benefits exceeded their likely costs, and charged OMB with responsibility for review and comment on agency preliminary or final regulatory impact analyses of proposed rules. This charge did not permit OMB to rewrite proposed agency rules, but it did permit recommended changes, additions, or deletions prior to their issuance. The order also contemplated that serious OMB-agency disagreements could be appealed to the president's task force and ultimately to the president if necessary.[15]

As with previous efforts, although somewhat more boldly, the Reagan order straddles a fine line between creation of a genuine centralized presidential rules review process within OMB and existing statutory and Administrative Procedure Act requirements that agency heads exercise final authority over all rule-making decisions for purposes of administrative appeal and judicial review. While it is still too soon to determine the ultimate effect of the compromise struck by the Reagan initiative, its practical administrative result may have been to give OMB de facto final say over the issuance of proposed rules which agency heads do not consider sufficiently important to appeal to the president or his task force.

In such circumstances, it is difficult to determine whether OMB's negative response to a proposed rule effectively subverts the intent of the Administrative Procedure Act and other legislation by causing the responsible decision maker to cancel or modify a rule under administrative pressure. What data exist suggest that a major share of the proposed rules rejected by OMB are thereafter permitted to die by the agencies which proposed them. Of the 52 proposed rules returned to agencies for revision by OMB between February 17 and April 30, 1981, for example, only 17 were changed and resubmitted. The remainder died.[16] Each of these never-published rules may have been inefficient regulatory initiatives of great potential cost and little potential benefit to society, as OMB's reviewers believed, and therefore were rightly sent to an early grave. But critics question if it is the place of OMB's analysts to effectively overrule the best judgment of knowledgeable and accountable agency administrators.

The rules review effort obviously represents a fertile source for controversy, raising as it does questions whose answers may ultimately turn upon interpretations of the nature and the extent of executive authority under the Constitution. For OMB as an institution, however, the effects of this foray into a new arena of responsibility are more concrete. First, the process has clearly conferred a new measure of power and authority upon OMB. Equally clear, however, is the fact that that power is very largely negative in character. All executive agencies must now undertake rule making in the knowledge that OMB will review and possibly stymie their initiatives. OMB emerges as an institutional curmudgeon of a peculiar sort, for it undertakes its review aware of the relative insecurity of its authority and the tension—sometimes explicit, often implicit—between its central review role and agency statutory responsibilities. Second, the current OMB regulatory role and the criteria by which it makes its review decisions are very largely the product of a political ideology which lays great emphasis on reducing the federal role within society. One may speculate on what would happen to this institutional function should a national administration ardently committed to a decrease in federal regulatory activity enter office in coming years.

PROFESSIONALISM AND POLITICS

It was suggested in an earlier section that since the late late 1960s, OMB has moved sporadically in the direction of greater political responsiveness with somewhat less emphasis upon non-partisan neutrality and professional competence. One might have expected that the Reagan presidency would accelerate this tendency. After all, the new administration espoused a massive turnaround in governmental philosophy and policy, and it had loudly and repeatedly criticized the career bureaucrats as co-conspirators with the Democratic politicians in bringing about the allegedly sorry state of the State.

But in regard to what is usually labeled the "politicization" of OMB, the recent record is mixed. There has been no increase in the number of political positions; in fact, the two new offices of executive associate directors (responsible for budget, and reorganization and management respectively), set up under President Carter, were not refilled. The qualifications of the Stockman appointees in terms of education and relevant experience were at least the equals of those of his predecessors and differed mainly in that several had worked with him in Congress. Some civil servants have left voluntarily—or with management encouragement—as in past transitions; and very possibly more would have gone had employment been more possible and attractive elsewhere.[18] Stockman has publicly praised the dedication and work of the career staff in support of the Reagan program. Quite apart from their individual political attitudes about the president's policies, the staffs themselves have been influenced by several institutional factors. First, the preeminence of OMB in both the executive and legislative aspects of the Reagan budget added standing and prestige to the professionals in OMB, always a proud group in Washington bureaucratic circles. Second, there has long—if not always—been a predisposition among OMB personnel that agency budgets are padded and that some programs should be severely cut or even eliminated. As suggested earlier, the Reagan administration provided support for many things the examiners in OMB wanted to do anyway.

But against these inducements has been an argument among certain OMB professional personnel relating to the making of decisions "on high" by non-career people without benefit of sophisticated analyses and recommendations. Some expressed the feeling that the top-down approach to decision making is negating creative professional work. Others emphasized that the present concern with outcomes of the whole budgetary process, not simply the professional quality of the budget analyses and decisions, made the work of OMB far more effective.

Probably the feature of the Stockman OMB most threatening to its performance and reputation for neutral competence however, has been the posture, the *modus operandi* of Stockman himself. As indicated earlier, he has been projected by the administration as its up-front leader in domestic affairs. His name and picture were on the front pages of the newspapers almost continually. He testified before virtually all of the congressional committees and many of the subcommittees, as the outward symbol of the Reagan domestic program who "took the heat" for that administration. He was and remains a policy and political leader. With Reagan, the budget became the number one political issue and Stockman its number one protagonist. The degree to which he could operate in such a position without his political prominence brushing off upon his agency and without the agency's coloration brushing off upon its career staff is an open question. A few knowledgeable persons, both within and outside of OMB, were asked whether they thought the politically neutral reputation and credibility of the agency could survive Stockman. Some responded that they thought it could, but not if he were succeeded by two or three more like him; that is, more persons who would enter the political limelight. (All doubted that there are any more persons with the qualities of Stockman sitting in the wings.)

A further set of questions is presented when one considers the posture of individual professional employees of an agency whose role is partly or primarily political. Is one more professional if he or she pursues with all efforts and persuasion the intentions of the agency, or if he/she quietly recedes from the struggle or even resigns when not in agreement? Does professionalism mean endorsement of social goals or the projection of "truth" as defined by the profession in its literature? Or does it mean going along with the organization which employs one? Questions of this kind have no doubt plagued BoB-OMB budget examiners since 1921. But never could they be more acute than in the last two years when federal programs have been under such fire. That is, can or should career employees at high levels provide maximum support for or against measures in which they have deep intellectual, personal, political, or ideological stakes against the positions of their agencies? Aid for the handicapped? protection of clean air? development of the B1 bomber? baring of a threatening drug? maintenance of food stamps at current levels? Can or should an OMB economist who is a convinced Keynesian give his or her intellectual all in support of supply side proposals? Still another question: will an OMB budget examiner who is now working enthusiastically for elements of the Reagan program be able to apply these energies with equal enthusiasm to essentially opposite programs in 1985 if an Edward Kennedy is elected president?

The answers to questions like these were sometimes muffled or qualified, but were on the whole surprisingly affirmative. The rationale leaned heavily upon theories of constitutional democracy: the president was properly elected by the people, he is being held responsible by the people to decide upon and carry out polices; it is our duty to do our best to help him do what he was elected to do in the most effective manner possible. We must not let our personal beliefs and political predilections interfere with doing the job for the president, and, besides, we may be wrong.

One of those interviewed referred favorably to a top OMB staffer as a "real pro." But he was not using the word "pro" the way most academics do: as one who thinks and acts with some degree of autonomy in "taking the abstractions of science (or other systematic knowledge) and applying them to the concrete and practical affairs of men."[19] Yet it is a certain kind of professionalism, epitomized by the legal profession: advocacy. In this sense, civil servants can be thoroughly professional and neutral while working for a totally political institution for completely partisan causes. This is probably what the civil service reformers of 100 years ago must have contemplated had they thought the matter through. It is also what the budget reformers 60 years ago must have contemplated—with the proviso that any thinking person of whatever political persuasion would favor maximum economy in government.

THE IMPACT OF THE REAGAN OMB

The problems of professionalism and politics suggested above are certainly not new; they hail back to the earliest skirmishes against the spoils system and to the problems of the central budget agency 50 years ago. In fact, the same might be said with respect to many of the changes credited to Reagan and Stockman. On the substantive side, many of their initiatives were, at least in their gross dimensions, accelerations and extensions of trends already under way. President Carter was increasing the amount and proportion of federal resources allotted to defense; Reagan approximately doubled Carter's proposed increases. Carter proposed cutbacks in domestic programs; Reagan greatly increased them. Both shied away from major changes in the biggest entitlement programs, most notably social security. Federal grants-in-aid reached a peak and began to decline in the late 1970s, and Regan accelerated the drop. He also proposed fundamental changes in decision making and funding responsibilities in the federal system. But these had in fact begun more than a decade earlier with revenue sharing and state-local participation in regional grant administration.

The sharpest break from the earlier trends was the massive tax reduction enacted in 1981; Carter had considered tax reduction but decided against it. Concern about federal regulation had been growing for at least 15 years, and the first official steps to counter their alleged burdens were taken by President Nixon. Every administration since has moved to strengthen the central restraints, and Regan has probably backed them more forcefully than his predecessors. But it is not a new idea—no more so than the central control of paperwork. The decline of management activities had continued for a dozen years, barring a short-lived effort at federal reorganization in the late 1970s. And the concern about fraud and mismanagement in government had begun years before and was recently manifested in the establishment of inspectors general in most of the major federal agencies during the Carter administration.

On the surface, therefore, there was nothing much really new about these OMB undertakings expect emphases and effort. Beneath the surface, however, there were many targets of discretion and choice: the recipients of programs which should be cut; the beneficiaries of various kinds of tax reductions; the industries or the business practices which should be freed from regulation. Most political scientists would agree that these kinds of issues are essentially and properly political and should be decided by politically responsible officials. OMB has proved itself a knowledgeable and pliable mechanism for making those determinations effective. As such, it remains an almost invaluable cog in our political system. Furthermore, it has demonstrated an unusual capability to provide effective service to administrations with widely disparate perspectives and views.

Have the first months of the Reagan administration brought real and lasting changes to the influence of OMB in our governmental system and to the nature of the agency itself? The prediction here is that it has, although not wholly because of Reagan and Stockman. ZBB was dropped and will probably not be revived. There has been no complete assessment of the value of the approaches and differences of ZBB from historic justification processes, but its requisite paperwork did not appeal to the agencies. More permanent, and probably more important, is the centralization of budgetary decision making in the OMB, which began almost immediately upon Reagan's inauguration. This has been due in substantial part to the political situation and to the strength of the executive leaders, but it has also been partly a product of the congressional budget process. If Congress is to have a relatively unified budget position, so must the administration. Departments and agencies cannot go off in their own directions. They must be disciplined to the administration's directions, and the only agency equipped to perform this role is OMB. The Reconciliation Act of 1971 was not a Reagan invention; it was first used the previous year in connection with Carter's last full budget cycle. But reconciliation had never been used on so massive a scale and may well become a fixture in the federal budget process. If so, it could intensify the centralizing effect. There has also been a centralizing influence within OMB with somewhat less participation by the career analysts and examiners in the OMB decision process. This may be a step in a long-range direction toward greater dominance by political officials.

The most striking change in the posture and performance of OMB since January 1981 has been a consequence of the person of its director: his knowledge, ability, and drive; his aggressiveness both in the executive branch and the president's high confidence in him. Over a longer pull, a Stockman or a series of Stockmans might bring about a real change in the office, but without that, OMB continues to be a resilient, adaptive, flexible agency which rolls with the punches and provides a force for stability and continuity for the federal government as a whole.

NOTES

1. We are indebted to A. James Reichley's perspective analysis of the Reagan program and philosophy in "A Change in Direction" in Joseph A. Pechman (ed.), *Setting National Priorities: The 1982 Budget* (Washington, D.C.: The Brookings Institution, 1981).

2. Ronald Reagan, "Inaugural Address," *Congressional Quarterly 1981 Almanac* (Washington, D.C.: Congressional Quarterly, Inc., 1982), 12-E. Boston College Professor Samuel Beer in a recent article entitled "The Idea of a Nation" in *The New Republic,* 187, 3 (July 19 and 26, 1982), pp. 23–29.

3. This proposition may be argued in the case of ZBB, but it is clear that the model was Georgia as that state had applied a private sector initiative, and it reached Washington via a president and the budget director he brought from Georgia. In most of the other cases, origination and modeling were in the Department of Defense, sometimes stimulated from the private sector.

4. In Dawes' book, *The First Year of the Budget of the United States,* (New York: Harper and Brothers, 1923), pp. 8–9.

5. Stockman's interest in the content of the federal budget dates at least to 1975 when he authored an overview of that processes whose premises closely resemble those he has pressed as OMB director. See David A. Stockman, "The Social Park Barrel," *The Public Interest,* 39 (November 1975), pp. 3–30. It is also significant that Stockman was only the second budget director in American history who had prior congressional experience and the first one in nearly 40 years—the last was Lewis W. Douglas, Franklin Roosevelt's first budget director, who held the post from March 1933 to August 1934.

6. The increased concern for the outlay consequences of budgetary decisions is reflected in the Budget Review Division's recent effort to install a CBMSU or Computerized Budget Management System Unit. This unit is responsible for computerized tracking of congressional and executive actions which might affect final budget outlays.

7. Many budget directors were highly influential within the executive branch, and some carried weight in Congress. But most worked quietly and with a low profile so far as the public was concerned. A few might have emerged as political leaders and spokesmen if they had served longer terms: Bert Lance, Roy Ash, George Shultz, even Dawes himself. But none "came on" immediately as did Stockman.

8. Specifically, Sections 301(b) (2) and 310 of that Public Law 93–344 of July 12, 1974.

9. As reported by Allen Schick in his *Reconciliation and the Congressional Budget Process* (Washington, D.C.: American Enterprise Institute, 1981), p. 6.

10. The idea of the phrase as an "elastic" one is Schick's. Ibid., p. 10; the relevant section of the Act is 301(b) (2).

11. Ibid., pp. 30–32.

12. See William Greider, "The Education of David Stockman," *The Atlantic Monthly* 248, 6 (December 1981), pp. 27–54. It surprised some, including these authors, that Stockman could survive his admissions and allegations of mistrust and misstatement about the Reagan economic and budget program on the part of himself and others high in the president's hierarchy. A number of people in Washington explained to us that no one else had the knowledge and the acumen to take his place. Yet Stockman himself had admitted in the article that "none of us really understands what's going on with all these numbers" (p. 38).

13. For example, a blue ribbon committee under the auspices of the National Academy of Public Administration, in a report prepared for the winner of the 1980 presidential election, *A Presidency for the 1980s,* laid heavy stress on strengthening the management activities of OMB. A later panel of the same Academy,

which consisted almost entirely of OMB and Bureau of the Budget alumni, was even more emphatic in its 1981 report: "Strengthening OMB's Role in Improving the Management of the Federal Government."

14. See Section 3504(b) (1) of *The Paperwork Reduction Act of 1980,* Public Law 96–511 of December 11, 1980.

15. U.S., President, Executive Order 12291, *Federal Register,* 46 (February 17, 1981), p. 13193.

16. This information is drawn from House Oversight and Investigations Subcommittee data obtained under subpoena and is reported in Michael Wine's excellent overview of the Reagan regulatory effort in "Reagan's Reforms Are Full of Sound and Fury, But What Do They Signify?" *National Journal* (January 16, 1982), pp. 92–98 at p. 93.

17. Ibid., p. 93.

18. We were unable to obtain comparative turnover data, but the impression of those with whom we talked was that voluntary turnover had not significantly changed.

19. Quoted from Don K. Price, *The Scientific Estate* (Cambridge, Mass.: Harvard University Press, 1965), p. 122.

CHAPTER 9

THE SHIFTING ROLES OF STATE BUDGET OFFICES IN THE MIDWEST
Gosling Revisited

KURT THURMAIER AND JAMES J. GOSLING

Guy Peters notes that governance in the 1980s and 1990s has involved two difficult problems.[1] First, governments have struggled to fund their policy commitments. This has been especially difficult given the recessions in the early years of each decade. Second, governments have struggled with the fundamental question of the legitimacy of government as a problem-solving mechanism for society. Candidates increasingly run on platforms to cut government expenditures and taxes, preferring to let private markets have a larger role in shaping society. These problems are related and compounded by the growing realization that policy problems facing governments are increasingly seen as intractable. Policy options do not seem to offer "easy" avenues for government action; the problems are too complex.

Budgetary decisions are integral to the choices governments are making as they struggle with these issues. As such, budgetary decisionmakers are a subset of the administrative decisionmakers who formulate and implement public policies. Unfortunately, there is a paucity of empirical studies of budgetary decision making with respect to policy making. This article contributes to the empirical literature by comparing data on decision making in the central budget offices in three midwestern states with data gathered nearly a decade earlier. The focus of the comparison is on the role that the central budget analysts (CBAs) play with respect to making public policy in these states. First we analyze the general orientation of the budget offices toward policy making, which provides the context for CBA roles. Then we analyze the roles of the CBAs with respect to their assigned agencies. The results from the comparison or the 1985 and 1994 studies raise several issues that bear on budget theory and practice.

STAGES OF BUDGET OFFICE EVOLUTION

In a 1996 article, Schick noted that decision making reforms have been the history of budgeting in this century. He described the evolution of budget offices from an emphasis on controlling expenditures with the advent of the executive budget process (1920–50), to an emphasis on managing agencies and performance budgeting (1950s), to a planning orientation launched by Program-Planning-Budgeting (PPB) system (1960s). He noted that all three orientations have a role in budgeting, but that the emphasis on one or another changed over time: "In the matter of orientations, we are dealing with relative emphases, not with pure dichotomies. The germane issue is the balance among these vital functions at the central level."[2]

Schick argued that a *control orientation* deals with a narrow range of concerns, mainly activities that bind operating officials to the expenditure ceilings set by the legislature and chief executive as budget policies (such as position controls and line transfers). A *management orientation* deals with issues such as organizational arrangements to accomplish a specific task, and staffing alternatives. A *planning orientation* focuses on a broad range of issues, including how long range goals and policies are related to particular expenditure choices; and which programs should be initiated, terminated, expanded, or curtailed. Although Schick focused on changes at the federal level, he noted that states largely followed the changes at the national level.

Schick used program budgeting, and PPB specifically, as the example of budgeting with a planning orientation. He argued that "as a policy device, program budgeting departs from simple engineering models of efficiency" to a macro-analytic approach where the "accent is on comprehensiveness and on grouping data into categories that allow comparisons among alternative expenditure mixes."[3] The budget thus becomes a statement of policy, and budgeting becomes an allocative process among competing claims. In later work, however, Schick argued that PPB failed in its promise to integrate policy analysis and budgeting.[4] While it introduced long-range plans into budgetary procedures, policy analysis did not assume a central role in the PPB system implemented at the federal level. Among the reasons for such failure, according to Schick, was that the budgetary conflict inherent in PPB trade-offs was itself in conflict with the conflict-avoidance norms of budgetary incrementalism, and until conflict was more acceptable in budgeting, something like PPB decision making did "not stand much of a chance of affecting budget outcomes."[5]

The cutback budgeting initiated in many states during the recession of 1981–83 disrupted budgetary incrementalism and its norms of conflict-avoidance. Controlling expenditures once again became the dominant orientation of central budget offices. Conflict could not be avoided under the extended periods of budgetary stress, and states were forced to make budgetary—and policy—trade-offs.[6]

Such generalizations, however, obscure significant differences in how states were oriented to grapple with these budgetary challenges. A study by Gosling in the mid-1980s compared the policy contributions of state budget offices in the neighboring states of Iowa, Minnesota, and Wisconsin.[7] Gosling's research found that the Wisconsin office had developed a strong policy analysis orientation toward state budgeting. The comparative study found that the three states ranged on a continuum from little policy making in the Iowa budget office to strong policy making in the Wisconsin budget office, with the Minnesota budget office in transition from the accounting and control orientation found in Iowa toward the Wisconsin model. Gosling's work raises the possibility that Schick's "Stages of Budgeting" framework can be extended to include a policy orientation stage of budget office evolution.

In his remarks to his staff of New York State budget examiners, budget director Paul Appleby noted that the budget office has a distinct point of view regarding government operations, that the budget office makes "quite a lot of policy," and that the budget analysts are somewhat removed from the political pressure of budgeting, although they are "in the midst of a highly-charged web of political currents."[8]

The remarks of practitioner Appleby shed light on the seminal question of budgeting raised by V.O. Key a decade earlier: on what basis does one give X dollars to this program and only Y dollars to another?[9] Appleby notes that values are always in play in budget decisions, and the play of forces in the process determines whose values will be supported financially, and to what degree. The foundation for decision is the "budget point of view" developed by analysts. Appleby notes that the analysts are not void of values either, personal or professional. His remarks highlight the importance he placed on his budget staff analyzing budget issues from the "peculiar" perspective of the budget office.

Based on Gosling's description of the Wisconsin model, budget offices may be said to have a policy orientation when CBAs are encouraged to conduct a wide variety of policy analysis activities, which often (but not always) include quantitative analysis. Gosling notes that the key issue regarding policy influence is the extent to which the budget analysts exercise "discriminating policy choice."[10] More specifically, this involves the "extent to which they are encouraged and actually review policy alternatives in response to agency requests, and whether they initiate policy proposals where no agency requests have been made."[11] To various degrees, depending upon their agency assignments, the budget analysts define policy problems, evaluate alternatives, and recommend options (including funding levels). Understanding the general orientation of the state budget office toward policy analysis provides an important context for understanding the "budget point of view" of CBAs as they make budget decisions.

METHODOLOGY

Both the earlier (1985) Gosling work and the 1994 research questioned most of the analysts and supervisors, and all three budget directors in the three states.[12] Iowa has significantly restructured its budget office since 1985 such that they no longer have supervisors between the analysts and the budget director. The 1985 study has a sample of 44 compared to 49 subjects in the 1994 study. The 1985 study used structured interviews, while the 1994 study used a loosely structured interview protocol.[13]

CHANGING ORIENTATIONS OF STATE BUDGET OFFICES

In 1985, the Wisconsin state budget office exhibited a policy analysis orientation, the Iowa state budget office exhibited a control orientation, and the Minnesota state budget office was beginning a transition from a control orientation to a policy orientation. In 1994, the analysts in these offices were asked whether they would characterize the general orientation of their offices toward agencies as a "control orientation, management orientation, planning orientation, [or] policy orientation?" Table 9.1 presents a tabulation of their responses. The total number of responses exceeds the number of analysts because several subjects in each state identified more than a single orientation.

About 92 percent of the subjects (45 of 49) in the sample characterize their budget office as having a policy analysis orientation. The policy orientation is the modal response in all three states. Analysts rarely cite the management orientation; those who do describe it as the macro-management level of inter-agency coordination as opposed to micro-management of agencies. They generally characterize micro-management activity as providing technical assistance to the smallest agencies, usually at the agency's own request. The 15 percent of staff noting a planning orientation is primarily from the budget directors and team leaders who see this perspective as rather unique to their levels in the budget office and their responsibility for financial management planning for the entire state.

The number of "policy" responses is almost triple the number of "control" responses. Surprisingly, the only state with a significant share of "control" responses is Wisconsin, where two-thirds of the staff also cite control as an important role in the budget office. As Gosling found in 1985, they usually

Table 9.1

Budget Office Orientation, 1994, by State

State	Control	Management	Planning	Policy	State N
WI Total	13	2	2	18	19
IA Total	2	0	3	11	11
MN Total	1	2	3	16	19
Grand Total	16	4	8	45	49

Note: State N indicates the number of subjects interviewed in 1994. The number or responses to each question varied. For example, only eighteen responses were recorded for this question in Wisconsin.

discuss control as a secondary orientation, subordinate to policy analysis. Aside from the Wisconsin responses, only three analysts view control as a budget office orientation. Almost every analyst in Iowa and Minnesota reported that their office was moving away from control and toward something else (usually policy analysis). This is not a common qualifying statement of the Wisconsin staff, and it raises questions about the nature of control in a policy orientation, an issue that we investigate when we begin a more detailed comparison of each state in 1985 and 1994 later in this article.

Before we move to the in-depth analysis of each state, however, we pause to describe the array of budget analyst roles identified in the 1994 interviews. The traditional characterization of analysts is that they serve as the gatekeepers, the ones who say "No." They are the watchdogs of the treasury, making sure that departments "tow the line." However, as seen in Table 9.2, only a minority of analysts characterize their role as adversarial."[14]

Table 9.2 reports 1994 responses to the open-ended question: "How would you characterize your role with respect to your agencies in the budget process? Would you say you are an antagonist, adversary, advocate, something else?" The response categories in Table 9.2 capture the more frequent types of responses. The modal response for analysts characterizes their role as an Advocate for their agency needs (26). Only 18 percent of the sample characterize their role as being an Adversary, and many of them report to be so only at certain periods of the process.

One of the important findings is that analyst roles are not mutually exclusive; some analysts report multiple roles that vary with the phase in the budget process or with different departments. For example, an Iowa analyst responded:

> I would say that my role is to check for the reasonableness of a request, do a lot of the background footwork to determine which new requests are really worthy of funding in such tight economic times. For instance, one of the most valuable things to look at is salaries and how they spend those budgeted salary dollars. Then we'll ask some hard questions. If you really need these positions, then why aren't they being filled?

> Interviewer: Would you characterize this role as being antagonistic to the department?

> To an extent it probably is. We have to ask those hard questions. On the other hand, once we've talked with department and have heard what they have to say about a particular program that they want or a particular spending pattern, and if we're convinced that that's the way it should be, then we're, like I said earlier, an advocate for the department up until the governor says yes or no.

A Minnesota analyst had a similar story:

Table 9.2

Budget Analyst Roles, 1994, by State

State	WI	IA	MN	Total
Advocate	11	9	6	26
Adversary	2	3	4	9
Conduit	1	1	5	7
Facilitator	5	5	1	11
Policy Analysts	6	1	5	12
Other	5	1	7	13
State N	19	11	19	49

> [It] depends on the situation. In general I think there's this continuum where agencies can have too much power and not provide information. For instance there was a computer system that was developed a few years ago. They ended up running significant deficits without providing information to some of the people here who should have known. In that case I'd be an antagonist. Sort of, the power's swung too far. On the other hand, sometimes people will get into a chopping frenzy and will just snap at programs or administrative budgets without understanding the repercussions on the people that are ultimately getting served. In those cases I have to swing back to sort of a different, more protagonist, defender of the agency.

Minnesota differs from the general sample in several respects. The modal response of Minnesota staff is "Other," and three of those responses are from staff who do not want to say Adversary and choose "critic" instead. Had these been coded as Adversary responses, then Adversary would become the modal response for the Minnesota office.

Analysis of budget office orientations and budget analyst roles in Tables 9.1 and 9.2 provide the context for the more complicated analysis of the interaction between the two dimensions in each state. We are also interested in the effect, if any, that changing the budget office orientation has on analyst roles. The next section provides a more complete view of the budget office in each state.

THE WISCONSIN STATE BUDGET OFFICE: STILL ROUTINIZED POLICY

A decade ago, Gosling found a routinized policy role for analysts in the Wisconsin state budget office. The policy process required early identification of policy issues by analysts so that issues could be prioritized and studied as preparation for the next budget development period. Policy development within the office was especially important for non-cabinet agencies, such as education and natural resources. These independent agencies generated their own policy priorities for legislative consideration. This meant that the governor turned to the state budget office to develop his own policy initiatives in those areas.

The 1994 interviews reveal that this aspect of Wisconsin budgeting has changed little. All eighteen of the staff who responded to the orientation question say policy is a primary orientation of the Wisconsin state budget office. As one senior analyst notes,

> In terms of policy development, I don't know that it's really changed that much. We continue to be asked, sometimes independent of agencies, to develop governor's policy initiatives. We have to react to initiatives proposed by the agencies. Inevitably we're asked to prepare

alternatives to something. We're asked to provide the same amount of service for less money in lots of cases or do more with the same amount of money. So that really hasn't changed.

In all cases, budget development for Wisconsin agencies requires continuous dialog and close cooperation between the analysts and the governor's policy staff. According to the current budget director, the two groups should have a relationship that is "very close and very good."

> One of the things that I'll say to analysts when they start in the budget office and to [the governor's] policy people when they start is, "You should develop a very good relationship with each other." The way I look at it, our analysts should be constantly talking to the governor's policy analysts who are their counterparts to have feedback going back and forth. If a governor's policy analyst is going to talk to a legislator, they're going to have to know the substantive background before they go in and make political commitments. The need to call up and ask the budget analyst, what are the facts here before I go in and have to deal with this person, so I can respond and so I don't commit to something that is going to cause a problem.

In this respect, the budgeting hierarchy in Wisconsin is very flat, and the budget director encourages direct communication, specifically avoiding an intermediary role. In his view, "I don't think that logistically everything can go through me. The bottleneck would be too tremendous. They have to be talking directly . . . When things get moving, it's got to go analyst to analyst, or we just won't be able to keep up with things." He continues:

> That's also the way they'll learn what the governor's politics are and that's the way the governor's analysts will learn in depth what the policy implications are. The governor's policy analysts and the budget analysts have to have two somewhat different perspectives, but they both have to know the other person's perspective if they're doing a good job. The two perspectives aren't mutually exclusive. It really is important that the budget analysts develop recommendations which are grounded in good public policy and which also take into account the governor's views on an issue.

The Wisconsin state budget office analysts see a close connection to the governor, regardless of who happens to be in office. When asked "whom do you work for?" as opposed to "who is your boss?" nine of the budget director's fourteen staff (64 percent) say the governor, and three more (21 percent) say the Secretary of Administration (who is also known in Wisconsin as the second governor). Analysts have a good feeling for the governor's perspective because they each brief him, and sit in meetings where he makes his views known. They also read newspapers and otherwise keep abreast of his public statements. This is a strong tradition in Wisconsin budgeting and may help to explain the strong policy role of Wisconsin state budget office. Governors know what this strong policy role has done in the past and what it can do for them. As a senior staffer notes.

> Whether you agree with him in terms of where his policies have taken the state or not, I think you do have to really give [the governor] a lot of credit for using the powers at his disposal to try to get some place. You can always disagree on the direction you're headed, but he has really used the tools at his disposal, whether it be vetoes or staffing or the Budget Office as somebody that serves the governor . . . We've been asked to do lots of things under previous governors. I think that we may have been asked to do things more independently

of agencies under Thompson, part of which is, because coming in at least, there were still some holdovers from the previous administration running certain commissions and where their terms exceeded the term of [former] Governor Earl.

Paradoxically, serving "the governor" is also what helps keep them nonpartisan in their work; their reputation for "neutral competence" continues to be respected. Underlying a sensitivity for the governor's perspective is a professional culture that values "going to the wall" for a department's request, even in the face of anticipated opposition in the governor's office. Every Wisconsin budget analyst says that this is an important part of the job, and most can cite recent examples of the practice. Even if the entire request is not ultimately accepted, often the stage is set for acceptance in the next budget round, and often some portion of the request will be incorporated into the governor's current budget if money is available and the policy aspect is not totally rejected by the governor.

The role responses of the Wisconsin analysts represent a subtle shift in role perception from the 1985 interviews. Then, analysts saw themselves more as agency critics, similar to the policy analyst response in 1994, but far from an advocacy role for agency requests. One explanation for the shift might be the difference in the governors and their administrations. The 1994 analysts saw themselves serving a popular two-term governor with a lock on reelection. There is a comfortable relationship between the governor and his cabinet, and the state budget office is aware of that and is part of the team. The analysts still have a critical perspective about agency budgets, but they also are willing to advocate agency needs. This compares with the one-term governor analysts served in 1985; he was in reelection trouble and had not been able to solidify the relationship between the governor's office and the cabinet agencies. The analysts were therefore more critical of agencies, trying to enforce the governor's priorities and policies. We might hypothesize that the longer the governor's team is together, the more willing is the budget office staff to advocate team-player needs. This hypothesis should be explored in future research.

The most surprising result of the question concerning budget office orientation in 1994 is that 68 percent of the staff say control is also an important emphasis in the Wisconsin office. Further discussion of this response reveals a consistent feeling that the governor has a definite set of goals and priorities, which require the Wisconsin state budget office to tightly control expenditures (especially positions) in low priority programs so that any discretionary money can be allocated to the governor's priorities. In this sense, the control orientation in Wisconsin is seen mainly as a policy control role more than a financial control role. As a senior supervisor notes:

> I think that there's a certain amount of a need in this administration, a certain amount of desire for exercising some control over the big picture and making sure that agencies are on the same page and carrying out the policies of the chief executive. Perhaps a little bit more so than an other administrations. I think we have also, though, wanted to get out of micro-managing agencies. Sometimes we're probably not entirely consistent with the thought, but . . . some of our instructions, I think, reflect a desire to delegate more to the agencies. This freeze policy that has just come out now, essentially it leaves it up to the agencies to determine which positions they need to fill and which they could do without, as opposed to having everything come to the budget office. So that's probably an example of where we have tried to give the agencies some flexibility to manage.
>
> You have the need for financial control no matter who's governor because the budget process tends to impose some discipline and restraints no matter who's governor. You only have so much money. You could go in for a tax increase, but that's usually a no-no. So you

Table 9.3

Matrix of Wisconsin Responses to Role and Orientation

Role Responses	Control	Management	Planning	Policy	Total Role Responses	T1 Staff (in Table 9.2)
Advocate		1	2	11	23	11
Adversary		1	0	2	5	2
Conduit		0	0	1	2	1
Facilitator		0	1	4	8	5
Policy Analyst		0	0	6	8	6
Other		0	1	5	10	5
Total Col R	2	2	4	29	56	
T1 Col n (in Table 9.1)	1	2	2	18		

always have more demands and more requests than you have money available, so that's automatically going to give the budget office some license to start making priorities and determining what's more important and where cuts should be made. But I think that there was a real effort to, in the governor's words, to sort of turn some things around. So I think Governor Thompson just felt that he wanted to marshal the resources of the state and move the state in a certain direction. To do that required a certain amount of policy control as well as fiscal control.

The feat of integrating a strong policy orientation with a visible control component is not easily picked up by new analysts. One of the newest analysts expresses uncertainly about what the budget office orientation is:

I think I'm going to have to be here a little bit longer. But just based on the kinds of interview questions they asked me, I think it's trying to strike a balance between trying to oversee and control, if you will, how agencies go about spending their resources. And the balance on the other side is policy, which is philosophically "this is where we're headed here." I sense that they're trying to strike some balance here.

The need to balance policy and control may again reflect changes in the political environment between 1985 and 1994. The conservative Republican governor in 1994 tried to exert budgetary and policy control while facing a Democratic majority in the legislature with a liberal leadership; whereas the Democratic governor in 1985, working with a large Democratic majority, placed a greater emphasis on getting things done rather than exerting control.

As seen in Table 9.3, the identification of orientation does not have a significant influence on the role perception of the Wisconsin state budget office staff. The principal comparison is between the control and policy orientations, and between the advocate and adversary roles. It might be expected that those who see a control orientation of the office might view their role as an antagonist to their assigned agencies, and that those who see a policy orientation might view their role as an advocate for agency programs that are "good public policy." Bearing in mind the high number of Wisconsin responses that are bipolar with respect to orientation, it is not too surprising that there is little difference in role perception between the two orientations.

Only two of the staff describe their roles as agency antagonists, compared to eleven that see the role as somewhat of agency advocates. In fact, these two analysts see multiple roles, depending on the point in the cycle or other factors, and both also see themselves as agency advocates at times. Six of the staff view the analyst role as being a policy analyst, of which two of the budget analysts also identify a control orientation. Another third view the role as being a conduit (1) or facilitator (5), and all but one of those see both a control and policy orientation.

Wisconsin analysts see multiple dimensions of their office and their roles. Over half of the staff identify an advocacy role, regardless of their views on the general office orientation. Finally, there is no discernible role pattern to differentiate between those who describe a control and those who describe a policy orientation for the Wisconsin state budget office.

MINNESOTA STATE BUDGET OFFICE, STILL IN TRANSITION

Policy agenda setting in Minnesota in 1985 was largely the preserve of the governor's ad hoc policy council composed of top officials from the three executive staff offices, including the state planning office, the finance department, and the governor's office. The recommendations from the state budget office were screened by the council, and the governor personally considered only the relatively few that had major policy or financial significance. Although the Minnesota analysts were encouraged to "incorporate a sense of the political implication of choice into their analyses," and "to assist the governor and his staff in the review process," they were discouraged from "working the legislature." Once the governor's budget shifted to the legislative arena, the politics of budgeting was in the hands of the budget director and other top officials, as deliberation focused "less on the public policy elements of choice and more on political accommodation and coalition building."[15]

In 1985, the Minnesota state budget office was also in the early stages of a significant change from an accounting and controllership orientation to one focusing more on policy. Instrumental in the change was a decision to recruit and hire the new budget director from among the Wisconsin budget office team leaders. The new director, Nellie Johnson, turned the Minnesota budget office activities toward the Wisconsin budget office model in several ways. The title of the analysts was changed from controller to executive budget officer (EBO), symbolic of a basic change in orientation from a control to a policy role. Analysts were also given the new task of conducting policy issue studies and recommending alternatives to the governor's policy group.

The change got mixed reviews among the analysts in the 1985 interviews. Minnesota had a tradition of long tenure in the state budget office, with analysts averaging 8.7 years on the job. The senior analysts expressed concern that the state budget office had swung so far to the policy role that the financial management (control) role was neglected. They also complained of undue politicization of the office because of its close association with gubernatorial partisan politics, jeopardizing their "neutral competence."[16] Moreover, the veteran controllers expressed concern that they were not trained to do policy analysis, and they were "unsure of the appropriate balance between policy analysis and daily financial management."[17] In what seemed to be an effort to bolster the policy role of the analysts, the new budget director recruited new analysts "with the expectation that they would reflect a new policy orientation." Thus the former practice of hiring accountants was dropped in favor of social science backgrounds.

The Minnesota responses in Table 9.1 suggest that as of 1994 the transformation has been successful, as only one of the sixteen analysts and none of the supervisors indicate that the office has control as a primary orientation. In fact, 81 percent of the analysts indicate that the office has primarily a policy orientation. Yet behind these number lies a much more complicated story, indicating that the Minnesota state budget office is still in transition.

Table 9.4

Matrix of Minnesota Responses to Role and Orientation

Role Responses	Control	Management	Planning	Policy	Total Role Responses	T1 Staff (in Table 9.2)
Advocate	0	0	1	5	6	6
Adversary	0	0	1	1	2	4
Conduit	0	1	0	3	4	5
Facilitator	0	0	0	0	0	1
Policy Analyst	1	0	1	5	7	5
Other	0	1	2	6	9	7
Total Col R	1	2	5	20	28	
T1 Col n (*in Table 9.1*)	1	2	3	16		

In 1994, new analysts in the Minnesota office find it difficult to characterize the orientation of the budget office, noting that there seem to be two camps within the staff. The new analysts describe the senior staff, who began their tenure in the budget office as controllers, as having a stronger control orientation, while the junior analysts are characterized as management and policy analysts with a more flexible approach with respect to agencies. The junior analysts are also attracted to the job because it presents a chance to influence policy development. The senior staff do not seem interested in policy development and are skeptical of its frequency within the office. The "dual-camp" perspective is reinforced by stories new staff hear from agency personnel about the strong adversarial relationships in the past between budget controllers and agency fiscal staff.

Senior analysts also acknowledge the different perspectives of the junior and senior camps, sometimes complaining that the newer staff does not appreciate the importance of control activities and their value in helping learn the details of budgeting. Yet, for all their emphasis on the importance of control activities, they acknowledge that the orientation emphasis today is certainly policy analysis—for better or worse. They point to the Nellie Johnson years as pivotal in changing the orientation. They note that the attempt to adopt the Wisconsin model was reinforced by hiring another Wisconsin budget office team leader as budget director to replace Johnson when she was promoted to assistant commissioner of the Department of Finance. Given the near unanimity of the "dual-camp" perspective in the interview discussions, the analysis of responses below is surprising.

As seen in Table 9.4 only one respondent in Minnesota sees the state budget office as having a control orientation, while sixteen see a policy orientation. As compared to the majority of Wisconsin responses, only a third of the Minnesota responses describe the analyst role as being an advocate for agency positions. Only two of the responses describe the role as being adversarial, and these fall in either the policy or planning orientations.[18] Another third describe the role as being a policy analyst, including the respondent who describes a control orientation for the office. Nearly half of the role responses fall into the "other" category, including roles such as consultant, catalyst, and "friendly critic." The latter description is echoed by the budget director, who wants the analysts to avoid being agency advocates and antagonists, but wants them to provide professional critical analysis of agency requests and programs.

At first blush, there seems to be a paradox of role and orientation perspectives in the Minnesota office. Most of the staff say that a division of perspectives exists, but it is not apparent when we tally their responses to the questions in 1994. One explanation for the paradoxical situation is that the budget director has tried to make the staffing patterns of the office play to the strengths of the different analysts. The result is that agencies with high policy content such as welfare and education are predominantly staffed by junior analysts, while the lower policy content agencies and budget operations are dominated by the senior analysts. This pattern is not apparent in the Wisconsin office, and it is the reverse of the situation in Iowa, where senior staff dominate the high policy agencies and junior staff dominate the lower policy assignments, reflecting, as we shall see, Iowa's strong swing from a control to a policy orientation.

On balance, the Minnesota office is still in transition to a unified perspective about analyst roles and office orientation. Unlike in Wisconsin, where the tally disguises a fairly cohesive view of the budget office orientation in practice, the opposite seems to be true in Minnesota, where budgeting in practice seems to be more diverse within a general notion that the office should increasingly have a policy rather than control orientation.

THE IOWA STATE BUDGET OFFICE: SOMETHING NEW

Gauged by the opportunity for "discriminating policy choice," the 1985 study found that the staff of the Iowa state budget office had a relatively minor, if any, policy role in the budgetary process. As part of the Iowa Comptroller's Office, the staff were paid to "manage the state's finances." Their summers were periods of low activity as they waited to receive the departmental budget requests in September. Using a target-based budgeting process in a difficult fiscal climate, department directors had some flexibility in determining their budget requests, as long as their budget did not exceed the target.

In 1994, however, the office has a radically different face and routine, reflecting significant changes that eclipse the reorientation of the Minnesota state budget office. Rather than merely reacting to requests, Iowa analysts now spend their summers working closely with the departments' budget staffs and top leadership to develop the budget requests that analysts will review when agencies formally submit their requests in September. Some are busy on interdepartmental task forces on mental health or job training to develop polices which will be reflected in the next round of budget requests. Needless to say, there have been some significant changes.

First, the budget office is now part of the Department of Management, which includes the state budget office, the state planning office, and the state's local budget review office.[19] The department was created as part of a 1986 reorganization of Iowa government that consolidated over sixty agencies and boards into about twenty. The average tenure of the Iowa budget staff in 1994 is eight years. Many of the current analysts were brought into the budget office as part of the reorganization in 1986. What is remarkable is how they are much more congruent on the orientation of the state budget office and the appropriate role of the staff with respect to their agencies than are the Minnesota staff, which have been in transition longer.

Every Iowa analyst indicated that the office had moved decidedly away from a control orientation toward a policy orientation, especially since 1991. Much of the transformation is credited to the new director of the Department of Management and the budget director. Both have been state budget analysts in the past. The crux of the office transformation is an approach that follows the prescriptions for re-engineering and total quality management. The department has a "vision statement" and two of its tenets appear in the dialogues of the budget staff.

Iowa Department of Management Vision Statement

The department is increasingly facilitative rather than controlling—that is, it strives to help make things happen rather than to prevent things from happening.

In its oversight role, the department establishes accountability for results rather than on the specification and review of means. Departments and local governments are given as much flexibility as possible to achieve desired outcomes. Our expertise is in outcomes measurement.

Central to the vision for the department is a concerted effort to change budget analyst roles from agency antagonists to facilitators, consultants, and even advocates for "real" agency needs. Coming after several cycles of cutting base budgets, this means that department directors have significant flexibility in how they achieve required cuts, or wish to reallocate their base budgets. Although Iowa still uses quarterly allotments, they are rarely adjusted or denied, and the budget office no longer exercises line transfer control within agency budgets.

According to the Department of Management director, "I think it fits with our changing role. We're constantly looking for, 'where's the value added in this?' The value is not added in comparing travel this year to comparing travel last year. The value added is in being able to assess how different alternatives meet, achieve different outcomes." The director wants analysts focusing on key issues. "We have said, your role as budget analyst is to sort through all this mass of information and pull out the key decisions that need to be made. Identify those, put them on a piece of paper, and bring with you the charts and the graphs and whatever relevant information needs to be there to support that decision. But let's zero in on those key decision. I don't really want to hear about the rest of it. The governor doesn't want to hear about the rest of it."

This new perspective is consistently echoed by the budget staff, including a senior staffer who note that,

> When I first started, it was the Comptroller's Office and extremely controlling. . . . But we're trying to get more to a policy operation. We want to be facilitative as much as we can . . . We've tried to be even more cooperative with the departments. We still have to ask the hard questions because we have a budgetary responsibility. We're more involved with the budget preparation at the department level. We don't want until the budget's on our desk and then go through it. We work with the departments as they prepare their budgets; we try and give them advice, what we believe will be best received by the governor, best received by the legislature.

Table 9.5 shows that all eleven of the Iowa staff identify the Iowa state budget office as having a policy orientation. Moreover, nine of the eleven identify and advocacy role for analysts within the policy orientation, the highest response rate for that cell of the three states. Only three of the staff see an adversarial role for analysts, and these fall across the control, planning, and policy orientations. The second highest role response is for a facilitator role, which is a response of almost half of all staff (five analysts). The strong emphasis on advocacy and facilitator roles reflects the radical transformation of the budget office and its role perspective in the last decade. Having moved from the Office of the Comptroller to the Department of Management, the staff reflects a highly cohesive perspective about their role with respect to agencies in Iowa budgeting. This description is typical:

> In the actual development phase of their budget, we're actually working with [the agencies], we're giving them the insight that we have as far as how revenue projections are looking, the information, the feeling that we got from the prior legislative cycle on where the governor's priorities seem to be leaning. Basically as they put their budget requests together, we are kind of an advocate for them. Not to let them go totally wild and put everything including the kitchen sink in their budget. What I try to do anyway is keep them on the course that I

Table 9.5

Matrix of Iowa Responses to Role and Orientation

Role Responses	Control	Management	Planning	Policy	Total Role Responses	T1 Staff (in Table 9.2)
Advocate	2	0	3	9	14	9
Adversary	1	0	1	3	5	3
Conduit	1	0	0	1	2	1
Facilitator	0	0	3	5	8	5
Policy Analyst	0	0	1	1	2	1
Other	0	0	0	1	1	1
Total Col R	4	0	8	20	32	
T1 Col n (in Table 9.1)	2	0	3	11		

think the executive branch is going to be looking at. Not to be overboard, but certainly not to say don't put something in. If you really feel it's important, do it, but I'll tell you what I think will happen to that based on what information I have now.

Once that budget is formally submitted to us, then our role changes. Then we're an information source and a sounding board for the executive branch as they begin to make their budget decisions. The process comes down to what the governor actually submits to the legislature. That puts us in a rather unique position. At least I think it does in my own case because I work with the department in developing their budget and in most cases, I feel comfortable that they have submitted a valid, legitimate budget. Then it becomes, kind of from my standpoint, I've got to go to bat for them to the governor's office. Once the governor's finally made his decision and he submits his budget to the legislature, then we switch hats again and then we're up there to explain and support the governor's budget to the legislature. It changes about three times.

Analysts seem to be striving to establish much better working relationships with agencies, trying to build a level of trust based on that. One analyst cites an example of how much progress had been with his agencies:

I attended a full day retreat with [a department] about a month ago. I spent a full day, was involved with the division administrators, the department head, deputy, and two other key people. It was very informative. I guess I felt good about it in the sense that they let me sit in on it and have input and thanked me for coming and said I was even helpful in raising issues. And sometimes on those retreat kind of things a department's going to get primarily focused on the things that they want and that they want to do. As somebody told me, it was helpful having the gentle reminders of the reality checks, that they aren't the only department in the world, not everything they want is necessarily a priority of the executive branch or the legislative branch, and there is a limitation on dollars, and gentle reminders of "what is your highest priority?"

As noted earlier, Schick's stages of budgeting framework suggest an evolutionary path of budget office development, paralleling the changing scope of demands on government and changing technology. The Iowa budget office is an example of a state that skipped the management and planning stages in Schick's framework and leaped to a policy orientation. The staff is remarkably cohesive in their new role perspective, avoiding the schism apparent in the Minnesota office.

Table 9.6

Undergraduate Degrees of Budget Staff, 1994

Undergraduate Degree	IA	MN	WI	Grand Total	IA%	MN%	WI%	Grand Total%
None	1	0	0	1	9	0	0	2
Social Science	4	9	18	31	36	47	95	63
Humanities	0	2	0	2	0	11	0	4
Phys/Natural Sciences	1	2	1	4	9	11	5	8
Business	4	6	0	10	36	32	0	20
Accounting/Finance	1	0	0	1	9	0	0	2
Grand Total	11	19	19	49	100	100	100	100

DISCUSSION

These three midwestern budget offices are no longer broadly arrayed on the continuum from a control to a policy orientation. In a relatively short three to five years, the Iowa office has leaped to the strong policy orientation found in Wisconsin, bypassing a management or planning phase. The Minnesota office, in contrast, remains in a transition toward a policy orientation that began a decade ago. From her perspective, the Minnesota budget director argues that the office is definitely emphasizing a policy orientation, although control remains an important budget office function. While our analysis of responses supports her view, there are strong undercurrents within the staff that suggest something less than a unanimous "budget point of view."

There are two plausible explanations for the different experiences of the Iowa and Minnesota budget offices' transformations. First, the literature suggests that educational backgrounds might be an important factor in reorienting an office from a control to a policy emphasis.[20] Gosling found in the 1985 interviews that the different orientations of the three budget offices were also reflected in the backgrounds of the people hired as budget analysts. He noted the emphasis on hiring accounting backgrounds in Iowa contrasted sharply with the emphasis on hiring MPA and social sciences backgrounds in Wisconsin. In Minnesota, the staff were also traditionally from MBA and accountant backgrounds, and he noted that the efforts of the Minnesota budget director to reorient the staff to a policy analysis orientation in 1985 were proving difficult, as the staff resisted their new involvement in "the politics" of budgeting, preferring the financial accounting work of budgeting.

The 1994 analysis of the analyst's educational backgrounds provides some support for this hypothesis. At one extreme is Wisconsin, with 95 percent of the staff holding a social science BA and none with a business degree (Table 9.6). At the other end is Iowa, with 45 percent holding an undergraduate degree in business, accounting, or finance, and only 36 percent with a social science BA. Minnesota is in between, with only 32 percent holding a business-related undergraduate degree and 47 percent holding a degree in the social sciences.

Disaggregating the educational backgrounds by the tenure of the analysts in each budget office yields some interesting findings. First, Iowa and Minnesota have each hired only one analyst holding a business undergrad degree in the last 5.5 years; 75 percent of the Iowa and 90 percent of the Minnesota hires in this period have been non-business degrees. The nine non-business Minnesota hires in the period account for 47 percent of the 1994 Minnesota staff, compared to the last three non-business hires in Iowa which account for only 27 percent of the staff. Iowa and Minnesota are also different in that 26 percent of the Minnesota staff with more than ten years in the budget office have a business degree, compared with only 18 percent of the Iowa staff.

Table 9.7

Graduate Degrees of Budget Staff, 1994

Undergraduate Degree	IA	MN	WI	Grand Total	IA%	MN%	WI%	Grand Total%
None	5	6	4	15	45	32	21	31
Social Sciences	1	0	2	3	9	0	11	6
MPA/MPPA	5	8	11	24	45	42	58	49
Business	0	4	0	4	0	21	0	8
Other (JD, MSW)	0	1	2	3	0	5	11	6
Grand Total	11	19	19	49	100	100	100	100

Thus, one explanation for the difference between the Iowa and Minnesota experiences may be the larger share of senior staff with business backgrounds in the Minnesota office, juxtaposed with a large group of junior staff with a non-business background. The Iowa office does not have the wide gulf in educational backgrounds found in Minnesota. On the other hand, since there is a greater number of business backgrounds in the Iowa office, we might expect the transition to a policy orientation to be more difficult. Moving the analysis to the graduate degree level reveals why this may not be the case.

As seen in Table 9.7, Wisconsin's office continues its tradition of emphasizing MPA degrees in its staff. Only 21 percent of the staff do not hold a graduate degree, and none holds a graduate degree in business (MBA). Slightly over half of the Iowa budget staff have graduate degrees, and none is in business. Minnesota presents a different case; it is the only office where analysts hold graduate degrees in business, accounting for 21 percent of the Minnesota budget staff. Analysis of graduate degrees by tenure in the budget office further elucidates differences in the offices. Of the four people hired in Iowa in the last 5.5 years, 75 percent have a graduate degree, and each of them holds an MPA degree. In contrast, the Minnesota budget office hired ten people in the same period, and while 90 percent have a graduate degree, 20 percent hold MBA degrees.

Thus, it would appear that the overall perspectives of budget analysts may be influenced by their educational backgrounds. The Wisconsin staff is uniformly lacking business education backgrounds, and is dominated by MPA degrees. Iowa's staff is increasing the proportion of staff with MPA degrees and none holds a graduate degree in business. Minnesota, on the other hand, has a core of staff with graduate degrees in business, and continues to hire people with that background. None of the budget directors interviewed in 1994 would exclude someone from the budget staff solely because she or he had a business degree background, but the Iowa and Wisconsin directors emphasized the benefits of analysts who understood government and public policy. Their recent hires are evidence of their perspectives.

A more intriguing explanation for the coherence of perspectives in the Wisconsin and Iowa offices relative to the Minnesota office is the degree to which staff perceive some affiliation with the governor. The 1994 study measures this is several ways: by how often analysts personally brief the governor budget decisions, the degree to which they anticipate the reactions of the governor and budget director (often perceived as speaking for the governor or at least guarding the governor's interests), and the degree to which they feel they "work for" the governor as opposed to their immediate supervisor or the budget director.

There is a stark contrast in briefing practices between the states. In Wisconsin, nearly all of the staff (analysts and team leaders) briefs the governor often. Minnesota present nearly the opposite case, with only two of the thirteen staff having ever briefed the governor; even the Minnesota team leader rarely briefs the governor.

In between these cases is Iowa, where only one new analyst hand never personally briefed the governor, but had attended the briefing on her budgets and also attended regular (monthly) "update" meetings with the governor and agency directors. During the final stages of the budget cycle, the usual practice in Iowa is for the budget director and the director of management to present the budget office recommendations to the governor, and the analysts attend the briefing to answer detailed questions. Certain analysts, especially senior staff, brief the governor personally.

As noted above in our analysis of the Wisconsin budget office, briefing the governor is a key ingredient to ensure that analysts know the governor's viewpoints in Wisconsin. Briefing the governor is part of learning the ropes in the budget office. It is learning what are the governor's parameters, what are the secretary's parameters, and then how to develop options within those parameters that are well thought out. The budget director sees them as valuable training programs:

> Certainly when we have a new analyst, and the team is going over to brief the governor, I'll say to the new analyst, "stay in the room while other members of the team are briefing. That will give you an opportunity to watch the process and that's how you'll get a feel for it. When your particular part of the briefing is done, you don't need to jump up and run out of the room. It's to your benefit to sit there and listen to the rest of the analysts."

The Wisconsin staff is quite clear about their partisan political neutrality and their distinction from the governor's partisan policy staff. Yet, they value the frequent interactions with the governor in various briefings and meetings because it keeps them informed of his priorities and policies. At the same time, they are comfortable enough in their relationship with the governor to present arguments that they "know" he may not agree with. That is their job, and they are strongly encouraged to present their independent and objective analysis of their assigned agencies and issues.

The Iowa experience with briefing the governor is much weaker. This description from an analyst is typical:

> [The governor's] goals have remained the same pretty much the whole time I've been with the state. Right now I've got a pretty good feel for what would fit well the governor's priorities. We don't always pick them very well. Gretchen [Department of Management director] and Janet [budget director] both have a pretty good grasp of what's going to fit within the governor's priorities. In the first round the analysts will take a shot at what they feel best suits the governor's program. Then we'll sit down and go over those budgets with Janet and she may take some out, she may put some in. Then we'll meet with Gretchen. After Gretchen, then we all sit down and meet with the governor and say this is where the Department of Management is at. Where would you like any changes? This is why we're here; are there any changes you'd like to see?
>
> We are in on the meeting to answer any detailed questions that he may have Gretchen or Janet, for the most part, present that to the governor. Sometimes we will make a presentation on a program that we've recommended so that the governor has a better background on what that program's about. But the governor's pretty well informed, knows a lot of those things beforehand. So he's able to ask a lot of good questions.

Although they attend the budget briefings and the monthly progress meetings, they are less participants and more observers. Their investment in the meetings is much smaller than their Wisconsin counterparts. They are prepared to answer questions, and sometimes will make a presentation, but that is the exception rather than the rule. Still, this frequent contact allows them to listen to the governor express his views and concerns, and observe the politics of his inner circle. This gives them a foundation and context for their negotiations with their assigned agencies, as explained by one analyst:

> When I see a budget request, I look at the things that they're asking for and see how it would relate to what the governor's policy is, what he is looking at for the overall program or the kinds of things that I know he supports or that I know he doesn't support. There hasn't been at the beginning of the budget process, a formal "this is what the governor's going to endorse." But after you've been here for a while and if you've worked with that department for awhile, you kind of get a feel.
>
> It takes awhile. I don't know. I would say it would take two to three years before you really feel comfortable making those decisions. It's all kind of second nature to me now. The departments that take up more of my time I've had for so long, that it's just kind of there. I know what the issues are, I know what issues have come up in the past, I know where the governor is on those issues.

Finding out the governor's position on an issue is more difficult for Minnesota analysts, due in part to the absence of personal contact with the current governor. As a senior analyst who has briefed previous governors notes, "That's been a feature of our role that has really gone up and down. With [former governor] Perpich we used to sit in the basement of the mansion and go through stuff, really small steps, inch by inch. With the existing governor in the current biennium . . . when he was new, we certainly briefed him directly on many issues. But in the last biennium I swear I don't remember being across from him. Now we were meeting with him on [an issue] type of things [but not on budget recommendations]."

Measured in terms of analysts' affiliation with the governor, the Minnesota staff has the most distant relationship. Only 6 percent of the Minnesota analysts agreed that they "work for" the governor (as distinct from their boss, their immediate supervisor). The responses below are representative of their views when asked directly, "Why wouldn't you say you work for the governor, since you put together his budget?"

> I don't see myself as working for the governor. It is the governor's budget, [but] other than emergencies only, deficiencies only, I didn't have a clear sense of what the governor's budget preferences were in that supplemental budget process. There was very little, if any, interaction with the governor's staff, other than the commissioner. So I guess I work for the commissioner. (respondent 1)
>
> It's true but most of those preferences get filtered through other people whether it's the commissioner or the assistant commissioner; the legislative LRD. But that's really sort of where I get those messages. Those are the people who sort of carry back those actual political or policy things. (respondent 2)
>
> In the regular budget cycle we had this thing called the executive budget team that would involve usually the budget director and the commissioner and a couple more people from the governor's office and some various assorted and sundry folks. They were supposedly making a recommendation to the governor. It wasn't always clear who was speaking for them. (respondent 3)

And the distance from the governor is just fine for some analysts:

Table 9.8

Analyst Affirmation Rates for Recommendations, 1994 and 1985

Affirm Rate %	IA		MN		WI		Grand Total	
	94	85	94	85	94	85	94	85
50–69	1		2	1	0	1	3	2
70–79	1	2	1	2	0	3	2	7
80–89	4	1	3	2	2	5	9	8
90–99	1	4	5	6	8	8	14	18
100	0	0	1	0	0	0	1	0
Grand Total	7	7	12	11	10	17	29	35
Average	75		78		84		83	

No, I don't work for the governor. He has his own staff up there at the capitol. No, I don't work for the governor. I think that we hear about his priorities and certainly all of us read in the newspaper. I mean, I find out a lot about what the governor's doing by reading the newspaper! I think some of that is that we hear about that in meetings and things, but it's just like with the agencies. We're not supposed to be an advocate of the agency and I don't see myself as that. And the same thing, I don't see myself *per se* as an advocate of the governor. I think that that's contrary to our role because if we did that then he in effect or the commissioner or the budget director wouldn't get the analysis that they need. However we do work for the executive.

The staff in Iowa and Wisconsin more readily identify with the governor and his policies and priorities. About 55 percent of the Iowa and 60 percent of the Wisconsin analysts (and 75 percent of the Wisconsin team leaders) respond that they "work for" the governor. The utility of briefings in nurturing a policy analysis perspective is supported by further analysis of the data from the three states, which indicates that frequency of briefings is positively correlated with a "work for" affiliation with the governor ($r = 0.349$, prob. ≤ 0.023). Frequency of briefings is also negatively correlated with the control orientation response for the budget office ($r = -0.567$, prob. ≤ 0.0001).

Table 9.8 presents the last evidence indicating that a closer relationship with the governor influences the perspectives (and perhaps decision making) of budget analysts. While Wisconsin staff estimate in 1994 that an average 84 percent of their recommendations are affirmed by the budget director, the averages in Iowa and Minnesota are lower (75 percent and 78 percent, respectively). A comparison of the affirmation rates between 1994 and 1985 is problematic, since there has been considerable turnover in staff in all three offices, and the fiscal and political environments have changed as well. However, it is interesting to note that the Wisconsin average has increased (80 percent of the staff report rates between 90 and 99 percent), while the Minnesota rate is about the same and the Iowa rate has surely dropped somewhat. Although it is possible that the change in rates in the Iowa and Minnesota offices is due to the relatively new phenomenon of higher staff turnover in recent years, none of the three budget directors attribute the affirmation rate to tenure on the job, beyond perhaps the first budget cycle. Rather, they suggest that either someone is good at putting recommendations together, or they are not.

On the other hand, part of what makes a good recommendation in their view is analysis that is comprehensive, including known political complications (such as interest group opposition), congruence with the governor's policies and priorities *or* a good argument for an exception. As we have just discussed, learning to analyze the multi-faceted budget problems requires experience on the job. And as the Wisconsin director noted, sitting in on budget briefings is a great way "to get the feel" for the issues.

CONCLUSIONS

The findings from this study suggest that another stage should be added to Schick's 1966 framework to account for the evolution of some state budget offices to a policy orientation, distinct from his planning orientation. The nexus between budget making and policy making has been more pronounced in recent years than it was even under PPB. As policy problems have become more complex, it appears that more governors are turning to the central budget staff to analyze policy options that are fiscally sound, while consistent with gubernatorial priorities. The effectiveness of this relationship seems to be enhanced by personal interactions between governors and CBAs.

The results reported in this article raise questions about the extent to which governors themselves influence budget offices' orientations and roles, and the extent to which that influence largely comes from a secretary or budget director who crafts what she or he believes best serves a governor. A related question is how successfully governors' perspectives are filtered through budget directors. Further investigation could also help illuminate the personal relationships between budget analysts and governors, including the extent to which personal affinities are created from regular briefings with the governor, and how that influences the recommendations of the analysts.

NOTES

1. B. Guy Peters, "Introducing the Topic," *Governance in a Changing Environment,* B. Guy Peters and Donald J Savoie, eds. (Monreal: McGill-Queen's University Press, 1995). 5–9.

2. Allen Schick, "The Road to PPB The Stage of Budget Reform," *Public Administration Review* 26(4) (Dec 1966): 244–45.

3. Schick, op cit., pp. 250–51.

4. Allen Schick, "A Death in the Bureaucracy. The Demise of Federal PPB," *Public Administration Review* (March/April, 1973): 150.

5. Ibid, p. 155.

6. This is not to argue that policy-driven conflict did not exist in the 1970s Governors in many states instituted programs for school aid equalization, state-financed property tax relief, and other initiatives. Incrementalism was not at all uniform. On the other hand, the generally steady incremental increases in budget revenues during this period provided the wherewithal for such initiatives since these involved new programs rather than trade-offs in the budget.

7. James J. Gosling, "The State Budget Office and Policy Making," *Public Budgeting and Finance,* 7 (Spring 1987): 51–65.

8. Paul Appleby, "The Role of the Budget Division," *Public Administration Review,* 17 (Summer 1957): 157.

9. V.O. Key, "The Lack of a Budgetary Theory," *American Political Science Review,* 34 (December 1940): 1137–40.

10. Ibid, p. 54.

11. Ibid.

12. The 1994 interviews included 100 percent of the Iowa budget staff (11/11), 89 percent of the Minnesota staff (16/18), and 81 percent of the Wisconsin budget staff (21/26). This coverage is comparable to Gosling's 1985 interviews, details of which can be found in his Table 1, p. 53. All three offices had reduced staffing since the 1985 interviews (by two in Iowa, two in Minnesota, and three in Wisconsin).

13. The interview protocol is available from the authors upon request.

14. Adversary, antagonist, or similar role identifications are reported in the tables as Adversary. Similarly, the Advocate category includes responses such as "protagonist."

15. Gosling, "The State Budget Office," pp. 57–58.

16. Ibid, p. 58.

17. Ibid, p. 62.

18. Two of the staff have missing values for the orientation variables and are thus excluded from this analysis.

19. This is a unique feature of Iowa's state-local relationships which involves a state review of each local government budget.

20. Robert D Lee, "Educational characteristics of budget office personnel and state budgetary processes," *Public Budgeting and Finance* 11 (Fall 1991) 69–79; and Thurmaier, "The Multiple Facets of Budget Analysis: Focusing on Budget Execution in Local Governments," *State and Local Government Review,* 27 (2) (Spring 1995) 102–117.

CHAPTER 10

COURTS AND PUBLIC PURSE STRINGS
Have Portraits of Budgeting Missed Something?

JEFFREY D. STRAUSSMAN

Do judges make budget decisions? At one time the question would have seemed preposterous. No formal constitutional role exists for the courts in the budget process, nor do various portraits of budgeting include a place for the judicial branch. Yet, few would argue that disputes have come before the courts in which resolution has required forms of budgetary action. Consider two easily recognizable illustrations:

The federal courts have been particularly active in the area of prison reform—especially the issue of prison overcrowding. Arkansas was the first state to have its corrections system judged to be in violation of the Eighth Amendment prohibition against cruel and unusual punishment beginning with *Holt v. Sarver* in 1969. Since then 35 states have experienced similar litigation against their prison systems. Research has indicated that state spending for corrections has been affected by court decisions; capital expenditures have tended to increase in the years immediately following a court judgment, and corrections spending as a percentage of the total state budget has increased after a court order.[1]

This form of court involvement—usually referred to as "institutional reform litigation"—has also involved constitutional challenges to the conditions found in state psychiatric institutions and in facilities for the mentally retarded. In 1972 litigation was initiated against the State of New York by the New York Association of Retarded Children, the American Civil Liberties Union, and parents of persons institutionalized in a state facility known as Willowbrook. The suit charged that the conditions in the facility were violations of constitutional rights. The litigation resulted in a consent decree which included a policy of "deinstitutionalization" of patients, improved staff-client ratios, and improved services to the newly deinstituitionalized population. The budgetary impact was extensive for the rest of the decade.[2]

Do judges known what they are doing—in a budgetary sense, that is? Cooper's case studies of *Bradley* v. *Milliken* (1971) and *United States* v. *City of Parma, Ohio* (1980), point out that judges are not oblivious to the budgetary dimensions of their remedial decrees. He notes that the judges in both cases urged the respective governments to seek federal funds as a way to soften the financial ramifications of their decisions.[3] Similarly, Judge Frank Johnson assumed that changes

From *Public Administration Review,* vol. 56, no. 4 (July/August 1986), 345–351. Copyright © 1986 by American Society for Public Administration. Reprinted with permission.

brought about in the psychiatric institutions in Alabama in the aftermath of the *Wyatt* decision would permit the state to qualify for medicare and medicaid funds—thereby easing the budgetary impact of his decree.[4] In general, judges have rejected the claim by defendant agencies that financial-exigencies do not permit remedial action to correct constitutional violations. Therefore, if budgets reflect policy preferences, then it would seem important to determine how judges may influence budgetary decisions. How would a judicial presence challenge current assumptions about the nature of public budgeting?

ENTER THE COURTS: A CHALLENGE TO INCREMENTALISM?

While the budgeting literature is practically devoid of references to litigation and the courts, conventional notions of how the process operates provides "rules of thumb" from which judicial-administrative interactions may be anticipated. Consider a frequently observed behavioral pattern of agency budgeting—the principle that agencies adopt strategies aimed at budgetary expansion.

Budgeting has been described by a number of participants as a series of disaggregated decisions that take place in a limited time frame with a few basic constraints. These include: the number of total players, formalized "rules," and fiscal constraints. By and large these constraints simplify an otherwise complicated process and provide budgeting with a degree of stability. Decisions are made by a set number of participants; the budget *cycle* is invariant over time. Strategy often centers around the effort to expand one's budget since expansion is equated with prestige and other perquisites of office. While other strategies (like the desire for budgetary stability) may sometimes compete with the goal of budget maximization, some research studies have shown that agency heads who pursue aggressive strategies have, on the whole, been successful.[5]

How might an administrator use the actual, or even better, the potential intervention of the courts to achieve budget expansion? Consider just one possibility drawn from Wildavsky's "crisis technique." As Wildavsky notes: "A number of agency officials are famous in budgetary circles for their ability to embellish or make use of crises. By publicizing a situation, dramatizing it effectively, and perhaps asking for emergency appropriations, an agency may maneuver itself into a position of responsibility for large new programs."[6] The threat of a lawsuit and subsequent judicial intervention in the budgetary process is one example of the kind of situation calling for the crisis technique.

An agency head may claim that prior funding has been inadequate. As a consequence, service levels are below what is considered "acceptable"—thereby providing the potential for litigation. Notice that the administrator need not admit failure. Rather, he or she simply argues that services are provided efficiently, but that the funding is inadequate. If the level of service is not raised (or services are not improved), the administrator suggests that the agency will most likely be sued. The crisis can be ameliorated (that is, the probability of a lawsuit may be lowered) if the appropriations for the agency are increased.

It is important to realize that the crisis could be either real or manufactured. The agency head may sincerely believe that, given the current funding, the probability of litigation is high. On the other hand, the agency head may exaggerate the situation. In either case, assume that the legislature has less than perfect information and therefore interprets the administrator's estimate of the probability of litigation as being reasonably accurate. Consider, now, how litigation *may* affect budgetary strategy:

When the administrator faces the legislative sponsors, an initial expectation by all involved is that the new budget level will be a fair share increase over last year's appropriation. This follows from incremental theory. Call this budget level F1. The threat of a successful lawsuit implies a higher *court mandated* budget. Call this level F3. Between these two levels is a budget level that the administrator may wish to obtain through the use of the crisis technique. This may be considered the "threat" level—F2. The three levels are obviously related in the following way: F1 < F2 < F3.

An important part of the administrator's strategy is specifying the likelihood of a successful suit. If the threat of a suit is to be effective in producing an appropriation above F1, the agency head would most likely tie agency performance to the budget level. The relationship need not be linear, nor need it be the same for all agencies that may be the target of litigation. Nevertheless, it is necessary that some claim be made that differential budget levels produce different performance levels. In this way the legislature is in a position to influence the agency's performance by its control of the purse strings. It then follows that the legislature may be able to affect the probability of a lawsuit by changing the agency's level of funding.

The administrator's strategy is clear—identify the existence of the threat of a suit and then try to convince the legislature to "buy" a reduction in the likelihood by identifying the probability at the F1 funding level and the expected reduction that an F2 level will produce. The administrator then asks for the F2 level.

The legislature does not, of course, automatically concede and give the agency head a higher (F2) budget. After all, the legislature, like the agency head, also has objectives that influence appropriations levels. Three are particularly relevant: (a) the legislature wants to control aggregate levels of spending and cannot, therefore, routinely grant all funding requests that are predicated on "crises," (b) the legislature may want to retain its power over budget making (rather than letting it slip into the hands of the courts), (c) the legislature has policy goals that may or may not be in agreement with the courts. These three objectives are not necessarily consistent with one another at a given point in time; their individual or joint impact on the legislature's likely response to the agency head's claims about the prospects of litigation are probably uncertain.

Essentially the legislature wants to know whether to provide an F2 budget, and if so, how large the F2 level should be. Obviously the legislature can choose to reject the administrator's threat. The legislature may do this because the lawmakers simply think that the administrator is wrong; they perceive no serious likelihood of a suit. If this happens, obviously the question of the size of F2 is irrelevant. If the legislature believes that the threat of a suit is credible, it need not accept the estimates provided by the agency head. Room still exists to negotiate over the size of F2 since the analytic question is the amount of reduction in the likelihood of a suit that different F2 levels will buy.

Does budgetary strategy and negotiation really unfold in this way when the threat of judicial intervention in agency operations is present? Diver, discussing institutional reform litigation, observed, "the lawsuit gives the operating manager unprecedented leverage to obtain additional resources. A judicial decree weakens the resistance he usually encounters in seeking funds."[7] The logic, of course, follows from the crisis technique; in additional, more general expectations of the "natural" inclination of administrators to expand budgets would certainly lead one to the strategic use of litigation outlined above. It is understandable, however, that few administrators would actually acknowledge that they in fact have adopted such a budgetary stance toward litigation—and only a smattering of anecdotal evidence even hints that the scenario outlined is plausible.[8]

From the standpoint of budgetary behavior, incrementalism is very much intact in this revised standard model. The courts may influence strategic behavior, but the process is largely unaltered. This is so because budgeting is still carried out largely by addition—adding modest amounts to the budgetary base of the agencies with little concern for the aggregate. While this portrait of the budget process has always received some criticism, it is nevertheless fair to say that, in the past, budgeting was usually described as a series of disjointed "bottom-up" decisions with little explicit attention to fiscal limits. In a positive sum budget atmosphere where all agencies *appear* to be winners, judicial intervention merely facilitates that strategic game for some of the players.

When increments are no longer guaranteed, the game is altered. Fiscal scarcity alters the game even without the intervention of the courts. In particular, the major features of incrementalism—compartmentalized budgetary roles, negotiation strategies, marginal adjustments to a previous year's budgetary base, and stability—are jeopardized by a deteriorating fiscal climate. As the fiscal environment worsens, the ability to sustain incremental features of the process erodes. For example, marginal adjustments are no longer guaranteed, the value (or importance) of negotiation strategies becomes diminished since there is less to negotiate about, and perhaps most important, the budget process becomes less predictable.[9] Even a casual glance at the federal budget process over the past five years would provide several illustrations of these observations.

Courts are likely to aggravate the situation. Judges, after all, are not fiscal managers; unlike governors, the judiciary operates with no balanced budget constraint. In fact, judges have said that defendant agencies cannot offer lack of funds as a reason for failure to remedy constitutional violations. The involvement of the courts in developing policy in a deteriorating fiscal environment *could* be profound. After all, if fair share adjustments are no longer guaranteed, court-mandated spending puts judges in a budgetary Robin Hood position. When the court dictates budgetary winners by requiring injunctive relief for the plaintiffs, there *must* be budgetary losers (given the budget constraint imposed by fiscal austerity). Are all agencies that face the wrath of judges inevitable budgetary winners? The next section identifies three factors that are likely to determine the strategic position of the agency: the fiscal climate, the probability of litigation (or the passage of time since the initial litigation), and agency agreement with the policy intent of the judicial decision. Using these three factors, conditions are described which lead to budgetary environments that differ from patterns expected from incremental behavior.

JUDICIAL-BUDGETARY ENVIRONMENTS: ALTERNATIVE STRATEGIC EXPECTATIONS

The previous section specified a revised model of budgetary incrementalism in an environment with some likelihood of litigation. The portrait of budgeting included a few restrictive assumptions. First, some probability of a lawsuit exists. Second, the administrator is willing to use that probability to try to extract a budget larger than the one otherwise anticipated by using the crisis technique. Third, the expected value of an expanded budget is greater than either the cost of being caught bluffing by the legislature or the budget office *or* the cost of a judicially imposed policy change which is unacceptable to the agency. This situation is a particular judicial-budgetary environment with the following characteristics:

- judicial activity was present or anticipated prior to the agency's use of the threat strategy;
- agency actually used the threat as part of the budget submission;
- agency is positive or at least neutral with respect to the likely policy outcome of litigation (assuming that agency, as defendant, should lose the suit).

This portrait of the judicial-budgetary environment is similar to Diver's description of "litigation as a bargaining game."[10] The image of litigation as a bargaining game is useful because it shows how, under certain (restrictive) conditions, the budget process *could* be used as a vehicle for substantive policy changes pertaining to due process rights, The determining condition of this first environment is the willingness of the agency to use the threat of a lawsuit as a budget ploy.

Consider a *second* environment. Here, litigation has already developed to the point that a court has rendered a judgment against the defendant agency. *If* the agency is in agreement with the policy enunciated by the court, the policy has a high probability of being implemented because the court's objective—*compliance*—and the agency's objective—*budget expansion*—seem to be compatible. Frequently, a judge facilitates negotiations between the parties, often resulting in a consent decree where the judge authorizes the implementation of some variation of the plaintiff's demands.

The time frame is one to three years after a court decision has been reached in this second situation. The agency asks for increased budget levels to implement the court's decision. The agency is expected to be either in agreement or, at minimum, neutral with respect to the policy direction of the court's decisions. Also, the agency expects a net increase in the budget beyond any anticipated fair share so that compliance with the court order does not take budgetary resources away from other programs managed by the agency.

Prison conditions in Rhode Island in the late 1970s illustrate this second environment. In August 1977, a district court judge found conditions in the state's maximum security facility to be in violation of the Eighth Amendment. After some initial resistance, the state began to implement the court's decision. Among the explanations offered for the state's compliance was the governor's general agreement with the policy implications of the court decision. Also, legislative resistance was softened by federal funds from the Law Enforcement Assistance Administration (LEAA) that would be used to defray some of the increased budgetary costs of compliance.

The *third* situation follows logically from the second. In many cases, a court decision, after a period of three or more years, has not been implemented to the satisfaction of the court. Accounts of well known institutional reform litigation cases such as *Holt* and *Willowbrook* have described this situation. The agency, as defendant, becomes embroiled in protracted litigation that takes place over several years. Sometimes the level of judicial involvement intensifies over the life of the litigation as the court searches for ways to enforce compliance. If the year that the decision was first announced is "t," what impact would judicial involvement have on the budgetary character of the agency in, say, t + 3 (or more) years—assuming that the agency *still* accepts the policy implications of the court's actions? From the vantage point of budgetary strategy only, the agency is unlikely to be in an advantaged position. First, the agency can obviously no longer use the threat of judicial sanction as a ploy in budget formulation. Second, the passage of time provides the legislature and the budget office with the opportunity to assess the consequences of noncompliance. Third, factors not related directly to the litigation may impinge on implementation. These may include the intergovernmental dimension of the dispute and the budgetary options available to the state. In a nutshell, both compliance *and* budgetary expansion are now made more problematical.

Many institutional reform cases probably fall into this third environment. The following observation by M. Kay Harris and Dudley P. Spiller, Jr. concerning the problems implementing the *Holt* v. *Sarver* (1969) decision in Arkansas is instructive: "The massive changes ordered in *Holt* required expenditure of funds in excess of the amount then in the control of the defendants. Although the defendant correctional administrator was not explicitly required to raise or spend additional revenues, as a practical matter compliance required that additional revenues be raised and spent. . . . The administrator at the time the implementation process began, who had welcomed the litigation as tool to make needed reforms, was unable to persuade the legislature to appropriate required funds."[11] A judicial-budgetary environment may offer options—as well as restrict options—for administrators and legislators. For example, in Alabama, Judge Johnson nudged the state toward a position of budgetary opportunity in *Wyatt* because improvements in mental health facilities would permit that state to become eligible for federal funding. However, when compliance requires large increases to an agency's operating budget (rather than expansion through capital spending), resistance is likely to be strong.

A *fourth* situation is one in which possible litigation is a threat to the agency. Unlike the first environment, the agency is *not* in agreement with the policy which the court would hand down in the event that the defendant agency lost the suit. Now, the administrator's self-interest principle—defined as budgetary maximization—is not self-evident. While the prospects for budget expansion still exist, nonbudgetary concerns of the agency, particularly judicial "encroachments" on executive terrain, may likely override the budget maximizing objective. An earlier study of administrative reactions to judicial decisions in California found that some prison officials resented what they felt was judicial interference in their administrative responsibilities.[12] While this does not completely obviate the feasibility of the crisis technique outlined in the first environment, it means that the costs associated with the unsuccessful use of the tactic are likely to be higher. Consequently, high risk administrators may still act *as if* the situation is like environment one, whereas risk averse managers may choose to marshall support against the court's involvement in the administration of their agencies even if some gains may be made from such judicial involvement.

Ohio's prison case, *Chapman* v. *Rhodes* (1977), is illustrative of this fourth environment. The director of Correction and Rehabilitation in Ohio at the time of *Rhodes* was opposed to the policy direction being taken by the federal courts in prison reform cases. The director believed that judges were not the allies of beleaguered corrections administrators in their struggles with the budget office or the legislature. On the contrary, the director generally had difficulties trying to increase his operating budget while, at the same time, developing a capital budget construction program. He felt that judicial involvement would only exacerbate his negotiations with the legislature. From his point of view, *Rhodes* provided no budgetary bonanza.[13]

A *fifth* situation may arise one to three years after the onset of litigation. Unlike environment two, in this situation the defendant agency finds the court mandated policy objectionable. Notice that nonbudgetary considerations may override simple budget-maximizing objectives. What are some of the agency's likely responses? First, *delay* would probably be related to the severity of the policy objections *and* the extent of judicial involvement. Second, the degree of resistance may be influenced by alternative programmatic options that are available to the agency. And third, the agency's responses may be affected by the type of budgetary consequence that is likely to follow. For instance, if judicially mandated improvements to facilities can be funded by intergovernmental grants, resistance may be less than in a situation requiring funding through a redistribution of the agency's operating budget. Perhaps the cases that best reflect these general conditions are those involving school desegregation where delay became routine political responses to judicial decisions. Two insiders in the Boston school desegregation saga summarized their view of the fiscal ramifications of desegregation in the following way: "It is avoidance, ineptitude, confusion, and then conflict, that give rise to the costliness of desegregation in some cities."[14] One need not reach the same harsh judgment to appreciate that both antipathy to the policy direction of the courts *and* the anticipated adverse effect on the fiscal environment have combined to produce delay and resistance in this environment.

A *sixth* environment follows logically from the one above. This is a situation three or more years after the onset of litigation. Like the previous environment, the agency is opposed to the policy direction of the court. The agency's resistance is expected to be high. Similarly, the legislature and/or executive tends to resist implementation *unless* the court's threat to take over political functions is considered highly credible.[15] In general, the larger the policy shift and the larger the reallocation of resources, the stronger the resistance will be. In this environment the prospects for successful judicial implementation are low.

Overcrowding conditions in local jails often reflect this environment. An Advisory Commission on Intergovernmental Relations study on jails included the observation, "In the race for local budgetary eminence, jails have long been functional losers."[16] Litigation has complicated the budgetary problem. While some local governments with inadequate jail facilities have responded by initiating capital budget projects, legislatures have been reluctant to put additional funds into existing structures while construction is planned or in progress. Judges have not turned a blind eye to the conditions in existing facilities merely because improvements are anticipated in the future. In this environment agency and/or legislative resistance is likely to be protracted as illustrated by the conflict between the courts and New York City and the State of New York concerning unconstitutional conditions of facilities located in the city.

WHEN THE INCREMENT IS MORTGAGED THROUGH JUDICIAL INVOLVEMENT

Judicial intervention in the budget process *may* not necessarily alter budget routines. If it cannot be shown that budgetary *methods* have been visibly altered as a result of judicial involvements in taxing and spending decisions, it can at least be argued that the courts have, on occasion, become none-too-silent forces in the budget process. Since participation of the courts requires litigation, and since litigation must be initiated by plaintiffs seeking injunctive relief, it follows that judicial involvement in budgeting is difficult to predict. What consequence does this loss of predictability have?

From the vantage point of the principal actors in the budget process, the unanticipated involvement of the courts impinges on the ability of actors to calculate the likely results of their strategic behaviors—and the responses expected from others to their behaviors. Since judicial behavior is not random, at this level we could say that the involvement of the courts in the budget process increases complexity and uncertainty—and thereby makes calculations more difficult. Does this make incrementalism obsolete? Not necessarily. Increased complexity and uncertainty make calculation more difficult; however, this is not likely to affect the entire process. Rather, budgeting is made more unpredictable for only those agencies influenced by litigation.

Can a budget process, then, be *partly* incremental? That depends where one looks. Surely agencies unaffected by litigation may utilize the standard model, except in conditions of budgeting stringency. But this pertains only to budget formulation up to the legislative phase of the budget cycle. A factual problem may exist. If fiscal conditions are deteriorating *and* courts are mandating improvements in one or more agencies, can it be assumed that incremental methods will remain unaffected in the review and appropriations phases of the cycle? Or can it be inferred that top-down influences will alter incremental methods? If so, with what results?

Answers depend on the aggregate size of the increment. This is, of course, a different use of the concept, one more conventional though analytically vacuous. This refers to the real year-to-year increases in a government's budget. A handy classification of different levels of fiscal scarcity has been suggested by Schick.[17] To use his terminology, under conditions of "chronic" scarcity (or worse), budget managers are inclined to try to dampen agency spending appetites since requests will necessarily exceed available resources. In such instances of fiscal stringency, Schick says that incremental methods and processes cannot prevail. The hard choices in a scarcity or cutback environment become aggravated by judicially mandated spending. The logic is simple enough; in this situation courts mortgage the modest budgetary increments. Both positive and normative consequences follow.

Positive consequences pertain to institutional regularities that are altered as a result of external conditions, such as the fiscal environment, that affect the budget process. Research on budget processes in environments of fiscal austerity has shown that basic patterns of strategy, negotiation, and accommodation are constrained by fiscal limits.[18] The impact of judicial intervention outlined here, however, is not a mere variation on the fiscal stress theme. Jurisdictions that can anticipate fiscal stringency fit Wildavsky's description of "poor and certain."[19] Poverty, in a budgetary context, is self-explanatory. Certainty refers to strategy and calculation. The process, in broad strokes, is essentially incremental. Judicial intervention in the process can alter these conditions.

Consider, first, the growth motive. Is it conceivable that agency heads could be in a position to resist budgetary expansion? Models of budgetary growth do not easily incorporate such a perverse possibility. But when resources are scarce, managers may not want to be responsible for expanded programs, facilities, or activities with which they are not in agreement—even if budgets grow. How might a manager actually *avoid* budget expansion when such expansion is predicated on judicial policy that is anathema to the manager? It depends on the implementation options available to the defendant agency. For example, injunctive relief to ameliorate prison overcrowding has been implemented in some states by moving prisoners out of state correctional facilities to country jails. While obviously a temporary approach, it has been used as a way to reduce overcrowding. Neither option neatly fits a model whereby the courts may be used as administrative leverage to pursue budgetary objectives.

The problem with the courts—from a budgetary perspective—is that they do not go away. This implies that short-term palliatives that produce incomplete implementation responses are unlikely to satisfy courts. Judges seem to have great staying power, as the history of institutional reform in Alabama prisons and psychiatric facilities under the watchful eyes of district court judge Frank Johnson demonstrates. When agencies welcome the courts, it is not difficult to interpret budgetary behavior; the "crisis technique" is relatively straightforward. But judicially mandated spending requires interpretation that does not easily come from basic models of what drives budgets—and how they are controlled.

From a political standpoint judges may be in positions to mortgage budgetary increments. The consequence is not trivial *if* a government in an austere fiscal climate finds that an agency is advantaged by judicial intervention. For instance, the budgetary climate in the City of New York has improved considerably since the financial crisis of 1975; nevertheless spending control is still heavily emphasized. Yet, because of judicial decisions concerning prison overcrowding, the corrections department has found itself in a relatively favored position (compared to other city agencies). This is not due to budgetary skill on the part of the agency's managers; rather, the court has, in effect, mortgaged part of the modest budgetary increment. The same observation could be made about judicial involvement in the areas of the homeless and special education in which advocacy groups foster litigation. From a conceptual standpoint, the interaction between the fiscal climate and judicial intervention wrecks havoc with the traditional stability that once enhanced understanding of public budgetary processes.

A RETURN TO V.O. KEY'S BASIC BUDGETARY QUESTION

Is this bad? It depends on what is expected from budgeting. This analysis supports V.O. Key's classic question concerning the basis for allocating budgetary resources among competing purposes.[20] Of course, Key posed the question in terms of a principle, or a set of principles, of nonmarket alloca-tion. Such principles, to the extent that they exist, are found in the application of microeconomics to public budgeting. But few would argue that, for example, the Paretian principle helps much in analyzing government budgets. This is one reason why budget researchers continue to pursue Key's query about the basis for allocating to activity x versus activity y.

Economists may rail at the suggestion, but political scientists have done no worse—and perhaps they have done a bit better at answering the question. Pluralist roots of incremental budgetary theory have served fairly well in the past to explain—post-hoc, to be sure—why there have been budgetary winners and budgetary losers. As long as the notion is accepted that competing purposes within a constrained budget force choice, the analytic problem—whether from the vantage point of microeconomics or even pluralism—is established. The major difference is that the normative underpinnings of microeconomics are easier to detect; political scientists have always been a bit squeamish about revealing their value-based presuppositions—partly because nothing rivals, say, the efficiency argument in allocation decisions.[21] But this may be pushed too far. After all, many reasons are offered for the general failure of budgetary reforms which attempt to make the process more "rational"—a code word for taking politics out of budgeting. One explanation is that the goal of making allocation decisions on the basis of efficiency sometimes conflicts with the norm of reciprocity.

Fiscal stringency does not automatically alter the normative dimensions of the allocation decision. However, most observers of budgeting would concede that zero-sum outcomes are more unpleasant than the "budgetary illusion" of positive sum (the term budgetary illusion is used since, even with real growth, some lose in terms of their *relative* share of the growth dividend). But even a casual glance at federal budgetary politics in FY1986 highlights the rudiments of pluralist budgetary politics—though they are somewhat constrained by top-down fiscal management decisions.

Little if any of this seems to fit budgetary situations which are impacted by court actions. Judges need not worry about either the analytics or the normative bases of allocation decisions. The protection of rights often seems divorced from fiscal limits and other organizational constraints. Advocates of due process protection could probably mount a strong argument that fiscal constraints *are* irrelevant. Logically, however, if a court mandates a change that must be funded within a budgetary constraint, the decision forces budgetary redistribution. Unlike redistribution that takes place, say, during the appropriations process—where claimants can attempt to exert their influence—those affected adversely by the budgetary fallout of the court's decision have no obvious place to turn.

The intervention of the courts in the budget process, then, requires taking Key's question to the high ground of political debate. Perhaps the search for budget theory has always been misplaced. Positive approaches to budgeting, after all, are really derived from propositions about individual and collective behavior that are said to be generalizable beyond the confines of public budgeting. Can budget theory be imagined without Simon and Lindblom?[22] When the spectre is raised of allocation decisions influenced by the courts, that likewise raises fundamental issues of constitutional and representative democracy—the degree to which decisions reflect constitutional fundamentals and/or electoral preferences—and discrepancies between them.

NOTES

The author acknowledges helpful comments on previous drafts from Jesse Burkhead, Phillip Cooper, Irene Rubin, Aaron Wildavsky, and anonymous referees. Financial support was received from the Center for Interdisciplinary Legal Studies, College of Law, Syracuse University.

1. Linda Harriman and Jeffrey D. Straussman, "Do Judges Determine Budget Decisions? Federal Court Decisions in Prison Reform and State Spending for Corrections," *Public Administration Review,* vol. 43 (July/August 1983), pp. 343–351.

2. Robert Martiniano, "The Willowbrook Consent Decree: A Case Study of the Judicial Impact on Budgeting" (Rockefeller College of Public Affairs and Policy, New York Case Studies in Public Management, September 1984).

3. Phillip Cooper, "Between the Legal Rock and the Political Hard Place: Interactions of Federal District Court Judges and State and Local Officials" (presented at the Annual Meeting of the American Political Science Association, Chicago, September 1–4, 1983).

4. Phillip Cooper, "Pressure Point: A Comparative Case Analysis of Federal District Court Equitable Decrees" (Presented at the Annual Meeting of the Western Political Science Association, Sacramento, April 12–14, 1984), p. 33.

5. See, for example, Lance T. LeLoup and William B. Moreland, "Agency Strategies and Executive Review: The Hidden Politics of Budgeting," *Public Administration Review,* vol. 38 (May/June 1978), pp. 232–239.

6. Aaron Wildavsky, *The Politics of the Budgetary Process,* fourth edition (Boston: Little, Brown and Company, 1984), p. 119.

7. Colin Diver, "The Judge as Political Broker: Superintending Structural Change in Public Institutions," *Virginia Law Review,* vol. 65 (February 1979), p. 85.

8. See, for example, Allen L. Ault, "Resource Utilization in Corrections," *Corrections Today,* vol. 42 (July/August 1980), p. 13.

9. For an extended argument see, Barry Bozeman and Jeffrey D. Straussman, "Shrinking Budgets and the Shrinkage of Budget Theory," *Public Administration Review,* vol. 42 (November/December 1982), pp. 509–515.

10. Diver, *op. cit.,* pp. 64–88.

11. M. Kay Harris and Dudley P. Spiller, Jr., *After Decision: Implementation of Judicial Decrees in Correctional Settings* (Washington: American Bar Association, November 1976), p.13.

12. Note, "Judicial Intervention in Corrections: The California Experience—An Empirical Study," *UCLA Law Review,* vol. 20 (February 1973), pp. 452–580.

13. Phillip Cooper, *Hard Judicial Choices: Federal District Judges and State and Local Officials* (New York: Oxford University Press, forthcoming).

14. Robert A. Dentler and Marvin B. Scott, *Schools on Trial* (Cambridge: Abt Books, 1981), p. 216.

15. William A. Fletcher, "The Discretionary Constitution: Institutional Remedies and Judicial Legitimacy," *Yale Law Journal,* vol. 91 (March 1982), pp. 635–697.

16. Advisory Commission on Intergovernmental Relations, *Jails: Intergovernmental Dimensions of a Local Problem* (Washington: ACIR, 1984).

17. Allen Schick, "Budgetary Adaptations to Resource Scarcity," in Charles H. Levine and Irene Rubin (eds.), *Fiscal Stress and Public Policy* (Beverly Hills: SAGE, 1980), pp. 113–134. Also, Allen Schick, "Macro-Budgetary Adaptations to Fiscal Stress in Industrialized Democracies," *Public Administration Review,* vol. 46 (March/April 1986), pages pending.

18. Naomi Caiden and Aaron Wildavsky, *Planning and Budgeting in Poor Countries* (New York: Wiley, 1975); see also, Jane Massey and Jeffrey D. Straussman, "Budget Control Is Alive and Well: Case Study of a County Government," *Public Budgeting & Finance,* vol. 1 (Winter 1981), pp. 3–11.

19. Aaron Wildavsky, *Budgeting* (Boston: Little, Brown and Company, 1975), pp. 114–116.

20. V.O. Key, "The Lack of a Budgetary Theory," *American Political Science Review,* vol. 34 (December 1940), pp. 1137–1144.

21. See Richard R. Nelson, *The Moon and the Ghetto* (New York: Norton, 1977), pp. 41–47.

22. Herbert A. Simon, *Administrative Behavior,* 3d. ed. (New York: The Free Press, 1976); Charles E. Lindblom, "The Science of 'Muddling Through,'" *Public Administration Review,* vol. 19 (Spring 1959), pp. 79–88.

CHAPTER 11

FEDERAL AGENCY BUDGET OFFICERS
Who Needs Them?

HERBERT G. PERSIL

WHAT DO THEY DO?

Little has been written about how recent legislation and changes in Congress have affected the work of agency budget officers, budget offices, and internal agency procedures. Practitioners of many years, no doubt, have been aware that budget issues with which they must deal today are different from those of the past, but their perceptions have not been documented.

In the first place, little has been written specifically about what these practitioners do, particularly agency budget officers, such as the nature of the work they perform and their responsibilities, so that the effects of the changes have not attracted much attention. Descriptions of budgeting in federal agencies usually do not dwell at length on the role of the agency budget officer. Perhaps, it has been simply accepted without elaboration that the official is responsible, somehow, for making the budget process function: initiating and prodding the formulation and preparation of the budget; obtaining or preparing adequate justifications of the budget request; serving as a resource person during the budget's progress through the executive and the legislature; and administering the enacted budget. An official full description of the typical role and responsibilities of the central budget officer in a federal agency does not appear to exist, although, no doubt, inside each agency there is an understanding based on tradition and practice of what that official does.[1]

ARE THE OLD TIME BUDGET OFFICERS EXTINCT?

One practitioner, on the basis of his concept of the agency budget officer, has lamented that changes in the budget process have diminished the budget officer's status and influence. Albert Kliman, in his article in the Spring 1997 issue of *Public Budgeting and Finance*, claims that the old-time federal agency budget officer has become a "dinosaur," an extinct species. He attributes this extinction not to a meteoric disaster but to events, beginning with the Congressional Budget and Impoundment Control Act of 1974, and to the increasing politicization of senior manage-

From *Public Budgeting and Finance,* vol. 18, no. 4 (Winter 1998), 114–122. Copyright © 1998 by Public Financial Publications, Inc. Reprinted with permission.

ment positions in the last two decades. These "catastrophic" events deprived the ancient beasts of their natural habitat and all but extinguished them. Today's altered species comprises members who no longer are seen as masters of financial management, but are regarded as "serfs," possibly supervisory, in the bureaucratic feudal system. These once proud creatures have lost their role as major contributors to the making of policy and, instead, are now relegated to make-work and technical functions.

Kliman acknowledges that this characterization is an overstatement, but this is his lead-in to argue that changes in the budget process, in fact, really have diminished the federal agency budget officer's role. Not everyone will agree with his gloomy assessment and, in fact, it may be premature to regard budget officers of the past as collections of ancient bones suitable only for being wired together and displayed in the Smithsonian Institution. There are indeed many indications that today's budget officers are alive, weary, and well, an active species that has adapted to survive in current environmental conditions. Just the same, it may be useful to examine his assertions and their relevance.

What was the nature of the old-time budget officer as seen by Kliman? In his view, this person had extraordinary responsibilities that extended beyond merely developing and distributing budget justifications and briefing management officials. A budget officer was an intimate participant with political appointees in the formulation of strategies to accomplish programmatic goals, working out their logic, defending them technically and giving them credibility during their advance through congressional consideration. The budget officer also supervised execution of the budget to ensure that programs were carried out in accordance with the law and desires of the agency head. He or she enjoyed this position because the agency head was this official's true supervisor, notwithstanding the location of the budget office in the organization structure. As long as the budget officer retained the full support of the agency head, he or she had the ability to authoritatively communicate policy and budget directives to bureau chiefs and program managers.

The budget officer was advisor, also, to congressional appropriations (and authorizing) committee staff on how to implement strategies, whether or not they conformed to those of the agency head. Providing such "technical advice" helped maintain the credibility of the agency budget staff and, at the same time, helped the committees avoid technical mishaps that could result in problems later for them and the agency. Appropriations committee staff have tended to view budget offices as their special proprietary resource and sometimes helped protect the budget officer from being stripped of power within the agency bureaucracy.

The budget officer so described was a powerful career official whose influence affected major program policies and execution of programs of the agency.[2] Retaining career status in that position required the ability to delicately balance a careerist's neutral detachment with providing full support and advice to policymakers. One consequence of that precarious position was a frequent effort by political appointees, particularly after a change in administration, to take control of the budget office. Kliman referred to these attempts as "power grabs." An example would be the effort by the budget officer's nominal supervisor in the organization, such as an Assistant Secretary for Management, to assert authority and intervene in the official's contacts with the agency head and bureau chiefs. The old time budget officer usually could rely on the agency head to reinforce his or her authority and set the matter straight with other department officials.

A situation might occur, perhaps because of a fundamental difference of views, whereby an agency head desires to replace a budget officer who does not want to be removed. Appropriations committees, on learning of the threat, may attempt to protect the person and insist that he or she be left alone. Kliman could have added that committee retaliation when its instructions are ignored can be prompt and severe, and there are examples in which this has occurred in the form of appropriations cuts, staff reductions, or statutory restrictions on the agency head's power and perquisites.

Whether or not this model of old-time budget officer was typical of the kind found in all federal agencies is not known. Considering the many differences and variations among federal agencies in the complexity of their programs and funding, size, and organization, it is unlikely. More probable is that most budget officers shared some of the attributes he described, but very few possessed all of them.

The most serious consequence of the changes in the budget process, in Kliman's view, is that they have diminished the budget officer's political role, so that he or she no longer is a political and a policy player in the agency. He cites as an example the insertion of an additional organizational layer where a budget officer is placed directly under the supervision of a political appointee, such as a "deputy assistant secretary for budget," who might then be regarded as the "official" budget officer.[3] The budget officer is left to focus mainly on technical matters, lacking the status to influence the policy process, and unable to prevent the filtering or altering of advice and identification of programs before being given to the agency head.

It is true, as he says, that legislative changes affecting federal budgeting have made it more complicated and have added extensive workload. As if to add further insult, there are efforts underway to reduce the size of budget offices in the government based on the recommendations of the Vice President's National Performance Review.

BUDGET REFORMS AND THE WORK OF BUDGET OFFICERS

Notwithstanding Kliman's view, an argument can be made to support the opposite case, that the current requirements of the budget process have enhanced, not diminished, the important role of budget directors and budget officers. The skills of the budget officer may be more important than ever for informing and assisting policymakers in reaching decisions within today's technical demands and the budget timetable. This extends to the budget officer's continuing communication with congressional appropriations committees, budget committees and the Congressional Budget Office, as all seek assistance and agreement on applying the complex new rules. A brief review of the effect on budget officers of some of the statutory reforms will illustrate the point.

The Congressional Budget and Impoundment Control Act of 1974, regarded here as the point of departure for changes in the budget process, was enacted, understandably enough, without budget officers in mind. The intent of the legislation was to expand the ability of Congress to consider the budget in total, applying priorities in terms of the entire budget rather than as separate unconnected appropriation acts. By creating the House and Senate budget committees and the Congressional Budget Office (CBO) for its assistance in this purpose, Congress hereby also added to the number of "clients" of agency budget offices, as the new entities naturally have looked to agency budget offices for data and information, explanations and, sometimes, briefings on agency programs and the budget. Because the appropriations and authorizations committees turn to the Congressional Budget Office for analyses of budget authority and outlays, to calculate the budget impact of committee proposals, and to validate agency estimates, CBO staff may often meet with agency budget staff to verify data and discuss the validity of assumptions used.

Currently, because of the strict budget ceilings on budget authority and outlays, the assumptions on which the estimates for some programs are based are no longer merely "technical." The estimates directly affect policy choices, program levels and funding to be appropriated, so these discussions may involve agency political persons as well as the budget officer. Fundamental program changes may have to be considered in order to accommodate the ceilings, the effects of which should be agreed upon by the agency and the CBO. It is difficult to make a convincing argument that the "burden" on budget offices and the participation of political persons in critical discussions illustrates a diminution of the budget officer's role.

The Budget Enforcement Act of 1990, and its amendments, has had a profound effect on decision making and the budget process in agencies. It codified an agreement between the president and Congress to achieve budget reductions into future years in the hope that a balanced budget would be achieved. The Act contained statutory ceilings on budget authority and outlays of "discretionary" programs for five years into the future, extended in subsequent budgets, so that any program increases had to be offset elsewhere in order to remain within the ceiling. It also created a category of "mandatory" spending to include programs in which budget authority and outlays did not require action by appropriations committees but continued because of permanent authorizing legislation. In this case, under "PAYGO" rules, increases in budget authority and outlays resulting from new legislation had to be offset by decreases from other legislation.

The Act had several consequences that greatly affected the work of budget officers. First, budget outlays had to be given closer scrutiny than before because once the rate of spending was established ("spendout rate"), they could not be changed, either in the annual budget or in the appropriations committees, except under specific rules. Outlays could no longer be changed to a more favorable level by simply changing the estimated rate of spending under rosier assumptions. Second, seriously complicating options under the ceilings, outlays in some programs do not take place in the same year budget authority is enacted but occur in later years. For example, budget authority for major construction activities or for subsidized housing programs could be enacted under the budget year ceiling so that contract commitments (obligations) could be made that year. However, outlays will occur in the future, perhaps over many years, in such programs, beyond control under outlay ceilings because treasury funds are actually expended in the progress of construction work or payment of subsidies. Choices laid out by budget officers have to be made between those programs spending quickly or those spending slowly, whatever other priorities may be under consideration. In agencies such as the Department of Housing and Urban Development, where over ninety percent of outlays in any year are derived from obligations made in previous years, the problem is exceptionally acute.

The third consequence was because of the ceilings, or "caps," on discretionary budget authority and outlays that were provided to each agency by the Office of Management and Budget (OMB) for guidance in the preparation of the annual budget. These caps, which declined each year in accordance with the total ceilings, were rigid and left little room for negotiation, with the result that there were significant changes in the way decisions were reached in agencies. In previous years, even in "tight" ones, bureaus within agencies could at least propose budget increases in the hope that they could be favorably negotiated with OMB. The budget process itself was structured to offer an opportunity to discuss priorities in which increases could be proposed. Under the current environment, no increases could be discussed unless offsets could be set forth in both budget authority and outlays, which few bureau chiefs were eager to volunteer. In order to make the hard choices, some agency heads suspended their usual budget process by not requesting the usual estimates from their bureau chiefs. This helped bureau chiefs avoid political problems caused by recommending reductions in programs vocally supported by interest groups. Some agency heads reached their budget decisions through a top-down process by preparing alternative budget proposals with minimal participation by agency managers.

The Act's consequences, as illustrated above, call for a budget officer and staff that is informed, flexible and resourceful. The budget officer's presence is needed to explain the implications of spend-out rates, the effect of alternative program and budget authority proposals on outlays, and potential sources of savings that might reduce outlays. To be able to do these, the budget officer must be more than a competent technician but must be able to extend that skill to the presentation of materials which clearly show program implications. The budget officer's participation in this way is what one would expect it to be and is not typical of someone layered out of the process to mere technical status.

The Federal Credit Reform Act of 1990 provides additional illustration of how reform legislation has added to the work of budget offices. Credit reform seeks to place federal direct loan and loan guarantee (including insurance) programs under control through the budget and in appropriations acts. Appropriations acts, which previously only limited program volume and administrative costs of credit programs, now include appropriations (budget authority) for the purpose of covering the cost of potential loss to the federal government. This recognizes that some loans do fail, and some loan guarantees must be utilized, and insurance claims may have to be paid leading to a loss to the treasury. The potential cost to the programs is now visible and must be provided for through appropriations instead of being hidden from view.

Agencies having direct loan or loan guarantee programs found preparation of the annual budget complicated enough before credit reform. Credit reform created the need to accumulate additional data, some not available before, and new accounting records so that historic losses could be tracked, new loss calculations entered for the budget, and provide a basis for fund control after appropriations are enacted. Preparation of the initial credit reform budgets was nightmarish as program staff, budget staff, and accountants wrestled with new concepts and terminology and endeavored to apply the requirements to their specific programs. The budget officer was responsible for assuring that agency managers understood the significance of the changes and how these affected program control and budget presentations.

1994 CONGRESSIONAL ELECTIONS

Another event, not statutory in nature, affecting budget officers across the government was the change in congressional leadership after the 1994 elections. The appropriations committees, like other committees, were assigned new chairpersons, and new chairpersons were also assigned to each subcommittee. The committee staff was also replaced, with new persons appointed by the new chairpersons of the ruling party. This ended long years of relative stability in committee staff and broke up long standing professional relationships between agency budget officers and the staff. The new staff, some of whom were inexperienced in the work of appropriations, naturally looked to agency budget officers, as their predecessors had done, as their routine link with the agencies. New understandings and procedural assumptions on such matters as providing information and justifications of agency programs had to be formulated. In this, budget officers have continued to carry out their traditional roles in working with the committee staff.

BUDGET OFFICERS STILL NEEDED IF NOT LOVED

These brief illustrations show how some of the budget reforms enacted by Congress, and the change in Congress itself, have added more work and responsibility to budget officers. They also show the increased importance of budget officers to agency heads as technical revisions to the rules have affected the program choices that must be made for the budget. They do not appear to be the basis for arguing that the status of budget officers has been diminished. They do not make for the increased politicization of the budget process, except to the extent that the increased involvement of political appointees in budgetary decisions can be so described.

Indeed, considering how the reforms have affected policy choices, participation by political appointees in discussions with staff of the appropriations committees, CBO and the OMB may often be essential. If the budget officer has less to say at such discussions, it does not reduce that person's status or relevance.

Any discussion of agency budget officers today should recognize that a common description in all details is not likely where the person's role in the policy process is concerned. One reason lies in the divergent management styles exercised by agency heads. Where there is an agency head who wants to be involved in the budget's details and have a budget expert close at hand, another agency head may prefer avoiding details, relying on an intermediary, and dealing with the budget officer infrequently. One agency head may be greatly interested in past experiences and call on the budget officer to explain how previous programs and policies worked or failed. Another agency head may not wish to be concerned with the past, especially if it was dominated by the party opposition, and proceed with new programs and a clean slate. An agency head may enjoy large meetings attended by top managers and senior staff to discuss policies in a collegial setting. Another may prefer meeting with only two or three people, having minimum discussion and making decisions on the spot. Obviously, the budget officer is subject to the preferences of the agency head, which may change from one administration to another.

A budget officer's effectiveness may also depend on personality and ability to work with and earn the confidence of intermediaries. Typically, budget officers work much of the time through an intermediary, such as chief of staff, executive assistant, special assistant, or some other individual close to the agency head. The intermediary will guide the decision process during budget formulation and govern the format preferred by the agency head for presenting issues for decision. The budget officer's acceptance and effect on policies may depend more on his or her relationship with the intermediary rather than on the frequency of contact with the agency head. Needless to say, the budget officer's own assertiveness in making sure important matters are brought to the agency head or intermediary is a collateral requirement.

Considering the many elements affecting the part budget officers may play in the policy making of an agency, it becomes difficult to argue that their status is elevated or diminished. Is there a standard, such as a model of the old-time budget officer, which can be applied among agencies to ascertain if the budget officer is being appropriately utilized? If there is a standard, it cannot be other than that used by the agency head to determine if he or she is satisfied with the budget processes in the agency. As said above, the attainment of that satisfaction begins, ultimately, with the management style and preferences of the agency head. In that case, to mourn the passing of the old-time budget officer is pointless, except to fulfill a nostalgic yearning for a return to simpler days. What works today is what gets the job done as desired by the agency head, using staff in a manner congenial to him or her.

This discussion has relied on the writer's own observations and experience rather than an empirically based study. Whether or not such a study could produce a standard for budget officers is not known, but unlikely in this writer's opinion. The absence of a budgetary theory, and the questionable prospect that one will be found, makes dim the possibility of a universal model budget officer, even if some individuals argue that dinosaur fossils indicate that sometimes in the past one did exist.

NOTES

1. The following description applicable to local government would probably fit a common perceptions of a federal agency budget officer, as well:

The budget division occupies a position of paramount importance in the overall functioning of a municipality or county. . . . [T]he head of the budget division usually becomes one of the principal aides to the chief administrator. . . . [H]e or she is usually placed in the office of the chief administrator to ensure a direct line of communication. Because of the wealth of knowledge that is acquired in the course of preparing that budget, the budget officer may well know more about governing operations than any other local officials, including the manager or the mayor. The budget officer typically possesses expertise extending beyond purely fiscal concerns, and he or she often contributes to studies and proposals involving administrative organization and management planning. Once the budget has been approved by the council, the budget officer and his or her staff assist the chief administrator in administering the budget.

From Leonard I. Ruchelman, "The Finance Function in Local Government," in J. Richard Aronson, (ed.) *Management Policies in Local Government finance,* 4th ed. Washington, D.C.: International City/County Management Association, 1996, p.27.

2. Kliman may have regarded the late John M. Frantz, the budget officer of the old Housing and Home Finance Agency and the first budget officer of the new Department of Housing and Urban Development, as the model. Frantz clearly was trusted and respected by the Department's top management and the appropriations committees until his retirement in January 1969. Kliman and this writer were privileged to be part of Frantz's staff.

3. In his article, he also regards the insertion of a political layer, the Program Associate Director, between the budget examiners and the Office of Management and Budget Director during the 1970s as part of the politicization of the budget process.

CHAPTER 12

THE BUDGET-MINIMIZING BUREAUCRAT?
Empirical Evidence from the Senior Executive Service

JULIE DOLAN

In a representative democracy, we assume the populace exerts some control over the actions and outputs of government officials, ensuring they comport with public preferences. Since the founding of the United States, public control over government spending has been at the top of the list of public concerns (Stabile 1998). After their colonial experiences and cries of "taxation without representation," the framers placed the power to tax and spend within the Congress, the branch expected to be most closely aligned with and controlled by the people (Oleszek 1996; Rossiter 1961). In doing so, the expectation was that government officials would heed public demands for taxing and spending or would face electoral repercussions.[1] However, the growth of the fourth branch of government has created a paradox: Unelected bureaucrats now have the power to affect government budget decisions (LeLoup 1977; Wildavsky 1964).

Concern over bureaucratic behavior stems from the increasingly important role that public administrators play in American governance. If they neutrally executed policy decisions made by their political superiors without personal involvement, their attitudes and values would be of marginal concern, as we would not expect them to affect the decision-making calculus. However, it is widely recognized that bureaucrats, especially those in executive positions, do engage in policy making (Aberbach, Putnam, and Rockman 1981; Meier 1993; Rourke 1984). Because these individuals hold unelected positions protected by civil service personnel regulations, how can the public be certain their decisions will comport with the public interest? Can substantial bureaucratic involvement in governance be reconciled with democratic ideals?

Focusing specifically on budgetary preferences, this article addresses how well the top ranks of the federal civil service represent the demands and preferences of the American citizenry. I empirically assess the competing claims of representative-bureaucracy and budget-maximization theories by focusing on members of the Senior Executive Service (SES), those employed within the top career ranks of the federal government. Because SES members are career civil servants who are intimately involved in policy making, focusing on how well their attitudes reflect public sentiments provides important information about the representative nature of the top ranks of the fourth branch of government.

From *Public Administration Review,* vol. 62, no. 1 (January/February 2002), 42–50. Copyright © 2002 by American Society for Public Administration. Reprinted with permission.

BUREAUCRATIC POLITICS AND FEDERAL SPENDING PRIORITIES

Competing theories in the bureaucratic politics literature lead us to different expectations about whether public administrators can be expected to heed public demands on budgetary matters. On one hand, some scholars claim that the federal bureaucracy will make broadly representative decisions, on budgetary matters as well as on other issues, because it is a representative institution itself (Kranz 1976; Krislov and Rosenbloom 1981; Long 1952; Nachmias and Rosenbloom 1973). Thus, because public administrators are drawn from the population they serve, their values and attitudes are likely to resemble those of the larger public, thereby ensuring democratically accountable decisions on their part. Along these lines, a number of works demonstrate that a demographically representative bureaucracy produces policy that is responsive to the citizenry. Although very little research focuses specifically on government spending, scholars have examined government outputs such as Farmers Home Administration loans, decisions to move Equal Employment Opportunity claims forward, and a variety of educational rewards and sanctions, to produce convincing evidence that public administrators at all levels of government heed the preferences of a variety of social groups and produce government outputs in accordance with their wishes (Hindera 1993; Hindera and Young 1998; Meier 1984; Meier and Stewart 1992; Meier, Stewart, and England 1991; Selden 1997; Stewart, England, and Meier 1988).

However, very little existing research focuses specifically on budgetary behavior and whether bureaucrats heed public preferences for government spending. A notable exception is Lewis' (1990) work, which focuses specifically on budget preferences. Using General Social Survey data from 1982 to 1988, he compares spending attitudes among federal, state, and local public administrators with those of the general public and finds remarkably few differences between the two groups. As such, he concludes that "government employees are no more likely than the average citizen to favor bigger government budgets" (222) and thus are relatively in sync with the public's demands for government spending. As such, elite administrators can be trusted to accurately represent public demands for government spending.

Conversely, other scholars theorize that administrators attempt to preserve their own self-interests by inflating public demands for spending, so as to secure better working conditions and perquisites for themselves (Buchanan 1977; Downs 1967; Niskanen 1971, 1975, 1991). In his seminal book *Bureaucracy and Representative Government* (1971), William Niskanen claims that bureaucrats are primarily self-interested individuals attempting to maximize their own utility through larger budgets, or larger discretionary budgets, as he later argues (Niskanen 1975). As such, they cannot be expected to legitimately represent public demands for government spending. Anthony Downs (1967) similarly reasons that bureaucrats are driven primarily by self-interest, and he is skeptical that the bureaucracy performs as a broadly representative institution. Referring to the behavior of bureaucratic officials, he argues "the pressure on them to seek representative goals is much weaker than the pressure of their own personal goals or those of their bureaus" (233).[2]

A number of studies have empirically verified that bureaucrats attempt, directly or indirectly, to maximize their own budgets.[3] Using National Election Studies (NES) data from 1982 to 1986, Garand, Parkhurst, and Seoud (1991a, b) find evidence that government employees are more likely than their private sector counterparts to favor policies that are consistent with expanding the public sector. They compare the federal-spending priorities and political behavior of government employees and private-sector citizens and find that government employment is generally associated with preferences for higher government spending and more leftist leanings. Similarly, Blais, Blake and Dion (1991) compare public- and private-sector voting behavior and vote choice, also using NES data, and find public-sector employees more supportive of left-wing political candidates. They even go so far as to suggest the existence of a public–private sector gap, similar to the gender gap, where public-sector individuals vote more often for Democratic candidates than do private-sector employees. Such electoral support, according to the authors, is given with the expectation that Democratic and left-wing candidates will be more likely to press for greater public spending, thereby improving working conditions for public-sector employees. Examining ideological orientation and policy attitudes among public- and private-sector employees in Great Britain, the Netherlands, and the United States, Blake (1991) concludes, "[W]henever significant differences appear between public sector and private sector employees, they show the former to be more left wing, more supportive of government spending and nationalization policies, and more opposed to tax cuts" (236). Aberbach, Putnam, and Rockman (1981) also confirm greater leftist leanings among federal executives compared to the public. Strong attitudinal and behavioral evidence demonstrates that public administrators are out of sync with public preferences for government spending, preferring greater spending than the median voter.

One reason that previous studies have reached such contradictory conclusions is that they have examined public officials employed in different positions and arenas of government. With the exception of Garand, Parkhurst, and Seoud (1991b), these studies rely on a combination of local, state, and federal employees, but the survey questions inquire only about federal-spending priorities, calling into question the validity of using state and local employees' expressed attitudes to predict their behavior within their own governments. Although government employees in all locales prefer relatively greater spending than the public on a variety of issues, state and local employees diverge from the public more than do federal employees (Garand, Parkhurst, and Seoud 1991b). In other words, state and local government employees prefer relatively greater federal spending than do individuals who actually work for the federal government. Self-interest may be at work here, in that state and local government workers perceive increased federal spending as relatively less costly than do their federal counterparts, expecting to reap benefits without increasing state or local taxes. Second, Niskanen's theory is written with senior bureaucrats in mind, but most studies lump all public administrators together without regard for their position within the organizational hierarchy.[4] An obvious problem with this approach is that we cannot be confident that those in lower positions will ever be in a position to influence budgetary matters for their organizations. Third, previous studies make no attempt to correlate bureaucrats' areas of expertise with their preferences for specific policies or program areas of government spending. So, whether a social worker's preferences for government spending on environmental protection, or a schoolteacher's attitudes on defense spending are appropriate measures for estimating future behavior is unanswered. Recognizing this limitation, Garand, Parkhurst, and Seoud (1991a) suggest that future research should attempt to correlate issue areas with specific spending issues. As such, this study attempts to add to and improve upon the existing body of work by focusing solely on SES members and by accounting for their substantive areas of issue expertise to estimate their spending preferences and behavior.

EXPECTATIONS AND HYPOTHESES

If the budget-maximizing theory is correct, public administrators should prefer greater spending than the public on issues that are likely to affect or come under their agency's jurisdiction. Attempting to secure larger budgets for their own organizations may not affect their preferences for spending issues outside their department's jurisdiction, however. Perhaps government employment is correlated with higher preferences for government spending across the board. If budgeting across the federal government is perceived as a zero-sum game where one agency's losses are another's gains, administrators should favor relatively greater spending on their own policies and programs while showing less support for spending on other government programs. But if administrators represent the policy attitudes of the public, they will not prefer greater spending than the average citizen. These conflicting theories lead to three testable hypotheses:

Budget-maximizing hypothesis: Compared to the public, public administrators prefer greater spending in areas that are likely to come under their organization's jurisdiction.

Zero-sum game hypothesis: Compared to the public, public administrators prefer less spending in areas that do not fall within their organization's jurisdiction.

Representative-bureaucracy hypothesis: Compared to the public, public administrators prefer similar levels of government spending.

These hypotheses allow me to assess how well senior executives represent the spending priorities of the general public while accounting for the possible affects of self- interest. If the SES is broadly representative of the American public, I expect these senior executives will demonstrate attitudes similar to public attitudes. On the other hand, if government employment inflates one's preferences for the provision of government services, we should find SES members unrepresentative of the public and leaning toward greater public-sector spending.

DATA AND METHODS

I empirically assess the link between public opinion and senior executives' attitudes by comparing their federal-spending preferences on a variety of policy issues. The data are drawn from three surveys: the 1996 American National Election Studies (NES) the 1996 General Social Survey (GSS), and the 1996 Survey of Senior Executives (SOSE). The NES and GSS are administered every other year and are widely regarded as valid and reliable instruments for assessing American public opinion on a variety of issues. The 1996 NES survey was based on interviews with 1,714 individuals and the 1996 GSS study included 2,904 respondents, of which approximately half were asked the relevant federal-spending questions. I developed the SOSE especially for this research and reproduced a number of federal-spending questions from the NES to make comparisons possible between the two samples.[5] It was mailed to a random sample of 1,000 SES employees between November 1996 and January 1997 and yielded a final response rate of 57 percent (n=570). The survey inquired about SES members' perceptions of influence, job responsibilities, and attitudes on spending and other issues.[6]

The Survey of Senior Executives reproduced a number of questions from the NES surveys, providing an excellent vehicle for making meaningful comparisons between the attitudes of SES administrators and the general public. The questions were reproduced verbatim, since even a slight variation in wording can produce marked differences in results.[7] The replicated questions asked respondents to indicate if they would like to see spending increased, decreased, or stay the same for a variety of government programs (for exact wording, see appendix 12A).[8] All tests of significance are based on the chi-square statistic, comparing the percentages of those who agreed that spending should be increased across each item.

The organization of the rest of the article is as follows: First, I compare SES members' government-spending priorities with public attitudes to assess the overall attitude congruence between the two groups. Second, I look more closely at bureaucratic attitudes on spending issues that are likely to come under the jurisdiction of their government department. Because I did not oversample individuals from any one department, only the Department of Defense and Department of Health

Table 12.1

Federal-Spending Priorities Among Senior Executives and the General Population

Federal-spending issue	Favor increasing spending (percent)		Difference (percent)
	Senior executives[1]	General population[2]	
Public schools	53.4	67.6	−14.2***
Protecting environment	45.4	41.1	4.3*
Dealing with crime	44.0	69.3	−25.3***
Child care	34.0	51.9	−17.9***
AIDS research	33.7	56.1	−22.4**
Health care*	31.6	64.1	−32.5***
Homelessness	31.5	57.2	−25.7***
Financial aid for college students	30.9	54.5	−23.6***
Foreign aid[3]	22.5	5.4	17.1***
Programs that assist blacks*	13.4	27.4	−14.0***
Aid to big cities*	11.4	26.4	−15.0***
Social Security	7.3	47.2	−39.9***
Defense*	6.9	17.5	−10.5***
Welfare programs	6.3	10.8	−4.5***
Food stamps	5.8	10.2	−4.4***

Note: The chi-square statistic for differences between SES members and the general public is significant at ***$p < 0.001$; **$p < 0.01$; *$p<0.05$.

[1]Source: Survey of Senior Executives, n = 570.

[2]1996 NES, n = 1,714, or 1996 GSS, n = 1,179–1,372, depending on question (GSS items marked with an asterisk).

[3]Between 1994 and 1996, the NES slightly changed the wording on one question. In both years, all questions began with, "If you had a say in making up the federal budget this year, for which of the following programs would you like to see spending increased and for which would you like to see spending decreased?" The wording in the foreign aid question changed from "foreign aid to countries of the former Soviet Union" to "foreign aid" between 1994 and 1996. In 1994, 7.1 percent of the NES respondents agreed that spending on "foreign aid to countries of the former Soviet Union" should be increased.

and Human Services contain sufficient numbers of senior executives to realistically estimate their preferences for programs under their jurisdiction (n=119 for Defense, n=44 for Health and Human Services).

FINDINGS

Overall, there is some evidence of attitude congruence between the general public and senior executives, lending tentative support to the representative-bureaucracy hypothesis. Examining the percentage of senior executives and the general public who agree that spending should be increased, Table 12.1 shows that the two groups largely resemble one another in their priorities for government spending. Public schools, crime, and the environment are policy areas ranked highly by each group, while food stamps, welfare, and defense spending are accorded relatively low priority.

Closer examination reveals that public administrators are more frugal and less inclined to favor increased government spending than the general public, lending tentative support to the zero-sum-game hypothesis (see Table 12.1). Contrary to the popular portrayal of the budget-maximizing bureaucrat (Niskanen 1971), these federal bureaucrats actually prefer *less* spending than the public on almost all broad spending categories. The largest difference between the two groups is their

Table 12.2

Differences in Spending Priorities, Department of Health and Human Services and General Public

	Agree spending should be increased (percent)		
	Department of Health and Human Services (n = 44)	General public[1]	Difference (percent)
Public school	65.9	67.8	−1.9
Health care*	52.5	64.1	−11.6**
Protecting environment	48.8	41.2	7.6
Child care	47.5	52.3	−4.8*
Financial aid for college students	41.0	54.7	−13.7*
Dealing with crime	40.5	69.2	−28.7***
Homelessness	37.5	57.5	−20.0***
AIDS research	33.3	56.4	−23.1**
Programs that assist blacks*	24.3	27.4	−3.1*
Food stamps	20.0	10.3	9.7***
Welfare programs	19.5	10.9	8.6*
Aid to big cities*	15.0	26.4	−11.4*
Social Security	11.9	47.3	−35.4***
Foreign aid	11.9	5.4	6.5***
Defense*	0.0	17.5	−17.5***

Note: The chi-square statistic for differences between SES members and the general public is significant at ***p < 0.001; **p < 0.01; *p < 0.05.
[1]1996 NES, n = 1,714, or 1996 GSS, n = 1,179–1,372, depending on question (GSS items marked with an asterisk).

support for Social Security spending. While almost half of the general population (47 percent) prefers more Social Security funding, less than 10 percent of SES members do. Further, greater than 20 percent more members of the public are likely to support funding increases on crime, AIDS research, health care, homelessness, and financial aid for college students.[9] Senior executives prefer more spending on only two issues: the environment and foreign aid.[10]

Although these findings suggest senior executives do not inflate government budgets for personal gain, their attitudes on spending issues that are likely to come under their jurisdiction are more suitable for these purposes. After all, if self-interest compels bureaucrats to seek larger budgets, we would expect them to favor increased spending on their own agency's programs above all else. Comparing bureaucrats within the Department of Health and Human Services (HHS) with the general public provides little support for the budget-maximizing hypothesis. These senior executives prefer significantly less spending than the public on three out of four policy areas that fall under the department's jurisdiction (health care child care, and AIDS research; see Table 12.2).[11] Further, executives in this department also rate public schools as more worthy of increased funding. If they behaved as self-serving budget maximizers, we would expect to see greater discrepancies between their preferences for their own policies and those administered elsewhere in the federal government. The only finding that is consistent with budget-maximizing expectations is found for welfare spending, where approximately 9 percent more senior executives prefer increased spending. But in a similar vein, these administrators also prefer devoting greater funds toward food stamps, a program administered by the Department of Agriculture. Thus, they appear more concerned with supporting programs that help the indigent rather than fattening their own budgets

Table 12.3

Differences in Spending Priorities, Department of Defense and General Public

	Agree spending should be increased (percent)		
	Department of Defense (n = 119)	General public[1]	Difference (percent)
Dealing with crime	57.1	69.2	−12.1***
Public schools	42.9	67.8	−24.9***
Protecting environment	31.9	41.2	−9.3*
AIDS research	31.1	56.4	−25.3***
Homelessness	25.2	57.5	−32.3***
Foreign aid	25.2	7.1	19.8***
Child care	24.4	52.3	−27.9***
Health care*	23.5	64.1	−40.6***
Financial aid for college students	20.8	54.7	−33.9***
Defense*	15.1	17.5	−2.4***
Programs that assist blacks*	7.7	27.4	−19.7***
Aid to big cities*	4.3	26.4	−22.1***
Social Security	3.4	47.3	−43.9***
Food stamps	1.0	10.3	−9.3**
Welfare programs	1.0	10.9	−10.9***

*** = The chi-square statistic for differences between SES members and the general public is significant at ***$p < .001$; ** = $p < .01$; * = $p < .05$.

[1] 1996 NES, n = 1,714, or 1996 GSS, n = 1,179–1,372, depending on question (GSS items marked with an asterisk).

for personal gain. Senior administrators at HHS are clearly more liberal than the overall sample of senior executives, but still less enthusiastic than the general public about increasing funds for their own programs.

Similarly, the findings from the Department of Defense fail to support the budget-maximizing hypothesis, as defense executives are no more likely to advocate increased defense spending than the general public, and they rank nine other programs as more deserving of increased funds than defense (Table 12.3). Resembling the larger sample of SES members, senior executives at the Defense Department continue to prefer less spending on almost all federal government programs than does the public and advocate greater spending on only one issue, foreign aid. Such evidence might be construed as consistent with the zero-sum-game hypothesis, except that most foreign aid programs are carried out under the auspices of the State Department, not the Defense Department. Further, defense administrators favor relatively less funding for defense than does the public. We cannot simply conclude that defense administrators inflate their own budgets at the expense of other government programs; rather, they appear to support less government spending on almost all programs.

These findings question the assumption that bureaucrats uniformly prefer larger budgets. On the contrary, they are more likely to advocate decreased government spending. Even on issues where they are likely to benefit most from increased spending, SES members are seldom more likely than the public to advocate increased spending.

What can explain these budget-minimizing tendencies among bureaucrats? Frugality on the part of senior executives may be a function of a number of factors. First, real fiscal pressures may simply loom larger in the minds of senior executives. When Niskanen wrote in 1971, annual deficits rarely exceeded $5 billion per year and were not an issue of public concern. By 1996, the U.S. government had been operating under a deficit for 27 consecutive years, with deficits exceeding $100 billion since 1982 (OMB 2000, 20). In an era of decreasing discretionary spending and increasing public concern over the size of the budget deficit—evidenced by the attention the issue received in the 1992 presidential elections—SES members' opinions may simply reflect the austere fiscal conditions under which they work.[12] Perhaps public officials have grown accustomed to doing more with less, and their responses simply reflect this reality. If so, Niskanen's budget-maximization theory may have less predictive validity when administrators are faced with spiraling deficits.

Second, and related to the first possibility, actual involvement in making budgetary decisions makes it highly probable that public servants possess greater knowledge about current federal spending levels and political realities than the general public. The public's inflated impression of actual foreign aid spending is instructive here. As polls have shown, the public believes that foreign spending consumes a much greater share of the federal budget than it actually does (Morin 1996), and such misinformation may carry over to their estimates of spending for other public programs. As such, senior executives' attitudes may be tempered by a more realistic assessment of actual spending levels. Third, senior bureaucrats may be more concerned with program-specific spending than broad spending levels, a possibility I cannot assess here. While individual bureaucrats may agree that overall spending could be cut within their departments, they may still prefer greater infusions of funds for particular programs within the department. Without survey questions written at the programmatic level, it is not possible to determine if this dynamic is at work. Fourth, it is possible that administrators were less than entirely truthful in their responses, fearing repercussions from a skeptical public that is rarely enthusiastic about bureaucrats or bureaucracy. Considering that politicians often run against the bureaucracy to get elected (Michaels 1997), senior executives may fear that anything they do or say, even filling out a confidential survey, will come back to haunt them. I encouraged honesty by assuring all respondents absolute confidentiality, and the 57 percent response rate leads me to believe that those who responded did not feel particularly threatened by sharing their views. Further, only a small portion of the survey dealt with federal-spending issues, so it is doubtful that most senior executives perceived these questions as being the focus of the survey. The combination of these factors gives me hope that deliberate falsification was kept to a minimum.

CONCLUSION

This article compares public executives' demands for public spending with those of the general public to determine whether the public can trust elite bureaucrats to make decisions that reflect their demands for government services. In contrast to previous attempts to assess the budget-maximizing behavior of public administrators, this research improves upon earlier attempts in a number of ways. First, Senior Executive Service employees make more appropriate units of analysis than do lower-ranking administrators, because they hold discretionary positions and are intimately involved in federal-budgeting matters. Second, by focusing specifically on items that are likely to be relevant to these government officials, that is, federal spending priorities, there is greater likelihood that responses are applicable to their work experiences. Further, accounting for potential self-interest in one's own program area by focusing on departmental spending issues ensures greater validity of findings.

Taken together, these findings do not support any of the originally specified hypotheses. Federal employment does indeed exert some influence on senior executives' federal-spending priorities, but in the opposite direction than is usually assumed. Senior executives are less likely than the general public to favor increased spending on the vast majority of government programs, contrary to assumptions about self-interested bureaucratic behavior. Further, there is little evidence that administrators act in a zero-sum fashion, inflating spending in their own programs while decreasing funds for competing programs. In both the Defense and Health and Human Services departments, senior civil servants advocate less spending on their own programs than does the public, and they rank other programs as being more deserving of increased funding. The representative-bureaucracy hypothesis is not supported, either. While senior executives and the public generally prefer increased or decreased spending for the same types of programs, senior administrators clearly prefer less spending than the public. To be consistent with representative-bureaucracy theory, federal bureaucrats would actually need to inflate their own preferences to truly represent public demands for federal spending.

It is possible, however, that senior executives' attitudes approximate true public demands for federal spending, more so than is reflected here. Public opinion polls report that the vast majority of Americans think government is wasteful and inefficient, while more than half agree that federal taxes are too high (Morin and Balz 1996). Yet when asked about their spending preferences for a variety of programs, they hardly demonstrate fiscal prudence. Rather, majorities advocate increased spending for nearly half of the programs. Thus, national surveys may provide slightly misleading information about true public-spending preferences, but they remain our best available estimate of public attitudes.

In sum, the budget-minimizing tendencies of federal administrators reported here suggest that self-interest is not as powerful a motivator as previously believed and, they suggest we should revise out theories about self-interested bureaucrats inflating government budgets for their own gain.

ACKNOWLEDGMENTS

The author would like to thank David H. Rosenbloom, Kenneth J. Meier, Gregory B. Lewis, Richard W. Waterman, Katherine C. Naff, and Anirudh V.S. Ruhil for their helpful comments on earlier versions of this article.

NOTES

1. The electoral consequences, we may infer, were more likely to be directed at the members of the House, as Senators were elected by the state legislatures until 1913.

2. Other scholars maintain that bureaucrats attempt to increase their own budgets to fulfill the policy mandates of their agencies and departments, not necessarily for personal gain (Fenno 1966; LeLoup 1977; Simon 1957; Wildavsky 1964). I am interested in assessing whether bureaucrats prefer greater spending than the public, not in pinpointing the specific motivations behind these attitudes.

3. In fact, Blais and Dion (1991) edit an entire volume of essays dedicated to empirically assessing Niskanen's budget-maximizing claims.

4. Lewis (1990) and Blake (1991) attempt to separate respondents according to broad occupational categories. Doing so does not guarantee, however, that they isolate only those with budgetary discretion.

5. To assure verbatim question wording on the surveys, I consulted the 1994 version of the NES, since the 1996 version was not yet available to the public. The 1996 NES did not reproduce all of the questions from the 1994 version, so I have supplemented my analysis with data from the 1996 GSS. The wording of the federal-spending priorities is slightly different on the GSS, however. Rather than asking respondents whether they would like to see spending increased, decreased, or remain the same, the questions ask whether the respondents believe we are spending too much, too little, or about the right amount. Certainly the questions are getting at the same issues, rendering them suitable substitutes. For the NES responses, I report the percentage of those who agree that spending should be increased, while I report the percentage of those who respond we are spending too little from the GSS. The policy issues are also phrased slightly differently on the

two surveys. While the NES asks about defense spending, the comparable GSS phrase is "national defense." Question wording varies slightly for the following items, so comparisons between senior executives and the general public should be interpreted with caution: defense, programs that assist blacks, aid to big cities and health care. See appendix 12A for the exact question wording.

6. The resulting sample of senior executives is representative of the entire SES. See Dolan (2000) for further information.

7. The NES began randomizing the order in which the federal-spending questions were asked in 1996 to minimize any question-order effects. Without knowing this in advance, no attempt was made on my part to randomize question order on the SOSE. However, the 1996 randomization does not appear to present any serious methodological problems. When comparing how NES respondent in 1994 (nonrandomized question order) and 1996 (randomized question order) ranked the spending issues in question, their two lists are virtually identical (see appendix 12B). Both groups indicated that dealing with crime is most deserving of increased spending while foreign aid is least deserving of increased funds. Between these two issues, the order in which the rest of the items fall is identical, with only two exceptions. Homelessness and public schools ranked second and third in 1994, while the order is reversed in 1996. AIDS research ranked much higher in 1996 than it did in 1994 (fourth in 1996, seventh in 1994). It is difficult to determine whether this difference reflects greater public support for AIDS research funding in 1996 or whether it is a function of the randomization process first used in 1996. Nonetheless, the relatively few differences between the two years suggest question order effects are minimal.

8. One question on the 1996 ANES differs ever so slightly from earlier versions. Asking respondents about their preferences for foreign aid spending, the 1994 survey asked about "foreign aid to countries of the former Soviet Union" while the 1996 version asked about "foreign aid," entirely omitting the clause about the Soviet Union. Because the SOSE was sent into the field prior to dissemination of the 1996 ANES results, the 1994 wording was used. As such, comparisons between senior executives and the general public are reported for both 1994 and 1996.

9. The Senior Executive Service, created in 1978 by the Civil Service Reform Act (CSRA), is composed primarily of career executives, although political appointees may hold up to 10 percent of the total positions and 25 percent of the positions in any one agency (Huddleston and Boyer 1996, 104). Because career civil servants are the intended subjects of representative-bureaucracy and budget-maximization theories, I removed political appointees from the sample and reran the results. Doing so did not alter the original results.

10. The average age of senior executives in the SOSE sample was 51.7 years with a standard deviation of 6.5 years, while the average age of the general public in the 1996 ANES sample was 45.5 years with a standard deviation of 16.9 years. Further, senior executives are more highly educated than the public, with 80 percent having at least one graduate degree, while only 10 percent of the general public in the NES sample does. Noting these differences, I regressed support for government spending against age, education, and whether one is employed within the SES to control for any effects of these variables. Age and education are negatively associated with a preference for increased spending across virtually all of the spending items, such that older and more educated respondents are significantly less supportive of increased spending. This is true for all issues except foreign aid, where age and education are positively (but not statistically significantly) associated with a preference for increased spending. Even controlling for age and education, federal executives remain less supportive of increased funding for AIDS research, crime, financial aid, homelessness, and Social Security. As before, executives continue to advocate relatively greater funding for the environment and foreign aid. The only change appears for welfare spending and food stamps, where executives now favor slightly greater spending. Considering the small size of the original differences, this is not particularly surprising. Thus, controlling for age and education does little to alter the original findings.

11. SES members at HHS also prefer significantly less spending on Social Security, an issue that fell under the department's jurisdiction until the Social Security Administration became an independent agency in 1995.

12. In the few years since the survey was administered, the U.S. government has enjoyed yearly surpluses. However, the survey was administered in 1996, when a deficit still existed.

REFERENCES

Aberbach, Joel D., Robert D. Putnam, and Bert A. Rockman. 1981. *Bureaucrats and Politicians in Western Democracies.* Cambridge, MA: Harvard University Press.

Blais, Andre, and Stephane Dion, eds. 1991. *The Budget-Maximizing Bureaucrat: Appraisals and Evidence.* Pittsburgh, PA: University of Pittsburgh Press.

Blais, Andre, Donald E. Blake, and Stephane Dion. 1991. The Voting Behavior of Bureaucrats. In *The Budget-Maximizing Bureaucrat: Appraisals and Evidence,* edited by Andre Blais and Stephane Dion, 205–30. Pittsburgh, PA: University of Pittsburgh Press.

Blake, Donald E. 1991. Policy Attitudes and Political Ideology in the Public Sector. In *The Budget-Maximizing Bureaucrat: Appraisals and Evidence,* edited by Andre Blais and Stephane Dion, 231–56. Pittsburgh, PA: University of Pittsburgh Press.

Buchanan, James. 1977. Why Does Government Grow? In *Budgets and Bureaucrats: The Sources of Government Growth,* edited by Thomas A. Borcherding, 3–18. Durham, NC: Duke University Press.

Dolan, Julie. 2000. The Senior Executive Service: Gender, Attitudes and Representative Bureaucracy. *Journal of Public Administration Research and Theory* 10(3): 513–29.

Downs, Anthony. 1967. *Inside Bureaucracy.* Boston, MA: Little, Brown.

Fenno, Richard F., Jr. 1996. *The Power of the Purse: Appropriations Politics in Congress.* Boston, MA: Little, Brown.

Garand, James C., Catherine T. Parkhurst, and Rusanne Jourdan Seoud. 1991a. Bureaucrats, Policy Attitudes, and Political Behavior: Extension of the Bureau Voting Model of Government Growth. *Journal of Public Administration Research and Theory* 1(2): 177–212.

———. 1991b. Testing the Bureau Voting Model. A Research Note on Federal and State-Local Employees. *Journal of Public Administration Research and Theory* 1(2): 229–33.

Gawthrop, Louis C. 1969. *Bureaucratic Behavior in the Executive Branch.* New York: Free Press.

Hindera, John J. 1993. Representative Bureaucracy: Imprimis Evidence of Active Representation in the EEOC District Offices. *Social Science Quarterly* 74(1): 95–108.

Hindera, John J., and Cheryl Young. 1998. Representative Bureaucracy: The Theoretical Implications of Statistical Interaction. *Political Research Quarterly* 51(3): 655–71.

Huddleston, Mark W., and William W. Boyer. 1996. *The Higher Civil Service in the United States: Quest for Reform.* Pittsburgh, PA: University of Pittsburgh Press.

Kranz, Harry. 1967. *The Participatory Bureaucracy: Women and Minorities in a More Representative Public Service.* Lexington, MA: D.C. Heath.

Krislov, Samuel, and David H. Rosenbloom. 1981. *Representative Bureaucracy and the American Political System.* New York: Praeger.

LeLoup, Lance T. 1977. *Budgetary Politics: Dollars, Deficits, Decisions.* Brunswick, OH: Kings Court Communications.

Lewis, Gregory B. 1990. In Search of Machiavellian Milquetoasts: Comparing Attitudes of Bureaucrats and Ordinary People. *Public Administration Review* 50(2): 220–27.

Long, Norton E. 1952. Bureaucracy and Constitutionalism. *American Political Science Review* 46(3): 808–18.

Meier, Kenneth J. 1975. Representative Bureaucracy: An Empirical Analysis. *American Political Science Review* 69(2): 526–42.

———. 1984. Teachers, Students, and Discrimination: The Policy Impact of Black Representation. *Journal of Politics* 46(1): 252–63.

———. 1993. *Politics and the Bureaucracy: Policy Making in the Fourth Branch of Government.* Pacific Grove, CA: Brooks/Cole Publishing.

Meier, Kenneth J., and Lloyd G. Nigro, 1976. Representative Bureaucracy and Policy Preferences: A Study in the Attitudes of Federal Executives. *Public Administration Review* 36(4): 458–69.

Meier, Kenneth J., and Joseph Stewart, Jr. 1992. The Impact of Representative Bureaucracies: Educational Systems and Public Policies. *American Review of Public Administration* 22(2): 157–71.

Meier, Kenneth J., Joseph Stewart, Jr., and Robert E. England. 1991. The Politics of Bureaucratic Discretion: Educational Access as an Urban Service. *American Journal of Political Science* 35(1): 155–77.

Michaels, Judith E. 1997. *The President's Call: Executive Leadership from FDR to George Bush.* Pittsburgh, PA: University of Pittsburgh Press.

Morin, Richard. 1996. Who's in Control? Many Don't Know or Care; Knowledge Gap Affects Attitudes and Participation. *Washington Post,* January 29, A6.

Morin, Richard, and Dan Balz. 1996. Americans Losing Trust in Each Other and Institutions: Suspicion of Strangers Breeds Widespread Cynicism. *Washington Post,* January 28, A1.

Nachmias, David, and David H. Rosenbloom. 1973. Measuring Bureaucratic Representation and Integration. *Public Administration Review* 33(6): 590–97.

Niskanen, William A. 1971. *Bureaucracy and Representative Government.* Chicago: Aldine Atherton.
———. 1975. Bureaucrats and Politicians. *Journal of Law and Economics* 18(3): 617–44.
———. 1991. A Reflection on *Bureaucracy and Representative Government.* In *The Budget-Maximizing Bureaucrat: Appraisals and Evidence,* edited by Andre Blais and Stephane Dion, 13–31. Pittsburgh, PA: University of Pittsburgh Press.
Oleszek, Walter J. 1996. *Congressional Procedures and the Policy Process.* 4th ed. Washington, DC: Congressional Quarterly Inc.
Rosenstone, Steven J., Donald R. Kinder, Warren E. Miller. 1999. American National Election Study, 1996: Pre- and Post-Election Survey [Computer file]. 4th release. Ann Arbor, MI: University of Michigan, Center for Political Studies.
Rossiter, Clinton. 1961. *The Federalist Papers.* New York: Penguin Books.
Rourke, Francis. 1984. *Bureaucracy, Politics, and Public Policy.* 3rd ed. Boston, MA: Little, Brown.
Selden, Sally Coleman. 1997. *The Promise of Representative Bureaucracy.* Armonk, NY: M.E. Sharpe.
Simon, Herbert A. 1957. *Administrative Behavior.* 2nd ed. New York. Macmillan.
Stabile, Donald R. 1998. *The Origins of American Public Finance: Debates Over Money, Debt and Taxes in the Constitutional Era, 1779–1836.* Westport, CT: Greenwood Press.
Stewart, Joseph Jr., Robert E. England, and Kenneth J. Meier. 1988. Black Representation in Urban School Districts: From School Board to Office to Classroom. *Western Political Quarterly* 41: 287–305.
U.S. Office of Management and Budget (OMB). 2000. *Historical Tables. Budget of the United States Government, Fiscal Year 2001.* Washington, DC: Office of Management and Budget.
Wildavsky, Aaron. 1964. *The Politics of the Budgetary Process.* Boston, MA: Little, Brown.

APPENDIX 12.A. WORDING OF FEDERAL-SPENDING SURVEY QUESTIONS

Wording on National Election Studies and Survey of Senior Executives (1996)

If you had a say in making up the federal budget his year, for which of the following programs would you like to see spending increased and for which would you like to see spending decreased?

1. Improving and protecting the environment
2. Foreign aid to countries of the former Soviet Union (1994); Foreign aid (1996)
3. AIDS research
4. Social Security
5. Welfare programs
6. Food stamps
7. Public schools
8. Solving the problem of the homeless
9. Child care
10. Dealing with crime
11. Financial aid for college students
12. Health care (not asked on 1996 NES)
13. Aid to big cities (not asked on 1996 NES)
14. Programs that assist blacks (not asked on 1996 NES)
15. Defense (not asked on 1996 NES)

Respondents were allowed the following choices:

a. Decrease spending
b. Increase spending
c. Keep spending about the same

Wording on General Social Survey (1996)

We are faced with many problems in this country, none of which can be solved easily or inexpensively. I'm going to name some of these problems, and for each one I'd like you to tell me whether you think we're spending too much money on it, too little money, or about the right amount. Are we spending too much, too little, or about the right amount on . . .

1. Health
2. Assistance to big cities
3. Assistance to blacks
4. National defense

Respondents were allowed the following choices:

a. Too little
b. About the right amount
c. Too much

APPENDIX 12.B. GOVERNMENT-SPENDING PREFERENCES AMONG THE GENERAL PUBLIC, 1994 AND 1996

1994
1. Dealing with crime
2. Homelessness
3. Public schools
4. Financial aid for college students
5. Child care
6. Social Security
7. AIDS research
8. Protecting environment
9. Welfare programs
10. Food stamps
11. Foreign aid to countries of the former Soviet Union

1996
1. Dealing with crime
2. Public schools
3. Homelessness
4. AIDS research
5. Financial aid for college students
6. Child care
7. Social Security
8. Protecting environment
9. Welfare programs
10. Food stamps
11. Foreign aid

Note: Issues are ordered from top to bottom according to each group's level of spending preferences. Thus, those at the top of the list have the highest percentages of respondents agreeing to increase spending, and those at the bottom have the fewest respondents agreeing to increase funds.

—3.4 Incrementalism—

CHAPTER 13

POLICE BUDGETING
Winning Strategies

CHARLES K. COE AND DEBORAH LAMM WEISEL

Police departments are big players in the municipal budgeting arena. According to the most recent data, U.S. police departments spent $20.9 billion (U.S. Department of Commerce 1991/92). In competing for limited resources, police departments can play an ace in the hole: crime. Arguably, no other urban issue is as emotionally charged as crime. As the recent spate of school shootings illustrates, no community can immunize itself against the devastating effects of violent crime. Thus, protecting the public safety resonates with the public. Despite steeply falling crime rates nationwide, most police departments continue to increase their federal, state, and local funding, though not all police departments are equally successful. Indeed, while many police budgets are rising at meteoric rates, a few are being cut.

The focus of this research is the budgetary strategies of police departments. Beginning with Wildavsky's pathbreaking study of federal budgeting (1964), researchers have plumbed the strategies that agencies use during the budget process. This study continues that line of inquiry by asking three questions: First, what explains the success of police departments that are able to increase their budgets significantly? Second, what strategies do police departments use successfully, and what are the caveats of using these strategies? Finally, which successful strategies uniquely apply to police departments, and which apply to other local government departments as well?

METHODOLOGY

The methodology was both quantitative and qualitative. In 1998, a survey was sent to the total population of local police departments serving populations over 50,000 (n = 490). The focus of the research was on large police departments for which a population of 50,000 served as a logical breaking point. The response rate was 61 percent.

In April 1999, a one-day focus group was held with professionals from five police agencies. Four criteria were used to select the participants: their departments (1) had substantially increased their budgets during the study period, of fiscal years 1997 and 1998; (2) represented different forms of local government, including the council-manager, county executive, and strong-mayor forms;

Table 13.1

Changes in Police Operating Budgets

Changes in Operating Budget, 1997–98

	Number of agencies	Percent
Decrease	24	11.6
No change	1	.5
0.001–2.99%	29	14.0
3–4.99%	45	21.7
5–7.99%	41	19.8
8–9.99%	32	15.5
10% or more	35	16.9
Total	207	100.0

Changes in Operating Budget, 1996–97

	Number of agencies	Percent
Decrease	17	8.3
No change	2	1.0
0.001–2.99%	30	14.7
3–4.99%	35	17.2
5–7.99%	52	25.5
8–9.99%	22	10.8
10% or more	46	22.5
Total	204	100.0

[1]Two factors account for the difference between the number of responding jurisdictions (299) and the number of jurisdictions reported here: not all jurisdictions responded to the question, and 16 percent did not have separate capital improvement budgets. Instead, they budget capital improvements in their operating budget. These

(3) were geographically diverse; and (4) were diverse with respect to population. The participants are profiled in Appendix 13.A.

The questions asked in the focus group were based on major themes revealed by the questionnaire. Those questions can be found in Appendix 13.B. There was one trained facilitator and two observers. The session was tape recorded, transcribed, and given to the respondents to check for accuracy.

EXPLAINING BUDGETARY SUCCESS

Agencies gauge their budgetary success in two ways: whether they have kept a harmonious working relationship with the chief executive and budget staff, and whether they have expanded their prior year's base budget or, in times of fiscal retrenchment, defended their base against cuts. Duncombe and Kinney (1987, 27) find that state agency heads believe that keeping good relationships is more important than increasing appropriations. Still, getting budget requests funded is an important barometer of budgetary success. Table 13.1 shows the changes in budgets in the surveyed agencies between FY 1996–97 and from FY 1997–98. Ninety-one percent of the agencies reported budgetary increases in FY 1996–97, and 88 percent reported increases in FY 1997–98. Not all police budgets increased, however; over the two-year period, budgets declined in 41 states.

How successful were police departments? Generally, they fared very well. The average budgetary increase over the two-year period for responding police departments was 6.4 percent, significantly

Table 13.2

Jurisdictions with Police Budget Expansions of 20 Percent or More, 1996–98

Jurisdiction	State	Number of sworn officers	Percent increase
Vancouver	WA	132	60.08
Omaha	NE	702	58.66
Cheektowaga	NY	129	44.84
West Valley City	UT	158	42.10
Prince George's County	MD	1,310	36.70
Chandler	AZ	220	35.11
Reading	PA	205	34.34
Murfreesboro	TN	144	32.14
Largo	FL	131	30.25
Brick Township	NJ	111	28.91
Decatur	IL	159	27.20
Rio Rancho	NM	104	26.99
Scottsdale	AZ	293	26.06
New Orleans	LA	1,700	25.81
Plano	TX	279	25.07
Coral Springs	FL	176	24.84
Las Vegas	NV	1,627	24.79
Charlotte-Mecklenburg	NC	1,386	24.66
Waltham	MA	141	24.39
Concord	CA	158	23.91
Denton	TX	112	23.22
Mesa	AZ	652	22.99
Naperville	IL	164	22.97
Killeen	TX	144	22.37
Laredo	TX	263	22.26
Fayetteville	NC	298	21.39
Orange County	CA	145	20.00
Dothan	AL	155	20.03

higher than the 2.8 percent increase in the Consumer Price Index (CPI) during the same period.

Many police departments were successful, but some were *extremely* successful. For example, 29 police agencies reported large gains averaging 20 percent or more for the two-year period [see Table 13.2].

In statistically comparing the 29 departments with large budget gains to the average department, no significant differences were found with respect to the tenure of the police chief, agency size, political structure, crime rates, or calls for service. The findings for crime rates and calls for service differed from that of Hudzik et al. (1981), who reported that agency budgetary growth was highly related to production norms including calls for service, crime rates, traffic accidents, response times, and special events.

Very successful departments significantly differ from other departments with respect to *population growth*. Population growth often occurs when middle-class persons move into a city's existing area or into newly annexed areas. Middle-class persons do not typically experience high crime rates, so a corresponding increase in staff might not be expected. On the other hand, middle-class citizens are informed customers and may demand services, including police. Moreover, annexation formulas sometimes dictate how much police staffing should grow; some police departments automatically receive more staff as the population increases.

Table 13.3

Policy Objectives and Budgetary Outcomes

Policy objective	Large-budget increase departments, (n = 29) percent	Average-budget-increase departments, (n = 204) percent
Increase general responsiveness to community	52	60
Community policing	55	74
Modernize	45	22
Increase staffing	45	23
Increase technology	35	40
Professionalize	27	38
Increase automation	17	24
Increase responsiveness to the minority community	3	9

Apparently, the argument for more staffing is persuasive. Twenty-five percent of departments reported a major increase in population (10 percent or more) from 1992 to 1997. Of these departments, 52 percent experienced large budgetary gains of 20 percent or more over fiscal FY 1997–98.

Police agencies' objectives may also affect their budgetary success. The survey asked respondents to indicate up to three policy objectives of the agency's chief executive. The results are reported in Table 13.3. Very successful agencies were less likely to report community policing as a key policy objective, perhaps because they already had a community policing program. On the other hand, very successful departments often wanted to increase agency staffing and modernize the department.

SUCCESSFUL BUDGETARY STRATEGIES

Wildavsky (1964) first discussed the strategies used by federal agencies to defend and increase their budget requests. Since then, considerable scholarship has concentrated on budgetary strategies and tactics at all levels of government. With the notable exception of Meyers' (1994) examination of federal budgeting agencies' strategies to devise advantageous budgetary structures, research has chiefly looked at government-wide strategies, giving scant attention to the strategies of *particular* agencies. The successful strategies employed by police departments are discussed below, namely:

- Use crime and workload data *judiciously*
- Capitalize on sensational crime incidents, *preferably* those occurring outside your community
- Get your message out *effectively*
- *Carefully* mobilize interest groups
- *Strategically* plan
- Play the federal grant process, *but* beware of feds bearing gifts
- Work *closely* with the chief executive and elected officials
- *Involve* all departmental levels

The strategies are drawn from survey results and the observations of the focus group participants. Care should be taken not to draw any broad conclusions based on the comments of the focus group participants. Their comments are merely suggestive and intriguing, but neither explanatory nor firmly prescriptive.

USE CRIME AND WORKLOAD DATA *JUDICIOUSLY*

Chief executives and police professionals have received considerable guidance regarding measuring and evaluating police performance. For example, in its "Greenbook" on police, the International City/County Management Association (ICMA) explains and recommends measures of patrol services, investigations, traffic services, drug control, and crime prevention (Geller 1991). Hatry et al. (1992, 71–91) propound measures of effectiveness for crime-control services, and Ammons (1996, 184–204) suggests performance benchmarks for police departments. Finally, criminal justice researchers discuss how to measure community policing, drug enforcement, and overall police effectiveness (Hoover 1996).

How do performance indicators relate to budgetary outcomes? The answer requires a distinction between crime rates and other workload indicators. Chief Terrence Sheridan (Baltimore County, MD) noted that only 19 percent of his department's 485,000 calls for service in 1997 were for crime-related issues. Likewise, Chief Jerry Bloechle (Largo, FL) estimated that 20 percent–25 percent of his department's calls were crime-related. Far more often, calls for service are order-maintenance concerns. The focus group participants agreed that calls for service are a much more accurate indicator of staffing needs than crime rates. Chief Douglas Bartosh (Scottsdale, AZ) divides officers' time into calls for service (47 percent), administrative duties (20 percent), and community-based policing (33 percent) and uses these statistics rather than the crime rate to justify staffing requests.

Still, the focus group participants recognized that crime rates can be a powerful rationale for making budget requests. Chief Bloechle pointed out that the crime rate has an emotional element and can be used to scare decision makers. Even when the crime rate is decreasing, graphically violent crimes may fuel citizens' and politicians' fears. The reporting of gory crimes in Charlotte, North Carolina, in 1996 prompted the governing board to offer the department 100 more officers. The chief had to respond: "We can't use them yet. Wait a while."

Promising a crime-rate reduction may backfire. Chief Don Carey (Omaha, NE) noted that the amount of crime is underreported. His mayor wanted to promise to reduce the crime rate. Chief Carey cautioned the mayor that as the police department successfully improves policing, the public will feel more confident in the department's ability and report more crimes, increasing the crime rate initially. Eventually, the crime rate will level off and decline, but not initially.

Writing in a period of increasing crime, Greene, Bynum, and Cordner (1986, 537) found that *both* the crime rate and increased workload significantly contributed to an increase in positions. This study did not replicate that finding, however, perhaps because crime rates were falling during the period studied. Table 13.4 shows that only 31 percent of agencies with large budget increases had an increase in crime. Surprisingly, 42 percent of successful agencies had a *decrease* in crime.

These data do not mean, however, that crime rates are an altogether unimportant budgeting factor. Table 13.4 shows that 31 percent of successful departments had an increase in crime, compared to only 19 percent of all departments.

The focus group participants agreed that targeting police efforts to *specific* types of crimes in particularly "hot" areas may convince policy makers to spend more on crime reduction. For example, Chief Sheridan accumulated crime data showing that one-third of all violent crime is committed by juveniles. After presenting the data to the county executive and the governing board, additional monies were appropriated to hire school resource officers and to build recreation centers.

Table 13.4

Crime Events and Budgetary Outcomes

Crime-related event	Large-budget-increase departments, (n = 29) percent	Average-budget-increase departments, (n = 204) percent
Major crime event	65	62
Gangs	65	60
Shooting	27	19
Increase in crime	31	19
Decrease in crime	42	33

Consequently, juvenile crime declined significantly. Likewise, the department identified a high number of crimes being committed in the county's seven commercial corridors. The budget was increased to harden targets with the cooperation of the business community, tc reassign officers to foot and bike patrol, and to increase staffing. Subsequently, arrest-clearance rates increased appreciably and crimes decreased.

Similarly, Chief Bloechle targeted resources to reduce vehicle accidents. In his community, he found that over several years only 15 homicides had occurred, compared to 77 vehicular deaths. He obtained resources to improve conditions at very dangerous intersections, worked closely with the public to increase safety awareness, and installed safety control devices. As a result, accidents and fatalities dropped precipitously.

Sometimes a picture speaks a thousand words. Chief Sheridan had two outdated, piston-driven, two-seater helicopters with limited fuel capacity. The department wanted jet turbine, Bell Jet Ranger helicopters equipped with a thermal imagery unit that could track persons fleeing on foot and by vehicle. Chief Sheridan showed the governing board videotapes of what this equipment accomplishes. The need for dangerous, high-speed pursuits is often eliminated. If a pursuit is required, the department has a visual record to evaluate procedures taken. The board members were thoroughly convinced by the videotape.

CAPITALIZE ON SENSATIONAL INCIDENTS, PREFERABLY THOSE OCCURRING *OUTSIDE* YOUR COMMUNITY

Tragically, sensational crime incidents are all too common, and they have seared the national psyche. Who was not shaken by such events as the Rodney King incident, the O.J. Simpson case, the spate of school shootings, and the day-trader massacre? Some high-profile violent crimes may not have national recognition, but still upset the public in a particular state or local jurisdiction. What is the effect of such sensational incidents on police funding? Research on this question has been limited and the results mixed. One survey indicates that critical incidents are not a significant factor in budgetary success (Greene, Bynum, and Cordner 1986, 537). However, in follow-up interviews, the same study finds that critical incidents, such as killings of police officers, were responsible for a "massive infusion of resources into the problem area despite economic conditions, public ideology, or political considerations" (Hudzik et al. 1981, 198).

Respondents to this survey indicated that sensational crime events *may* result in large budgetary increases. Table 13.4 shows that 65 percent of successful departments experienced a major crime event. Such an event does not, however, automatically lead to increased funding, for 62 percent of all departments also had a major crime event. Likewise, 65 percent of successful departments had a high amount of gang activity, which is often publicized, but so did 60 percent of the typical departments.

The focus group participants shed more light on how sensational incidents may factor into funding decisions, observing that three types of sensational events may be influential: national incidents, crimes localized to a particular state or region, and incidents within one's own jurisdiction. Examples of national incidents in the 1990s included the Rodney King beating, the O.J. Simpson murder investigation, the Louima police brutality case in New York City, and the Littleton High School shooting. Taking the O.J. Simpson case as an example, many police departments received more funding for crime-scene analysis and technical investigative equipment because of the mistakes made by the Los Angeles police department. Similarly, the National Institute of Justice received $20 million to improve its labs and develop training materials.

Chief Bloechle cited two examples of localized incidents. After riots in St. Petersburg, his and other departments in Florida received more funds for helmets, riot shields, and riot training. Likewise, his department received more funds for disaster preparedness after the devastating effects of Hurricane Andrew in south Florida.

In both instances, the police department received needed funds without directly experiencing the negative effects of the incidents. This is the best-case scenario; however, a sensational incident *must* occur in a particular police jurisdiction, and the public's perception of that police department usually suffers as a consequence. For example, the inability of the Los Angeles Police Department to protect the O.J. Simpson crime scene and the Rodney King beating cast that department in a negative light.

Similarly, Deputy Chief Jack Boger (Charlotte-Mecklenburg, NC) noted that the occurrence of sensational events within one's city can be a double-edged sword. Charlotte-Mecklenburg had 10 unsolved serial murders of women. The homicide unit had been substantially under-staffed. Because of the murders, the unit's budget was increased by 150 percent. The murderer was apprehended, but the department's reputation was hurt nonetheless because the murders were not solved quickly.

GET YOUR MESSAGE OUT *EFFECTIVELY*

Working effectively with the media creates a good public image of the department and enhances police performance, which may result in the chief executive officer and governing board viewing budget requests positively. To create good working relationships with the media, police administrators should understand the different needs of the press and television. Television reporters want someone to talk on camera; therefore, officers should be trained to talk to reporters and to handle potentially damaging and embarrassing questions "live and in color." The Omaha police department, for instance, trains its officers to think and talk in sound bytes, saying nothing longer than seven seconds.

Generally, television reporters do not follow up on the story of the day. Print reporters, though, have the luxury of time and can follow a story in more depth. Often, print reporters come from journalism schools with a well-honed mistrust of policing, and developing a trusting relationship with these reporters may take some time. Spokespersons should not unnecessarily stonewall reporters: They should make clear which questions are acceptable and which are out of bounds and why.

The media can effectively assist ongoing investigations by publicizing wanted suspects and by supporting new policing initiatives. For example, when Chief Carey went to Omaha, he wanted to have very visible successes to build confidence in law enforcement. Among other issues, he focused on traffic safety. He met with media representatives, not just reporters but also assignment editors, bought them lunch, and explained the new initiative. He then took them out to interstate overpasses to explain how laser technology would detect speeders. The media played up the story, using videos to show how the laser technology worked and how the department was changing driving behaviors. Average speed decreased 11 miles per hour, 25,000 speeding tickets were issued in the first month, and accidents declined 79 percent.

Chief Bartosh noted that effective image building should go beyond the media. Scottsdale has a city cable program, a quarterly magazine, and a Web site. Crime information is posted monthly on the Web site, enabling citizens to know what crimes occurred in their neighborhood. Chief Sheridan said that the public has enthusiastically responded to his agency's Web site. Baltimore County also has a telephone number by which citizens can get crime statistics for their area. If a specific crime problem is occurring in a neighborhood, the phone system automatically calls homes with listed numbers in the area to alert them to the trend.

CAREFULLY MOBILIZE INTEREST GROUPS

Government agencies commonly mobilize interest groups to leverage support for their budget requests. Wildavsky and Caiden (1997, 57–8) note that federal agencies influence policy makers by finding a clientele and then serving, expanding, and securing feedback from it. Agencies form either "iron triangles" or "issue networks." An iron triangle is a fixed relationship between legislative committees, the agencies they oversee, and their allied interest groups. Issue networks, on the other hand, are loose-knit, changing relationships between interest groups, involved citizens, experts, and agencies concerned with a particular issue (Heclo 1979, 102). One study found that police departments tend to form issue networks, not iron triangles. Hudzik et al. (1981) found that law enforcement agencies form relationships with particular constituents to secure funding, but that such relationships are highly transitory, rising to support an agency one year and disappearing the next.

Police departments have always had a natural constituency of neighborhood groups, civic organizations, and business groups concerned about crime. Moreover, the widespread adoption of community policing has greatly expanded police departments' ties to the community. Examples of continuing, permanent relationships include:

- Serving schools by stationing school resource officers in public schools, creating continuing ties to educational administrators, teachers, students, and parents.
- Routinely meeting with established neighborhood organizations.
- Routinely meeting with civic groups, business groups, and victims organizations.

In addition to these permanent relationships, police officers form temporary issue networks with community groups to address particular problems, often identified by the citizens themselves. Once the problem has been solved, the coalition dissolves.

Table 13.5 indicates the types of interest groups active in the budgetary process. The most active type of group is neighborhood organizations, followed by business groups, civic groups, minority groups, tax-accountability groups, local businesses, education groups, and victims organizations.

The focus group participants stressed the importance of keeping close ties to citizen groups. Having open and trusting communication with the community is a fundamental tenet of community policing, but arrangements for doing so differ. For example, Charlotte-Mecklenburg has district boards that regularly meet with the police department. Baltimore County gives $200,000 annually to 105 police community relations councils throughout the country. Scottsdale works each year with a citizens budget advisory group that reviews and supports its budget, operates "citizen academies," has regular contact with block watch captains, and holds meetings in citizens'

Table 13.5

Types of Police Interest Groups

Type of interest group	Percentage of groups active in the budget process (n = 299)
Neighborhood organizations	68
Business groups (such as chambers of commerce)	42
Civic groups	34
Minority groups or advocates for minorities	28
Tax-accountability groups	20
Locally owned businesses	16
Victims organizations	16
Education groups	15
Other groups	20

homes attended by city council members. Finally, Largo develops its annual goals and objectives by meeting with citizens groups.

Because police departments are so visible and because crime is so emotionally charged, police departments have considerable public support, which may be manifested in the budget process. For example, police departments have effectively blocked funding cuts by taking their case to the public (Greene, Bynum, and Cordner 1986). Likewise, police departments can mobilize interest groups' support for more funding.

The focus group participants observed that community policing has resulted in substantially more contact with community groups. Chief Bloechle noted, however, that having such extensive contact with the citizenry is a politically delicate matter. Governing board members take their responsibility to serve as conduits and advocates for the public very seriously. They are especially sensitive to the extensive contacts that police officers have with citizen groups. In effect, police departments are engaged with the public 24 hours a day, seven days a week. Accordingly, Chief Bloechle is careful not to overuse interest groups. For example, the department has 140 volunteers eager to lobby for police funding. Chief Bloechle has to rein in their enthusiasm. Similarly attuned to the sensibilities of governing board members, the Charlotte-Mecklenburg police department sends reports of police-community meetings to governing board members representing the districts in which the meetings were held.

Interest groups may choose inside or outside lobbying strategies (Wilcox 1998). Inside strategies persuade governing board members personally, while outside strategies mobilize the general public to pressure policy makers. Table 13.6 indicates that the interest groups worked both inside and outside. Outside strategies include testifying or speaking about police matters during hearings on the budget, submitting letters of support or opposition on police issues, and generating large turnouts at budgetary or council meetings. The most common inside strategy is to directly lobby council members or the mayor.

Strategically **Plan**

Strategic planning explores policy alternatives, emphasizing the future implications of present decisions (Bryson 1995, 5). A strategic plan is a statement of long-range goals and objectives. Strategic planning should occur *before* the budget cycle (Halachmi and Boydston 1991). A long-range strategic plan enables governing board members to make better one-year, operating-budget policy decisions.

Table 13.6

Types and Incidence of Interest Group Strategies

Strategy	Method	Percentage using the method (n = 299)
Outside strategy	• Testify or speak at public hearings on the budget	62
	• Submit letters of support or opposition on budget increases	41
	• Generate large turnouts at budgetary hearings or council meetings	16
Inside strategy	• Lobby council members or the mayor directly	59

Bryson (1995, 152) surmised, however, that most budgets are formed without strategic thought.

The survey did not ask when in the budget year strategic planning occurs, but 55 percent of respondents reported they had a written strategic plan. Strategic plans usually span a three- to seven-year period. Sixty-one percent of police departments had a five-year strategic plan:

- One or two years   14 percent
- Three to four years   18 percent
- Five years   61 percent
- More than five years   7 percent

Fifty percent of the strategic plans were disseminated to the public, while the other half were for internal use only. One can only speculate why some strategic plans are not disseminated. Sometimes the absence of transparency is a result of fear of misrepresentation. Rubin (1998) finds that some mayors do not want performance targets published because they fear their political opponents would unfairly dwell on missed targets.

Police departments' strategic plans are typically part of a city's overall strategic-planning process. Scottsdale, Largo, and Charlotte-Mecklenberg follow a citywide strategic-planning process. The strategic plan is updated annually, and its results drive the budgetary process. Governing boards principally fund initiatives that are identified during the strategic planning. In Charlotte-Mecklenburg, strategic goals cross organizational boundaries. For example, the police department has joint goals with both the Building Inspections and Neighborhood Development departments. In the last budget year, the police departments successfully advocated additional resources for these departments to address crime issues. Interagency cooperation is useful in Charlotte-Mecklenburg, as it is in many communities, because other agencies often resent the police departments' large share of the budget pie. Going to bat for other agencies reduces this tension, resulting in a smoother, more coordinated attack on the root causes of crime.

PLAY THE FEDERAL GRANT PROCESS, *BUT* BEWARE OF FEDS BEARING GIFTS

Operating budgets tell only one part of the budgetary story. Eighty-four percent of the respondents (251 police departments) had a separate capital improvement program in which capital expenditures were budgeted.

Police departments purchased a variety of capital items. The most common types of communications technology included 800 MHZ radios, dispatching systems, mobile data terminals, and

Table 13.7

Funding Sources for Police Agencies

Funding source	Number of departments receiving funds (n = 299)	Low range	High range
Bureau of Justice Assistance	155	$1,231	$28,277,320
Office of Community Policing Services	200	$2,622	$99,317,610
U.S. Department of Housing and Urban Development	88	$3,366	$62,682,000
National Highway Traffic Safety Administration	67	$1,049	$6,680,701
Foundations	24	$500	$242,760
Businesses	30	$414	$7,641,214
Discretionary grants	139	$6,161	$21,620,099
Other sources	130	$5	$64,892,873

laptops for police vehicles. Capital budgets also included expenditures for buildings (75 percent of respondents), vehicles (59 percent) and property (48 percent). The cost of these commitments ranged from $20,000 to $176 million. The more expensive items were typically funded by bonds, and the less expensive items by grants, general funds, or asset-forfeiture funds.

Police departments can access a variety of external funding sources, including state and federal grants, foundations, and business groups. Table 13.7 indicates the number of police departments that received such funds, amounts received, and the granting organizations. The Office of Community Policing Services was the largest source of funding; of the 299 respondents, 200 reported receiving such funds (ranging from $2,622 to $99,317,610 in New York City). Likewise, a large number of cities (155) received funds from the Bureau of Justice Assistance. The U.S. Department of Housing and Urban Development contributed $85,641,000. A large number of departments (139) also received discretionary grants from sources such as the Office of National Drug Control Policy, the Drug Enforcement Administration, the Victims of Crime Act, the Bureau of Alcohol, Tobacco, and Fire Arms, and other (mostly federal) sources. In addition, 130 police agencies reported other amounts ranging from $5 to more than $64 million from such diverse sources as investment revenue and contributions.

Although it is a less common funding source, departments tap nongovernmental funding. Twenty-four agencies reported grants from private foundations in amounts ranging from $500 (Prince William County) to $42,760 (Omaha); 30 agencies received grants from local businesses or corporations in amounts ranging from $414 (Yakima) to $7,641,214 (New York City). In addition, police departments received non-cash, in-kind assistance from businesses. For example, Charlotte operates four rent-free substations in shopping centers, and businesses donated land to build a police station in Scottsdale.

Some police departments fared better than others in the grants arena. By summing grants from all outside funding sources (Bureau of Justice Assistance, discretionary grants, U.S. Department of Housing and Urban Development, Office of Community Policing Services, National Highway Traffic Safety Administration, foundations, and corporations), the amount of funding per capita in each jurisdiction was calculated. Police departments ranged from $1 to $32 per capita, with 42 agencies reporting grants of $10 or more per capita.

Obtaining outside funding may be related to having a full-time grants seeker on staff. Twenty-eight percent of respondents had at least one full-time grants seeker, but 38 percent of agencies with

$10 or more per capita had at least one or more grants person. Fifty-one percent of respondents had different individuals in the agency seeking grants. Twelve percent of agencies with $10 or more per capita either had a unit (such as research and planning) working on grants or employed a consultant to secure grants.

Sophisticated technology is highly valued; however, the focus group participants pointed out that buying equipment with grants should be done *cautiously.* Some equipment clearly serves as a force multiplier, freeing up police officers' time. Such equipment increases *efficiency* by reducing costs. An example of a force multiplier is a dictation system. Officers can dictate in less than 10 minutes what takes more than 30 minutes to type on a laptop. Tapes can be entered by fast-typing clerical personnel, who are paid much less than police officers.

Other equipment, however, *increases* operating costs because the equipment requires ongoing support. For example, laptops and mobile data terminals in cars allow officers to check license plates expeditiously. *Effectiveness* increases, but efficiency decreases (costs go up) because such equipment requires support personnel. Sensitive to this distinction, Chief Bloechle had the opportunity to use grant funds to buy laptops at $5,000 apiece, but he decided to buy personal digital assistants at a unit cost of $700, thereby avoiding hiring additional support personnel.

Not all police chiefs and governing boards are sensitive to this distinction, however. Sometimes, chiefs are not fully aware of the additional price tag. Understandably, vendors are not always completely forthcoming about the full costs. At other times, governing boards simply do not want to hear chiefs' admonitions. With appetites whetted by federal grants, they take a bite of the federal apple, forgetting that equipment needs repair, upgrading, and software support.

Another caveat is that sometimes high-tech systems do not work as promised for various reasons. First, vendors are not always candid about failed systems in other jurisdictions. Second, some systems are so new that there is little or no track record to evaluate them. Third, simply calling other departments to get information about systems usually does not work. Charlotte learned the hard way about the necessity of going on the road to see how systems *really* operate in other jurisdictions. Fourth, purchasing regulations often dictate buying the lowest-priced system, even if it is not the most effective. As a remedy, local governments should ensure their purchasing regulations are flexible enough to buy the best-suited (often not the cheapest) high-tech equipment.

Local governments can bite from the federal apple for operating as well as capital purposes. Since 1994, $8.6 billion in funding from the Office of Community Policing Services has paid for 100,000 positions in police departments.[1] Departments receiving the funds committed themselves to funding these positions with own-source revenues three years after funding. Departments are now having to pay the piper.

WORK *CLOSELY* WITH THE CHIEF EXECUTIVE AND ELECTED OFFICIALS

The focus group participants stressed the importance of creating and sustaining a close working relationship with the chief executive and elected board members. Chief executives have varying interest in policing. With those for whom crime is an overriding concern, establishing rapport is easy. The Baltimore County executive, for instance, is a former prosecutor who is very supportive of police initiatives. Sometimes chief executives have special contacts. The mayor of Omaha, formerly a congressman for 10 years and president of the Republican Governors' Association, now chairman of the public safety committee of the National League of Cities, has been able to secure substantial grants for the police department. Omaha ranked twelfth in the country in government grants per capita and led the country in grants per capita from foundations.

Reporting arrangements may indicate a police chief's relationship with the chief executive. For example, Scottdale's police chief is the only operating department head who reports directly to the city manager; other operational department heads report to assistant city managers.

The focus group participants stressed the importance of responding to the needs of elected board members. The relationship with governing board members depends on the form of government, on the election of board members at-large or by district, and on the amount of partisanship. For example, Omaha is a strong-mayor city in which all council members are elected by district. Moreover, the mayor has veto power and is in the party opposite to a majority of the council. Because of this strained political situation, Chief Carey has developed a close working relationship with *each* board member. He is especially sensitive to each board member's particular needs and priorities. He sends a monthly report over the Internet to the council and meets monthly with the council's public safety committee.

Taking their direction from the city or county manager, police chiefs in council-manager cities may have less direct contact with elected officials, but they, too, must be sensitive to their wishes—transparency is essential. Chief Bartosh noted that if governing board members are not fully informed about police matters, they will get information—often misinformation—from other sources such as the media or disgruntled employees.

Responding quickly and accurately to governing board members' concerns is critical. Governments should have an expeditious way of routing concerns to all departments, including police. Chief Sheridan noted that his department responds quickly to such concerns by getting back to council members as soon as possible.

INVOLVE ALL DEPARTMENTAL LEVELS

Police departments are a bit schizophrenic. On the one hand, they are quasi-military organizations with a distinct chain of command and very detailed rules and regulations. For example, to be accredited by the Commission of Accreditation for Law Enforcement Agencies, agencies must comply with more than 400 standards. On the other hand, research has conclusively demonstrated the high degree of personal discretion exercised daily by police officers. Furthermore, community policing demands that officers creatively work with citizens to solve unique problems.

If police chiefs principally follow an authoritarian, top-down managerial model, they limit participation in the budget process to relatively few managers at the top of the organization. But if they subscribe to an empowering management model, they involve all levels in budgeting. Participation encourages accountability, promotes more buy-in, and fosters commitment to organizational goals. Charlotte found that when officers had no input into budgeting, those with good ideas would simply look at a budgeted line item, assume it could not be changed, and not even share their creative ideas. Now that officers know what goes into the budget, they feel empowered to recommend changes.

CONCLUSION

Police departments in communities experiencing high population growth tend to have commensurate budget increases. Police departments employ different strategies to gain budget approval. Some of the strategies may be used by all local government agencies, while others are unique to police departments. The types of workload data, interest groups, strategic plans, relationships with the media, organizational structures, and working relationships with managers and governing boards experienced by police departments differ from those of other agencies with different missions. Therefore, further research should look at the specific strategies used by other government agencies.

Each local government department may have particularized tactics. Staffing norms, professional standards, real and imagined mandates, benchmarks, accreditation, and surveys all help agencies to justify budgets (Ammons 1996). Just as police strategies have nuances, so do these and others. Researchers might well focus on the strategies employed by agencies with a significant budget impact, such as fire service, road maintenance and construction, health and welfare, solid waste collection and disposal, and parks and recreation.

ACKNOWLEDGMENTS

This article was based on data from the study, "A National Assessment of Police Chiefs' Experience in the Budgetary Process," supported by Grant #97-LB-VX-KOOB, Office of Science and Technology, National Institute of Justice, Office of Justice Programs, U.S. Department of Justice to the Police Executive Research Forum. Points of view expressed in the article are those of the authors and do not necessarily represent the official position or policies of the U.S. Department of Justice.

NOTE

1. This is the figure claimed by the Clinton administration; some critics argue it is inflated.

REFERENCES

Ammons, David N. 1996. *Municipal Benchmarks.* Thousand Oaks, CA: Sage Publications.
Bryson, John M. 1995. *Strategic Planning and Sustaining Organizational Achievement.* 2nd ed. San Francisco, CA: Jossey-Bass.
Duncombe, Sydney, and Richard Kenney. 1987. Agency Budget Success: How It Is Defined by Budget Officials in Five States. *Public Budgeting and Finance* 7(1): 24–37.
Geller, William A., ed. 1991. *Local Government Police Management.* 3rd ed. Washington, DC: International City/County Management Association.
Greene, Jack R., Tim S. Bynum, and Gary W. Cordner. 1986. Planning and the Play of Power: Resource Acquisition among Criminal Justice Agencies. *Journal of Criminal Justice* 14(4): 529–44.
Halachmi, Arie, and Robert Boydston. 1991. Strategic Management with Annual and Multi-Year Operating Budgets. *Public Budgeting and Financial Management* 3(2): 293–316.
Hatry, Harry P., Louis H. Blair, Donald M. Fisk, John M. Greiner, John R. Hall, Jr., and Phillip S. Schaeman. 1992. *How Effective Are Your Community Services?* Washington, DC: Urban Institute.
Heclo, Hugh. 1979. Issue Networks and the Executive Establishment. In *The New Political System,* edited by Anthony King, 87–124. Washington, DC: American Enterprise Institute.
Hoover, Larry T., ed. 1996. *Quantifying Quality in Policing.* Washington, DC: Police Executive Research Forum.
Hudzik, John K., Tim S. Bynum, Jack R. Greene, Gary W. Cordner, Kenneth F. Christian, and Steven M. Edwards. 1981. The Environment of Manpower Decision Making. In *Criminal Justice Manpower Planning: An Overview,* edited by John K. Hudzik, 180–208. Washington, DC: U.S. Law Enforcement Assistance Administration.
Meyers, Roy T. 1994. *Strategic Budgeting.* Ann Arbor, MI: University of Michigan Press.
Rubin, Irene S. 1998. *Class, Tax and Power: Municipal Budgeting in the U.S.* Chatham, NJ: Chatham House.
U.S. Department of Commerce, Bureau of the Census. 1991/92. *Expenditures of Municipal Governments by Function and Character and Object,* vol. 4, no. 4. Washington, DC: U.S. Government Printing Office.
Wilcox, Clyde. 1998. The Dynamics of Lobbying the Hill. In *The Interest Group Connection,* edited by Paul S. Herrnson, Ronald G. Shaiko, and Clyde Wilcox, 89–99. Chatham, NJ: Chatham House.
Wildavsky, Aaron. 1964. *The Politics of the Budgetary Process.* Boston, MA: Little, Brown.
Wildavsky, Aaron, and Naomi Caiden. 1997. *The New Politics of the Budgetary Process.* 3rd ed. New York: Longman.

Appendix 13.A

Focus Group Participants

Participant	Jurisdiction	Population	Number of personnel	Form of government
Chief Jerry Bloechle	Largo, FL	68,038	219	Council-manager
Deputy Chief Jack Boger	Charlotte-Mecklenburg, NC	612,095	1,808	Council-manager
Chief Terrence Sheridan	Baltimore County, MD	485,000	1,990	County executive
Chief Douglas Bartosh	Scottsdale, AZ	190,500	464	Council-manager
Chief Dan Carey	Omaha, NE	358,209	880	Strong-mayor

Appendix 13.B

Focus Group Questions

Theme	Questions
Strategic priorities	• Is your current budget a statement of your priorities for policing and public safety? Why or why not? • If the budget reflects your strategic priorities, what are some examples? • If the budget does not reflect your strategic priorities, are there some other avenues for accomplishing this? • How does your budget format (line-item, program, zero-based, or combination) help or limit you in reflecting strategic priorities in the budget? • What are some examples of strategic priorities, which you have pursued through the budgeting process by tapping local funds?
Budget strategies	• What factors have contributed to your recent budgetary successes, e.g., national or local crime trends, big crime events, population increases, fiscal conditions, etc.? • What has been the role of local politics in the process, e.g., elections, media, advocacy groups, other? • What role do personality and reputation play in the process? • How have you "sold" strategic priorities to get funding? • To what extent has planning been a factor in securing funding?
Technology	• What are some examples of technological priorities, which you have pursued through the local budgeting process? • Are local funding options the only or first avenue for funding technological innovations? • What factors make it difficult for you to secure funding for strategic priorities or technological innovations? What strategies do you use to overcome or address these factors?
Community groups	• What has been the role of the public in setting budget and strategic priorities? • What key community groups have been active in the process? • Do you ever take your case to the public? If so, how?
Media	• Do you ever take your case to the media to get support for funding for strategic objectives? If so, how?

CHAPTER 14

AARON WILDAVSKY AND THE DEMISE OF INCREMENTALISM

IRENE S. RUBIN

Aaron Wildavsky, *The New Politics of the Budgetary Process* (Glenview, IL: Scott-Foresman/ Little Brown, 1988), 468+xxiv pp.; cost pending.

Aaron Wildavsky, *Budgeting: A Comparative Theory of Budgetary Processes* (New Brunswick, NJ: Transaction Books, 1986), 403+xii pp.; $34.95 hardcover, $18.95 paper.

Aaron Wildavsky's theory of budgetary incrementalism dominated the mainstream of American budgeting for decades. He argued that department heads drive the budget process, that only the increments from a well defined base are examined by the legislature, and that conflict is controlled and change is limited. From his perspective, governmental budgeting was an annual repeated process, the result of bargaining between individuals who had gotten to know each other through budgetary activities.

Wildavsky's model of budgetary decision making could not account for entitlement programs, which, over time, took up an increasing proportion of the budget. Nor could incrementalism deal with or explain top-down budgeting that bypassed the departments and bureaus. It could not deal with cutbacks because they made the definition of the base questionable. It did not deal much with interest groups, and it treated the environment of budgeting as an exogenous variable, not part of the real budget process, Most important, incrementalism was based on a theory of human nature. Thus it was argued that incrementalism had to hold at all times, in all places, and under all conditions. It did not allow for variation.

The mainstream remained loyal to Wildavsky, but many budget scholars began to defect from the orthodoxy in the 1970s. Gradually, Wildavsky himself dropped his well-known theory. The two books reviewed here, *Budgeting: A Comparative Theory of Budgetary Processes* and *The New Politics of the Budgetary Process,* document this intellectual evolution.

Wildavsky hinted at the passing of incrementalism in 1984. In the final edition of the old *Politics of the Budgetary Process,* he argued that the conditions necessary for incremental budgeting had disappeared. He did not otherwise change the book, but warned that it did not describe cur-

---

From *Public Administration Review,* vol. 49, no. 1 (January/February 1989), 78–81. Copyright © 1989 by American Society for Public Administration. Reprinted with permission.

rent budgeting. Some readers may have bemoaned this authoritative passing of incrementalism; others may have welcomed its long delayed demise. But readers of both stripes must have been frustrated at Wildavsky's reluctance to reconceptualize the book once he acknowledged that it was no longer descriptive.

Professor Wildavsky has only gradually let go of incrementalism. In 1986, he published his revised *Budgeting: A Comparative Theory of Budgetary Processes*. That book mixed substantial chunks of incrementalist theory with a more incisive, analytic, and contemporary theory. *The New Politics of the Budgetary: Process* relegates incrementalism to a single chapter. In a forthcoming book with Joseph White, *Battle of the Budget* (anticipated publication 1989), incrementalism disappears completely. As incrementalism falls away, the books get more complex, more interesting, and less internally contradictory.

The New Politics of the Budgetary Process is the better of the two books reviewed here. It is narrower in its scope and hence more satisfying on many levels. In addition, *The New Politics* is much richer and more complex than the old *Politics of the Budgetary Process*. It allows for many more budget actors, more flexible roles for the actors, and changes in budget process and format. Wildavsky acknowledges in the *New Politics* that there are different sorts of budget resources, that most federal budgeting takes place outside the appropriation committees, and that entitlements conflict with the traditional essence of budgeting which involves choice between competing programs. While his earlier writing emphasized bottom-up budgeting, in the *New Politics* he describes top-down, bottom-up, and in-between budget processes.

Wildavsky's attempts to explain the significance of entitlements in chapters 7 and 8 may be the most creative and important contribution of the book. He argues that entitlements lock in benefits for some and that there is a drive towards elevating benefits to the level of entitlements whenever possible. Open-ended expenditures allow flexible adaptation to changing conditions, but they present an intrinsic obstacle to budgetary balance.

In chapter 8, Wildavsky describes the history of three different groups of entitlement programs, fast growing, stable, and declining. He used Medicare and Medicaid as examples of fast growing programs, Black Lung and End State Rental Disease as examples of programs holding their own, and Title XX of the Social Security Act and Revenue Sharing as examples of programs either declining or terminated. On the basis of these examples, he argues that entitlement claims can be of different strengths and can be reversed, even if not in the annual appropriations process. Wildavsky notes, however, that the largest, most expensive programs have had the strongest claims and hence have had a destabilizing effect on expenditures.

In addition to the entitlements, Wildavsky also wrestles with military expenditures in the *New Politics of the Budgetary Process*. He describes the formal system of budgeting in defense and then claims that reality does not work that way. He notes a number of problems in defense budgeting, such as the competition between branches of the military pushing up prices for new equipment and reducing coordination, cost overruns on ship and weapons contracts, and waste in general. Many of his conclusions are not satisfying. On the competition between the branches, he says, "whether more will be gained through central control than is lost through uniformity remains to be seen" (p. 356). On the discussion of whether the military goes after weapons that are too expensive and beyond reason, he concludes, "it is not easy to discern where wisdom lies" (p. 357). On cost overruns, Wildavsky writes, "that elusive yet vital quality called good judgment is hard to find" (p. 361). On waste, "the price of achieving a worthwhile objective is to fund some unworthy items" (p. 363). Clearly, the best analysis in the book is in the entitlements section.

While Wildavsky has been hesitant to express firm opinions on what should be done about problems in the military, he has been exuberant about expressing his opinions in other areas. For example, Wildavsky states that high employment is not a legitimate public sector goal, that the public sector should not grow at the expense of the private sector, that balance should be linked to expenditure constraints (not revenue increases), and that a constitutional amendment to limit expenditures is a terrific idea.

There are good discussions on particular topics that students of all ages may find enlightening, such as on military reprogramming and the potential pitfalls of a line item veto for the President. Wildavsky raises the key issue of budget tradeoffs between defense and domestic spending and also the interesting issue of "black" or secret funding. Budget tradeoffs are nonincremental in that policies and their supporters change, and that the concept of "fair shares" has little to do with outcomes. People outside the bureaucracy can fight over policy and hence over the budget.

Despite its strengths, however, the *New Politics* probably should not replace the old Politics as an undergraduate text, especially at the freshman-sophomore level. Budgeting is more complicated and seemingly without pattern than it used to be. Wildvsky should be congratulated for not trying to reduce what is essentially complicated to misleading simplicity. But the increased complexity will probably make the *New Politics* less appealing for teaching lower level undergraduates than the old *Politics*.

In short, this book is useful and thought provoking. It is worth reading, thinking about, and arguing about. The *New Politics* is unlikely to become a new orthodoxy, and so it ushers in a new period of intellectual ferment in budget theory.

Budgeting: A Comparative Perspective was a transitional book for Wildavsky, with elements of both incremental and nonincremental thought. The book's fundamental premise is not incrementalist; it argues that budgeting differs across time and space and that explaining that variation is a key task of budget theory. Wildavsky recognizes in this book that tolerance for conflict is a cultural variable and that conflict can be expressed or channeled in a variety of ways in budgeting. The argument that budget processes are variable, depending on the level of resources, the level of uncertainty, and the local culture, is well made. Wildavsky also makes a convincing case that history matters because the changing economic and political environment of budgeting matters.

A number of chapters recapitulate earlier lines of thought. Chapter 5, on budgeting in poor countries, which relies on his work with Naomi Caiden,[1] is successful because the work still seems applicable. It emphasizes the impact of wealth and uncertainty on budgeting, two themes that remain important to budget theory. In chapter 3 (written with Michael Dempster), which describes the evolution of quantitative budget models, the result is only partly satisfying. In the later models, the time frame for the analysis stretches out, and environmental factors are brought into account for change. These are improved quantitative models of budgeting. The fact that the models have to cover long time periods to be meaningful and that the environment of budgeting plays a major role in the outcomes is contrary to early incremental theory. Wildavsky ends the discussion as if these studies said nothing theoretically divergent from his starting point.

An additional problem throughout the book is that the chapter titles are misleading. For example, chapter 3 is entitled "From Qualitative to Quantitative Models," but it deals only with incrementalist-inspired quantitative models. There has been a mushrooming of nonincrementalist quantitative literature in recent years, some of which is theoretically arresting, especially the literature on trade-offs, but this literature is not even footnoted here.[2]

In chapter 10, on budget reforms, Wildavsky reiterates his old argument [3] that budget formats should not be reformed. He argues that line-item budgeting is a hardy perennial, the most adaptive form of budgeting, and that other forms of budgeting have been tried and have failed. In his view, traditional budgeting, with its norms of annularity, balance, and comprehensiveness, has prevailed. Not only is this position factually dubious, since numerous units of government have gone to various hybrid forms of budgeting, but elsewhere in the chapter and elsewhere in the book Wildavsky notes that annularity, balance, and comprehensiveness have suffered collapse. Faced with this apparent contradiction, Wildavsky temporizes, "both are true when applied to different spheres" (p. 329). He distinguished between the form in which the budget is voted in the legislature (presumably line item and incremental) and different ways of thinking about budgeting (presumably more program oriented.) It is not clear if he is arguing that format has no influence over thinking (if so, he is factually incorrect) or if he has something else in mind, but he is clearly tangled in contradictions because of his tenacious tie to the argument that reform is bad for budgeting.

At times Wildavsky develops alternative hypotheses to explain the same phenomenon, without attempting to reconcile them or to explain how they might go together. In one part of the book, he argues in accordance with his traditional theory that incrementalism always survives because it is functional (p. 328). Elsewhere he argues from his newer perspective that incrementalism is not a constant, but a variable dependent on resource levels (p. 16). Yet, he also maintains that incrementalism reflects local culture, which he defines as hierarchical, sectarian, or market oriented, and that some cultures may not support incrementalism (p. 24). There may be a way of putting some or all of these insights together: the matter simply requires more thought. Wildavsky stops short of a synthesis of his ideas, which creates a choppy feeling from chapter to chapter.

Budgeting: A Comparative Theory is both thought provoking and occasionally frustrating. It is thought provoking when Wildavsky formulates new measures and complex hypotheses about the effects on budgeting of wealth, certainty, culture, the relative growth of the public and private sectors, and aspects of politics. These hypotheses are the intellectual core of the book. The book is frustrating because of its inability to present evidence for many of its key points.

For example, in chapter 9, Wildavsky hypothesizes that, when economic growth outstrips taxation, the result is incremental budgeting with "fair shares" (p. 302). The argument is tantalizing. Wildavsky gathered evidence on budgeting in each of the countries about which he writes. Yet he concludes his argument with the hypothesis and never compares it to his evidence. One could easily conclude the opposite, that the availability of large increments of politically acceptable revenues would encourage nonincremental budgeting, with planning and new programs and some existing programs growing faster than others. The reader is left with considerable uncertainty about the size of the increment that breeds incrementalism and the impact of the political acceptability of new taxes on the existence of incrementalism.

In a recent book,[4] Terrence McDonald argues that purposely created scarcity of revenue leads to incrementalism. There is a politically imposed choice to keep taxes and spending down and to insulate the wealthy from taxation. The result is a pattern of incremental decision making that insulates the city from needs and demands. This pattern may vanish if a coalition forms to resolve severe municipal problems. This is quite a different interpretation than Wildavsky places on similar data. McDonald's argument does not depend on regime types (Wildavsky's hierarchical, sectarian, or capitalist types) nor does it depend on the actual level of wealth. It depends on current choices about the desired level of spending, and it suggests that incrementalism may reflect and serve the interests of particular social or occupational groups and that if the groups involved should lose power or municipal crisis should forge a new coalition, incrementalism passes. In its extreme version, incrementalism is a plot of the wealthy who impose their definition of the limits of taxable wealth on the majority. One wonder how Wildavsky would respond to such an interpretation of the relationship of incrementalism to politics.

A number of stylistic problems are found in this book, including loose definitions; unsupported global generalizations (he argues the British make the least of their social cleavages, p. 303); overstatements (the implementation of Zero Based Budgets is equivalent to overthrowing a political regime, p. 339); and occasional foolishness ("Perhaps the Japanese know themselves better than outsiders do," p. 308). These problems are not serious, but they are distracting.

Somewhat more seriously, Wildavsky sometimes poses questions that may be puzzling to him, but are unlikely to be puzzling to other scholars. For example, he wonders why dependence on government has grown since the industrial revolution, when it is clear to him that conditions in general have improved for most workers (p. 364). He seems to have little grasp of the kinds of changes wrought by industrialization that might make a labor force more dependent on government. He never refers to the deskilling of the labor force or to the growth of unemployment and the successive private attempts and failures to deal with widespread joblessness during long depressions.[5]

Overall, this book has some strengths and weaknesses, as one might expect from a transitional book. It is especially useful when it theorizes in nonincrementalist terms, and it would be useful in a budgeting or politics class where the students could grapple with his hypotheses, design studies to test them, or weigh his arguments.

The gradual acknowledgment by Wildavsky that incrementalism is no longer useful or descriptive has opened the way for new directions in budget theory. Budget theory has moved away from describing the budget process as a set of fixed roles and uniform repeated procedures, and it has moved toward exploring the varieties of budget process across space and their evolution across time. The emphasis has changed from describing the commonalities to explaining the variations. Budget theory that once blithely ignored the environment now focuses on its role.

Recent budget theory has expanded its scope from an exclusive focus on appropriations to one that includes the politics of revenues, the organization of the decision-making process, attempts to balance and rebalance the budget, and the implementation of budgets once they are passed. Recent work has changed the view of budgeting as the allocation of dollars to the allocation of a variety of resources, including loans, subsidies, insurance, and grants. And it has concentrated on the variety of ways that programs can be delivered, including direct provision of services, contracts, entitlements, and public enterprises. Each resource and each system of program delivery has different political and budgetary characteristics. Ideally, future budget theories will accommodate and integrate all this complexity and variety, and they will specify the conditions under which their generalizations hold.

NOTES

1. Naomi Caiden and Aaron Wildavsky, *Planning and Budgeting in Poor Countries* (New York: Wiley, 1974).

2. See, for example, Frederick Pryor, *Public Expenditures in Communist and Capitalist Nations* (Homewood, IL: Irwin, 1968); Bruce Russett, "Who Pays for Defense," *American Political Science Review,* vol. 63 (June 1969), pp. 412–426; Bruce Russett, "Defense Expenditures and National Well-Being," *American Political Science Review,* vol. 76 (December 1982), pp. 767–777; Jerry Hollenhurst and Gary Ault, "An Alternative Answer to Who Pays for Defense," *American Political Science Review,* vol. 65 (September 1971), pp. 760–763; David Caputo, "New Perspectives on the Public Policy Implications of Defense and Welfare Expenditures in Four Modern Democracies: 1950–1970," *Policy Science,* vol. 6 (December 1975), pp. 423–426; Harold Wilensky, *The Welfare State and Equality: Structural and Ideological Roots of Public Expenditures* (Berkeley: University of California Press, 1974); Kathleen Peroff and Margaret Podolak-Warren, "Does Spending on Defense Cut Spending on Health," *British Journal of Political Science,* vol. 9 (January 1979), pp. 21–39; William Domke, Richard Eichenberg, and Catherine Kelleher, "The Illusion of Choice: Defense and Welfare in Advanced Industrial Democracies, 1984–1978," *American Political Science Review,* vol. 77 (September 1971), pp. 760–763; K. Dabelko and J.M. McCormick, "Opportunity Costs of Defense: Some Cross National Evidence," *Journal of Peace Research,* vol. 14 (June 1977), pp. 145–154; Barry Ames and Ed Goff, "Education and Defense Expenditures in Latin American: 1948–1968,"

in *Comparative Public Policy,* Craig Liske, William Loehr, and John McCamant, eds., (Beverry Hills: Sage Publictions, 1975).

3. Arnold Meltsner and Aaron Wildavsky, "Leave City Budgeting Alone," *Financing the Metropolis: Public Policy in Urban Economics,* John P. Crecine, eds, *Urban Affairs, Annual Review #4* (Beverly Hills: Sage Publications, 1970), pp. 311–358.

4. Terrence McDonald, "San Francisco: Socioeconomic Change, Political Culture, and Fiscal Politics, 1970–1996," *The Politics of Urban Fiscal Policy,* Terrence McDonald and Sally K. Ward, eds. (Beverly Hills: Sage Publications, 1984).

5. Alexander Keyssar, *Out of Work: The First Century of Unemployment in Massachusetts* (Cambridge: Cambridge University Press, 1986).

CHAPTER 15

DECISION STRATEGIES OF THE LEGISLATIVE BUDGET ANALYST
Economist or Politician?

KATHERINE G. WILLOUGHBY AND MARY A. FINN

Current understanding of public budgeting recognizes the confusing and complex nature of process and outcome (see, for example, Rubin 1993; Kiel and Elliot 1992). *Process* involves budget development and the interaction of numerous players, often with competing values, experiences, and allegiances. *Outcomes* reflect policy execution as supported by appropriations. Interest in both facets of budgeting remains high because of continued fiscal stress at all levels, institutional fragmentation, and citizen skepticism about the ability of government to handle budget and policy matters responsibly (consider the 1996 budget impasse at the national level.

In this environment, budgetary outcomes are certainly less suspect if process is at least perceived by the public as objective and equitable. Therefore, research efforts that dissect budgetary process and further specify individual and group decision-making behaviors become very important. Along such lines, this research empirically examines the decision behavior of legislative budget analysts involved in the familiar and routine task of reviewing agency spending plans for state legislators. The purpose of this research is to focus on the decisions of budget and fiscal analysts who are important staff of modern state legislatures; to examine budgeting strategies of these analysts and classify them; to characterize decision orientations of analysts demographically; and to compare the decision orientations of these analysts to their executive counterparts.

This work replicates that by Willoughby (1993a and 1993b) about executive budget analysts and their budgeting strategies. Her research uses decision task simulation and social judgment analysis to examine the spending strategies of 131 central budget bureau analysts from ten southern states. Her findings support the premise that spending decisions of public budgeters do not rely on a single rationality. That is, most analysts in this study take advantage of a mix of two or three cues predominantly when they review agency spending plans.

Willoughby's results show that the largest number of analysts (63 percent) can be classified as *mixed value* in their decision orientation, weighing political and economic factors about equally when they consider agency spending requests. The second largest group of analysts (27 percent), labeled *politico,* ascribe predominant weight to one or more political factors (gubernatorial di-

From *J-Part,* vol. 6, no. 4 (1996), 523–546. Copyright © 1996 by Public Management Research Association. Reprinted with permission.

rection, primarily) when they make budgetary recommendations. The smallest group of analysts are labeled *incrementalists* (6 percent) and *rationalists* (4 percent), those who depend solely on agency acquisitiveness or performance measures, respectively, when they analyze agency budget requests. These findings buttress modern notions that incrementalism is an inadequate explanation of public budgeting behavior.

Willoughby distinguished the four groups of analysts according to other factors. Her results indicate that the spending policies of analysts are best characterized by the fiscal environment of the state government and the age of the analyst. That is, economic factors (agency workload and efficiency of operation) carry greater weight in the budgetary decisions of younger analysts working in less fiscally stable environments.

Subjected to the same experiment, how will legislative budget analysts behave? The following hypotheses will be tested:

H$_1$: The decision strategies of most legislative budget analysts will reflect the mixed value spending orientation common to executive analysts. Since they are different from executive analysts, however, it is expected that institutional affiliation of legislative budget analysts will manifest itself in their predominant weighting of legislative agenda (as opposed to gubernatorial agenda) relative to other cues when they make spending recommendations.

H$_2$: Given the these analysts have more than one boss (as opposed to a governor), it is expected that, on average, they will weigh economic or objective cues more heavily than do their executive counterparts. This assumes that executive budget staff receive more focused policy direction from one governor than legislative budget staff receive from numerous legislative members, each with special and/or constituent interests at heart.

H$_3$: Given the fiscal constraints of the budgets in all state governments visited in 1992, it is expected that the least number of analysts will be classified as incrementalist, or characterized as using current base as the sole or most heavily weighted factor in determining future spending.

H$_4$: Assuming that more seasoned analysts (those who have a longer tenure in the position) are more cognizant of the politics of budgeting, it is expected that they consider political factors more heavily than do novice analysts when they make spending recommendations to legislators.

LITERATURE REVIEW

The Vital Role of the Legislative Fiscal and Budget Analyst

Research is limited about legislative process and staff at the state level. According to Oppenheimer (1983, 570, 577), "In a comparison with the extensive literature on how Congress shapes policy and budgets, the work on state legislatures and policy outputs is dwarfed. . . . Some of the research is indeed very fine, but the gaps in the literature are large." Studies that do consider state government legislative process and staff are often case analyses of efficiency and/or organization, or they are aggregative analyses of expenditures or number of bills passed as a proxy measure of policy output (BeVier 1979; Frost 1961; Milstein and Jennings 1973; Rosenthal and Forth 1978; Steiner and Gove 1960; Worman 1975).

The efforts of legislators to enhance their policy control over executives is evidenced in their advancing professionalism, however (Balutis and Butler 1975; Heaphey and Balutis 1975; Jones 1992; Oppenheimer 1983; Rosenthal 1981 and 1990; Skok 1980; Welch and Peters 1977). Longer sessions; higher salaries for elected and appointed positions; an increased number of staff aligned with individual legislators, committees, and the institution as a whole; changing committee structure; and improved facilities and technological capabilities all have contributed to the modern legislative environment. Mooney (1995, 48) points out that increased professionalism enhances legislative capacity "to perform its role in the policymaking process with an expertise, seriousness, and effort comparable to other actors in that process."

Nevertheless, in an environment that promotes the career legislator, "some 30 percent of the legislators taking their seats are new" (Gurwitt 1993, 29). This is explained in part by a poor revenue environment, greater fragmentation of power and the subsequent conflict over policy, and dwindling public opinion about legislative character. Such an environment only empowers legislative staff, those with the potential to serve and influence many different legislators over time. With budgets continuing to drive state politics, the influence of legislative fiscal staff intensifies given their role as information providers. Mooney (1991, 445) emphasizes that "those who can successfully supply information to decision makers will have their interests better represented in the legislative process than those who cannot." Gosling (1985) concurs that much of the power of a legislature vis-à-vis the executive rests with its proactive interpretation of the governor's recommended budget, often an interpretation that legislative analysts initially provide to legislators.

Decision Behavior of Legislative Budget Analysts

This study extends a growing body of literature that uses empirical research methods to decipher legislative and budgeting behavior. Examples of this type of research include Mooney's analysis of the information sources of legislators from three states. In this study, he finds that legislators weigh information sources differently depending upon their task. "Legislators deciding on their votes use more insider information, those persuading their colleagues use more middle range information, and those writing bills use more outside information than do those participating in the other subprocesses" (Mooney 1991, 451).

Similarly, Stanford (1992) considers the factors that are the most influential to legislators when they evaluate state agency budget requests. Her findings confirm two aspects of budgeting behavior that are assumed in the present research effort. First, Stanford successfully distinguishes the decision orientations of legislators, labeling such as control, management, planning, or funding. These results support the notion that the specialized activities of public budgeters generate routine behaviors that can be modeled effectively. Second, she finds that seven of the eight variables defined as important decision factors "significantly influenced the decision calculus of legislators at the deliberative stage of budget review" (p. 24). Her point here relates to the demise of incrementalism as an adequate explanation of modern public budgeting.

Like Willoughby's work, Thurmaier's (1995) analysis of the spending decisions of practitioners and graduate students of public administration is another example of the application of experimental design to the study of budgeting by analysts. In this study, subjects are placed in treatment and control groups. Individuals in each category are given various pieces of hypothetical budget information from which they must determine a recommended expenditure limit. Thurmaier (1992) and Willoughby (1993a) incorporate experimental design a bit differently, yet they arrive at the same conclusions. For instance, both find that budgeters take advantage of a limited number of factors when they make decisions about expenditures. Also, budgeters tend to weigh political cues more heavily than economic cues, even though economic factors play a significant role in the analysts' decision process. Both find that personal and/or environmental factors influence budgeters' interpretation and weighting of different budgetary cues.

Exhibit 15.1   Decision Model of the Legislative Budget Analyst

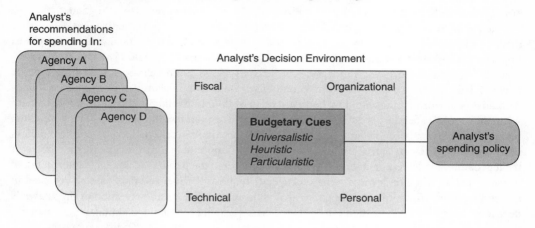

A final work of note is that of Bretschneider, Straussman, and Mullins (1988) in which graduate students of public administration and business administration were given revenue forecast information along with other financial, political, and demographic data about a hypothetical city and asked to decide on a maximum expenditure limit for the upcoming budget. The authors found that budgetary role and individual characteristics influence decision orientations of subjects. Perhaps the weakest aspect of this experiment is that all subjects were students and not "real actors" in the public sector.

This research is based on an understanding that the role and activities of the legislative budget analyst are specific and routine. It is understood that such activities are conducted in a very complicated and changeable environment as explained by Rubin (1993) in her real-time budgeting model. Yet, while her work addresses macrobudgeting decision making in a very fluid environment, this research analyzes microbudgeting decision making conducted at a particular point in the budget cycle. Barber (1966) describes this *insular* quality of such decisions in his experiment involving local board of finance members by noting that budgeters focus almost exclusively on their own community and its unique budgetary situation when they deliberate about spending. This research analyzes the contained setting of the analyst engaged in reviewing agency budget requests to make spending recommendations to legislators before passing the appropriation bill or bills.

Exhibit 15.1 illustrates the decision scenario of the typical legislative analyst involved in the familiar activity of reviewing agency budget requests and developing spending recommendations or options for legislators.

According to this model, the analyst may receive agency budget requests directly from the agency early in the development of the governor's recommended budget (at the same time as executive budget staff) or may receive such indirectly in the governor's recommended budget just prior to the start of the legislative session. The analyst's decision environment is characterized by fiscal, institutional, and personal factors. The fiscal environment is defined overwhelmingly by the revenue estimate for the particular budget year in question and indirectly by the long-term fiscal health of the state government, often indicated by its bond rating. Institutional factors include the organizational environment defined by the location of the legislative budget office; the appointment of its director; and its primary mission or orientation, staff size, and budget format. Such factors also include the technical environment as it relates to the computer hardware and software and other technological capabilities afforded to the analyst for the conduct of work. The personal environment of the analyst includes educational and work experiences, age, and gender.

The decision environment represented in Exhibit 15.1 is based on normative and descriptive theories of public budgeting that consider rational, incremental, and political process factors as important determinants of government spending (Babunakis 1982; Grizzle 1985 and 1986; Lindblom 1959; Premchand 1983; Simon 1957; Wildavsky 1992). Such factors include those that are universalistic (rational), represented by economic or objective measures of performance. Incrementalist behavior is represented by heuristic rules of thumb that analysts traditionally consider when they look at spending requests from year to year (for example, the amount of increase to the budget from current base that an agency requests). Particularistic criteria include political factors related to the agency, its activities, and the agendas of important budget players, like members of the legislature, the governor, agency personnel, clients, and the public. An analyst's interpretation of these factors when reviewing numerous agency requests for legislators is then represented in a spending orientation or judgment policy that is the cumulative characterization of the analyst's decision strategy. Such orientation can be characterized as more economic, traditional (incremental), or political, depending on the analyst's interpretation and weighting of the different cues.

DATA SOURCE

Data for this study was collected from nine state legislatures in the southeastern region of the United States in 1992.[1] Approximately 89 of 109 analysts (82 percent) eligible to participate in the project completed the questionnaire.[2] According to Exhibit 15.2, the typical legislative budget analyst can be characterized as male, about thirty-nine years old, and earning over $45,000 per year. On average, the legislative analyst has served in his present position almost six years and has been employed in state government for over a dozen years. He is most likely to hold an advanced degree, probably in business or public administration.

METHODOLOGY

Social judgment theory (SJT) and analysis is used to measure the spending decisions of these analysts. SJT is a method of analyzing individual choice behavior that has been used with success in the social and other sciences (Adelman, Stewart, and Hammond 1975; Al-Tabtabai and Diekmann 1992; Dell'Omo 1990; Dhir 1987; Grizzle 1985; Hammond et al. 1987; Stewart and Gelberd 1976; Whorton, Feldt, and Dunn 1989; Willoughby 1993a; see also, Waller 1988 for a historical review of the use of SJT in accounting and auditing research). This method of analyzing human decision behavior requires subjects to perceive multiple cues and discern their importance when they make a decision. Rather than ask subjects what factors are most important to them when they are involved in specific decision tasks, social judgment analysis presents a carefully defined decision task to the subject and requests a choice. The manner in which subjects take advantage of various factors included in the decision tasks and the consistency with which they make choices among a number of decision scenarios can be quantified using multiple regression.

The father of social judgment theory, Egon Brunswik (1956), developed a lens model to illustrate what he terms the *behavioral episode,* as a distal stage (goal), proximal cues, and individual judgment. According to this model, a *zone of ambiguity* exists between individual judgment and distal state. The behavioral episode (or judgment) is a probabilistic process of adapting to the environment. The use of cues is functional; not all cues are needed, and some are more dependable than others to a particular individual in a specific decision task (Hammond et al. 1977). The

Exhibit 15.2

Personal Characteristics of Legislative Budget Analysts

Value Label	Frequency	Valid percent
Present Job Title		
Deputy director	9	10.1
House fiscal officer	1	1.1
Senior legislative analyst	22	24.7
Legislative analyst	55	61.8
Other[a]	2	2.2
	89	100.0
Previous Employment		
Legislature	12	13.5
State agency	37	41.6
Municipal government	6	6.7
Federal agency	2	2.2
Private sector	14	15.7
Directly from school	8	9.0
Other[b]	10	11.2
	89	100.0
Level of education completed		
Some college	1	1.1
College graduate	21	23.6
Some graduate work	17	19.1
Master's degree	42	47.2
Doctoral/professional degree	7	7.9
Otherc	1	1.1
	89	100.0
Gender		
Male	55	62.5
Female	33	37.5
Missing	1	missing
	89	100.0
Income		
$20,000–$25,000	2	2.3
$25,000–$30,000	8	9.2
$30,000–$35,000	9	10.3
$35,000–$40,000	9	10.3
$40,000–$45,000	14	16.1
$45,000	45	51.7
Missing	2	missing
	89	100.0

[a]The two participants in this category listed their job titles as chief economist and economist. They are employed in the legislative budget office in their state and have four and three years service as a legislative budget analyst in that office, respectively.

[b]This category includes participants previously employed in an executive budget office; a university; a county budget office or agency; or a court system.

[c]This category includes a participant who completed doctoral courses only (ABD).

zone of ambiguity can be defined by several measures: the weight or importance placed on each cue by the individual; the form of the functional relationship between each proximal cue and the distal state; and the organizing principle of the individual.

In this study, the lens model is transformed (see Exhibit 15.1). Individual judgment is an analyst's recommendation regarding each of forty hypothetical state agency budget request profiles. Proximal cues are the criteria typically used by these analysts when they make judgments regarding specific budget requests. Distal state is the analyst's overall judgment policy that reflects individual dependence on and usefulness of cues among numerous budgetary decisions.

According to Exhibit 15.1, the independent variables include the decision cues, along with fiscal climate, organizational and technical aspects, and personal characteristics. Judgment policy is dependent on an analyst's particular weighting of the specified criteria in his/her fiscal, institutional, and personal settings. The dependent variable is the analyst's decision-making orientation or spending policy.

The survey instrument is the same one that Willoughby (1993a) administered to executive budget analysts and includes task definition and cue specification.[3] The instrument comprises one section including the decision task simulation and one section regarding demographics. Analysts' responses to the simulation serve as the data for this study, along with information about their education, work background, and other personal characteristics.

The simulation comprises forty hypothetical agency budget requests profiles measured on seven factors or cues considered by these budgeters when they reviewed spending plans. The profiles had been generated randomly on microcomputer and then displayed in this section of the questionnaire so that each analyst received the same profiles in the same order to review. The first two factors presented in the each profile, agency workload and efficiency of operation, serve as proxy measures of economic cues. Acquisitiveness of the agency head (request compared to current budget) serves as proxy measure of a heuristic cue, incrementalism (consideration of the base for future spending levels). Gubernatorial and legislative agendas, agency head trustworthiness regarding spending, and public support serve as proxy measures of particularistic or political cues.

While the laboratory quality of the simulation is noted (analysts were provided complete information for an incomplete list of cues that make up each profile), the information taken collectively within the analyst's working environment was not necessarily unrealistic.[4] Hammond et al. (1980, 186) note that SJT "emphasizes the concept of representative design." Stewart (1988, 58) suggests that "[t]he goal of judgment analysis in the context of SJT is to derive a useful description of the judgment process and not necessarily to reproduce faithfully all the properties of the process itself."

RESULTS

The analyst's organizing principle is mathematically represented by a second degree polynomial equation:

$$\hat{Y} = b_{11}X_1 + b_{12}X^2 + \ldots b_{n1} X_n + b_{n2}X^2 + c$$

where,

$\hat{Y}$ = analyst's predicted spending orientation or policy
$b_{11\text{-}n1}$ = regression coefficients for the value of cues
$b_{12\text{-}n2}$ = regression coefficients for the square of the value of cues
$X_{1\text{-}n}$ = the scored budge cues
X^2 = the square of the scored budget cues
c = a constant value

Quadratic terms are used to allow for the generation of curvilinear function forms in cases where an analyst's use of a cue is best represented by a utility curve. Each regression produces partial coefficients for each cue and its square, along with standard errors and t scores. Partial regression coefficients are standardized to indicate the relative influence of each cue to each analyst. Standardized coefficients, or beta weights, provide a measure of the percentage of variability in an analyst's judgment policy that can be explained by each cue. Each beta weight is divided by the sum of all beta weights for an analyst to determine relative weight of each cue to each analyst. In the final regression model for each analyst, relative weights sum to 100.

The multiple correlation coefficient or predictability score calculated for each analyst provides a measure of the comparability of an analyst's predicted judgments with his/her actual spending recommendations. This measure provides both an indication of the fit of the regression model to an analyst's actual behavior and the consistency with which an analyst makes recommendations across all forty budget request profiles. Predictability scores from .70 to .90 are common in judgment analysis; scores of .80 and above are considered *good* (Stewart 1988).

Graphic depiction of analysts' consideration of cues is represented using function forms. These forms illustrate an analyst's subjective use of cues when making spending recommendations. The graphs portray the manner in which an analyst takes advantage of each factor and are considered in conjunction with relative weights.

Individual Cognitive Styles

Exhibit 15.3 illustrates the function forms for three analysts representing different spending policies. The vertical axis of each form represents an analyst's recommendations for each of the forty profiles, scored on a scale from 1 to 20.[5] The horizontal axis represents the scores applied to specific cues within each profile, on a scale from −10 to +10, or from 0 to +10 in the case of *acquisitiveness*. Agency acquisitiveness has a possible score from 0 to +10 because, barring specific gubernatorial directives to make cuts, it is rare that an agency head will ask for less than current base when requesting FY + 1 funds. Relative weights are found in the lower right corner of the function forms. Multiple correlation coefficients are found at the bottom of each spending policy.

Distinctiveness of spending policy is evident when function forms are considered along with relative weights. For instance, analyst A considers legislative agenda predominantly when making spending recommendations. Forty-three percent of the variability in this analyst's spending judgments can be explained by his/her consideration of the agenda of important members of the legislature.

Statistical significance of the quadratic term for *legislature's agenda* attests to the positive, slightly curvilinear manner in which this analyst takes advantage of this cue. That is, as an agency's budget is more positively endorsed or supported by important members of the legislature, the more strongly the analyst favors inclusion of the request in the total budget package. In this case, agency efficiency and gubernatorial agenda also are significant ($p < 0.005$), although they are not relied upon by the analyst as heavily as legislative agenda (weights of 12 and 16, respectively). Consideration of this analyst's predictability score (0.96) attests to the consistency with which he/she makes recommendations based on the interpretation of the political factor, *legislature's agenda,* predominantly and helps to explain the significance of the other two cues.

Analyst B takes advantage of several political cues and one analytical cue in a more balanced manner than analyst A. This analyst weighs agency head reputation, legislative agenda, and agency efficiency almost equally when making spending recommendations. The t scores that correspond to these cues are significant ($p < 0.005$). The predictability score of 0.84 indicates a good fit of predicated to actual spending recommendations. This analyst consistently focuses on these three factors when making spending recommendations for the forty budget profiles presented in the simulation.

Exhibit 15.3   **Judgment Policies of Three Legislative Budget Analysts**

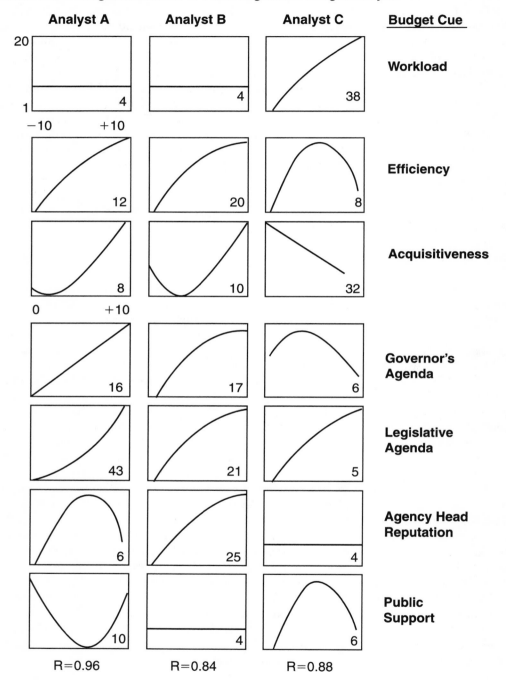

Analyst C considers agency workload and acquisitiveness most heavily when reviewing budgets. Thirty-eight percent of the variability in this analyst's spending policy can be attributed to his/her consideration of agency workload. The function form for this cue indicates that as workload increases, the analyst more strongly favors inclusion of the agency's request in the total budget package. On the other hand, this analyst ascribes almost equal weight (32 percent) to the cue, *acquisitiveness,* considering this factor in a negative, linear manner. He/she confers weaker recommendations to include an agency's spending request in the total budget package as requests increase compared to current budget.

These results illustrate the complexity and uniqueness of information processing exhibited on the part of legislative budget analysts engaged in a familiar decision task and are similar to distinctiveness of budgeting strategy exhibited by executive budget analysts (Willoughby 1993a). For example, whereas analyst A takes advantage of one political cue predominantly when reviewing agency budget requests, analyst B considers a mix of political and analytical factors, and analyst C considers analytical and traditional ones.

Classification of Analysts by Spending Policy

Analysts' spending policies are grouped into clusters. This involves a two-step process. First factoring produces an analysis of the similarities among observation—that is, among the recommendations by the subjects for each of the forty budget request profiles. Second, cluster analysis considers the similarities among cases—that is, among the spending policies of the eight-nine analysts.

In this case, factor analysis is used for exploratory purposes "to achieve economy of description through data reduction" (Goddard and Kirby 1976, 14). The objective of using factor analysis is to reduce from forty the number of variables upon which analysts' judgment policies will be measured. Resulting factor scores are then used in the clustering procedure to determine if analysis' judgment policies can be grouped (Gorsuch 1983).[6] A seven factor solution results from this first step to classify analysts. Seven scores are calculated for each analyst and saved in an active file that is accessed when the cluster procedure is conducted.

Cluster analysis follows the factoring procedure and involves the classification of objects or units into groups whereby within-group homogeneity and between-group heterogeneity is maximized (Zapan 1982, 4). The analysts' spending policies are grouped according to the values of their factor scores produced in the previous step.

Clustering can be accomplished in a variety of ways. Two types of clustering include the non-hierarchical (single level) and the hierarchical (multilevel) procedures. The first method partitions entities into clusters by an iterative process, while the latter classifies entities into groups either through agglomerative or divisive means. The agglomerative procedure begins with all objects as single entities and the combines them by level until all objects are included within one group (Lorr 1983, 19–20). The hierarchical, agglomerative technique is the most commonly used cluster procedure and is used here to group analysts' spending policies.

Several agglomerative methods exist, distinguishable by the definition of distance considered between an entity and a cluster or between two clusters (Mezzich and Solomon 1980, 20–21). In this case, Ward's minimum-variance method is used. Zapan (1982, 25) elaborates on the distance measure (squared Euclidean) endorsed by Ward's method and its usefulness, noting that this method is "very efficient, but favors the grouping of small clusters."[7]

Clustering produced a data matrix along with an agglomeration schedule. Exhibit 15.4 represents the dendrogram, which graphically displays this schedule—analysts clustered according to similarity of spending policy. Case and group numbers are listed along the bottom of the graph.

Exhibit 15.4   Dendrogram Using Ward Method: Hierarchical Cluster Analysis

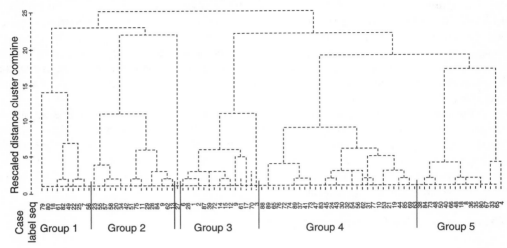

Five clusters are highlighted in Exhibit 15.4, although more could have been acknowledged.[8] The decision about how many clusters or groups to acknowledge is a subjective one. Usually, the distance values represented on the vertical axis of the dendrogram are consulted to determine the least number of well-defined clusters (Romesburg 1984, 213–15). In this case, the five clusters illustrated each contain a healthy number of cases and, as will be shown, represent distinctive between-group characteristics.

Graphic interpretation of average spending policy by group is presented in Exhibit 15.5. This information was developed by calculating the mean recommendation for the forty budget request profiles by group and then conducting multiple regression to produce an average judgment policy for each cluster of analysts. According to results, only 18 percent of the legislative budget analysts weight direction from important members of the legislature most heavily (group 2). Alternatively, 70 percent of analysts weight the economic criteria, agency workload, and efficiency of operation most heavily when they review agency budget requests (group 3, 4, and 5). Virtually all groups indicate the significant influence of one or both of these cues when they review agency budget requests for legislators.

Another notable result is that acquisitiveness of the request (consideration of the base) is not the sole or most heavily weighted cue for any of the groups. This cue is considered second to workload for the seventeen analysts in group 5 and is moderately important to the twenty-five analysts in groups 1 and 3.

Looking at the function forms, it is noteworthy that analysts tend to utilize most cues in a positive, linear, or slightly curvilinear manner. As the agency workload increases, the more positive the endorsement is for full funding of the request by the analyst; the greater the efficiency of the agency's operation, the more positive the endorsement; the more the agency's budget is positively promoted by various budget players—legislators, the governor, the public–the more positive the analyst's endorsement; the more trustworthy an agency head is in terms of equating requests with the spending needs, the more positive the endorsement.

However, the interpretation of agency acquisitiveness is quite distinctive, depending upon the group, Note differences in the consideration of this cue across groups 1, 3, and 5. (This cue is not

Exhibit 15.5   **Average Spending Policy by Group**[a]

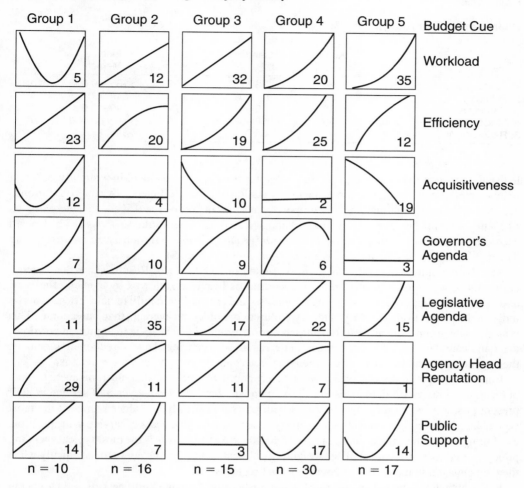

[a]Mean weights of budget cues are presented in the lower right corner of each function form for each group.

significant to analysts in groups 2 and 4.) Analysts in group 5 consider agency acquisitiveness rather heavily, second only to agency workload, when they review agency spending plans. These analysts negatively consider any requests above current budget. Analysts in group 3 interpret agency acquisitiveness somewhat as do those in group 5, although not as heavily. Finally, analysts in group 1 consider agency acquisitiveness to be slightly more important than do those in group 3, and less important than do those in group 5. Analysts in group 1 provide weaker endorsements of agency budgets that exhibit relatively small increases in the base; they react more positively to agency budgets that exhibit relatively large increases in the base.

The graphic presentation in Exhibit 15.4 allows for the comparison across groups that may seem similar based on their cue weightings alone, yet they vary when the manner in which cues are utilized is exhibited. For example, analysts in groups 2 and 4 weigh agency efficiency and

Exhibit 15.6

Characteristics of Analysts by Group

Group # and Name	Age in Years	Gender %M/%F	Years in Position	Income Median	n
1. Bureaucrat	34	33/67	4.90	>$35–40,000	10
2. Politico	39	100/-0-	5.16	>$45,000	16
3. Rationalist	39	40/60	4.21	>$40–45,000	15
4. Mixed Value	39	60/40	5.11	>$40–45,000	30
5. Rationalist/incrementalist	42	65/35	8.35	>$45,000	17

legislative agenda rather heavily, yet they interpret the cues, on average, in a slightly different manner. Notice also the distinction in the interpretation of agency efficiency by analysts in groups 1, 2, and 4; the interpretation of public support by analysts in groups 1 and 5; and the interpretation of agency workload by analysts in groups 3 and 5. Based on these results, analysts can be labeled according to their spending policy as *bureaucrat* (group 1); *politico* (group 2); *rationalist* (group 3); *mixed value* (group 4); and *rationalist/incrementalist* (group 5).

The demographics for each group are presented in Exhibit 15.6. Results show that bureaucrats—those who weigh agency head trustworthiness heaviest, followed by agency efficiency, and then public support—are the youngest analysts and are predominantly female. These analysts indicate the lowest average salary category. Politicos are older, on average, than bureaucrats. This is an all-male group, with analysts having served an average of five years in their present positions, and it indicates the highest salary category. These analysts weigh legislative direction most heavily, then agency efficiency of operation, when they determine budgetary recommendations.

Rationalists (predominant consideration of economic factors) are also older, on average, than bureaucrats. This group comprises mostly women who have the fewest years of service in their present positions when they the compared with other groups. Mixed values represent the most typical legislative budget analyst—male, thirty-nine years old, five years of service in the position, and falling within the annual salary range of $40,000 to $45,000. This is the most typical spending policy as well (n = 30), with analysts weighting political and economic cues almost equally when they are engaged in the review of agency budget requests.

Rationalists/incrementalists are most distinguished by their age and years of service, being older, on average, than analysts in the other groups and having significantly more years of service in their present positions (8.35 on average) than other analysts. This group is predominantly male and indicates an annual salary range above $45,000.

Results from a chi square test of independence (gender and spending policy) and analyses of variance (age, years of service, and income with spending policy) indicate that of the demographic variables, only gender and income are statistically related to analysts' decision orientation.

Comparison with Executive Budget Analysts

Exhibit 15.7 compares frequency distributions of cue weights by executive and legislative analysts. Legislative analysts are more likely to consider agency workload and efficiency of operation significant (cue weight of 20 or greater) than do executive analysts. Also, legislative analysts are less likely than are executive analysts to ascribe predominant weight to one (political) factor. While 63 percent of executive budget analysts weigh the governor's agenda heavily (cue weight of 20

Exhibit 15.7

Frequency Distribution of Weights of Budgetary Cues by Executive Budget Analysts (EBA)[a] and Legislative Budget Analysts (LBA), in Percent

Weight	Workload		Efficiency		Acquisitive		Governor's Agenda		Legislator's Agenda		Agency Head Reputation		Public Support	
	EBA	LBA	EBA	LBA	EBA	LBA	EBA	LBA	EBA	LBA	EBA	LBA	EBA	LBA
0.9	26	20	17	25	48	48	8	58	49	21	36	42	65	42
10–19	43	33	53	38	40	42	28	40	43	43	56	45	28	38
20–29	22	29	24	31	8	9	37	1	8	17	7	11	5	16
30–39	8	16	5	6	2	1	21	0	0	13	0	0	2	3
40–49	<1	1	2	0	2	0	3	0	0	3	<1	2	0	1
50–59	<1	1	0	0	0	0	2	0	0	2	0	0	0	0
Total	101	100	101	100	100	100	99	99	100	99	100	100	100	100
Total N	131	89	131	89	131	89	131	89	131	89	131	89	131	89

[a]Data presented concerning executive budget analysts is from Willoughby 1991a, page 142, Table 4.5: *Frequency Distribution of Weights on the Seven Criteria for the 131 Budget Analysts' Judgments.*

or greater), only 35 percent of legislative analysts weigh legislative agenda as heavily when they make agency budget recommendations. Results in Exhibit 15.7 indicate that legislative analysts are more likely than executive counterparts to consider a broader range of factors as significant. For example, legislative analysts are more likely than executive analysts to consider legislative agenda, agency administrators, and public support important when they prepare spending recommendations.

Exhibit 15.8 compares the percentage of executive and legislative analysts as grouped by spending policy. These results indicate that while the largest group of legislative analysts can be classified as mixed value—heavily dependent upon legislative direction and objective measures of performance when they review agency spending plans—most do not conform to this orientation. Indeed, results show that 47 percent of analysts depend most heavily on factors *other than* legislative agenda when they prepare spending recommendations (includes bureaucrats, rationalists, and rationalists/incrementalists). Also, budget base does not serve as the sole or most heavily weighted cue of any group of legislative analysts. This compares with the 6 percent of executive analysts labeled incrementalist who do weigh agency acquisitiveness most heavily of all cues. Finally, 82 percent of legislative analysts, compared to 67 percent of executive analysts, weigh the economic factors of agency workload and/or efficiency heavily when they make spending recommendations (includes bureaucrats, mixed values, rationalists, and rationalist/incrementalists).

DISCUSSION AND CONCLUSION

These results indicate that support for H_1 is mixed. While the legislative analysts classified as mixed-value in orientation do reflect their institutional affiliation in the weight that they ascribe to the agenda of important members of the legislature, as opposed to that of the governor (an insignificant cue for almost all legislative analysts), most do not fall into this category of spending policy (strongest consideration of the cue *legislature's agenda* and the economic factors *workload* and *efficiency*). On the other hand, there is support for H_2—82 percent of legislative analysts consider workload and efficiency significant when they review agency spending plans, compared to 67 percent of executive analysts. Support for H_3 is also mixed. Legislative analysts are different from executive ones in that none are categorized as strictly incrementalist in orientation. However, for 19 percent of the legislative analysts, agency acquisitiveness is an important budgetary cue, considered second to agency workload.

Support for H_4 is more ambiguous. For instance, it is clear that those who are least likely to take advantage of legislative direction when they review budgets (bureaucrats) are younger, female, have fewer years of service, and are in the lower annual salary range. On the other hand, those who are most likely to predominantly consider either the political factor or legislative agenda (politicos) or to predominantly consider agency acquisitiveness in conjunction with economic factors (rationalist/incrementalists) when they review budgets tend to be male, have the longest tenure as analysts, and fall within the highest annual salary range.

Concerning politicos, perhaps men feel more comfortable within majority male legislative institutions, and that accounts for their heavy consideration of the agenda of important legislators. Maybe their work experience contributes to a greater appreciation of the politics of budgeting. Women tend to have fewer years of service, on average, than do men, both in the workforce and in the analyst position (see Willoughby 1991b). Maybe female analysts are less familiar with such politics, and this explains their heavier reliance on agency administrators and objective measures of performance when they consider budget plans. The relationship between salary level and orientation may be more straightforward. Given the employer-employee relationship involved, it is

Exhibit 15.8

Executive Budget Analysts (EBAs)[a] and Legislative Budget Analysts (LBAs) Grouped According to Policy Type, in Percent

Policy Type	Predominant Use of Budget Cues	EBAs	LBAs
Bureaucrat	Agency workload and/or agency efficiency, and agency head reputation	0	11
Politico	Gubernatorial agenda, legislative agenda, agency head reputation, and/or public support	27	18
Mixed value	Gubernatorial agenda or legislative agenda, and agency workload and/or agency efficiency	63	34
Rationalist	Agency workload and/or agency efficiency	4	17
Rationalist/ incrementalist	Agency workload and agency acquisitiveness	0	19
Incrementalist	Agency acquisitiveness	6	0
	Total	100	100
	N	131	89

[a]Data presented concerning executive budget analysts is from Willoughby 1993b, page 115, Table 5.4: *Analysts Grouped According to Policy Type.*

expected that analysts who make higher salaries would consider legislative agenda more heavily than would those who make lower salaries.

The distinctiveness of the rationalist/incrementalist orientation is interesting. This group ascribes heaviest weight to agency workload, then acquisitiveness, with other significant factors including legislative agenda, public support, and agency efficiency, in that order. In other words, concerns of important members of the legislature are not ignored by these analysts.

In light of their heavier reliance on economic factors and broader consideration of political factors, legislative budget analysts can be characterized as more objective than executive budget analysts. In fact, aside from the sixteen who are labeled *politico,* most consider legislative agenda a secondary, or more often an unimportant, cue (for example, bureaucrats). Unlike their executive counterparts who are typically aligned with one chief executive, legislative analysts have a number of legislators, in addition to other budget players, to consider. It is interesting that while legislators themselves may consider gubernatorial agenda rather heavily when they deliberate about appropriations (Duncombe and Kinney 1986), legislative staff indicate significantly less consideration of this factor when they make recommendations to legislators. On the other hand, in a discussion of the use of performance-based information for budgetary decision making, Broom (1995, 14) points out that provision of such, "while not transforming the decision process, is adding value to deliberations." She alludes to a greater "comfortableness" on the part of legislators concerning the interpretation and use of performance measures in their budgetary deliberations. Accordingly, it seems legislative analysts serve a important role in communicating an objective perspective on budget matters, one that is useful to those with the final say.

NOTES

1. The nine states include Alabama, Florida, Georgia, Kentucky, Louisiana, Mississippi, North Carolina, South Carolina, and Virginia. Six states have legislative budget offices or fiscal committees that serve both houses (Alabama, Georgia, Kentucky, Louisiana, Mississippi, and North Carolina). Three states have separate

budget review staff under Senate Appropriations or Finance Committees and House Appropriations or Ways and Means Committees (Florida, South Carolina, and Virginia).

2. The sample was drawn from the population of analysts in these legislatures with primary responsibility for agency budget review for recommendation to the legislature, and from those who have been employed for at least one fiscal year by their legislative budget office. The survey instrument was administered to analysts by one or both researchers in a group setting. Each researcher followed a typed protocol in administering the questionnaire to analysts. Administration of the questionnaire to analysts was usually preceded by a face-to-face interview with the budget office director or deputy director. Information about office organization, mission, budget format, and technological capabilities was collected at this time. Also, directors were asked about the role of analysts, staff relationships to legislators and committees, recruitment, turnover, and future concerns.

3. This instrument is discussed in detail and an example profile is exhibited in Willoughby (1993a).

4. As noted previously, these cues are consistently mentioned in the public budgeting literature as important to budgeters when they are making spending decisions. In addition to previous exposure to executive analysts (see Willoughby 1991a and 1993a), as a validity check, several legislative analysts from states not included in his study were asked to assess the decision exercise for completeness and relevance. Their comments indicate that such in exercise is reasonable, given the repetitive nature of budget review activity required of legislative budget analysts

5. A recommendation of 1 indicates very weak endorsement by the analyst for inclusion of the budget request in the total budget package for FY+1. A recommendation of 20 indicates very strong endorsement by the analyst for inclusion of the budget request in the total budget package for FY+1.

6. Factor analysis begins with development of a correlation matrix for all variables to be included in the model. Standard scores are calculated for all original recommendations by analysts and these scores are factored. This step insures the development of a standardized data matrix, which is necessary for the subsequent cluster procedure (Romesburg 1984, 78–92). The matrix represents the correlations among the recommendations provided by the subjects for each of the forty budget request profiles.

Three measures are used to assess the appropriateness of using the factor model. The Bartlett Test of Sphericity indicates whether to reject or not reject the null hypothesis that the population correlation matrix is an identity. If this measure is large, with a very small significance level, the null hypothesis can be rejected and the factor model is an appropriate one to use. The Barlett Test of Sphericity for this data equals 2961.73 ($p = 0.0000$) and suggests the appropriateness of using the factor model. A second indicator that the factor model is an appropriate one considers partial correlation coefficients. When factor assumptions are met, partial coefficients should near zero. The anti-image correlation matrix provides the negative of the partial coefficients, and if the proportion of low correlations is high, use of the factor model is appropriate. In this case, the factor model is appropriate as only 0.8 percent of the off-diagonal elements of the anti-image correlation matrix are greater than 0.09. Finally, the Kaiser-Meyer-Olkin Measure of Sampling Adequacy provides an index that compares observed correlation coefficients to partial correlation coefficients. Kaiser (1974) suggests that KMOs of 0.80 or above are meritorius, indicating that factoring is appropriate. The KMO for the data from this project equals 0.82, indicative of the appropriateness of the model for data reduction (see also, Norusis 1986 for a step by step approach to factoring for reduction).

The next step in factor analysis involves extraction to determine the number of factors necessary to adequately describe the raw data. The principal components method of extraction is used to produce a new set of variables or dimensions that are orthogonal or independent of one another. Results produce a first component that accounts for the greatest amount of variance in the sample, a second dimension that accounts for any variance not accounted for by the first component, a third dimension that accounts for any further variance, and so on (Rummel 1970).

Several thresholds can be considered to determine the appropriate number of factors to include in the final solution. The Kaiser or eigenvalue criterion (where the eigenvalue is greater than or equal to one) is a common rule-of-thumb used to determine the appropriate number of factors to extract (Kim and Mueller 1978, 49). Using this criterion, results indicate a seven factor solution, a reduction from forty, "to overcome the difficulty of clustering too many variables" (Everitt 1980, 10).

This solution is substantiated by examination of the plot of eigenvalues or *scree*—where the slope of large factors begins to trail off. In this case, the scree begins at the seventh factor, again suggesting a seven factor solution (Kim and Mueller 1978). Because factoring is conducted for data reduction purposes, it is unnecessary to seek the definition of the dimensions produced (Adelman, Stewart, and Hammond 1975; Rohrbaugh and Wehr 1978; Romesburg 1984).

Finally, the quartimax method of rotation is conducted for better distinction among factors. According to Rummel (1970, 120), it is particularly desirable when factor scores will be used to provide input for further analyses.

7. As with factoring, clustering involves several steps. Using the seven scores resulting from factor analysis for each analyst, a *resemblance* or distance data matrix is developed, which provides measures of the similarity or dissimilarity among pairs of subjects. Ward's method of clustering necessitates the use of the squared Euclidean distance coefficient as its distance measure. This is a dissimilarity coefficient whereby the smaller the value of the coefficient, the more similar the subjects (Romesburg 1984, 11–13).

After the data matrix is produced, clustering by step commences. An agglomeration schedule provides distance coefficients and the stages at which clusters are developed. This schedule can be used to help determine the number of clusters to consider in further analyses. A dendrogram provides a graphic display of clustering by stages and is more easily interpretable than the schedule.

8. Case number 27 is an example of an outlier that does not fall within any group using the distance measure shown. It is interesting that this case has a predictability score of 0.75, indicating a lack of consistency by the analyst in interpreting the budgetary cues across all forth budget request profiles. When using social judgment analysis, predictability scores below 0.80 suggest that the arithmethic model of the individual's judgment policy is rather poor.

REFERENCES

Adelman, Leonard; Stewart, Thomas R.; and Hammond, Kenneth R. 1975 "A Case History of the Application of Social Judgment Theory to Policy Formulation." *Policy Sciences* 6:137–59.

Al-Tabtabai, Hashem, and Diekmann, James E. 1992 "Judgmental Forecasting in Construction Project." *Construction Management and Economics* 10 (Jan.):19–30.

Babunakis, M. 1982 *Budget Reform for Government: A Comprehensive Allocation and Management System.* Westport, Conn.: Quorum Books.

Balutis, Alan, and Butler, Daron, eds. 1975 *The Political Pursestrings: The Role of the Legislature in the Budgetary Process.* New York: Wiley.

Barber, James D. 1966 *Power in Committees.* Chicago: Rand McNally.

BeVier, Michael J. 1979 *Politics Backstage: Inside the California Legislature.* Philadelphia: Temple University Press.

Bretschneider, Stuart; Straussman, Jeffrey D.; and Mullins, Daniel. 1988 "Do Revenue Forecasts Influence Budget Setting? A Small Group Experiment." *Policy Sciences* 21:305–25.

Broom, Cheryle A. 1995 "Performance-Based Government Models: Building a Track Record." *Public Budgeting and Finance* 15 (winter): 3–17.

Brunswik, Egon. 1956 *Perception and the Representative Design of Experiments.* Berkeley: University of California Press.

Dell'Omo, Gregory G. 1990 "Capturing Arbitrator Decision Policies Under a Public Sector Interest Arbitration Statute." *Review of Public Personnel Administration* 10 (spring): 19–38.

Dhir, Krishna S. 1987 "Formulating Management Policies for Value Engineering/Value Analysis." *IEEE Transactions on Engineering Management* 34 (Aug.):161–71.

Duncombe, Sydney, and Kinney, Richard. 1986 "The Politics of State Appropriations Increases: The Perspective of Budget Officers in Five Western States." *Journal of State Government* 59 (Sept./Oct.): 113–23.

Everitt, Brian. 1980 *Cluster Analysis,* 2d ed. New York: Halsted Press.

Frost, Richard T., ed. 1961 *Cases in State and Local Governments.* Englewood Cliffs, N.J.: Prentice-Hall.

Goddard, John, and Kirby, Andrew. 1976 *An Introduction to Factor Analysis.* London: Institute of British Geographers.

Gorsuch, Richard L. 1983 *Factor Analysis,* 2d ed. Hillsdale, N.J.: Lawrence Erlbaum.

Gosling, James J. 1985 "Patterns of Influence and Choice in the Wisconsin Budgetary Process." *Legislative Studies Quarterly* 10 (Nov.): 457–82.

Grizzle, Gloria. 1985 "Performance Measures for Budget Justifications: Developing a Selection Strategy." *Public Productivity Review* 9:328–41.

Grizzle, Gloria. 1986 "Does Budget Format Really Govern the Actions of Budget Makers?" *Public Budgeting and Finance* 6 (spring): 60–70.

Gurwitt, Rob. 1993 "Legislatures: The Faces of Change." *Governing* 6 (Feb.): 29–32.

Hammond, Kenneth R.; Hamm, Robert M.; Grassia, Janet; and Pearson, Tamra. 1987 "Direct Comparison of the Efficacy of Intuititve and Analytical Cognition in Expert Judgment." *IEEE Transactions on Systems, Man, and Cybernetics* 17 (Sept./Oct.): 753–70.

Hammond, Kenneth R.; McClelland, Gary H.; and Mumpower, Jeryl. 1980 *Human Judgment and Decision Making: Theories, Methods, and Procedures.* New York: Praeger Publishers.

Heaphey, James J., and Balutis, Alan P., eds. 1975 *Legislative Staffing: A Comparative Perspective.* New York: Wiley.

Jones, Rich. 1992 "The Legislatures." *The Book of the States, 1992–1993,* ed. 29. Lexington, Ky.: Council of State Governments, 124–32.

Kaiser, H.F. 1974 "An Index of Factorial Simplicity." *Psychometrika* 39:31–36.

Kiel, L. Douglas, and Elliot, Euel. 1992 "Budgets as Dynamic Systems: Change, Variation, Time, and Budgetary Heuristics." *Journal of Public Administration Research and Theory* 2:2:139–56.

Kim, Jae-On, and Mueller, Charles W. 1978 *Introduction to Factor Analysis.* Beverly Hills, Calif.: Sage.

Lindblom, Charles. 1959 "The Science of Muddling Through." *Public Administration Review* 19:79–88.

Lorr, Maurice. 1983 *Cluster Analysis for Social Scientists.* San Francisco: Jossey-Bass.

Mezzich, Juan E., and Solomon, Herbert. 1980 *Taxonomy and Behavioral Science: Comparative Performance of Grouping Methods.* London: Academic Press.

Milstein, Mike M., and Jennings, Robert E. 1973 *Educational Policy-making and the State Legislature: The New York Experience.* New York: Praeger.

Mooney, Christopher A. 1991 "Information Sources in State Legislative Decision Making." *Legislative Studies Quarterly* 16 (Aug.): 445–55.

Mooney, Christopher A. 1995. "Citizens, Structures and Sister States: Influences on State Legislative Professionalism." *Legislative Studies Quarterly* 20 (Feb.): 47–67.

Norusis, Marija J. 1986 *Advanced Statistics SPSS/PC +.* Chicago: SPSS, Inc.

Oppenheimer, Bruce I. 1983 "How Legislatures Shape Policy and Budgets." *Legislative Studies Quarterly* 8 (Nov): 551–97.

Premchand, A. 1983 *Government Budgeting and Expenditure Controls: Theory and Practice.* Washington, D.C.: International Monetary Fund.

Rohrbaugh, John, and Wehr, Paul. 1978 "Judgment Analysis in Policy Formation: A New Method for Improving Public Participation." *Public Opinion Quarterly* 42 (winter): 521–32.

Romesburg, H. Charles. 1984 *Cluster Analysis for Researchers.* Belmont, Calif.: Lifetime Learning.

Rosenthal, Alan. 1981 *Legislative Life.* New York: Harper and Row.

Rosenthal, Alan. 1990 *Governors and Legislatures: Contending Powers.* Washington, D.C.: CQ Press.

Rosenthal, Alan, and Forth, Rod. 1978 "The Assembly Line: Law Production in the American States." *Legislative Studies Quarterly* 3:265–91.

Rubin, Irene S. 1993 *The Politics of Public Budgeting,* 2d ed. Chatham, N.J.: Chatham House.

Rummel, R.J. 1970 *Applied Factor Analysis.* Evanston, Ill.: Northwestern University Press.

Simon, Herbert A. 1957 *Administrative Behavior,* 2d ed. Glencoe, Ill.: Free Press.

Skok, James E. 1980 "Federal Funds and State Legislatures: Executive-Legislative Conflict in State Government." *Public Administration Review* 40 (Nov./Dec.): 561–67.

Stanford, Karen A. 1992 "State Budget Deliberations: Do Legislators Have a Strategy?" *Public Administration Review* 52 (Jan./Feb.): 16–26.

Steiner, Gilbert Y., and Gove, Samuel K. 1960 *Legislative Politics in Illinois.* Urbana: University of Illinois Press.

Stewart, Thomas R. 1988 "Judgment Analysis: Procedures." In Berndt Brehmer and C.R.B. Joyce, eds. *Human Judgment: The Social Judgment Theory View.* Holland: Elsevier, 41–74.

Stewart, Thomas R., and Gelberd, Linda. 1976 "Analysis of Judgment Policy: A New Approach for Citizen Participation in Planning." *American Institute of Planners Journal* (Jan.): 33–41.

Thurmaier, Kurt. 1992 "Budgetary Decisionmaking in Central Budget Bureaus: An Experiment." *Journal of Public Administration Research and Theory* 2 (Oct.): 463–87.

Thurmaier, Kurt. 1995 "Responsive and Responsible Budgeteers: An Experiment in Budgetary Decisionmaking." *Public Administration Review* 55:5:448–60.

Waller, William S. 1988 "Brunswikian Research in Accounting and Audting." In Berndt Brehmer and C.R.B. Joyce, eds. *Human Judgement: The SJT View.* Holland: Elsevier, 247–72.

Welch, Susan, and Peters, John G. 1977 *Legislative Reform and Public Policy.* New York: Praeger.

Whorton, Joseph W. Jr.; Feldt, James A.; and Dunn, Delmer D. 1989 "Exploring the Values Underlying

Evaluation of Research: A Social Judgment Analysis." *Knowledge in Society: International Journal of Knowledge Transfer* 1 (winter); 40–55.

Wildavsky, Aaron. 1992 *The New Politics of the Budgetary Process,* 2d ed. New York: HarperCollins.

Willoughby, Katherine G. 1991a "The Decision Making Orientations of State Government Budget Analysts: Rational or Intuitive Thinkers?" Ph.D. diss., University of Georgia.

Willoughby, Katherine G. 1991b "Gender-Based Wage Gap: The Case of the State Government Budget Analyst." *Review of Public Personnel Administration* 12:33–46.

Willoughby, Katherine G. 1993a "Decision Making Orientations of State Government Budget Analysts: Rationalists or Incrementalists?" *Public Budgeting and Financial Management* 5 (winter): 67–114.

Willoughby, Katherine G. 1993b "Patterns of Behavior: Factors Influencing the Spending Judgments of Public Budgeters." In Thomas D. Lynch and Lawrence L. Martin, eds. *Handbook of Comparative Public Budgeting and Financial Management.* New York: Marcel Dekker, 103–33.

Worman, Michael A. 1975 "Role Consensus and Conflict in Legislative Staffing." In Heaphey and Balutis, eds.

Zapan, Jure. 1982 *Clustering of Large Data Sets.* Chichester, U.K: John Wiley.

PART 4

THE BUDGET PROCESS

While it is not always clear exactly what the goals of particular budget processes were supposed to be, or whether the goals were achieved in full or in part, there is widespread agreement among budget scholars, staff, and elected officials, that process matters, and that process changes are important. In fact, participants may overemphasize the ability of process to influence outcomes and recommend process changes when other policy choices would be more effective.

The first three pieces in this part describe three successive major changes in budget process at the national level, what they were supposed to achieve, and how they were supposed to achieve it. One deals with the Congressional Budget Reform Act of 1974, one with Gramm-Rudman-Hollings deficit reduction act in 1985, and the third with the Budget Enforcement Act of 1990. Read together, they suggest that budget process is responsive to major problems, perhaps with some lag time, despite the reluctance of those who wield budget power to give it up. These descriptions of budget process help flesh out the argument made by Joseph White in the opening essay of Part 1, that budgets do not always grow because there is a complex budget process with many checks and balances in it.

In the fourth selection, Gloria Grizzle addresses the question of what difference does it make how information is laid out for decision makers in the budget. Does the format of the budget, subject of so many budget reforms, influence the outcomes? This question has been difficult to answer, because such a large variety of factors influence budget outcomes. How can one sort out the impact of the format from these other factors? Grizzle argues that format does make a difference to how budgets are discussed and analyzed, a sort of intermediate effect. Format reforms make the budget more transparent and agencies more accountable to elected officials and the public. Whether they affect the totals or distribution of expenditures remains an open question.

Jerry McCaffery and John Bowman look at process a little differently. They illustrate the direct role of citizens in the budget process through initiative and referenda, with the example of Proposition 13 in California, a watershed event that changed state and local relations and that became an icon for lower taxes and reduced scope of the public sector. Proposition 13 was a citizen rebellion against increasing property taxes as the value of homes rose in California, a vivid testimony to the effects of years of public officials not listening to the voters. It was thus an example of democracy in action, citizens taking control. But Proposition 13 may not have been a good policy choice, and the exercise of direct democracy may be more effective as a threat than as a fact. If elected officials don't listen, citizens will vote for tax limits. The message was not lost on thousands of elected officials throughout the country.

CHAPTER 16

TEN YEARS OF THE BUDGET ACT
Still Searching for Controls

LOUIS FISHER

The Budget Act of 1974 has led a charmed life. Rarely has a statute missed goals by such wide margins without being repealed or severely amended. Modifications have occurred in practice, of course, and yet the statute remains virtually untouched. Only in recent years has the Act encountered unfavorable reviews. For most of its existence it has been treated with respect, if not reverence.

It is this sacrosanct quality that makes analysis of the Budget Act so difficult. Even when members of Congress were appalled by the results of the budget process, most of them rallied to its defense. For much of the early years, "protect the process" functioned as an all-purpose talisman. Recent years have given rise to a different and wholly contradictory defense. If budget results are too dreadful for anyone to condone, we now learn that the results stem not from the process but rather from outside political pressures. In the language of a cliché now making the rounds: the process is not the problem; the problem is the problem.

This won't do. If the process is not the problem, why did we make such fundamental changes to the congressional budget process in 1974? No one at that time thought of explaining deficits and late appropriations by "outside forces." Such an excuse or rationalization would have been transparently lame. Congress selected a process that it thought could deal best with political forces, both internal and external.

It is not necessary, or possible, to place the "whole blame" on the Budget Act of 1974. Nor is it acceptable to absolve the Budge Act of all responsibility. The Budget Act made a difference. We can disagree on what those effects have been, but we should not now describe the Budget Act process as inconsequential. We cannot at the same time argue that the Budget Act is not responsible for deficits and late appropriations and then oppose repeal or modification because the Budget Act offers the last best hope for discipline and accountability.

We need to break with this decade-long defensiveness. We should be able to look at the original objectives of the Budget Act and determine the extent to which they have been satisfied. We should reexamine those objectives and make a judgment as to whether they make sense in terms of the institutional strengths and weaknesses of Congress. Perhaps the original objectives were misguided and yet the Budget Act, as it has evolved, offers significant benefits unforeseen by those who drafted and passed the Budget Act. If so, we should say that. But let's be candid about where we are and where we want to go.

The first part of this article reviews the general record of the Budget Act: its use as a macroeconomic tool and the growing complexity of budget resolutions. The second part identifies and evaluates nine objectives of the Budget Act.

MACROECONOMIC POLICY

The history of the Budget Act divides into two broad periods. From 1975 to 1978 a fledgling process struggled for survival. To gain the votes necessary to pass a budget resolution, the newly created House and Senate Budget Committees played an essentially accommodating role among the established authorizing, tax, and appropriations committees of Congress. At the macro level, Congress used the process principally to stimulate the economy and reduce unemployment. It deliberately subordinated the goal of budgetary restraint to economic recovery. The record on deadlines looked promising. Congress generally adhered to the Budget Act's timetable for adopting budget resolutions and passing the regular appropriations bills.

The years since 1978 have witnessed mounting deficits, inflation, and high interest rates. Citizen groups across the country advocated curbs on public spending and supplied momentum for a constitutional amendment to balance the federal budget. Congress responded by adopting a number of procedures, including reconciliation, to constrain the growth of federal domestic programs. These techniques, combined with the application of budget resolutions to credit activities and to outyears, exacerbated relations between the legislative and executive branches and within Congress itself. Budget resolutions and appropriations bills were delayed, estimates for outlays and revenues became increasingly unrealistic, and members of Congress complained that the budget process had become so time-consuming and complex that it side-tracked other essential legislative duties.

Congress first attempted a "dry run" of the budget process in 1975 (for fiscal 1976). Both houses agreed that it was important to gain experience with the main features of the Budget Act, even though full implementation would not be required until fiscal 1977. After President Ford sent his fiscal 1976 budget to Congress, the two Budget Committees prepared a first budget resolution restricted to the five aggregates: revenues, budget authority, outlays, deficit, and public debt. The committee reports subdivided the aggregates for budget authority and outlays into 16 functional categories. The breakdowns by functional category would be placed in future budget resolutions.

Both Houses of Congress adopted budget resolutions designed to stimulate the economy—the House more so than the Senate. As part of a deliberate anti-recession strategy, Congress accepted the need for a deficit higher than recommended by Ford. The congressional priority favored economic recovery over budgetary restraint. The same legislative preference was applied the next year to Ford's budget for fiscal 1977 (Table 16.1).

Final figures for budget authority greatly exceeded the estimates in the first and second budget resolutions. Nevertheless, outlays fell short of congressional expectations. This discrepancy became known as "shortfalls" in spending. Congress at first welcomed the development, accepting the news about shortfalls as evidence that the Budget Act was contributing to budgetary discipline. But shortfalls had been a chronic problem for years, reflecting a systematic and persistent bias on the part of agencies to overestimate outlays. Late congressional action on supplemental appropriations bills also made it difficult for agencies to spend available budget authority. In some cases Congress was too optimistic about the ability of agencies to implement new federal programs and expand existing ones. Finally, Congress had an incentive under the Budget Act to overestimate outlays.

Table 16.1

Congressional Action on Ford's Budgets ($ billions)

	President's Budget	First Budget Resolution	Second Budget Resolution	Actual
Fiscal 1976				
Budget Authority	$385.8	$395.8	$408.0	$415.3
Outlays	349.4	367.0	374.9	364.5
Receipts	297.5	298.2	300.8	298.1
Deficits	51.9	68.82	74.1	66.4
Fiscal 1977				
Budget Authority	$433.4	$454.2	$451.55	$465.2
Outlays	394.2	413.3	413.1	400.5
Receipts	351.3	362.5	362.5	355.6
Deficits	43.0	50.8	50.6	44.9

A high figure provided a cushion against unanticipated expenses (supplying valuable "running room") and therefore lessened the need for a third budget resolution.[1]

Under the first two years of the Carter administration, Congress continued to use the Budget Act to stimulate the economy and combat unemployment. One of its first actions, in February 1977, was the adoption of a third budget resolution for fiscal 1977 to accommodate an economic stimulus bill. The purpose of the third resolution, said the House Budget Committee, was "to arrest the sharp decline in economic activity since adoption of the second budget resolution in September [1976]."[2] Carter revised Ford's budget for fiscal 1978 to make room for the economic stimulus package. His revised budget added $6.2 billion in outlays and reduced receipts by $4.7 billion, increasing the size of the projected deficit from $57.2 billion to $68 billion. Congressional action on budget resolutions closely tracked the aggregates requested by Carter.

Carter's budget for fiscal 1979 was still basically expansionary. His message to Congress explained that his budget "provides for a continuing recovery of the nation's economy from the 1974–75 recession."[3] To provide stimulus, the budget called for an increase of $38 billion in outlays and a deficit of $61 billion. The high level of the deficit reflected his decision to reduce taxes by $25 billion "to help assure continued economic recovery and reduction in unemployment."[4]

The first budget resolution for fiscal 1979 gave Carter what he wanted in aggregates for budget authority and outlays. Because of a higher estimate for revenues by Congress, the deficit projected in the resolution was $10 billion lower than the president's budget. In the second budget resolution, Congress reduced the aggregates for budget authority, outlays, and deficit, while keeping revenue estimates at the same level (Table 16.2). The Budget Committees expressed concern about inflation, but predicted a range between 6 and 7 percent for fiscal years 1978 and 1979.[5] Inflation was much higher than 7 percent for fiscal 1979, pushing taxpayers into higher brackets. Ironically, this increased the amount of receipts and brought a reduction in the deficit.

Beginning with Carter's budget for fiscal 1980, both branches became more concerned about inflation and the need to restrain spending. Carter's budget message referred to fiscal constraint as "an imperative if we are to overcome the threat of accelerating inflation."[6] Whereas earlier reports from the House Budget Committee had placed the spotlight on unemployment and economic stimulation, the focus now fell on spending restraint, inflation control, and concern for a balanced budget. The Committee noted that the consumer price index had jumped to an annual rate of 8.8

Table 16.2

Congressional Action on Carter's Budgets ($ billions)

	President's Budget	First Budget Resolution	Second Budget Resolution	Actual
Fiscal 1978				
Budget Authority	$507.3	$503.45	$500.1	$501.5
Outlays	459.4	460.9	458.2	448.4
Receipts	401.6	396.3	397.0	399.6
Deficits	57.75	64.65	61.25	48.8
Fiscal 1979				
Budget Authority	$568.2	$568.85	$555.65	$556.7
Outlays	500.2	498.8	487.5	491.0
Receipts	439.6	447.9	448.7	463.3
Deficits	60.6	50.9	38.8	27.7
Fiscal 1980				
Budget Authority	$615.5	$604.4	$638.0	$658.8
Outlays	531.6	532.0	547.6	576.7
Receipts	502.6	509.0	517.8	517.1
Deficits	29.0	23.0	29.8	59.6
Fiscal 1981				
Budget Authority	$696.1	$697.2	$694.6	$718.4
Outlays	615.8	613.6	632.4	657.2
Receipts	600.0	613.8	605.0	599.3
Deficits	15.8	(+)0.2	27.4	57.9

percent from July to October 1978, requiring a switch from sustaining economic growth to restraining inflation.[7] The first budget resolution projected budget authority at $11 billion below Carter's budget, outlays at approximately the same level as Carter's, about $6 billion more in receipts, and therefore a deficit $23 billion instead of Carter's $29 billion estimate.

Comments during floor debate on the first budget resolution reinforce the impression that 1979 was indeed a turning point for the budget process. Robert Giaimo, chairman of the House Budget Committee, described the resolution as putting "an end to the spending pattern of recent years, when program after program year after year was given a sizeable incremental funding increase, almost regardless of its effectiveness."[8] A year later he told his colleagues: "This budget marks a departure from past years. It is not a 'spending as usual' budget. It is not loaded with fiscal sweeteners to please this group or that group or this member or that member."[9]

Although the Budget Committees assumed the posture of fiscal restraint, Congress found it difficult to control spending or the size of the deficit in fiscal years 1980 and 1981. As a means of imposing discipline, the Senate Budget Committee proposed reconciliation in the second budget resolution for fiscal 1980, requiring seven committees to cut outlays and the budget deficit by $4 billion. The House resisted, producing a deadlock that delayed adoption of the second budget resolution until November 28, more than two months past the statutory deadline. The two houses eventually agreed to strike the reconciliation instructions.

Results for fiscal 1980 were disappointing. The budget deficit ended up not at the $23 billion anticipated by the first budget resolution, or the $29.8 billion in the second resolution, or the $46.95 billion in the revised second, but at $59.6 billion. Even for fiscal 1981, when Congress for the first time enacted a full-scale reconciliation bill, budget deficits could not be controlled. Carter initially recommended a deficit of $15.8 billion, revised that two months later to $16.5 billion, and Congress (largely on the basic of higher revenue estimates) adopted a first budget resolution that called for a surplus of $200 million. As the fiscal year unfolded, the surplus evaporated and was replaced by increasingly higher predictions of deficits. Despite a reconciliation effort that reduced the deficit by about $8 billion (through a mix of spending cuts and tax increases), the final deficit soared to $57.9 billion. Total revenues were not as high as expected, while outlays far outpaced the estimates in the budget resolutions (Table 16.2).

President Reagan reworked Carter's budget for fiscal 1982 by cutting domestic spending, increasing military spending, and reducing federal taxes. The estimate for outlays was cut by $44 billion, budget authority by $37.4 billion, and receipts by $54 billion. As a result, the projected deficit rose from $27.5 billion to $45 billion. Despite major retrenchments in the Reconciliation Act of 1981, which reduced fiscal 1982 outlays by $35.2 billion, the budget continued to grow. The first budget resolution, which basically endorsed the aggregates requested by Reagan, was so out of date by the summer of 1981 that Congress preferred to adopt a pro forma second budget resolution that simply reaffirmed the numbers in the first resolution.

The Budget Committees recognized that the numbers being reaffirmed were unrealistic. When the House Budget Committee began its markup on the second resolution, it estimated the deficit at $87.2 billion.[10] The outlook for fiscal 1982 continued to deteriorate. By the time the fiscal year was over, receipts were far lower than expected, outlays had climbed $33.1 billion above Reagan's budget, and the deficit reached $110.7 billion.

Budgetary miscalculations also marred the record for fiscal 1983. Reagan's budget continued his objective of restraining domestic spending, as did the two Budget Committees (although their figures for budget authority and outlays were somewhat higher). Because of section 7 in the first budget resolution, the identical figures for budget aggregates took effect on October 1 as the second resolution without any further action by Congress. The same procedure was adopted for fiscal 1984 and fiscal 1985, allowing language in the first budget resolution to automatically trigger the second resolution if Congress failed to act by October 1. In effect, Congress eliminated the second resolution.

The recession of 1981–82 cut deeply into revenues. Outlays increased because of costs associated with unemployment compensation and other recession-related programs. Despite the cutbacks achieved through another reconciliation effort, outlays were about $50 billion above the President's budget. Congress passed a special tax bill to bring in additional revenues. Even so, the combined effects of declining receipts and rising outlays more than doubled the deficit, pushing it from the $91.5 billion estimated in Reagan's fiscal 1983 budget to $195.4 billion (Table 16.3).

In submitting his fiscal 1984 budget, President Reagan confronted new power relationships on Capitol Hill. House Democrats had picked up 26 seats during the 1982 elections, while Republican senators were hastily distancing themselves from the White House. Reagan's projected deficit of $188.8 billion triggered another attempt at reconciliation. Committees were directed to cut spending by $12.3 billion and to increase taxes by $73 billion over a three-year period. By the end of the year, however, the deficit reduction plan was derailed because of disagreements between the House and the Senate. Legislation was passed to cut outlays by $8.5 billion over the three-year period, but neither house approved tax increases to meet the reconciliation requirement.[11] The budget resolution anticipated a deficit of $169.9 billion for fiscal 1984; the actual deficit came to $185.3 billion.

Reagan's budget for fiscal 1985 produced a major stalemate. Both Houses of Congress regarded his deficit projections as unacceptable: a deficit of $180.4 billion for fiscal 1985, with higher levels

Table 16.3

Congressional Action on Reagan's Budgets ($ billions)

	President's Budget	First Budget Resolution	Second Budget Resolution	Actual
Fiscal 1982				
Budget Authority	$772.4	$770.9	$770.9	$779.9
Outlays	695.3	695.4	695.4	728.4
Receipts	650.8	657.8	657.8	617.8
Deficits	45.0	37.65	37.65	110.6
Fiscal 1983				
Budget Authority	$801.9	$822.4	$822.4	$866.7
Outlays	757.6	769.8	769.8	796.0
Receipts	666.1	665.9	665.9	600.6
Deficits	91.5	103.9	103.9	195.4
Fiscal 1984				
Budget Authority	$900.1	$919.5*	$919.5*	$949.8
Outlays	848.5	849.5*	849.5*	851.8
Receipts	659.7	679.6	679.6	666.5
Deficits	188.8	169.9	169.9	185.3
Fiscal 1985				
Budget Authority	$1,006.5	$1,021.4	$1,021.4	$1,064.9 est.
Outlays	925.5	932.1	932.1	959.1 est.
Receipts	745.1	750.9	750.9	736.9 est.
Deficits	180.4	181.2	181.2	222.2 est.

* Excludes reserve fund amounts.

after that. Although both houses fought for months over reductions in defense spending and enacted a deficit reduction act (producing a "downpayment" of about $150 billion over a three-year period), the budget resolution adopted on October 1, 1984 called for a deficit of $181.1 billion for fiscal 1985 followed by larger deficits in fiscal years 1986 and 1987.

Over the first six years of the Budget Act, Congress and the president were generally accurate in estimating receipts (even underestimating them in fiscal 1979 when inflation pushed taxpayers into higher brackets). The record since then has been one of massive overestimates. President Reagan overestimated receipts by $33 billion in fiscal 1982 and by $65.5 billion in fiscal 1983. Congress also overestimated receipts for those years. Outlays have generally exceeded the projections of Congress and the president. This pattern of overestimating receipts and underestimating outlays resulted in deficits far above presidential and congressional projections.

GROWING COMPLEXITY OF BUDGET RESOLUTONS

The legislative history of the Budget Act suggests that budget resolutions were meant to be used for two purposes: debating macroeconomic policy and deciding broad issues of budgetary priorities. Congressman Richard Bolling, serving as House floor manager for the budget reform bill, said that the budget resolution "does not get into particular programs, agencies, appropriations, or projects. To do so would destroy the utility of the congressional budget process as an instrument for making national economic policy."[12]

Despite Bolling's admonition, budget resolutions became a means of voting (at least indirectly) on specific programs and activities. The preparation and review of budget resolutions opened the door to duplication of effort and to conflict among committees. Much of this was inevitable and predictable. Congressman George Mahon, who objected that the House Budget Committee had invaded the jurisdiction of his Appropriations Committee, admitted that it was "certainly appropriate for the [budget] committee to have an awareness of individual spending programs in order to arrive at its recommendations."[13]

The budget process presents many opportunities for the Budget Committees to consider program details. First, the authorization and appropriations committees supply program details in their March 15 reports to the Budget Committees. Second, testimony at Budget Committee hearings covers program details, even though the legislative history of the Budget Act suggests that the Budget Committee hearings should concern "economic conditions and national priorities at a high level of aggregation."[14] Third, votes within the Budget Committees on amendments to the proposed budget resolutions often focus on specific program interests. Fourth, the Budget Committee reports permit discussion of program details, as do amendments offered on the floor during action on budget resolutions. Fifth, although budget resolutions are restricted to aggregates and functional categories, every member of Congress has access to committee markup documents or computerized backup sheets to determine whether a particular program is covered by a budget resolution. Members are basically program oriented and want to know if a budget resolution allows room for projects and programs of interest.

With each passing year the debates on budget resolutions descended ever more deeply into program details. The number of floor amendments offered to budget resolutions increased each year. On the House side, the number of floor amendments submitted for the first budget resolution climbed from 6 in fiscal 1976, to 16 for each of the fiscal years 1977 and 1978, to 26 for fiscal 1979, and to 50 for fiscal 1980. The House responded by adopting restrictive rules to limit floor amendments. These rules, in turn, became increasingly complex as the House attempted to balance two conflicting needs. There was a need to expedite action on budget resolutions, but members also insisted on an opportunity to offer alternative packages. Both Houses of Congress spent increasing amounts of time debating budget resolutions.

Budget resolutions grew longer and more complex. At first restricted to aggregates and functional categories, they added sections on outyears, reconciliation, deferred enrollment, federal credit, and other objectives. Section 301(a) of the Budget Act permits the first budget resolution to include (in addition to aggregates and functional categories) "such other matters relating to the budget as may be appropriate to carry out the purposes of this Act." Section 301(b)(2) also allows the Budget Committees to place in the first budget resolution any procedure "which is considered appropriate to carry out the purposes of this Act."

Aggregates and Functional Categories

The first two budget resolutions, adopted for the "dry run" in fiscal 1976 and the transition quarter (July 1 to September 30, 1976), included only the five aggregates. The resolutions did not subdivide the aggregates into functional categories. For fiscal 1977, Congress implemented the Budget Act in full by providing in the budget resolutions a breakdown of budget authority and outlays into 17 functional categories.

Beginning in fiscal 1980, the first budget resolution added a multi-year perspective by adopting aggregates for fiscal years 1981 and 1982. The second budget resolution not only established aggregates for those years but provided functional subtotals as well. Budget resolutions now supply a detailed breakdown for four years: the current year, the upcoming year, and two years beyond that. Each functional category, for the four years, contains dollar amounts for new budget authority, outlays, and credit operations. The budget resolutions for fiscal 1977 ran about four to five pages. Contemporary resolutions are now ten times that long.

Reconciliation

The first budget resolution for fiscal 1980 asked committees to recommend savings and suggest ways to reduce unobligated and unexpended balances. It also identified the need to control off-budget spending. As part of a reconciliation effort, the Senate adopted instructions in the second budget resolution to direct seven committees to cut $3.6 billion in spending. The House refused to go along, arguing that its committees had already made substantial cuts to meet the targets of the first resolution and that it would be unreasonable to ask them to redo their work at such a late stage. As finally adopted, the second resolution resolution merely reiterated the request for legislative savings.

This experience convinced both houses that reconciliation could not work as the Budget Act intended. Reconciliation was supposed to come in the fall, after action on the second budget resolution, and was actually used that way for the second resolution for fiscal 1976, which directed the tax committees to reduce revenues by $6.4 billion. However, the effort in fiscal 1980 to use reconciliation in the fall to cut spending was so unsuccessful that Congress conceded that full-scale reconciliation had to be timed for the first resolution in the spring.

Reconciliation instructions, itemizing for each committee the proposed reductions in budget authority and outlays, began with the first budget resolution for fiscal 1981. House and Senate committees were directed to cut spending and raise revenues. Some of the savings resulted from pushing spending from fiscal 1981 to the next year. To counter this kind of tactic in the future, the Budget Committees decided to require reconciliation savings over a multi-year period. For example, the first budget resolution for fiscal 1982 included reconciliation instructions for fiscal years 1982, 1983, and 1984. Similarly, the first budget resolution for fiscal year 1983 applied reconciliation to fiscal years 1983, 1984, and 1985.

Reconciliation instructions for fiscal 1984 reached out to fiscal years 1985 and 1986, but Congress became deadlocked over the amounts, particularly the requirement of $73 billion in revenues. The end of the year arrived without action by Congress to implement reconciliation, although legislation in April and July 1984 achieved some of the outlay savings.

Credit Budget

Congress initiated a "credit budget" in the first budget resolution for fiscal 1981. The credit budget included both the loans made directly by the federal government and the loans it guarantees. The first budget resolution established dollar limits for new direct loan obligations and for commitments on new primary loan guarantees. It also divided new direct loan obligations into two categories: off-budget and on-budget, placing dollar ceilings on each. The second budget resolution for that year established dollar levels for new direct loan obligations, new primary loan guarantee commitments, and a third element of the credit budget: new secondary loan guarantee commitments. New direct loan obligations were again divided into off-budget components. For both the first and the second budget resolutions, the aggregates for the credit budget represented targets rather than binding ceilings.

In adopting a credit budget for fiscal 1982, Congress allocated the three basic aggregates of the credit budget among 19 functional categories. Limits (expressed as a sense-of-Congress resolution) were placed on the operation of the Federal Financing Bank and the off-budget and on-budget portions of new direct loan obligations. The second budget resolution for fiscal 1982 was passed in form identical to the first.

The credit totals for fiscal 1982, even though subdivided by functional category, were advisory rather than binding. For fiscal 1983 Congress attempted to impose mandatory limits on federal credit. It did this by incorporating in the front part of the first resolution (covering new budget authority and outlays for each functional category) specific dollar levels for three aspects of the credit budget: new direct loan obligations, new primary loan guarantee commitments, and new secondary loan guarantee commitments. On October 1, those figures were automatically adopted as part of the second budget resolution, and that practice has been followed for fiscal years 1984 and 1985. However, the procedure has yet to produce binding and enforceable ceilings on federal credit.

Off-Budget Spending

Closely associated with the credit budget are the efforts to control off-budget spending, most of which consists of lending programs. For example, off-budget outlays result from the transactions of the Federal Financing Bank and the Rural Electrification Administration, both of which have been excluded from the unified budget. The first budget resolution for fiscal 1980 recommended that "a way be found within the congressional budget process to relate accurately the estimates of off-budget federal entities and capital expenditures in the unified budget." The second resolution for that year reaffirmed the commitment to relate the outlays of off-budget federal agencies to the congressional budget. It estimated that off-budget outlays (and hence off-budget deficits) were about $16 billion for fiscal 1980.

In initiating a credit budget, the first budget resolution for fiscal 1981 divided the target ceiling for new direct loan obligations into its off-budget and on-budget components. After increasing the dollar amounts for each component, the second resolution reiterated the limits for off-budget and on-budget direct loan programs.

For fiscal 1982, the first budget resolution established the sense of Congress that the president and Congress, through the appropriations process, should limit the off-budget lending activity of the federal government to a level not to exceed $17.73 billion. In its second budget resolution for fiscal 1982, Congress reaffirmed the first resolution.

When Congress incorporated credit figures in the front part of the first budget resolution for fiscal 1983, it did not separate direct loan programs into off-budget and on-budget. It did state, later in the resolution, that it was the sense of Congress that budget resolutions should reflect "the full range of fiscal activities of the federal government" and that each resolution, beginning with the first resolution for fiscal 1984, "shall list, for each functional category, the off-budget activities associated with that category, as well as the new budget authority, outlays, new direct loan obligations, new primary loan guarantee commitments, and new secondary loan guarantee commitments associated with that category." On October 1 the first budget resolution for fiscal 1983 automatically became the second resolution for that year. That material was not included in the budget resolutions for fiscal 1984 and fiscal 1985.

Deferred Enrollment

Under section 301(b)(1) of the Budget Act, the first budget resolution may require that all or certain bills and resolutions providing new budget authority, or providing new spending authority described as entitlements, shall not be enrolled until the second budget resolution has been agreed to. Moreover, if reconciliation is required under the provisions of a second budget resolution, enrollment may be delayed until Congress has completed action on reconciliation.

In the spring resolution for fiscal 1981, Congress for the first time prohibited the enrollment of bills that exceeded the budget authority allowed by that resolution until Congress completed action on the fall resolution and any reconciliation required. Congress also delayed the enrollment of bills that would reduce federal revenues in fiscal 1981 by more than $100 million. Deferred enrollment was used again in the first budget resolution for fiscal 1982. In prohibiting the enrollment of bills that provided new budget authority or entitlements in excess of the budget resolution, Congress specifically selected as ceilings "the appropriate allocation or subdivision made pursuant to section 302" of the Budget Act. Enrollment of bills in excess of those ceilings could not occur until Congress completed action on the second budget resolution and any reconciliation required.

The House Budget Committee included deferred enrollment in the first budget resolution for fiscal 1983, tightening the process still further by selecting as ceilings "the allocations or subdivisions required by section 302(b) of the Budget Act." The effect was to adopt not merely the 302(a) allocations by committee but the 302(b) allocations by subcommittee. Congressman Jamie L. Whitten, the chairman of the House Appropriations Committee, successfully offered an amendment to delete the deferred enrollment procedure. He objected that it put another obstacle in the way of timely action on appropriations and placed unreasonable controls on discretionary spending while exerting little control over entitlement programs.[15]

A SCORECARD FOR THE BUDGET ACT

How well has the Budget Act performed over the years? To what degree has it met its objectives? To some the answer is self-evident. The House Rules Committee noted in 1984: "Critics of the budget process often forget what fiscal decision-making was like prior to the adoption of the Congressional Budget Act."[16] The apparent message: "It's bad now but you should have seen it before." Clearly the contemporary record is bad; it is less clear that the record ten years ago was worse. That must be demonstrated by comparing the two periods. Nevertheless, there are those who question whether the Budget Act contains goals tangible enough to measure.[17] Such a position makes the Act virtually immune either to praise or criticism; it would be incapable of evaluation. However, the objectives of the Budget Act are sufficiently well-defined by the statutory language and its legislative history.

Restrain Spending

Several studies conclude that the Budget Act was meant to be neutral toward spending. They claim that the process could be used for higher or lower spending, bigger or smaller deficits.[18] It would seem difficult to argue that Congress overhauled its budget process, set up new committees, and created new institutions, such as the Congressional Budget Office, simply to make the process neutral toward spending. The overwhelming motivation was to restrain the growth of federal spending. The legislative record on spending had produced, by the campaign year 1972, an acrimonious battle between President Nixon and Congress. They found themselves locked in a collision course over a spending ceiling of $250 billion for fiscal 1973. In an unusual attack on the internal procedures of a co-equal branch, Nixon criticized the "hoary and traditional procedure of the Congress, which now permits action on the various spending programs as if they were unrelated and independent actions."[19] In a nationwide radio address he warned that "excessive spending by the Congress might cause a congressional tax increase in 1973."[20]

The premise of congressional irresponsibility led to the creation of the Joint Study Committee on Budget Control in October 1972. Given the political climate from 1972 to 1974, it is incongruous to characterize the Budget Act as neutral toward spending. There was a clear expectation that it would give Congress more effective ways to restrain spending. Congressman Robert Giaimo, testifying as the chairman of the House Budget Commieee, offered this perspective in 1978. "We don't need a Budget Act to enable us to spend more. We need a Budget Act in order to impose a discipline on ourselves, which was the very purpose of the Budget Act, to establish and change priorities, but within an overall discipline, within overall limitations."[21] Four years later, speaking now as a private citizen, he described the Budget Act of 1974 as "basically a contract whereby Congress agreed to curb its undisciplined spending habits and the president gave up his impoundment powers.[22]

This link between spending constraint and impoundment control is important to understand. The history of impoundment legislation reinforces the view that the Budget Act was meant to restrain federal spending. Each house had passed legislation in 1973 to limit the president's authority to impound funds. However, members were reluctant to present a bill to the president because such legislation had a "pro-spending" quality. The public would interpret the bill as another effort by Congress to spend more than the president wanted, offering further proof of uninhibited congressional spending. A statutory control on impoundment would be politically acceptable only if Congress attached it to a measure that promised greater congressional control and responsibility over spending. That union was achieved by making the Impoundment Control Act the final title of the Budget Act.

Has the Budget Act restrained spending? No one can predict what would have resulted without the Act, but a number of procedures associated with the Act have encouraged higher spending; the preferred status of entitlements (more on that later); the March 15 estimates that invite greater advocacy from congressional committees; the existence of the Budget Committees as another access point for members of Congress and lobbyists rebuffed by the authorization and appropriation committees; the use of "current services" and "current policy" to adjust the spending levels of every program for inflation (a giant hold-harmless procedure); and the adoption of generous aggregates in budget resolutions to serve not as ceilings on congressional spending but as floors. The process allows members of Congress to justify amendments to increase appropriations by arguing that the higher spending would still be within the totals sanctioned by the budget resolution. Instead of keeping within the president's aggregates, members can vote on bountiful ceilings in budget resolutions and then tell their constituents that they have "stayed within the budget." Which budget—the president's or Congress'—is never made clear.[23]

The growth of federal spending has not been slowed by the Budget Act. Taking the Office of Management and Budget's figures for budget outlays computed in constant fiscal 1972 prices, outlays climbed from $183 billion to $266.4 billion from fiscal 1966 through fiscal 1975, or an annual increase over that ten-year period of 4.2 percent. This period is distorted by the buildup in fiscal years 1967 and 1968 to finance the Vietnam War, and the years immediately following that benefited from decreases in national defense spending (Table 16.4). It also includes the 11.9 percent increase for fiscal 1975, which reflected a dramatic rise in payments to individuals. Over the next decade, from fiscal 1976 through fiscal 1985, outlays rose from $279.5 billion to an estimated $397 billion, or an average annual increase of 4.2 percent.

Reduce Deficits

By curbing spending, Congress hoped to limit the size of federal deficits. The Joint Study Committee began its report by noting that the federal government had been in a deficit position 37 times in the 54 years since 1920. Of the 16 years of budget surplus, 10 occurred before 1931. In the 43 years since 1931, only six years yielded surpluses. Other than the World War II years, the largest

Table 16.4

Budget Outlays in Constant Fiscal 1972 Prices

Fiscal Year	Outlays ($ billions)	Dollar Increase	Percent Increase
1960	143.3	—	—
1961	149.9	6.6	4.6
1962	162.4	12.5	8.3
1963	163.0	0.6	0.4
1964	170.4	6.6	4.0
1965	166.8	−3.6	−2.1
1966	183.0	16.2	9.7
1967	207.6	24.6	13.4
1968	224.7	17.1	8.2
1969	220.3	−4.4	−2.0
1970	220.3	—	0.0
1971	222.7	2.4	1.1
1972	230.7	8.0	3.6
1973	233.3	2.6	1.1
1974	238.0	4.7	2.0
1975	266.4	28.4	11.9
1976	279.5	13.1	4.9
TQ	69.9		
1977	286.3	6.8	2.4
1978	300.2	13.9	4.8
1979	304.4	4.2	1.4
1980	324.4	20.0	6.6
1981	337.1	12.7	3.9
1982	346.1	8.7	2.6
1983	360.1	14.0	4.0
1984	366.3	6.2	1.7
1985	397.0	30.7	8.4

Source: Office of Management and Budget, *Historical Tables: Budget of the United States Government, Fiscal Year 1986*, Table 6.1

deficits had appeared in recent years. Not only were deficits a fixture of contemporary budgets, they were growing larger. Deficits reached $23 billion for fiscal years 1971 and 1972 and $14.8 billion for fiscal 1973. For their time (though not for ours), the deficits were immense. The Committee concluded that the "constant continuation of deficits plus their increasing size illustrates the need for Congress to obtain better control over the budget."[24]

In the ten years from fiscal 1966 through fiscal 1975, deficits averaged $14.8 billion a year. For the decade from fiscal 1976 through fiscal 1985, the average annual deficit increased to about $100 billion a year (Table 16.5). The future looks worse. The budget resolution adopted on October 1, 1984, called for deficits of $192.7 billion for fiscal 1986 and $207.6 billion for fiscal 1987, based on rather optimistic assumptions about economic growth. Any slowdown or downturn in the economy would push those figures much higher.

Voting on Aggregates

The Joint Study Committee concluded that "the failure to arrive at congressional budget decisions on an overall basis has been a contributory factor" in the continuation of deficits. No committee

Table 16.5

Budget Deficits

Fiscal Year	Deficit ($ billions)	Fiscal Year	Deficit ($ billions)
1960	+0.3	1975	45.1
1961	3.4	1976	66.4
1962	7.1	TQ	13.0
1963	4.8	1977	44.9
1964	5.9	1978	48.8
1965	1.6	1979	27.7
1966	3.8	1980	59.6
1967	8.7	1981	57.9
1968	25.2	1982	110.6
1969	+3.2	1983	195.4
1970	2.8	1984	185.3
1971	23.0	1985	222.2 est.
1972	23.4		
1973	14.8		
1974	4.7		

was responsible for deciding "whether or not total outlays are appropriate in view of the current situation . . . As a result, each spending bill tends to be considered by Congress as a separate entity, and any assessment of relative priorities among spending programs for the most part is made solely within the context of the bill before Congress."[25]

The Budget Act supposedly supplied the antidote for the fragmented splintered system that had operated up to 1974. "It is almost inconceivable," said the House Rules Committee a decade later, "that Congress would return to the old system of acting independently on each piece of budgetary legislation and then adding up the results and calling that a budget."[26] A study that same year claimed that prior to the Budget Act "Congress examined programs and considered appropriations individually, so that it had neither a coherent view of aggregate levels of federal spending nor a view of how individual programs fit into those aggregate spending levels."[27]

These descriptions of conditions before 1974 are overdrawn and incorrect. Such stereotypes are used to exaggerate the virtues of the new system over the old. In fact, the "old system" was not nearly so fragmented, incoherent, and irresponsible. The Joint Committee on Reduction of Federal Expenditures prepared "scorekeeping reports" and circulated them on a regular basis. These reports were printed in the *Congressional Record*. Members of Congress therefore knew, from month to month, how legislative actions compared to the president's budget. Through informal techniques, Congress managed to coordinate its actions and change the shape of the president's budget without exceeding its size. The results reveal a systematic pattern, not chaos. This is apparent by examining the five-year period immediately preceding the Budget Act. From fiscal 1969 through fiscal 1973, appropriations bills were $30.9 billion below the president's budgets. Over that same period, backdoors and mandatory entitlements exceeded the president's budgets by $30.5 billion.[28] Basically, Congress was cutting defense and foreign assistance while adding to such programs as Labor-HEW and environmental protection. The totals, however, remained within the ballpark of the president's budget. Congressional spending was not widely out of control.

The Budget Act assumed that members of Congress would behave more responsibly if they voted explicitly on budget aggregates and faced up to totals, rather than deciding spending actions in "piecemeal" fashion on separate appropriations and legislative bills. Members presumably

Table 16.6

Dates for Adopting Budget Resolutions

Fiscal Year	First Budget Resolution (May 15 Deadline)	Second Budget Resolution (September 15 Deadline)
1976	May 14	December 12
1977	May 13	September 16
1978	May 17	September 15
1979	May 17	September 23
1980	May 24	November 28
1981	June 12	November 20
1982	May 21	December 10*
1983	June 23	**
1984	June 23	**
1985	October 1	**

* The second resolution merely "reaffirmed" the figures in the first resolution.
** No second resolution was adopted for these years. The first resolution automatically became binding as the second resolution on October 1.

wanted to vote on budget totals and be responsible for them. However, the behavior of Congress has been increasingly one of irresponsibility. Congressman David Obey recently remarked:

> Under the existing conditions the only kind of budget resolution you can pass today is one that lies. We did it under Carter, we have done it under Reagan, and we are going to do it under every president for as long as any of us are here, unless we change the system, because you cannot get members under the existing system to face up to what the real numbers do. You always wind up having phony economic assumptions and all kinds of phony numbers on estimating.[29]

Members have discovered a number of ingenious methods to avoid a vote on aggregates, especially deficits. First they adopted a second resolution in 1981 that "reaffirmed" the totals in the first resolution, even when everyone knew that the earlier figures were wholly unrealistic. In a burst of euphemism, supporters of the Reagan administration quite charitably called the figures "noncurrent economic assumptions." A second step away from responsibility was the automatic device that triggered the second resolution in 1982, 1983 and 1984, thus dispensing with the need to vote on higher deficits. The aggregates in the spring resolution, no matter how unrealistic or discredited, become the fall resolution if Congress does not act by October 1 (Table 16.6). It is evident that Congress has no intention of debating and passing a second resolution that will reflect the conditions of the fall months. Still another step toward unaccountability was to tuck the higher deficits into a revised second resolution adopted the following spring. No separate vote or debate on the higher deficits is conducted because by that time Congress turns its attention toward the upcoming year.

In 1979 the House figured out a way to handle increases in the public debt limit without voting on them. Instead of taking a separate vote on a debt limit bill, the new procedures lifts the public debt limit from the first budget resolution and places it in a joint resolution, which is then "deemed" to have passed the House. The only House action is to incorporate by reference the debt limit in the budget resolution. This may seem an efficient system, since one vote serves two purposes, but the public debt limit rarely commands much attention or interest during debate on the budget resolution, and recent budget resolutions have been notoriously unrealistic about deficits.

Another step away from accountability occurred in 1983 when the House Budget Committee advocated an "adjustment resolution" that would raise budget totals to take into account "technical and economic adjustments." This category included changes in economic assumptions and technical estimates, such as inflation and unemployment rates. The adjustment resolution would have been handled with fast-track procedures and limited time for floor debate. Fortunately, the Senate refused to go along, partly because the vagueness of "technical estimates" invited misuse and escapist budgeting. The availability of an adjustment resolution could serve as an incentive for adopting unrealistic and overly optimistic figures in the first resolution, with realism inserted at some later stage, where it would have less visibility and accountability.

Coordinate Appropriations and Revenues

Congress adopted two strategies in 1974 to control deficits: placing restraints on spending and consciously relating outlays to revenues. The Joint Study Committee condemned the failure to decide congressional budget decisions on an overall basis. To correct this deficiency, the Committee proposed that each house create a Budget Committee to review the budget on a comprehensive basis. The House committee would have 21 members, the Senate committee 15. In both cases, one-third of the members would be drawn from the Appropriations Committees, one-third from the tax committees, and one-third from the legislative committees.

In essence, the Joint Study Committee wanted the Budget Committees to play a coordinating role between the interests of the appropriations and tax panels. The Budget Act, however, followed a different course. Instead of the appropriations and tax committees having 14 of the 21 seats on the House Budget Committee, the number dropped to 10 out of 23. The allotment of 10 seats remained fixed as the Budget Committee grew to 25 members in 1975, 30 members in 1981, and 31 members in 1983. The two-thirds control therefore declined over the years to one-third. In the case of the Senate Budget Committee, the Budget Act did not provide specific quotas for the Appropriations and Finance Committees.

Allen Schick concluded that the "most far-reaching dilution of Budget Committee power came as a by-product of the shift from coordinative to representative committees." If the Joint Committee recommendations had prevailed, the Budget Committees "would have operated as agents of the revenue and Appropriations Committees, not as independent power centers," and their position would have been strengthened "by the status of these powerful committees."[30] A coordinative approach might have forced the two money committees to keep spending and revenues in better balance, avoiding the extraordinary deficits of the decade following 1974.

The Joint Study Committee also wanted a tax surcharge imposed if receipts plus the "appropriate deficit" (as specified in the concurrent resolutions) did not equal estimated expenditures in the final concurrent resolution. The surcharge would not have been triggered unless the discrepancy exceeded one percent.[31] This procedure was omitted from the Budget Act.

The years since 1974 have not been characterized by close coordination between appropriations and revenues. The Budget Committees never recruited a staff capable of dealing with the jurisdiction of the tax committees, which consists of far more than revenues. Because of such programs as Social Security, Medicare, as well as interest on the public debt, the tax committees are responsible for as much spending as the Appropriations Committees. As late as 1982, Congressman Leon Panetta could testify that Congress had created "almost a hemorrhage" on the revenue side by adopting various tax credits and deductions: "We are just now beginning to look at the whole picture, and the whole picture includes revenues. . . ."[32] During the Reagan years, reconciliation became the means of reaching the expenditures within the jurisdiction of the tax committees. Over half of the spending reductions in the reconciliation acts of 1981 and 1982 were within the jurisdiction of the House Ways and Means Committee and the Senate Finance Committee.[33]

Control Backdoors

The Joint Study Committee expressed alarm about the "splintering" of the appropriations process. Of the spending estimated for fiscal 1974, the Committee reported that only 44 percent was associated with items to be considered in appropriations bills. [34] Even some of that amount was pro forma, since entitlement legislation required the Appropriations Committees to provide whatever amounts were necessary to meet legal obligations. Another form of backdoor spending was contract authority, which allowed agencies to obligate funds prior to receiving appropriations. The Appropriations Committees must later provide funds to "liquidate" these obligations. Congress passed the Budget Act shortly after the Clean Water Act of 1972, which provided $18 billion in contract authority over a three-year period. The third backdoor was borrowing authority, allowing agencies to borrow from the Treasury Department or from the public without coming to Congress for appropriations.

The Budget Act of 1974 placed controls on new backdoors. New forms of contract or borrowing authority would function essentially as ordinary authorizations. Agencies could not enter into obligations without an appropriation. Title IV of the Budget Act therefore puts new contract and borrowing authority through the front door. However, Title IV does not apply to certain types of spending authority which were exempted, such as 90 percent self-financed trust funds or outlays of government corporations. Entitlements, then, were given preferred treatment, even though the drafters of the Budget Act recognized that entitlements represented the most explosive growth area of the federal budget. [35]

Although the Budget Act has helped curb new backdoors, the growth of entitlement spending continued to undermine the position of the Appropriations Committees. In 1970 the Appropriations Committees had responsibility for two-thirds of gross outlays; other committees had responsibility for only one-third. The responsibility is now almost evenly divided. If we take into account the entitlements that are subject to annual appropriations, an exercise that is purely ministerial and mechanical on the part of the Appropriations Committees, the other committees are now responsible for more than half of budget outlays. The bulk of this consists of Social Security, Medicare, and interest on the public debt, which are within the jurisdiction of the tax committees. [36]

Debate Budget Priorities

The Joint Study Committee anticipated that its proposals would lead to "an improved congressional system for determining relative funding priorities." [37] One of the five declared purposes of the Budget Act is "to establish national budget priorities." To permit decision and debate on priorities, Congress adopted the system of functional categories used for decades by the executive branch.

Functional categories represented a compromise between the extremes of budget aggregates (total outlays and total budget authority) and specific line items for programs and projects. With the Budget Act it was contemplated that Congress would consider the budget in terms of 16 broad categories, such as national defense, income security, health, and agriculture. The number of functional categories has fluctuated over the years.

The choice of functional categories was partly compelled by political and practical considerations. To allocate the budget by committee jurisdiction might have exacerbated conflicts among committees. Functional categories blurred the lines, requiring "cross-walking" to convert functional allocations to committee jurisdiction. But the choice of functional categories came at a cost. For example, the functional category "Commerce and Transportation" is too broad and diffuse to allow a member of Congress to know whether the amount is too large or too small. Even the subfunctions (water transportation, ground transportation, and air transportation) are too abstract to permit reasoned debate over budget priorities. Members of Congress and their constituents do not think in such terms. Instead, the debates are framed in terms of mass transportation versus private automobiles, the deregulation of air fares, the cost of seat belts and air bags, and other specific policy questions.

Functional categories have not provided a happy medium by which members can alter budget priorities. "Transfer amendments" (proposing that funds be taken from one functional category and placed in another) are rarely successful. Members seem to follow the time-honored principle: never openly do harm. Under the old system, budget priorities could be altered indirectly by reporting an appropriations bill with less than the administration wanted, while adding more to a different appropriations bill. Members could trim the defense appropriations bill and add to the Labor-HEW appropriations bill without ever explicitly taking money from one department and giving it to another.

In short, it might have been easier to change budget priorities under the older fragmented, decentralized system than under the Budget Act of 1974. In 1980 Allen Schick estimated that Congress did more reordering of budgetary priorities "before it had a budget process than it has since."[38] More recently he remarked that "the more Congress is organized to make redistributive decisions, the less capable it is of doing so."[39]

Enact Appropriations on Time; Eliminate Continuing Resolutions

In reporting the Budget Act, the House Committee on Rules said that one of the "visible disabilities of the existing congressional budget process is the failure to complete action on appropriations bills prior to the start of the new fiscal year." The legislative schedule would be even more demanding because of action on budget resolutions. The Committee concluded that the fiscal year would have to be moved forward by three months—from July 1 to October 1—"to put an end to the continuing resolution practice."[40] The Budget Act included this change for the fiscal year.

Part of the delay in passing appropriations was related to the growth of annual authorizations. To accelerate action on appropriations, the Joint Study Committee recommended that authorization bills be enacted a year in advance of appropriations.[41] Authorizing committees found this proposal unacceptable. As a substitute procedure, the House Rules Committee established a deadline of March 31 for the enactment of authorizing legislation, reserving for itself the consideration of waivers for emergency authorizations. Authorizing committees regarded this requirement as wholly unrealistic. As modified by the Senate and the conference committee, Section 402(a) of the Budget Act adopted a deadline of May 15 for reporting authorization bills. The Act also required passage of all regular appropriations bills by early September.

The conferees on the Budget Act believed that "in the future it will be necessary to authorize programs a year or more in advance of the period for which appropriations are to be made." They expected Congress to develop a pattern of advance authorizations for programs that would be authorized on an annual or multi-year basis.[42] In recent years there has been a push for biennial budgeting—particularly for authorization bills. Nevertheless, there has been no uniform trend toward advance authorizations or two-year authorizations. In fact, most of the direction has been toward shorter cycles: converting programs authorized on a permanent basis to a two-year cycle or moving two-year authorizations to an annual review.[43]

For the first few years after the Budget Act, the record of action on appropriations bills looked promising. For fiscal years 1977 and 1978, most of the appropriations were passed by the House in June and enacted by October1. The record slipped a bit in fiscal 1979 and has grown worse ever since.[44] Before the Budget Act it was highly unusual if all twelve months of a fiscal year went by without passing the regular appropriations bills. It is now a common occurrence.[45] From fiscal 1968 through fiscal 1975, only two appropriations bills were under a continuing resolution for an entire fiscal year. From fiscal 1976 through fiscal 1985, that figure jumped to 27.[46]

Congress has fallen into the habit of placing entire appropriations bills in a continuing resolution.

For example, the giant continuing resolution (P.L. 98–473) passed at the end of the 98th Congress contains the full text of five regular appropriations bills: Interior, Military Construction, Foreign Assistance, Defense, and Transportation. This is a phenomenon that is entirely post-1974.

The timetable is now far behind what it was before 1974, even with the additional three months gained by changing the fiscal year. The Appropriations Committees used to blame late authorizations for their failure to pass appropriations on time. Now they have a multitude of new explanations: late action on budget resolutions, late action on 302(a) and 302(b) allocations, and the deferred enrollment process. Appropriations bills are also delayed because of the prospect of contentious legislative riders on such issues as abortion, school prayer, and school busing.

To eliminate some of these excuses, the House of Representatives could resolve the present conflict between the Budget Act and House Rule XXI. The Act merely requires that authorizations be reported by May 15. Under House rules, appropriations bills may not be reported unless authorizations have been enacted. It would be helpful to allow appropriations bills to come to the floor after a certain date, such as June 1, regardless of progress on authorization bills and budget resolutions. The Appropriations Committees can be expected to stay within the dollar amounts recommended by authorizing committees in the most recent phase of their deliberations: committee markup, the reported bill, the bill passed by the House, or the amount provided in a conference report. A June 1 go-ahead date would encourage authorizing committees to move more quickly.

Independent Institutional Expertise

The Joint Study Committee recommended that the Budget Committees be provided with a joint staff headed by a legislative budget director. The director and the staff would be "highly trained, professional and nonpartisan" to give Congress "its own center of congressional budgetary operations. . . ."[47] The Budget Act created staffs for each of the Budget Committees, established the Congressional Budget Office, and directed the General Accounting Office to redouble its efforts on program evaluation. These steps were meant to offset the technical advantage of the Office of Management and Budget and the agencies.

The process established by the Budget Act supplies more information and a better understanding of macroeconomic developments, but improvements in these areas do not automatically translate into more responsible or intelligent decisions on the budget. Information can clarify; it can also confuse. Congressman John Dingell offered this observation in 1984:

> What we have done over the past decade is to create a budget process that is so complex as to be incomprehensible to almost everyone. Most of the members do not understand it beyond a superficial level. The press does not understand it. The business community does not understand it. The financial community does not understand it. And most important of all, the public does not understand it.[48]

The power of the purse is not merely a means by which Congress controls the executive branch. It is also the way the public controls government. Any process that confuses legislators and the public, no matter how much it may delight the conceptual dreams of technicians, is too costly for a democracy. In a critique of the obfuscation practiced by the legal community, Justice Cardozo warned that "justice is not there unless there is also understanding."[49] Similarly, without comprehension no budget process is worth maintaining.

The Budget Act has encouraged multi-year budgeting, an approach that began decades ago. Congress enacted legislation in 1956 to require five-year estimates by the executive branch.[50] The

Legislative Reorganization Act of 1970 also required five-year estimates.[51] Congress discovered in 1980 that a multi-year approach was needed for reconciliation to prevent committees from meeting their assigned cuts by pushing costs from the current year to the next year. However, information needed for a multi-year focus can also foster irresponsibility. Instead of confronting reality in the current year and making hard choices, Congress can salve its conscience by concocting rosy projections for the outyears. These figures give members momentary peace of mind but never materialize. They are figments in the purest sense. Outyear projections invite procrastination. The aggregates required for a balanced budget are never in the current year, or upcoming year, but always three to five years out.

Control Presidential Impoundment

The Nixon administration's attempt to withhold appropriated funds sparked a series of confrontations during the 92d and 93d Congresses.[52] Members of Congress protested that the administration was using impoundment to substitute its sense of budget priorities for those enacted and funded by Congress. The Impoundment Control Act of 1974 (Title X of the Budget Act) narrows the president's authority to accumulate budgetary reserves. The Act recognizes two types of impoundment: rescissions and deferrals. If the president wants to rescind (cancel) budget authority, he must obtain the support of both houses within 45 days of continuous session. If he wants to merely delay the obligation of budget authority, either house could disapprove at any time.

This latter control, the one-house legislative veto, is now invalid as a result of the Supreme Court's decision in *INS* v. *Chadha* (1983). But Congress had already begun to disapprove deferrals by placing language in the regular or supplemental appropriations bills. Since this type of disapproval is included in a bill sent to the president for his signature, it is permissible under Court's test.

The effect of Title X has been to regularize the impoundment process, giving the administration a solid base of legal support while allowing Congress to overturn deferrals it disagees with. Significantly, the rescission process puts the burden on the president to secure the support of both houses within a limited number of days. Otherwise, the congressional priorities are to be respected and carried out.

Suggestions have been made in recent years to change the burden of the rescission process by requiring Congress to enact a joint resolution of disapproval to prevent the president from rescinding funds. Of course the president could veto the joint resolution, placing on Congress the additional burden of mustering a two-thirds majority in each house for the override. Besides altering the balance between the branches, this reform would entail multiple votes and extraordinary majorities to restate a budgetary choice already expressed in a duly enacted statute. Congress might have to act four times: enacting an appropriation bill which the president then vetoes; overriding the veto; passing a joint resolution to disapprove a rescission; and voting to override this veto. Members of Congress have regarded this repetition of a congressional preference as demeaning to their institution.[53]

CONCLUSIONS

Some of the objectives in 1974 could have been achieved without creating a complex procedure dependent on the passage of budget resolutions. Title IV has been effective in restricting new backdoors. Title X has been helpful in resolving impoundment disputes between Congress and the president. The Congressional Budget Office has established itself as a valuable agency for estimating the cost of pending legislation, performing scorekeeping tasks, and making macro-economic projections.

Authorization bills have been speeded up somewhat because of the May 15 deadline for reporting. Congress could accelerate action on appropriations bills by allowing them to be reported for floor action after June 1. This change would resolve the present inconsistency between the Budget Act and House Rule XXI. A June 1 green light would make it possible to complete action on appropriations bills before the start of the fiscal year. As matters now stand, the delays resulting from the adoption of budget resolutions and Section 302 allocations make it practically impossible for Congress to complete action on other than a handful of appropriations bills by October 1.

What purpose is served by passing budget resolutions? They appear to encourage spending, delay appropriations, confuse the members and the public, and invite escapist, irresponsible budgeting. It is time to rethink the rationale behind budget resolutions and determine whether the liabilities far exceed the benefits. The risks are high when an inherently decentralized Congress tries to imitate the president by producing a budget. As Mark Kamlet and David Mowery warn:

> The organizational requirements of comprehensive budgeting and fiscal policy formulation are quite different from those of representation, accessibility, and pluralism that have historically (although not consistently) been characteristic of Congress. The U.S. Congress is not an institution whose sole mission is the preparation of the annual budget; as such, it is unrealistic to expect Congress to adhere to the same complex procedures as those employed in the executive branch institutions whose primary responsibility is the preparation of the annual budget.[54]

Without budget resolutions, committees would not have to spend time producing March 15 reports; there would be more floor time to act on authorizing, appropriations, and tax bills; members would not have a reason to offer amendments to bring appropriations up to the ceiling provided by a budget resolution; and the phrases "below budget" and "above budget" would once again have meaning. Congressional performance could be scored unambiguously against a single benchmark: the president's budget.

As matters stand now, there is chronic confusion about which budget is the budget: the president's, the first budget resolution, the second budget resolution, the second budget resolution revised, or a succession of reestimates, updates, and revised baselines. Dozens of legislators are able to put together their own "budgets," complete with aggregates and breakdowns for functional categories. Elimination of budget resolutions might reinvigorate the president's budget, which has become increasingly irresponsible since 1974. It may well be that the politics of congressional budgeting has undermined the central tenet of the Budget and Accounting Act of 1921: the president's responsibility to submit and stand behind an executive budget.

Some members continue to support budget resolutions, despite misgivings about their contents, because they fear that a failure on the part of Congress to pass a resolution would send a signal to the country that Congress was incapable of controlling the budget. These fears might be misplaced. There is little evidence that the public (or even the "attentive public" or the "opinion leaders") have much more than a vague notion about the mechanics of the Budget Act. But the public can comprehend the bottom line: deficits of enormous size. Using the Budget Act to reduce the deficit from $200 billion to $150 billion a year will not be enough to win public support or confidence.

Doing away with budget resolutions need not return us to the Dark Ages (or to the "Old System"). Budget Committees can continue to monitor backdoors, issue "early warning reports" to alert Congress to budgetary excesses, and propose improvements in the budget process. The Budget Committees can be reshaped to perform as explicit agents of the party leadership. They could be made responsible for coordinating the spending decisions of the authorizing committees (entitlements), for coordinating appropriations and revenues, and exploring action needed in such areas as permanent appropriations, tax expenditures, federal credit, and off-budget agencies. Without having to propose and pass budget resolutions, the Budget Committees might play a more important role in recommending fiscal policy and pursuing multi-year strategies.

NOTES

1. Congressional Budget Office, "Estimates of Federal Budget Outlays," Staff Working Paper, February 1978. See also CBO's "Analysis of the Shortfall in Federal Budget Outlays for Fiscal Year 1978," Staff Working Paper, March 1979, and House Committee on the Budget, "Federal Budget Outlay Estimates: A Growing Problem," Committee Print, April 1979.

2. U.S., Congress, House, H. Rept. No. 12, 95th Cong., 1st sess., 1977, p. 4.

3. *The Budget of the United States Government, Fiscal Year 1979* (Washington, D.C.: Government Printing Office, 1979), p. 3.

4. Ibid., p. 4.

5. H. Rept. No. 1456, 95th Cong., 2d sess., 1978, p. 12; U.S., Congress, Senate, S. Rept. No. 1124, 95th Cong., 2d sess., 1978, p. 13.

6. *The Budget of the United States Government, Fiscal Year 1980* (Washington, D.C.: Government Printing Office, 1980), p. 3.

7. H. Rept No. 95, 96th Cong., 1st sess., 1979, p. 21.

8. 125 *Congressional Record* 9028 (1979).

9. 126 *Congressional Record* 8809 (1980).

10. H. Rept. No. 369, 97th Cong., 1st sess., 1981, p. 6.

11. House Committee on the Budget, "A Review of the Reconciliation Process," Committee Print (October, 1984), pp. 40–45.

12. 120 *Congressional Record* 19673 (1974).

13. 121 *Congressional Record* 36155 (1975).

14. S. Rept. No. 579, 93d Cong., 1st sess., 1973, p. 19.

15. See Whitten's statement in "Congressional Budget Process," *Hearings* before the House Committee on Rules, 97th Cong., 2d sess., 1982, pp. 311–12.

16. H. Rept. No. 1152, pt. 1, 98th Cong., 2d sess., 1984, p. 5.

17. John W. Ellwood, "Budget Control in a Redistributive Environment," in *Making Economic Policy in Congress,* Allen Schick, ed. (Washington, D.C.: American Enterprise Institute, 1983), p. 73.

18. Allen Schick, *Congress and Money* (Washington, D.C.: The Urban Institute, 1980), pp. 72–74; John M. Plaffy, "The Congressional Budget Process," in *Mandate for Leadership II* (Washington, D.C.: Heritage Foundation, 1984), p. 388.

19. *Public Papers of the Presidents of the United States. Richard Nixon, 1972* (Washington, D.C.: Government Printing Office, 1974), p. 742.

20. Ibid., p. 964.

21. U.S., Congress, Senate, "Can Congress Control the Power of the Purse?," *Hearings* before the Senate Committee on the Budget, 95th Cong., 2d sess., 1978, p. 13.

22. "Congress Must Get Serious," *The Washington Post* (June 4, 1982), p. A19.

23. For more on the incentives for higher spending provided by the Budget Act, see Louis Fisher, "The Budget Act of 1974: A Further Loss of Spending Control," in W. Thomas Wander et al., *Congressional Budgeting: Politics, Process and Power* (Baltimore, Md.: Johns Hopkins University Press, 1984), pp. 170–189.

24. H. Rept. No. 147, 93d Cong., 1st sess., 1973, p. 1.

25. Ibid.

26. H. Rept. No. 1152, pt. 1, 98th Cong., 2d sess., 1984, p. 5.

27. Charles S. Konigsberg, "Amending the Congressional Budget Act of 1974," *Journal of Legislation* 11 (Winter 1984), p. 94.

28. H. Rept, NO. 147, 93d Cong., 1st sess., 1973, p. 30.

29. U.S., Congress, House, "Congressional Budget Process," pt. 1, *Hearings* before the House Committee on Rules, 97th Cong., 2d sess., 1982, p. 239.

30. Schick, *Congress and Money,* p. 84.

31. H. Rept. No. 147, 1973, p. 7.

32. "Congressional Budget Process," pt. 1, *Hearings* before the House Committee on Rules, p. 27.

33. Ibid., p. 345.

34. H. Rept. No. 147, 1973, p. 10.

35. Ibid., pp. 12–13.

36. Statistics are provided by James L. Blum, Assistant Director for Budget Analysis in the Congressional Budget Office, reprinted in "Issue Presentations Before the Rules Committee Task Force on the Budget Process," prepared by the House Committee on Rules, 98th Cong., 2d sess., 1984, pp. 25–26.

37. H. Rept. No. 147, 1973, p. 4.

38. Schick, *Congress and Money,* p. 332.

39. Allen Schick, ed., *Making Economic Policy in Congress* (Washington, D.C.: American Enterprise Institute, 1983), p. 4.

40. H. Rept. No. 658, 93d Cong., 1st sess., 1973, p. 31.

41. H. Rept., No. 147, 1973, p. 30.

42. H. Rept. No. 1101, 93d Cong., 2d sess., 1974, p. 56.

43. Louis Fisher, "Annual Authorizations: Durable Roadblocks to Biennial Budgeting," *Public Budgeting & Finance* 3 (Spring 1983), pp. 25–30.

44. See the author's chart reprinted in "Issue Presentations Before the Rules Committee Task Force on the Budget Process," p. 81.

45. Ibid., p. 83.

46. H. Rept. No. 1152, pt. 1, 98th Cong., 2d sess., 1984, p. 43.

47. H. Rept. No. 147, 1973, p. 3.

48. "Congressional Budget Process," *Hearings* before the House Committee on Rules, 1984, p. 161.

49. Anon Y. Mous, "The Speech of Judges: A Dissenting Opinion," *Virginia Law Review,* 29 (1943), p. 638.

50. 70 Stat. 652 (1956).

51. 84 Stat. 1140, 1169 (sec. 221), 1173–74 (see. 252) (1970).

52. Louis Fisher, *Presidential Spending Power* (Princeton: University Press, 1975), pp. 175–201.

53. See remarks by Senator Sam Ervin, Jr., 119 *Congressional Record* 15236 (1973).

54. Mark S. Kamlet and David C. Mowery, "The First Decade of the Congressional Budget Act: Legislative Imitation and Adaptation in Budgeting," unpublished manuscript, January 1985, p. 18.

CHAPTER 17

DEFICIT POLITICS AND CONSTITUTIONAL GOVERNMENT
The Impact of Gramm-Rudman-Hollings

LANCE T. LELOUP, BARBARA LUCK GRAHAM, AND STACEY BARWICK

The 1985 Balanced Budget and Emergency Deficit Control Act, known as Gramm-Rudman-Hollings or simply as Gramm-Rudman, is one of the most controversial and misunderstood acts of Congress in recent years. It not only proposed fixed deficit targets and required mandatory budget cuts if targets were not met, but included the most far-reaching changes in congressional budget procedures since the passage of the Budget and Impoundment Control Act of 1974. It also raised serious constitutional issues of separation of powers and the relative roles of Congress and the president in guiding the fiscal affairs of the nation. Despite the fact that the law's rapid passage and tumultuous first year provide limited grounds for generalization, we believe that Gramm-Rudman is more than an isolated event. It can be understood more accurately as the most dramatic in a series of procedural adaptations by a frustrated Congress in response to increasing policy and political constraints.

In an article published in the Autumn 1986 volume of this journal, Harry Havens reviewed the origins of Gramm-Rudman, the deficit reduction machinery, and the actual sequester of $11.7 billion in early 1986.[1] In this article, we address an overlapping but essentially different set of issues: the relationship of the adoption of the law to recent political and fiscal trends, constitutional issues surrounding the role of Congress and the president, and the impact of the law on Congress itself. We review the emergence and the passage of the bill in 1985, mandatory deficit reduction and budget process changes, budget politics in 1986, and the effect of court decisions on Gramm-Rudman. We conclude by assessing the impact of Gramm-Rudman, considering both the short-term prospects for change as well as possible long-term consequences of the law. We begin by examining the changes in national budgeting over the past decades that created the context for such an experiment to be launched.

INCREASING CONSTRAINTS AND GROWING INSTABILITY IN THE CONGRESSIONAL BUDGET PROCESS

For half a century the congressional appropriations process was a model of stability and predictability.[2] Since the late 1960s, however, congressional decisions on taxing and spending have been characterized by instability, adaptation, and experimentation. The Budget and Impoundment Control Act of 1974 was the major statutory change, but budgeting procedures have remained in flux in subsequent years. Gramm-Rudman is the most radical experiment. Congressional performance in budgeting over the past two decades can be explained on the basis of several theoretical factors: the behavioral motivations of members of Congress, perceptions of constitutional imbalance between legislative and executive branches, and fundamental changes in the structure of the budget itself. A full examination of these factors is beyond the scope of this study, but attention to some of the underlying forces is essential to understand deficit reduction efforts.

Gramm-Rudman-Hollings emerged as a result of increasing political and policy constraints that have destabilized the budget process, particularly in Congress. Policy constraints have increased the pressure on the legislature while narrowing members' discretion. The result has been procedural instability: changes in rules, timing, voting alignments, committee roles, leadership actions, and coalition building strategies. Ultimately, we believe, these political and policy constraints led a frustrated Congress to try a mandatory process in an attempt to check burgeoning budget deficits. Four constraints in particular served to reduce flexibility and help explain the volatility in congressional budgeting.

1. *Growing inflexibility caused by changes in budget composition.* Changes in the composition of the budget, the growth of entitlements and multiyear spending commitments have rendered the federal budget increasingly inflexible for decision makers.[3] These well-documented changes in the composition of the budget created both political and technical constraints. With outlays composed largely of social security, health entitlements, interest on the debt, and a growing defense share, the range of expenditures available for annual manipulation has been sharply reduced. The shrinkage in the 1980s of the so-called nondefense discretionary portion of the budget from 25 percent to around 17 percent has exacerbated the situation. Not only does a smaller component remain to be cut, but congressional resolve not to make further domestic spending cuts has hardened.

2. *The increasing vulnerability of budget totals of changes in aggregate economic performance.* National budgeting has increasingly become a multiyear process based on projections and estimates. Budget totals are increasingly vulnerable to changes in aggregate economic performance. For example, a decrease in annual GNP growth of one percent below the estimate can increase deficits by a total of $90 billion in five years. Estimation errors between projected and actual economic growth since 1976 have averaged 1.15 percent for OMB and .98 percent for CBO.[4] Difficult cuts achieved at high political costs can evaporate overnight when aggregate economic performance and the resulting budget baselines are reestimated.

3. *Historically large, chronic structural budget deficits.* The deficits themselves have become the dominant policy constraint. The five year revenue loss from the Economic Recovery Tax Act of 1981 (ERTA) of $635 billion was not compensated by expenditure reductions, leading to the chronic structural budget deficits that ensued. By late 1981 economic and budget projections revealed rapidly growing outyear deficits exacerbated by a recession. Table 17.1 compares deficit estimates in the presidential and congressional budgets with actual deficits. Congress and the president found themselves chasing a moving target as actual deficits consistently exceeded policy expectations. The growing deficits and decreasing flexibility in spending and revenue totals began a series of ad hoc budget process changes in the 1980s.

4. *Actions taken by the president to reduce congressional options.* The actions of the president in the 1980s increased policy inflexibility, further exacerbating procedural instability in congressional budgeting. While the proposals and the pronouncements of the president have long been recognized as a key determinant of congressional decision making,[5] the establishment of tight presidential parameters in concert with deficits, problematic economic projections, and growing outlay inflexibility created a uniquely restrictive setting for congressional budgeting in the 1980s.

Table 17.1

Comparison of Annual Deficits ($ billions)

FY	President's Budget	Binding Congressional Budget Resolution	Actual
1986	180.00	171.90	220.70
1985	180.40	181.20	212.30
1984	188.80	169.90	185.30
1983	91.50	103.90	195.40
1982	45.00	37.65	110.60
1981	15.80	27.40	57.90
1980	29.00	29.80	59.60
1979	60.60	38.80	27.70
1978	57.75	61.25	48.80
1977	43.00	50.60	44.90
1976	51.90	74.10	66.50

Source: Congressional Research Service: Congressional Budget Office, 1986.

Instead of maintaining an active budgetary role throughout his presidency, after 1981 Ronald Reagan engaged in a series of changing political strategies, varying levels of White House participation in an attempt to achieve administration objectives.[6] Using the executive budget, the veto threat, and other actions, the president established additional constraints prior to congressional consideration, most notably a fixed rate of real growth for defense and a non-negotiable stance on revenue increases. While the president, like the Congress, is subject to the limitations imposed by structural deficits and mandatory spending, the Reagan administration was more concerned about long-term ideological goals than the deficits. Congress, more short-term oriented, struggled with its procedures and processes in an attempt to control the deficits.

In the face of these growing political and policy constraints, the congressional budget process showed the signs of strain. Because the budget process created by the 1974 Budget Act remained unpopular with many members of Congress, particularly key committee chairs, reformers were leery of formally revising the law. As a result, much of the procedural adaptation in the 1980s was informal but highly significant. Perhaps most important was the shift of reconciliation towards the beginning of the procedure and its institutionalization as a regular part of the budget process.[7] In addition, the second concurrent resolution which had proved to be ineffectual, was effectively dropped after 1982. Provisions were added to the first resolution specifying that it would become binding if no second resolution was passed.

While these two changes may arguably be seen as strengthening the process, many of the procedural developments clearly reflected an unraveling of the process.[8] Supplemental appropriations were increasingly used to avoid discipline or replace cuts. Fewer appropriations bills were passed on time, leading some to conclude that the situation was worse than it had been before 1974. As a result, more spending bills, both authorizations and appropriations, were lumped together in huge omnibus packages. These massive spending bills not only invited nongermane amendments of every description, but were increasingly difficult to pass. Shutdown of the federal government often seemed to be the only way to break an impasse. Some authorization bills were never passed, leading to an increase in appropriations not authorized by law, a violation of House and Senate rules.[9] Finally, procedural controls and enforcement mechanisms seemed to weaken while waivers to the budget act increased.

Leaders in the House and Senate continued to complain about the constant budget and deficit crises while considering ways to improve congressional control. Numerous committees and task forces reviewed the budget process and recommended changes. Perhaps the most comprehensive review of the congressional budget process was conducted by Representative Anthony Beilenson (D-CA) whose House Rules Committee Task Force recommended a comprehensive revision.[10] Those recommendations, largely ignored in 1984, would prove important when Congress struggled with Gramm-Rudman-Hollings the next year.

Despite dissatisfaction with the budget process, Congress actually made substantial budget cuts in the 1980s. Although deficits remained in the $200 billion range, without several major budget-tightening measures passed in the 1980s, deficits would have been in the $300 billion range. These difficult and divisive decisions only heightened frustration. Greater attention to macrobudgeting, shifting strategies, and informal changes in the budget process had failed to dent the deficit problem. Late in the session in 1985 a group of Senators fixed upon an idea to force deficit reduction, finally making it the top priority of Congress.

DEFICIT POLITICS: FORGING A MANDATORY SOLUTION

The Original Gramm-Rudman-Hollings Plan

When Senators Phil Gramm (R-TX), Warren Rudman (R-NH), and Ernest Hollings (D-SC) introduced their mandatory budget-balancing amendment to the debt ceiling extension (H.J.Res. 372) on 25 September 1985, they probably did not anticipate the degree to which the issue would dominate Congress for the rest of the year. As the deficit continued to grow and the budget stalemate of 1985 dragged into late summer, both Rudman and Gramm's staffs were working on extraordinary methods of forcing deficit reductions. Hollings had long advocated a budget "freeze" as a means to control the deficit. Coordinating their efforts, they fell in line behind Gramm's proposal for fixed deficit targets and a mandatory sequester—across-the-board cuts—if Congress failed to meet those targets on their own. Congress had five years to reduce the deficit to zero. The philosophy of the mandatory approach, as explained by the sponsors, was not actually to resort to indiscriminate cuts. Rather, the process was to serve as a forcing mechanism, creating such an unattractive alternative that Congress would reach deficit targets on their own. In case they did not, the sponsors found the automatic cuts preferable to huge deficits.

The Gramm-Rudman-Hollings amendment had several other key provisions. It exempted social security from automatic cuts, but specified that half of the cuts would come from entitlements and other federal retirement programs. The other half would come from other programs including defense procurement. The amendment called for changing the congressional budget process, advancing the timetable, and attempting to increase enforcement mechanisms. Finally, the plan specified a process to trigger automatic cuts based on estimates made jointly by OMB and CBO.

Deficit reduction was an issue no one could be against. Although many senators were suspicious of such a mechanical approach, Senator Gramm had found a legislative vehicle—the debt ceiling extension—that had to pass the Senate. Several years earlier, the House had adopted a plan whereby the debt limit was extended automatically as part of the budget resolution. In the Senate, however, separate legislation was needed to enable the federal government to borrow to meet its obligations. The sponsors did not intend to allow a debt extension without their deficit reduction plan.

Despite the mixed reviews received by this plan, leaders quickly recognized its unstoppable political momentum. Democratic Senators Robert Byrd (D-WV), the minority leader, and Lawton Chiles (D-FL), the ranking minority member on the Budget Committee, offered an alternative that would reach the deficit targets by equal amounts of defense cuts, domestic cuts, and tax increases.[11] When this alternative failed to gain support, they worked with Majority Leader Robert Dole (R-KS) and Budget Committee Chair Peter Domenici (R-NM) to make the original amendment more palatable. In a comment to reporters he later regretted making, Senator Rudman called his bill, "a bad idea whose time has come." This seemed to sum up well the reaction of most senators who on October 9 approved it by a vote of 75–24.[12]

The House Response

Across the rotunda in the House of Representatives, the dominant reaction of majority Democrats was frustration and anger. Animosity towards Phil Gramm, who had helped orchestrate Reagan's 1981 budget plan before he switched parties, remained high. Many members felt that the plan allowed the president to avoid all responsibility for the deficits. Some felt their own Democratic leaders had failed to seize the initiative on deficits and had been left completely on the defensive. Serious opposition to the Gramm-Rudman-Hollings plan centered on several key elements:

The programs subject to automatic cuts. Opponents felt that the plan as passed by the Senate was unfair and unbalanced because cuts would fall disproportionately on domestic social programs. Few were anxious to throw social security into the pool of vulnerable programs, but felt that revenues and other exempt programs should be considered for reducing the deficit as well.

The impact on defense. The actual share of cuts to be levied on defense was in dispute. Members feared that cuts would be "irrational," shielding slow-spending weapons procurement while damaging fast-spending categories such as personnel, operations and maintenance. If the president declared a national security emergency to avoid defense cuts, it was not clear whether the cuts would be made up on the domestic side.

The impact on the economy. The original amendment provided that in the case of a recession (negative or no real growth for four consecutive quarters), the automatic cuts would not take effect. Opponents, however, felt this exemption was inadequate and would eliminate the ability of the government to use discretionary fiscal policy to manage the economy.

The power of the president. Opponents feared that one result of the plan was a massive transfer of budgetary power from the Congress to the president. While proponents disputed this charge, it was uncertain in the original amendment exactly how much discretion the president would have.

The constitutionality of the plan. Members questioned if it was constitutional for one Congress to bind the hands of future Congresses—whether it was within the doctrine of separation of powers for the legislature to pass a law mandating that the executive make certain cuts. It was also not certain that if part of the law were determined to be unconstitutional, other parts would remain operative.

Despite the concerns, having extended the debt ceiling two months earlier, the House opted to move directly to conference with the Senate. House leaders agreed in principle with some form of automatic cuts; so it was clear from early October 1985 on that some sort of dramatic new process would be enacted. The first conference convened on October 16 amidst vast publicity and high levels of emotion. It was a strange reversal of the legislative process. Gramm-Rudman had never been subjected to legislative hearings or committee markup; the conference was the first opportunity to examine some of the details of the plan. House leaders appointed forty-eight conferees to negotiate with the nine Senate managers.

The speed with which Gramm-Rudman appeared on the political landscape not only caught the House unprepared, but the White House as well. The administration quickly endorsed the concept, but various officials expressed reservations. OMB Director James Miller raised several constitutional issues in his appearance before the committee while supporting the basic approach. Secretary of Defense Caspar Weinberger was less enthusiastic, indicating that he had grave doubts about the impact of Gramm-Rudman on national defense. "We can't have our defense and our security policy be a total prisoner of a rigid formula designed to reduce the budget."[13] Nonetheless, on the highly charged issue of the deficit, the administration was in no better position to oppose Gramm-Rudman than the House Democrats.

The conference committee was simply too large to resolve the divisive issues. As the negotiators remained in deadlock at the end of October, facing default by the government on November 1, each set of conferees reported separate versions back to their respective houses. The House passed its own version of a mandatory deficit reduction plan in a near party-line vote of 249–140.[14] Even liberal Democratic members who opposed the plan voted for it to prevent passage of the Senate version. The House version altered the deficit targets and allowed fewer cuts if real economic growth slipped below an annual rate of three percent. The Senate adopted a revised version of its own. Concerned over the constitutional role of CBO, the revised Senate plan introduced the Comptroller General of the GAO into the trigger process to certify the OMB/CBO figures and issue final sequester instructions to the president.

Although each body continued to insist on its own version, the partisan rhetoric obscured the fact that the House and Senate already were in agreement on the broad outlines and most of the details of mandatory deficit reduction. This was particularly true of the far-reaching changes in the congressional budget process which had been included in the legislation. Many of the recommendations of the Beilenson plan had been incorporated into both versions. With imminent threats of government default and headlines about draconian budget cuts, these important procedural developments were largely overlooked. Differences between the House and Senate remained on protection of Medicare, the FY 86 deficit target, the technical question of whether deficit targets would be scored on budget authority or outlays, and the severability of any unconstitutional portion of the new process.

Compromise and Final Passage

As the next date for default, November 15, neared, and as President Reagan prepared to leave for Geneva to meet Soviet leader Mikhail Gorbachev, combatants on both sides agreed to yet another temporary extension of borrowing authority. The treasury calculated that the next default would occur on December 12. Following the early November votes, a second, smaller conference was appointed. Most of the real progress was made, however, by a select group of negotiators working behind closed doors. House Majority Whip Thomas Foley (D-WA), House Democratic Caucus Chair Richard Gephardt (D-MO), Senate Finance Chair Robert Packwood (R-OR), and Senate Budget Chair Domenici hammered out the key compromises. The break in the impasse came when Senate negotiators offered to split mandatory cuts equally between defense and domestic programs. House leaders accepted and in turn agreed to delay the FY 86 cuts until March and backed off on their insistence that if any part of the bill was found to be unconstitutional, the entire process would be negated. They also agreed to the role of GAO, which many believed would solve the constitutional separation of powers issue raised by the involvement of CBO. Although a few difficult issues remained, the deadlock had been broken.

House Democrats were reassured when conferees agreed that if defense cuts were blocked by the president for national security reasons, no cuts would be made in other programs. On December 11 both chambers approved the compromise plan. After full day of floor debate, the Senate approved by a 61–31 margin.[15] While proponents continued to extoll the virtues of the plan, opponents like Senator Patrick Moynihan (D-NY) called the bill a "suicide pact." After Senate

Table 17.2

Revised Budget and Deficit Reduction Process Under Gramm-Rudman-Hollings

Action	To Be Completed By
President submits budget	Monday after January 3
CBO report to Congress	February 15
Committees submit views and estimates to budget committees	February 25
Senate Budget Committee reports budget resolution	April 1
Congress passes budget resolution	April 15
House Appropriations Committee reports appropriations bills	June 10
Congress passes reconciliation bill	June 15
House passes all appropriations bills	June 30
Initial economic, revenue, outlay and deficit projections made by OMB and CBO	August 15
OMB and CBO report tentative contents of sequester order to GAO	August 20
GAO issues deficit and sequester report to the president	August 25
President issues sequester order	September 1
Fiscal year begins and sequest order takes effect	October 1
OMB and CBO issues revised projections based on subsequent congressional action	October 5
GAO issues revised sequester report to president	October 10
Final sequester order becomes effective	October 15
GAO issues compliance report on sequester order	November 15

Source: Balanced Budget and Emergency Deficit Control Act of 1985.

passage, the House approved by a 271–154 vote; 153 Republicans and 118 Democrats voted for the bill.[16] The next day, despite some apparent misgivings, President Reagan signed the bill, noting that it was "an important step toward putting our fiscal house in order." Just hours after the bill was signed into law, Representative Mike Synar (D-OK) filed suit in federal district court for the District of Columbia challenging the constitutionality of the law. He would later be joined in the suit by a dozen other members and a public employees union, and still later, found his challenge supported by the United States Justice Department.

THE BALANCED BUDGET AND EMERGENCY DEFICIT CONTROL ACT OF 1985

Gramm-Rudman-Hollings as finally passed by Congress and signed by the president, retained the fundamental forcing mechanism devised by the sponsors. It set maximum deficit levels in both the executive and legislative budget of $171.9 billion in FY 86, $144 billion in FY 87, $108 billion in FY 88, $72 billion in FY 89, $36 billion in FY 90, and no deficit by FY 91. If the estimated deficit exceeded the targets by more than $10 billion, the mandatory sequester process would take effect. A special timetable and procedures were provided for FY 86 as well as a limit on the total amount that could be sequestered.

Revision of the Congressional Budget Process

Table 17.2 shows the revised budget and deficit reduction timetable that went into effect in 1986 for FY 87 and subsequent years. Advancing the timetable, moving reconciliation to the beginning of the process, dropping the second budget resolution, and strengthening enforcement procedures in both chambers were among the most important procedural changes. The changes promised to continue the uncertainty in the relative powers and responsibilities of the money committees in Congress.

Key dates from the submission of the president's budget to the passage of spending bills were advanced. Perhaps the most important changes were the April 15 date for passage of the first resolution, the June 15 date for reconciliation, and the June 30 date for appropriations bills. The May 15 deadline for reporting authorizations, long an irritant to the standing committees, was eliminated altogether. In an attempt to force themselves to meet the deadline, Congress adopted language that attempted to prevent adjournment for the Independence Day holiday if action on spending bills was not completed.

In addition to advancing the timetable, Congress attempted to strengthen enforcement of budget reduction requirements to facilitate the goal of deficit reduction. First, totals and subtotals in the budget resolution were made binding as opposed to targets under the old process. Second, committees are given ten days to publish their internal allocations of outlays, budget authority, entitlements, and credit among its subcommittees (Section 302(b)). Legislation emanating from committees that have not done so are made subject to a point of order on the floor. This requirement allows the Budget Committees and party leaders to more closely monitor compliance with overall totals. Third, no legislation providing new budget, entitlement, or credit authority may come to the floor until a budget resolution is passed. Exempt from this constraint are bills taking effect in the next fiscal year, and House appropriations bills after May 15. Fourth, no budget resolution is in order in either house of Congress if it would exceed the maximum allowable deficit. Fifth, legislation from any committee—even committees that have made 302(b) allocations—may be subject to a point of order if it would cause the committee's allocation to be exceeded. In the House, budget, credit, and entitlement authority are covered. In the Senate, this is applied to budget authority and to estimated outlays. Finally, in the Senate, waivers of these restrictions can only be adopted with a three-fifths majority vote. In the House, waivers of conference reports, budget resolutions or reconciliation bills exceeding targets must also receive a three-fifths majority. All other provisions may be waived by a simple majority in the House.

With the exception of exempting social security and moving it "off-budget," Gramm-Rudman-Hollings moved to make the federal budget more comprehensive and realistic. Previously off-budget entities were moved on-budget; credit authority in the form of direct and guaranteed loans were made party of the president's budget. Social security, while excluded from overall totals, is included for purposes of calculating the deficit.

On the surface, the revisions of the budget process accomplished through the passage of the Gramm-Rudman plan appear to strengthen and further centralize congressional taxing and spending decisions. Both budget committees would appear to have increased their power relative to authorizing and appropriations committees. As experience with congressional budgeting in recent years has indicated, however, it takes more than legislation to change procedures and power bases in Congress. Spending committees found many ways to circumvent restrictions under the previous system. Actual enforcement continues to depend on the will of the House and Senate to use the parliamentary procedures made available to them.

The Deficit Reduction Process

House Democrats had wanted to make cuts in the FY 86 budget immediately after adoption primarily for anticipated shock value. They finally conceded this point in conference, agreeing to postpone the first cuts to 1 March 1986, and capping the total reductions. As a result, Gramm-Rudman spelled out a separate process and timetable for FY 86 and one for subsequent years. Only 7/12s of the excess deficit could be sequestered up to the maximum of $11.7 billion dollars in 1986, because only 7 months of the fiscal years remained.

The act specifies how an excess deficit is determined and the procedures for reducing it. A joint OMB/CBO report is issued in August, estimating the deficit for the coming fiscal year based on assumptions specified in the law. The Comptroller General was required under the original law to review the data, assumptions, and methodologies of the report, making a final determination of the figures in the joint OMB/CBO report.

If an excess deficit is identified, the president is required by September 1 to issue a sequestration order. The law as enacted allowed the president no flexibility in determining cuts except for a limited number of defense accounts in 1986.[18] The deficit timetable provides a month that allows, but does not require, Congress to achieve the required reductions by some other means. OMB, CBO, and GAO revise their budget and deficit estimates based on any subsequent congressional action, and GAO issues the final report to the president by October 10. The president's final sequester order goes into effect by October 15. The Comptroller General reports to Congress on compliance with the order by mid-November.

Allocating and Calculating the Reductions

Gramm-Rudman introduced the concept of "budgetary resources" to describe the budget, entitlement, and borrowing authority on which outlays are based. Since mandatory reductions are triggered by outlays, which are not directly controlled by Congress, the sequester order, must reduce budgetary resources to lower outlays by the requisite amount. Unobligated defense balances were made subject to sequestration.

As agreed in conference committee, half of the total reduction would come from defense, the rest from all other programs. Exempt programs include: interest; social security; railroad retirement; veterans' compensation and pensions; aid to families with dependent children (AFDC); supplemental security income (SSI); women, infants, children (WIC); child nutrition; food stamps; medicaid; and several other trust and claims payments and funds. Special rules for making reductions were written for unemployment, federal pay, student loans, child support enforcement, foster care and adoption assistance, and the Commodity Credit Corporation (CCC). Programs with automatic spending increases could be reduced only to the extent of reducing or abolishing the cost of living adjustments (COLAs). Percent limits on cuts were applied to health programs: medicare, veterans' medical care, community health, migrant health, and Indian health facilities and services. The controversial medicare cuts were limited to 1 percent in FY 86 and 2 percent in subsequent years.

Defense reductions are made by first calculating the savings achieved by abolishing military retirement COLAs which occur in the nondefense portion of the budget but are counted in the defense half of the cuts under Gramm-Rudman. The remaining cuts are made by computing a fixed percentage reduction in defense outlays from new budget authority and unobligated balances. Outlays from prior obligations, about 40 percent, are not subject to sequestration.

The Balanced Budget and Emergency Deficit Control Act of 1985 attempted to provide an alternative to budget stalemate. A speedier budget process with more enforcement muscle replaced the ten-year-old congressional budget process to help Congress reach its goal of a balanced budget. Yet the future of the plan very much depended on the courts, the economy, the president, and how Congress would adapt to the new requirements.

IMPLEMENTING GRAMM-RUDMAN-HOLLINGS IN 1986

As members returned to begin the second session of the 99th Congress, OMB, CBO, and GAO had already begun preparing estimates of the deficit reductions that would have to be made in the FY 86 budget. Committees geared up to attempt to meet the new deadlines in the revised congressional budget process. It was to be a session where Gramm-Rudman affected almost every operation of Congress.

Making Mandatory Reductions for FY 86

Economic and budget projections in January of 1986 confirmed that the deficit that year would exceed $220 billion—far above the fixed target in Gramm-Rudman. CBO and OMB each reported their version of the cuts on January 15, filling an entire volume of the Federal Register.[19] GAO resolved the relatively minor differences between the two estimates. On February 5 the House rejected a Republican resolution to force Congress to come up with an alternative to avoid the mandatory cuts, insuring that the new deficit reduction process would go into effect.

Harry Havens has carefully documented how the fiscal 1986 cuts were calculated using the methods described in the previous section.[20] Details of that process and the actual cuts are not reported here, but several factors bear special attention. When exempt and partially exempt programs were removed from the calculations, only 20 percent of outlays were subjected to the across-the-board cuts. The cuts fell heavily on defense personnel, operations and maintenance, procurement and research accounts. On the domestic side, cuts fell on education, health, housing, natural resources, and the activities of independent agencies. The across-the-board cuts were 4.9 percent in defense accounts and 4.3 percent in domestic accounts. Potential mandatory cuts in the FY 87 budget would be even more severe. CBO estimated that under their February estimate for a deficit of $166.6 billion, cuts for FY 87 would be 6.2 percent for defense and 8.4 percent for domestic programs. If the economy performed worse than expected, however, the deficit could rise to $194 billion requiring cuts of 14.2 percent in defense and 20.9 percent in domestic spending.[21]

On February 7 a three judge federal district court panel ruled the automatic trigger provision of the Gramm-Rudman-Hollings law unconstitutional because of the role of GAO. The lower court finding, however, cast further doubt among members about the viability of the process. Standing committees struggled to meet the new February 25 date for views and estimates to meet the earlier deadline for the budget resolution. And on 1 March 1986, cuts totaling $11.7 billion were ordered for the programs not exempted from the Gramm-Rudman scalpel.

Effects on the Congressional Budget Process

One of the first test votes on the enhanced enforcement capability under Gramm-Rudman came in March when the Senate voted 61–33 not to exempt additional loans for farmers from the Gramm-Rudman restrictions.[22] The Senate Budget Committee moved quickly under the new timetable, reporting a budget on March 19 that differed significantly from the president's. Its inclusion of significant new revenues evoked quick opposition from the White House. The Budget Committee's report was to be the last semblance of timeliness in what would become a year of missed deadlines. As April 15 passed, the new date for the concurrent resolution on the budget to be adopted, the Senate had taken no floor action. The House Budget Committee prepared its own version while waiting for the Senate to act. With bipartisan support, Senate leaders passed a $1 trillion budget on May 2, despite White House opposition. The Senate budget projected a deficit of $144 billion, the exact Gramm-Rudman target.

One of the key effects of Gramm-Rudman-Hollings became apparent during Senate consideration of the 1987 budget and the sweeping tax reform package. The new larger majorities required to waive provisions of the budget act combined with additional restrictions created the need for "offsets." This effectively meant that all amendments offered on the floor had to be "deficit neutral"; increased spending had to be compensated by outlay reductions or revenue increases somewhere else. While not eliminating all amendments, this had a dramatic impact on Senate floor procedures, making it much more difficult to amend either the budget or the tax bill.

The House followed its own tradition of partisan budgets when it adopted a budget resolution specifying a deficit of $137 billion, savings were based on sharp cuts in defense and some modest revenue increases. While funding increased for selected social programs, President Reagen labeled the House version a "radical anti-defense budget."[23] Gramm-Rudman proved to be a mixed blessing for the president and a formidable weapon for House and Senate leaders. Because of the 50–50 split in mandatory defense and domestic spending, failure to reach an alternative package of cuts would result in even greater defense cuts. Senate leaders linked acceptance of some tax increases with continuation of the president's desired defense buildup. In conference, however, House Democratic negotiators refused to approve additional revenues without some sign of acceptance from the White House. The result was a deadlock that left the congressional budget process stalled.

Despite the breakdown of the revised timetable, Gramm-Rudman was having a significant effect on committees. The appropriations committees in particular found themselves under greater restrictions than in the past.[24] Under the 302(b) allocations, unlike past practice, the full appropriations committees could not adjust subtotals internally to keep within the overall cap. This increased conflict within subcommittees during mark-up. Scoring the deficit on outlays, not budget authority, had a noticeable effect on the appropriations committees. Senate appropriations are subject to a point of order if their bills exceed outlay allocations, and House leaders tried to enforce the same procedure. This hit defense appropriations particularly hard because of differences in the rate that programs convert budget authority into outlays. The revised budget process seemed to give the budget committees and party leaders greater control over the appropriations committees because of the specificity of the 302(b) allocations. It also precluded the president's using the sympathetic defense authorization and appropriations process to override cuts made by the budget committees.

With no budget resolution, the June 15 deadline for reconciliation was missed and it was obvious that no spending bills would be passed by June 30. The new prohibition against recessing for the Independence Day holiday in this case was quietly waived on June 19 by the Congress. House and Senate conferees finally reached a compromise, and on June 26 enacted the budget resolution for FY 87. It envisioned a deficit of $142.6 billion based on outlays of $995 billion and revenues of $852 billion. Most of the budget savings came from defense, some $28 billion below the president's request. Congress had given in to the president on taxes but placed deficit reduction over defense. As members left Washington for the Fourth of July, spending bills, reconciliation, and extension of the debt ceiling all remained. Before they would return, the Supreme Court would settle some of the constitutional issues surrounding the controversial deficit reduction law.

GRAMM-RUDMAN-HOLLINGS AND THE COURTS: THE CONSTITUTIONAL FLAW

The deficit reduction plan raised constitutional questions from the start. The key question presented to the courts was whether certain provisions of the Gramm-Rudman-Hollings Act were constitutional under the principle of separation of powers. This doctrine, more accurately described as one of separated institutions sharing powers, creates indistinct boundary lines that permit each branch of government to participate to some degree in the principal activities of the others. In the 1970s, the Supreme Court adopted a more relaxed interpretation of the separation of powers principle.[25] However, in *INS v. Chadha* (1983), the Court employed a formalistic model of separation of powers in striking down the legislative veto. This strict interpretation was again utilized in the case of *Bowsher v. Synar* decided on 7 July 1986.[26] Despite some sweeping constitutional issues, the finding that Gramm-Rudman violated the Constitution was restricted to a narrow, technical question: whether Congress has chosen the wrong official to carry out the trigger function of the mandatory budget cuts.

Both Congress and the executive expressed doubts about the constitutionality of the automatic trigger mechanism.[27] Anticipating an immediate challenge to the act, a fallback procedure was added to take effect in the event that any of the reporting procedures described in the law were invalidated. The fallback procedure called for the report prepared by the directors of OMB and CBO to be submitted to the Temporary Joint Committee on Deficit Reduction instead of the Comptroller General. This committee, composed of the entire membership of the budget committees of both houses of Congress, must report a joint resolution in five days to both Houses. Congress then must "certify" the cuts by voting on the resolution under special rules. The resolution, if passed and signed by the president, serves as the basis for the presidential sequestration order.

The District Court Challenge: *Synar v. United States*[28]

A special three-judge district court panel was convened in early 1986 to consider three principal issues:[29] (1) whether the plaintiffs had standing to challenge Gramm-Rudman, (2) whether the Gramm-Rudman-Hollings Act violated the delegation doctrine, and (3) whether the role of the Comptroller General in the deficit reduction process violated the doctrine of separation of powers. In a unanimous *per curiam* decision the District Court held that the plaintiffs had standing to challenge certain provisions of the Gramm-Rudman-Hollings Act.[30] However, the court found that the section of the act that delegated the Comptroller General broad power in the deficit reduction process was unconstitutional because he can be removed by Congress. The court observed that the Comptroller General, while appointed by the president and confirmed by the Senate, is removable not only by impeachment but also by joint resolution of Congress for specified causes.[31] According to the court, the purpose of the removal provision was to make the Comptroller General, an officer of the legislative branch, subservient to Congress. Under separation of powers, the court concluded that Congress may not retain the power of removal of an officer performing executive functions. On this point, the court recognized that

> Once an officer is appointed, it is only the authority that can remove him, and not the authority that appointed him, that he must fear and, in the performance of his functions, obey. Giving such power over executive functions to Congress violates the fundamental principle expressed by Montesquieu upon which the theory of separated powers rests: "When the legislative and executive powers are united in the same person, or in the same body of magistrates, there can be no liberty; because apprehension may arise, lest the same monarch or senate should enact tyrannical laws, to execute them in a tyrannical manner."[32]

The plaintiffs also argued that the Gramm-Rudman-Hollings Act delegated broad, if not excessive powers to administrative officials in making economic calculations that determined the estimated deficit which required budget cuts in violation of Article I of the Constitution. The District Court ruled that it did not have to consider this question since the law was unconstitutional on other grounds. In *obiter dicta*[33] however, the court was not persuaded by the plaintiffs' argument on why Gramm-Rudman violated the delegation doctrine and concluded that the delegation made by the Act was constitutional. This was a defeat for Synar who argued that Congress had declined to make hard political choices by authorizing excessive power to administrative officials such as the directors of OMB and CBO to affect spending levels for a range of federal programs.

The Supreme Court Review: *Bowsher v. Synar*

The District Court's ruling was automatically appealed under a provision in the law that granted expedited review to the Supreme Court. *Synar v. United States* provided much of the reasoning for the Supreme Court's final ruling in the case. In affirming the District Court decision, the Supreme Court in a 7–2 decision struck down the automatic trigger mechanism in Gramm-Rudman-Hollings, employing a strict interpretation of the separation of power doctrine. The majority opinion, written by Chief Justice Burger, concluded:

> Congress cannot reserve for itself the power of removal of an officer charged with the execution of the laws except by impeachment. To permit the execution of the laws to be vested in an officer answerable only to Congress would, in practical terms, reserve in Congress control over the execution of the laws. . . . The structure of the Constitution does not permit Congress to execute the laws; it follows that Congress cannot grant to an officer under its control what it does not posses.[34]

According to *INS v. Chadha* (1983)—the controlling precedent—the majority further stated that, "To permit an officer controlled by Congress to execute the laws would be, in essence, to permit a congressional veto. Congress could simply remove, or threaten to remove an officer for executing the laws in any fashion found to be unsatisfactory to Congress."[35] Based on their ruling in *Chadha,* the Court found this kind of control over the execution of laws constitutionally impermissible. Bowsher, the Comptroller General, argued that rather than striking down the automatic cut mechanism, the appropriate remedy would be to nullify the 1921 statutory provisions that authorized Congress to remove the Comptroller General. The Court declined to take such a step, referring to the language of Gramm-Rudman-Hollings that creates fallback provisions that take effect if any of the procedures in the law are invalidated. Burger also argued that invalidating the removal provision would be contrary to congressional intent in the 1921 law that created the GAO.

In concurring in the Court's judgement, Justice Stevens, joined by Justice Marshall, disagreed with the majority's view on why the Constitution prohibits the Comptroller General from exercising his power under Gramm-Rudman. They argued that neither the removal power of Congress nor the Comptroller General performing executive functions is the real question.[36] They argued that the issue is a matter of delegating to an officer of Congress power to make national policy. Justice Stevens argued that "It is, in short, the Comptroller General's report that will have a profound, dramatic, and immediate impact on the government and on the nation at large."[37] When Congress legislates, it must follow the procedures set forth in Article I—enactment by both Houses and presentment to the president.

The separate dissenting opinions by Justices White and Blackmun expressed the view that the constitutional flaw in *Bowsher* did not justify the remedy it imposed. Justice White argued that the majority imposed an overly formalistic view of the separation of powers doctrine. He stated that the 1921 law for removal of the Comptroller General has never been used, is of minimal practical significance, and should be regarded as a triviality. He rejected the argument that the removal of the Comptroller General by Congress imposes subservience on the part of the Comptroller General since removal must take place by joint resolution and the president plays a substantial role. Justice Blackmun argued, as did Justice White, against invalidating one of the most important federal enactments of the past several decades in order to preserve a 65-year-old removal of power that has never been exercised and appears to have been all but forgotten. Blackmun concluded that the 1921 law calling for the removal of the Comptroller General should have been struck down.

How would Congress respond? Would the Court's decision mark the end of Gramm-Rudman's only effective way of forcing action on the deficit? Would the backup procedure work or could the law be amended to make it constitutional?

RESOLVING THE FY 87 DEFICIT AND THE CONSTITUTIONAL FLAW

As they had the year before, Senators Gramm, Rudman, and Hollings viewed the debt limitation as the legislative vehicle for repairing their mandatory deficit reduction scheme. Their initial option for fixing the constitutional flaw was to eliminate the power of Congress to remove the Comptroller General. This option, however, quickly encountered opposition. Representative Jack Brook (D-TX), Chair of the House Government Operations Committee that oversees the GAO, was against any such change.

Congress quickly disposed of another problem caused by the Supreme Court's decision, however. On July 17, both the House and Senate approved resolutions certifying the March 1 cuts in FY 86 spending that had been invalidated by the Court. The fallback procedure was employed with slight parliamentary modification to retain the resolution's privileged status in the Senate. Members seemed unwilling to reopen the question of cuts already made and approved by large majorities in both bodies.

By the time the Senate reported the debt ceiling extension, proponents had chosen a second method: empowering OMB to determine the scope and distribution of spending cuts to achieve the deficit targets. Under the revised process proposed by Senators Gramm, Rudman, and Hollings, GAO still played a role in formulating the estimates, but OMB would issue the final report to the president. OMB discretion would be limited by barring the agency from making changes between the preliminary reports except to reflect changes in laws approved by Congress or regulations. The date for the president's budget was moved back to February from the earlier date, and a provision was included to revert to the original process if the Comptroller General was made an executive branch official. "Gramm-Rudman II," as it was dubbed by some, also met with strong opposition in the House and only grudging acceptance by the White House because of the limitations on OMB. Nonetheless, the amendment was adopted by the Senate on July 30 by a 63–36 vote. But the effort to fix the constitutional flaw bogged down as members prepared for an August 15 recess. House leaders wanted to rely on the backup procedure without any changes. Other members wanted to defer decisions until the August deficit reestimates were released. Despite the efforts of Gramm and his allies to prevent passage of any debt ceiling legislation, Congress agreed to a temporary extension without the Gramm-Rudman amendment.

The early August estimates by OMB and CBO confirmed what many had feared: the deficit for FY 86 and the projected deficit for FY 87 were much larger than expected. OMB's estimate of the FY 86 deficit had jumped $27 billion in six months. On August 20, CBO estimated the deficit for the coming fiscal year at $170.6 billion while OMB estimated it at $156.2 billion. Without the GAO to reconcile differences, the average was taken: $163.4 billion. The cuts outlined in the congressional budget would be insufficient to reach the deficit targets. The deficit target suddenly became $154 billion rather than $144 billion, taking advantage of the fact that sequestration would not be ordered unless Congress missed the deficit target by more than $10 billion. An additional $9.4 billion in cuts or revenue increases were needed to avoid a vote on mandatory cuts.

Most members agreed that despite the disappointing budget numbers, across-the-board cuts should be avoided for FY 87 at all costs. Still lacking appropriations bills and reconciliation, the congressional budget timetable was in shambles. As leaders focused on preparing an omnibus spending bill and making additional cuts to reach the $154 billion deficit target, the Gramm-Rudman amendments were again postponed. The package of additional cuts agreed to by both parties and the administration was a solution no one seemed to like but was considered better than all the alternatives. Relying primarily on revenues from the one-time sale of government assets such as Conrail, legislators proposed "golden gimmicks" worth around $13 billion using "smoke and mirrors."[38] As many had predicted early in the year, the critical FY 87 budget decisions were finally made in late night sessions in early October, after the fiscal year had begun. Another deadline was missed when the deficit reduction package was not enacted before October 1. As Congress struggled with continuing resolutions to keep the government running, a $576 billion omnibus spending bill, deficit reductions, debt extension, and the Gramm-Rudman-Hollings amendment, many noted that the congressional budget process looked pretty much the same in 1986 as it had in recent years.

Congress finally completed action on the budget with a deficit estimated at around $151 billion, below the target specified in Gramm-Rudman-Hollings. Despite attempts to block extension of the government's borrowing authority unless the bill contained their amendment to repair the deficit reduction process, Senators Gramm, Rudman, and Hollings were unsuccessful. Senate leaders, however, agreed to only a six month extension so that on May 15, 1987, proponents could once again attempt to remedy the constitutional flaw and make the process mandatory.

GRAMM-RUDMAN-HOLLINGS: AN ASSESSMENT

The Balanced Budget and Emergency Deficit Control Act of 1985 was both hailed as the salvation of the republic and condemned as a testament to the failure of budgeting in a democracy. Obviously, it is neither as good as its proponents nor as bad as its opponents claimed. Just as no single factor can explain its adoption, no single judgment can accurately assess its effect after one year. Like other policies, it has elements of success and failure.

The case that Gramm-Rudman-Hollings was a failure is relatively easy to document. Virtually without exception, every date in its ambitious new timetable for congressional budgeting was missed and missed badly. The Supreme Court ruled that the crucial trigger mechanism designed to make cuts automatically was unconstitutional. Congress failed to repair the constitutional flaw. Gramm-Rudman proved no panacea to the legislative-executive deadlock that has characterized budgetary politics in the 1980s. Congress struggled with the same issues in the same climate of internal discontent over its budget procedures. Budget decisions in 1986 dramatized a basic flaw in the time table: legislators are increasingly unlikely to make difficult choices on anything other than final budget baselines. Unless the basis of decision making can be made more certain, incentives to miss deadlines and delay the tough decisions until September or October will be compelling.

Beyond the prominent features of Gramm-Rudman's failures lies perhaps an even more serious indictment. Despite its claim to make Congress more attuned to deficit reduction as a long-term problem, it only emphasized Congress' short-term and short-sighted instincts as an institution. It did not eliminate expediency in budgeting; it exacerbated expediency. The $10 billion cushion allowed in the law to account for estimation error and economic changes was simply added to allow a larger deficit. The package of reductions adopted on October of 1986 to technically meet the target will significantly increase the deficit in outyears.[39] Advanced revenue collections and delayed outlays in FY 87 will have a similar effect on future deficits.

Many of the flaws of Gramm-Rudman-Hollings noted by critics at the outset remain. The process is an essentially irrational approach to budgeting. It has potentially damaging effects on both domestic and defense programs because of the way it cuts current year outlays. It threatens the health of the economy by eliminating the countercyclical potential of the budget, threatening to make cuts or raise revenues at precisely the wrong time. The recession escape clause would come into effect long after the crucial decision-making time had passed. Despite the Court decision, many broader questions of legislative-executive power remain unsettled. While provisions of the law may be within the letter of the Constitution, they seem to be counter to the spirit of the Constitution which gave Congress ultimate responsibility for decisions on taxing and spending.

Despite the negative case, Gramm-Rudman had some positive effects. Its goal of making federal deficits the top legislative priority was achieved; it simply could not legislate away the factors which had made deficits chronic in the first place. Gramm-Rudman permeated almost every facet of the second session of the 99th Congress. And despite the unenviable record detailed above, Gramm-Rudman communicated to the public congressional resolve to deal with deficits. Its failures, however, may make voters even more cynical.

Gramm-Rudman provided the initiative to reexamine and reform the congressional budget process. Despite the failure to meet the timetable, other changes served to centralize and strengthen macrobudgeting in Congress. The spending committees exhibited more discipline as a result of being subjected to greater accountability for budget totals. The budget committees and party leaders were strengthened. Reconciliation, for all the controversy surrounding it, was acknowledged as a crucial element of congressional budgeting. Enforcement under new rules was enhanced, especially in the Senate. The provisions requiring offsets to preserve deficit neutrality had a profound effect on the legislative process in 1986. The results were evident in the sweeping tax reform that passed and in a reduction in the amendments to the omnibus spending bill. Despite all the criticism, budget growth between FY 86 and FY 87 was the lowest in decades. While not balancing the budget, many of these changes may have a long-term positive impact on the ability of Congress to make fiscal decisions.

Victory by the Democrats in the Senate in the 1986 election will only make the task of those seeking to restore the mandatory provisions of the law in 1987 more difficult. Recall, however, that Gramm-Rudman-Hollings garnered significant Democratic support in numerous Senate votes in 1985 and 1986. Economic forecasts may be a greater obstacle than Democratic control. Estimates in late 1986 suggest that the deficit will far exceed $151 billion in FY 87 and that cuts as high as $70 billion may have to be made to reach the target of $108 billion for FY 88. Such results would seriously threaten the Gramm-Rudman approach. Many economists predict disastrous results for the economy if such drastic cuts are made.

Congress has several options for dealing with Gramm-Rudman-Hollings, none very appealing. First, the mandatory process could be restored by fixing the constitutional flaw in the original version by methods already proposed or others. Second, Congress could try to meet the original deficit targets but simply rely on the backup method to certify cuts. Third, Congress could amend the law to add a more sophisticated economic escape clause, changing the deficit targets by formula based on aggregate economic performance. This is similar to an amendment proposed by Representative David Obey during consideration of the bill in 1985, but not adopted. Fourth, Congress could simply amend the targets, restating their commitment to a balanced budget but adopting a more gradual phaseout that recognizes economic reality. Finally, Congress could simply scrap Gramm-Rudman by ignoring it as they do other statutes such as the Humphrey-Hawkins Act of 1978. Despite their antipathy to Gramm-Rudman, Democratic members in particular are suspicious of this approach, and fear handing the Republicans a ready-made campaign issue for 1988.

Whatever course Congress chooses for the future, Gramm-Rudman is one more milestone in its struggle to exercise its constitutional power of the purse. Despite some positive effects, Gramm-Rudman reveals once more that choosing one problem to solve does not make related problems disappear. As long as Congress faces increased policy and political constraints, procedural instability and high levels of conflict will result. With budget totals that remain inflexible to manipulation but vulnerable to the economy, it will continue to be difficult to budget with certainty. While deficits remain high, Congress will continue to seek some method to deal with the budget that still accommodates their other policy and political objectives. Gramm-Rudman-Hollings is a fascinating example of that search.

NOTES

This research was made possible in part through a grant from the Everett M. Dirksen Endowment for Legislative Research and a grant from the University of Missouri Weldon Spring Endowment. Their support and assistance is gratefully acknowledged.

1. Harry S. Havens, "Gramm-Rudman-Hollings: Origins and Implementation," *Public Budgeting and Finance* 6 (Autumn, 1986): 4–24.

2. Richard Fenno, *The Power of the Purse* (Boston: Little Brown, 1965) and Aaron Wildavsky, *The Politics of the Budgetary Process* (Boston: Little Brown, 1964).

3. Lance T. LeLoup, *Budgetary Politics* (Brunswick, Ohio: Kings Court Inc., 1986), 33–37.

4. Louis Fisher, Congressional Research Service, *Statement Before House Committee on Government Operations,* (October 17, 1985), Table 1.

5. Wildavsky (1964).

6. Allen Schick, "The Budget as an Instrument of Presidential Policy," in Lester M. Salamon and Michael S. Lund (eds.). *The Reagan Presidency and the Governing of America* (Washington, D.C.: Urban Institute Press, 1985), 91–125.

7. Lance T. LeLoup, "After the Blitz: Reagan and the U.S. Congressional Budget Process," *Legislative Studies Quarterly* 7 (August 1982): 331–339; Allen Schick, *Reconciliation and the Congressional Budget* (Washington, D.C.: American Enterprise Institute, 1981).

8. Louis Fisher, "Ten Years of the Budget Act: Still Searching for Controls," *Public Budgeting and Finance* 5 (Autumn 1985): 3–28.

9. House Rule XXI, clause 2(a) and Senate Rule XVI.

10. U.S. House of Representatives, Committee on Rules, *Report on the Congressional Budget Act Amendments of 1984* (October 1984), 98th Cong., 2nd sess.

11. *Congressional Record,* October 5, 1985, S12730–12732.

12. *Congressional Record,* October 9, 1985, S12988.

13. *Congressional Quarterly Weekly Reports,* October 26, 1985, 2148.

14. *Congressional Record,* November 1, 1985, H9615.

15. *Congressional Record,* December 11, 1985, S17444.

16. *Congressional Record,* December 11, 1985, H11903.

17. This section is based on Public Law 99–177. The Balanced Budget and Emergency Deficit Control Act of 1985.

18. Allen Schick, "Explanation of the Balanced Budget and Emergency Deficit Control Act of 1985," prepared for Congressional Research Service (December 1985), 9–13.

19. *Federal Register,* vol. 51, no. 10, book 2, (January 15, 1986).

20. Havens (1986): 15–20.

21. Congressional Budget Office, *The Economic and Budget Outlook: Fiscal Years 1987–1991,* Report to the House and Senate Committees on the Budget, Part I (February 1986).

22. *Congressional Quarterly Weekly Reports,* March 15, 1986, 315.

23. *Congressional Quarterly Weekly Reports,* May 17, 1986, 1079–1081.

24. Stephen Gettinger, "Spending Panels Confront Life After Gramm-Rudman," *Congressional Quarterly Weekly Reports,* June 7, 1986, 1258–1261.

25. *United States v. Nixon* 418, S.Ct. 683 (1974), *Train v. City of New York* 420, S.Ct. 35 (1975), and *Buckley v. Valeo* 424, S.Ct. 612 (1976).

26. *Charles A. Bowsher, Comptroller General of the United States v. Mike Synar, Member of Congress et al.,* 106 S.Ct. 3181 (1986).

27. For example, Trent Lott (D-Ms.) asked the American Law Division of the Congressional Research Service to prepare a constitutional analysis of the controversial provisions. The CRS responded by finding that Gramm-Rudman did not violate the Constitution on the four areas in question. See *Congressional Record,* October 24, 1985, E4793–4795.

28. Eleven members of Congress subsequently joined Synar's suit. This case was consolidated with *National Treasury Employees Union v. United States,* a virtually identical suit. In the case, the National Treasury Employees Union sued because Gramm-Rudman suspended a 3.1 percent cost of living increase its members were to have received in retirement benefits on January 1.

29. *Synar v. United States,* 626 F. Supp. 1374 (D.D.C. 1986).

30. The opinion was signed by all three judges, Scalia, Johnson, and Gasch, but the author of the opinion was not identified. It was widely speculated that Antonin Scalia, formerly of the U.S. Court of Appeals for the District of Columbia and currently Associate Justice of the Supreme Court, wrote the opinion, See *Wall Street Journal,* "Supreme Court Ruling Clouds the Outlook for Deficit Reduction," July 8, 1986, 27, col. 3; and Richard Cohen, "Judicial Whim," *National Journal,* July 26, 1986, 1863.

31. The causes for removal of the Comptroller General are impeachment or joint resolution of Congress after notice and an opportunity for a hearing only for: permanent disability, inefficiency, neglect of duty, malfeasance, or a felony or conduct involving moral turpitude (626 F. Supp. at 1391, 1986).

32. *Synar v. United States,* 626 F. Supp. at 1401–1402.

33. In this instance, the District Court provided its views on this question so that the Supreme Court, in case it decided to address this issue, would have the benefit of the lower court's views and would not result in delay if it were necessary to remand the case.

34. *Bowsher v. Synar* at 10 (slip opinion).

35. *Bowsher v. Synar* at 11 (slip opinion).

36. Justices Stevens and Marshall took a broader view of the separation of powers doctrine in *Bowsher.* They argued that the majority's question that the Comptroller General performs executive functions rests on an unsound premise based on distinct boundaries between the three branches of government. Their view is the functions performed by the Comptroller General are legislative.

37. *Bowsher v. Synar* at 19 (slip opinion).

38. *Congressional Quarterly Weekly Reports,* September 20, 1986, 2179.

39. Elizabeth Wehr. "Gramm-Rudman Both Disappoints and Succeeds," *Congressional Quarterly Weekly Reports,* November 15, 1986, 2879–2882.

CHAPTER 18

THE BUDGET ENFORCEMENT ACT AND ITS SURVIVAL
Congress Hears from Experts

PHILIP G. JOYCE

The Budget Enforcement Act of 1990 (BEA) established a new budget process highlighted by categorical spending limitations and a pay-as-you-go discipline covering revenue reductions and mandatory spending increases. The environment in Congress has been less than welcoming, however, during the first year of the agreement. Support for the new process, never strong, has waned in light of the recession, recent international events, and continuing record budget deficits. This has led many members of the Congress to introduce legislation that would change the BEA, and several congressional committees convened hearings to consider the future of the BEA during the first session of the 102nd Congress.

In the Spring 1991 issue of *Public Budgeting & Finance,* Naomi Caiden reflected on the extent to which politicians listen to experts when formulating budget policy.[1] It is interesting to follow this point, by examining the extent to which Congress sought out such experts when considering the future of the BEA, and, further, to review the advice given. Two hearings, held in October and November of 1991, exemplify both the kinds of choices facing the Congress and the type of advice that members have been receiving. The first, held on October 10, was a hearing before the House Budget Committee's Task Force on Budget Process, Reconciliation, and Enforcement. The second, on November 6, was a hearing before the Subcommittee on Legislation and National Security of the House Committee on Government Operations.

The remainder of this article reviews the testimony given the two committees by four witnesses with established knowledge of federal budgeting. The witnesses include current Congressional Budget Office (CBO) director Robert Reischauer, past CBO director Alice Rivlin of the Brookings Institution, Urban Institute scholar Isabel Sawhill, and Professor Allen Schick of the University of Maryland. Each assessed the successes and limitations of the BEA, critiqued the proposals for amending it, and offered other general advice concerning the budget process and deficit control. In each of these cases, written statements provided to the two committees have been briefly summarized.

From *Public Budgeting and Finance,* vol. 12, no. 1 (Spring 1992), 16–22. Copyright © 1992 by Public Financial Publications, Inc. Reprinted with permission.

VIEWS OF ROBERT REISCHAUER—HOUSE BUDGET COMMITTEE (OCTOBER 10) AND HOUSE GOVERNMENT OPERATIONS COMMITTEE (NOVEMBER 6)

The discretionary spending limits and pay-as-you-go regime are making an important contribution to controlling the federal deficit. Large budget deficits continue to be a major obstacle to raising living standards and expanding opportunities, however. Sooner or later the administration and Congress should take further steps to reduce the deficit, and any revisions to the BEA should be designed to contribute to that goal.

Two factors are causing a reassessment of the discretionary spending limits for 1993. First, the international situation has changed, causing many to ask whether further reductions in defense spending may be desirable. While reductions in nuclear weapons do not necessarily result in lower defense spending, the savings could be substantial if these reductions are followed by reductions in forces and programs.

Second, the discretionary spending caps will prove more restrictive in the future than they have so far. The 1992 appropriation bills have used devices such as delayed obligations, in order to comply with the 1992 spending caps by pushing outlays into 1993. In addition, the domestic caps must be adjusted downward in the president's 1993 budget because of lower than expected 1991 inflation. Finally, a greater than expected portion of Operation Desert Storm spending will spill over into 1993, where it will crowd out other defense spending under a fixed discretionary limit.

Beyond 1993, the caps get much tighter. The implications of this are displayed by viewing two scenarios to illustrate the size of the reductions that might be required to meet the caps in 1994 and 1995. If the president's FY 1992 defense request (a 3 percent annual real reduction) is accepted, the nondefense side of the budget would have to undergo real reductions of about 7 percent in 1994 and another 3 percent in 1995. On the other hand, if nondefense programs are maintained at their real 1993 level (such that all of the needed cuts come from the defense budget), the defense budget would be cut by 8 percent in 1994 and another 6 percent in 1995. Defense reductions of this size would be easier if the president's budget for defense was cut beginning in 1993.

Proposals from specific members of Congress have focused on amending the BEA to remove the walls between defense and domestic discretionary spending. Representative John Conyers, chairman of the House Government Operations Committee, is the author of one such proposal. The Conyers bill would replace the three separate limits on domestic, international, and defense spending with a single cap for all discretionary spending, beginning in 1993.[2] Others have advocated a more indirect approach, through funding certain items—say NASA or aid to the Soviet Union—from the defense budget.

In any case, experience with previous versions of the Balanced Budget Act suggests that, when targets become too tough to meet, the targets get raised. The 1994 and 1995 targets will not get easier to meet merely through switching funds from one discretionary category to another, although the Congress may still wish to rearrange the spending caps in 1993. Establishing a single cap will not by itself contribute to economic growth by reducing the deficit. Future living standards might be improved, however, by a reallocation of discretionary spending toward investment activities that could add to productivity and growth.

Come 1993, the budget will certainly return to the top of the political agenda, for several reasons. First, the public debt is likely to reach its statutory limit by early 1993. In addition, by the time of the 1994 budget, large sequestrations may again be a real possibility. Although the BEA does not require additional deficit reduction until at least 1994, the budget deficit remains a serious economic and social problem. Low saving in the 1980s is already causing the economy to pay a heavy price, and large continuing deficits will continue to constrain economic growth.

Because projected deficits are even higher today than they were when the first of the laws specifically designed to control them was enacted in 1985, many believe that these laws have been a failure. As high as the deficits have been, however, they would have been even higher without the BEA and its predecessors. Even though the BEA seems to be working, there is a necessity for more budget reductions. It is relevant to wonder how the budget process can be strengthened. First, some version of the caps and the pay-as-you-go discipline should be extended past 1995, to offset the temptation to avoid the limits by delaying spending until 1996 or later. Second, ways must be devised to slow the growth of mandatory spending, especially for health care services. Third, consideration should be given to establishing targets for deficit reduction, rather than targets for the deficit. Under this type of scenario, the law could require a fixed amount of deficit reduction each year. It would be important that this objective be backed up by a more convincing threat than the current sequestration, which exempts 95 percent of mandatory programs in whole or in part. One possibility would be to trigger an automatic surcharge on personal or corporate income tax payments, if the required level of deficit reduction were not achieved.

VIEWS OF ALICE RIVLIN—HOUSE BUDGET COMMITTEE (OCTOBER 10, 1991)

The next few years will be extraordinarily challenging for federal budgeteers. The crumbling of the Soviet empire will spark debate in how best to redirect defense and international spending to enhance the chances of peace and stable international development. Growing domestic problems will also force a thorough rethinking of the federal domestic role. Business-as-usual budgeting, in which marginal changes are made in a generally accepted portfolio of federal activities, will no longer be possible. This will be particularly difficult because the starting point of the debate is a huge federal deficit and expanding debt, the existence of which both constrains choices and demands a large fraction of annual federal revenue.

As you examine whether any process changes can make these big decisions even a little bit easier, I would encourage you to keep in mind several points.

First, the most important single thing you can do to strengthen the economy over the long haul is to get the deficit down. A policy of moving the federal budget (including Social Security) from deficit to surplus would eventually reduce the debt held by the public, put downward pressure on interest rates, create a healthy climate for investment, and even allow the United States to become a capital-exporting nation again.

Second, even if the discretionary caps and the pay-as-you-go rules of the current process continue to be enforced, the budget is not now on a track to a long-run surplus or even balance. Thus, any changes in the budget process that make it easier to shift priorities must avoid loosening the overall budget discipline.

Third, any budget process changes should be designed to make it possible to recognize shifting priorities and accelerate budget deficit reduction at the same time. A reasonable first step would be to move forward to 1993 the merging of defense, international, and domestic into a combined cap. This would permit military budget savings to begin as soon as possible, and the Congress could decide whether to use these savings for nondefense spending, for deficit reduction, or for some of each.

Fourth, the BEA, complex as it is, has proved far more workable than the Gramm-Rudman-Hollings procedures it replaced. I would not recommend overhaul of these procedures in the near term, and certainly not until a workable alternative has been worked out.

Finally, for the longer run—even if a unified surplus was achieved—the budget process should retain the notion that priorities can and should change, but budget discipline should not be abandoned. While it would not be good economic policy to try to keep the budget deficit at a specific figure year-by-year (as in Gramm-Rudman-Hollings), nor to enshrine such a figure in the Constitution, prudent budgeteers must recognize that public services are not free. Public services, like private services, must be paid for.

VIEWS OF ISABEL SAWHILL—HOUSE GOVERNMENT OPERATIONS COMMITTEE (NOVEMBER 6, 1991)

The immediate issue being considered by the Committee is whether to amend the Act to eliminate separate caps for defense, international, and domestic discretionary spending. In general, I have supported the principle of deficit-neutral budgeting as a mechanism for keeping the budget deficit on a downward track. However, the fire walls between categories have never been needed for this purpose and may be inappropriate given the change in the international situation. Indeed, taking down the walls between discretionary categories may not be sufficient. It may be useful to modify the agreement to enable discretionary spending increases to be financed through higher taxes and lower entitlement spending.

Assuming that defense spending can be cut significantly beyond what is currently implicit in last year's budget agreement, the current inside-the-beltway debate suggests that there are a number of competing uses for these savings. They include (1) deficit reduction, (2) public investment, (3) middle class tax relief, and (4) everything else (such as long-term health care). My personal view is that we should devote any additional funds to some combination of deficit reduction and public investment.

First, deficit reduction is an important way of promoting the long-term growth of the economy. Last year's agreement moves us in the right direction. Although the deficit is ballooning to unprecedented levels, this primarily is a result of the recession and the savings and loan crisis which are less important over the long-term than the legislative actions that Congress took last year. While more deficit reduction is necessary, I would not advocate it as early as FY 1993, given current weaknesses in the economy.

In the long run, I would also not put all of our eggs in the private investment basket. Public and private investment are complementary. We cannot march into the twenty-first century on one foot. We need more up-to-date factories *and* better roads, communications, education, and training. These investments are so critical because all of the evidence suggest that they have powerful payoffs. The rate of return to investment in human resources has been rising because (1) we work in an increasingly globalized economy, in which people are the only unique resource a nation has to offer, and (2) because the United States is becoming a more service-oriented, knowledge-based economy. In short, we are devoting fewer of our resources to education, training, and investment in children at a time when the need to devote more is greater than ever.

Let me turn to taxes. Political pressures to cut taxes are mounting. While arguments are made that tax cuts are needed to stimulate the economy and get us out of recession, almost all economists agree that they would be too little and come too late to have much effect. As a long-term proposition, tax cuts don't look much better. We have not fully paid for the tax cuts of 1981, and it may be time to stop consuming and start investing in the future either by reducing the deficit or making sound public investments.

VIEWS OF ALLEN SCHICK—HOUSE BUDGET COMMITTEE (OCTOBER 10, 1991)

I regard BEA as a seriously flawed deal, even if it was the best that the two warring branches of government could do under the difficult circumstances that they faced a year ago. The BEA's flaws were driven by expedience, as the negotiators were more agreed on what should be avoided—imposition of harsh, Gramm-Rudman-Hollings cutbacks—than on the objectives that should be accomplished. Compared to Gramm-Rudman-Hollings, BEA has been a big improvement, mainly because it is more flexible and fosters more honest budgeting than Gramm-Rudman-Hollings. Nonetheless, BEA has serious shortcomings, including excessively detailed technical rules, the legitimized inattention to the deficit, spending caps that are not sufficiently responsive to new developments and changing priorities, and a double standard that caps discretionary spending while permitting entitlements and other direct spending to rise without limit.

Although the BEA was billed a year ago as the "deal of the century," which would enable the president and Congress to get on with the business of government, the projected deficit is now bigger than it was before BEA took effect. This is in part because of the deteriorating economy, but also because BEA did not produce $500 billion in genuine savings. While approximately 40 percent of the total savings were in defense, there is strong reason to believe that these savings would have been realized absent BEA, because of changing international conditions.

Even more remarkable than the deterioration of the deficit outlook is that it has occasioned no response in either the legislative or the executive branches. The age of no-fault budgeting has arrived. Nobody is to blame for the deficit, and nobody has to do anything about it. In fact, one of the side effects of BEA has been to suspend the reconciliation procedure at the very time that the deficit has surged above budgeted levels. It is very likely that, in the absence of BEA's no-fault rules, Congress would have taken some reconciliation action during the 1991 session.

Further, budget priorities have been frozen by BEA, and mandatory programs escape serious budgetary review. The paralysis in budgeting is reflected in both discretionary and PAYGO categories. BEA has called a halt to virtually all domestic discretionary initiatives, by barring tradeoffs between discretionary spending and mandatory spending or revenue changes. The bias is even stronger on the PAYGO side, where new initiatives can only be funded by producing additional revenue, obtaining an emergency designation, or finding other mandatory offsets. While priorities have been frozen, discretionary and mandatory programs are not treated equally. PAYGO expenditures are permitted to float upwards without limits, as required by current policy, discretionary spending is capped at fixed amounts. This means that a program classified as PAYGO will likely do a lot better than one that is subject to the caps. This creates both incentives for congressional committees to shift favored programs from discretionary to PAYGO, and effectively removes almost 60 percent of federal spending from budgetary control.

At this point, it should be apparent that just tinkering with the discretionary caps will not suffice, it is necessary to make more fundamental changes in BEA procedures. The following recommendations are intended to address the aforementioned deficiencies of BEA.

1. The discretionary caps should be established as limits, not as floors. Increasingly, the caps are seen as the minimum that must be spent regardless of the condition of the budget or other program needs. BEA should be clarified to make sure that there is no requirement that funds be provided up to the cap.
2. The reconciliation process should be applied each year that the BEA agreement remains in effect.
3. Budget savings should be based only on structural changes in programs, all temporary provisions should be excluded. BEA overstates deficit reduction by including various bookkeeping tricks and temporary provisions in the budget baseline.
4. The president and congressional leaders should periodically meet to discuss modifications of BEA rules. While these meetings might be convened at the initiative of the two

branches, they should take place whenever there is a significant rise in deficit projections. In an age of divided government, it is important to build bridges between the two branches. Further, changes are likely to be enacted only pursuant to presidential-congressional negotiations.

5. PAYGO would be changed to require that at least a portion of revenue increases be allocated to deficit reduction. A consequence of the PAYGO linkages between revenues and mandatory spending is that increased revenues are seen only as a way of financing additional spending, and not as a way of ameliorating the deficit.

6. The discretionary spending caps should be retargeted to reflect changed budget priorities. The defense caps should be lowered and a portion of the savings should be made available to other budget needs. A portion of these savings should also be allocated to deficit reduction.

7. Savings from cutbacks in defense should be channeled into a special national priorities fund, and Congress should decide how much should be allocated to reducing the deficit, aiding other countries, and financing domestic alternatives. Congress would then allocate any peace dividend among various national needs, as opposed to the normal method by which every program gets its "fair share" of any incremental increase.

8. Congress should establish a process for terminating low-priority programs and recycling the funds for other uses. It is remarkable that despite "tight" budgets, not a single significant domestic program has been terminated in the past few years. Congress should establish a procedure to spur such terminations. This process could, as was the case with the base-closing process in defense, rely on outside experts and be designed to reprogram funds, not cut expenditures.

9. Congress should study the means of reducing the portion of the budget locked into mandatory programs, as well as the means of making such programs more responsive to budget conditions. At present, federal programs are either annual or permanent. A middle ground should be vigorously pursued, with the specific goal of building more flexibility (and controllability) into existing mandatory programs.

CONGRESS AND EXPERTS—LOOKING TO THE FUTURE

These experts generally believe the BEA to be a desirable, but not sufficient, step toward the eventual control or elimination of federal deficits. It is clear to each that further deficit reduction is necessary. In addition, the ability to control the growth of entitlement spending is central to further progress on deficit reduction. As we move toward possible amendment of the BEA in an election year, or perhaps another wholesale revision of the budget process, it will be interesting to see whether the debate centers around these issues and whether further actions of the kinds recommended by these and other experts become a reality.

NOTES

The author is grateful to Robert Reischauer, Alice Rivlin, Isabel Sawhill, and Allen Schick for reviewing summaries of their testimony prepared for this article. Marvin Phaup, Robert Hartman, James Blum, and Rita Hilton provided other helpful comments.

1. Naomi Caiden, "Do Politicians Listen to Experts? The Budget Enforcement Act and the Capacity to Budget," *Public Budgeting & Finance* 11 (Spring 1991) 41–49.

2. The Conyers proposal is embodied in H. R. 3732.

CHAPTER 19

DOES BUDGET FORMAT REALLY GOVERN THE ACTIONS OF BUDGETMAKERS?

GLORIA A. GRIZZLE

BUDGET FORMATS, DELIBERATIONS, AND DECISIONS

Beginning in 1917 with the Bureau of Municipal Research's recommendations on format for the New York City budget, one can trace a series of authors who hold that the format in which a budget is cast importantly affects the ensuing budget deliberations and ultimately the allocation of funds.[1] With the advent of program or performance budgeting in the 1950s, both Burkhead and Mosher noted the importance of format.[2] In his study of performance budgeting in the U.S. Department of the Army, Mosher concluded that the way in which information is classified importantly affected the "kinds of treatment and kinds of decisions that can be made at various levels" because the classification framework "conditions our subsequent perspectives, understandings, and decisions made within the framework."[3]

In thinking about how the organization of data might affect budget decisions, it is useful to conceptualize a two-step process. In the first step, the format in which the proposed budget is cast would influence the content of discussions that budget makers hold during the budget review process. Anton emphasizes this influence in his description of the Illinois state budgeting process. He reports that the budgetary discourse was shaped by the informational categories established by the line-item format that Illinois used. In his words, "because these categories reflect a desire to know how much money was or will be spent for which things, budget presentation and review is rarely accomplished in any terms but these."[4]

In the second step, the content of budget deliberations, that is, "the nature of budgetary discourse," would influence the budget decisions that determine how much money is appropriated for what purposes. The planning-programming-budgeting system (PPBS) is perhaps the best known budget reform for which format was believed to affect budget decisions. For example, in studying the introduction of PPBS into the federal government's budgeting process, Fenno, Schick, and Wildavsky have stated that the budget format affects budgeting decisions.[5] Perhaps Schick expressed it most cogently when he said, "the case for PPB rests on the assumption that the form

From *Public Budgeting and Finance,* vol. 6, no. 1 (Spring 1986), 60–70. Copyright © 1986 by Public Financial Publications, Inc. Reprinted with permission.

Figure 19.1 **Two-Step Process Envisioned by Budget Reform Proponents**

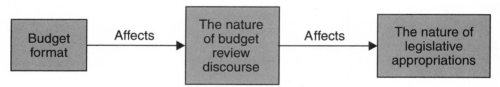

in which information is classified and used governs the actions of budgetmakers and conversely, that alterations in form will produce desired changes in behavior."[6]

Thus, the two-step process envisioned by budget reform proponents can be diagrammed as seen in Figure 19.1. Some practitioners, however, do not agree that budget format has an important effect upon budget deliberations, especially where the legislature's deliberations are concerned. They believe that legislators base their budget decisions on "politics" and that changing budget format will not change legislative decisions. In his study of the Georgia zero-base budgeting (ZBB) process, Lauth reports that 84 percent of the agency budget officers and 88 percent of analysts in the governor's office believed that the appropriations committees rarely or never took evaluation measures into account in making budget decisions.[7] In their survey of state budget directors, Ramsey and Hackbart reported that legislatures often act as barriers to real change in budgetary emphasis because they insist "on knowing how specific monies are being spent and what is being bought with these monies."[8] Juszczak, a budgeter in the federal government, concluded that the structuring of supporting schedules is more important than the overall budget format.[9]

Only recently have students of budgeting attempted to quantify the ways in which new formats introduced through budget reform have in fact changed appropriations. Three studies of state budgeting systems have attempted to relate format to appropriations directly without examining in what ways, if any, format affected the intervening budget review deliberations. Two of these studies examine the change over time in the proportion of the total budget allocated to broad functions. Examining these proportions for Arkansas during a five-year period after the introduction of its priority budgeting system (a variant of ZBB), Carr concludes that budgetary decisions are incremental and that the budget format had no effect upon budgetary decisions.[10] In looking at Virginia's change to a program budget format, Hickman concludes that format is one of many factors that influence budget decision. He cites economic and demographic changes as more influential than format in causing shifts over time in the proportion of the total budget allocated to broad functions, such as education.[11]

Stutzman, in the third study, examines the extent to which the Michigan legislature's departmental appropriations agreed with the governor's recommendations over a 15-year period. She found that changes in budget format affected legislative behavior in a surprising way. During those years of major budget format change, the legislators reacted by making appropriations that departed radically from the governor's budget recommendations.[12]

While these studies represent a commendable step in moving from descriptive case studies to assessing quantitatively the effects of budget reforms, looking only at formats and appropriations for broad functions may leave several important questions unanswered. First, studies at such high levels of aggregation cannot capture programmatic shifts that may have taken place within broad functional areas. It is possible that format could have influenced how much was appropriated to particular programs within these broad functions.

Second, to demonstrate convincingly that a change in format did or did not change appropriations when studying a single state requires a time series of budget decisions that occurred both before and after the budget reform, as well as evidence that refutes other plausible causes of appropriation changes. To their credit, the Virginia and Michigan studies do take other causes into account. The Virginia study concludes that other factors are more important influences on budget decisions than format, and the Michigan study goes further by providing sufficient evidence to discount the other factors examined as being the cause of disagreement between gubernatorial recommendations and legislative appropriations.

Third, studies that focus only upon format and legislative appropriations leave unexplored the budget review process that occurs after proposed budgets are formatted and before the legislature appropriates funds. If we are to advocate budget formats as instruments of budget reform, we need to understand better the intervening process by which formats influence appropriations. Budget reforms are, we are told, expected to center legislative attention "on integrated related activities or programs rather than line-item objects of expenditure."[13] To what extent does format "center legislative attention"?

Case studies reported in the literature do give some attention to this intervening process. In studying the change from a line-item to a performance budget format in Los Angeles, Sherwood and Eghtedari concluded that the unanticipated effect was that legislators opted not to participate rather than to focus on broad policy.[14] In contrast, Hickman concluded that Virginia's shift to a program format resulted in more direct involvement by the legislature in shaping budget outcomes.[15] Based upon interviews with budget directors in five cities, Cope concluded that city councils used the parts of the format with which they were familiar or comfortable and ignored the rest.[16] Hrebenar reports a similar tendency on the part of the Washington Senate.[17] In sum, these case studies report conflicting results about the effect of format upon legislative deliberations.

In conclusion, we cannot, from the studies mentioned above, make any generalizations about how, or to what extent, budget format affects the nature of legislative deliberations. We might learn more about how the organization of the budget influences appropriations decisions if we would undertake a few studies that directly test Fenno's proposition that " . . . the form of the budget determines what the conversation will be about."[18] The sections below report one such study that compares the deliberations of legislative appropriations committees that used different budget formats.

ANALYTICAL FRAMEWORK FOR DESCRIBING BUDGET DELIBERATIONS

Surely the best known work asserting the influence of budget format on the character of the budgeting process is contained in Schick's "The Road to PPB."[19] The three classic orientations described in this article—control, management, and planning—provide appropriate analytical categories for classifying the nature of budget deliberations. The control orientation is believed to dominate budget reviews that use line-item formats. The management orientation best characterizes the performance budget; and the planning orientation best characterizes the program budget. Each of these orientations, and the content of deliberations expected to occur when they are used during the budget review process, is briefly described below.

A budget format containing detailed classification of objects of expenditure conforms to the control orientation. The range of concerns to which this format responds includes holding agencies to spending ceilings set by the legislature and chief executive, providing reporting that will enforce the propriety of spending, limiting an agency's spending in terms of the objects to be bought (e.g., equipment, office space, and personnel).

A budget format organized around a government's activities conforms to the management orientation. It focuses upon the work that operating units do and how efficiently they do it. Performance measures associated with this orientation include the quantity and quality of output and the unit cost of that output. The range of concerns includes how much work is to be done, how best to organize to accomplish the work to be done, and which grants and projects should be funded.

A budget format organized by program conforms to the planning orientation. The range of concerns includes long-range goals and policies and how these relate to initiating, terminating, expanding, or curtailing particular programs. Performance measures associated with this orientation include program outcomes, cost-effectiveness, and the extent to which program objectives are achieved. Cost-benefit studies, systems analyses, and long-range forecasts are sources of information expected to be associated with the planning orientation to a greater extent than with management and control.

Schick notes that "it should be clear that every budget system contains planning, management, and control features. A control orientation means the subordination, not the absence, of planning and management functions. In the matter of orientations, we are dealing with relative emphases, not with pure dichotomies."[20]

In a 1974 survey of 88 cities, Friedman found the control orientation to be most prevalent, as evidenced by scoring the presence of institutional practices related to each budgeting type for each city. The average presence of institutional practices related to each type of budgeting was 70 percent for control, 60 percent for management, and 42 percent for planning. He found that "one or another budget-making purpose tends to dominate and assume paramount importance in most cities. Although they are compatible, the three patterns of budgeting are not necessarily co-equal."[21]

Friedman's survey confirmed Axelrod's contention that the three orientations are not mutually exclusive and that governments have improved their budgets by strengthening management and planning without abandoning control.[22] As an illustration of the hybrid nature of budgeting in practice, note a Fort Worth budget participant's description of that city's "performance" budget:

> Actually, the Fort Worth budgetary process is one which includes the elements of all three traditional types of budgets. It is a line-item budget, particularly in the control aspects, in that specific appropriations are made for each line item, and operating department heads are accountable by line item for variances between appropriations and actual expenditures. Elements of a performance budget are present because activity appropriations are based loosely on work to be performed, at least in the planning stages of the budget. However, the Fort Worth budgetary system could best be described as primarily a program budget because inputs to the process each year are defined in terms of existing, expanded, or reduced programs, and detailed descriptions of each program are provided in the budget document.[23]

Similarly, Howard, in reviewing state budgeting, finds it "virtually impossible to classify states' budgeting processes in unambiguous categories. The simple question—Is your state doing object-of-expenditure budgeting, program budgeting, PPBS, or zero-base budgeting?—cannot be answered simply. State budget systems are hybrids rather than purebreeds, distinguished by the adopted and adapted parts of recent reforms as well as by state-specific practices."[24]

Thus, we would not expect to find pure forms of budget formats in state or local governments. We can, however, characterize the extent to which a given government's budget format conforms to the three orientations and compare formats that differ in their dominant orientations.

HOW DO FORMATS INFLUENCE "WHAT THE CONVERSATION WILL BE ABOUT"?

Ideally, one would like to address this question by exposing each of several budgeting groups to different budget formats (in their pure forms) and then comparing the nature of deliberations under the different formats. Barber's method of eliciting decision criteria from legislative groups would be useful, given such an experimental design. He was able to induce local government boards of finance to spend a half hour in a small-group laboratory on a budget-reducing task. He tape recorded and analyzed their deliberations and categorized them by the decision criteria used.[25] However, the laboratory approach has two serious disadvantages. First, gaining executive or legislative participation in such an experiment is unlikely. Moreover, budgeting behavior in a short laboratory exercise might differ from behavior in the budgeters' natural environment.

A more practical way of learning about the relationship of format to the nature of deliberations would be to compare deliberations according to format variations as they naturally occur in the real world. This approach is more likely to produce information of direct relevance to practitioners. State governments have two advantages in this regard. First, states vary considerably in the formats they use. Second, a number of states tape record (but do not transcribe) their legislative appropriations committee meetings. The discussions in these meetings can be analyzed to compare the dominant orientations of legislative deliberations under different budget formats. The study reported below takes this approach, using the control, management, and planning orientations discussed above.

Florida and North Carolina were the two states selected for study. Appropriations committees for both houses of the legislature in both states were included in the analysis. During the 1979 and 1981 legislative sessions, the period included in the analysis, Florida appropriations committees used the organizational-unit format described below.

North Carolina is a particularly interesting state to study because its appropriations committees used two quite different formats. After the governor's recommended budget changed to a program format in the early 1970s, some appropriations committees used that format for a few years. Other committees, however, insisted that the governor provide them with a detailed line-item format. By 1981, all the committees used the line-item format. The North Carolina committee meetings examined occurred during the 1975, 1977, and 1981 legislative sessions.

A Description of the Budget Formats Studied

Table 19.1 summarizes the features of each budget format studied.[26] In order to illustrate how a department's budget would be structured under each format, we compare the structure used for a single department—the Department of Corrections. The program format presents pages for each of nine corrections programs. These programs are classified into 22 subprograms. Six of these 22 subprograms are further broken down into 16 program elements. Finally, four of the 16 elements are themselves broken down into 10 subelements. In contrast, the line-item budget is first classified by three accounting funds. One fund includes pages for each of 18 purposes; the second, for 11 purposes; and the third, for a single purpose. The organizational format presents pages for each of eight budget entities. Four entities are departmental divisions and four are organizational units one level below the division level.

None of these formats is a pure type. The program format described, for example, does not cut across departmental lines. However, the formats are sufficiently different from each other that we would expect them to influence deliberations differently.

Table 19.1

A Comparison of the Characteristics of the Budget Formats Studied

	Format		
Characteristic	Program	Line Item	Organization
Overall structure of information	Program	Fund: purpose	Organizational unit
Dominant information focus	Lowest level of program structure	Purpose's detailed objects	Division's summary objects: issues
Narrative	Descriptions at each level of program structure	Brief descriptions of each purpose's function	None
Objective	For each program component	For some purposes	None
Statistical information presented	Lowest level of program structure	Each purpose	None
Comparative financial data presented	Last year's actual; this year's appropriation; governor's recommended	Last year's actual; this year's appropriation; governor's recommended	This year's estimate; agency request; governor's recommended
Separation of continuation level funding from expansion funding	None	For each fund, purpose, and object	For each division
Funding source classification	Each program component; 3 categories	Each purpose; detailed itemization	Each division; 2 categories

Given our descriptions of the three formats, we would expect budget deliberations using the program format to focus on the range of concerns defined by the planning orientation. We would expect the deliberations using the line-item format to focus on those concerns included within the control orientation. Although the organizational-unit budget is not a performance budget, we would expect its focus on divisions and subdivisions to result in a greater management orientation than would the other two formats.

Analysis and Findings

For each of the three budget formats, 10 appropriations committee meetings were selected for analysis.[27] For each of these meetings, questions that legislators asked and comments they made during the meeting were coded according to their orientation. In addition to Schick's planning, management, and control orientations, a fourth category was added to capture funding-oriented questions. Frequently legislators wanted to know how an expenditure was to be funded. Would state funds be matched by federal funds? What proportion of the cost would be supported by user fees? Was state money required? Would state general fund revenues be required in the future?[28]

Table 19.2 distributes the questions by budget format and orientation. As expected, the program format deliberations contain a higher proportion of planning-oriented remarks by legislators than do the other two formats. Both the program and organizational-unit formats contain about the same proportion of management-oriented remarks, but substantially more than occur with line-item format deliberations. There is also a marked difference in the proportion of remarks that are control-oriented, with deliberations using the line-item format dominated by this orientation to a much greater extent than are program and organizational-unit format deliberations. Finally, all

Table 19.2

Percentage of Legislator's Remarks Fitting Each Orientation, by Budget Format

Orientation	Format		
	Program	Line Item	Organizational Unit
Planning	9%	1%	3%
Management	69	40	70
Control	4	51	13
Funding	18	8	13

Table 19.3

Proportion of Variation in Orientations across Meetings that Budget Format "Explained"

Orientation	Proportion (Eta Squared)	Significance (F Value)
Planning	.20	3.46*
Management	.32	6.24*
Control	.64	23.59*
Funding	.10	1.49

*Indicates explanation is statistically significant at the .05 alpha level.

the committees demonstrate some concern for funding, but this concern does not dominate any committee's deliberations and variation across the three format types is not marked.[29]

There is an additional observation about the data in Table 19.2. The planning orientation does not dominate deliberations under the program format. In spite of this format, the management orientation dominates. Planning ranks third, after management and funding concerns. It appears that legislators do seek out additional information they believe important when a given format does not provide it.

To what extent does program format account for, or "explain" in a statistical sense, the variations in orientation that occurred among the 30 meetings? To address this question, we analyzed this variation across the committee meetings. As Table 19.3 shows, budget format was not a statistically significant factor in explaining the extent to which different committee meeting deliberations emphasized the funding orientation. Format did account for some significant proportion of the variation for the other three orientations. Format accounts for 64 percent of the variation in how much emphasis a committee placed upon control. It accounts for 32 percent of the variation in management emphasis and 20 percent of the variation in planning emphasis.

CONCLUSION

These findings indicate that format is, as budget reform proponents have assumed, an important factor influencing the nature of budget deliberations. As Hickman suggested when analyzing the Virginia experience with program budgeting, format is not the only factor and, at least in this study, does not explain a majority of the variation in orientation among legislative appropriations committee meetings. Clearly, however, format did influence "what the conversation was about" during the legislatures' review of these states' proposed budgets.

Further research, extending this analytic approach both to executive as well as legislative delibera-tions and to additional states, might yield answers to questions this single study necessarily leaves unresolved. For instance, to what extent and in what direction do other formats influence legislative deliberations? To what extent do factors other than budget format affect the nature of the deliberations? For example, do deliberations differ in growth compared to no-growth or retrenchment years?

Once this intervening link between budget format and appropriations decision is better under-stood, a second step will be to link deliberations under different formats to appropriations deci-sions, controlling for other factors that influence appropriations. Eventually, we should be able to identify not only the ways in which format affects budget review, but also how these effects vary in the presence of other factors, such as fiscal condition and demographics. The practitioner could then be better guided in choosing the format that best suits the situation. Or, should it turn out that in many situations formats do not make much difference one way or the other, budgeting theory could be redirected toward more fruitful lines of inquiry.

NOTES

1. New York Bureau of Municipal Research, "Some Results and Limitations of Central Financial Con-trol in New York City," *Municipal Research* 81 (1917). See also W.E.F. Willoughby, *Principles of Public Administration* (Washington, D.C.: Brookings, 1927), p. 454.

2. Jesse Burkhead, *Government Budgeting* (New York: John Wiley, 1956), p. viii; Frederick C. Mosher, *Program Budgeting: Theory and Practice* (Chicago: Public Administration Service, 1954).

3. Mosher, pp. 5 and 83.

4. Thomas J. Anton, *The Politics of State Expenditure in Illinois* (Urbana: University of Illinois Press, 1966), p. 73.

5. Richard F. Fenno, "The Impact of PPBS on the Congressional Appropriation Process" in *Information Support, Program Budgeting, and the Congress,* Robert L. Chartrand, Kenneth Janda, and Michael Hugo, eds. (New York: Spartan, 1968), p. 183; Allen Schick, "The Road to PPB: The Stages of Budget Reform," *Public Administration Review* 26 (December 1966), p. 257; Aaron Wildavsky, *The Politics of the Budgetary Process,* 2d ed. (Boston: Little, Brown, 1974), p. 136.

6. Schick, p. 257.

7. Thomas P. Lauth, "Performance Evaluation in the Georgia Budgetary Process," *Public Budgeting & Finance* 5 (Spring 1985), p. 72.

8. James R. Ramsey and Merlin M. Hackbart, "Budgeting: Inducements and Impediments to Innova-tions," *State Government* 52 (Spring 1979), p. 69.

9. Thad Juszczak, "Designing Budget Formats for Analysis" (presentation at the 1983 meeting of the American Society for Public Administration).

10. T.R. Carr, "An Evaluation of the Impact of the Priority Budgeting System of Arkansas on Budget Out-comes" (paper presented at the 1983 meeting of the American Society for Public Administration), p. 13.

11. Richard E. Hickman, Jr., "The Effect of Virginia's Program Budget Format on Budget Outcomes" (paper presented at the 1983 meeting of the American Society for Public Administration), p. 8.

12. Mary Patrick Stutzman, "Changing the Format of Budget Documents: The Effect on Budgeting Out-comes" (paper presented at the 1983 meeting of the American Society for Public Administration), p. 15.

13. Eli B. Silverman, "Public Budgeting and Public Administration: Enter the Legislature," *Public Finance Quarterly* 2 (October 1974), p. 477.

14. Frank Sherwood and Ali Eghtedari, "Performance Budgeting in Los Angeles," *Public Administration Review* 20 (Spring 1960), p. 66.

15. Hickman, "Virginia's Program Format," p. 8.

16. Glen Hahn Cope, "The Architecture of Budget Requests: Does Form Follow Function?" (paper pre-sented at the 1983 meeting of the American Society for Public Administration), p. 11.

17. Ronald J. Hrebenar, "State Legislative Budgetary Review Processes: Utilization Patterns of Alternative Information Sources," *Midwest Review of Public Administration* 9 (April–July 1975), p. 140.

18. Fenno, "Impact of PPBS," p. 68.

19. Schick, "Road to PPB," pp. 245–256.

20. *Ibid.,* p. 245.

21. Lewis C. Friedman, "Control, Management, and Planning: An Empirical Examination," *Public Administration Review* 35 (November/December 1975), p. 627.

22. Donald Axelrod, "Post-Burkhead: The State of the Art or Science of Budgeting," *Public Administration Review* 33 (November/December 1973), p. 577.

23. Charles W. Binford, "Reflections on the Performance Budget: Past, Present and Future," *Governmental Finance* 1 (November 1972), p. 30.

24. S. Kenneth Howard. "State Budgeting" in *The Book of the States 1980–81,* vol. 23 (Lexington, Ky.: Council of State Governments), p. 199.

25. James David Barber, *Power in Committees: An Experiment in Governmental Process* (Chicago: Rand McNally, 1966), pp. 34–46.

26. Appendix A contains a more detailed description of the three budget formats studied.

27. Early in the appropriations process information sessions are held. Agency personnel give presentations and committee members ask questions. Later the process is more oriented to deciding how much the committee will recommend that the House and Senate appropriate for each program, budget entity, or line item. Meetings for each format were balanced in terms of the phase of the appropriations process in which they occurred.

An attempt was also made to examine deliberations in several different program areas. Meetings selected using the organizational-unit format were education, corrections, and human resource programs. Program-format meetings were education, human resource, transportation and general government programs. Line-item format meetings were education, human resources, and corrections.

28. A total of 1321 questions/comments were coded by type of concern expressed and then categorized by the orientation related to that concern. For example, questions about program goals, outcomes, and cost-effectiveness were categorized as planning orientation. Questions asking for justifications of individual objects of expenditure were categorized as control orientation. Questions about a department's activities, the amount of work to be done, and the efficiency of agency operations were classified as management oriented.

29. A contingency table analysis showed these differences to be statistically significant at the .001 level. Chi square for the raw frequencies table was 310.06. Cramer's V, representing the degree of association between format and orientation was moderately positive, .34 (the possible range is .00 to 1.00). Because of differences in cell sizes, Chi square and Cramer's V were also calculated for a standardized contingency table. The calculations were similar to those for the raw frequencies table. Chi square was still significant at the .001 level, and Cramer's V was .36.

CHAPTER 20

PARTICIPATORY DEMOCRACY AND BUDGETING
The Effects of Proposition 13

JERRY MCCAFFERY AND JOHN H. BOWMAN

Perhaps the most spectacular attempt at budget control through tax limitations is represented by the passage of Proposition 13,[1] the Jarvis-Gann Initiative, in California on June 6, 1978. Limitations on taxes are not new.[2] However, Proposition 13 has some unique features and special impacts which make it all the more interesting since it quickly became the prototype for limitation attempts in other states. This article explores the complexities of Proposition 13 in the context of fiscal policymaking. One of the major issues to be kept in mind in what follows is that the initiative as an electoral device is generally classified as one of the package of reforms growing out of the Progressive movement of the early 1900's; it permits direct democratic participation. Yet the study of Proposition 13 raises serious questions about the feasibility of participatory democracy in a policy area which commonly has been dominated by experts.

Even the smallest governmental unit exists in an inter-governmental context with diverse revenue structures at its own level and multiple sources of monies and controls stemming from other levels of government. Proposition 13's "meat-axe" approach to taxing—and budgeting—disrupted many of these relationships. What was headlined in petitions as a "property tax limitation"[3] evolved into a complicated and extensive set of consequences. These include a property tax reduction of major proportions (spread unevenly over California's governmental structure), and property tax relief captured only partially by Californians, serious problems of taxpayer equity, and a restructuring of intergovernmental relationships in California. Furthermore, the stringency of that "simple" property tax limit raises the prospect of defaults on certain non-voted debts and may greatly limit the use of general obligation debt instruments. Moreover, the stringency of the limit also will have a direct impact on many of California's cities which have traditionally underfunded pension plans, since these past obligations now must compete with current services for significantly reduced revenues. Ironically, this simple tax limit jeopardizes California's solution to the *Serrano vs. Priest*[4] school finance case. Finally, given the initiative's two-thirds voting requirement for passage of new and/or increased taxes at both state and local levels, what has been done electorally will be even harder to undo. Each of these points will be discussed in more detail below.

INITIAL LOCAL RESPONSES AND STATE BAIL-OUT

In February, 1978, the staff of the California Assembly Revenue and Taxation Committee estimated that passage of Proposition 13 would cost local governments $7 billion out of an anticipated $33.9 billion in total local revenues—a drop of 20.8 per cent.[5] The $33.9 billion figure represented the controller's estimate of a 17.7 per cent increase over the actual 1976–77 total of $28.8 billion for local revenues; the $7 billion reduction threatened to cut local revenues almost $2 billion below the 1976–77 dollar base. Consequently, in the middle of the 1977–78 fiscal year, local government budgeters knew that passage of Proposition 13 would not only cut property taxes nearly 60 per cent and total revenues 20.8 per cent below the levels otherwise expected to be available for the *next* (1978–79) budget year, but that it would put them 6.6 per cent below the base of the *previous* (1976–77) year.

Thus, direct democratic participation limiting the property tax would impose a severe revenue cut on local governments, and a 7 per cent inflation rate for government goods and services made the bite even deeper.[6] Not only would there be 20.8 per cent fewer dollars than expected, but last year's dollars would buy only 93 per cent of what they purchased in 1977–78 and about 86 per cent of what they had purchased in 1976–77. For the 1978–79 budget year, therefore, the total decrease approximated a cut of 26 per cent. On June 6, 1978, the handwriting on the wall was no longer something that could be wished away. Proposition 13 was passed by about as large a majority as those which had squelched two previous tax limitation attempts.[7]

Andrew Glassberg[8] argues that there is a difference between small or incremental declines in available resources and substantial or "quantum" decreases. If there is an expectation that the cut can be restored by resorting to proper strategies, then the cut may be treated as incremental. Quantum cuts are defined by size and a low leadership expectation of revenue restoration; consequently, says Glassberg, " . . . post-crisis managers are operating in a fundamentally different environment . . ." and their familiar strategies for dealing with incremental changes " . . . are unlikely to be applicable . . . ," although many of their initial reactions " . . . will be of the traditional sort developed to deal with incremental budget declines. . . ."[9] Clearly, California local governments faced a quantum revenue decrease, although with a well-publicized state surplus of some $5–6 billion and a legislature in session, an obvious strategy was to replace local revenues with state revenues.

The size of the potential revenue reduction forced local governments to respond immediately. Changes were made to both sides of the revenue-expenditure equation. New budget estimates were called for; increased fees, lay-offs, and service cuts were threatened and often implemented. The largest immediate service reduction occurred in education;[10] in 70 southern California school districts surveyed by the *Los Angeles Times,* about two-thirds eliminated or sharply curtailed summer school.[11] Los Angeles, the biggest school district in the state, not only eliminated summer school, but also closed down its regional occupational training centers and slashed summer recreation by about 60 per cent. Additionally, 10,000 clerical employees, who normally worked on an annual basis, were laid-off for two months. Since schools were major users of the property tax, most had prepared a budget in anticipation of the passage of Proposition 13. In its "doomsday" budget, the Long Beach school board had slashed all interscholastic sports, eliminated adult education, drastically cut the length of the school day and sent lay-off notices to nearly half of its 2,916 teachers.[12] Nor did schools eschew raising or creating new fees and charges of various kinds aimed at community use of school facilities, including swimming pools, racquet ball courts, playing fields, and classrooms for night meetings, adult education, driver education, public lectures, and student health services. At El Camino College, the school catalog now costs $1.00. The San

Diego school board decided to charge community groups $70 for use of the school auditorium and the Los Angeles Community College system set a fee of $1.00 an hour for the use of tennis courts and $2.00 if the lights were on.

Cities, counties, and special districts were not idle during this period. Proposition 13 would become law on July 1. After that date local governments would need a two-thirds popular vote to raise taxes, fees and charges. Consequently, for the remainder of June most local governments concentrated on raising various fees, charges, and other non-property taxes. Some also made cuts in services, but service reductions could always be made later in the summer. After July 1, the tax structure would be very difficult to change. The League of California Cities estimated that over a quarter of the state's 417 cities had raised or were considering raising fees and charges during June.[13] The most popular increase seemed to be business licenses, followed by increases in various utilities, e.g., water, gas, electricity, telephone, cable television, but no source of income was too small to be overlooked.

Seal Beach, which has a long and pleasant beach front, increased beach parking fees from $2 to $3; it also increased business license taxes by 100 per cent. San Francisco raised its zoo admission from $1 to $2 for adults and from 50¢ to 75¢ for children and eliminated free days.[14] Moreover, museum admissions also were increased. The large cities, although they talked about disastrous cuts, tended to wait for state action. Los Angeles froze salaries for 18 elected officials and 44,000 municipal employees. In June, Los Angeles County had laid off only 67 flood control workers. San Diego rescinded its four per cent pay raise and San Diego County established user fees for the flood control district, raised transit district fares by five cents, and eliminated most night service. Some of the communities raised fees and charges dramatically. Beverly Hills' commercial rental tax jumped from $1.25 to $23.50 per $1,000 of gross receipts. Baldwin Park boosted license fees by 40 per cent and raised fees for issuing and processing various city permits by 50 per cent. Buena Park established a $40 paramedic fee for residents and $50 for out-of-towners. Inglewood enacted a fire service fee which included a levy against any structure requiring more fire protection capability than a home. Laguna Beach increased animal and business license fees by almost 100 per cent. Lynwood, in a series of moves that was not atypical, established a fee for almost everything: sewers, fire clearance, fire service, water turn-on and turn-off, the city dump, tree trimming, and sidewalks. Business license fees were increased, as were water rates. Recreation, park maintenance, tree trimming, and sidewalk repair services were reduced. Finally, twenty-six employees were laid off.

Rancho Palos Verdes took out an insurance policy by adding an inflation clause to the existing fee structure. Arcadia provided for street sweeping charges based on front footage of properties. Oakland adopted several new taxes, including a five per cent admission tax on entertainment events; it also increased the real estate transfer tax by 50 per cent and raised the annual business license tax from 90 cents to $14 per $1,000 of gross revenues. The business tax rate on auto dealers was increased from 30¢ to 60¢ per $1,000 of gross receipts. On the service side, the transit district reduced schedules and personnel by 40 per cent. Downey doubled its dog license charge from $5 to $10. Sacramento increased the 18 hole golf fee from $3.50 to $4.50 and raised parking meter fees from 10¢ to 25¢ an hour. Inglewood instituted a "tipplers tax," a 10 per cent surcharge on drinks served at bars. Localities with harbor or marina facilities either created or increased fees and charges. Orange County more than doubled charges for guest slips, moorings, and boat storage at Dana Point and Newport Beach,[15] as well as for the county's 14 regional parks, beaches, and campgrounds. Newport Beach also froze salaries of all public employees and cut trash collections from twice to once a week.

Actions taken by communities during the month of June also included cuts in services. For example, Camarillo extinguished 1,000 street lights; Cerritos eliminated school crossing guards; Compton eliminated its public information and centralized purchasing offices, reduced its senior citizens and recreation activities by 80 per cent, cut its public works crews by 30 per cent, and closed 25 per cent of its fire stations. Covina cut its library staff in half and reduced hours, eliminated crossing guards, and reduced street sweeping from a weekly to monthly basis. Monrovia eliminated most free recreation programs, cut library hours from 56 to 30 a week, and reduced counter time for the public at the planning, building, and safety counters from nine to six hours. Needles closed its city park and recreation department, and transferred the workers to other jobs. Pasadena reduced library hours and maintenance of streets and recreation buildings. Petaluma cut its swimming pool season from eleven months to six. Piedmont eliminated its summer playground program. Riverside imposed fees on swimming pool use and reduced community center hours.

For special districts primarily financed through the property tax (non-enterprise), Proposition 13 was a disaster. About 80 per cent of the expenditures of California's 3,407 non-enterprise districts were made by fire (23.0 per cent), flood (17.7 per cent), planning (29.3 per cent), and parks (9.9 per cent) districts.[16] The property tax accounted, on average, for funding of 89 per cent of the expenditures of fire protection districts, 77 per cent of flood control districts, and 71 per cent of the funding of recreation and parks districts, while planning districts relied on property taxes for less than 1 per cent of their revenues. With the passage of Proposition 13 the total revenues available to the fire, flood, and parks districts would be reduced 51 per cent, 44 per cent, and 41 per cent respectively. These districts now would either have to be supported by other units or get legislative authorization to use a new fee, charge, or tax to replace the property tax revenue loss. Those districts which were able to impose special charges for their services (enterprise districts) tended not to rely heavily on the property tax for revenue. Although the average reliance (14 per cent) for these districts was low, some used it as a major revenue source. Moreover, all would suffer some reduction. Consequently, while some waited to see if the state would make up for the property tax loss, others began to shift more of the burden to their fee structure. For example, the Los Angeles Metropolitan Water District took steps, only a day or two after Proposition 13 passed, to shift its revenues to sales and away from the taxing power. This involved a hearing and rate setting procedure. It was estimated that the District's 12 per cent fee increase would represent a 75 per cent to 100 per cent increase by the time it reached consumers.[17]

In sum, immediately after its passage Proposition 13 was producing visible fee increases and service cutbacks, many of which affected leisure time activities in the season when leisure is most valued, as local governments, large and small, attempted to cope with the prospect of drastically reduced revenues and uncertainty about what the state would do to help them. As Glassberg suggests, even in time of a perceived quantum decrease, they relied mainly on familiar mechanisms, which by and large have some theoretical underpinning, be it an ability-to-pay test (rate based on gross receipts) or economic efficiency (user charges). Meanwhile, threatened cuts in vital services and estimates of Proposition 13 lay-offs continued to appear. On July 1, the Employment Development Division estimated that as of June 28, 3,252 lay-offs had occurred as a result of Proposition 13, with 1,104 occurring in the week of June 21–28. Future lay-offs were estimated to be as high as 165,000.[18]

The State's response came near the end of June. Senate Bill 154 drew upon the large state surplus to provide California local governments with about 90 per cent of what they had expected before the tax limitation (Table 20.1). However, restrictions accompanied the money. Cities were required to use the state aid " . . . first to ensure continuation of the same level of police and fire protection as was provided in 1977–78."[19] However, cities were authorized to effect cost savings so long as they did not impair the protection provided. The same stipulation was applied to

counties. Additionally, counties which accepted any bail out money were barred from disproportionately reducing health services, and their budgets were to be reviewed by the state director of
health services. The largest part of the county aid went for a variety of health and welfare related
programs ($1 billion), not including a one-year waiver of the state's 10 per cent matching require-
ment for the mental health, alcohol, and drug abuse programs. Money for special districts was
distributed to the county boards of supervisors for allocation to the special districts within each
county.[20] Most of the money went to fire protection districts, while those districts with authority
to levy fees and charges were encouraged to do so. Again, fire and police protection levels were
given the highest priority. A $2 billion block grant was extended to school districts to guarantee
an average of 90 per cent of estimated 1978–79 budgets, but it incorporated a sliding scale so
that high spending districts would be guaranteed 85 per cent of their 1978–79 budgets and low
spending districts 91 per cent of theirs. The county office of education also was given a 90 per
cent budget guarantee, primarily for special education and vocational education service provision,
and community colleges were guaranteed 85 per cent of their 1978–79 budgets. A $900 million
state emergency loan fund was created as a loan of last resort, and finally, a very strict local pay
raise control was written in which allowed local discretion only in merit increases and legitimate
promotions, but lock-stepped state and local cost-of-living raises (if state employees received
no cost-of-living raise, neither would anyone else). Those who had voted for Proposition 13 in
an effort to trade-off property tax increases for part of the state surplus had succeeded, but their
victory set in motion a chain of events which would have serious repercussions among taxpayers
and for the state and its subunits.

EFFECTS OF PROPOSITION 13

Property tax controls typically affect other aspects of government finance (e.g., grants, revenue
diversification),[21] and California's Proposition 13 is no exception. Indeed, a bewildering array
of consequences is traceable to the deceptively simple 400-odd-word initiative. The following
discussion illustrates the pervasiveness of the effects in California.[22]

Proposition 13 drops 1978–79 California property taxes some $7 billion (nearly 60 per cent
below what they otherwise would have been (see Table 20.1). This sharp reduction is perhaps the
most unique—and newsworthy—feature of Proposition 13,[23] although the feature may soon spread
to other states. The severity of the property tax cut is quite uneven, both among counties and among
types of governments. Intercounty variation occurs because pre-Proposition 13 county-average tax
rates per $100 of assessed value ranged from $4.75 to $13.15 (average of $11.19) compared to the
new limit of $4.00 (net of bond-service levies).[24] Variation among types of governments occurs
because local governments have relied on property taxes to differing degrees (Table 20.1) and
because Proposition 13 stipulates that constituent units within a county share in the new, lower,
county-collected property tax "according to law," a phrase defined by the legislature to mean previous years' (one year for schools, 3-year average for others) relative property tax shares.[25] The
first-year legislative response to Proposition 13 matches increased state assistance closely to lost
property taxes, however, so that the overall loss of revenues averages about 10 per cent for each
of the major types of local governments (Table 20.1).

Because the increased state aid for 1978–79 comes from accumulated state surpluses, local
governments' property tax losses should translate into tax savings (ignoring for now local revenue adjustments). Not all of the property tax cuts, however, will be captured by Californians.
The portion of the $7 billion reduction most likely to remain largely within the state is that on
owner-occupied residences, which accounts for about 35 per cent of the total (or roughly $2.5

Table 20.1

Effects of Proposition 13 and S.B. 154 Aid on California Local Government Finances, 1978–79 (dollars in millions)

Government Type	Total Revenues—All Sources	Property Tax			S.B. 154 Aid	Net Loss	
		Before Prop. 13	After Prop. 13	Prop. 13 Revenue Loss		Amt.	As % of Total Revenues
Cities[a]	$ 5,292	$ 1,348	$ 542	$ 806	$ 250	$ 556	10.5
Counties[a]	7,740[b]	3,801	1,565	2,236	1,480	756	9.8
Schools	12,125	6,468	2,929	3,539	2,267	1,272	10.5
Sp. Districts (Non-Enterprise)	961	388	172	216	125	91	9.5
(Enterprise)	4,407	443	196	247	0	247	5.6
TOTALS:	$30,165	$12,448	$5,404	$7,044	$4,122	$2,922	9.7

Source: California, State Legislature, *Summary of the Conference Report on S.B. 154 Relative to Implementation of Proposition 13 State Assistance to Local Governments* (Sacramento; June 23, 1978; processed), p. 1.

[a]The independent city of San Francisco is included with the counties.

[b]Excludes $1.911 billion in federal aid attached to AFDC received at the state level and subsequently sent to the counties for disbursement to recipients.

billion).[26] A significant part of this will redound to the federal government in the form of higher income taxes resulting from reduced property tax deductions.[27] The remaining 65 per cent will go in the first instance to business, including owners of residential rental units, agriculture, and public utilities. How much of this will remain in California is difficult to estimate. Depending upon a variety of circumstances (e.g., extent of market competition, mobility of resources), the property tax—and property tax cuts—may rest with the owners of taxed property (shareholders, in the case of corporations), be passed forward to consumers through prices, and/or be passed backward to labor (and other resource suppliers) through wages. The combination of these three tax treatments practiced by California businesses and the representation of Californians in the three groups which ultimately bear taxes jointly will determine the extent to which Californians will share in the business tax reduction, and solid data on these points do not exist. Additionally, the property tax cut will lower California's tax effort and, thereby, its share of federal revenue sharing (with a lag of a couple of years);[28] matching monies for attracting other federal grants also will be harder to come by. In short, Californians may find that a major part of the property tax cut will leak out of the California economy.

Tax savings also will be less to the extent that replacement revenues are raised at either the local or the state levels. It will be difficult, however, to raise taxes for two reasons. One is that the post-Proposition 13 mood at the state level favors tax *cuts*—the legislature enacted a $1 billion state income tax cut in late August, featuring increased personal credits and inflation-index brackets.[29] Indexing will slow the growth of the income tax (and the state surplus). Moreover, Proposition 13 imposes a two-thirds vote requirement for new and increased state and local taxes. For local units, however, it provides that "special taxes" may be imposed with the approval of two-thirds of a jurisdiction's "qualified electors." Neither of these terms is used in California law, so the meaning is not clear.[30] With regard to "special taxes," possible interpretations range from opening to localities revenue sources not previously authorized by the state (e.g., income taxes) if the voters will approve them to removing from local officials the right to adopt or increase the rates of taxes previously authorized by the state.[31] In either case, though, the two-thirds vote requirement may be insuperable. The hurdle would be most easily cleared if "qualified electors" is interpreted to mean those actually voting,[32] but a case can be made for interpreting this to mean those registered to vote, or even those *eligible* to vote—whether registered or not.[33] Interestingly enough, although Proposition 13 is generally said to have received "overwhelming" public support, it would not have passed under any of the above possibilities: those voting yes on Proposition 13 amounted to only 64.7 per cent of those voting (the yes vote exceeded 66 per cent in only 26 of the 58 counties), 42.3 per cent of the registered voters, [34] and perhaps only one-fourth of all potentially eligible voters.

As noted above, many local governments already have turned to new and increased fees and charges to make up part of their revenue losses. It is both appropriate and possible to exact from users the revenues necessary to support some types of publicly provided services, and in these cases greater reliance on user charges should be considered a positive result of Proposition 13, producing improvements in both allocative efficiency (either under- or over-supply can result from divorcing payments from benefits) and equity (non-beneficiaries do not have to subsidize beneficiaries).[35] For other types of services, however, it is either not technically feasible or not desirable (on distributional grounds) to link payments and benefits.[36] These services must be funded from general tax revenues, such as the property tax. Unfortunately, Proposition 13 will present some serious equity problems. One of these results from the large cut in the level of property taxes: there is some evidence that higher levels of taxation are associated with greater assessment uniformity (equity).[37] This source of diminished equity, however, is certain to be dwarfed by inequities resulting from shifting of tax shares among classes of property owners. Proposition 13 requires that new or transferred properties be valued for tax purposes according to their market values at the time of construction or transfer (sale or otherwise), while properties not exchanged since 1975 are valued at 1975 prices, adjusted upward by the lesser of the rate of the state consumer price index increase or 2 per cent per year. (These values constitute "full cash value," on which the tax cannot exceed 1 per cent). This guarantees inequities—on the standard presumption that current market value is the best measure of value for tax purposes—because only recently-sold properties can be valued at market value. In some assessment systems, reassessments between mass re-appraisals in fact are triggered by sales, but California has the dubious distinction of being first to require this method, while precluding ever putting all properties on the same footing through mass reappraisal—and by constitutional provision! The effect is to make the "property tax" more dependent upon mobility and property turnover than on property value, and to cause newcomers to a community to bear a disproportionate share of the cost of local services. Because business properties sell less frequently than residential properties, this same provision will cause residential properties to bear an increasing share of the property tax over time—probably not a result contemplated by the typical supporter of Proposition 13. Some offset to this business-to residential tax share shift is provided by the fact that Proposition 13's valuation provisions (although not its rate limitations) apply only to real property, for in California the only tangible personal property that is taxable is that of business, and it is revalued annually.[38] The offset is unlikely to be complete, however, since tangible personal property accounted for less than 15 per cent of taxable property values before Proposition 13.[39]

Relationships among governmental units, as well as among taxpayers, are affected by Proposition 13 and the state legislation implementing it. In general, the changes are toward greater centralization and decreased local control.[40] At the root of the changes, of course, is the nearly 60 per cent reduction of the property tax which dropped this tax's share of total 1978–79 revenues for California local governments from 40 per cent to 18 per cent.[41] The argument has been made by some that, because of the historically high reliance of local governments on property taxation and the notion that this tax is better suited than other major taxes to local use, anything that weakens the property tax weakens local government (and conversely for strengthening the tax).[42] In California, this tendency of the property tax reduction itself has been reinforced by several provisions of S.B. 154, the statute clarifying Proposition 13 and providing for state assistance to make up much of the revenue loss. State-local and inter-local relationships both are affected. Whereas nearly 6,300 units of local government had imposed property taxes,[43] now only the 58 counties (including the independent city of San Francisco) can levy a property tax because Section 1 of Proposition 13 provides that the property tax is " . . . to be collected by the counties and apportioned according to law to the districts within the counties" and S.B. 154 gives meaning to this by stipulating that the counties also *levy* the tax and then divide the proceeds on the basis of historic shares of property tax collections.[44] This greatly reduces the ability of local units to effect their own fiscal policies; the county and state roles have increased at the expense of all other units formerly having authority to levy property taxes. This is particularly true for special districts, whose tax-replacement aid goes first to county governments. Each county will receive an allocation of money for special districts (based on the counties' shares of special district property tax losses), but "the county will have complete discretion in allocating the assistance [within state-prescribed] guidelines."[45] While many government "reformers" will applaud this apparent victory of the elected generalists over the special-purpose units,[46] the change will not necessarily be for the better in all cases; special-purpose units with boundaries differing from those of the multi-purpose units often will permit clear equity and efficiency gains—e.g., better correspondence between actual and desired service levels and between benefit and financing areas.[47] Moreover, if "fiscal pressures" are a poor basis for determining the assignment of functional responsibilities,[48] it is not clear that the pressure produced by Proposition 13 will produce the optimal functional re-alignment.

The advent of uniform county-wide property taxes[49] will have other effects, as well. For example, intra-county tax rate differentials which may distort locational decisions[50] will be eliminated. Another *potentially* beneficial effect would be the reduction of fiscal capacity disparities and the consequent removal of one source of expenditure variation,[51] but as long as the proceeds from these levies are distributed on the basis of prior years' property tax collections, this gain cannot occur (except to the extent that *future* decisions that would have worsened matters are averted). The current combination of uniform tax rates within a county and allocation among units based on historic tax patterns means that rural areas (where taxes generally have been relatively low) will tend to subsidize urban areas (where tax rates generally have been higher), a result that may be either desirable or undesirable depending upon the circumstances of a particular situation (and, of course, the criteria used to evaluate such a shift). Other results more obviously tend to be undesirable. For example, rapidly growing areas will have no control over their property tax revenues and may be unable to serve expanded populations and/or new properties (e.g., factories, shopping malls) without lowering the overall level of service; growth in a *single* small unit will translate into increased revenues for the entire county area and for *all* units within the county (other than special districts) in proportion to pre-FY 1979 tax shares. This is Twin Cities-style tax-base sharing carried to the extreme.[52] This may affect special districts with no revenue source other than property taxes (and property tax replacement aid) the hardest—e.g., many fire protection districts—but cities and school corporations could fare worse, however, due to the inflexibility of current (S.B. 154) aid distribution provisions; special districts at least have the opportunity to press their cases for increased revenues with the county, which determines intra-county special district tax-replacement shares.

In addition to the largely inter-local effects discussed above, the post-Proposition 13 situation also changes previous state-local relationships. As already noted, the major property tax replacement funds to date have come from an accumulated state surplus, and increased state funding has brought increased state control. Thus, for example, no local unit can receive state tax-replacement aid or loan funds under S.B. 154 if it grants cost-of-living pay increases for 1978–79 to its employees, welfare recipients, or others, in excess of those granted to state employees; the state's police powers are invoked to render "null and void" any contractual provisions to the contrary, and these provisions also " . . . supersede any inconsistent provisions in the charter of any county or city."[53] Other "strings" attached to increased state aid, already noted, include the requirement that counties, cities, and appropriate special districts give first priority to police and fire service so that local units will not drop below 1977–78 levels of *service* in these functional areas; provisions concerning health service reductions; provisions which make special districts dependent upon overlying general-unit discretion for tax-replacement distributions (which could provide leverage for other county- or city-initiated controls); and various provisions pertaining to education finance.

Proposition 13, as noted, threatened to undo the legislature's response to the California Supreme Court's demands in *Serrano vs. Priest* for school finance restructuring, a further intergovernmental problem. The Assembly Education Committee argued that the tax limits would preclude high-wealth district tax increases which were to transfer money to the state starting in 1978–79 as part of the equalization provisions, make it impossible for districts to raise the local share of foundation-program funding, and render revenue limits meaningless.[54] S.B.154's education provisions, described earlier, represent the initial reworking of the *Serrano* solution, and it appears that the state's guarantee of a higher percentage of estimated 1978–79 budgets for low-spending districts than for high-spending districts (91 per cent vs. 85 per cent)—combined with the Proposition 13 tax limits—will cause per pupil expenditure disparities to be reduced more quickly than otherwise.[55]

In short, Proposition 13 has served as the vehicle for some extensive changes in California intergovernmental relations, including structural and functional adjustments as well as increased centralization of both decision-making authority and financing.

Other effects of Proposition 13 are numerous (and some no doubt have not yet been identified), but only a few more can be noted here. The Assembly Revenue and Taxation Committee notes that, "Many cities have seriously under-funded employee pension and retirement systems, . . ."[56] This situation may mean even deeper cuts in current services than otherwise would be necessary, for current services must compete for strictly limited (and reduced) revenues with unliquidated obligations from prior years. The competition between current services and debt service also is intensified. Outstanding debt issued without voter approval (unlike voted debt approved before July 1, 1978) does not entitle the issuing jurisdiction to property taxes in excess of those available under the new general limits. For units with such debt, an already tight fiscal situation is made even tighter. Possible outcomes include one or more of the following: further cuts in current services, default, and New York-style state and/or federal rescue. Future debt issues, whether voted or not, must be serviced within the Proposition 13 tax limitation. This means general obligation borrowing may be infeasible in many—perhaps most—instances in the future,[57] especially if tax-replacement aid is reduced and/or continues to be tied to historic property tax shares. In any event, the fact of property tax reduction and limitation is likely to result in higher bond interest rates.

CONCLUSION

The complexities associated with Proposition 13 provide a lesson in the hazards of fiscal policymaking through direct voter participation. While the full effects of Proposition 13 are not yet known, it is clear that it has reshaped California local government finance overnight. The financing role of property taxes has been cut from 40 per cent to 18 per cent for local governments on average. Furthermore, the tax now can be levied by only 58 counties at a county-wide uniform rate (excluding levies for old debt) rather than by some 6,300 local units, although these other units still share in property tax revenues on the basis of prior years' levies. Even if a community within a county were to agree unanimously to increase property taxes, it now has no authority to do so. Moreover; within any county this new system will fail to target increased revenue to units with rapidly increasing needs, and the tax-base incentive for cultivating new business development is diminished. Ironically, it appears that much of the property tax savings from this reduction will flow outside California. Homeowners clearly will enjoy some relief from recent high property taxes, but the extent of relief going to renters remains uncertain. In addition, mass reappraisals are now barred and all reassessments (other than an across-the-board increase of up to 2 per cent are triggered by transfer. of property or new construction. Over time, this will shift an increasing share of property taxes toward homeowners (and within this group, those who change residences) and guarantee inequities because only recently sold properties can be valued according to current market value; thus, the tax increasingly will become a tax on mobility.

The diminished role of this traditional local tax work-horse dramatically increases the importance of state aids. At least in the first year, increased state aids have meant increased state control over local government finances and structures—a development that is not likely to be reversed.

A huge state surplus played a role that cannot be over-estimated. On the one hand, the surplus may have contributed strongly to the passage of Proposition 13. On the other hand, it was essential to an orderly transition. The essential question is whether a surplus of such magnitude will continue to be available for future rescue operations.

NOTES

1. Briefly, Proposition 13 sets the maximum property tax rate at 4 per cent of assessed value, limits to no more than 2 per cent per year the assessed value increase for any real property with unchanged ownership, and requires that both state and local tax increases receive two-thirds approval. These provisions are developed more fully below.

2. Advisory Commission on Intergovernmental Relations (ACIR), *State Limitations on Local Taxes and Expenditures*, A-64 (Washington: Government Printing Office, 1977).

3. As presented on the sheet covering the Jarvis-Gann initiative petitions [California, Assembly Revenue and Taxation Committee, *Facts About Proposition 13: The Jarvis/Gann Initiative*, revised edition (Sacramento; February 21, 1978, processed), Appendix 1, p. 56] (hereafter cited as *Facts*).

4. 487 P. 2d 1241, 96 *California Reporter* 601 (1971).

5. *Facts*, p. 41.

6. Increases in the state-local government purchases deflator were 9.1 per cent, 6.2 per cent, and 6.8 per cent for 1975, 1976, and 1977, respectively [U.S., Department of Commerce, *Survey of Current Business*, 57 (January, 1977), Table 27, p. 17; 58 (June, 1978), Table 27, p. 14].

7. The 1968 and 1972 Watson Initiatives were defeated by percentages of 69 per cent and 65.9 per cent (*Facts;* p. 1). Proposition 13 passed with a 64.7 per cent majority according to voting statistics from the California Office of the Secretary of State (Sacramento; June 9,1978; processed).

8. Andrew Glassberg, "Organizational Responses to Municipal Budget Decreases," *Public Administration Review,* 38 (July/August, 1978), pp. 325–332.

9. *Ibid.,* see discussion pp. 327–328.

10. "Many School Districts Cancelling Summer Classes," *Los Angeles Times,* June 9, 1978, Part I, pp. 1, 16.

11. "Schools Scramble to Make Up Lost Funds," *Los Angeles Times,* Part I, p. 3, July 3, 1978. Unless otherwise cited, the information on schools is drawn from this source, pp. 3 and 16.

12. The state bail-out money made many such actions unnecessary. On average, it was expected that most school districts would be provided with more money than they had the previous year, but less than what they had expected to have in 1978–79 [*ibid,* p. 16].

13. Ronald Soble, "Local Fees and Taxes Grow Under Prop. 13;" *Los Angeles Times,* July 3, 1978, Part I, p. 1.

14. "Prop. 13 Impact This Year Still Uncertain," *Los Angeles Times,* July 3, 1978, Part I, pp. 3, 12–14, is the source for information on cities and counties, unless otherwise cited.

15. Soble, *loc. cit.*

16. California, Legislative Analyst, *An Analysis of Proposition 13: The Jarvis-Gann Initiative* (Sacramento; May 1978; processed), Tables V-34 and V-35, pp. 155–56. (hereafter cited as Legislative Analyst report).

17. "Legislature Passes Prop. 13 Rescue Bill," *Los Angeles Times,* June 24, 1978, Part I, pp. 1, 24–25.

18. *Los Angeles Times,* July 3, 1978, Part I, p. 3. June was a month of sabre rattling. There were some scarce headlines concerning actions which never materialized and other actions were taken and rescinded. Finally, the count of persons who actually lost jobs varied. On June 8, Los Angeles said it would have to fire 8300 workers; by July 8, no one had been laid-off [*Los Angeles Times,* June 8, 1978, Part 1, pp. 1, 20, and July 8, 1978, Part II, p. 1]. School districts started cancelling summer classes on June 9, with some expressing doubt about their ability to open on schedule in the fall, without aid, [*Los Angeles Times,* June 9, 1978, Part I, pp. 1 and 17] or to stay open beyond December [*Los Angeles Times,* June 10, 1978, Part I, p. 28]. The state first claimed that as many as 450,000 Proposition 13 lay-offs would occur. On June 11, it cut this figure in half [*Los Angeles Times,* June 11, 1978, Part I, pp. 3 and 22]. The Congressional Budget Office estimated a total of 60,000 jobs would be lost as a result of Proposition 13 [*Los Angeles Times,* July 7, 1978, Part I, p. 1]. On July 13, the Governor's office estimated that 8327 Proposition 13 lay-offs had occurred. The number is and will be hard to determine, due to such factors as early retirements and higher attrition rates caused by diminished pay increases.

19. California, State Legislature, *Summary of the Conference Report on SB 154 Relative to Implementation of Proposition 13 and State Assistance to Local Governments* (Sacramento; June 23, 1978; processed),

p. 4, This report is the source of information on the state response to Proposition 13 in the balance of this section.

20. Conversations with legislative staff disclosed that giving the money directly to counties for apportionment to special districts was an attempt at regaining administrative integrity within counties, by making special districts compete with other units for resources.

21. See, for example, the description of Indiana's program in Donald W. Kiefer, "The 1973 Tax Package," *Indiana Business Review,* 49 (October, 1974), Special Tax Issue, pp. 3–31; ACIR, *Limitations,* for a more general treatment of several states' programs; and Helen F. Ladd, "An Economic Evaluation of State Limitations on Local Taxing and Spending Powers," *National Tax Journal,* 31 (March, 1978), pp. 1–18.

22. For excellent analyses of the wide range of effects, see *Facts* and Legislative Analyst report, cited above.

23. Limits typically seek to control future tax growth. Where cuts have been made, however, the state—as an integral part of the program—generally has replaced local revenue losses. For example, see Kiefer, op. cit., p. 3; and Robert J. Kosydar and John H. Bowman, "Modernization of State Tax Systems: The Ohio Experience," *National Tax Journal,* 25 (September, 1972), p. 379.

24. The rates are for 1976–77 [California, State Board of Equalization, *Annual Report 1976–77* (Sacramento; State of California, December, 1977), Table 14, p. A-19.].

25. *SB 154 Conference Report,* p. 2.

26. Figures of the Legislative Analyst as cited in George Skelton, "Major Loss of Property Tax Saving Seen," *Los Angeles Times,* June 13, 1978, Part I, pp. 1, 27.

27. *Facts,* p. 72.

28. *Ibid.,* p. 48, and Legislative Analyst report, pp. 55–56.

29. George Skelton, "State's Biggest Tax Slash Becomes Law," *Los Angeles Times,* August 31, 1978, Part I, pp. 1, 24.

30. *Facts,* p. 27.

31. *Ibid.,* pp. 27–29, presents a discussion.

32. Legislative Counsel advises this interpretation is likely because the literal requirements probably could not be met [Legislative Analyst report, p. 42].

33. *Facts,* p. 27.

34. Voting statistics from the California Secretary of State.

35. Selma Mushkin, ed., *Public Prices for Public Products* (Washington: The Urban Institute, 1972), is an excellent source of information on user charges.

36. See Mikesell, this symposium.

37. John H. Bowman and John L. Mikesell, "Uniform Assessment of Property: Returns from Institutional Remedies," *National Tax Journal,* 31 (June, 1978).

38. *Facts,* p. 17, and California, State Board of Equalization, Assessment Standards Division, *Proposition 13, Jarvis-Gann Initiative* (Sacramento; June 8, 1978; processed), pp. 3, 20. The latter suggests implementation procedures to county assessors.

39. Based on assessed values for 1977–78 [State Board of Equalization, *Annual Report 1976–77,* Table 4, p. A-4].

40. Major intergovernmental effects are summarized well by David B. Walker, "Proposition 13 and California's System of Governance," *Intergovernmental Perspective* 4 (Summer, 1978), pp. 13–15.

41. The figures, respectively, are from the Legislative Analyst report, p. 13, and *SB 154 Conference Report,* p. 1. Reliance on the property tax varies considerably among governmental units; based on pre-Proposition 13 data (the 40 per cent average), counties got from 32–40 per cent of their revenues from the property tax; cities, from 0–6 per cent; school districts, from. 20–90 per cent and special districts, 0–100 per cent [*Facts,* p. 8]. The variation will continue, given the historically-based allocation of property taxes under S.B. 154, although at lower overall percentages.

42. See Richard P. Nathan, "Is Local Control the Loser in Jarvis Vote?," *Wall Street Journal,* June 8, 1978, p. 18; and Glenn W. Fisher, "Property Taxation and the Political System," in Arthur D. Lynn, Jr., ed., *Property Taxation and Public Policy.* TRED 8 (Madison, University of Wisconsin Press, 1976), pp. 5–22.

43. Legislative Analyst report, p. 11.

44. *SB 154 Conference Report,* p. 2. Other possible approaches are discussed in *Facts,* pp. 13–16.

45. *SB 154 Conference Report,* p. 7. Exceptions are multi-county districts (which will receive aid directly from the state) and city subsidiary districts (which will be subject to city council funding decisions).

46. Walker, *op. cit.,* p. 14.

47. For discussions of pertinent considerations, see: Wallace E. Oates, *Fiscal Federalism* (New York: Harcourt Brace Jovanovich, 1972), ch. 2, pp. 31–53; Robert L. Bish, *The Public Economy of Metropolitan Areas* (Chicago: Markham, 1971), ch. 3, pp. 35–62; and Gordon Tulluck, "Federalism: Problems of Scale," *Public Choice,* 6 (Spring, 1969), pp. 19–29.

48. ACIR, *Governmental Functions and Processes: Local and Areawide,* A-45 (Washington: Government Printing Office, 1974), pp. 19, 122–25.

49. In addition to the basic rate ceiling of 1 per cent of full cash value (4 per cent of assessed value, given the state's 25 per cent assessment standard), property taxes to service debt authorized by voters before July 1, 1978, also can be imposed at rates differing among areas as debt loads vary relative to the tax base. As a result, the statewide average property tax rate for 1978–79 is expected to be 5 per cent although this will approach 4 per cent over time as these earlier debt issues are retired [*Facts,* p. 13]. Richard O'Reilly, "Tax Cut Will Be Less Than Many Expect," *Los Angeles Times,* August 24, 1978, Part I, pp. 3, 22, discusses Los Angeles County effects.

50. Roger W. Schmenner, "City Taxes and Industry Location," in *Proceedings of the Sixty-Sixth (1973) Annual Conference on Taxation* (Columbus, Ohio: National Tax Association-Tax Institute of America, 1974), pp. 528–32.

51. John H. Bowman, "Tax Exportability, Intergovernmental Aid, and School Reform," *National Tax Journal,* 27 (June, 1974), pp. 163–73.

52. Under 1971 state legislation, communities in the seven-counties of the Minneapolis-St. Paul SMSA share 40 per cent of commercial and industrial assessed value increases [see Gene Knaff, *Tax Base Sharing: The Minnesota Program After Two Years* (St. Paul: Metropolitan Council of the Twin Cities Area; December, 1977; processed); and Walter H. Plosila, "Metropolitan Tax-Base Sharing: Its Potential and Limitations," *Public Finance Quarterly,* 4 (April, 1976), pp. 205–224]. In California 100 per cent of the assessed value increase from *all* assessed value increases in a county is shared throughout the county in proportion to pre-FY1979 tax levies.

53. *SB 154 Conference Report,* p. 12.

54. *Facts,* pp. 50, 53, and Legislative Analyst report, pp. 140–41.

55. Equal spending and equal educational opportunity, of course, are not synonymous; sometimes higher spending is necessary to give some pupils needed services. A nationally-syndicated column focused late in July on effects of Proposition 13 budgetary pressures (15 per cent cut below previously planned level) in San Francisco schools " . . . where school children speak 17 different tongues as their First language, . . .": special programs are being cut (e.g., 200 non-tenured bilingual education program teachers are being terminated) to preserve most programs affecting larger numbers of students [Jack W. Germond and Jules Witcover, "Politics Today: Prop. 13 Squeeze Already Felt in 'Frisco's Schools," Bloomington, Indiana, *Herald-Telephone,* July 27, 1978, p. 8].

56. *Facts,* p. 43.

57. *Ibid.,* pp. 16, 29–30, and 45–47, discusses these and other debt-related matters. Bonds threatened with default include "assessment" bonds (issued for street lighting and similar localized improvements), "tax increment" bonds (e.g., those issued by redevelopment agencies to be repaid from higher tax revenues resulting from redevelopment), and "lease/purchase" bonds (for facilities financed by government and then leased). This last type is in increased danger of default only if the lessee is another government dependent upon property taxes for lease payment funds.

PART 5

CONSTRAINTS

Budgeting is characterized by constraints, as illustrated by the Proposition 13 citizen referendum, and the top down budgeting represented by the Budget Enforcement Act and its spending caps. Those are only two of the many legal constraints on budgeting. State and local levels of government have to deal with intergovernmental constraints, in the form of requirements for the receipt of grants and mandated services and service levels. Local governments are not free to establish functions or taxes unless the state level government says they can. Even home rule, which gives somewhat broader powers to local governments, grants only limited autonomy. A further constraint has to do with earmarking, which may limit particular revenue sources to particular items of expenditure, and the establishment of floors, minimum amounts of spending for favored programs.

In this part, four types of constraints are discussed. One results from intergovernmental relations, where a higher level of government mandates spending or service levels or provides grants for particular services or for general revenue. Grants often come with strings attached, which reduce the budgetary flexibility of the recipient. Mandates order state or local governments to provide a service at a particular minimum level but may not provide the funding, setting up additional constraints. A second major source of budgeting constraints is the growth of entitlements. Entitlements are a form of direct spending that goes up automatically when there are more people eligible for funding. If there is only so much money, and entitlements are increasingly expensive, they push out other forms of spending. Elected officials might want to spend more on education or road improvements, but they can't because they have to pay whatever the entitlement programs end up costing. What is left can go to other programs. A third form of constraint comes from tax and expenditure limitations, such as Proposition 13. These may be in the form of constitutional amendments, making them especially difficult to change. A fourth constraint is litigation, the result of courts making judgments. These settlements, like entitlements, take priority in the budget, overruling whatever preferences elected officials or citizens might have. Money for court settlements must be paid first. Note that courts redressing wrongs and enforcing rights is part of a democratic structure, as is citizen direct democracy as seen in some tax and expenditure limitations.

One theme in this part is that federalism in the United States has provided a changing rather than a fixed structure of operations for state and local governments. George Break puts the issue of central government power versus the power of the state and local governments in historical and political context, noting the willingness of Democratic administrations to use the power of the central government to achieve social ends and the determination of Republicans to decentralize power back to the states, and the alternation between parties and policies that has marked the period from the Great Depression of the 1930s onward. Break examines the Reagan administration's New Federalism proposals of the early 1980s in this context.

Ray and Conlan examine the emotional issue of mandates and how much they really cost. They find the costs not as overwhelming as had been claimed and conclude that much of the emotional response to mandates lies in its ability to preempt state and local priorities, to curtail autonomy, rather than in the actual dollar impact. Since Ray and Conlan published their piece on mandates, the federal government passed a law restricting the federal government's ability to impose unfunded mandates on state and local governments. While the law is not ironclad, it seems to have increased congressional awareness of the burdens they have often shifted to the states, and may have reduced the tendency to add new burdens.

In the subpart on entitlements, Ysander and Robinson describe what entitlements are and how they reduce discretion in budgeting, and propose some possible solutions. In the United States, however, no solutions have yet been worked out, and entitlements remain a major constraint on U.S. budgets, a kind of first call on revenues. Only after entitlements are funded is money available for other purposes, which creates problems when there is a defense buildup. Those problems are exaggerated when defense is building up during a period of reduced taxation. The result has to be either cutbacks in other services and programs or deficits, or both. Joe White addresses the issue more broadly of how budgeting for entitlements differs from budgeting for other kinds of programs and how both policy and budget theory have to adapt to this very different kind of expenditure.

The subpart on tax and expenditure limitations addresses the issue of popular support for such limits and the consequences of passing them. These two selections were published in 1982, reflecting the passage of Proposition 13 in California in 1978, and the passage of major tax limitations in other states at around the same time. After 1982, the movement toward tax and expenditure limits slowed down in the states, but the ones that were passed generally remain in place, providing formidable constraints on budgeting. The possibility that such limits might be passed frames budgeting even in states that did not pass such measures.

Caiden and Chapman describe what happens to budgeting when revenue constraints such as Proposition 13 in California are filtered through the state level to the local level, resulting in magnified uncertainty and repetitive budgeting, as budget numbers shift from day to day and month to month. Cope and Grubb examine the variety of tax limits imposed in Texas, concluding that what triggers these popular tax limitation movements is the property tax rather than all taxes, and tax increases rather than the absolute level of taxation. It matters less whether the level of taxation is high or low than it does whether it is increasing rapidly. These authors confirm for Texas what Caiden and Chapman contend in their piece on California, that limitations on revenue (including bonds) result in the fragmentation of government at the local level.

Tax limitation movements focus on revenue constraints, but courts can make judgments in a variety of areas. They can decide that a particular revenue source is illegal and has to be given back to the taxpayers; they can decide that a particular expenditure is mandated and that local governments have to provide it, regardless of local priorities. The courts often get into budgeting when rights are involved. They may judge that schools with primarily black children are underfunded compared to schools with primarily white students and that the school districts must equalize the physical facilities or the per pupil spending. Or they may judge that a state spending formula to equalize spending on all students unfairly penalizes school districts where parents choose to tax themselves more heavily to give their children a better education. Jeffrey Straussman and Kurt Thurmaier, in the essay reprinted here, discuss court cases based on overcrowding of prisons, and the disproportionate and cruel punishment that results. Straussman has developed this idea of rights-based budgeting in several other articles as well. In a democratic society, where there are constitutional rights of citizens, courts may become budgeters by reorienting priorities to assure that those rights are respected.

CHAPTER 21

CHANGES IN INTERGOVERNMENTAL FISCAL PATTERNS

GEORGE F. BREAK

If the Reagan Administration's intention to shift some measure of fiscal responsibility away from Washington and place more decision-making power in state capitals inspires a sense of déjà vu, it happens not only because the package label, "the New Federalism," has a well-worn look born of earlier usage, but also because the decentralization concept has been recycled through every Republican administration elected within the last half century. The basic issue, indeed, is as old as our federal republic.

The implicit constitutional recognition of the central government as one of delegated and limited powers was given explicit clarification in the Tenth Amendment, which rounded off the Bill of Rights with the ringing assurance that all powers not delegated to the federal government nor constitutionally disallowed to the states belong to the states or to the people. Although this apparent guarantee of a rather wide range of state power—and responsibility—was a major issue in the 19th century, leading to many arguments over what was "implied" by the assigned powers, the focus in recent years has largely shifted to the other end of the spectrum. There attention has been so concentrated on trimming the authority of the states over areas such as civil rights, which they have handled inequitably or inadequately, that the Tenth Amendment, to some observers at least, has seemed to be more honored in the breach than the observance. Yet it lingers as an issue, and the question of its importance may be the greatest ideological difference separating Republicans from Democrats.

What is this thing called Federalism? In the heat and misery of the Great Depression a reluctant Democratic administration, seeing human need and perceiving the fiscal ineptitude (or incapacity) of state and local governments, established direct and unprecedented links between Washington and the places of need, thereby bypassing the old forms and superimposing new architecture on the old structure of American government. Every Republican administration since then (save perhaps the brief troubled one of Gerald Ford) has tried, at least nominally, to restore some of the old structural outlines, but those efforts have tended to encounter irresistible forces that thwarted the attempts. Eisenhower endorsed the Kestnbaum Commission's recommendations and proclaimed his support for returning powers and fiscal responsibilities to the states. Yet overwhelmed by the shock of Sputnik and the pressure of the baby boom, his administration inaugurated the first major outpouring of federal aid to

From *Public Budgeting and Finance,* vol. 2, no. 4 (Winter 1982), 42–57. Copyright © 1982 by Public Financial Publications, Inc. Reprinted with permission.

local school districts. Pushed by General Motors and the boom in automobiles, the same administration accelerated the effusion of federal money for highways, creating an interstate highway program with a federal matching portion of 90 percent. Instead of diminishing the federal role, Eisenhower's legacy made for heavier dependence of state and local governments on Washington.

Nixon's call for a "New Federalism" came in the wake of the tidal wave of categorical federal grants unleashed by Johnson's Great Society, which had extended direct federal support not only to a whole spectrum of state and local government agencies, but also to a wide new circle of "para-governmental" groups formed to awaken the political consciousness of formerly inactive segments of the society. Nixon's plan was to replace many of these categorical outlays with a dual system of federal revenue sharing that would give important distributional responsibility to the states. Some of the federal money was to be aimed at specified general problems (the term "Special Revenue Sharing" was later replaced simply by "block grants"), while some was to be unrestricted (General Revenue Sharing). Despite the enactment of some portions of the proposed program, Nixon's New Federalism certainly did not separate functions or tidy up the structure of government. The attempt to streamline and consolidate the maze of categoricals produced a few block grants, but they tended to suffer from a deeply rooted Washington disease known as "hardening of the categories," and most of them came out of Congress looking more like knobby bundles of old parts than like carefully articulated new vehicles. Even General Revenue Sharing did disappointingly little to "return decision-making power to the states," insofar as it was hobbled by a grotesquely complex and controversial set of distribution formulas and given a limited life span and a meager budget; in practice, moreover, it was subject to the same far-reaching set of congressionally mandated restrictions and regulations that governed other federal grants.

With the relatively conservative instincts of a Southern Democrat, even Carter made a campaign issue of the need to simplify and reorganize the tangled world of the federal bureaucracy, but he too succeeded only in enlarging the scope of Washington's fiscal responsibility—or, as conservatives saw it, Washington's "intrusion" into affairs of state and local jurisdictions.

Against this background, Reagan's blueprint for a "New Federalism" can be seen either as simply the newest version of an old and outmoded design or as an exciting means of restoring the venerable outlines of an ancient but heavily overlaid federal structure. To those who argue that there is no reason to think that this proposal for remodeling will be more successful than the last, one possibly significant rejoinder can be made. That ultimate arbiter of structural revision, the Supreme Court, may well be undergoing an important change of attitude. The addition of Justice O'Connor has apparently reinforced the efforts of Justice Rehnquist to breathe new life into the Tenth Amendment and reverse the tide of federal government expansion. Any further Reagan appointees could accelerate that trend.

In the final analysis, of course, it is the people whose support, indifference, or opposition will determine the eventual fate of Reagan's New Federalism proposals. These would bring about three major changes, spread out in varying degrees over the next ten years—sharply reduced support levels for federal aid to state and local governments, structural alterations in the federal grant system toward greater use of block grants, and some major reassignments of spending and operational responsibilities in the U.S. federal system.

LOWER SUPPORT LEVELS FOR FEDERAL AID

For federal grants-in-aid, fiscal 1981 may well turn out to have been a critical watershed year. The amounts did increase from $91.5 billion in 1980 to $94.8 billion in 1981, but that percentage increase (3.6) was the smallest in 20 years, and in purchasing power it represented a decline of more than four percent. Such a sudden reversal of past trends was hard enough for recipients to adjust to, but worse still was the prospect, presented in the Reagan Administration's 1982 budget proposals, that federal grant monies would decline to $91.2 billion in 1982 and to $81.4 billion in 1983. At projected inflation rates, that would represent a decline in real grant funds of 25.7 percent in two years. No wonder there has been distress and dismay in states and localities. And there may be much more to come.

These changes, however, do not occur in isolation, and it is important to view them in their proper context. A lower level of spending on federal aid implies some accompanying change in the federal budget. Although the precise nature of those changes can never be specified, three possibilities deserve discussion in the present economic environment—higher defense spending, lower federal taxes, and lower budget deficits.

Time-Lag Effects of Budget Shifts

That future increases in defense spending will come, at least in part, at the expense of federal aid to state and local governments seems virtually certain. Such a substitution represents not only a functional realignment of federal spending priorities but also a regional reallocation of federal money flows (Advisory Commission on Intergovernmental Relations (ACIR), June 1980). Some states will gain on balance, while others lose. It is extremely difficult to estimate the geographic incidence of defense spending because of the problems involved in tracing the purchase goods and services by prime defense contractors from subcontractors and other businesses in different states. Available estimates do, however, give a rough picture of the kinds of regional reallocations involved. In 1974–76, for example, California received 20 percent of military outlays other than compensation of personnel, but only 10 percent of federal aid to state and local governments. For New York State the two percentages were 8½ and 11½ respectively (ACIR, June 1980, pp. 84–85). Even states that stand to gain about as much in increased defense spending as they lose in federal aid can expect to feel some important economic effects. Initially these will derive simply from timing. Since the cutbacks in federal aid are scheduled to occur quickly while the growth in defense spending will come much more slowly, many states will face reduced federal money flows in the short run, whatever their long-term prospects from the program substitution may be. The additional fact that during that period lower federal aid implies lower federal budget deficits introduces a combination of effects to be discussed later.

Flypaper Effects

The second-stage effects of the Reagan budget shifts, hinging on how and where the money is spent once it begins to circulate in the economy, may be of even greater significance. A state that gains as much in its private sector income from higher defense spending as it loses in public sector income from lower federal aid can, experience tells us, be expected to end up spending less on government services than before. Even though total state income remains unchanged, the shift from one sector to another is most likely to make a difference. Money tends to stick where it lands, and empirical studies of these flypaper effects confirm the strong propensity of public officials to spend more of an income gain on government programs than do private individuals when they receive the income gain directly (George F. Break, 1980, pp. 91–93; Edward M. Gramlich, 1977).

Federal Tax Reduction or Stabilization?

As important as the shift of federal priorities from domestic to defense spending among the Reagan fiscal initiatives was the Economic Recovery Tax Act of 1981 (ERTA). This early product of

Figure 21.1   Individual Income Taxes as a Percentage of Taxable Personal Income

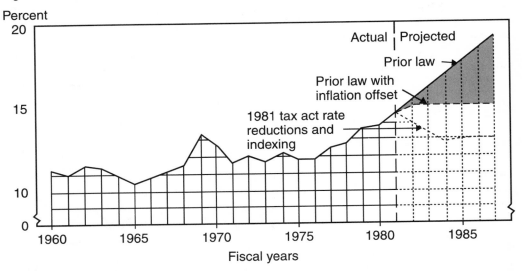

Source: United States Congress, Congressional Budget Office, *Baseline Budget Projections for Fiscal Years 1983–1987* (Washington, D.C.: U.S. Government Printing Office, February 1982), p. 32.

the new administration has often been described as the largest tax reduction in U.S. history. And indeed it was, compared to what could have happened had it not been passed and had no other changes been made in the federal tax laws. Compared to the level of tax burdens existing before it was passed, however, its accomplishments are much more ambiguous. Measurement is complicated, for one thing, by the effects of inflation on federal income tax burdens. Under prior tax law, individuals with constant real incomes were steadily pushed into higher and higher tax-rate brackets. Adopting the assumption that the appropriate standard for comparisons is a constant level of real tax burdens on individuals, Congressional Budget Office projections show that ERTA tax rate reductions and inflation indexation lowered individual income taxes from 15 percent of taxable personal income in 1981 to 13 percent in 1987, as compared to a 19 percent burden level that would by that time have prevailed under the old (prior) tax law (Figure 21.1). On that basis, in other words, two-thirds of ERTA's total tax reduction represents a stabilization of 1981 real tax burdens and one-third a reduction in such burdens. Of course, if the proper comparison is with the level of individual income tax burdens prevailing during the 1960s and most of the 1970s, ERTA represents no tax reductions at all, as Figure 21.1 shows.

A second complication stems from the effects of the new Accelerated Cost Recovery System (ACRS) on business tax burdens. In an inflationary economy, tax depreciation that is based on historical cost, as it is in federal income taxes, overestimates taxable profits and thus produces excess tax burdens. This bias can be countered by accelerating the rates at which historical costs can be recovered. How well such adjustments work depends on what rates of inflation and real rates of interest happen to prevail. In general, as Martin Feldstein (1981) has demonstrated, at moderate rates acceleration approximately offsets the deficiencies of historical cost depreciation, while at lower rates it overcorrects and at higher rates undercorrects. The effects of the new ACRS depreciation rules on business tax rates, then, depend critically on how successful the government is in reducing the inflation rate. Indeed, combined with the present investment tax credit, ACRS produces negative tax rates on most kinds of equipment at inflation rates as high as six to nine percent (Jane G. Gravelle, 1982). The desirability of such subsidies for new business investment, and particularly their highly uneven incidence, will be a major tax reform issue during the next few years. In any case, analysts of the New Federalism should take full account of the effects of dramatically lower federal tax rates on business income.

A final ambiguity concerning the direction in which the whole spectrum of federal tax rates is moving emerges from the role of the payroll tax for social security. As long as this tax is regarded as a form of personal saving for future benefit entitlements, the payroll tax increases now occurring, and programmed to occur in the future, impose no significant burdens on federal taxpayers. While this view is reinforced by the benefit characteristics of social security, the system has also taken on many ability-to-pay elements. Those elements have caused many workers (and economists) to regard the payroll tax as simply a tax, and recent public discussion of the prospective insolvency of the trust fund and the possibility of reduced benefit levels has certainly strengthened that point of view. Weighed against the combined tax burden increases imposed by inflation's impact on individual incomes and the continuing rise in payroll taxes, the tax rate reductions of the 1981 Act look puny indeed to many low- and middle-income workers.

Federal Tax Reduction as State-Local Fiscal Support

How much lower federal tax burdens will be in the next few years, then, is very much an open question. Nonetheless, the basic philosophy of the New Federalism clearly combines lower federal taxes with increased state-local government spending responsibilities, at least in the long run. The main question then becomes the extent to which the lower federal taxes will strengthen the revenue-raising powers of state and local governments. Three well-known hypotheses, taken together, suggest a pessimistic answer to that inquiry. While all three have been challenged by critics, who question both their relevance and their validity, these propositions deserve consideration.

The "flypaper effects" hypothesis, as already noted, predicts that equal reductions in federal aid and in federal taxes will lower the level of state-local government spending. The problem here is to decide which level of spending—the higher grant-supported level or the lower self-supported level—is more consistent with voter tastes. Resolution of this issue requires consideration of the other two hypotheses.

The "taxpayer revolt" hypothesis, which vaulted into prominence with the passage of Proposition 13 in California in 1978, predicts that no state or local politician will lightly propose tax increases to the electorate. If that is the case, federal tax reductions will add little or no strength to state-local revenue-raising powers. It might help if the federal reductions were to be billed not as long-overdue alleviations of excessive tax burdens but as a means of financing a decentralization of governmental spending responsibilities, but that strategy has so far been a more implicit than explicit aspect of the initiatives. The staying power of the taxpayer revolt is certainly open to question. It is one thing for taxpayers to favor cuts that are expected to reduce government waste and quite another to vote for cuts that are expected to lower the quality of government services. The latter kind of choice was only beginning to surface in California in 1981. That it had not reached the point of quelling the tax revolt, however, was clearly demonstrated by the vote of Californians in June 1982 to eliminate state inheritance taxes and to index the individual income tax fully for inflation. If nothing else, these developments suggest that it is a poor time to expect state and local governments to undertake new fiscal responsibilities.

While the first hypothesis could be irrelevant and the second short-lived in its effects, the third, which deals with the abilities of state and local governments to raise revenue, has great and continuing relevance, which, unlike the first two, cannot be so neatly pinned down. Statisticians would state the interactions among competing tax systems in two alternative ways for purposes of testing. The "tax room" hypothesis argues that since all levels of government draw on the same economic base for their tax revenues—namely, the nation's total income, output, and wealth—reduced reliance on that base by any one level will open opportunities for greater use of the base by other levels. The alternative hypothesis holds that intergovernmental tax competition within the U.S. economy is so strong that state and local governments are much less able to draw on available economic bases than is the federal government. Verification of either proposition has proved difficult.

The theoretical and empirical evidence for and against the "tax room" hypothesis is highly mixed. Although it is widely assumed to be a political virtue for any jurisdiction to have tax rates at least as low as those elsewhere, economic studies of business locational decisions have so far failed to establish relative tax burdens as a major determinant (ACIR, March 1981). For interregional moves, nontax factors such as wage and transportation costs consistently show up as the most important considerations. For interlocal moves, where nontax differentials are typically smallest, the tax differentials (as well as government expenditure differentials) are likely to be capitalized into offsetting land price differentials (Break, 1980, pp. 210–213). However, variations in tax and expenditure levels may have more importance for households. The quality of an area's educational system clearly matters to many, and highly paid skilled and professional workers are very likely to pay attention to the top marginal income tax rates imposed by state and local governments.

Whatever real difference taxes may make to business and household locational decisions, interjurisdictional tax competition is indisputably a game in which many state and local governments now participate. The unsettled question is whether that competition is more attributable to inescapable features of the environment in which state and local governments operate, such as the openness of their economies, than it is to avoidable characteristics of their fiscal systems. It would be of special policy interest to know how much the situation might be altered by moving income-support programs such as welfare entirely to the federal level and by relating state and local tax systems more closely to the benefit model of taxation (Break, 1980, pp. 226–237). Such changes should lessen the chances that tax increases desired by local residents to improve public services would nevertheless be deterred by fears that any tax increase might have adverse economic consequences. Any move that made such risks seem insignificant should increase the ability of federal tax reduction to play a strongly supportive role in encouraging local initiative to raise service levels. In the present world, marked by the strong ability-to-pay orientation of state and local fiscal systems, the validity of the tax-room hypothesis is less certain. Lower federal tax rates, for example, increase the importance of intergovernmental differentials in any tax that is deductible from the federal tax base and may, therefore, have a discouraging effect on state-local tax increases. On the other hand, by reducing the overall burden of taxation in the country, cuts in federal taxes may make people more amenable to state and local tax increases that are seen to promise better government services. This reaction is likely to be more prevalent in fiscal systems with a strong tax-benefit nexus.

Lower Federal Budget Deficits

Lower support levels for federal aid to state and local governments, if not accompanied by higher federal spending of other kinds or by lower federal taxes, must result in smaller federal budget deficits (or larger surpluses). The major economic effects of smaller federal deficits are lower interest rates and lower inflation rates. By itself the former would help such interest-sensitive industries as housing and automobiles, and the interregional impacts of such a stimulus are well known. Taken together, lower interest and inflation rates would help state and local governments in the short run by strengthening the recovery from the 1981–82 recession and in the long run by raising the economy's rate of economic growth.

Conclusion

The much-discussed direct costs of lower support levels for federal aid to state and local governments are only the beginning of the story. Less spending on grants necessarily creates offsetting changes in other parts of the federal budget, and these changes in turn will alter the fiscal environment in which state and local governments operate. Only when these indirect benefits are combined with the direct costs will the true image of the New Federalism begin to come into focus. Nor is that all. The structural shift away from categorical grants toward block grants represents far more than a change in format. It is clearly intended to be a major step toward decentralizing governmental decision making by making more states responsible for the ways in which money is spent.

FROM CATEGORICAL TO BLOCK GRANTS?

For more than a decade Republican administrations have been seeking to reduce the dense and tangled forest of categorical grants and their corresponding Washington bureaucracy by shifting much of the intergovernmental expenditure load to the simpler and more decentralized block grant format. The hope is to reduce the administrative machinery and overlapping which have grown up with the maze of small federally administered programs of specific intent and to locate authority over expenditure decisions closer to where the money is spent. Though it is not clear whether the ultimate aim of this move is to make for greater efficiency or for gradual reduction of the scope of the federal government and perhaps of government in general, the block grant format has much operational appeal. Unfortunately for those attracted to it, strong forces legislate against the inherent shift of power which it represents.

One of the most basic of those forces is the "fingerprints" theorem of government expenditure, by which legislators who appropriate money want their marks to be clearly displayed on it when it gets to their constituents. Categorical grants are the legislator's dream, since they have the advantage of specificity and bear the clear imprint of the authorizing body. Block grants, in contrast, dull or even obliterate the distinguishing marks of the creators by giving much of the control over allocation of the funds to authorities at a lower level of government.

Another deterrent to effective block grants is the pressure from interest groups which have enjoyed privileges and protection under the terms of categorical funding. In the relatively few instances in which Congress has brought itself to consolidate categoricals into the larger, less restricted block grants, such groups as have found (or imagined) their concerns to be shortchanged in the shift have usually succeeded in getting new guidelines, set-asides, and other constraints added to the enabling legislation. Sometimes the end result has simply been a restricted grant with a broader program base; sometimes the new block grant has languished for lack of funding while new categoricals have been created around it in closely related program areas (Norman J. Ornstein, 1982).

The consequence of such pressures is that of the 20 major block grant proposals made between 1965 and 1980, only five were enacted. (Timothy J. Conlan, 1981.) These are the Partnership for Health (1966), the Law Enforcement Assistance Act (1968), the Comprehensive Employment and Training Act (1973), the Community Development Block Grant program (1974), and the social services grants under Title XX of the Social Security Act (1975). Conlan's analysis of the major factors associated with the successful enactment of these programs gives rise to little optimism about their reappearance, and Ornstein is similarly pessimistic. The Reagan proposals for FY 1982 were to consolidate 83 categoricals into six block grants. Congress responded by converting 57 categoricals into nine blocks. The administration's plan for FY 1983 is to amalgamate 41 narrow-based aid programs into seven broad-based ones. Congress' mood by mid-summer 1982 had not grown noticeably cooperative.

Whatever the prospects for block grants may be, the important question is whether an expanded role for them would improve the federal grant system. Analysts typically place block grants somewhere in the middle of an aid spectrum that stretches from restricted categorical grants with their fiscal and economic efficiency goals at one end to unrestricted general revenue sharing grants with their redistributive, equity goals at the other. As David R. Beam (1981) has vividly demonstrated, however, federal rules and regulations have been no great respector of the principle of nonrestrictiveness. Regulatory federalism, as he terms the current trend, has developed a new set of orders and constraints that apply equally to all federal grant programs. If the money is raised by one level of government, in other words, the fingerprints will be there. Escape from such requirements might be possible under a program of tax sharing, designed to harness the superior taxing powers of the federal government to the service needs of state and local authorities, but the temptation to combine constraints with the return money flow would still be there. Only federal tax reductions and turnbacks are forms of assistance that are completely free of federal interference.

The theoretical case for block grants rests on their ability to incorporate some of the strengths of the other two main grant forms (categoricals and general revenue sharing) while minimizing their weaknesses. At the very least, therefore, the Reagan proposals provide an excellent opportunity for reexamination of existing federal programs at both ends of the aid spectrum.

Categorical Grants: The National Interest Test

For categorical grants two broad normative tests may be suggested. The first is that federal aid is justified when the national interest in a particular public program is significant but not dominant. If the national interest is dominant, as many fiscal experts feel it is for Aid to Families With Dependent Children and Medicaid, for example, categorical grants should be replaced by federal operation of the program. If the national interest is insignificant, categorical grants should simply be discontinued, as is planned in the transitional trust fund arrangement to be discussed in the next section. Only if the national interest is significant but not dominant is some restricted form of federal aid appropriate. Such programs should then be submitted to the second normative test.

Categorical Grants: The Operational Efficiency Test

The economic goal of categorical grants is to expand the operation of state and local governmental programs with benefit spillouts to their socially optimal levels. It is by no means easy to translate this general objective into operational terms (Break, 1980). Experience indicates that the aided program must be a tightly defined one, and if federal matching is to be used, its amount should reflect the relative strength of the national interest. In that regard it may be useful to distinguish programs in which the national interest is distinctly a subsidiary one from those in which the federal and state-local governments are, or should be, more or less equal partners. For the former type of program an open-end matching grant would be appropriate and for the latter a closed-end, participatory matching grant.

U.S. experience with open-end matching grants, unfortunately, provides little useful evidence of their potential accomplishments. Beam's "pessimistic findings on 'optimizing' grants" are very much to the point here (1980). They are based on six major kinds of weaknesses that such grants may exhibit. The first is fiscal uncontrollability and rapid growth. Since open-end matching grants place program controls firmly in the hands of grantees, they can succeed only when grant recipients have enough of their own funds in the program to care strongly about total program costs and to wish to administer the program efficiently. A good working rule might be that the federal matching share should be well below 50 percent. Both AFDC and Medicaid have matching shares that are much too high by this test. Indeed, those shares create a prima facie case for full federal responsibility for the programs in question.

The next two criticisms are that optimizing grants typically create inequitable interstate spending differentials and allocate federal funds inequitably among rich and poor states. These are important concerns for programs such as AFDC and Medicaid, but they represent a criticism of the federal use of open-end matching grants rather than of the instrument itself. Optimizing grants are aimed at economic efficiency not equity, and no policy instrument can serve two different goals well. Federal equity goals should be sought either by direct transfers to individuals or by block and revenue sharing grants.

The fourth potential weakness of optimizing grants—that the funds may be diverted by recipients to unintended uses—is one that applies to all grants other than completely unrestricted ones. The open-end feature, of course, makes it particularly important that the aided program be defined so that qualified expenditures can readily be distinguished from unqualified ones. Early experience with social service grants provides a vivid illustration of what not to do (Martha Derthick, 1975).

Federal open-end grants have been subject to disturbingly high error rates in defining eligible beneficiaries, as well as to outright fraud. As Beam notes, experience strongly suggests that federal matching rates were set too high in the AFDC and Medicaid programs. The risks that "free" money will erode ordinary incentives for operational efficiency have been stressed in intergovernmental grant literature for some time. Empirical evidence that supports these fears, derived from studies of state aid for public libraries and school bus services, has recently been presented by Richard Silkman and Dennis R. Young (1982). Moreover, high grantor matching may well bring excessive red tape, which is the last of Beam's criticisms, as a controlling device. In principle, low-matching, well-defined, open-end grants should need few federal controls other than the usual auditing of fund uses. Where the federal and state-local interests in the program are more or less equal, however, the need for controls, or better still joint operation, is much greater.

How useful optimizing grant theories can really prove to be when applied to the federal aid system is far from clear. Nevertheless, they offer a means by which President Reagan's New Federalism proposals can be turned into a systematic evaluation of federal categorical grants. If few meet the two tests suggested here, the case for a major reallocation of program responsibilities within the federal system would be much strengthened. In such an environment the equity goals of federal aid are likely to acquire increased importance.

Unrestricted Grants: The Equity Goal

A better distribution of income and wealth may be sought through the use of a wide variety of fiscal instruments. The two of interest here are direct transfers to individuals, to be discussed in the next section, and unrestricted formula grants that allocate federal support to jurisdictions according to their relative program needs and revenue-raising capacities. General revenue sharing is the obvious instrument here, but many block grants are likely to be close substitutes because of the high fungibility of the money distributed under them. Compared to GRS, such block grants would have two advantages. Their distribution formulas could be directed to the relative grantee fiscal needs in the broad program area chosen for aid, and the relative amount of federal money appropriated for each block would reflect federal spending priorities. Block grants of this sort could be used in conjunction with program turnbacks to help alleviate the distributional effects of those devolutions on state and local governments.

RESPONSIBILITY REASSIGNMENTS

The most dramatic part of Reagan's New Federalism is the proposed set of program trade-offs and turnbacks. Originally, the main trade-off involved full federal assumption of Medicaid costs in return for full state-local responsibility for food stamps and AFDC, but this was later changed to leave food stamps in the federal sector. All of these programs belong in what Richard Musgrave has called the "distribution" branch of government (1959), and both he and other fiscal economists have long argued that in the modern world responsibility for that branch should rest in the hands of the national government. The reason is that there are few self-contained communities left with populations so stable that the welfare of the poor retains a strong local dimension. In a highly mobile society taxpayers receive more or less the same utility from helping the poor and disadvantaged who live in other parts of the country as from helping those nearby. In economic terms the benefits generated by the distribution branch are a national public good. This is not to deny the presence of local benefits from income-support programs, but rather to argue that their proper role is that of supplementing a uniform national program operated and financed by the federal government. To assign them a greater role is to risk the proliferation of suboptimal benefit levels resulting from the real or imagined fears of the adverse fiscal effects of relatively generous state or local welfare programs.

This logic leads to the broad policy recommendation that food stamps be kept at the federal level and that both Medicaid and AFDC be gradually moved to full federal financing. These changes, which have been recommended by the ACIR for some time (April 1969, p. vi; June 1981, p. 111), would provide an excellent opportunity for a coordinated reform of the different programs aimed at uniform national support levels, involving both in-kind and money transfers, and at the establishment of implicit marginal tax rates—i.e., integrated benefit-reduction rates for all income-tested support programs—that did not unduly discourage work effort. One immediate barrier to these changes is a federal budgetary cost that would be both significant and inconsistent with some key aspects of the Reagan program, since their enactment would presumably necessitate either tax increases or defense spending reductions not now contemplated.

Less obvious, but potentially much more serious barriers are presented by the complex set of distributional effects implicit in the program transfers. These would include:

- The interstate and interregional gains and losses generated by the changes in federal expenditures and taxes.
- The gains and losses of low-income families in different states resulting from the shift to a uniform national pattern (supplemented or not by state-financed increments) from existing independently determined patterns—in 1979 familes of four with no outside income qualified for monthly AFDC benefits of over $500 in Hawaii, Vermont, and Wisconsin, as compared to only $120–140 in Mississippi and Texas (Edward M. Gramlich and Deborah S. Laren, 1982, pp. 161–171).
- The gains and losses of state and local taxpayers and spending program beneficiaries from the budgetary reactions of those governments to the changed federal financing patterns for AFDC and Medicaid.

These reactions would be a mixture of income and price effects that work in opposite directions. The shift of existing state-local costs of AFDC and Medicaid benefits to the federal government would stimulate state-local spending in general, but the elimination of open-end matching grants would raise state-local costs of providing benefits to their own residents—from an average of 42 cents to provide an additional dollar of AFDC benefits to one dollar (Gramlich and Laren, 1982, p. 169)—and hence would discourage own-financed state or local welfare and medical benefits. So far as those programs alone are concerned, one would expect the price effect to dominate any potential stimulus from the income effect, and empirical studies confirm that expectation. Larry Orr's study of the AFDC program (1976), for example, estimated that a shift to a federally financed AFDC benefits floor that eliminated federal matching at the margin but held constant, or even increased, the federal share of total benefits would reduce those levels, on the average, by 16 percent. Since federal Medicaid and AFDC matching now varies inversely with per capita state incomes, low-income states would experience smaller income gains and larger price increases than high-income states from federalization of the two programs. Gramlich and Laren's hypothetical simulations for 1979 AFDC benefits, based on Orr's findings, show the Wisconsin benefit for a family of four falling from $510 to $414, while Mississippi's benefit would fall from $120 to $86.

It appears, then, that low-income families might have much to lose regardless of whether AFDC responsibilities are turned back entirely to the states, as Reagan proposes, or moved mainly up to the federal level, as others recommend. Federalization could, of course, set the national floor high enough to protect the majority of AFDC beneficiaries from any loss of purchasing power, even if their own states withdrew entirely from the program, but such a policy would entail high federal budgetary costs. A period of fiscal stringency is not the best of times in which to contemplate a major reform of the nation's welfare system. But it is also not the worst of times in which to propose a turnback of federal responsibilities to the states, since in that way reduced federal support levels can at least be accompanied by fewer federal constraints.

The Reagan turnback plan has three main features:

- Identification of those federal grant programs in which the national interest is too weak to justify their continued existence (originally 44 programs but later reduced in number).
- Establishment of a transitional trust fund to which specified federal taxes would be transferred and from which states could draw funds either in the same amounts and with the same strings as before or in the form of super revenue sharing without strings. Beginning in fiscal 1988, the trust fund would gradually be phased out as the federal taxes financing it were discontinued—the gasoline tax in 1988, alcoholic beverage taxes in 1989, telephone excises in 1990, and tobacco excises in 1991.
- The gradual assumption by state and local governments of full financial responsibility for the turned-back programs, accompanied by whatever pickups of the discontinued federal taxes they wished to enact.

Such a broad devolution of power and responsibility raises several important questions. One concerns the strength and nature of the national interest in each of the programs selected for turnback. Even if accomplishments here fall far short of expectations, much may be learned in the process of the debate about the nature of our federal system. Those categorical grant programs that survive are likely to be more firmly based on principle, others may better be consolidated into block grants, and still others may best be discontinued altogether. A second question concerns the relative merits of specific tax turnbacks, such as those proposed for inclusion in the transitional trust fund, and of general federal tax reductions, such as those enacted in the 1981

Economic Recovery Tax Act. Specific tax turnbacks send out clear signals of intent—one level of government is vacating a certain tax field with the expectations that another level will pick it up. General tax reductions normally give no such signals. However, the 1983 individual income tax rate reductions enacted by ERTA, which have been much criticized for their potentially adverse budgetary and macroeconomic effects, could be reaffirmed and readvertised for their state-local revenue strengthening, microeconomic effects. State income tax increases might or might not be as politically salable as state pickups of discontinued federal excises. Even if they are, there would still be concerns about the distributional effects of the exchange.

Fiscal devolutions, like tax reform, may be unattainable unless there is a large group of potential gainers and few, if any, significant losers. In assessing their positions under the Reagan proposals, every state and local government in the country will be counting up the costs of their new responsibilities and balancing them against the additional resources likely to be available to them. A wealth of information on these questions has already been provided in an ACIR staff working paper (December 1981). It includes simulations of the state-by-state net fiscal effects of a large number of turnback packages, each combining the discontinuance of specific federal grant programs with hypothetical revenue replacements sufficient to make up for the total amount of federal aid lost in the nation as a whole. For all 50 states and the District of Columbia, in other words, the net fiscal effect of each package is zero. Individual state net per capita effects are then positive for gainers and negative for losers, and the standard deviation of these estimates is used as convenient summary measure of the degree of fiscal mismatch implicit in each of the devolution packages. Two of the many findings are of interest here.

One of the packages with a 1980 federal cost of $7.9 billion involves the turnback of 205 federal grants in a wide variety of functional areas other than income support. If the states were to take over this additional cost and finance it by picking up federal excises on cigarettes and alcohol, the mismatch measure (standard deviation of net per capita fiscal effects) would be $12.87, but if the federal income tax were used instead, the measure would rise to $14.82. What this indicates about the distributional superiority of the excise tax turnback is surprising, and it illustrates the value of empirical simulations of alternative devolution packages.

The other set of interesting findings involves the larger turnback of 283 federal grant programs with a 1980 federal cost of $20.5 billion. If this devolution were financed by allocating an equal amount of federal income tax revenues to the states, the absolute value of the mismatch standard deviation would be $26.54, but relative to the size of the turnback package it would be only 29 percent, as compared to 43 percent for the smaller package discussed above. Some states would be heavy losers, however. The largest net losses would be imposed on Mississippi, the state with the lowest ACIR 1979 tax capacity rating (71 percent of the national average). According to the simulations, Mississippi's net loss would be $89 per capita, producing a total loss of 9.4 percent of its own-source revenue. Significantly, when the package's net fiscal effects were recomputed substituting per capita revenue sharing for the income tax as a financing source, the mismatch standard deviation fell to $18.24 and although Mississippi remained as a major loser, its losses fell to $51 per capita and 5.4 percent of own-source revenues.

These impact simulations illustrate some of the most important and controversial trade-offs inherent in any decentralization of political and fiscal responsibilities. Program devolutions will increase the freedom of U.S. governments to respond to diverse tastes for public goods in different states and localities but at some sacrifice of equity. If tax turnbacks are relied upon, rich jurisdictions can pick up their additional responsibilities with less sacrifice than poor jurisdictions. If per capita revenue sharing were used instead of tax turnbacks, the equity losses would be less, but that financing policy would risk the addition of federal fingerprints to the monies distributed and might also weaken the accountability of state and local officials to their constituents.

SOME HOPES FOR CHANGE

The Reagan Administration's New Federalism proposals have led a rather sheltered early life, much overshadowed in the public eye by the prospects and problems created by rapidly rising defense expenditures, greatly changed federal income tax rates, and huge budget deficits. Yet even in their first ten months of existence, something was accomplished (David B. Walker, Albert J. Richter, and Cynthia Cates Colella, 1982), and much more is promised. It may well be that a period of resource limitations and budget stringency, such as appears to be in prospect, is a good time in which to attempt these moves. Certainly the postwar years of economic ease and rapid growth are as often cited for their failures as for their accomplishments in the intergovernmental finance area. As a result of its 11-volume study of The Federal Role in the Federal System: The Dynamics of Growth, for example, the ACIR concluded that the intergovernmental aid system had become overloaded with too many separate programs and too much federal control and regulation (December 1980). A few years of austerity may sharpen public appreciation of the need for reform and interest in the best ways of accomplishing it. In such an environment the New Federalism proposals are a welcome initiative, inviting supporters to perfect their designs for structural reforms and challenging critics to come up with better alternatives.

REFERENCES

Advisory Commission on Intergovernmental Relations, *State Aid to Local Government*, Report A-34 (April 1969).
————, *Regional Growth: Flows of Federal Funds, 1952–76*, Report A-75 (June 1980).
————, *The Federal Role in the Federal System: The Dynamics of Growth*, In Brief Report B-4 (December 1980).
————, *Regional Growth: Interstate Tax Competition*, Report A-76 (March 1981).
————, *The Federal Role in the Federal System: The Dynamics of Growth, An Agenda for American Federalism: Restoring Confidence and Competence*, Report A-86 (June 1981).
————, *Changing the Federal Aid System: An Analysis of Alternative Resource/Responsibility Turnbacks and Program Trade-Offs*, Staff Working Paper (December 1981).
Beam, David R., "Economic Theory as Policy Prescription: Pessimistic Findings on 'Optimizing' Grants," in Helen M. Ingram and Dean E. Mann (eds.), *Why Policies Succeed or Fail* (Beverly Hills, Calif.: Sage Publications, 1980), pp. 137–162.
————, "Washington's Regulation of States and Localities: Origins and Issues," *Intergovernmental Perspective* (Summer 1981), pp. 8–18.
Break, George F., *Financing Government in a Federal System* (Washington, D.C.: The Brookings Institution, 1980).
Conlan, Timothy J., "Back in Vogue: The Politics of Block Grant Legislation," *Intergovernmental Perspective* (Spring 1981), pp. 8–17.
Derthick, Martha, *Uncontrollable Spending for Social Services Grants* (Washington, D.C.: The Brookings Institution, 1975).
Feldstein, Martin, "Adjusting Depreciation in an Inflationary Economy: Indexing Versus Acceleration," *National Tax Journal* (March 1981), pp. 29–43.
Gramlich, Edward M., "Intergovernmental Grants: A Review of the Empirical Literature," in Wallace E. Oates (ed.), *The Political Economy of Fiscal Federalism* (Lexington, Mass.: Lexington Books, 1977).
———— and Deborah S. Laren, "The New Federalism," in Joseph A. Pechman (ed.), *Setting National Priorities: The 1983 Budget* (Washington, D.C.: The Brookings Institution, 1982).
Gravelle, Jane G., "Effects of the 1981 Depreciation Revisions on the Taxation of Income from Business Capital," *National Tax Journal* (March 1982), pp. 1–20.
Musgrave, Richard A., *The Theory of Public Finance* (New York: McGraw-Hill, 1959).

Ornstein, Norman J., "Chipping Away at the Old Blocks," *The Brookings Bulletin* (Winter–Spring 1982), pp. 11–15.

Orr, Larry L., "Income Transfers as a Public Good: An Application to AFDC," *American Economic Review* (June 1976), pp. 369–371.

Silkman, Richard, and Dennis R. Young, "X-Efficiency and State Formula Grants," *National Tax Journal* (September 1982).

U.S. Congress, Congressional Budget Office, *Baseline Budget Projections for Fiscal Years 1983–1987* (February 1982).

Walker, David B., Albert J. Richter, and Cynthia Cates Colella, "The First Ten Months: Grant-in-Aid, Regulatory, and Other Changes," *Intergovernmental Perspective* (Winter 1982), pp. 5–22.

CHAPTER 22

AT WHAT PRICE?
Costs of Federal Mandates Since the 1980s

MARCELLA RIDLEN RAY AND TIMOTHY J. CONLAN

Federal mandates became the leading cause of intergovernmental friction in the early 1990s. While nonhealth-related federal aid declined in relative importance over the previous 15 years, the number of federal regulations affecting state and local governments grew at a rapid pace. According to one study, regulatory enactments increased by 75 percent during the 1980s (Conlan, Beam, and Colella 1993).

The financial costs of such requirements have concerned many state and local officials. According to the former head of the National Conference of State Legislatures, "federal mandates are putting a stranglehold on state budgets" (Martin 1991). Such sentiments generated mounting opposition to unfunded mandates by the nation's mayors and governors and prompted introduction of numerous bills in Congress to restrict enactment and/or reimburse costs of new intergovernmental regulations.[1] After two years of intensive intergovernmental lobbying—and the Republican electoral landslide in 1994—Congress responded in early 1995 by enacting the Unfunded Mandate Reform Act of 1995.[2]

Despite landmark legislation to curb the practice of imposing unfunded federal mandates, accurate information about the fiscal dimensions of the mandate problem remains surprisingly limited. Recent estimates have ranged as high as $500 billion in total costs (Fabricius 1991, 1) and as low as $8.9 billion (Conlan, Beam, and Colella 1993, 65), but all estimation efforts to date have been sharply limited in scope, quality, timing, and methodology. Although Congress has already acted to limit the costs of future mandates, a truly effective legislative solution may require a more precise and comprehensive understanding of the effects of federal mandates on state and local governments.

EXISTING RESEARCH

Intergovernmental regulation emerged as a major public policy concern in the late 1970s and early 1980s. In 1980, New York City Mayor Edward Koch argued that a "mandate millstone" was beginning to choke off the vitality of American cities. Soon after, Ronald Reagan became the first president to give federal mandates prominent attention in federal policy debates (Presidential Task Force 1982).

In this same period, scholarly research into the legal foundations, political development, and

From *State and Local Government Review,* vol. 28, no. 1 (Winter 1996), 7–16. Copyright © 1996 by Carl Vinson Institute of Government, University of Georgia. Reprinted with permission.

Table 22.1

Estimated Costs of Unfunded Federal Mandates to Selected Cities and Counties, Fiscal Year 1993

Program	Total Costs to	
	Cities	Counties
	(millions)	
Clean Water Act/Wetlands	$3,613	$1,186
Solid Waste Disposal/RCRA	882	646
Safe Drinking Water Act	562	164
Clean Air Act	404	302
Americans with Disabilities Act	356	294
Fair Labor Standards Act	212	262
Underground Storage Tanks	161	176
Endangered Species Act	37	120
Asbestos Removal (AHERA)	129	NA
Lead-Based Paint Removal	118	NA
Immigration Act	NA	1,536
Bond Arbitrage Restrictions	NA	78
Superfund amendments	NA	43
Davis-Bacon Act	NA	11
Total	$6,473	$4,817

Sources: U.S. Conference of Mayors: Price Waterhouse 1993. Table 1; and National Association of Counties: Price Waterhouse 1993, Table 1.

administrative implementation of intergovernmental regulation expanded dramatically.[3] Research into the fiscal effects of federal mandates has been more limited, however. A study by the Urban Institute in the late 1970s concluded that federal mandates imposed "substantial" costs, averaging about $25 per capita (Muller and Fix 1980, 327). This finding was based on only six major regulations in seven jurisdictions, however, and it is now seriously out of date.

More recently, the Environmental Protection Agency (EPA) attempted to estimate total yearly costs of complying with national environmental standards. State government costs were estimated at $3.0 billion in 1987, increasing to a projected $4.5 billion (in constant 1987 dollars) in the year 2000 (EPA 1990, 2–6). Local government spending necessary to comply with federal environmental requirements was estimated to increase from $19.2 billion in 1987 to $32.6 billion in 2000, a 68 percent increase in 13 years.

Although environmental regulations impose some of the most costly burdens on state and local governments, they are not the only source of mandated expenditures. Other expensive regulations involve health care services, access for the physically disabled, and employee pay and working conditions. Table 22.1 presents cost estimates for 14 such mandates developed by the U.S. Conference of Mayors (USCM) and the National Association of Counties (NACo). These organizations compiled regulatory compliance data from 314 cities and 128 counties. The resulting estimates totaled $6.5 billion when extrapolated to all cities and $4.8 billion for all counties (USCM 1993, 2; NACo 1993, 2). The quality of these estimates was limited by several factors, however, including the absence of independent verification of local submissions, a nonrandom sample of participating jurisdictions, a small sample of regulatory programs, and the absence of data on state expenditures (U.S. Senate Committee on Environment and Public Works 1994).

One other effort to examine the costs of federal regulations on both state and local governments was undertaken for the U.S. Advisory Commission on Intergovernmental Relations (ACIR) in 1993. This research utilized Congressional Budget Office (CBO) "fiscal notes" prepared during the 1980s to develop a more comprehensive estimate of the financial costs imposed by federal regulatory enactments on both state and local governments. Since 1983, CBO has attempted to estimate the intergovernmental fiscal impacts of proposed federal legislation. During the 1980s, the office produced state and local cost estimates on more than 3,500 bills and amendments, including 457 estimates for bills that were enacted into law. ACIR's analysis of these data indicates that new regulatory statutes adopted between 1983 and 1990 imposed cumulative estimated costs of between $8.9 billion and $12.7 billion on states and localities, depending on the definition of man date that is used.

Unfortunately, these CBO data only provide a rough and conservative estimate of the fiscal magnitude of federal mandates. CBO estimates are usually prepared at an early stage of the legislative process, long before the promulgation of actual administrative rules and requirements that impose specific compliance responsibilities on affected governments.[4] The resulting estimates are often inaccurate. Moreover, the CBO data do not include the impact of major regulations enacted in the decades before development of the CBO process. Nor do they include a number of mandates enacted during the 1980s for which CBO was unable to prepare a cost estimate.

USING IMPACT ANALYSES TO ESTIMATE MANDATE COSTS

This article presents findings derived from an alternative source—the regulatory impact analyses prepared by federal agencies during the rule-making process. Beginning in 1981, Executive Order 12291 required that federal agencies estimate the anticipated fiscal impacts of newly proposed regulation on other governmental entities, businesses, or the overall economy.[5] If the impact was likely to be major (defined as an annual impact of $100 million or more) then agencies were generally required to prepare a regulatory impact analysis (RIA) that detailed anticipated costs and benefits of the proposed requirements. Because these analyses were made later in the rule-making process, when specific regulatory requirements could be analyzed in greater detail, they were not subject to some of the limitations inherent in CBO's fiscal notes. They could be used to generate a relatively comprehensive, albeit incomplete, portrait of federally imposed expenditures by state and local governments.

Method

Our research focused on final regulations promulgated by seven federal departments and agencies from 1981 through 1992. These 12 years represented the first extended period for which systematic data was available for estimating the costs of proposed federal regulations. The specific federal departments selected were Labor (DOL), Interior (DOI), Education (DOE), Health and Human Services (HHS), Housing and Urban Development (HUD), Transportation (DOT), and EPA. Previous research indicates that most federal regulatory actions affecting other levels of government are generated by these seven federal agencies (Conlan, Beam, and Colella 1993).

Two search methods were employed to identify major rules that impose significant costs on state and local governments. One search utilized the *Unified Agenda of Regulations*. Every federal agency prepared a semiannual agenda of forthcoming regulatory actions during the test period, published each April and October in the *Federal Register*. Final regulations identified by a federal agency as "major"—due to a projected adverse fiscal impact upon state and/or local government—were isolated, the subsequent final rule making was examined in the *Federal Register,* and the associated RIA or its summary was analyzed. Costs for each regulation, as projected in the RIA by the agency, were examined for magnitude and the expected time period during which the impact would be felt.

One hundred sixty-eight agendas were reviewed in detail to identify major regulations that were expected to impose significant costs on states and localities. The abstracted information provided in the *Unified Agenda* was frequently incomplete, however, and often varied by agency and by year. Thus, a second search technique was utilized as a backup. The on-line database of the *Federal Register* provided by LEXIS was used to search for regulations designated by each agency as "major" and having an impact on state or local governments. A common search request format was adhered to in order to isolate major, final rules that were likely to affect state or local governments.[6]

Findings

For the 12-year period from 1981 through 1992, the seven federal agencies we examined issued 15 major final rules that imposed significant financial costs on state and local governments (Table 22.2). Two-thirds of these rules were issued by the Environmental Protection Agency. All but 1 of the 15 rules were completed after 1985, suggesting an acceleration of regulatory activity during the last half of that decade.

For the entire group of regulations, the estimated costs to be imposed on states and localities were substantial. Costs projected for the regulations for which data were available totaled $30.2 billion in 1992 dollars (Table 22.3).[7] The estimated costs for individual rules ranged from $133 million for EPA's 1987 Hazardous Substance Listing and Planning Requirements to $6.9 billion for DOT's nondiscrimination rules for the handicapped in mass transportation.

This overall figure is somewhat misleading, however, because federal agencies employed different assumptions when estimating the costs of different regulations. The costs for some rules, such as School Asbestos Removal, were projected over a 30-year period, while others, such as Community Right-to-Know Requirements and National Contingency Plan Requirements for Hazardous Substances, were estimated for only 5 or 10 years.

Accordingly, in Table 22.4, the authors attempt to standardize such discrepancies by totaling only those regulatory costs incurred during a common 12-year implementation period (1983–94). These estimated costs are also converted into consistent 1992 dollars. Using this method, combined costs incurred during this period for all 14 regulations totaled an estimated $10.85 billion.[8]

How do such mandates compare to overall levels of federal regulatory activity? The seven agencies examined issued a combined total of 3,292 final rules during the 12 years studied, but the vast majority of these rules, considered singly, had relatively minor estimated impacts. On average, for all federal agencies, OMB data suggest that fewer than two percent of all final rules meet the government's cost and economic criteria as major rules. Extrapolating this percentage to our sample of seven agencies, we estimate that approximately 50 rules met this threshold during the time examined. A majority of these rules were aimed at private sector entities, however, such as manufacturers, airlines, and utilities—leaving a subset of approximately one-half of one percent of all final rules that imposed major cost burdens on state and local governments.

Discussion and Limitations

Measuring the costs of federal mandates by using agencies' regulatory impact analyses has clear advantages over using data generated by individual jurisdictions or the CBO. It is more uniform

Table 22.2

Major Rules, 1981–1992, Projected to Have Adverse Fiscal Impact on State and Local Governments

No.	Year	Agency	Title
1.	1982	EPA	National Oil and Hazardous Substances Pollution Contingency Plan Amendment
2.	1986	DOT	Nondiscrimination on Basis of Handicap (Mass Transit Programs)
3.	1987	EPA	Extremely Hazardous Substances List and Threshold Planning Quantities; Emergency Planning and Release Notification Requirements
4.	1987	DOL	Application of the Fair Labor Standards Act to State and Local Government Agencies
5.	1987	EPA	Asbestos-Containing Materials in Schools Rule
6.	1987	EPA	Emergency and Hazardous Chemical Inventory Forms and Community Right-to-Know Reporting Requirements
7.	1988	HUD	Lead-Based Paint Hazard Elimination
8.	1988	EPA	Underground Storage Tanks Containing Petroleum: Technical Requirements
9.	1988	EPA	Underground Storage Tanks Containing Petroleum: Financial Responsibility Requirements
10.	1989	EPA	Criteria for Filtration and Disinfection of Surface Water and National Primary Drinking Water Regulations for Micro-biological Contaminants
11.	1990	EPA	National Oil and Hazardous Substances Pollution Contingency Plan Revisions
12.	1991	HHS	Medicare and Medicaid: Requirements for Long-Term Care Facilities
13.	1991	DOT	Transportation for Individuals with Disabilities
14.	1991	EPA	Maximum Contaminant Level Goals and National Primary Drinking Water Regulations for Lead and Copper
15.	1992	EPA	Criteria for Municipal Solid Waste Landfills

Note: DOL = Department of Labor; DOT = Department of Transportation; EPA = Environmental Protection Agency; HHS = Health and Human Services; and HUD = Housing and Urban Development.

and comprehensive than the local information and more accurate than the CBO data. At the same time, this technique is dependent on the availability and quality of regulatory impact analyses. If agencies do not classify a rule as major, or if they fail to prepare an RIA for some other reason, then this method does not capture the costs of such requirements. Even if an RIA is prepared, the technique used here allows little independent judgment as to the quality of the estimates prepared. Finally, even though we utilized two overlapping search procedures, we may have overlooked or miscategorized rules during the search process because of the large volume of rules and the complexity of specific regulations. Each of these limitations is explored in more detail in the following sections.

A Conservative Approach

The cost-estimating technique we have employed in this research is systematically biased in a conservative direction. It represents a low-range estimate for the costs of federal mandates, although the full extent of this bias is impossible to estimate.

There are several reasons why this approach is prone to underestimate the total costs of federal

Table 22.3

Total Lifetime Projected Cost Estimates for 15 Federal Mandates

Rule No.	Title	Cost Estimate in 1992 dollars
1.	National Oil and Hazardous Substances Pollution Contingency Plan Amendment	$ 172,909,000
2.	Nondiscrimination on Basis of Handicap (Mass Transit Programs)	5,357,040,000
3.	Extremely Hazardous Substances List and Threshold Planning Quantities; Emergency Planning and Release Notification Requirements	132,627,200
4.	Application of the Fair Labor Standards Act to State and Local Government Agencies	1,447,380,000
5.	Asbestos-Containing Materials in Schools Rule	2,507,774,900
6.	Emergency and Hazardous Chemical Inventory Forms and Community Right-to-Know Reporting Requirements	316,940,000
7.	Lead-Based Paint Hazard Elimination	Not Available
8.–9.	Underground Storage Tanks Containing Petroleum: Technical and Financial Responsibility Requirements	2,550,269,500
10.	Criteria for Filtration and Disinfection of Surface Water and National Primary Drinking Water Regulations for Microbiological Contaminants	3,294,637,200
11.	National Oil and Hazardous Substances Pollution Contingency Plan Revisions	651,249,600
12.	Medicare and Medicaid: Requirements for Long-Term Care Facilities	402,393,000
13.	Transportation for Individuals with Disabilities	6,911,354,000
14.	Maximum Contaminant Level Goals and National Primary Drinking Water Regulations for Lead and Copper	2,312,072,000
15.	Criteria for Municipal Solid Waste Landfills	4,166,547,000
	Total	$30,223,193,400

mandates. To begin with, it excludes all rules that federal agencies consider nonmajor. Consistent with OMB guidelines for implementing Executive Order 12291 (now E.O. 12866), agencies commonly use the threshold of $100 million in annual costs to define a major rule, but these calculations may be inaccurate or flawed. Smaller rules are generally excluded, even though the cumulative costs of such rules may be substantial.

Additional omissions from our list include larger mandates that agencies deem to be nonmajor because they are associated with some form of grant funding. Medicaid has been the most rapidly growing component of many state budgets in recent years, due at least in part to congressionally mandated expansions of coverage during this period. By some estimates, these mandates added $2.5 billion to the states' Medicaid tab by 1992 (Rovner 1991). Yet our search techniques did not trigger cost estimates for any of these Medicaid expansions, which may technically be considered part of a cooperative program in which state participation is considered voluntary.

Finally, our study's limited time frame omits potentially costly regulations which are outside the 12-year window of study. Among the excluded regulations are those promulgated before Executive Order 12291's cost-estimating procedures were initiated in 1981—including costly requirements associated with federal wastewater treatment regulations, education of handicapped children, and wage standards in federally subsidized construction. Also missing are regulations that were pending when our research window closed; such regulations include rules resulting from legislation passed in the late 1980s or early 1990s but which had yet to be issued in final form. Table 22.5 contains

Table 22.4

Mandated Expenses: Standardized Cost Estimates of 14 Federal Mandates over 12 Years

Cost Estimates from Year of Implementation

Rule No.	Base Year	1983	1984	1985	1986	1987	1988	1989	1990	1991	1992	1993	1994	Total	Total in 1992 Dollars
						(in millions of dollars)									
1.	1981	13	12	11	10	9	8	7	7	6	5	5	5	98	140
2.	1983					200	194	189	183	178	173	168	163	1,448	1,920
3.	1986					16	15	13	12	11	10	9	8	94	115
4.	1984					216	310	103	93	85	77	70	64	1,018	1,305
5.	1987						204	185	168	153	139	127	115	1,091	1,295
6.	1986						39	35	32	29	26	24	22	207	252
8–9.	1987							106	103	100	97	95	92	593	704
10.	1987								296	269	245	223	202	1,235	1,466
11.	1989									130	123	117	119	489	540
12.	1987										339			339	402
13.	1990										628	571	519	1,718	1,823
14.	1988										112	97	94	303	348
15.	1990											256	249	505	536

Grand total: $10.85 billion (1992 dollars).

Note: Rule numbers are as assigned in Table 22.2. Estimated costs for Rule 7 were not available.

Table 22.5

Estimated Costs Associated with Other Recent Federal Regulations

Other Recent Regulations	Estimated Costs
Americans with Disabilities Act	Less than $1.0 billion over 5 years
Clean Air Act Amendments of 1990	$250–300 million annually
Medicaid expansions in 1990 budget agreement	$870 million over 5 years
National Voter Registration Act of 1993 ("Motor Voter")	$100 million over 5 years

Sources: CBO cost estimates, various years.

a list of several recent regulatory enactments that are not included in our table of cost estimates, along with CBO estimates of their likely fiscal impact.

As indicated earlier, the Congressional Budget Office also developed cost estimates for many other intergovernmental statutes enacted during the 1980s, including several significant mandates for which agency RIAs are unavailable. A rough attempt to combine estimates from both agency and CBO sources yielded a total lifetime estimate of $42.2 billion while estimated costs for 1991 alone totaled $4.2 billion. However, the lack of consistency between the two sources of estimates makes this at best an uncertain, though still conservative, approximation.[9]

Estimation Issues

The fiscal impact of a regulatory action is frequently hard to anticipate and compute for several reasons. In the first place, highly different entities may be affected, and the regulatory impacts will often vary greatly from one jurisdiction to the next.

Another reason is that the sheer complexity of regulatory issues can defy accurate cost estimation. For example, issues involved in the regulatory impact analysis prepared for the Community Right-To-Know rules (Items 3 and 6 in Table 22.3) included:

- What is the appropriate baseline? Should conditions and remedies already taken by communities prior to the final rule be part of the analysis?
- How does one calculate what might have been spent independent of federal requirements?
- How should affected entities be identified and with what criteria?
- Are alternative solutions to be considered and on what basis?
- Should regulated activities vary with the size or type of an entity?
- Should cost impact be calculated on an assumption of full implementation?
- How should social costs and benefits be computed?
- Should efforts be made to ascertain duplicative costs created by different regulations?[10]

Similarly, the Department of Labor discovered a marked lack of consensus about how the costs of the rule, Application of the Fair Labor Standards Act to State and Local Government Agencies, should have been computed. These regulations affected wage levels and overtime compensation in every state and in 83,000 different counties, townships, municipalities, school districts, and special districts. Estimates from such entities as the National League of Cities, the International City Management Association, the American Federation of State, County, and Municipal Employees, and the Congressional Budget Office ranged from $500 million to $3 billion per year.

Data Limitations

Finally, a set of limitations affecting the data used in this study arise out of the search technique rather than the cost estimates themselves. Some regulations contain a complete cost or economic analysis, but most contain only summaries or highlights that omit important information about how cost estimates were derived. For the purposes of our research, four items of information were sought: the base year for the calculations, the discount rate used, the length of the discount period, and the expected total cost impact upon state and local governments. None of the 15 rules contained all four items of information. The reader of federal regulations is often left to guess, infer, or to seek alternate sources of information about the agency's method and rationale for projecting the impact of a regulation.

Moreover, reporting practices vary across agencies and over time. DOL clearly listed the assumptions and the data sources used to reach its estimate for the rule, Application of the Fair Labor Standards Act to State and Local Government Agencies, as well as the actual steps used in its estimation. In contrast, HUD did not relay any information in its Lead-Based Paint Hazard Elimination regulation about calculations of impact costs or what led to the determination that this is a major rule.

CONCLUSION: MORE THAN MONEY?

Our research has attempted to utilize a relatively new body of regulatory information in order to generate more reliable estimates of federally induced regulatory costs. Utilizing regulatory impact analyses prepared by federal agencies as part of the rule-making process, we identified 15 major intergovernmental regulations promulgated during the 1980s. Based on the combined regulatory cost estimates accompanying these rules, we estimate that state and local governments were required to spend at least $10.85 billion on federally mandated activities during the period between 1983 and 1994, and they were committed to a projected total of $30.2 billion by the year 2019.

Viewed as a whole, these regulations represent substantial costs on affected state and local jurisdictions. Nevertheless, costs of this magnitude fall short of the crushing burden often claimed by some participants in the mandate cost debate. For example, the National Conference of State Legislatures has estimated that bills directly attributable to federal mandates can account for up to 25 percent of a state's annual general fund budget (Wnuk 1993,13). And the Williamsburg Resolve, adopted by the 1994 Republican Governors Conference, states that unfunded mandates will commandeer one-fourth of all local revenues by 1998 (Hittinger 1995). In contrast, the 15 programs we examined imposed combined costs totaling less than one percent of state and local revenues in 1992.

How should we account for such disparities? It is important to recognize, first, that efforts to quantify the financial costs of federal mandates are fraught with difficulty. Currently available estimates vary dramatically, depending on the definition of mandate that is used, the specific expenditures that are included, the method of estimating those expenditures, the quality of those estimates, the jurisdictions included in the sample, and other factors. To date, most attempts to quantify federal mandate costs have been incomplete or open to serious question.

Recognizing these difficulties, the estimates we have generated are almost certainly too low. Our figures do not include a number of smaller, nonmajor regulations for which cost estimates were not available. Nor do they reflect other costly regulations that were imposed before or after our period of study, such as clean water requirements from the 1970s or the Clean Air Act Amendments of 1990.

Because we believe our estimated total is conservative, we can attempt to compensate by making generous adjustments for the most notable omissions. To offset limited data on clean air and clean water regulations, we can add to our total $18.45 billion, representing 90 percent of all state and local spending for pollution abatement in 1991 (the last year for which such data are available) (U.S. Bureau of the Census 1994, Table 374). Combined with the environmental compliance costs already included in our earlier regulatory estimate, this new figure assumes that, in the absence of federal requirements, state and local governments would spend nothing to reduce air, water, and solid waste pollution. If we also assume that one-half of total state and local spending on Medicaid in 1992 ($25 billion) was federally mandated—rather than encouraged by generous matching incentives—the combined total still equals only 4.6 percent of total state and local general expenditures in 1992 (ACIR 1994,120).

This is an impressive (and probably generous) sum. It is in the same range as another recent assessment of the relative fiscal burden imposed by federal mandates (Dearborn 1994). But we question whether costs of this magnitude could inspire the tremendous outpouring of state and local opposition to intergovernmental regulation that occurred in the early 1990s. Our interpretation is that unfunded mandates acquired symbolic importance far beyond their direct financial costs. For many of the nation's governors, mayors, and county officials, mandates may have come to represent a more profound concern over their dwindling authority and policy independence. If this is true, however, then the mandate problem cannot be cured with a financial fix alone.

NOTES

This research was supported by grants from the Fenwick Library Fellowship and the graduate research assistantship programs at George Mason University. In addition, portions of this research were made possible by the LEXIS on-line data service of the Mead Data Central Corporation. The authors express their appreciation to Mead Data Central and to Philip C. Berwick of the George Mason University Law Library for their help in making this service available. An earlier version of this research was presented to the 54th National Training Conference of the American Society for Public Administration, in San Francisco, on July 18,1993.

1. For example, 32 mandate relief bills were introduced in the first session of the 103d Congress, including 9 that required federal reimbursement or waiver of some or all of the costs of federally mandated activities. For a discussion of some economic issues involved in constructing a program of mandate reimbursement, see Whitman and Bezdek (1989).

2. Pub. L. 104–4. This act is intended to: 1) give Congress and federal agencies more and better information about the costs and benefits of proposed federal mandates and regulations; 2) create procedural barriers to the enactment or promulgation of unfunded mandates and regulations; and 3) establish a process for examining the fiscal effects of, and possible modifications to, existing federal mandates.

3. See Lovell et al.(1979); Beam et al.(1984); Zimmerman (1992); and Posner (1995).

4. For a more detailed discussion of these problems, see Gullo (1990).

5. In 1993, this executive order was superseded by Executive Order 12866, Regulatory Planning and Review.

6. The actual search protocol was as follows: "State or local government W/50 [within 50 words on either side of] Executive Order 12291 or Regulatory Flexibility or Paperwork Reduction Act or Cost Impact or Major Rule or Regulatory Evaluation and Final Rule and Department of _____ and Date After (01–01–19 __ and Date Before (12–31–19__)." This search for key phrases was administered for each of the seven sample federal agencies for each of the 12 years reviewed.

The review by LEXIS was complicated by two factors, however. One was the lack of standard nomenclature used by the various agencies in writing rules and regulations. Thus a completely consistent search protocol was not always effective in identifying the pertinent regulations.

A second complication involved discrepancies between LEXIS entries and the *Unified Agenda.* Crosschecks between printed copy of the *Unified Agenda* and the LEXIS database found discrepancies in the time period in which completed regulations were reported in the two sources. Reconciliation of such discrepancies was possible in most, but not all, cases.

7. HUD did not publish its cost estimates for Lead-Based Paint Removal when it issued this rule. In other cases, rules applied to private as well as public sector entities. Additional information concerning specific cost estimates and assumptions made in allocating such costs is available directly from the authors.

8. This is a conservative estimate of the total costs of federal mandates. For reasons discussed, the actual figure is likely to be much higher.

9. Cost estimates for federal statutes were obtained from Congressional Budget Office estimates prepared for legislative consideration.

10. See work papers on file in EPA Dockets Office.

REFERENCES

ACIR. *See* U.S. Advisory Commission on Intergovernmental Relations.

Beam, David R., Timothy Conlan, Cynthia Cates Colella, and Margaret Wrightson. 1984. *Regulatory federalism: Policy, process, impact, and reform.* Washington, D.C.: ACIR.

Conlan, Timothy J., David R. Beam, and Cynthia Cates Colella. 1993. *Federal regulation of state and local governments: The mixed record of the 1980s.* Washington, D.C.: ACIR.

Dearborn, Philip M. 1994. Assessing mandate effects on state and local governments. *Intergovernmental Perspective* (Summer-Fall): 22–26.

Fabricius, Martha. 1991. *Fiscal impact of proposed mandates from the 102nd Congress.* Washington, D.C.: National Conference of State Legislatures.

Gullo, Theresa A. 1990. Estimating the impact of federal legislation on state and local governments. In *Coping with mandates.* Michael Fix and Daphne A. Kenyon, eds. Washington, D.C.: Urban Institute Press.

Hittinger, Russell. 1995. Power to the people: States and local communities battle the feds for the ball. *The American Enterprise* (March/April): 27–34.

Koch, Edward L. 1980. The mandate millstone. *The Public Interest* 61 (Fall): 42.

Lovell, Catherine, et al. 1979, Federal and state mandating to local governments. University of California at Riverside. Mimeograph.

Martin, John. 1991. *Federal Action Monitor* 11, no. 36 (September 6). (Oklahoma State Senate newsletter.)

Muller, Thomas, and Michael Fix. 1980. The impact of selected federal actions on municipal outlays. In *Government regulation: Achieving social and economic balance,* vol. 5 of *Special study on economic change.* U.S. Congress, Joint Economic Committee. Washington, D.C.: GPO.

National Association of Counties: Price Waterhouse. 1993. *NACo unfunded mandates survey.* Washington, D.C.: NACo.

Posner, Paul. 1995. The politics of federal mandates: Congress on the frontiers of federalism. Columbia University, New York. Unpublished dissertation.

Presidential Task Force on Regulatory Relief. 1982. *Reagan administration achievements in regulatory relief for state and local governments: A progress report.* Washington, D.C.

Rovner, Julie. 1991. Governors ask Congress for relief from burdensome Medicaid mandates. *CQ Weekly Report* 16 (February):417.

U.S. Advisory Commission on Intergovernmental Relations (ACIR). 1994. *Significant features of fiscal federalism,* M-190–2. Washington, D.C.: ACIR.

U.S. Bureau of the Census. 1994. *Statistical abstract of the United States.* Washington D.C.: U.S. Department of Commerce.

U.S. Conference of Mayors: Price Waterhouse, 1993. *Impact of unfunded federal mandates on U.S. cities: A 314 city survey.* Washington, D.C.: USCM.

U.S. Environmental Protection Agency (EPA). 1990. *Environmental investments: The cost of clean: A summary.* Washington, D.C.: EPA.

U.S. Senate Committee on Environment and Public Works. 1994. *Staff report: Analysis of the unfunded mandates surveys conducted by the U.S. Conference of Mayors and the National Association of Counties.* Washington, D.C.: U.S. Senate.

Whitman, Ray D., and Roger H. Bezdek. 1989. Federal reimbursement for mandates on state and local governments. *Public Budgeting and Finance* 9 (Spring): 47–62.

Wnuk, Christine. 1993. Foiling federal mandates. *State Legislatures* 19, no. 5: 13.

Zimmerman, Joseph F. 1992. *Federal statutory preemption of state and local authority,* A-121. Washington, D.C.: ACIR.

CHAPTER 23

THE INFLEXIBILITY OF CONTEMPORARY BUDGETS

BENGT-CHRISTER YSANDER AND ANN ROBINSON

Public budget makers in the western industrial countries are facing new tasks. Instead of a redistributing and reserving for public use part of an anticipated rapid growth of affluence, they are now often left with the much more difficult and unpleasant task of halting the expansion of public expenditure and of reallocating resources within a stagnating and inflation-ridden economy. Moreover, they can no longer rely on the accuracy of economic forecasting. In trying to tackle these new tasks they often come to realize that the welfare strategies and planning methods hitherto used have entrapped them in a rather rigid system of commitments and responsibilities with little leeway for intramarginal adjustments and reorientations. This has intensified the search for new ways to create flexibility, new strategies and planning methods that are better designed for the needed adjustment to a changing environment.

In this article we will spell out more clearly the various reasons behind this need for flexibility in public budgeting. We start by taking a longer view of the trends in public expenditure and finance, pointing at some major adjustment problems of budget policy that grew out of the construction and expansion of the "welfare state." This potential need of budgetary flexibility was, however, first made acute and generally acknowledged by the experience of economic stagnation in recent years. We therefore also look closely at the present situation, where so much of budget policy is involved in fighting, and/or adjusting to, economic stagflation.

While economic development calls for flexibility, the development of bureaucracies, political institutions, and voter attitudes seem bound in the opposite direction—towards an increasing rigidity in decision-making and spending patterns. In a second article, we review these political trends and discuss to what extent the tendency towards institutional rigidity can also be viewed as arising out of the new budgeting tasks.

Most of the problems we discuss are common to all western industrial economies, although the extent to which they are critical—and generally perceived—may vary. We have throughout used the following eight countries as a common frame of reference: Canada, France, Italy, The Netherlands, Sweden, U.K., U.S.A., and West Germany.

From *Public Budgeting and Finance,* vol. 2 (3) (Autumn 1982), 7–20. Copyright © 1982 by Public Financial Publications, Inc. Reprinted with permission.

FROM COLLECTIVE TO INDIVIDUAL SECURITY

How much flexibility you need in public budgets is a question of what external and internal changes you must be ready to adjust to and how well foreseen these changes will be. From the point of view of this public "risk-taking," public budgets have radically changed over the last half century.

In the old "guardian state" a main task of the state was concerned with collective security, minimizing and insuring against the risk of external or internal assaults on society by defense and foreign policy and by the judiciary and other control systems of central administration. Besides these expenditures on collective security—what the economists usually call pure collective goods—another major category of expenditure was investments in roads and in other kinds of infrastructure. In economic jargon, the investments were concerned with "semi-collective goods," characterized by a high proportion of fixed cost, long economic life span, and large returns to scale, which made them natural candidates for tax financing.

With public budgets dominated by these ambitions and kinds of expenditures, flexibility was needed only to adjust to changes in the national security situation and to long-term trends in internal migration and urbanization, etc.

Other kinds of risks, whether arising from changes in the economic conditions or from the vicissitudes of families and enterprises, were born by the individual unit directly affected. It was still the individual firm or the individual household that had to do most of the adjusting, not the public budgets.

The development over the last half century from the "guardian state" to the "welfare state" has meant a shift of emphasis from collective security to social and individual security. The major and growing part of public budgets in the western industrial countries is now aimed at ensuring reasonable standards for the individual household. To a growing extent, public budgets are thus acting as buffers or insurance against the individual lifecycle or family situation, against unemployment and ill-health, against the cost of bringing up children and the cost of growing old. This fact that much risk taking has been moved upwards from the individual household—and sometimes also from the individual firm—to government creates new needs for flexibility in public budgets. Social risk sharing is not a zero-sum game where one individual's fortune may be expected to even out another's misfortune. Demographic mutations and changes in the economic environment may require drastic changes not only in total public resource use but also in the allocation of resources between different purposes.

How difficult it may be to attain the needed flexibility will depend on the form given the individual standard guarantees. The government can guarantee income by transfers to individual households or firms, or it may instead guarantee the availability of certain social services directly by publicly producing the services and distributing them free of charge or heavily subsidized, i.e., as public consumption. Public consumption may for other reasons be a preferred way, but from the point of view of flexibility it certainly has the disadvantage of creating further commitments and adjustment problems for the public budget makers.

When it comes to demonstrating trends and tendencies involved in public expansion, Sweden is usually a good example, since the relative expansion of public expenditure and tax financing has here been carried further than in any other industrialized country (Klingman and Peters, 1980; Ysander, 1981a). Figure 23.1 shows how the Swedish "welfare strategy" developed during the period 1950–1980. All public expenditure of a non-business, non-contractual nature has been grouped in two main categories: collective security and social security. Under the general heading of collective security, all current and investment expenditure for defense and foreign policy, general administration, judiciary system, and fire service have been counted. All other expenditures

Figure 23.1   **The Swedish Welfare Strategy—The Use of Taxes 1950–80**

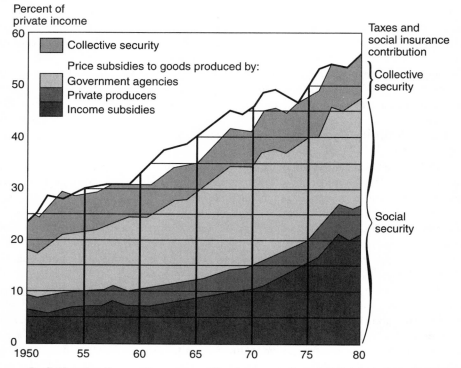

Source: B.-C. Ysander, *Fem avgiftsargument* (Five Arguments for Public Pricing), *SOU* 1979:23 (Royal Commission Report), Stockholm; and *Offentlig ekonomi i tillvxt* (Expanding the Public Economy), The Industrial Institute for Economic and Social Research, Stockholm, 1981.

are subsumed under the heading of social security, and are assumed to be mainly concerned with guaranteeing or preserving individual standards. Social security expenditures have been further broken down into two categories: "income subsidies" or direct transfers to households, and "price subsidies." There are, finally, two kinds of price subsidies. The major part, called public consumption and related investment in the national accounts, goes to government agencies, producing various types of social services in education, health, social welfare, roads, etc. The rest are subsidies for current or investment expenditures within the private sector, e.g., for housing and food, to public utilities, or to ailing industries.

A thick line at the top shows the development of income from taxes and social insurance contributions. All budget items are displayed as shares of private income.

The figure shows a very striking development pattern. The share of income used for collective security has remained more or less constant over the whole period, around 10 percent. The dramatic expansion of the public budget share has entirely been due to the increase in social security expenditure. This has more than tripled its share during the 30 years. The proportion in social security expenditures of public consumption and related investments as well as of income subsidies has remained fairly unchanged during the period. The share of price subsidies to private producers has expanded at a slower rate than other social security expenditure, in spite of the considerable increase of industrial support measures in recent years.

The role played by capital formation in general and infrastructure investment in particular in the Swedish public budget is also diminishing. The GNP share of public capital formation is now less than it used to be 30 years ago.

Welfare strategies vary among different countries. Compared to Sweden, most OECD countries have experienced a less rapid total expansion of public budgets and are also relatively less dependent on price subsidies in general and public consumption in particular. This is particularly true for countries like Italy and France, where social security expenditures have traditionally been dominated by income transfers to households. The relative dependence on public consumption is relevant to the question of budget flexibility. It seems reasonable to argue that welfare strategies which depend more on public consumption, involving relatively more of public production and employment, tend to make it harder both economically and politically to adjust downwards, at least in the short run.

Whatever the differences in welfare strategy, certain main traits are common to public budget development in the different countries. The share of total incomes channeled through public budgets has been growing everywhere. The relative role played by expenditures for collective security has been continuously dwindling, particularly rapidly during the 70s. Finally, a diminishing share of public expenditures is used for capital formation.

SOCIAL INSURANCE THROUGH PUBLIC BUDGETS

Social security expenditures can to a large extent be construed as a means of "insuring individual standards." One way of studying what public budgets do for the individual household is to look at their impact on the anticipated life income of a young individual. The expectations of future standards for the individual will be determined by life cycle changes, by the need for educational services for the individual and any future children, old age care, etc., and by various kinds of risks of ill health or unemployment. The existence of public budgets may affect this anticipated life income in two ways. In part, the public budget may be construed as an obligatory group insurance policy with premiums computed from average probabilities for the various social events. The other kind of impact will be direct changes in the individual's real income prospects.

The part of the impact that can be construed as an insurance of life income or standards affect individual expectations in at least two ways. First, it redistributes the resources available over time in proportion to the expected needs in different phases of life. Here government can be said to act as a substitute for a perfect credit market, making it possible for individuals to lend and borrow in proportion to their needs. Second, it changes the variance of the anticipated real income or standard in different years. Social security here assumes the role of a pure risk insurance, compensating for various kinds of economic and family vicissitudes.

Changes in real income prospects through public budgets may again be characterized in two different ways. Collective and social security may shift the levels of expected life income by affecting available resources or by changing incentives. It may also redistribute expected life incomes between individuals and households. Besides these redistributions that are openly accounted for in the tax and transfer system, there are also "disguised" redistributions due to the difference between the collective and obligatory "insurance contracts" involved in social security and the insurance individuals would voluntarily have contracted. A healthy, talented, and well-educated individual may run less risk than another individual and may value security differently.

Open redistribution between expected life incomes seems in fact to play a marginal role in public budget systems. The dominant part of the social security budget can be interpreted as an insurance of individual lifetime standards or income. Thus the actual redistribution is not from rich to poor so much as between age cohorts of the general population: a "lifetime" redistribution. This has obvious implications for the study of government risk taking and the need for flexibility or adjustment in public budgets. Public budget makers must be ready to adjust to various kinds of demographic and economic changes, and most such adjustments will affect a majority of voters.

DEMOGRAPHIC CHANGES

Since so much of government expenditure is concerned with insuring individual standards, one major reason for requiring flexibility and adjustment in the public budget is the prospect of demographic changes. The goods and services needed by a household vary a great deal with the composition of the household, the number and age of adults and children, etc. If social security is interpreted to mean the insurance of certain standards for each type of household, population changes that entail drastic changes in the age structure, or in the pattern of migration and localization, may obviously require a corresponding adjustment and reallocation of budgetary resources. The adjustment problem will often be further magnified by the fact that the population changes also affect the proportion of people in active ages constituting the productive basis—and the tax base—for society. A low and stabilized death rate contrasts against a still volatile, but in the long-term declining, birth rate. The birth rate which has declined sharply since the mid-60s is in most countries expected to remain low also during the remaining decades of the century. Historical experience tends, however, to show that no great reliance can be put on predictions of birth rate. There seems to be no assurance of stability in birth rates in the mature industrial society where fertility is controlled according to the changing desires and economic circumstances of successive parental generations. Within the overall pattern of aging populations, we may also in the future have to deal with the various problems raised by fluctuating child populations.

Although the aging process may be more or less advanced in the different countries, all are characterized by a declining rate of population increase, and by reproduction rates that imply long-term population decrease and an ongoing shift upwards in the age structure, with relatively more old people and fewer children. This "aging" of the population is in most cases expected to continue at least over the next decades. According to United Nations' population statistics and projections, there were in 1950 in the more developed regions of the world almost nine individuals in active age (15–64 years), for each person over 65. The projected ratio for the year 2000 is only five to one. In Western Europe this ratio is now only four to one and still declining.

Since Sweden constitutes an extreme example of the common trends, the adjustment problem implied by population changes may be exemplified by Swedish data. Figure 23.2 shows the Swedish population development 1925–2025 according to an official projection made some years ago. The figure demonstrates the two common traits of population change that we emphasized above: the high degree of uncertainty and the long-run tendency towards a declining and aging population.

Both the uncertainty and the aging have obvious consequences for the economy. The constant ebb and flow in the number of children passing through school and young adults coming of age to join the labor force, marry, and establish new households has unsettling effects on the functioning and development of the educational system, the labor market, and the demand for housing and consumer durable goods. The increasing number of old people creates economic, social, and political problems of meeting the needs of the aged for income maintenance, medical care, and housing, etc.

As an example of these possible consequences for public budgets, we recount in Table 23.1 some estimates of consumption patterns for different age groups in Sweden in 1975. It should be emphasized that no attempt has been made here to estimate independently the private consump-

Figure 23.2 **The Swedish Population 1925–2025**

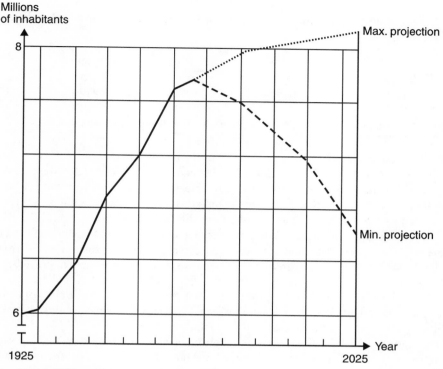

Source: National Central Bureau of Statistics (1976).

tion costs of children. The figure for this in the table is simply the sum of those public transfers to households that are specially ear-marked for the private consumption of children. The actual distribution of private consumption within the family has thus been left open. What is of interest to us here is the fact that, although the total consumption of older people was estimated to be some 20 percent below that of people in active ages, their consumption of publicly produced service—roughly equivalent to that of children—was twice as large as that of people in the active ages. The transfer of an individual from active to retirement age not only means that his or her total consumption cost, only slightly reduced by retirement, now has to be borne by the remaining income earners; it also means a radical reshuffling of the "consumption basket," with a heavy emphasis on various kinds of social services.

CHANGES IN THE ECONOMIC ENVIRONMENT

Another major reason for the need for flexibility in public budgets has to do with changes in the economic environment and uncertainty surrounding these changes. Technological changes and shifts in competitive or bargaining positions change the relative prices and with that the real income of individual households and firms, as well as that of countries. The experience of the industrial countries in the 70s affords dramatic examples of this. Two big oil price hikes entailed a considerable worsening of terms-of-trade for many oil importing countries and affected the competitive position and profitability of many branches of industry. The discovery of new natural resources

Table 23.1

Private and Public Consumption per Capita for Different Age Groups in Sweden, 1975
(Swedish croners)

	0–14 years	15–64 years	65 + years	Total
Private consumption	2,200	26,700	14,900	18,200
Public consumption	11,500	6,600	11,900	8,700
Total consumption	13,700	33,200	26,900	27,000

Source: A. Nordin and C.J. Aberg, *Befolkning och ekonomi*, Trygg-Hansa, Stockholm, 1977.

in some cases led to a devaluation of the old and to changes in the relative wealth of nations. The increasing competition from newly industrialized countries helped to initiate a long-term decline and stagnation in many of the traditional industrial branches of the western countries. An unusually severe and well-synchronized recession coupled with rising trends in inflation rates created stabilization problems which in many countries are still far from solved.

Altogether, the uncertainty surrounding industrial and macroeconomic planning has undoubtedly increased compared to the first postwar decades, which now in retrospect seem to exhibit an unusually stable and orderly economic development—at least for the western industrial countries. The Bretton Woods system of fixed exchange rates, the highly regulated capital markets, and the international cooperation and planning for reconstruction and trade liberalization all contributed to make the world relatively safe for economic planners. This experience may well prove to have been historically unique and is now definitively a thing of the past.

During earlier periods, without the safety net of social security, most of the adjustment responsibility would have been borne by the individual household or the firm directly affected. The changing fortunes of competition would be registered in the varying factor incomes, and from the income earners the effects would spread to dependents by way of intrafamily transfers. To the extent that a social security budget means insuring individual standards, much of this economic risk taking has now been taken over by the government.

The adjustment needed by way of public budgets not only means redistributing the gains and losses, using profits from expanding parts of the economy to compensate the welfare losses of ailing industries and regions and of adversely affected households. Another and perhaps even more difficult task is the adjustment of overall levels of domestic consumption.

Long-term changes in terms of trade and in the competitive position of a country sometimes require considerable downward adjustment of consumption levels and trends. The major responsibility for enforcing these overall adjustments and ensuring that the consequences are fairly distributed among the various segments of the population today falls on public budget makers. This is a task for which they are often ill prepared, which may be one major explanation why so many countries have failed in carrying through effective stabilization policies in recent years.

There is another important but more controversial side to government risk taking. Economic adjustment does not only mean tightening the belt and persevering through hard times. It also means successively restructuring the economy, getting resources out of declining industries and production areas into expanding production sectors, and new innovative efforts. When the individual standards are to a certain extent guaranteed by the government and expected gains and losses are evened out, the personal inducements to move, and to take new initiatives and new risks may be adversely affected. This could be true of subsidized industrial firms as well as of subsidized households, and could reduce the mobility of both capital and labor and, *ceteris paribus,* introduce new rigidities in the whole economy. To the extent that this is true, it means that more and more of the responsibility also for initiating change and affecting mobility will be placed with the government. Increasingly active labor market and industrial policies could then be viewed as an unavoidable sequence to a matured social security system.

Increased government intervention in this sense, however, also increases the flexibility requirements for public budgets since, e.g., with a limited labor supply, workshops somehow must be closed before new ones can be opened. Another example of this need for flexibility, by now experienced by most countries, is concerned with wage policy. On the one hand, economic adjustment in market economies presupposes a certain degree of flexibility in nominal wages. On the other hand, the claims to guaranteed standards, rooted in the social security system, coupled with union solidarity, tend to make relative and absolute adjustment of nominal wages hard to achieve. To accommodate simultaneously both these contrary claims may require a fine-tuned continuous adjustment of the tax and transfer system. How far it is possible to go in this direction is, however, still a controversial question.

That public budgets in the future need a lot more built-in flexibility is incontestable. What we still do not know, and where different views and ideologies still sharply differ, is to what extent public budget adjustments can be substituted for individual adjustments without losing the efficiency gains of a decentralized economy.

RETARDED GROWTH

It is usually much easier to adjust when resources are expanding than to do so in a stagnating climate where expansion for one category of expenditure can only be bought at the price of contracting another kind of expenditure. This partly explains why so much attention is focused on the question of budget flexibility right now in a time of industrial stagnation. However, quite apart from the present tendencies towards declining industrial productivity, there are good reasons to suppose that future budget makers will have to operate within much narrower growth limits than during the first postwar decades. This is simply due to the existence in the economy of several sectors with different rates of productivity increase.

It seems reasonable to assume that the more labor intensive service sectors will always on the average register a lower productivity increase than those prevailing in industry. Given this assumption, even a balanced growth of industrial production and service production will require that successively more people are moved from the industrial sector into the service sectors, while the overall rate of productivity increase in the economy will decrease, tending in the long run towards that of the service sector with the least increase in productivity. If we also want to have the consumption of goods and services for each type of household show a balanced growth—not an unnatural norm in a welfare state—then obviously, with an aging population, the shift of labor into service sectors and the decline of the overall productivity increase will be even more rapid, everything else being equal. If, on top of that, we add the fact that only dramatic increases in intercontinental migrations now seem to be able to prevent a long-term decline of the labor supply in the western industrial countries, it seems fairly certain that future public budget makers will have successively fewer new resources to play with and will have to fall back more on internal savings.

The growth of recorded gross domestic production (GDP) will in fact tend to show an even more marked retardation than that which is actually happening in total domestic production. One reason for this could be a relatively expanding "black and grey" sector of the economy, i.e., an increasing share of productive activities that goes unrecorded due to illegal tax evasion or because they are performed within the household and never marketed. Another and less specu-

Figure 23.3 **The Statistical Uncertainty—Swedish GNP 1950–80 under Alternative Assumption**

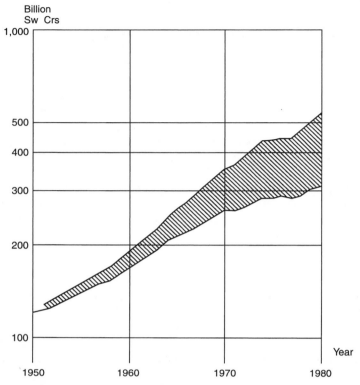

Source: B.-C. Ysander, *Offentlig ekonomi i tillväxt* (Expanding the Public Economy), The Industrial Institute for Economic and Social Research, Stockholm, 1981.

lative reason is the accounting conventions used in national accounting and in our definition of GDP. As long as we treat public consumption by definition as a sector with a zero increase in productivity, any growth of public consumption implies that official figures of GDP will show an exaggerated retardation.

Figure 23.3 exemplifies this accounting illusion from Sweden, the country with the largest and fastest increasing share of public consumption. The lower curve shows the actually recorded growth of GDP in Sweden for the period 1950–1980. The upper curve shows how this growth would have been recorded if instead we had used the alternative convention of assuming that the productivity increase in the public sector was the same as that of the private sector. As the figure shows, this alternative assumption would have meant that total production increased five times during the 30 years instead of three times as actually recorded. If we neglect the possibility of an actual decrease in productivity in the public employment, it means that we would expect the actual increase of productive capacity to lie somewhere within the shadowed area in the figure. Wherever it lies exactly, it is a reasonable assumption that the retardation of recorded growth of GDP, already noticeable during the first three postwar decades, will continue in the future. It is therefore futile to hope that the present concern with budget flexibility can soon again be forgotten in a new sustained wave of economic affluence and expansion.

MACROECONOMIC CONSTRAINTS ON BUDGETARY ADJUSTMENT

There are other factors besides the tendency towards retarded growth that make it more difficult than before to effectuate the needed budgetary adjustment. The share of total incomes that is channeled through the public budgets has grown in all countries during the last two decades—in the case of Sweden, doubling since 1961. The same is true of public employment. In the extreme case of Sweden, public employment now tends to surpass employment in the manufacturing industries. The elasticity of government receipts relative to GDP, as estimated over the last two decades, ranges from 1.08 in Germany to 1.32 in Sweden. This rapid expansion of the relative importance of the public sector in the economy also means that considerations of macroeconomic effects and consequences for the private sector must play an enlarged and constraining role in calibrating and timing the adjustments in public budgets. Let us just here note some of the best known instances of these macroeconomic constraints on budgetary adjustment.

Taxes play an increasingly important role in determining the cost of producing goods and services. Tax increases, unfortunately timed, may contribute to an upward "cost push" effect on domestic inflation, directly by way of commodity prices or indirectly by way of their influence on wage settlements. To the extent that the tax increases also squeeze profits and disposable incomes, they may also restrict effective supply both in the factor and the commodity markets. High taxes and the concomitant high degree of tax consciousness therefore tend to make tax adjustments a very delicate operation even without stagflation.

On the expenditure side, the macroeconomic constraints mostly discussed are concerned with the influence of government budgets on factor markets. With government as both a dominant employer and a dominant borrower on the capital market, the rate of public expenditure increase must necessarily affect the cost situation for producers within the private sector. Saying this does not mean that one has to subscribe to the simplified picture of government and private firms competing directly on a homogeneous labor market or a market for loanable funds. Even if public employment is to a certain extent "segregated" from the industrial labor market, the rate of increase in public employment will undoubtedly affect the overall development of wage cost in the economy. Even if the capital market is partly rationed by the government itself and the availability of capital funds mainly determined by monetary policies, an increasing deficit in the public budgets will in the end tend to push up the price of capital—the interest rate. If the deficits grow large enough, not even the best intended monetary policy will be able to avoid some of the deficits spilling over into inflationary additions to the liquidity in the economy. It should perhaps be emphasized that these constraints refer to the timing and rate of budgetary adjustments, *not* to the level or relative size of the public sector.

As a further and final example of the stability constraints on budget adjustment, we can use the problem of capitalization. If, as in Sweden, two-thirds of all incomes are channeled through public budgets and one-third of disposable incomes derive from public transfers, it would indeed be remarkable if income expectations and capital values were not largely determined by the tax and transfer system. This means that drastic changes in taxes and transfers may lead to speculative instability on the markets concerned, entailing large windfall profits and losses for the capital owners. Housing policies in Western Europe during the postwar period afford many good illustrations of this problem.

What examples show is simply that with the growing importance of the public economy, budget policy becomes an integral and indeed often a major part of general economic policy. This places constraints on the possible rate and timing of budgetary adjustments.

INDUSTRIAL STAGNATION AND DEFICIT SPENDING

The question of budget flexibility has in recent years acquired a new urgency and new dimensions by the stagflation developments in the western industrial countries. The average rate of annual inflation in these countries has more than doubled over the last ten years. At the same time, industrial production and investment are stagnating and resource utilization and employment are still far below normal levels in most countries. As can be expected, industrial stagnation and high unemployment in most countries go together with a public budget deficit. The demand for social security expenditures rises, while at the same time there is a shrinking of the base for direct taxes and for social security contributions.

In trying to find a policy against stagflation, the governments in the western countries seem to have been faced with two policy options, both with undesirable side effects and neither of which has so far proved efficient. One option is to keep up employment by a cautious expansion of domestic demand, while at the same time trying to contain the budget deficit by finding new and less inflationary sources of tax finance. You pay the risk of increased inflation and a mounting deficit in the hope that if you manage to hibernate a couple of more years, the world inflation will be dampened by outside efforts.

The contrary option is to focus on the fight against inflation, accepting the risk of rapidly rising unemployment. Restrictive monetary policies are combined with a relative shrinkage of both taxes and public expenditures in the hope of dampening inflation by simultaneously restricting public demand and expanding private supply. The risk involved is that if the second effect does not materialize, all you are left with is unemployment. Alternative measures have also been tried, including selective incentives for industrial expansion and income and price policies directed towards the goal of breaking inflationary expectations.

Whichever option is tried, one experience seems to be common to all present-day public budget makers. The limits on real resource growth and tax financing are now effective and generally acknowledged to a much greater extent than ever before. Whatever the long-term view and the political priorities, most parties involved in public budget making now seem to concede the fact that growth both of public consumption and of total public expenditures during the remaining years of the 80s will be slow. This means that part of the necessary new public expenditures for the rapidly rising number of older people, etc., will have to be provided by more strictly economizing with already existing public resources and more cautiously "marketing" existing social services.

PRICE EXPECTATIONS AND INFLATION ADJUSTMENT

The high rate of inflation has also brought attention to a number of questions concerning the management of public budgets in an inflationary economy. The problems involved are both political and technical. They have to do both with the rapid rate of price change and with the increased uncertainty surrounding these changes.

There are really two main questions. The first concerns to what extent there should be adjustments for inflation. A second group of questions concerns how such adjustments should be made. To adjust completely to inflation by "indexing" the whole budget—taxing real instead of nominal incomes and fully compensating on the expenditure side for all additional costs due to price movements—could at best be interpreted as an attempt to keep the public budget neutral in the fight against inflation. Instead of trying to break or change price expectations in private markets, public budget makers accept and accommodate them. In the worst case it could mean superimposing a new inflationary spiral by partly compensating for the effects of earlier compensations, by lessening the resistance against price and wage increases, and by running up a bigger deficit because of the rising relative cost of public services. There is a reasonable argument for limiting the extent of inflation adjustment in the hope of breaking price expectations and price movements.

There are also many different questions concerning the most efficient way of indexing various budget items. The current tax rules in most countries exhibit a perplexing mixture of nominal and real terms. The indexing of tax scales is a fairly simple first step that has by now been taken in most countries. To further approach a consistent real tax system is, however, a very complicated business which cannot be discussed in isolation from the problem of indexing the credit market and of inflation accounting in the rest of the economy.

On the expenditure side, inflationary adjustment involves a series of questions concerning the criteria to be used in deciding the suitable degree of compensation and the choice of the price index to be used in adjusting the various expenditure items. Once these decisions have been made, one is still left with the difficult problem of making estimates for the adjusted budget. Price expectations must be built into the budgetary process in a consistent way. The basic tool for such estimates—a model of price determination in the economy—is still lacking in most treasuries.

Inflation also affects budgetary planning in other ways. One of the main reasons for the increasing unreliability of macroeconomic models is probably connected with the fact that most of these models do not take price expectations explicitly into account. If price expectations may radically change behavior and by that also the economic outcome, and if these expectations cannot in any simple way be explained in terms of the recent development of economic aggregates, then the models will fail to produce accurate forecasts. This forecasting failure has obvious and important implications for budgetary flexibility. It forces the government to shorten its perspective in budgetary planning and makes it necessary to find ways of reviewing and changing budgetary decisions with short notice, to make the whole process of budgetary decision making more flexible and less drawn out in time.

REFERENCES

Klingman, D., and B.G. Peters (1980), "The Growth of Public Expenditures in Scandinavia 1875–1965," *Political Studies,* Vol. 28.

National Central Bureau of Statistics (1976), Information i prognosfrågor No. 3.

Nordin, A., and C.J. Åberg (1977), *Befolkning och ekonomi* (Stockholm: Trygg Hansa).

Ysander, B.-C. (1979), "Fem avgiftsargument" (Five Arguments for Public Pricing), *SOU* 1979:23 (Royal Commission Report), Stockholm.

———— (1981a), Offentlig ekonomi i tillväxt (Expanding the Public Economy) (Stockholm: The Industrial Institute for Economic and Social Research).

———— (1981b), "Oil Prices and Economic Stability: The Macroeconomic Impact of Oil Price Shocks on the Swedish Economy." *IUI Working Paper* No. 47 (Stockholm: The Industrial Institute for Economic and Social Research).

———— (1981c), "Taxes and Market Stability" in *Business Taxation, Finance and Firm Behavior,* C. Eliasson and J. Soderstein (eds.) (Stockholm: The Industrial Institute for Economic and Social Research).

CHAPTER 24

RE-ESTABLISHING BUDGETARY FLEXIBILITY

ANN ROBINSON AND BENGT-CHRISTER YSANDER

The build-up of the welfare state has increased the need for flexibility and adjustment in public budgeting. The postwar experience of public decision making has, however, exposed tendencies in the opposite direction—towards more inflexible budgets and less political control of public spending. This is not just an unfortunate coincidence. The political changes may be viewed as reflecting the new tasks assigned to the public sector in a welfare state. When the new tasks are tackled with planning methods more appropriate to the execution of public duties in a guardian state, the result will be increased rigidity.

To the extent that the impact of public programs is no longer national and collective, but limited to certain groups of individual beneficiaries, one would expect the organization of voters into interest groups. Instead of individual voters expressing their preferences on national interests in political elections, the voters will be represented by their various interest groups, competing and lobbying for public resources. The mandatory power of the political establishment will have to make trades with the mandatory power of interest organizations.

When the government commitments directly touch on the individual's private welfare, it is only natural that these commitments are perceived as social contracts, the obligations of which must be honored. No one is likely to sue the government for damage because it is postponing a weapons acquisition, a new courthouse, or a national road project. Any short-term tampering with the conditions for pensions or other social insurance benefits is, on the other hand, likely to cause a public outcry about infringement of rights and contractual obligations. The rigidity in spending plans this may lead to will tend to be further reinforced by the fact that any reduction is apt to be viewed as discrimination against a particular group of beneficiaries.

The new emphasis on distribution will also change the politician's role. Instead of trying to interpret the electorate's wishes in terms of a socially optimal amount of armaments or judiciary resource, he or she must now act as umpire in the midst of an unlimited amount of competing claims for the distribution of welfare. The demand for more policemen does after all have a limit, while there is no assured limit to the demand for a bigger slice of the common bounty. Ideology, in the sense of an arrangement of individual preferences along an undimensional scale of possible collective actions, will tend to become superceded by the politics of group interest, with each

Figure 24.1 **Two Models of Public Decision Making**

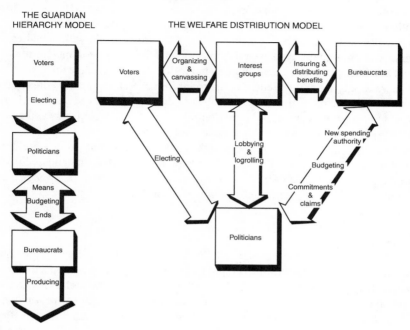

group appraising the budget impact by its own private standard. The fact that so much of social insurance concerns so many—a kind of lifetime redistribution—will serve, however, to secure a certain political stability and coherence.

When public budgets dealt mainly with collective security, the political establishment could in principle still retain the full responsibility both for interpreting the wishes of the voters and for translating them into detailed spending decisions. The budgeting dialogue between political decision makers and executive bureaucrats could then be viewed as simply a way of informing the politicians about technical possibilities and constraints. With the political role more and more turned into that of an insurance broker, with the taxpayers as more or less willing underwriters, politicans will often come to depend more on their bureaucratic agents, who must do the actual insurance adjusting. There will almost unavoidably be a decentralization of public spending and marketing. It will be the agents who will hear the claims and do the actual settling. It is through the agents that much of the needs and the wishes for more generous criteria and coverage in insurance will be channeled. The agents will present the final bill of earlier commitments and try—possibly with the support of entrenched interest groups—to compete for new spending authority.

The position of the bureaucrats or public agents will be further strengthened by increased government involvement in the production of welfare services. The demand for welfare service will not only be registered, but to a certain extent also regulated by the suppliers. Bureaucratic interests will be closely allied with the interest groups concerned, making political revisions of programs correspondingly more difficult. This may also have the unfortunate and unintended effect of further widening the gap between individual clients and political decision makers.

Thus, change in economic tasks and obligations is likely to cause a corresponding change in the conditions for public decision making. A very simplified picture of the "old" and the "new" model of decision making is shown in Figure 24.1 The "guardian hierarchy model"—in political science particularly associated with the work of Max Weber—is still used as a common frame of reference for much normative work on planning and budgeting methods, as instanced by the argumentation for PPBS systems. That the more complex "welfare distribution model" is closer to current practice would probably be acknowledged by most people with actual experience in public administration. Equally well established is the fact that as we continue to fit our planning methods and practices to the guardian hierarchy model, public budgeting in the welfare state tends to become increasingly inflexible, reducing the room for necessary political adjustments.

Economic and political developments of public budgeting in the welfare state thus appear to be intertwined but seemingly irreconcilable. Centralization of individual risk taking is not viable if no political room is left for the necessary central adjustments.

We will return in our concluding remarks to the possible ways of creating more flexibility for political control and budgeting. First, however, we shall try to trace the changing political roles and the increased rigidities in public decision making through the history of postwar Britain, dealing in turn with planning methods, bureaucrats, politicians, and voters.

THE METHODS OF BUDGETING

The history of the development and use of budgetary techniques reveals how politicians gradually come to realize that they need instruments of budget making expressly designed to fit current economic, environmental, and political needs. While they search for new tools, they continue to use old ones. When the old tools are not adapted to new conditions, rigidities appear in the processes of planning and control. In this section we show how the techniques employed in Britain in the expansionist phase of public spending from 1950 to 1975 have acquired characteristics that inhibit flexibility in a period of limited resources and rapid inflation.

In the old "guardian state," when governments were primarily concerned with collective security, simple methods of public expenditure planning and control could be employed effectively. The British system of "Treasury control" perfected in the 19th century under Gladstone was highly regarded as a shining example of executive budgeting. A system that provided on a yearly basis prior sanction by the finance ministry, parliamentary authorization of expenditures and taxes, and careful "post hoc" audit, sufficed for the era of limited government. But the expansion of public capital formation and the advent of the welfare state in the 1950s revealed deficiencies in this traditional "circle of control."

The deficiencies of annual appropriations and controls first came to light as governments embarked on large-scale capital projects. Highway construction and the building of hospitals and schools did not take place in the course of a single financial year. Plans made in one year entailed expenditures for many years ahead. Governments also realized that their open-ended commitments in the sphere of social welfare and insurance had a continuous impact on the shape of the public budget. Although continued expansion of the public sector was politically popular with the electorate, it carried economic dangers with it. Politicians could not proceed too fast with new schemes if they wished to avoid undue strains on the economy. Thus, budget makers came to recognize that they required some estimation of the long-term effects of their decisions on the total of future public expenditure and on the shape of the whole economy. Instead of annual budgets, they needed to make multiyear budgets.

In 1958 the Estimates Committee of the British House of Commons issued a report which demonstrated the inadequacies of annual budgeting in a period of expanding government expenditures. The Plowden Committee (1960) recommended the establishment of the Public Expenditure Survey Committee (PESC) which has operated since 1961. PESC's task is to survey all public services in

Britain—including local government and nationalized industries—and to project forward for five years the expected costs of current programs and agreed-upon decisions. Five-year forward looks had already been used for some departments, including defense, prior to 1961, but the novelty of PESC was that it covered the entire public sector in one exercise.

PESC itself is not a planning system, because it merely records the future financial effects of decisions already taken. But it is used as the basis on which plans for new spending initiatives are agreed. Armed with projections of economic growth over the same five-year period as the PESC estimates, ministers can put the two sides of the equation together. They can see how much of future economic resources will be absorbed by current commitments and how much room is likely to be left for further expansion of public services. They can then agree on how and when to introduce new programs. So long as the forecasts of future expenditures on current commitments are stable, that is, so long as inflation is correctly forecast and its effects are calculable, and so long as the forecasts of future economic expansion are accurate, PESC appears to provide an ideal basis for rational public expenditure planning. It appears to offer the prospect of making rational decisions about the desired changes to the total size of the public sector, and to encourage rational allocation of future resources among competing functions of government. However, the way in which PESC has been used by politicians, especially as economic circumstances have altered, has encouraged rigidities in expenditure programs instead of increasing the rationality of the planning process.

It was perhaps just bad luck that PESC was first used at the very time that Britain was moving from a period of postwar economic expansion and relatively low rates of inflation into a period of slow and uncertain growth coupled with increasing rates of inflation. But experience with the use of multiyear budgets in other countries reveals similar tendencies. A device that might work well under conditions of stable economic growth has limited governmental freedom of action and choice under conditions of scarce resources.

It is easy to blame the PESC instrument itself, the economic forecasters, or the politicians for the rigidities that have arisen from the use of this device. But it should be remembered that the way in which it was used merely reflected widely shared current attitudes and assumptions. In spite of warning signs, no one really wanted to believe that economic growth could come to an end. When PESC was first introduced, economic growth was expected to continue indefinitely and to bring only benefits. Politicians and public alike agreed on the advantages of economic growth. It appealed to both Conservatives and Socialists. It offered the attractive prospect of expanding public services and of creating a "humane" state without the accompanying pain of excessive taxation or overly harsh redistribution of income and wealth.

The relationship between economic growth and the development of a welfare state was elo-quently pursued in influential books by Anthony Crosland (1956), and J.K. Galbraith (1958). A developed and expanding economy, in their estimation, offered plenty of scope for collective provi-sion of public services without affecting the individual's prospects of personal affluence. Anyone who suggested, as did E.J. Mishan (1967), that growth might have concomitant disadvantages and that it might not necessarily increase welfare and happiness found himself swimming against a strong intellectual tide. Expectations of continued economic growth remained an underlying assumption of politicians and budget makers. PESC therefore simply acted as a handy tool for the realization of a dominant ideology—the ideology of growth. Indeed, many politicians still have not accepted that there are costs and limits to growth and hope that the current economic conditions under which they have to work are merely a severe example of a passing slump.

Even so, PESC might have proved a good basis for expenditure planning if the estimates of costs of current programs and the forecasts of future resources had generally been accurate. But the estimates of costs were always too low and the forecasts of future resources always too optimistic. Over-optimistic expectations of the room for new programs led politicans to overspend. They compounded this effect by their attitude toward the programs once they had been agreed in Cabinet. Once a new program has been agreed to and written into PESC, its status changes from that of proposal to that of commitment. Adjustments then become very difficult because they have to be presented as "cuts" even if they are simply cuts in projected increases.

There are other reasons why the way in which PESC was used encouraged rigidity in public spending. PESC became a part of the machinery for management of the economy. It recorded the long-term effects of commitments to public services. The economy had to be managed so that the promises could be kept. There were, of course, other important objectives of economic management—balance of payments, exchange rate stability, etc.—but the maintenance of the public sector gradually became more and more an effective constraint as the public sector grew in size.

In Britain since the war, the economy has generally been regulated through demand management. In theory, fiscal demand management can be carried out by making adjustments either to future and current public expenditure or to taxation. In practice, taxation, not spending, was generally the preferred tool of adjustment. Politically the firm commitments to expenditure programs, enshrined in PESC, discouraged the use of the spending tool. Alterations to social programs in particular proved politically risky in Britain, where the electorate widely accepted the Beveridge principles of the welfare state. Current spending on goods and services become particularly difficult to adjust, especially in periods of rapid inflation. Where governments were forced to make cuts in spending, they tried to concentrate on capital programs. Projected capital programs not yet started could always be postponed. Expenditure, however, has technical disadvantages as a tool of economic management. There are considerable time lags between the announcement of a change and its consequent effects on the economy. "Stop-go" in public spending creates disturbances and instability in administration and may even generate extra costs. So when adjustments have had to be made to accommodate disturbances in the path of economic growth, taxation has always been preferred. The all-party Expenditure Committee of the House of Commons, in its Ninth Report of 1974, concluded that:

> . . . changes in the level of public expenditure should be used only as a tool of last resort. . . . short-term management of the economy should primarily be carried out by changes in taxation.

In 1976, however, the British government was forced by an economic crisis to make very considerable budgetary adjustments: Constrained by the requirements of the IMF loan, it had to use both taxation and expenditure as tools. By now, however, governments had come to see that over reliance on multiyear budgeting under PESC had tied their hands too much. The figures in PESC had become firm commitments that they had no reasonable means of altering. New machinery was therefore required for the control of public spending. A device was required that would ensure that the Cabinet plans were adhered to in practice, and would permit year by year adjustments to spending programs as circumstances dictated. Thus "cash limits" were introduced in 1976 and now cover some 60 percent of public expenditure in Britain. They do not, significantly, cover social insurance such as unemployment benefits, which have expanded considerably during the recession. They are not, therefore, a universal tool for injecting control and flexibility into public spending. Cash limits tell departments and agencies of government how much money they can expect for the coming year in cash terms. They mark something of a return to the pre-PESC annual Treasury control, and PESC has accordingly been downgraded politically.

The successful implementation of cash limits as a device for greater flexibility and control in public spending depends largely on the attitudes of the departments and agencies. Some agencies, after five years of cash limits—but only two years of strictly applied limits without inflation adjustment—are beginning to respond by searching for flexibility in the use of their resources. But many others do not yet realize the import of Anthony Crosland's words in 1975 when he told British Local Authorities: "the party is over." Cash limits can only inject flexibility of response into government agencies if the agencies themselves are willing to look hard at their activities and goals. Cash limits are used by central government to tell agencies: "This is the amount of money that you have to spend—see what you can do with it." Earlier techniques of budget making were used by governments to say, "This is what we want you to do—see how much money you need to do it."

In the expansionary period of public spending, a whole constellation of associated budget-making techniques known generally as PPBS—planning, programming, budgeting system (program budgeting, output budgeting, cost-benefit analysis, management by objectives, program analysis and review)—were introduced into the governmental machinery of many countries, including Britain. First used successfully in the defense departments of the U.S.A., Britain, and Sweden, these new approaches to budget construction appeared to offer advantages that could be employed throughout the public service. Instead of costing services by their inputs—staff, materials, and services—the desired objective or goal of a government agency was first specified and then an analysis made of the best allocation of resources to achieve that end. The techniques of rational economic analysis were to be brought to bear on the needs of government. Properly applied, the system had two requirements. First, it needed clear specification of goals, and second, it needed well-researched and analyzed breakdown of likely costs (Robinson, 1972).

Initially, PPBS was welcomed and encouraged by central governments. In 1965 President Johnson decreed that it should be used throughout the U.S. federal government. Canada, Sweden, and Britain experimented with the system. Local authorities, as well as central governments, turned to the new approach. In 1970, the incoming Conservative government in Britain under Edward Heath issued a White Paper boldly entitled: "A new style of government." The new style was to include a greater use of rational budget-making techniques together with a reorganization and rationalization of the central Departments of State to pull the whole machine into one coherent whole. But in practice the PPBS approach to budget construction proved expensive and difficult to operate. Although it was technically feasible, higher levels of government soon became disenchanted with it. They found the strain of assessing needs and setting clear objectives beyond them. It gradually disappeared from the central government machinery. Even in the U.S.A., where the greatest enthusiasm for the approach was exhibited, the wholesale use of it was abandoned. But it left behind an intellectual residue. Its effect was much greater on the periphery of government than at the center. It transformed the way in which budget makers within departments, agencies, and local authorities construct their annual requests for money. Bureaucrats, even if their agency does not indulge in a full-scale "program budget" or "output budget" exercise each year, find it convenient to continue to think in terms of fixed programs and objectives when planning their requests for funds. In the absence of machinery for the clear political specification of goals, the use of PPBS and related techniques at the lower levels of government has merely served to encourage a tendency towards rigidity.

The experience of the use of techniques for budget construction—PESC, PPBS and cash limits—illustrates that it is no use devising good tools for budget construction if they are subverted by the attitudes and behavior of politicians. PPBS failed because central government failed to play its part, and cash limits may fail if agencies cannot respond to limitations. The first requirement of all budgetary techniques is that politicians should have a clear idea of what their goals really are. Politicians often have only a vague idea of what they want. Even when they get as far as writing down proposals in an election manifesto, they often have hardly considered what those proposals mean in practice. The relationship between political goals and governmental organization is not clearcut either. Each objective, even were it to be clearly specified, cannot necessarily be matched by a single agency to carry it out. Functions of government departments frequently overlap.

BUREAUCRATIC STRUCTURE AND BEHAVIOR

Most countries have acquired a large bureaucratic machine to deliver the services and benefits of the welfare state. The structure of the bureaucratic machine varies in some detail from country to country. Some countries are constitutionally more centralized than others. They have developed traditions of strong central control and a uniform provision of services. In other countries, decentralization is a more predominant characteristic. But there are some common features of structure that seem to have become essential in the welfare state. Most countries have a centrally determined standard of public service provision and a degree of decentralization in the delivery of those services to the public. Decentralization of delivery appears to be a necessary consequence of the large size of modern government and of the needs of regional variations.

The bureaucratic structure is also determined by the manner in which social insurances are delivered. Services can be provided either by a state monopoly or via insurance programs that cover the costs of provision in the private sector. Health services are provided by a state monopoly in Britain, but via insurance programs in France and Germany. There is obviously some inherent capacity for rigidity in the first model unless it has something to compare itself with. Comparison may be possible if there is a parallel private sector. In Britain, for example, private medicine exists side by side with the state system.

The degree of propensity towards rigidity of structure and organization is not simply a function of either centralization or monopoly power. Decentralized delivery systems can also become rigid if there is no mechanism for the constant re-evaluation of their goals. Decentralization of structure can encourage rigidity by removing the possibility of central or independent criticism of agency performance. Under the traditional hierarchical structure of the classical government department, a constant chain of command was maintained. Once agencies are decentralized, the chain of command is broken and agencies are more likely to develop a life of their own. As a result, agencies can be established by central government, go out into the field to perform their tasks, and continue to flourish for years even if their original function has long since disappeared.

Many organizations come to believe that they are better placed to interpret changing needs and requirements than are the politicians. After all, they deliver the services and are in day-to-day contact with clients. They believe that they, not the politicians, can best interpret society's needs. Thus they are able to generate goals related to public needs from within themselves. This claim by bureaucracies deserves closer investigation than it has hitherto received. Agencies make the claim that they respond to demands for services. But, in fact, they control the supply of services, and the public can only take what is offered to them. Agencies of government therefore often act more like firms supplying goods in the market than like simple service bodies responding to autonomously generated demand (Tarschys, 1975).

The position of the bureaucrat in the welfare state is strong vis-a-vis his or her political master, and it is strong vis-a-vis the general public. In particular, bureaucrats are often in a better position to press their claims upon government than are their clients by being well organized and represented by powerful unions. Perhaps, it might be argued, the consumer of public services is already perfectly well able to make his or her voice heard through the representation of interests in an elected Parliament. This comment would have some validity if elected Parliaments were primarily concerned to represent the individual elector's interests. Analysis of the current role of Parliaments and the behavior of their members does not bear this out. Parliaments not only channel demands from individual members of the electorate, they also channel demands from organized interest groups, among them the bureaucracy itself. Indeed, the channels of communication are used much more by organized groups than by individuals. Groups and bureaucracies, not the general public, come to determine the shape and content of public programs.

THE ROLE OF LEGISLATURES

The way in which modern legislatures represent "the national interest" has been modified by the existence of organized interest groups. Organized groups have many advantages over the individual elector. They have access to information and can provide material that is useful to elected members when they are making speeches or attending committee hearings.

The nature of the representative process has been changing considerably as the public sector has expanded. This change has been little understood. Those who studied the work of legislative bodies in the 1950s and 1960s thought that they had discerned the "decline of the legislature." A common pattern appeared in all countries. As the government's activities expanded, it seemed to be gaining power at the legislature's expense. A vast literature on the role and decline of legislative assemblies included books with emotive titles like *What's Wrong with Parliament?* and *Congress in Crisis.* They all added up to the conclusion that legislatures had lost their powers to the executive branch of government and that they were now only of minor significance in the determination of policy. They were most particularly apathetic in the field of public finance (Robinson, 1978).

It is perhaps not surprising that legislatures should have appeared particularly passive in determining the patterns of finance. Most legislatures work under constitutional restrictions on the extent to which they can alter their government's proposals for spending and taxing. The most extreme case is afforded by the British example, where government spending plans are never, and taxing plans are rarely, altered in any detail by votes in the House of Commons. At the other end of the spectrum is the U.S. Congress, which has considerable constitutional powers over the size and shape of the federal budget and has enhanced its powers considerably since the passage of the 1974 Budget Act. The various continental and Scandinavian countries fall somewhere in between the British and American models in the freedom of action that they permit their legislatures in altering the government's budget. In most cases their powers are considerably restricted and limited. But in practice even the powerful U.S. Congress in its most assertive mood makes only incremental adjustments to the executive's budget proposals. Why should such a powerful legislature restrain itself when it comes to the budget?

There are strong psychological forces at work that limit a legislative assembly's capacity to alter the executive budget. Politicians find that they are the captives of what they, and their predecessors, have already created. They consider that much of the government's budget is "uncontrollable" and therefore not open to adjustment. Past decisions embodied in legal requirements and entitlements now take up such a large proportion of existing budgetary resources that little room for flexibility exists (cf. Green, 1980). The main determinant of the size of this year's budget is the size of last year's budget. Changes can only take place at the margin. The precise degree to which any budget is, or is not, open to adjustment year by year depends in the last analysis on what is defined as a fixed commitment and therefore "uncontrollable." In most countries the commitments to social insurance are regarded as fixed. These items now form the bulk of the annual budget, and all other items—apart from defense—are regarded as residuals. Commitments to social insurance, however, are only commitments until the law is changed. Any legislature, if it wanted to do so and had a sufficient majority of votes, could stop or change any program. The commitment is not so much legal as psychological.

During the expansion of the welfare state, legislatures played a passive and limited role in one sense only. Certainly they have not played a very active part in the critical evaluation of existing programs and in making judgments of an allocative nature. Unlike their counterparts in the 19th century, they have not been greatly concerned with efficiency and effectiveness of government. But that is not to say that they have played no part in the expenditure process. The evidence from studies of legislative behavior reveals that their role has been that of an encouraging chorus providing background music to the main themes of government. They have called continually for new hospitals, schools, and roads, and better levels and coverage of social insurance. Many of them have thought that this was their proper role in the expenditure process. By and large, over the years they have found the results gratifying. The introduction of new programs has enabled them to claim that they have played their part by representing constituency and group needs. Few have displayed much interest in the detailed examination of the government's spending proposals or in the evaluation of the effectiveness and efficiency of services. Most problems, they imagine, can be solved by throwing more money at them. Thus they have allowed what constitutional powers they had over money to atrophy through lack of use.

For most parliamentarians, the task of careful sifting through detailed reports on the work of government departments is not their first priority. Apart from their constant pleas for higher spending, few elected representatives paid much attention to the budgetary process until the economic crises of the mid-1970s. They thought that this aspect of parliamentary procedure was on the technical fringe of politics, of little interest to them, their constituents, or the media. When they were given new opportunities for debate they did not use them. In Britain, where from 1970 regular debates were held on the PESC figures published as the Annual Expenditure White Paper, the response was deeply disappointing. The debates were lackluster and poorly attended.

The economic crises of the mid-1970's gave parliamentarians in many countries a shock. They discovered that their constituents and pressure groups continued to want more and better services, but they also wanted lower taxes. Once the tap of economic growth was turned off, expanding services could only be provided by increased taxation or borrowing. There appeared to be some limits to taxation. By the time that the welfare state had reached its full development, taxation had ceased to be a matter of redistribution between rich and poor, and had become a matter of redistribution between the bulk of the population at the various stages of its life-cycle. If services were to be retained or expanded in a period of non-growth, then everyone would have to pay. Thus politicians found themselves in the grip of a pincer movement. The public continued to press for better services, the bureaucracy supported them and defended itself from attack, yet the taxpayers wondered if they really wanted to pay more (Jay, 1976; King, 1978).

The new spirit of interest in parliamentary control of government expenditure embodied in the Congressional Budget Act of 1974, the Italian Reforms of 1978, and the developments of the British Select Committee system in 1970 and 1979 can be related to the representatives' perception of apparent changes in political attitudes among the electorate. The passage of Proposition 13 in California, the budgetary limitations imposed in many other U.S. states, and the formation of specific anti-tax parties for example, seemed firm evidence of a change in public attitudes. Britain in 1979 and the U.S.A. in 1980 elected governments pledged to cut public spending and taxes.

IN CONCLUSION—THE ART OF CREATING FLEXIBILITY

We have argued that the increased concern for budget flexibility is not just the result of present economic difficulties. The need for flexibility is a fundamental one, arising out of the very nature of the social security system that has been created in "the welfare state." Collective risk-sharing implies the need for collective adjustments as the needs of society and the economic conditions change. Even if the economies of the western world had continued to grow, the size and nature of the public sector would, ultimately, have required politicians to recognize that they would have to make budgetary adjustments.

In the first postwar decades the need for such adjustments was hidden or swamped by the fact that the public sector had not yet been fully developed, and by economic growth levels that permitted a uniquely rapid expansion of public budgets. Politicians were thus shielded from having to make really hard choices of an allocative nature. When, from time to time, economic circumstances dictated that they had to make some adjustments, they could always raise taxes. When that option became less open to them, they resorted to borrowing to pay for current services. That option has now been virtually exhausted.

Until recently, politicians never reached a point where they were required seriously to question their goals and to assess the effectiveness of existing programs. That moment is fast approaching in all countries, and in some it has already arrived.

Even if we should take the most optimistic view of the possibilities of future economic progress and expect to regain former rates of growth in industrial productivity, the sheer magnitude of the social security already attained and the unavoidable retardation of overall growth in the economy will mean that in the future more and more concern will have to be directed towards the adjustment of public budgets to demographic and economic structural changes. At present, our capacity to adapt budgetary thinking and techniques is being severely tested by the need to adjust to stagflation—and to the politics devised to combat stagflation.

The fundamental long-term requirements for public budget making are of both economic and political origin. From the economic point of view, new tools are needed that permit adjustments in a large public sector primarily concerned with risk sharing for individuals, in an economy with retarded growth, undergoing demographic and structural changes.

From the political point of view, new tools of budgetary planning must help politicians to perceive these economic needs for adjustment and the limits of possible further commitments. They must also assist politicians to communicate more clearly to the electorate the conditions and resource constraints under which public spending decisions have to be made. Budgetary tools should also encourage politicians to look more critically at their goals and objectives.

Finally, the tools of budgetary management ought to include the possibility of more effective countervailing forces that can provide independent evaluation and assessment of the performance of government services.

One obvious but rather drastic way of limiting the need for public adjustment would be to hand back part of the risk taking to households and firms by privatizing more of the social services. This could mean privatizing the production decisions by creating, e.g., more favorable conditions for private schools, medical units, and insurance companies. It could also, or instead, mean privatizing the purchasing decisions by making more use of market pricing for social services and income insurance, decreasing the subsidies in "public consumption," possibly compensating this by increased income subsidies. The political decision makers would then be able to avoid a number of difficult adjustment decisions, but there would be a price paid, almost by definition, in terms of less security for some individuals or firms.

A more substantial transfer to the private sector of the current public budget decisions is, however, hardly a realistic alternative in any country. We must then search for ways of creating more flexibility within the framework of existing public budgets. Flexibility would have to be introduced already in the design of decisions, programs, and organizations.

Increased budget flexibility may involve a general shortening of the life span or length of commitment of expenditure programs and contracts. More use could be made of so-called "sunset legislation," where a time limit or a time for an unconditional review of the program in question is explicitly stated in the original decisions. The possible scrapping of old programs may have to become as much a political concern as the initiating of new ones. This could involve a much more careful costing of programs in advance and a more serious and continuous attempt at evaluation of current programs by way of political reviews or a broader use of public pricing. Long-term expenditure decisions may also have to include conditional clauses about economic conditions and available finance.

We may have to prepare public resources—everything from agencies and civil service organizations to public buildings and public employees—for multiple use. This may involve making agencies less tailor-made for special tasks, more multifunctional and ready to compete for new programs and duties, and designing buildings and rewriting contracts accordingly. An important and necessary part of any such attempt must be a new design of government careers, rewriting employment contracts so as to create more mobility among different government jobs and between private and public employment.

You do not, however, usually get flexibility for nothing. Creating flexibility can imply sacrificing gains in efficiency and security that are only possible to realize with a long-term commitment. Civil servants may not enjoy the idea of a possible retraining, and multiple use of buildings tend to be expensive. This simply means that we also must try to minimize costs in the search for flexibility. There is, however, always the possibility that flexibility in public agencies in some cases may indeed be costless, increasing productivity by providing new incentives and by avoiding some stultifying effects of organizational aging.

To achieve greater budgetary flexibility in the long run requires more than the mere change of budgetary and planning techniques. It presupposes a new understanding and acceptance by the voters of the need for flexibility as a condition for making the social security system economically viable. One way of gaining that acceptance could be to bring as many as possible of the hard choices directly before the individual voter, which could imply an increased degree of political decentralization. Obviously there are limits to how far such a decentralization could be taken as long as the collective risk sharing and solidarity of the social security system extends beyond the borders of individual municipalities.

REFERENCES

Britten, S. (1975), "The Economic Contradiction of Democracy," *British Journal of Political Science*, Vol. 5.

Crosland, C.A.R. (1956), *The Future of Socialism* (London: Cape).

Downs, A. (1966), "Why the Budget Is Too Small in Democracy," *World Politics*.

Galbraith, J.K. (1958), *The Affluent Society* (London: Hamish Hamilton).

Green, D. (1980), "The Budget and the Plan," in *French Politics and Public Policy*, G. Casny and M.A. Schain (eds.) (London and New York: Methuen).

Heclo, H., and A, Wildavsky (1974), *The Private Government of Public Money* (London: Macmillan).

Jay, P. (1976), *Employment, Inflation and Politics* (London: Institute for Economic Affairs).

King, A. (1978), *Why Is Britain Becoming Harder to Govern?* (London: BBC Publications).

Lindblom, C.E. (1959), "The Science of Muddling Through," *Public Administration Review*, Vol. 19.

Mishan, E.J. (1967), *The Costs of Economic Growth* (London: Staples Press).

Mosher, F.C. (1978), *The G A O: The Quest for Accountability in American Government* (Boulder, Colorado: Westview Press).

Niskanen, W.A. (1973), *Bureaucracy: Servants or Masters* (London: Institute of Economic Affairs).

Robinson, A. (1972), "Prospects for PPBS: Some Macro Variables Examined in U.S.A., Canada and Britain," *Public Administration Committee Bulletin*, June.

———— (1978), *Parliament and Public Spending* (London: Heinemann).
Rose, R., and B.G. Peters (1978), *Can Government Go Bankrupt?* (New York: Basic Books).
Simon, H. (1957), *Models of Man* (New York: Wiley & Son).
Tarschys, D. (1975), "The Growth of Public Expenditures: Nine Models of Explanation," *Scandinavian Political Studies,* Vol. 10.
Wildavsky, A. (1964), *The Politics of the Budgetary Process* (Boston: Little Brown).
———— (1975), *Budgeting: A Comparative Theory of the Budgeting Process* (Boston: Little Brown).

CHAPTER 25

ENTITLEMENT BUDGETING VS. BUREAU BUDGETING

JOSEPH WHITE

As entitlements have become a larger part of the federal budget, they have received more attention in discussions of the federal deficit. That entitlements influence budget totals is well known (Bipartisan Commission, 1995, 1994; U.S. Congress 1997a, 1997b, 1995; Schick, 1995). What has been the effect of increased attention to entitlements on the process of federal budgeting? How can entitlements be incorporated into a theoretical understanding of budgeting?

In this article I will argue that for good programmatic reasons, budgeting for entitlements differs in basic ways from the traditional process of budgeting for bureaus. As a result, many of the practical and theoretical disputes familiar from the budgeting literature have little relevance to budgeting for entitlements. Moreover, measures to adapt budgeting to fit entitlements risk losing many of the functional merits of the traditional process of budgeting for bureaus. The challenge of entitlement budgeting, then, is not simply how to control the deficit with tools developed for budgeting different kinds of programs. It is also how and even whether to combine budgeting for two different kinds of programs in one process.

THE DECLINE OF "TRADITIONAL" BUDGETING

Budget theory once said little about entitlements. What has been called "traditional" budgeting includes a set of common institutions and goals that evolved from the late 18th century through the mid-20th. In Aaron Wildavsky's account, budgeting is annual, incremental, conducted on a cash basis in the form of line items. It serves purposes of accountability, control in many senses, pursuit of efficiency or effectiveness, economic management and planning (Wildavsky, 1978, 502).

Naomi Caiden emphasizes that the annual unified budget had goals of program information, efficiency and effectiveness; facilitating choice; directing allocations; reviewing policy; comparison; and control of the executive (Caiden, 1982, 517–518). In the American model, traditional budgeting includes an executive budget document, specialized appropriations or budget committees within the legislature, and specific budgeting legislation—all on an annual or, occasionally, biennial cycle.

From *Public Administration Review,* vol. 58, no. 6 (November/December 1998), 510–521. Copyright © 1998 by American Society for Public Administration. Reprinted with permission.

Control of deficits is only one among many functions of traditional budgeting (Caiden, 1982; Wildavsky, 1978; Schick, 1966; Ervin, 1980). In many ways, traditional budgeting was designed to serve administrative as much as policy ends (Schick, 1980b). The resulting institutions never satisfied a series of critics who sought to bring a more structured concern with objectives into budgetary choice, and the history of the attempts to reform budgeting and satisfy those critics is extensive (Axelrod, 1988, 280–303; Key, 1978; Schick, 1966, 1973; Wildavsky, 1978, 1984). In the late 1970s and early 1980s, however, students of budgeting also began worrying that the operating norms of the traditional process, such as annualarity and comprehensiveness, were progressively being ignored and perhaps outmoded. Naomi Caiden, for example, wrote about the "Myth of the Annual Budget" (Caiden, 1982).

The traditional focus on agency appropriations was always a limited view of what might be considered "budgeting." Most evidently, it did not include revenue decisions. Revenue decisions have just as large an effect on budget balances, and many economists have argued that any macroeconomic policy of demand management would be better pursued through raising or lowering taxes than by adjusting spending accounts (see Stein, 1996).

Nevertheless, the bulk of the politics of budgeting normally does focus on spending decisions. Even much budgeting discussion of revenues is often phrased in terms of spending, as in critiques of "tax expenditures." Caiden and others perceived an increasing share of government activity that did not work through, and so was not controlled by, the annual appropriations process. Tax expenditures and various credit programs, as well as entitlements and other "backdoor spending," could be included in the 1980s list of activities that were not in fact budgeted annually (Bennett and DiLorenzo, 1983; Ippolito, 1984; Schick, 1980a; Wildavsky, 1980). However, it proved possible to work some of these, such as credit programs, into the traditional framework.[1] The difficulties posed by entitlements are more fundamental.

DISTINGUISHING ENTITLEMENT FROM BUREAU BUDGETING

Bureau Budgeting

The budgeting that Wildavsky, Caiden, and other scholars defined as "traditional" was designed to finance bureaus that provide a service to the public or, more generally, perform some government function: policing, fire fighting, collecting taxes, medical research, space exploration, or whatever. In all these cases, the government establishes some set of goals and then provides a bureaucracy to pursue those ends. Government has not committed itself legally to a precise level of services. Rather, it has promised to provide a bureaucracy that it is to be hoped will provide an acceptable level.

Although a bureau's objectives may be defined and sold in personal terms, whether they are met depends on the performance of the bureaucracy in question. Thus, the federal government establishes the medical system of the Department of Veterans Affairs, from which services may be claimed, but what veterans receive depends on two factors—a separate decision about the bureau's funding, and how the bureau performs its tasks. Budgeting for those tasks is a process of deciding amounts to provide to each bureau. We can call this process bureau budgeting,

The traditional questions of budget control are questions about bureau performance and direction. Will the bureau use the money properly? Will Congress, the president, or the bureau's officials control the program? When budgeting added a focus on management to the interest in control, the issue was still the individual bureau's performance of its task (Schick, 1966; Ervin, 1980). Annual budgeting is a form of oversight of bureau officials.

This view of bureau budgeting is especially true of budgeting within the federal government because of the way Congress organizes itself. Within Congress, budgeting for bureaus has long been treated as a process separate from the normal policy-making routines. Without such a distinction, there would be no point to having appropriations committees separate from the authorizing, legislative committees. The division of labor between the authorizations and appropriations processes is, of course, hotly contested at the margins (Fisher, 1979; Rubin, 1988; White, 1993b). Virtually all politicians are interested in policy priorities and the distribution of benefits to states and districts, and those interests are pursued in both authorization and appropriations processes. Nevertheless, a sense that appropriations decisions should involve matters that are less likely to be considered in authorizations is extremely common.

The distinctions permeate statements by members and staff of the appropriations committees in off-the-record interviews. In one subcommittee chair's version, "Appropriations says the most efficient way to spend money. Some think the authorizations should say how to spend it, too. I think they should say what the need is." A sub-committee clerk distinguished "developing your basic legislation" from "get[ting] into how well a program is operating, particularly from a financial standpoint." One member who became a full committee chair after my interview declared that the separate processes "provide you with a check and balance." Another future chair explained that authorizers:

> should set goals they think would be good to reach to make the programs work in their area. Then have a later decision as to how to fit it in at that time, under the conditions of that Budget year. The authorizers should say what we need to face changing social circumstances. Appropriations should say what we can afford at the time, what programs are working.

Precisely because such distinctions provide part of the justification for their separate authority, appropriators make serious efforts to provide at least the appearance (and I would argue the reality) of attention to management and financial issues.[2]

Entitlement Budgeting

The process of making entitlement commitments within Congress, however, involves no distinction between the budgeting and legislative functions. Program design and spending commitments are identical, and the same committees have jurisdiction over each. While the congressional budget resolutions may set targets for changes in entitlement law, that is in principle no different from the same resolutions setting standards for a year's appropriations bills. Actual legislative changes in entitlements still must be reported by the authorizing committees.

In federal budget parlance, "entitlements" are the major category of "direct spending." All direct spending is "budget authority and ensuing outlays provided in laws other than appropriations acts, including annually appropriated entitlements" (Schick, 1995, 209–10). "Entitlement authority" in particular is "a provision of law that requires payments to eligible persons or governments"[3] (U.S. Congress, 1997a, 142).

The term "entitlement" developed out of the "new property" movement of legal thought that began in the 1960s, and was used by the Supreme Court in *Goldberg v. Kelly* (397 U.S. 254 [1969]). The General Accounting Office came to define the term as "legislation that requires the payment of benefits . . . to any person or unit of government that meets the eligibility requirements established by such law." The key is that "eligible recipients have legal recourse if the obligation is not fulfilled" (Weaver, 1985, 308–09).

In an entitlement program, the recipients—whether persons, legal persons (firms) or governments—are entitled by law to quantifiable benefits. Either the benefits are directly delivered to the beneficiary, or they are payments on behalf of the beneficiary for services purchased in a cash transaction from some third party.

In some exceptional cases, the entitlement is not to an amount of benefit but to a share of a capped total, as in the Title XX Social Services Block Grant. But the entitlements that have attracted the budgetary attention and involve the vast bulk of funds are open-ended. Annual spending for Social Security, or Medicare, or civil service pensions is the sum of specific benefits. Therefore, instead of directly allocating sums of money to individual accounts, entitlement budgeting involves estimating and attempting to influence the total of the payments determined by entitlement law.

Spending on open-ended entitlements rises or falls not because of discrete annual decisions about how much money to spend, but through the interactions of demographics, economics, and existing program law. Since Congress (presumably to its regret) cannot legislate demographic and economic conditions, altering entitlement spending then requires altering the underlying program law.

In entitlement budgeting, program beneficiaries are actually entitled to an amount of budget, and spending is the sum of services. In bureau budgeting, the budget is distributed to the program's operators, not to the beneficiaries, and services are what can be bought with the spending.

Since the real question is what a bureau will accomplish with its funding, the bureau itself is a major object of attention in bureau budgeting.[4] How much does the bureau "really need" to fulfill its legal obligations? How good an argument can be made that more (or less) input will lead to more (or not much less) output? Could the bureau operate more efficiently if it operated differently? In this context the primal meaning of the term "budgetary control" is not spending limits, but control of how the bureau spends its appropriation (Schick, 1966).

In entitlement budgeting, the main object of attention is the specific promise to recipients. There must be an administering bureau (the Social Security Administration for pensions or the Health Care Financing Administration for Medicare and Medicaid), but its personnel and performance normally are a secondary theme in budget disputes. Administrative campaigns to tighten eligibility determinations for nonuniversal programs (such as Supplementary Security Income or Disability Insurance) do occur. But even these efforts often require some tweaking of eligibility standards or review procedures, that is, basic program law. Medicare could indeed save money by better claims administration that reduced fraud. Yet the secondary nature of this theme is clear in policy discussion; indeed, the general public's focus on potential savings from such measures is commonly dismissed by the cognoscenti as evidence of insufficient public education (Blendon, et al., 1997).

Three Issues in Traditional Budgeting

The extent of the difference between budgeting for bureaus and entitlements may be further illustrated by considering three common concerns of traditional budgeting theory and practice; "coercive deficiencies," the level of detail in line items, and the conflict between focusing on inputs or "programs" in budget decisions. These concerns do not exist if the program involved has been designed as an entitlement.

The so-called Antideficiency Act has been called the "cornerstone of congressional efforts to bind the executive branch of government to the limits on expenditure of appropriated funds" (quoted in U.S. GAO, 1992, 6–9). Its terms as they have evolved address a problem that was especially significant in the 19th century: agencies might use up their budgets before the end of the fiscal year so that, faced with the prospect of operations being suspended, Congress might feel "coerced" to make up the deficiency. Although complex in operation, the basic principle of the law, as the GAO reports, is simple: "Government officials are warned not to make payments—or to commit the United States to make payments at some future time—for goods or services unless there is enough money in the 'bank' to cover the cost in full. The 'bank,' of course, is the available appropriation." (U.S. GAO, 1992, 6–11). But the assumptions behind this principle, namely that officials' discretion in program spending decisions can and should be limited by available budget authority, are false for entitlements.

If the agency administering an entitlement spends more than has been appropriated, that is either because (a) it paid the wrong recipients too much, or (b) the original estimate was wrong. In the first case the agency has misapplied the laws explicitly, which it should not have done regardless of the spending result or the availability of budget authority.[5] This is different from the normal coercive deficiency case, in which the "excessive" spending could be expected nevertheless to fit the bureau's basic mandate. If spending instead exceeds the estimate because the estimate was wrong, the agency is just doing its job, and there should be no suggestion that it is manipulating or coercing the legislature. Instead, the major remedy for deficiencies, coercive or otherwise, is apportionment of the appropriation over a shorter time period by some control agency, but this remedy is inappropriate. If costs were higher than expected, and the Office of Management and Budget (OMB) were to say, "sorry, we can't release more than thirty percent of the estimate for the year in any one quarter," it would violate the underlying entitlement.

Another traditional issue is the level of detail in line items. Does one want the control advantages of detailed specification or the management flexibility of broader terms? Yet this issue too is meaningless for entitlements. An entitlement program's rules are the program's rules; they cannot be funded at a higher or lower level of detail.

Many decisions in bureau budgeting involve the level of inputs (money for salaries, buildings, travel, etc.) needed to produce some level of output (medical care, arrests, or whatever). The attendant focus on inputs is continually criticized as leading to insufficient attention to the values of alternative outputs. The proposed reforms, which by various names call for greater emphasis on comparing alternative programs, have their own weaknesses (Wildavsky, 1978, 1984). Whatever the merits, this debate also has no meaning when applied to entitlements. The vast majority of the objects of expenditure are the actual outputs. The relationship between money and social security checks is not subject to the same kind of question as that between, say, military purchases and combat performance.

THE POLICY CHOICE BETWEEN PROGRAM FORMS

Much of the basic character of budget decisions for entitlement programs differs from the nature of decisions for bureau programs. Subsequent sections will discuss how budget conflicts differ according to the program type. First, however, we must consider why the two forms exist at all.

Budgeteers may instinctively see entitlements as a tactic to evade traditional controls. Yet there are strong policy justifications for the entitlement approach, just as there are programs for which the bureau approach seems more natural.

On the whole, an entitlement should be for a benefit that can be quantified and divided up. Protection from crime, a classic "public good," would be hard to deliver in this way.[6] Space exploration, the census—in short, most bureau programs in the real world—do not have benefits that can be divided so neatly. A pension, however, is quite precise. The likelihood that classic "public goods" do not make easy entitlements should not, however, be interpreted to mean that entitlements are not in the "public interest." For instance, although the direct benefits of Social Security go to individuals, its supporters should argue that its consequences for the community as a whole, in terms of fairness and a general sense of security and perhaps a greater sense of community, are major virtues of the program.

Social Security is one example of a wider class, social insurance programs. Social insurance programs displace uncertainty from individuals onto the government. Whether the risk is of unemployment, expensive illness, or a longer than normal life (so greater need for pensions), socializing risk protects individuals. But that protection would be less reliable if programs were not designed as entitlements, with predefined benefits for people in certain circumstances. If the point of a program is to provide certainty, making benefits subject to annual appropriations and bureau performance would be an inferior means toward the program's ends.

Entitlement promises may also be the better way to pursue policies in which a government seeks to encourage or reward specific behaviors such as interest paid in return for loaning the government money, veterans' benefits distributed in return for serving in the armed services, or pensions for current workers in the future in return for their paying for the pensions of current retirees now.[7] In this sense entitlements involve a form of contracting behavior between a government and members of the public, in which the entitlement form makes the promise of benefits sufficiently concrete to be credible.[8]

In some cases either the bureau or entitlement form is theoretically possible, but there are strong policy or political but nonbudgetary reasons to choose one or the other. Health care can be provided as an entitlement (as in Medicare or Canadian National Health Insurance) or through bureaus (as in American veterans' programs or the British National Health Service). The political reasons why Medicare had to be designed to reimburse existing physicians and hospitals, rather than as a national health service, are well-known. Why might the veterans' programs have been an exception? One likely factor is, when they were created, a sufficient supply of service-delivering institutions (e.g., hospitals, especially those capable of treating service-related conditions) did not exist. So creation of government-owned supply was much easier to defend than when, decades later, Medicare was created in a country that already had an ample supply of hospital beds. In any event, it should be clear that physicians' and hospital advocates' opposition to a national health service model for Medicare was not simply a budgetary strategy—though it surely increased costs!

To a substantial extent, therefore, the choice to have entitlement programs is a matter of policy design, to which budgeting must adjust. When we look at the difference between social insurance programs on the one hand, and activities such as armies and research institutes and the weather service on the other, we may go so far as to say (with one of this article's anonymous reviewers) that "the two types of programs that are the purview of these control systems represent two very different functions of the modern state." How, then, does entitlement budgeting work?

BUDGETING FOR ENTITLEMENTS IN THE FEDERAL GOVERNMENT

Entitlements and the Annual Budget

From the standpoint of entitlement budgeting, it is commonly argued, the annual budget is not only mythical but undesirable. Thus the Bipartisan Commission on Entitlement and Tax Reform (1995, 2) reported that "the first and most important of our recommendations" was to make "major spending and tax decisions" on a 30-year timeframe. "When discretionary spending was the largest share of our budget," the commission explained, "short term planning may have been appropriate." After all, agencies operate, relating inputs to outputs, in the short term. But that would not be appropriate for budgeting the massive social-insurance programs that are the major entitlements.

One may raise awkward questions about what budgeting on a 30-year horizon could possibly look like. Should programs be looked at every 30 years? Or should they be changed every year in response to any alterations in the (extremely unreliable) 30-year forecast? One might also remember that annual budgeting never looked *only* at the coming year. Bureaus do have to program spending for longer terms, if only to purchase items that take more than a year to build. In spite of these caveats, commitments to entitlements do, on the whole, require that budgeting for entitlements have a longer time frame than is used for bureaus.

Actual allocation of money to entitlements therefore is not made on an annual basis. For some programs that is extremely explicit: Social Security and Medicare Part A have permanent budget authority consisting of receipts to their trust funds. In other cases, such as Medicaid, money must be appropriated annually. Yet events in the 1980s made clear that this was not viewed as a matter for discretion—it is "mandatory" spending.

The Reagan administration continually proposed spending levels for such programs that assumed enactment of legislative changes that authorizing committees in fact refused to report. Appropriators did not believe they could themselves report those legislative changes.[9] Instead, they tended to report, and Congress to pass, appropriations that met the president's figures but therefore did not fund the commitments created by continuing law. It was presumed that the courts could order the government to make good those commitments (absent changes in the law), so the Reagan administration requested supplemental appropriations as the funding began to run out, and Congress always responded (though not without some close calls). The 1985 Gramm-Rudman-Hollings Act recognized that this process made little sense and formally took the appropriators out of the entitlement budgeting business by writing the distinction between "mandatory" and "discretionary" annual appropriations into congressional budget rules. So the appropriators now are expected to devote their attention to the discretionary (bureau) accounts.

New Institutions for Entitlement Budgeting

As the bureau budgeting process could not address entitlements, new institutions were developed. The rising share of mandatory spending within the federal budget was one reason for the "Seven-Year Budget War" described by Allen Schick and, thus, for passage of the Congressional Budget and Impoundment Control Act of 1974 (Schick, 1980a). Dissatisfaction with the 1974 act's procedures led to the invention of reconciliation on the first budget resolution in 1980 and the various overarching constraints produced in the 1985 Gramm-Rudman-Hollings and 1990 Budget Enforcement Acts (White and Wildavsky, 1991; Schick, 1995).

The key component in the new budget process for entitlements is reconciliation, which occurs on what might be called a quasi-annual cycle. Although the opportunity for reconciliation is annual, significant reconciliation legislation does not pass on anything resembling an annual basis. As the process was invented, bills were passed in 1980, 1981, and 1982. Since then, however, only the laws passed in 1984, 1987, 1990, 1993, and 1997 could reasonably be termed major—and in some years (e.g., 1983 and 1995, for very different reasons), ambitious instructions from the budget resolution failed to result in the planned legislation.

Are the years of inaction a budget choice comparable to appropriating to bureaus an amount adequate to maintain current services? Not really. Even if totals are straight-lined, appropriators make many changes in the details of agency proposals. Even more fundamentally, if annual appropriations do not occur, the affected programs are shut down. That is why the appropriations process cannot be allowed to fail, but reconciliation can. As Richard Fenno explained in his classic account, the expectation that appropriators "finance programs and projects" was prior to any expectation that they do so "economically" (Fenno, 1966, 7–8). Financing programs is the main activity of budgeting, the actual financing of entitlements simply is not annual, and reconciliation thus is not analogous to appropriations.

Reconciliations evolved from being scored over one year to three years, five years, and seven years.[10] Such evolution was needed to cope with some aspects of entitlement spending. Entitlement expansion can be phased in over time, or scheduled to occur at some future date, and program rules can be manipulated to create spending in future years even when there is an ostensible spending reduction in the coming year. Various tactics of hidden expansion do exist in bureau budgeting, but they are not so committing.[11] Revenues involve the same basic dynamics as entitlements, and the very size of the deficit required that anyone who wished to pursue a balanced budget had to adopt a longer time horizon (as in 1995). As entitlements became the major portion of spending, however, they alone became sufficient reason to extend the time-horizon of spending control beyond the norms of the annual budget.[12] Reconciliations, then, do not occur every year, and when they do, their scope is not confined to one year.

The reconciliation process makes changes in entitlement law so as to reduce projected deficits (though it could in theory also be used to increase deficits). Another new set of institutions, the "PayGo" points of order and sequesters, are designed to inhibit action by Congress on either entitlements or revenues that would increase the deficit (or, I suppose it is possible now to say, dissipate a surplus). These procedures and the underlying nature of entitlement programs lead to different strategies, tactics, and roles than in traditional budgeting as described by Wildavsky and others.

Strategies and Tactics of Entitlement Budgeting

In as much as budgeting is a political conflict, there will be similarities among cases of that struggle even when the program designs differ as broadly as between bureaus and entitlement programs. Constituencies with more resources will normally do better. Opponents of a program will seek to downplay, and supporters to exaggerate, the consequences of cuts. Efforts will be made to define the program base in a favorable way (Meyers, 1994; Muris, 1989; Schick, 1995). The federal government and state and local governments will seek to blame each other for disappointing constituencies. In short, all budgeting will involve power politics, blame avoidance, and attempts to manipulate knowledge.

Nonetheless, the programmatic characteristics of entitlements create differences in both tactics and roleplaying from what is common in bureau budgeting. Some of these differences follow from the concept of entitlement itself. Discourse about entitlement programs tends to involve a language of "rights," and the courts may become involved in the enforcement of those rights (Straussman, 1988). Because the legislature can alter statutory rights, however, the most important differences involve the need to effect changes in underlying law for entitlements, rather than just appropriate a spending total. Most of the tactics of entitlement spending controllers can be understood as weaker analogues of the tactics used in bureau budgeting.

For example, budget controllers often can give less money to bureau managers and assert that capable managers will be able to increase agency efficiency and still provide the same benefits. Controllers cannot really use the same tactic with the public agencies that manage entitlements, which makes it harder for controllers to deflect blame for the consequences of disappointing people about spending levels. In some entitlements, however, payments to *private* operators with a stake in a program may be reduced while budget cutters claim that benefits do not have to decline commensurately.

Medicare provides a good example of both the success and conditions for this tactic. Once someone (either a Republican president or Congress) puts cuts to Medicare beneficiaries on the table, someone else (a Democratic Congress or president) proposes payment reductions for hospitals, physicians, or other providers. Provider cuts are then possible because the issue is posed as either breaking the promise to beneficiaries or cutting providers, and because some politicians (to the glee of their opponents) have been willing to take the blame for proposing the former. While highly successful, this is not a model on which budgeteers can safely rely.[13]

In bureau budgeting, inaction leads to the money running out, so advocates may feel some need to compromise with budget controllers so as to get legislation at all. This is not normally the case for entitlements, with one exception—when programs that are financed from trust funds approach "bankruptcy" (Patashnik, 1997a). The annual reports by the trustees of the Social Security and Medicare Part A funds are used by advocates of budget control to raise fears that might impel program supporters to cede some ground. Crises of the Social Security trust fund in 1977 and 1982 did force action, and projections in recent years that the Medicare Part A trust fund would go broke provided the occasion for Republican claims that they had to cut Medicare in order to save it (Rich, 1996; Rosenbaum, 1996). Therefore some budgeteers who believe the distinction between Medicare's Parts A and B and a separate trust fund make no policy sense seek to preserve it so as to retain the action-forcing aspects of Part A trust fund shortages.[14]

Although trust funds can add impetus for action, imminent default does not happen very often. Moreover, impending default is not necessarily an impetus for spending restraint. It may equally encourage revenue increases. Thus if "budget control" is defined as "deficit control," then trust funds are a more desirable measure than if the person calling for "budget control" really wants to limit the total budget. So long as a trust fund is in surplus, its existence makes it particularly difficult to justify program cuts. Indeed, surpluses can be used to promote spending increases (Patashnik, 1997a; Derthick, 1979). Thus, trust funds do not provide an impetus for program advocates to compromise that is remotely comparable to the effect of annual appropriations.

The easiest way to reduce any program's burden on the budget or economy is to allow inflation to make stable or increasing nominal spending hide a real decline in a program's purchasing power and shares of the economy and budget. Unfortunately for budgeteers, however, entitlements lend themselves especially easily to indexation of benefits by including automatic inflation adjustments in the underlying law (Weaver, 1988). Moreover, beneficiaries will notice inflation-related losses more easily than the consequences of squeezed budgets for bureaus. So entitlements are less subject to control by erosion.

Given the disadvantages of the entitlement form, budget controllers often look for ways to make an entitlement operate more like a bureau program. The common proposal to "fix" Medicare by replacing its fee-for-service reimbursement with some form of voucher to buy insurance follows this logic (Aaron and Reischauer, 1995; Butler and Moffitt, 1995; Cutler, 1997; White, 1993a). What services a person actually received would depend, as with a bureau program, on an organization's performance—except that it would be a private organization, the managed care organization or insurer. Advocates of such proposals may or may not be correct in arguing that market competition provides an incentive for productivity that government bureaus do not enjoy. But even if this difference were real, the logic of budgetary control remains the same whether the bureau is public or private. Rather than pay per service, the government pays a fixed sum to an organization.

Some of the differences in tactics may also be perceived by asking about "guardian" and "claimant" roles, and how they might be played for entitlements. In this context, the questions would be who takes the role of "guardian of the purse" for entitlements, a role supposedly once taken by the appropriations committees for bureau budgets, and how the role is played (Fenno, 1966; Wildavsky, 1984).

Such role theory has limited use even for bureau budgeting, and one should not expect perfect role stability even in that case (Schick, 1980a; White, 1989; Cox, Hager, and Lowery, 1993). It may be far more useful to think in terms of controller and advocate positions being specific to individual disputes, rather than being personal identities (Meyers, 1994). Yet, however they are framed, the roles or positions of guardians and claimants should work differently for entitlements than for bureau programs.

Most evidently, the problem is different. Entitlements may expand automatically due to demographic or economic conditions or both, so "guardianship" may require positive action and "claiming," merely defensive action, rather than the reverse.

Moreover, the roles are not as easily separated as in bureau budgeting, even acknowledging the ambiguities in that case. The authorizing committees that are traditionally viewed as claimants also must be the major sources of law that "guards." Though members of the budget committees may claim to be guardians, they do not have the power to impose anything. Party leaders do not have the technical knowledge, and so, in practice, significant reconciliation legislation has frequently been designed and pushed by authorizing committee leaders such as former Senator Robert Dole (R-KS) and former Representative Dan Rostenkowski (D-IL).[15]

Guarding against entitlements spending increases requires somewhat different skills than for bureau spending. Instead of being explicitly asked for higher spending, politicians may be asked about a change in eligibility or some other provision whose spending effects cannot be seen without technical knowledge. In order to say "no" to requests for more bureau spending, it is nice to have a rationale, but technical knowledge is less important than political strength. Budget controllers have the option of telling an agency to work out its own plan within a lower total. In entitlement budgeting, the proper provisions to lower spending must be written into law so the politicians have to get the answers right.

Technical analysts are therefore more important in entitlement budgeting than in bureau budgeting. Some estimators (for example in agencies, or in the Office of Management and Budget if a president seeks a programmatic expansion) may act as claimants, underestimating costs so as to enable spending.[16] The Congressional Budget Office plays a version of the guardian role for entitlements that could not be played in the same way by other parts of Congress before. In fact, since it requires analytic credibility, it may have to be played by nonpoliticians in order to work.[17]

Overall, tactics for entitlement budgeting differ significantly from those for bureau budgeting. Previous sections of this essay showed that the purposes of the programs, the purposes of their budgeting, the time frame for budgeting and common disputes about how budgeting should be done also differ. Other than tactics, roles, purposes, issues, and time frame, budgeting for entitlements and bureaus are the same process.

CONCLUSION: AN UNEASY COMBINATION

The difficulties in applying traditional budgeting theories and practices to entitlement budgeting derive from the fact that they were developed to address a fundamentally different program type, bureau programs. A new entitlement budgeting pays little attention to the irrelevant traditional concerns. One might infer, therefore, that the two processes should be analyzed and proceed separately. Yet that is not conventional wisdom at all.

Instead, the bureau and entitlement budget processes are integrated in the budget resolution process. Multiyear reconciliation requires multiyear budget resolutions. Multiyear budget resolutions require multiyear figures for bureau budgeting. So the combination creates multiyear bureau budgeting.

Unfortunately, the standard decisions in bureau budgeting—what W. F. Willoughby called a "general and financial work plan" for agencies (Mosher, 1984, 21)—cannot logically be made on a schedule much longer than a year. Not enough is known about bureau operations and challenges and input variables such as the price of fuel. Commitment far in advance must sacrifice some of the goals that are balanced in bureau budgeting: legislative control, or efficiency, or flexibility for good management.

At one point this was a not a problem, since outyear figures for bureau spending were not taken seriously. Since 1990, however, the reconciliation legislation of 1990, 1993, and 1997 has put the outyear figures for discretionary (bureau) spending into law, as "caps" on bureau appropriations. Indeed, the savings scored from these caps have been a major component of the savings in the reconciliation acts of 1990, 1993, and 1997. Precisely because the legislature and executive do not have to specify the programmatic changes to enforce those caps, it is easier to project savings that way than through legislating entitlement changes (Reischauer, 1997).

Combining bureau and entitlement budgeting in one process, therefore, has created a strange form of multiyear bureau budgeting. Decisions about totals are supposed to be made on a multiyear basis, and decisions about details annually. The danger of this approach is that the decision about totals can be made without consideration of its consequences on the details.

Deciding separately on details and totals is bad budgeting. Budgeting should be a process in which details and totals are considered together, so preferences about one dimension can be refined by awareness of consequences on the other. Rather than such an iterative process of mutual adjustment, federal bureau budgeting is becoming a process in which targets are set one year and in later years politicians scramble to meet the targets. Such a process makes the traditional questions of control—how much is needed to achieve certain ends efficiently, or to guarantee that agencies pursue legislative intent—in essence irrelevant, supplanted by, "how on earth can we meet this target?" Politicians can only be less accountable for their decisions because they would not in fact be considering targets and their policy consequences at the same time. Those who set targets do not have to admit to policy consequences, and those who vote on details can blame previous politicians who set targets.

Current caps have values in the outyears that are extremely hard to justify for the usual purposes of bureau budgeting, or simply good public policy. (Reischauer, 1997) It is possible to imagine easier budgetary environments in which caps might be high enough to be basically meaningless.[18] Yet political controversy early in 1998 about possible uses of a budget surplus suggested that, once adopted, the device of long term caps on discretionary spending was proving a remarkably powerful way of deflecting attention from budget details. Raising the caps, somehow, was not on the agenda.

Under current circumstances, therefore, conflicts between the needs of entitlement and bureau budgeting raise severe doubt about the traditional norm of comprehensiveness. Meaningless caps are no more appropriate for a sensible budget process than are caps that are implausibly low. So is it really possible to budget sensibly, and simultaneously, for different time frames?

Logically, yes. The multiyear portions of budgeting could be combined with more flexible outyear targets for the bureau programs, Being a little less strict about totals for discretionary programs is more practical on fiscal and policy grounds than it would have been 30 years ago precisely because the bureau portion is becoming a smaller share of the total budget, so the same percentage variation would have less effect on either budget totals or the economy.

Such a flexible approach, however, requires acknowledging that budget totals in the outyears are not hard and fast policy. And if the totals are not hard and fast policy, why should supporters of entitlement spending accept programmatic changes that are justified, after all, by the supposed targets for budget control in the future? What ever the analytic merits, one may predict political difficulty selling a budget process that sought to combine multiyear entitlement spending control with bureau spending flexibility.

This article began by arguing that entitlement budgeting and bureau budgeting are different and have different needs. Aaron Wildavsky stated the difference nicely, but in terms of a budget dominated by the one or the other. In *The New Politics of the Budgetary Process,* he wrote that "whereas in earlier times government faced inward, doing and controlling its own programs, in our time government faces outward, to the people it must support" (1992, 274). Facing inward is bureau budgeting, and facing outward is entitlement budgeting. It is true that most of the budget is now entitlements so budgeting as a whole might be said to face "outward."

Yet the federal government still budgets half a trillion dollars for bureaus, and the traditional functions of bureau budgeting still have value. So this article ends with a conundrum. Budget process analysts should no longer believe that the conflict between entitlement budgeting and bureau budgeting is a matter of the former being an "evasion" of the disciplines of the latter, which was the analysis of the 1970s and early 1980s. Nor is it so obviously wise to subsume bureau budgeting into new structures invented to control entitlements, which has been the relatively unconscious trend of the 1990s. How, then, can they best be brought together, and what could be the norms and values of a process that recognized that their differences are necessary and legitimate?

ACKNOWLEDGMENT

I would like to thank the Brookings Institution, the Twentieth Century Fund/Century Foundation, and Carleton College for support in various ways at the time I was writing this article. I also would like to thank anonymous PAR reviewers, as well as Roy Meyers, John Ellwood, and Irene Rubin for comments on related drafts, and John Gilmour, Robert Hartman, and Susan Irving for comments when I presented a version at the 1997 meeting of the Association for Public Policy Analysis and Management, Washington DC, November 1, 1997. No one other than myself should be associated with any demerits of this argument, and many people, not limited to those above, contributed to any merits.

NOTES

1. In essence, budget authority must now be appropriated to cover the direct costs of any interest subsidies as well as discounted future costs of the estimated level of defaults. This does change the incidence of loan cost or the timing of when they compete for resources with discretionary appropriations. But, if anything, this reform, by smoothing the impact of loan programs, reduces the extent to which uncertainty from credit programs should destabilize other accounts. As in any process involving estimates, there is still room for some gaming and errors (see U.S. GAO, 1998).

2. Such work is performed mainly by staff, not legislators, but for purposes of justifying the institution of appropriations committees, that does not matter. See White (1989).

3. As the definition suggests, "annually appropriated entitlements" are not generally believed to be in fact provided by annual appropriations acts. See below for the evolution of that belief.

4. A reviewer of this article noted that the administering personnel are likely to be a more important factor in budget politics for bureau programs than for entitlement programs. This should certainly be true relative to dollars spent on programs because there ate likely to be more personnel per dollar in bureau programs.

5. Thus spending improperly for an entitlement for which budget authority is available, such as Social Security given the current balances in its trust funds, would be no less improper than spending improperly for an entitlement for which the money could therefore run out, such as Food Stamps.

6. As Roy Meyers said in a private conversation, states or localities could be entitled to a given amount of money for crime fighting, or to funding for a certain number of new police officers. But this is a step removed from citizens' concerns; there could be no comparable "entitlement" to safety for citizens at the local level.

7. Although interest on government borrowing is sometimes not counted as an entitlement, it should be evident that it fits all the conditions of entitlement budgeting and has none of the attributes of bureau budgeting.

8. Much of the case for the entitlement form in general also argues for indexing of benefits in particular. For instance, an intergenerational contract for pensions ought to have an inflation adjustment; otherwise, "the contract, by its nature being of a long-term character, becomes meaningless" (Musgrave, 1986, 110). Which is not to say that all entitlements are indexed or that a desire to ensure commitments is the only cause of indexing, as the story of Social Security indexing itself shows (Weaver, 1988).

9. It is perhaps conceivable that such legislation on appropriations bills could be approved with a liberal interpretation of the Holman rule in the House. The point of order also could be waived by a special rule when the appropriations bill is considered in the House, or waived on the Senate floor. In 1996, for example, a freeze on inflation adjustments to food stamp benefits was passed in the Agriculture Appropriations Act. Nevertheless, such legislation is decidedly not the norm.

10. Actually, the Senate has used ten-year scoring since 1993, but I use the shorter periods in House scoring because the shorter periods have in fact been the effective targets within budget debate.

11. Aside from the well-publicized "camel's nose" (Wildavsky, 1984), another form is to invest so much in a project that there comes a point where even people who do not like it want to finish it so as not to waste the investment. One close observer of the appropriations process commented that he was sure Mr. Whitten (House Appropriations Chair) and Mr. Bevill (House Energy and Water Appropriations Subcommittee Chair) knew exactly when spending on the controversial Tennessee-Tombigbee waterway (serving their states of Mississippi and Alabama) reached that point. But they still had to win the funding each year.

12. In confirmation of the importance of entitlements to a change in time-horizon, I should add that in spite of the supposed disappearance of deficits as of 1998, arguments for a long-term focus, based now almost entirely on entitlement concerns, remain prominent.

13. See White (1995c). The sequence of proposals and results from 1995–97 fits the argument fully.

14. My source for this report is personal conversations. This attitude towards trust funds is another difference between bureau and entitlement budgeting. In the former case, trust funds are traditionally seen as an evasion of control, as seen both in the traditional public finance case for a unified budget, and current disputes over the transportation trust funds.

15. Dole largely led development of the 1982 and 1984 reconciliations from his position as Senate Finance Chair, and Rostenkowski assisted in those efforts and in the end shaped much of the 1990 reconciliation (White and Wildavsky, 1991).

16. In personal conversations with CBO and GAO staff, and with other health care policy participants, I encountered a consensus that the Clinton administration's OMB has tended to estimate the baseline spending in state Medicaid programs generously so as to encourage coverage expansions through the Section 1115 waiver process. See Robert Wood Johnson Foundation, State Initiatives in Health Care Reform (July/August 1995), 7–9, 12.

17. Roy Meyers (1994) argues powerfully that technical knowledge is important to budget control in general, not just for entitlements. He is surely right that programs that appropriate discretionary budget authority but have unusual spending and financing patterns, such as revolving loan funds, require just as much technical skill for control as do entitlements. Yet the broad difference between the requirements for most bureau spending and entitlement spending still fits my description. Moreover, his own perspective as a former CBO analyst is a good example of the ways in which more technical budgeting requires a redefinition of any controller role.

18. An optimistic though plausible suggestion from John Ellwood.

REFERENCES

Aaron, Henry J., and Robert D. Reischauer (1995). "The Medicare Reform Debate: What is the Next Step?" *Health Affairs* 14(4): 8–30.

Axelrod, Donald (1988). *Budgeting far Modern Government.* New York: St. Martin's Press.

Bennett, James T., and Thomas J. DiLorenzo (1983). *Under-ground Government; The Off-Budget Public Sector.* Washington, DC: CATO Institute.

Bipartisan Commission on Entitlement and Tax Reform (1995). *Final Report to the President.* Washington, DC U.S. Government Printing Office.

———— (1994). *Interim Report to the President.* Washington, DC: U.S. Government Printing Office.

Blendon, Robert J., et al. (1997). "Trends: What Do Americans Know About Entitlements?" *Health Affairs* 16(5):111–15.

Butler, Stuart M., and Robert E. Moffitt (1995). "The FEHBP as a Model for a New Medicare Program." *Health Affairs* 14(4):47–61.

Caiden, Naomi (1982). "The Myth of the Annual Budget." *Public Administration Review* 42(6): 516–523.

U.S. Congress (1997a). Congressional Budget Office. *The Economic and Budget Outlook. Fiscal Years 1998–2007* Washington, DC: U.S. Government Printing Office.

———— (1997b). Congressional Budget Office. *Long-Term Budgetary Pressures and Policy Options* (March).

———— (1995). Congressional Budget Office. *The Economic and Budget Outlook: Fiscal Years 1996–2000.* Washington, DC: U.S. Government Printing Office.

Cox, James, Gregory Hager, and David Lowery (1993). "Regime Change in Presidential and Congressional Budgeting: Role Discontinuity or Role Evolution?" *American Journal of Political Science* 37 (February): 88–118.

Cutler, David M. (1997). "Restructuring Medicare for the Future." In Robert D. Reischauer, ed., *Setting National Priorities: Budget Choices for the Next Century.* Washington, DC: The Brookings Institution, 197–233.

Derthick, Martha (1979). *Policymaking for Social Security.* Washington, DC: The Brookings Institution.

Ervin, Osbin L. (1980). "The Functions of Budgeting: An Elaboration of the Schick Typology." *Midwest Review of Public Administration* 14: 119–130.

Fenno, Richard F., Jr. (1966). *The Power of the Purse: Appropriations Politics in Congress.* Boston: Little, Brown.

Fisher, Louis (1979). "The Authorization-Appropriations Process in Congress: Formal Rules and Informal Practices." *Catholic University Law Review* 29: 51–105.

Ippolito, Dennis S. (1984). *Hidden Spending: The Politics of Federal Credit Programs.* Chapel Hill: University of North Carolina Press.

Key, V.O. (1978). "The Lack of a Budgetary Theory." In Albert C. Hyde and Jay M. Shafritz, eds., *Government Budgeting: Theory, Process, Politics.* Oak Park, IL: Moore Publishing Co., 19–24.

Meyers, Roy T. (1994). *Strategic Budgeting.* Ann Arbor: University of Michigan Press.

Mosher, Frederick C. (1984). *A Tale of Two Agencies: A Comparative Analysis of the General Accounting Office and the Office of Management and Budget.* Baton Rouge: Louisiana State University Press.

Muris, Timothy J. (1989). "The Uses and Abuses of Budget Baselines." Working Papers in Political Science P-89-3. Palo Alto, CA: Hoover Institution.

Musgrave, Richard A. (1986). *Public Finance in a Democratic Society: Collected Papers of Richard A. Musgrave.* Vol. 2. Brighton, Sussex, England: Wheatsheaf Books.

Patashnik, Eric M. (1997). "Trust Funds and the Politics of Precommitment." *Political Science Quarterly* 112: 431–52.

———— (forthcoming). "The New Politics of Budgeting." In Mace Landy and Martin Levin, eds., *The New Politics of Public Policy,* 2nd ed.

Reischauer, Robert D. (1997). "The Unfulfillable Promise: Cutting Nondefense Discretionary Spending." In Robert D. Reischauer, ed., *Setting National Priorities: Budget Choices for the Next Century.* Washington, DC: The Brookings Institution, 123–54.

Rich, Spencer (1996). "Report Sets Clock Ahead on Medicare Insolvency." *Washington Post* 6 June, A12.

Robert Wood Johnson Foundation (1995). *State Initiatives in Health Care Reform.* (July/August): 7–9, 12.

Rosenbaum, David (1996). "Gloomy Forecast Touches off Feud on Medicare Fund." *New York Times* 6 June, Al.

Rubin, Irene S. (1988). "The Authorization Process: Implications for Budget Theory." In Irene S. Rubin, ed., *New Directions in Budget Theory.* Albany: SUNY Press, 124–147.

Schick, Allen (1995). *The Federal Budget: Politics, Policy, Process.* Washington, DC: The Brookings Institution.

———— (1980a). *Congress and Money.* Washington, DC: The Urban Institute Press.

———— (1980b). "Budgeting as an Administrative Process." In Allen Schick, ed., *Perspectives on Budgeting,* Washington, DC: American Society for Public Administration, 1–14.

————— (1973). "A Death in the Bureaucracy: The Demise of Federal PPB." *Public Administration Review* 33(2): 146–156.

————— (1966). "The Road to PPB: The States of Budget Reform." *Public Administration Review* 26(4): 243–258.

Stein, Herbert (1996). "The Fiscal Revolution in America, Part II: 1964–1994." In W. Elliot Brownlee, ed., *Funding the Modern American State, 1945–1995*. Washington, DC, and Cambridge, UK: The Woodrow Wilson Center Press and Cambridge University Press, 194–286.

Straussman, Jeffrey D. (1988). "Rights-Based Budgeting." In Irene S. Rubin, ed., *New Directions in Budget Theory*. Albany: SUNY Press, 100–123.

U.S. General Accounting Office (1992). "Availability of Appropriations: Amount." In *Principles of Federal Appropriations Law*. GAO/OGC 92–13. Washington, DC: USGAO, ch. 6.

————— (1998). *Credit Reform: Greater Effort Needed to Overcome Persistent Cost Estimation Problems*. GAO/AIMD-98–14. Washington, DC: USGAO.

Weaver, R. Kent (1988). *Automatic Government: The Politics of Indexation*. Washington, DC: The Brookings Institution.

————— (1985). "Controlling Entitlements." In John E. Chubb and Paul E. Peterson, eds., *The New Direction in American Politics*. Washington, DC: The Brookings Institution.

White, Joseph (1995a). *Competing Solutions: American Health Care Proposals and International Experience*. Washington, DC: The Brookings Institution.

————— (1995b). "(Almost) Nothing New Under the Sun: Why the Work of Budgeting Remains Incremental." In Naomi Caiden and Joseph White, eds., *Budgeting, Policy, Politics: An Appreciation of Aaron Wildavsky*. New Brunswick, NJ: Transaction Books, 111–32.

————— (1995c). "Budgeting and Health Policymaking." In Thomas E. Mann and Norman J. Ornstein, eds., *Intensive Care: How Congress Shapes Health Care Policy*. Washington, DC: The Brookings Institution, 52–78.

————— (1993a). "Markets, Budgets, and Health Care Cost Control." *Health Affairs* 12(3): 44–57.

————— (1993b). "Decision Making in the Appropriations Committees on Defense and Foreign Operations." In Randall B. Ripley and James M. Lindsay, eds., *Congress Resurgent: Foreign and Defense Policy on Capital Hill*. Ann Arbor: University of Michigan Press, 183–206.

————— (1989). "The Functions and Power of the House Appropriations Committee." Ph.D. diss., The University of California.

White, Joseph, and Aaron Wildavsky (1991). *The Deficit and the Public Interest: The Search for Responsible Budgeting in the 1980s*. Berkeley and New York: The University of California Press and The Russell Sage Foundation.

Wildavsky, Aaron (1992). *The New Politics of the Budgetary Process*, 2nd ed. New York: Harper Collins.

————— (1984). *The Politics of the Budgetary Process*, 4th ed. Boston: Little, Brown.

————— (1980). *How to Limit Government Spending*. Berkeley: The University of California Press.

————— (1978). "A Budget for All Seasons? Why the Traditional Budget Lasts." *Public Administration Review* 38(6): 501–509.

CHAPTER 26

CONSTRAINT AND UNCERTAINTY
Budgeting in California

NAOMI CAIDEN AND JEFFREY I. CHAPMAN

Constraint and uncertainty are the great shapers of budget processes and policies. Where they are low, budgeting tends to proceed incrementally, and budget reformers entertain dreams of planning and program techniques. Where they are high, quite different patterns of budgeting emerge. Budget structures are likely to splinter into special funds and jurisdictions. It is not possible to forecast revenues and expenditures beyond a short period, and budgets are made and remade throughout the year. Opportunism in taxing and spending replaces planning, and cash flow management assumes the greatest importance. The pattern of budgeting begins to resemble that of poor countries described by Caiden and Wildavsky, in which lack of redundancy prevents orderly budgeting and planning and forces participants into behavior dysfunctional for the system as a whole.[1]

But in California there is a crucial difference. California is not a poor country, but a rich state. Though governments in the state currently find traditional sources of revenue expansion severely constrained, they operate in an environment still rich in possibilities, not least of which is future economic growth. However, because state and local financial decisions are interconnected, uncertainties tend to reverberate through the system, growing in intensity as they are passed from state to locality down to program level. Meanwhile, resourcefulness and ingenuity are contributing toward altered patterns of revenues and expenditures presaging a more entrepreneurial and hard-nosed role for government.

This article analyzes the budgetary accommodations and adjustments which California governments have made to current constraints and uncertainties. We begin with the state budget, and trace how with the final disappearance of the built-up surplus of former years, unpredictability has dictated its repeated remaking throughout the year. We then turn to local governments and outline how these varied jurisdictions have coped with problems which stem in large part from forces outside their own control.

IMPONDERABLES IN STATE BUDGETING

California is famous, among other things, for the event which at least symbolically launched the most recent tax revolt in the United States. Proposition 13, approved in June 1978, stands squarely

---

From *Public Budgeting and Finance,* vol. 2, no. 4 (Winter 1982), 111–129. Copyright © 1982 by Public Financial Publications, Inc. Reprinted with permission.

349

as the conceptual marker dividing the lost land of good times from the troubled present. It was followed by other initiatives, but their effects were blunted for two years by the existence of a large state reserve which was used to "bail out" local government and allowed a measure of flexibility and redundancy for the state government. The exhaustion of the state surplus in 1981 coincided almost exactly with cuts in federal aid by the Reagan government and with the impact of the national recession. All these developments affected budgeting not only because they eroded the financial position of the state, but because no one could tell just what would happen at any given moment and because their timing interrupted orderly progress of the budget cycle.

Proposition 13 affected state budgeting because the state was called on to make good the revenue deficiencies its passage caused in local jurisdictions. Proposition 13 limited property tax rates to one percent of the market value and limited growth in assessed value to two percent annually. New local taxes could be imposed only with the consent of a majority of two-thirds of the voters. The effects of the amendment were not only to slash local revenues, but to broaden the gambit of state government as local finance became far more dependent on the state budget. The state government also assumed some local functions, assumed more responsibility for the future of education, and made arrangements to compensate the localities for property losses through a "bail out" formula for distribution of the state surplus.

For the first two years the state surplus sufficed to take care of what would otherwise have been deficits, but the state financial position was deteriorating steadily. Proposition 13 was followed by Proposition 4 in 1979, a limitation on public expenditure growth tied to increases in population and per capita income. Even more serious was the temporary indexing of the state personal income tax, which diminished 1981–1982 revenues by about $2.3 billion. Finally, in June 1982 voters approved an initiative permanently indexing the state income tax and abolishing the state inheritance and gift taxes.

By the time the budget for the 1981–82 fiscal year was under consideration, the financial position was already difficult. In early 1980 there were warnings that the remainder of the state surplus was running out and that from this point on the state would face potential deficits. Had there been no reserve, the shortfall for the 1980–81 budget would have amounted to $1.5 billion out of a total of $24.5 billion. The prospective narrow margin of solvency was diminished even further by proposals of the Reagan administration to change the equation of fiscal federalism, though their exact impact remained unclear. In April 1981 it appeared that the total loss for California during fiscal year 1981–82 (state, local, and individual) would amount to $1.8 billion with offsetting savings of about $82.3 million.[2] By September 1981 the figures were slightly more optimistic: $1.4 billion and $378.4 million respectively. For the following year, 1982–83, further cuts in federal aid were estimated to be even deeper, ranging from $1.5 billion to $2 billion. The significance of these cuts were not only in their considerable and damaging extent, but in the fact that at the time when the state budgets were being formulated, no one knew just how much they would be. Little wonder that arguments occurred on whether the crisis would be limited to a single year or was to be typical for the future.[3]

The real joker in the pack though was the state of the economy whose repercussions on the budget were to be the subject of a never-ending guessing game. The Department of Finance thought that it was being ultra-conservative when it estimated revenues for the 1981–82 fiscal year, only to find before a month was out that it had erred on the side of over-optimism. In July, revenues lagged by $55 million; in August, $84 million; and in September, $170 million. The December 1981 revision of the revenue outlook predicted a 1981–82 shortfall of $826 million, primarily because bank and corporate taxes and sales taxes were running far behind. In January 1982 realized tax revenues were again short of forecast tax revenues by about $130 million; by March the figure had increased to $350 million. Although the budget was balanced by the end of the year, the difficulties in producing accurate revenue estimates and the persistent and growing revenue shortfalls were alarming. For the following year, 1982–83, they promised to be even more serious. In May 1982 the Department of Finance predicted a revenue shortfall for that year of $805 million. This was significantly increased by the passage of the two new tax-cutting initiatives which will cost the state an additional $340 million in fiscal year 1982–83, and far more in the future.

Finally, expenditure estimates were also subject to shocks. Soon after the 1981–82 budget was passed, the Medfly appeared, probably costing the state from $50 million to $80 million. The refusal of the State Office of Administrative Law to approve emergency regulations drafted by the Department of Social Services to implement the Reagan administration cuts in AFDC cost the state an estimated $20 million as opposed to a projected $60 million savings.[4] There was a further shortage in the Medi-Cal area of about $200 million—$50 million from a federal shift and $150 million from an inaccurate forecast of savings and increased utilization. Other unanticipated costs (such as a larger number of forest fires than expected) and the passage of various pieces of legislation resulted in estimates for increased expenditures of over $170 million before the 1981–82 fiscal year was half over.

The result of all these developments was predictable: budgets which started off in formal balance were subject to constant re-estimates of impending deficits, though no one could be quite sure of the exact amount. Until the 1982–82 budget, this was not important, because, if a deficit did eventuate, it could be taken care of through the surplus. Now that the surplus had vanished, prospective deficits could no longer be viewed with equanimity, but required timely and sufficient responses to avert disaster.

MAKING AND REMAKING STATE BUDGETS

The response of the state administration and legislature to the uncertainties of budgeting over the past year bring to mind one of those old cliff-hanging serial movies: each episode ends in suspense about the fate of the hero or heroine, who is saved by a mind-boggling rescue in the succeeding sequence, only to fall victim almost immediately to some new near disaster. In the case of the state budget, the plot is complicated by the existence of two subjects, the budgets for fiscal years 1981–82 and 1982–83 respectively. To keep the story intelligible, their progress is separated and divided for analytical purposes into three sections covering the three major budget activities: initial work on the 1981–82 budget, changes in that budget during the 1981–82 year, and progress on the 1982–83 budget. It is important to remember, however, that during the 1981–82 fiscal year, work was proceeding concurrently on both the current and the following year's budget.

The First Round: Making the 1981–82 Budget

At the outset, the problem of incipient deficit in the 1981–82 budget was dealt with mainly by one-time responses. The governor's budget, presented in January 1981, was mangled by the legislature so that at the time of signing in June 1982, it stood at $734 million above its original $25 billion figure, or an increase of about 2.8 percent. The legislature, deprived of its customary surplus cushion, met the shortfall by temporizing, apparently hoping the situation would improve the following year. Its measures included the following:

1. The financing of capital outlays, previously funded through the general fund, by the one time only use of tidelands oil revenue.

2. Anticipation of increased federal funding of Supplemental Security Income/State Supplementary Payment (SSI/SSP) grant expenditures allowing for a decrease in general fund expenditures despite a 9.2 percent cost-of-living allowance to recipients.
3. A gain of $379 million in one-time revenues from taxes on the unsecured property roll accruing to school districts, for a reduction of $23 million in education expenditures by the state.
4. A similar $62 million one-time revenue gain from unsecured property rolls for community college districts, for a reduction of $7 million in state expenditures.
5. Suspension of the AB 8 deflator for one year.[5]
6. Permanent elimination of three local government subventions for a general revenue gain of $58 million.
7. One-time elimination of the motor vehicle license fee subvention worth $114 million to the state.
8. Reduction by $50 million of business inventory subventions to local governments.

Through these and other lesser actions the budget was balanced, with a Reserve for Economic Uncertainties of $475 million. But this feat was only achieved by one-time measures. One-time revenue increases totalled nearly $514 million; one-time expenditure cuts totalled $208 million. Even if they worked this time, these expedients could not be duplicated in later years; but before many months were out, it became evident that they were insufficient.

The Budget Is Made Throughout the Year: Remaking the 1981–82 Budget

By October 1982, unexpectedly high expenditures and low revenues were causing concern that the current year's budget would end in deficit. The governor's response was to reopen the 1981–82 budget. From this point on the budget would be made throughout the year in a series of ad hoc revenue and expenditure measures. Time after time it would be thought that the budget for the current year was in balance and could safely be left to its own devices. But each time it turned out preliminary estimates it had been too optimistic and it was necessary to devise new measures to ensure a satisfactory result.

The initial moves were made by the governor. First, he imposed a two percent across-the-board cut on all state operations with the exception of local assistance. In fact, the cut was really more than two percent, since it had to be implemented over the remaining three-quarters of the fiscal year. Second, the governor asked the Public Works Board and School Allocation Board to hold up capital outlays (with the exception of construction related to the clean-up of polychlorinated biphenyls and to health, fire, and safety). These cuts were expected to save about $460 million.

Despite these measures, new estimates in mid-October revealed a shortfall of $600 to $900 million. A change in federal tax laws could bring an additional shortfall of $300 million, though the state showed no inclination to conform, and to this end had failed to pass enforcement legislation. During November, the general fund borrowed over $900 million to meet cash obligations, and the governor called a special session of the legislature to deal with welfare reform. This, however, immediately degenerated into a squabble concerning voting reapportionment and initially made no contribution to solving the budget problem.

The December outlook was gloomy. Revision of the revenue outlook predicted a deficit of $826 million in 1981–82. Although revenue estimates now appeared more accurate, general fund revenues were still $14 million below the November forecast. It became apparent that the state would have to continue to borrow over the next three months, at interest costs which might be as much as $2 million.

January saw further deterioration in the budget outlook, making further expenditure cuts likely. The state comptroller asserted there was no money within the special funds from which the general fund had usually been able to borrow without payment of interest, so that interest payments on internal borrowing had reached $3 million. If things continued without any change it would be necessary to issue warrants at the end of the year instead of checks, effectively anticipating the following year's revenues—a tactic not used since the 1930s depression.

The special session of the legislature, therefore, turned its attention to raising additional revenues for the current fiscal year. Two measures were the focus of debate. The first would have increased the 1982 penalties for late payment of taxes from 6 percent to 18 percent for individuals, and from 12 percent to 18 percent for corporations. In later years, the penalty would be based on the federal income tax late penalty, which is in turn based on the prime rate. The second proposal was to increase the rate at which employers remit the withheld personal income tax of their employees to the state. Despite Republican resistance on the ground that both measures were fiscal gimmickry, the second of these measures, estimated to raise $180 million, was enacted.[6] But the fiscal position still remained shaky, although new reductions in spending had been implemented. The comptroller estimated there would be a shortfall of $150 million in the 1981–82 budget and realized tax revenues for January fell short of estimates by about $130 million.[7]

In February it seemed that light was beginning to show around the corner as the legislature was able to resolve its differences to enact several budget-saving expedients. First, tax revenues were increased by an estimated $165 million by additional penalties for late payment of all state taxes except for gift and inheritance. At least $100 million of this amount came from the speed-up of sales tax collections from corporations with monthly sales exceeding $4 million. This would shift a portion of tax liabilities from July to June, thus borrowing from the following year to help the current budget.

A second bill reduced expenditures by about $107 million by a combination of budget cuts, raids on untouched special funds, cancellations of tax refunds for the installation of energy-saving devices, cuts amounting to some $23 million in state reimbursements to local governments for workers compensation benefits, and a $36 million reduction in capital construction and energy and resources projects.[8] A third measure enacted a cut of $73 million in Aid to Families with Dependent Children payments, thereby bringing California into compliance with federal budget cuts. The effect was to deny benefits to nearly 20,000 recipients and reduce benefits to another 115,000. Altogether revenue and expenditure measures passed during the fiscal year had made more than a billion dollar change in the 1981–82 budget, and on February 17, the governor could at last announce a projected surplus for the year.

But the story was not yet over. Only two weeks later, the governor reconvened the legislature as a committee of the whole for a formal briefing on the state of the buget. The faltering economy had once again brought revenues well below forecasts, reversing the newly acclaimed surplus into a potential deficit. Thoroughly frightened by figures which predicted a $350 million shortfall in the current year and a possible deficit of $3 billion to $4 billion for the following one, Democrats and Republicans composed their differences to reach a compromise package to save the budget yet again.

The new budget legislation changed the budget by $481 million, again by a series of one-time measures.[9] The elimination of contributions by the state general fund and local school district to the State Personnel Retirement System during May and June saved $180 million. This move was legally possible because the fund earned more money than anticipated during the year from high interest rates. A further acceleration of sales tax revenues from more corporations brought in another $150 million, and the final $151 million was gained by scooping up nearly every unused dollar in the state treasury.

These Democrat-supported measures were not achieved without concessions to the Republicans. The compromise exacted a suspension of cost-of-living adjustments for virtually all budget categories for the first three months of the next fiscal year. This saving of about $350 million meant that those on welfare, the aged, blind and disabled, state employees, local governments, school districts, and medical providers would not receive full increases during 1982–83. Even with this concession, the budget bill barely passed, with no votes to spare in the Senate and a majority of only one in the Assembly.

Still, the budget had been saved. The governor made doubly sure by an executive order the same day he signed the budget bill, freezing all new state hiring, promotions, and transfers, for an additional saving of $10 million to $15 million. It could now be guaranteed that the state would finish the year in the black. With the help of further cut-backs in capital construction, a surplus of $67 million even seemed possible. There was still a chance that the year might end with a $17 million deficit for technical reasons, but by May, the uncertainties of the 1981–82 budget finally appeared resolved. But the means of resolution—a series of ad hoc measures—had done nothing to help the 1982–83 budget.

Estimates and Reestimates: The Making of the 1982–83 Budget

Much of the time that the governor and legislature were wrestling with the 1981–82 budget, they were also looking to the 1982–83 budget, whose prospects, if less immediate, seemed no less bleak and uncertain. To make it balance at all, the governor was forced to adopt several contentious assumptions. First, he assumed that two initiatives on the June 1982 ballot, fully indexing the state income tax and eliminating the inheritance tax, would be rejected by the electorate. As earlier noted, if they were approved, they could cost the state $340 million. Second, the state would save $450 million by reducing spending and shifting costs to local jurisdictions. Third, the governor projected an improved economy during the year, a highly doubtful prospect. Finally, he expected to be able to gain the agreement of the legislature to a one-time speedup of tax collections and increased penalties for slow tax payment.

These proposals were not received with equanimity in the legislature. The Republicans announced plans for an alternative budget, though at the time of writing this had failed to emerge. By February 1982, the budgetary assumptions were already beginning to unravel. The legislative analyst advocated nearly $700 million in budget cuts to balance the budget, while preliminary estimates of federal aid cuts of between $1.5 billion and $2 billion were hardly reassuring. So great were the difficulties with the 1981–82 budget that these problems received little attention beyond preliminary positions taken up by the parties in the legislature.

By May, however, when it seemed the current year's budget had finally been put to rest, the outlook for the 1982–83 budget could no longer be ignored. The Department of Finance estimated that a deficit of nearly $1.5 billion could be expected. Most of this deficit was the direct result of newly written legislation ($489 million) and a revised revenue shortfall ($805 million). If both tax reduction initiatives were approved in the June ballot (as actually happened), and if the legislature failed to pass the governor's proposals for service reductions, the deficit could reach over $3.3 billion.

In response to these problems, an informal "Wednesday Group" has been established, consisting of party leaders of both houses and representatives of the governor's office, often including the governor himself. The group discusses various ways of balancing the budget, and participants are in a position to implement their commitments. Various tentative proposals have been made, including a Democratic suggestion for a tax increase of between $1 billion and $2 billion (adamantly opposed by the Republicans) and Medi-Cal reforms estimated to save $500 million (opposed by the physicians' lobby). The impending election for state governor has made the position no easier and none of the potential candidates has come forward with a credible or viable budget strategy.

To cap off the struggle, the Assembly attempted to appropriate an additional $238 million for education. Unfortunately, this money did not exist, since it was supposed to be the 1981–82 surplus, which at the time was approximately zero. The State Senate, which had already adopted its version of the budget without the fictitious funds, adjourned for vacation rather than discuss the Assembly's version. The Assembly capitulated, and finally, on July 1, the governor was able to sign a $25.2 billion budget which was actually less, in current dollars, than the previous year's budget. The balance was achieved by cutting aid to cities by $221 million, eliminating all state employee salary increases, increasing student fees at all state universities and colleges, and cutting Medi-Cal by about $400 million.

It appears as though neither the legislative or executive branches of the state government are prepared to make a long-run commitment on budget problems. There has been no systematic response to the budget crisis, and perhaps none is possible given political differences among participants and a highly turbulent environment. In order to achieve a formally balanced budget, there has been resort to expedients—one-time ad hoc taxing and spending measures—which provide no lasting basis for sustained financial capacity. In fact a real annual budget cannot be produced at all; instead the budget is made and remade throughout the fiscal year in a desperate game of catch up to make the figures come out even at the end. The formal budget is subject to so many uncertain assumptions that budgeting seems to the outsider a kind of never-never-land whose relationship to reality is most tenuous. But to those who have to live by the decisions, however hasty, poorly timed, or ill-conceived, the state budget is only too real. In particular, the constraints and uncertainties of state budgets are transferred to local governments which must cope with their reverberations.

REVERBERATIONS AT THE LOCAL LEVEL

It was to be expected that the uncertainties of state budgeting would be reflected at the local level. A major, and at the time unforeseen, effect of Proposition 13 was to increase the dependence of local jurisdictions upon the state. The necessity for a state "bail out" of local governments following passage of the initiatives added to their existing dependence on state subventions from several taxes and state reimbursements for several important areas of expenditure. Options for local government were further constrained by the direct impact of economic recession upon local own-source revenues, the possibility of more tax-cutting citizen initiatives, the impact of inflation upon relatively fixed expenditures, and the cuts by the federal government. Local governments have been forced to respond to these constraints without any clear idea of their dimensions or future direction. In the ensuing uncertainty, public budgeting systems have become more volatile, and public managers have had to adopt flexible, opportunistic strategies. Their optimism that better times will come may not be realized; there may be continued budget cuts in service delivery and local capital infrastructure.

It is difficult to generalize about local government in California. Public authorities are woven together in a complex web of fragmented and overlapping jurisdictions. Counties, cities, and a multitude of special districts each have their own patterns of revenues and expenditures. Consolidated information is relatively difficult to obtain and where it does exist is likely to be misleading, since each jurisdiction seems to be unique into itself, shaped by its own revenue and expenditure policies, and its particular configuration of population, geographical land area, resources, and economy. In addition, the speed of recent changes quickly outdistances the observer.

Yet, despite their diversity, California local governments form part of a system, and that system is dominated by the state government. Local budgets vary in their dependence on the state. Enterprise funds and districts and quasi-autonomous public corporations are affected much less than cities, cities less than counties; school and community college districts are the most dependent of all. But within each category, there may be considerable variation, according to specific local policies.

Local financial dependence on state government predated Proposition 13 since by law local governments are the creatures of the state, but many jurisdictions maintained considerable autonomy through own-source revenues, in particular the property tax. Following Proposition 13, local authorities were inversely affected according to their dependence on the property tax. Enterprise districts and a few cities were almost entirely unaffected. But cities, nearly a quarter of whose revenue was derived from property taxes, and counties, over one-third dependent, felt substantial effects. Community college and school districts, where property taxes made up as much as half of revenue, were even harder hit, while some special districts had relied on property taxes for as much as 80 percent of funding. The effect of the property tax losses was to close a significant area of autonomous decision making to local governments. "Before Proposition 13," said one local official, "we used to set our own property tax rates; now all this is beyond our control." By restricting options, the property tax limitation made local governments more vulnerable to adversities on other fronts, and dependent on more volatile revenues sensitive to economic swings.

The distribution of the large state surplus staved off disaster by converting a probable 15 percent loss in revenues that year to one of less than 2 percent. But the price, in terms of increased dependence on the state budget, was high. The state had effectively taken over educational finance, as well as SSI/SSP. It had also, in accordance with the terms of the proposition, gained formal mastery of the property tax, since this was now to be allocated "according to law." The bailout itself was not only subject to state terms and conditions, but was distributed according to a formula which, in the absence of agreement on a permanent arrangement, changed each year.

As long as state revenues held, and there was a state budget surplus, the effects on local governments were relatively muted. Though budgets for the 1978–79 fiscal year suffered some cuts, the following two years were largely stable. But by fiscal 1981–82, the strength of the state budget had been eroded by political responses to perceived demands by the electorate, cutting inheritance taxes and indexing the income tax, as well as the economic recession. As noted, the state reacted with heavy cuts in local government assistance, reducing or eliminating several subventions or local shares of state taxes. For local governments now heavily dependent on state financing, the results were serious. Virtually all jurisdictions found themselves obliged to make sharp adjustments downward in their preliminary expenditure forecasts and to find revenues to make up the gap. Faced with doubtful prospects, local governments have exhibited a variety of responses—business as usual, efforts to maintain options, cutting budgets close, extending the budget cycle, cost allocation, innovative finance, bargaining with the private sector, and, of course, cutting service and capital expenditures. Description of these reactions is based mainly on interviews with a limited number of local government officials at different levels whose responses demonstrated a surprising, or perhaps unsurprising, degree of consistency.[10]

Business as Usual

Despite the repeated necessity to make budget cuts with the general erosion of spending power, few local authorities have established new budget techniques to deal with the situation. In typically small jurisdictions executives feel they have control of the line items and can use their knowledge to make cuts when and where necessary. Only exceptionally, and cautiously, are local governments continuing efforts to improve systemwide budget technology. This lack of innovation in hard times is consistent with the findings of a recent Rand study and Schick's analysis of the relationship between resource availability and the introduction of program budgeting.[11] There is no hurry to implement zero-base budgeting or "decremental" systems. Since the majority of those interviewed felt the present position was temporary, there seemed little point in investing in new processes.

Local government executives are also quick to find rays of light even in the present gloom. For example, the passage of Proposition H in June 1982 in the City of Los Angeles, allowing a cap to be placed on police and fire officer pension cost-of-living increases, has brought considerable relief to future budget prospects. A decision of the courts in favor of the City of San Gabriel, confirming the legality of a property tax to cover costs of public employee pensions mandated in the city charter, has raised hopes of similar possibilities both for pensions and even other mandated expenditures in other charter cities. There is also some feeling that the projections of the state department of finance are unduly pessimistic, extrapolating current trends which are in reality subject to considerable change and disturbance. Confidence runs high in the resilience of the California economy, the favorable effect of federal tax cuts, and the share of the state in defense expenditures. Emphasis is on strategies to deal with present predicaments, rather than to plan for a future of cutback management.

Maintaining Options

A major strategy to cope with uncertain revenues is to maintain options. This may be accomplished in two main ways. The first is to set out a budget, but require from departments a detailed list of priorities, indicating where cuts may be made if adverse conditions develop. Thus, in the City of Los Angeles, agencies have been asked to formulate budgets with different levels of spending, spelling out their implications in a detailed review of spending and a list of options: decision makers "can go in 16 different directions" according to how things fall out. Los Angeles County also requires preliminary reports from departments to identify areas for cuts. Another city manager anticipates starting out "with a budget we can manage, and then we expect to redirect funds in mid-year."

The opposition approach is also feasible. In San Bernardino County, a target budget for 1982–83 was adopted with a 15 percent cut in inflation-adjusted program costs. The aim was to create a contingency reserve which the Board of Supervisors might then be able to reallocate. Similarly, in Riverside County a budget of 90 percent of the previous year's appropriations without allowance for inflation was approved, again providing for a contingency reserve for possible restoration of at least some of the cuts. Another county made no attempt at all to develop a new budget and simply readopted the one from the previous year.

Cutting Things Close

One of the reasons for the relative stability of local governments in recent years has been the existence of revenues. Typically budgeters would aim for a fairly large positive balance at the end of the year. Now many find, in the words of one city manager, that they are "hitting awful close." The margin for error is small. For example, the City of Los Angeles in 1981–82 had only a six percent growth in sales tax revenues, instead of the previous years' 15–20 percent increase. In mid-year the state refused to reimburse certain accounts in the workers' compensation area, leaving a gap which had to be offset by accelerations in tax collections, a mid-year hiring freeze, and cancellation of equipment purchases. Once it had been customary to expect a one percent surplus at year's end; now a zero balance is likely.

Other jurisdictions report similar experience. In Los Angeles County, a surplus of over $160 million in 1978–79 has gradually been eaten away until budget authorities predict only "a razor thin" margin of $9.6 million for the current year, representing only 0.2 percent of the general county budget. In another city, an official reported it was no longer possible to budget for a surplus; the previous year it had been less than one percent of the general fund: "if you miss a revenue by one percent then you're in trouble."

To cope with diminishing reserves, authorities adopt defensive tactics by estimating revenues low and expenditures high. Typically, agencies are not expected to spend all of their budgets, but rather about 96 to 97 percent. Budget officials have always kept contingency reserves to smooth cash flow. Now these are used to cushion what are felt to be inevitable uncertainties during the budget year. They may also create some slack by not counting salary savings, so this amount also acts as an in-built cushion. Funds are carefully monitored on a day-to-day and month-to-month basis and adjustments made where necessary. In the City of Los Angeles only routine expenditures are allocated without further review; even if money has been allocated in the initial budget, new requests have to be approved by the mayor. Constant watchfulness is necessary to stay on top.

Extending the Budget Cycle

Local government officials have generally expected budget processes to take about six months, starting with preparatory work in December and ending with adoption of a budget by the beginning or end of June. The difficulty is that the state budget is completed (even if it is on schedule which is by no means always the case) at the beginning of July. It is therefore difficult, if not impossible, for localities to know what the state is going to do in relation to local assistance while they are working on or adopting their own budgets.

Where it is difficult to predict state actions, local budgets become preliminary documents only, which everyone knows will have to be redone. The introduction to the City of Riverside budget expressed the predicament: "Time constraints do not allow us the luxury of waiting for the conclusion of state budget deliberations; hence the necessity of proceeding with the information now available to us."[12] In Los Angeles County the 1982–83 budget recommendations were based on the governor's January proposed state budget, but they emphasized "These recommendations should be considered subject to further downward revisions in June," since they did not take into account subsequent projections of an additional state deficit of nearly $1.5 billion or passage of the June tax initiative. Even by April, it was "becoming increasingly apparent that the governor's January budget assumptions may not hold up."[13] The County of Riverside also started from the governor's January proposed budget, but four months later found it impossible to resolve continued uncertainties regarding such items as the motor vehicle in lieu revenue, reductions in annual cost-of-living adjustments in health-related programs, transfer of responsibilities from state to county level without full reimbursement, and changes in reimbursement practices for certain health programs.

Faced with unpredictability in a large part of their budgets, local governments have had to extend their own budget cycles. "We run two budgets a year," explained one city manager, "The process starts in January and the budget passes on June 1. Then we have to redo it all again in August when the state budget is through . . . we are doing the budget all year round." In Los Angeles County the 1981–82 budget required four consecutive documents to keep up with changing conditions. The lack of a stable and permanent funding mechanism for local government by the state is directly reflected in local budget processes. To quote from the Los Angeles County Budget Recommendations, "Because the state has chosen to make financing of local governments an annual exercise, we are unable to predict with any certainty the magnitude of next year's 1982 revenue shortfall . . . budget planning has become an annual crisis."[14]

Allocating Costs

The need to implement cuts and the threat of uncertain funding have produced increased consciousness of cost which has in turn impacted on financial mechanisms. Constraints on property taxes and uncertain state funding have produced incentives for local officials to maximize revenues in other areas. One manifestation is a slow growth in charges for current services (which have grown since 1978 from $490 million to $751 million, or from 8.2 percent to 10.5 percent of local budgets). Local governments have also tried to save money by contracting for services, with somewhat mixed results.

User fees are part of a widespread movement to allocate costs to service users, whether these are private individuals or units of the same jurisdiction. Cost allocation is a means of relieving pressure on the general fund by ensuring that other local government elements pay their full share of administrative overheads or other services. Usually the general fund is only one mechanism through which services are financed. In the City of Los Angeles, for example, only about one-half of expenditures are financed through the general fund. The remainder, including airport services, water, power, and sewers, comes from enterprise funds which operate on a fee-for-service basis. If utilities are counted, only about $33 million in a budget of over $175 million in the City of Riverside is financed through the general fund; the remainder is covered by no less than 18 other funds. The name of the game is to allocate as much as possible of general fund expenses to these other funds. To this end, cities and counties are increasingly adopting cost allocation plans, usually put together by outside consultants and requiring substantial computer capacity. These documents list for each unit full costs of the service it supplies, including space use, unbilled rent, equipment use, unbilled insurance, and utilities.

The increased awareness of costs may also be seen in recourse to special assessments in some jurisdictions. Some types of benefits assessment districts do not generally require electoral approval and they are being increasingly used, although the total revenues received through this process are still quite small. In special districts and certain circumstances a two-thirds vote is not necessary. For example, it was ruled that the Los Angeles Rapid Transit District could gain revenues from an increase in sales tax through a vote short of a two-thirds majority. Legislation to make the creation of special benefit assessments easier was recently defeated in the state legislature, but some localities have utilized the device. The City of San Bernardino has established five assessment districts in the last year, including two for landscaping in different parts of the city, a downtown parking district, and a street lights assessment. Under these arrangements, the city advances the sum necessary for the improvements and is gradually reimbursed from a special tax levy on the residents or users of the area involved. Other localities are thinking of special assessments for a variety of services including street lights, tree trimming, flood control, and standby fire services.

Innovative Finance

Necessity, it has been said, is the mother of invention, and in straitened circumstances public officials have often been resourceful. Because of the New York fiscal crisis, the term "creative finance" has come into disrepute, so we shall label these responses of California officials "innovative finance." Their methods are quite different from those used in New York, resembling them only in their novelty and departure from textbook precepts for public financial management.

The general attitude which lies behind adoption of innovative financial strategies has been well expressed by D. Gale Wilson in "A New Portfolio for the City Manager." "If we're going to be strong in this business," he writes, "we ought to follow a proactive stance and develop and obtain a degree of fiscal independence and integrity. As long as we have to lean on others and beg, we're going to go hungry." What he has in mind is "to generate new money by application of entrepreneurial techniques and enterprises."[15]

In fact, local officials have been employing innovative financial techniques for some time. A prime area is that of lease-backs, commonly used as a means for financing capital items without the need for floating general obligation bonds. A lease-back arrangement involves setting up a separate authority to borrow money to finance a structure which the parent government will then rent. Some schemes are quite complex, as the example of the City of Palmdale illustrates. The city created the Palmdale Civic Authority (PCA) as a financing device to build the city library. The PCA charges rent to the city for the use of the library equal to the principal and interest payments on its bonds. Actually the rent payments come from the Palmdale Community Redevelopment Agency, which signed an agreement with the city and PCA to pay them out of the tax increment from one of its redevelopment projects, in turn based on mortgage revenue bonds.[16]

The tax exempt nature of municipal bonds together with the depreciation provisions of federal tax law have provided local governments and private investors with new opportunities. For example, the City of Los Angeles recently financed replacement of a police station through a leasing arrangement in which title was signed over to a private firm. A bond issue, divided into $5,000 certificates of participation, was floated to pay investors 11.15 percent interest tax free over ten years. The city maintains full operational control of the facility which it will buy back for a nominal fee at the end of the lease.[17] In a well-publicized transaction, the City of Oakland sold its museum and auditorium to private investors, then leased it back. The proceeds of the sale will be invested and the income used to pay back Municipal Improvement Revenue Bonds and make lease payments. At the end of the lease period the facilities would be repurchased by the city using the remaining invested sales proceeds. The city secures immediate cash while the investors gain tax-exempt earnings and a useful tax shelter.[18] Other California local governments are looking at the "Oakland system" with interest and wondering how much their own city halls are worth. They are also considering how to take advantage of federal tax regulation changes, for example, in the areas of co-generation in power plants and equipment leasing.

Meanwhile local governments have not been idle. High interest rates mean high borrowing costs, but they have also given a new importance to cash flow management. Several cities have benefited from high interest earnings on unused cash reserves, although they realize that this flow is subject to the volatility of the credit market and cannot be counted on in the future. Some jurisdictions are deliberately exploiting their power to borrow on the tax exempt market through tax or revenue anticipation notes. They may borrow to the extent of their largest monthly deficit, which may provide them with cash beyond their immediate needs. This sum can be reinvested, with the difference (spread) between the tax exempt and market rates accruing to the city or county. The use of commercial paper is becoming popular; local authorities find it profitable to borrow at tax exempt rates while investing their own cash at market rates. At least one county has a deliberate strategy of relending the proceeds of revenue anticipation notes to other public bodies with credit ratings lower than its own, in effect filling a probable need for a public banking service.

Bargaining with the Private Sector

One seldom-mentioned consequence of Proposition 13 has been its effects on the issuance of local government general obligation debt. This debt had been backed by the property tax base of the local jurisdiction. Now, with the base and the rate out of the local jurisdiction's control, new general obligation debt, at the local level, has disappeared.

Thus, while in the past the local jurisdiction would provide infrastructure for new development financed by general obligation debt, now the jurisdiction negotiates and bargains with the developer. For private developers to obtain the set of permits, they must now provide infrastructure, cash, or other useful assets to the community. For example, the City of Santa Monica now receives $400,000 per year from a developer (in lieu of the Proposition 13 property tax loss) as a contribution from the revenues received from the new Santa Monica shopping mall. There are other examples. The developer may provide sewers or affordable housing; the city may take a profit position in the development.

Local governments, of course, find themselves in a "fiscal squeeze": revenues are rising, but are no longer keeping pace with inflation.[19] Their position is one of the "acute scarcity" described by Allen Schick in which "available resources do not cover the incremental rise in program costs."[20] In these circumstances, governments typically adopt short-term strategies which include cutting new demands, deferring postponable expenditures, and retrenching in the most vulnerable areas. With their reserves gone or nearly gone, California governments have resorted to all of these.

Yet it is difficult to come to grips with the real extent of the budget cuts. Unlike its obverse, incrementalism, decrementalism is suffused with uncertainty. First, there is no consistency in the bases used as measures for reduction. Jurisdiction may use last year's budget, this year's initial proposals, last year's expenditures, or this year's current service budget. Second, they may count cuts in dollars or positions. If the latter, it is not always clear whether these are real positions or budgeted positions, or whether contract employment is being substituted for direct employment. Third, budgeted cuts at the beginning of a year are subject to upward or downward revision during the year, depending on whether predicted revenue flows or inflation estimates are borne out, or whether some new funding source, such as a fee increase, is found. Fourth, the increasing fragmentation of local government makes it difficult to evaluate reductions for an entire jurisdiction. Finally, the real extent of cuts for the coming year's budget is always unknown.

Expenditure patterns have been confused, but it appears that many local governments initially responded to real revenue decline by cutting capital expenditure.[21] In some cases it was possible to take funds from proposed capital projects and use them for general purposes. New capital expenditures have been largely brought to a halt, and maintenance has been deferred. Long-term capital plans have been scrapped, and cycles for refurbishment of streets, parks, and buildings indefinitely deferred.

A second response has been to cut staffing. In the last four years the City of Los Angeles dropped 2,000 regular positions out of a total workforce of 28,000 and dismissed 4,000 CETA workers. In Los Angeles County a work force of nearly 80,000 was cut to less than 70,000 in 1981–82, and it is expected that a further 3,000 positions will be lost in the coming year. These cuts have translated into service reductions—longer waits for building permits, streets cleaned and repaired less often, trees left untrimmed, library hours cut, fire stations undermanned or closed, and neighborhood clinics shut. Cuts have not been allocated in any uniform way, but certain patterns may be detected. Areas which generate their own revenues have been protected unless these revenues have fallen below their requirements. Police and to a lesser extent fire departments have suffered less than other services: a ten percent across-the-board cut will translate into a five percent cut for police and fire services and 15 percent for the remainder.

Other local services have been more vulnerable, and, as might be expected, libraries and recreation budgets have been hardest hit. Most vulnerable of all have been the areas dependent on outside funding which have been directly affected by cuts at state and federal level—health, welfare, and education. Local governments have been quick to divest themselves of responsibility where possible. For example, Los Angeles County now requires a $700 deposit from noninsured patients at the county hospital.

Local budget officials appear to see federally funded services as beyond their control: federal funds are referred to as "soft" money or "entrepreneurial" money. Most direct federal aid at the local level is program specific, and if funding ceased, programs would simply disappear. If mandates were involved, many localities would probably turn to litigation. The probable future loss of federal revenue sharing is taken far more seriously, since these funds had often been used to help meet the cost of essential services. But it is still too soon to estimate the impact of the federal cuts.

The implications of prolonged uncertainty in local government financing go beyond these immediate responses. In a positive direction, emphasis on allocation of costs to services instead of to a general tax base may make for greater appreciation of local services previously thought of as "free." Reluctant taxpayers may now come to see just what they were receiving for the money they paid, and hidden subsidies to the business community may be evaluated. It is time that local governments had more expertise, explored alternative means of service delivery, and gauged the worth and efficiency of their operations.

But the more "businesslike" stance of local government may also have adverse implications for the role of local governments in carrying out public policy. There is a legitimate place for public enterprise and there is no reason why it should not contribute to the support of public services. The danger is that the creation of "public markets" based on the same principles of effective demand and profitability as private markets may overwhelm the general mission of local governments in protecting the public interest as a whole. Moreover, the mechanisms whereby local governments have sought to improve their position—special districts, leaseback arrangements, and so on—have tended to create confusing financial structures and to erode accountability. Local officials are tempted to obfuscate, not to clarify, to devise short-term responses to meet crises without pondering their future implications, to maintain flexibility to the abrogation of long-term policy making. Crisis budgeting might meet the needs of the moment, but its hidden costs may be much greater than apparent savings.

CONCLUSIONS

It is difficult to write about California budgeting at this moment. Not only is the immediate future cloudy, but the dimensions of the present are also uncertain. The perceptions of many officials may be accurate or the officials may be living in a fool's paradise. Others, particularly program officials who must actually implement the cuts, predict disaster, but they may also be wrong. Conclusions must be tentative.

The horizons of California budgeting at all levels have drawn closer. Unable to predict the future or comprehend the present, participants have resorted to short-term responses to try to keep afloat until a new wave of fiscal prosperity washes them once more high and dry. Decisions are made in ad hoc fashion, to maintain the status quo as far as possible and preserve the narrow ground of political consensus. But these temporary expedients in themselves constitute a pattern, whose effects may leave a lasting mark upon budget processes and policies. These longer-term effects include permanent changes in revenue structure, state-local relationships, and the nature of public services.

Given current uncertainties, the flexible and opportunistic stance of budget participants may be the only practical and appropriate response. But "mudding through" carries with it a heavy price in the public as well as the private sphere. Short-sighted decisions may be expensive in the long run. Deterioration in physical infrastructure must eventually be paid for. Cuts in social and educational programs may be translated into costs for criminal justice, welfare, and unemployment support. Degradation of the environment in city or county may be hard to reverse. If the present situation of routine crisis persists, no doubt resourceful politicians and officials will find ways to keep the ship afloat, but it is time to give greater thought to its direction.

NOTES

1. See Naomi Caiden and Aaron Wildavsky, *Planning and Budgeting in Poor Countries* (New Brunswick, N.J.: Transaction, 1980); and Howard Glennerster, "Social Service Spending in a Hostile Environment," in Christopher Hood and Maurice Wright (eds.), *Big Government in Hard Times* (Oxford: Martin Robertson, 1981), pp. 174–196.

2. The cuts included about $130 million from the food stamp program, about $240 million from Medi-Cal, about $250 million from Medicare, about $42 million from job training programs, about $87 million from social services and child welfare, between $400 million and $550 million from AFDC, about $26 million from child nutrition programs, and between $109 million and $114 million in education funds, Ellen Hume, "Budget Cuts Could Cost State $2 Billion," *Los Angeles Times,* February 8, 1982.

3. Kerry Drager, "The Post-13 Transformation in Local Government Lobbying" *California Journal,* Vol. 12, No. 8, pp. 285–286.

4. Douglas Shuit, "State Attempt at Welfare Cuts Stalls," *Los Angeles Times,* October 3, 1981.

5. AB 8 was the state's second-year bail-out bill providing aid to local governments. The deflator provision would have automatically cut the bail outs to all local jurisdictions if state revenues were not adequate. In 1981–82 they would not have been sufficient and so the cuts would have occurred by formula rather than through legislative activity.

6. Jerry Gilliam, "Bill to Speed Tax Collections Signed," *Los Angeles Times,* January 19, 1982.

7. Douglas Shuit, "Brown Signs Three Bills to Balance Budget," *Los Angeles Times,* February 18, 1982.

8. Ibid.

9. Douglas Shuit and Claudia Luther, "State Fiscal Rescue Bill Sent to Brown," *Los Angeles Times,* March 12, 1982.

10. It would of course be impossible in a short survey to do total justice to such a varied and dynamic scene. On the local level, views of the situation depend to a great extent on where the jurisdiction receives its revenues; for example, entities largely dependent on property taxes or intergovernmental sources are impacted quite differently from those which enjoy substantial autonomous income from fees. There is no attempt here at comprehensive analysis, but rather an attempt to report impressions from public material and interviews with public officials, mainly in Southern California. From these sources a fairly consistent picture emerges, but given the size and diversity of the public sector in California, exceptions to these general findings undoubtedly exist. These exceptions do not invalidate the conclusions here, but are manifestations of an ambiguous, constantly changing, and perpetually surprising environment. Interviews were conducted with budget officials in the Counties of Los Angeles, Riverside, and San Bernardino, and the cities of Los Angeles, Rialto, Riverside, and San Bernardino. The authors would like to thank these officials for their time and cooperation. Thanks are also due to Janet Chaney and Tremain Downey, graduate assistants in the Department of Public Administration at California State College in San Bernardino, who assisted in interviewing, and to other graduate students in the department who were generous with information and insights. However, the views and conclusions expressed in the article are solely those of the authors.

11. Warren E. Walker and Jan M. Chaiken, *The Effects of Fiscal Contraction on Innovation in the Public Sector* (Santa Monica: Rand, 1981); and Allen Schick, "Budgetary Adaptions to Resource Scarcity," in Charles Levine and Irene Rubin (eds.), *Fiscal Stress and Public Policy* (Beverly Hills: Sage, 1980), pp. 113–133.

12. City of Riverside, *Preliminary Program Budget, 1982–83,* p. I.

13. Los Angeles County, *Recommendations for the Proposed 1982–1983 Budget,* April 27, 1982, p. 8.

14. Ibid., p. 15.

15. *Western City,* March 1982, p. 14.

16. The authors are indebted to Alan London for bringing this example to their attention.

17. *Western City,* March 1982, p. 14.

18. "Oakland Sells the City Jewels," *Western City,* March 1982, pp. 6–7.

19. Charles Levine, "Organizational Decline and Cutback Management," in Charles Levine (ed.), *Managing Fiscal Stress* (Chatham, N.J.: Chatham House, 1980), p. 17.

20. Schick, op. cit., p. 123.

21. For example, Mark David Menchik, et al., *Fiscal Restraint in Local Government: A Summary of Research Findings* (Santa Monica: Rand, 1982), p. 15.

CHAPTER 27

RESTRAINT IN A LAND OF PLENTY
Revenue and Expenditure Limitations in Texas

GLEN HAHN COPE AND W. NORTON GRUBB

At first glance Texas is an unlikely candidate for inclusion in a symposium on resource limitations in state and local government. Texas is an affluent state, although some segments of the population have benefited little from the general prosperity. Texas cities are relatively young and most are growing, feeling few of the fiscal pressures that older industrial cities in declining regions are facing. For example, the Urban Institute's six-city study of urban infrastructure endorsed Dallas as having a sound capital plant, as well as being a possible model for urban management.[1] Although currently in a strong financial position which is projected to continue into the near future, Texas government is confronted with numerous pressures, including formal limitations, to restrain governmental expenditures and even to reduce them from the relatively low levels that now exist.

Historically, government in Texas has been limited. The state constitution was adopted in 1876 during a period of depressed economic conditions and reaction against the preceding Reconstruction government.[2] The constitution dictated weak public officials and included limitations on public debt, taxing, and spending powers. Many amendments proposed since then, of which over 200 have been adopted, were intended to restrict further the power of Texas officials.

Although the Texas economy has improved considerably since 1876, the general sentiment for limited government has remained. Texas is one of only four states with neither a personal nor a corporate income tax. Local governments are restricted constitutionally to property tax rates not to exceed 2.5 percent of assessed value for Home Rule and 1.5 percent for general law cities (though these limits have been approached only in the poorest cities) and several cities have passed more binding limits in recent years. State spending and taxing powers are also limited. The state constitution limits state spending for direct income assistance payments to individuals—in practice, Aid to Families with Dependent Children (AFDC)—to $80 million. A constitutional amendment adopted in 1942 requires that spending legislation not exceed the comptroller's revenue estimates without new tax legislation, except in emergency situations. An amendment passed in 1978 limits total state expenditure growth to the "rate of growth in the state's economy," defined by the legislature to be the rate of growth of personal income. The effect of these restraints has been to reaffirm the sentiment for low spending, even as the state's fiscal bases have been expanding rapidly.

From *Public Budgeting and Finance,* vol. 2, no. 4 (Winter 1982), 143–156. Copyright © 1982 by Public Financial Publications, Inc. Reprinted with permission.

STATE FINANCES

Texas' tax structure differs from that of many other states, both in its absence of income taxes and in its heavy reliance on gas and oil severance taxes. Thanks to OPEC's pricing policies, severance taxes in Texas grew by 558 percent during the 1970s. In 1982 severance taxes accounted for 28 percent of total state tax collections, compared to 14 percent ten years earlier.[3] Other state taxes grew at a lower but still impressive rate of 317 percent in the same period. The largest tax source other than severance taxes is the sales tax, which now accounts for 38.5 percent of total collections. A variety of smaller taxes—a motor vehicle sales tax, cigarette, alcohol, and tobacco taxes, a business franchise tax, and the like—comprise the remaining third of Texas' tax revenues. This is a relatively heavy reliance on selective sales and excise taxes, since similar taxes account for only about 18 percent of revenues in other states.[4]

Because of high income growth in the 1970s and increasing oil and gas prices, Texas now ranks fourth among the states in taxable capacity according to the Representative Tax System devised by the Advisory Commission on Intergovernmental Relations, compared to a ranking near the national average in 1967.[5] Because tax collections per capita are so low, ranking 43rd among the states in 1979, Texas' tax effort (tax collections divided by total taxing capacity) is the lowest in the nation at 63 percent of the national average[6] and has fallen consistently since the late 1960s. Furthermore, much of the burden of the oil and gas severance taxes falls on nonresidents.[7] Clearly, then, the State of Texas does not suffer any fiscal problems arising from an inadequate tax base; the low levels of taxation and spending are, more than ever, the result of political choice.

The historic distrust of government in Texas has been embodied in the budgeting structure of the state. The Texas constitution provides for numerous elected officials, in addition to the governor, as part of the plural "executive." No single official, including the governor, has the power to control state expenditures once appropriations have been made to the various state agencies. Each agency is nearly autonomous, responsible to either an elected department head, or to a commission, popularly elected or appointed by the governor for fixed, overlapping terms. This has tended to give the state legislature the only central control over expenditures, except that the elected comptroller has responsibility for accounting.

Even the budget process, frequently a source of policy direction and "power of the purse" for a governor, is shared in Texas with the legislature. The governor has been designated the chief budget officer of the state since 1931. The Legislative Budget Board (LBB), created in 1949, also has budgetary authority and must submit budget estimates to the legislature as well. Since 1973 the LBB has also been required to submit a performance report at the beginning of each biennial legislative session, including efficiency, workload, and other performance information for each agency. The same legislation required "fiscal notes" to be prepared by the LBB estimating the cost to the state of all nonappropriation bills and resolutions. These five-year projections are attached to the bills during consideration by the legislature. In the same year, Texas adopted zero-base budgeting, requiring all administrative agencies to submit budget decision packages at several levels, in order of priority, to the LBB and governor's budget office.

Texas' dual budgeting system, in which all agencies submit budget requests to both the LBB and the governor's office simultaneously and both develop budgets for consideration by the legislature, is relatively distinctive among the states. The two budget agencies coordinate their processes, sending out joint budget preparation instructions, and hold joint hearings on agency budget requests. The two budget documents are not necessarily similar, however. The governor's budget has traditionally been considered by appropriations committees as the one in which new program requests or changes would appear; the LBB budget has been the more conservative of the two, for the most part limited to existing agencies and programs.[8] In the past several years, since the dominant party in the legislature has been different from that of the governor, the governor has used his budget primarily as a policy document, indicating agency spending plans and possible veto areas. The actual bill considered by the legislature has been the LBB version.

The generally conservative nature of Texas politics, as well as anti-tax sentiments similar to those in the "Proposition 13" movement, have combined to produce a climate favorable to more formal limitations on taxation and expenditure than had existed prior to the 1970s. Following the success of Proposition 13 in California, the political pressure for property tax relief and reductions in government spending became irresistable. In a 1978 special session the legislature devised the Tax Relief Amendment, a package of unrelated constitutional amendments which benefited a large number of voters. To no one's surprise, the amendments were overwhelmingly approved by the voters in the November 1978 election.

One of the provisions included in the package was the constitutional limit restricting the growth rate of state expenditures. Because of biennial budgeting in Texas, the growth rate limitation first took effect in the 1982–82 biennium. By using the growth rate of total per capita personal income as the definition of "rate of growth in the state's economy," the limitation allows expenditures to keep up with income inflation and population growth. During the 1970s real per capita income in Texas had increased by 27 percent, or about 2.5 percent per year; thus, on the basis of historical experience, this spending limit would allow for a modest rate of growth in real per capita expenditures. In the first legislative session after passage of the Tax Relief Amendment the LBB prepared several forecasts of personal income growth using econometric and time series models. The growth rate finally chosen, 33 percent over the two years, was the highest of the estimated rates, and was slightly higher than the growth rates of about 28 percent prevailing for most of the previous decade.[9]

Allowing for a 33 percent growth over the 1982–83 biennium, state expenditures were limited to $15.220 billion. Expenditures from taxes dedicated to special funds—e.g., state sales taxes on gas and motor oil dedicated to highway expenditures and to several school funds—are excluded from the expenditure limitation. The conventional wisdom has been that the state's expenditure levels were unaffected by the existence of the limit on their growth, at least in the 1982–83 biennium. The evaluation appears to be incorrect, however. The final budget for the two years was only $24 million below the limit, after several gubernatorial vetoes reduced the legislative version. In addition, a special legislative session held in June 1982 to appropriate funds for state college and university construction projects and for improvement to the state's overcrowded prison system spent exactly as much as was allowed under the spending limit. Since state tax collections have been growing at a faster rate than per capita personal income, the state has accumulated a sizable surplus that cannot be spent under the expenditure growth rate limit. The personal income-related spending limit has therefore superseded the older, revenue-based "pay-as-you-go" limitation.[10]

The budgetary constraints imposed by the expenditure growth limitation present a number of obstacles to state fiscal policies that are only beginning to be understood. For example, in 1979 the newly elected governor, William Clements, proposed a program of property tax relief for local governments, especially school districts, beyond that of the 1979 Tax Relief Amendment. This would have reduced school district taxes by an average of 19 percent, but did not pass because of its own complexity.[11] Such a measure would now be included under the expenditure limitation and is therefore unlikely in the near future. Similarly, should the state wish to compensate local governments and citizens for declining federal revenues, those expenditures would also be subject to inclusion in the general fund limitation.

There now appear to be only three mechanisms for circumventing the expenditure limit in

Texas, none of them promising. The first is to increase the number or amount of dedicated taxes. The trend in Texas in recent years has been away from dedicated taxes, however, to give the state legislature more control over biennial allocation decisions. The second is for a majority of both the Senate and the House to declare an "emergency," a resolution that permits overriding the limit; while this provides a simple and potentially routine escape mechanism, it would probably be politically difficult and has not yet been tried. The third possible mechanism is to increase nontax revenues, also excluded from the limitation. These include income from licenses, fees, and user charges, which are a relatively small source of funds for the state (3.9 percent of total revenues) and have been declining, and federal funds, which also have been reduced. Even though Texas, with its low reliance on federal aid, may lose relatively less from federal cuts than other states,[12] there will be little help from federal sources in evading the expenditure limit.[13]

Reductions in federal revenues may also cause the $80 million welfare expenditure limit in Texas to become binding. (This limitation also prohibits state expenditures for AFDC without federal matching funds, a provision that may be troublesome if President Reagan's proposed welfare "swap" is enacted.) Even with Texas' extremely low benefit levels, state officials estimate that this limit will be exceeded between 1983 and 1985. To avoid reaching the ceiling, a constitutional amendment has been proposed for voter approval in November 1982 that would replace the dollar ceiling with a limit of one percent of state expenditures. Based on the 1981 budget, this would total about $114 million, and would continue to increase as long as state expenditures increase. In the absence of any major changes, the higher limit is unlikely to result in significantly greater welfare expenditures. Texas is now ranked 49th among the states in AFDC expenditures for a family of four, testimony to its unwillingness to support welfare spending even though the current limitation has not yet been reached.[14] If federal funds are reduced further or the proposed "swap" is implemented, this may force a substitution of state for federal funds that would make the welfare ceiling a serious constraint.

Texas faces no real resource problems in the coming decades. Personal income is projected to grow at a higher rate than the national average over the next 20 years; population and manufacturing employment are expected to continue to increase, though at declining rates after 1990.[15] The exhaustion of gas and oil reserves probably won't affect severance tax collections until after the year 2000.[16] Evidently, expenditure limitations at the state level have reflected not any past or future fiscal strains, but a historic philosophy favoring low taxes, limited government, and individual self-sufficiency. Even as Texas has developed into a wealthy urban state with a diversified economic base, this philosophy has kept state expenditures more consistent with those of a poor rural state dependent upon agriculture. The result may be to constrain the state from meeting the legitimate demands for spending that may arise in the coming decades.

LOCAL RESOURCE LIMITATIONS

One future demand on the state may develop in the areas of fiscal assistance to local governments, which is currently almost nonexistent in Texas (except for school aid). The tradition of home rule and local control is powerful in Texas, and Texas municipalities are more free from state authority than are municipalities in any other state.[17] One consequence of local control, however, is that the state provides very little financial aid to local government. Nonschool aid in Texas comprises less than one percent of local government revenues, while across the country about 11 percent of local government revenues come from state noneducation grants.[18] Local governments have responsibility for most of the governmental services that support the state's growing population and economy, but have access to fewer revenue sources than many older industrial states.

Among local governments including school districts, own-source revenues account for about 56 percent of all funds; local taxes are 35 percent of the total. Use of local resources varies greatly among the localities, however. School districts, which receive the most state and federal aid, generate only 44 percent of total revenues from their own sources. Special districts, on the other hand, rely on taxes and user charges for 89 percent of their funds. The major local revenue sources are the property tax, comprising about 84 percent of local tax revenues, and the sales tax, which provides municipalities with about 30 percent of their tax revenues, but is unavailable to other local jurisdictions. Property taxes provide a higher percentage of revenue to Texas localities than to local governments across the nation (for whom property taxes comprise 76 percent of local tax collections), primarily because of the absence of local personal or corporate income taxes and a lower reliance on sales taxes in Texas.

Tax rates and spending in Texas local governments are characteristically conservative. Local tax revenues per capita in 1979–80 were $331 and expenditures per capita were $1,027 in the same year, compared to national averages of $381 and $1,143, respectively. These figures include education expenditures, which in Texas are slightly higher than average. As a result, nonschool spending in Texas at $586 per capita is considerably below the national average of $787. Again, low tax and expenditure policies in Texas are not the product of fiscal stringency, except in occasional situations, but of Texans' conservative attitudes toward government.

Texas cities have enjoyed relatively strong fiscal positions in the past decade, primarily because of their population and economic base growth and low unemployment rates.[19] Cities in Texas have broad powers of annexation, which have aided them in avoiding some of the difficulties of older cities elsewhere in the country which lost economic bases to suburban areas. Texas cities can annex up to 10 percent of their land area per year if it is included in their "extra-territorial jurisdiction" (ETJ), an area extending five miles beyond their boundaries for large, home-rule cities. Incorporations of independent cities within that ETJ are allowed only after the residents of the proposed new city have requested annexation by the larger city and have been refused. Once annexed, an area must be provided with city services within a reasonable time period.

Not all cities in Texas have enjoyed the tremendous growth and wealth of Dallas and Houston, however. El Paso has a per capita income below the national average and high unemployment. San Antonio has also suffered from low income and unemployment. A number of small cities near the Mexican border are also depressed and in relatively worse fiscal positions than their wealthy sisters. In addition, within the larger cities the concentrations of low income and minority populations typical of northern cities also exist. These groups have enjoyed few of the benefits of economic growth, and they appear to be increasingly concentrated in the large cities. For example, between 1970 and 1980 Dallas' population increased from 33 percent minority to almost 42 percent and Houston's increased from 38 to 45 percent.

While sales and property tax rates in Texas cities have remained relatively low, growth has led to booming real estate markets and retail sales, and tax collections have generally increased at a rate greater than inflation. Assessment practices, however, did not always allow local governments to benefit from the higher property values. Prior to 1979 each of the approximately 2,000 jurisdictions appraised property within its area separately, generally at a level far below market value. Assessment ratios were set by each jurisdiction, usually far below 100 percent of appraised value. The result was a nonsystem of tax assessments in which a single piece of property could be taxed on several different values by the overlapping jurisdictions in which it was situated, and in which assessment ratios varied wildly among jurisdictions and among types of property. In 1979, for example, assessment ratios for counties averaged 16 percent and ranged from 4 to 35 percent; ratios for school districts averaged 45 percent and ranged between 2 and 86 percent.[20] In 1979 the Texas legislature enacted a new property tax code which established each of the 254 counties as a tax appraisal district (effective January 1, 1982), charged with the task of uniformly appraising all property. All taxing jurisdictions were required to use those uniform values. The law also established assessment ratios at 100 percent of appraised value. Since the new appraisal districts have begun reassessments and have brought taxable values close to 100 percent of market value, the constitutional limitations on tax rates have become even less binding than previously.

Several other tax relief measures have been enacted in recent years, however, which do limit local governments' taxing and spending powers. The Tax Relief Amendment of 1978 created a series of exemptions and abatements to the property tax, applicable statewide. All homeowners were given a $5,000 exemption applicable to school district tax levies, raised to $15,000 for elderly or disabled homeowners. Elderly homeowners, in addition, have their school taxes frozen at 1979 levels as long as they occupy their homes.

Agricultural and timber land was granted preferential taxation at "agricultural use value" based upon income generated rather than market value. This provision was intended to institutionalize the widespread underappraisal that had been in effect prior to the reform. In 1981 voters approved another series of exemptions whose actual amounts are determined by local option, designed to ease the burden that reappraisals may cause under the new law. Exemptions are permitted in any fixed proportion up to 40 percent of market value in 1982–84, 30 percent from 1985–87, and 20 percent after that. Elderly and disabled homeowners may be given an additional $3,000 exemption.[21] Another local option established by the tax changes allows cities and towns to designate "reinvestment zones" in blighted areas beginning in 1982. In these zones cities have two options: tax abatement for property owners who make improvements in conformity with a comprehensive plan; and direct investment in the areas to provide amenities or improvements, using tax increment financing to repay municipal bonds issued for that purpose. At this time a few cities have established reinvestment zones, and others are being considered, but none has been fully implemented.

The agricultural use and homestead exemptions already appear to have reduced taxable value in some jurisdictions. A Property Tax Board study concluded that the agricultural use classification, when fully implemented, would remove about 15 percent of market values from the tax rolls. This especially affects urban and suburban areas in which nonresidential land had been taxed at market value, but numerous developers and speculators have also received agricultural use assessments.[22] In school districts, homestead exemptions reduced residential property values by about 20 percent in 1979, the first year they were available, and by almost 8 percent in 1980. The effects of the exemptions varied considerably throughout the state; in 1980 some districts removed almost nothing from the tax rolls while others lost up to 81 percent.[23]

The long-term effects of local exemption options, tax abatements in reinvestment zones, and tax increment financing of development cannot be evaluated yet, since only a few cities have acted upon their new options. All of these measures have the potential to erode significantly the property tax bases of local jurisdictions.

In 1978 and 1979 the Texas legislature enacted several other measures intended to increase citizen knowledge and control of local tax burdens, and to limit local government spending. The Truth in Taxation Act passed in 1978 requires local taxing units to publish notices of proposed property tax rates if increases over 3 percent are under consideration. A public hearing on the higher tax rate must be held prior to the open meeting in which the increase is voted upon. These provisions were intended to increase citizen participation and to make it more difficult for local governments to increase taxes. Further revisions enacted in 1979 and 1981 allow voters to petition for a tax rate rollback if an annual tax level increase is over 8 percent. If 10 percent of the required voters sign petitions within 90 days of the announcement of the tax increase, a referendum must be held. If it passes, the tax increase is reduced to 8 percent. Unlike the situation for local governments in many other states, Texas voters do not have to approve tax rate increases proposed by city councils or the governing bodies of other jurisdictions; only general obligation bond issues must be approved by the voters. The disclosure and referendum requirements therefore make local governments more vulnerable to citizen dissatisfaction with taxes.

Local governments have not been immune to citizen tax initiatives, however. Between 1979 and 1981 over a dozen tax limitation proposals were placed before the voters in Texas cities. Of these, provisions were adopted to limit taxes or tax rate increases in eight cities. Many of the initiatives followed massive property tax reappraisals. Because of Texas' low assessment ratios and the rapid growth in real estate prices, reappraisals had the effect of considerably increasing the tax bills of many homeowners. The new exceptions, which applied only on certain classes of property, and the traditionally higher assessments on commercial and business property added to the perceived inequities in the property tax, since middle-income homeowners seemed to face the highest increases. As a result, most initiatives were designed to limit annual increases in tax collections. Some proposals also attempted to reduce the actual tax rate, and a few limited annual expenditure growth. Several limitations required reappraisal of the entire city in order to increase individual property value, except for improvements to the property. This was intended to stop the alleged practice of reappraising the growing, affluent areas of cities more frequently than the poorer sections. The possibility that poor areas may not have increased in value as dramatically as wealthier neighborhoods did not deter the "reformers."

Until 1982, local tax limitations had greater success in smaller cities and suburbs than in large cities. Proposals to limit tax increases and reduce property tax rates failed in Fort Worth, Dallas, and Amarillo. In Houston a tax rate limit of 50 cents per $100 assessed value for operating expenditures passed in August 1982, after several previous proposals had failed. Between 1979 and 1982, initiatives also passed in Corpus Christi, Baytown, El Paso, Galveston, Grand Prairie, Irving, League City, Victoria, and West University Place. The election in Irving was later declared invalid because the measure—an 8 percent limit on annual property tax increases for any individual and a 6 percent limit on total property tax collection increases—interfered with the city's ability to repay bonded indebtedness in compliance with bond covenants. A similar proposal in Lubbock was also declared invalid, keeping it off the ballot. After these experiences, the proposals passed in Houston, and several other cities specifically exempted that part of the tax levy used to repay bonds; a few cities like El Paso, without such exemptions, may still face legal challenges to the tax limits.

While voters in Dallas and Fort Worth have rejected local tax limitations, such initiatives have been proposed in all large cities except San Antonio and Austin. Of the possible explanations for the lack of taxpayer resistance in these two cities, the presence of a city-owned utility is the most powerful: San Antonio's gas and electric utility provides 18 percent of the city's revenues (compared to 15 percent contributed by the property tax), while Austin's municipal utility contributes 24 percent of total revenue, again slightly higher than the 23 percent from the property tax.[24] State and federal government officials accuse Austin of using high utility rates to "tax" their exempt property. Both cities have relatively low property tax rates, and in addition San Antonio has not had a property tax reappraisal within the past several years because of a court order prohibiting reassessments. Thus the evidence confirms for Texas what others have concluded in other states: the culprit behind tax limitations seems to be the property tax, rather than all taxes, and the growth of property taxes, rather than their absolute level.

In response to taxpayer pressures, some city officials in Texas have begun to revise their budgeting practices, both to keep expenditures in line before taxpayers begin to complain and to induce greater accountability by city departments. In Dallas, for example, a major revaluation of property in 1980 and a recession-related decline in new construction growth caused large property tax increases, which in turn prompted taxpayers to propose reducing the tax rate from 56.6 cents per $100 valuation to 40 cents and to limit annual tax increases to 5 percent. Although both measures failed, the city council was already bound by its own Financial Management Performance Criteria, adopted several years before, which had generally prohibited tax increases over 5 percent annually. Since this limit proved too low in 1981, the city council raised it to 8 percent, a level that matches the state tax increase number that triggers taxpayer referenda.

The necessity to raise taxes after a long history of tax stability precipitated various changes in the city's budget process. In 1982 Dallas began converting its predominantly line-item budget to a program budget, based on program goals and service objectives. Performance indicators had been included in Dallas budgets for some years, giving the appearance of performance-oriented decision making. These measures were not used effectively, however, and were unavailable in some crucial areas because of an inadequate management information system. Dallas has had a sophisticated revenue forecasting system for four years, however.[25] The new budgeting system will be based upon an upgraded information collection and analysis effort, and will be integrated with a similarly program-oriented accounting system. Implementation will take several years. Both the new budgeting and accounting systems are intended to provide better information to the city manager and city council so they can avoid the problems they had in 1981 when, for the first time, tough budgetary decisions were required which included tax increases. City officials hope that by tying budget decision making to service delivery, the new budgeting format in Dallas will improve decision making and their ability to justify those decisions to taxpayers.

Similar changes have taken place in Austin. In contrast to Dallas and other major cities, citizen dissatisfaction in Austin has been expressed by rejection of bond proposals intended to fund maintenance and construction of growth-related infrastructure, rather than imposition of tax limits. Until 1982 the city's capital improvement budget was developed from requests submitted by city departments and various advisory boards, a process that denied citizens and neighborhood groups real participation and seemed to promote growth-related bonds despite fears that Austin's "quality of life" would suffer. In 1982 budget staff expanded the capital budget process to include greater participation of neighborhood groups and citizens through public meetings, a process that has so far generated much more favorable citizen reaction. A second modification of the capital budgeting process has been intended to improve the evaluation of all proposals. Capital projects are now scrutinized for conformity with the city's master plan. Austin's capacity to absorb and repay additional debt within the existing tax rate is also considered.

Improved analytical procedures have not been confined to capital budgeting. The city's operating budget process traditionally has been very detailed, allowing the city council to make budgetary decisions about administrative minutiae but with little program analysis. After a move to a modified zero-base format in 1980, which retained the detail of the previous line-item budget, the city budget staff, under the direction of a new city manager, is converting to a program budget. The new process is designed to shift the council's focus from object-of-expenditure details to decision making on broad policy issues and programmatic goals. The new budget procedures also incorporate five-year fiscal projections, which the budget office began developing in 1980 in response to property tax revisions and "Truth-in-Taxation" requirements. The city has continued to rely on fees and user charges, in addition to sales and property taxes, in order to keep taxes low. As in Dallas, Austin officials hope that the combination of a more analytic, program and service-oriented approach to budgeting and a more open, participatory decision process for capital projects will forestall taxpayer revolts and prevent future voter rejection of bonds.

The inability to persuade voters to pass growth-related bonds may have serious negative consequences for the structure of local government in Texas. In Austin, for example, one response to the city's inability to extend sewer and water services to developing areas in the city's "preferred growth corridor" was to approve the establishment of a special Municipal Utility District (MUD) to provide those utilities to the area. A MUD can issue revenue bonds to pay for its capital improvements, to be retired from utility fees. The city will assume responsibility for the bonds whenever the area is annexed to the city. Such utility districts, including many special purpose water districts, have proliferated in other high growth areas of the state, and are responsible for the fastest growing category of local government debt in Texas.[26]

Growing numbers of special districts, while not causing the problem of tax base loss that has been the result of suburban incorporation elsewhere, still create enormous problems, especially in planning development and managing water resources. In the Houston area, for example, the MUDs have posed new environmental threats by increasing the rate of subsidence in coastal areas, and there is some evidence that developers have cut corners in construction costs and hired incompetent operators, errors that may at some point saddle the MUDs (or the cities which annex them) with huge capital costs long after the developers have left.[27] Increased special district debt also competes for funds with debt issued by other local governments, and may contribute to increasing interest rates. Finally, the democratic mechanisms and accountability procedures of these quasi-governmental districts are weak at best, since the resident voters who approve MUDs are the relatively few people, often friends of the developer, who live in the undeveloped areas. If the democratic processes that result in tax referenda and bond election failures can be circumvented, as the utility districts allow, this may portend serious difficulties in governance and water resource management in the future.

Growth has been a mixed blessing for local governments in Texas. Local governments are under relatively strict fiscal constraints, although their economic growth rates are relatively high and current spending levels are low by national standards. Modernization of the property tax appraisal system and increases in property values have led to taxpayer revolts and the imposition of fiscal limitations on local governments. The "costs" of prosperity are being borne locally without additional state aid, but with state-imposed tax limitations, optional homestead exemptions, and other tax abatements that erode the tax base. Tax limitations and abatements have the potential for preventing municipalities from generating the additional revenue necessary to keep pace with population and employment growth, to build the infrastructure necessary for the growth, and to prevent the further fragmentation of local governments by the proliferation of special districts. The expenditure limitation at the state level also makes assistance from that source less likely, even though Texas enjoys healthy state surpluses. The tax and expenditure limitations have had some positive consequences for Texas local governments, however. They have stimulated some cities to develop more participatory decision processes and have stimulated more careful, analytic approaches to budgeting. As a result, these cities may be better equipped to respond to fiscal challenges in the future.

LONE STAR LESSONS

Several conclusions emerge from this brief survey of Texas' response to resource limitations. First, budgetary and tax restraints do not necessarily occur only in situations of resource scarcity or high public spending. The tradition of fiscal conservatism and distrust of government in Texas has led to voluntary constraints, even though these may result in unspent surpluses at the state level and reduce the state's ability to respond to such changes as reduced federal funding and demands for property tax relief.

Second, at the local level the cities least affected by expenditure limits have been those funded by a broader base of revenue sources than the typical sales and property tax combination. City-owned utilities and broad use of fees and charges have made several cities less vulnerable to property tax limitations and voter dissatisfaction. Another factor diffusing voter dissent has been the stability of tax assessments in several cities that have not recently revalued property. As these cities begin to experience countywide reappraisals, their resistance to taxpayer initiatives may fall.

Third, the new constraints felt by city officials have resulted in a shift in budget processes. A movement away from control-oriented budget formats to those more amenable to broad policy and planning decisions has followed the imposition of local and statewide tax and expenditure limits. Although control is still necessary, these new budget processes should provide additional program and performance information with which city councils can make taxing and spending decisions; they are also designed to include taxpayers in some budgetary decisions to avoid further revolts.

Finally, the taxpayer rejection of bond issues and other constraints on capital improvement funds, including high interest rates on tax-exempt securities, may result in further fragmentation by way of special districts. Special districts may not dilute municipal tax bases as severely as suburbanization has elsewhere, but they tend to reduce the power of voters to determine their own tax and expenditure policies.

Texas has few revenue difficulties at present, except in isolated instances. There is potential, however, for future problems. Oil and gas revenues will begin to fall in the 1990s; some substitute for one-quarter of the state's tax collections will eventually need to be found. Local governments have few sources of revenue available, and state aid is made more difficult by limitations on expenditure growth. Federal fund reductions will affect Texas less than other states, but both local governments and the state welfare agency are constrained in their ability to make up the differences. Losses in areas such as welfare, transportation, and urban development grants may cause particular problems in the large cities.

The most serious problem created by the state and local limitations may not be strictly fiscal, however. These constraints, intended to maintain Texas' popular low tax and expenditure position, impose a rigidity on governmental activities that may become a serious future obstacle to responsible government. A proliferation of special districts at the local level reduces the flexibility of general-purpose local governments to respond to citizen needs; tax and spending limits have similar results. A strong state fiscal position that cannot be used to aid local governments or provide service increases in other needed areas because of an expenditure limitation does little to make government responsive or responsible. By curtailing its flexibility to adapt to the changing needs of its growing economy and population, Texas may have restrained not only its finances but also its potential for future development.

NOTES

1. Peter Wilson, "The Future of Dallas's Capital Plant," *America's Urban Capital Stock,* Vol. 4 (Washington, D.C.: The Urban Institute, 1980), pp. 41–42.

2. Clifton McClesky, Allan Butcher, Daniel E. Farlow, and J. Pat Stephens, *The Government and Politics of Texas,* 6th ed. (Boston: Little, Brown & Co., 1978), pp. 25–26.

3. Fiscal year 1981 figures are taken from the Comptroller of Public Accounts, *Annual Financial Report of 1981, State of Texas* (Austin: Office of the Comptroller, November 2, 1981). Earlier figures are from the U.S. Bureau of the Census, *State Tax Collections in 1971* (Washington, D.C.: U.S. Government Printing Office, 1971).

4. U.S. Bureau of the Census, *State Government Tax Collections in 1980,* Government Finances, Series GF80, No. 1 (Washington, D.C.: U.S. Government Printing Office, 1980), Tables 3 and 4.

5. *Tax Capacity of the Fifty States: Methodology and Estimates* (Washington, D.C.: Advisory Commission on Intergovernmental Relations, March 1982), Table 3, pp. 20–21.

6. Ibid., Table 7, pp. 44–45.

7. Stephen McDonald, "Who Pays Texas' Oil Severance Tax Now?" *Texas Business Review,* Vol. 54, No. 6 (November/December 1980), pp. 309–311.

8. For a more complete description of the Texas budget process, see Beryl E. Pettus and Randall W. Bland, *Texas Government Today,* rev. ed. (Homewood, Ill.: The Dorsey Press, 1979), pp. 338–349.

9. For the different calculations of possible growth rates, see Legislative Budget Board, "Tax Relief Amendment Implementation: Limit on Growth of Certain State Expenditures," *Texas Register,* Vol. 5, No. 8 (October 28, 1980), pp. 4272–4279. The range of estimates—from 24.9 percent to 33.9 percent—mattered considerably because the expenditure limit calculated by the highest and lowest limit differed by about $1 billion, or about 7 percent of state expenditure under the limit actually chosen.

10. Information on the operation of the spending limitations was obtained from Jack Huffman, Legislative Budget Board, and William C. Hamilton, Governor's Office of Budget and Planning.

11. Information on the relief measures was obtained from Tim Lewis, Governor's Office of Budget and Planning.

12. In 1979–80, Texas' per capita federal aid was $264.39, compared to the national average of $336.56. *Governmental Finances in 1979–80,* Table 24, pp. 90–99.

13. While Texas will suffer less than other states in the aggregate, the concentration of federal grants in precisely those areas where Texans have been the most reluctant to appropriate their own funds: welfare programs, social services, and education for pupils with special needs, means that these areas are likely to be more severely cut in Texas than in other states. On the dominance of federal funds in Texas, particularly for those programs benefiting poor children, see W. Norton Grubb, Patricia Griffin Heilbrun, and Christine Galavotti, *Far, Far to Go: Public Expenditures for Children and Youth in Texas* (Austin: LBJ School of Public Affairs, 1982).

14. See *Social Security Bulletin* 45 (June 1982), Table M-34 for December 1980 figures.

15. Thomas Plaut, "A Supply-Side Model of the Texas Economy: Detailed Forecasts to the Year 2000," *Texas Business Review,* Vol. 56, No. 2 (March/April 1982), pp. 49–55.

16. Texas Research League, "Public Revenues from Oil and Natural Gas in Texas: What Lies Ahead?" (Austin: Texas Research League, May 1982), pp. 23–20, and *passim.*

17. Advisory Commission on Intergovernmental Relations, *State and Local Roles in the Federal System* (Washington, D.C.: U.S. Government Printing Office, April 1982), Table 106, p. 262.

18. All data on local revenues and expenditure patterns are taken from the Bureau of the Census, *Governmental Finances in 1979–80,* since there are no other reliable sources of centrally collected information on local government finance in Texas.

19. See, for example, "Fiscal Trends in Large Texas Cities," *Fiscal Notes,* Texas Office of the Comptroller, Vol. 82, No. 1, December 1981; and Joseph Pluta, "Urban Fiscal Strain and the Health of Large Texas Cities," *Texas Business Review,* Vol. 53, No. 1 (January–February 1979), pp. 8–12.

20. *Assessment Practices of Texas School Districts, Counties, and Cities, 1979* (Austin: Texas Research League, March 1981). The data underlying this report, provided by the School Tax Assessment Practices Board (now the State Property Tax Board), comprise the only information available on assessment rates. These data may be inadequate, however, because the board lacks sufficient personnel to perform serious checks on local appraisers.

21. The structure of exemptions is more complex than described here. For more details, see the "Taxpayers' Rights, Remedies, Responsibilities!" published by the State Property Board and included in the *State Property Tax Board Statement,* Vol. 4, No. 7 (January 1982).

22. Daniel Brody, "Property Taxes: Relief, Reform . . . Revolt?" House Study Group Special Report No. 61, Texas House of Representatives, November 10, 1980. See pp. 86–93 for details of extraordinarily high exemptions under the agricultural use provisions, and pp. 98–100 for a discussion of the impact on school districts of the homestead and other exemptions.

23. Brody, op. cit., pp. 98–100. See also *Annual Report for Texas Year 1980* (Austin: State Property Tax Board, August 1981), Appendix C, "School District Report Data: 1980."

24. Information on city finances was obtained in interviews with budget and finance officials: David Black and Jan Hart, Dallas; Robert Gable, El Paso; Stu Summers, San Antonio; and Frank Rodriguez, Austin.

25. See Roy Bahl, Larry Schroeder, and C. Kurt Zorn, "Local Government Revenue and Expenditure Forecasting: Dallas, Texas," Occasional Paper No. 49 (Syracuse: Metropolitan Studies Program, The Max-

well School of Citizenship and Public Affairs, Syracuse University, August 1981), for a description of this process and its development in 1978.

26. Texas Municipal Advisory Service, *Public Debt in Texas, 1980,* Special Report No. 140, p. 2.

27. For a more thorough discussion of development districts in Texas and their possible consequences, see Virginia Lacy Perrenod, "Urban Fringe Special Districts Along the Upper Texas Gulf Coast: Accountability and Impact Upon the Environment," *Public Affairs Comment,* Vol. 27, No. 4 (August 1981).

CHAPTER 28

BUDGETING RIGHTS
The Case of Jail Litigation

JEFFREY D. STRAUSSMAN AND KURT THURMAIER

Judicial decisions are one element in the erosion of state and local government discretion. Litigation has included public personnel practices, environment policies, the liability of public employees, school desegregation and the constitutional rights of persons who are institutionalized in state and local facilities such as prisons, psychiatric centers, and institutions for the developmentally disabled. The budgetary significance of these rulings has not been sufficiently documented. While a few cost "guestimates" have been made about the administrative consequences of judicial decisions, the impact on local government discretion is more subtle than a cost estimate.[1] This article examines the impact of litigation concerning constitutional rights violations on the local budgetary process. The thesis is that the presence, or the threat, of this litigation alters the strategy and behavior of the participants in the budget process by shaping choices and narrowing options. This argument is illustrated with a case study of jail litigation in a single local government. The argument is then extended beyond the specific case to suggest how judicial activity, in general, is likely to affect the local government budgetary process.

JAIL LITIGATION AND THE PUBLIC PURSE STRINGS

An Overview

According to a 1982 National Sheriff's Association survey, of 2,664 jails responding, 285 were under court orders, 423 had been under court orders, and 529 were engaged in litigation at the time of the survey.[2] Plaintiffs frequently alleged that inmate overcrowding and/or the general conditions in local jails violated the eighth and fourteenth amendments of the Constitution of the United States. While the specific violations naturally varied from lawsuit to lawsuit, a common remedy sought—a reduction in overcrowding—encourages public officials to expand capacity. This is done in one of three basic ways: by building new facilities or expanding existing ones; by converting facilities originally designed for other purposes; or by placing prisoners in the jails of other jurisdictions.

If two things are reasonably clear about local jails and local budgets, they are: the cost of jails is high and jails are not a high priority for local political leaders. An Advisory Commission on Inter-governmental Relations (ACIR) study, now somewhat dated, reported that the cost of construction per bed in the northeast between 1978 and 1982 was $37,200. Operating expenditures per inmate in fiscal year 1977 were $5,253.[3] These capital and operating costs are probably underestimates for reasons other than the obvious inflationary adjustments that must be made to obtain current cost estimates of jail expansion. For example, total wage and non-wage compensation of new personnel should be added to capital cost projections since additional capacity will require more staff. Hidden costs of incarceration, including public assistance payments to families of inmates and lost taxes to state and local governments, would increase the full cost of incarceration.[4] Capital estimates invariably underestimate the inflationary costs of delay that accompany the political conflict over when and where to build.[5]

The politically acceptable price tag of incarceration, however, may well be lower than the real cost of maintaining a jail that satisfies constitutionally acceptable minimum standards. After all, inmates are not a preferred constituency group. Elected officials are often faced with the prospect of demonstrating the incompatible—that they are tough on law and order and, simultaneously, fiscally prudent. This means that jail administrators will have a dif-ficult budgetary obstacle to overcome when chief executives and local legislators divide the pie among education, parks and recreation, roads, police and the local jail. Few would be surprised to learn that the jail is frequently the budgetary loser. But is this an axiom of local government budgeting?

Not necessarily. Perhaps a subtle paradox exists in the local government budgetary process where some managers are better off—in a budgetary sense—when their discretion is seemingly eroded. Better off in this context means receiving budgetary resources greater than would other-wise had been the case in the absense of a lawsuit. Erosion of discretion refers to the restriction of options available to the public manager who must make budgetary choices. To explore this proposition, the next section of this article presents a model of the impact of litigation on the local budget process and interprets the plausibility of the model through a case study of jail litigation in a single county.

Loss of Budgetary Discretion: A Model

What happens when a defendant government agency loses a lawsuit and the court orders that un-constitutional conditions must be corrected? Phillip J. Cooper, in his book, *Hard Judicial Choices* presents a "decree litigation model" which outlines the major phases cases pass through when plaintiffs seek equitable relief from alleged unconstitutional conditions.[6] First, the case is triggered by an event or a threshold. The latter may be a level of overcrowding deemed intolerable by an advocacy group. Second, the judge must find the defendant liable; otherwise, the case would end at this stage. Third, the judge, in negotiation with both the plaintiffs and the defendants, fashions a remedy to the unconstitutional conditions. Fourth, in the post decree stage the remedy is refined and implemented.[7] The model, straightforward and parsimonious, provides a very useful way to track an equitable decree case in progress.

Consider a hypothetical case at the beginning stage of the remedy phase of the model—the phase where negotiation may unfold as a three-person game with the defendant agency, the court and the legislature. The judge wants compliance with the decision with minimal intervention in the actual administrative details of implementation. Despite criticisms of the so-called "imperial judiciary," judges have, by and large, recognized the inherent limitations of judicial intervention in the administration of government agencies and have therefore approached such intervention gingerly.[8] What will be the impact of the remedy to constitutional rights violations on the local budget? We expect the litigation to force a series of decisions that allocate resources to the rights-based population. Two corollaries follow:

1. Rights-based allocation decisions narrow the budgetary discretion of budget makers.
2. Paradoxically, some managers are "better off"—defined as the ability to protect and defend their budgets—when this discretion is reduced.

The hypothesis and corollaries presume the unfettered implementation of judicial remedies. But the likelihood of uncomplicated compliance is probably going to depend on factors that pertain directly to the agency and the legislature. These will include: (1) policy agreement with the suit by the relevant public officials such as the chief executive, key members of the legislative body, and appointed officials such as the administrator of the jail, (2) the fiscal condition of the jurisdiction, and (3) the passage of time from the trigger phase to the remedy phase. We expect these factors to interact so that, even in a relatively healthy fiscal climate, policy agreement with the suit will deteriorate as the time between the trigger phase and the remedy phase lengthens. The reason for this expectation is that time allows other options to surface. But is this expectation borne out in practice? We answer this question through an analysis of a case study of jail litigation in a county government and then suggest alternative interpretations of the impact of litigation on the local budgetary process.

Jail Litigation Comes to Standard County

The Public Safety Building (PSB) of the Standard County Sheriff Department includes the county's jail. The state Commission on Corrections established a rated capacity of 212 for the facility. According to guidelines established by the National Correctional Association, a local jail should not exceed 90 percent of its rated capacity so that professional criteria regarding the classification of detainees can be followed. Standard County was unable to satisfy this 90 percent guideline. The inmate population has increased from about 5,000 in 1983 to over 8,000 in 1986.[9] [See Figure 28.1.]

While the causes of this increase are not entirely clear, some of the increase is attributed to state prisoners that were temporarily housed in local jails to manage the state's overcrowding problem. Moreover, between 1982 and 1985 the county accepted prisoners from other counties in the state because they provided much needed revenues from a full charge-back system.

The jail division budget has followed an incremental pattern [see Figure 28.2]. Increases over a ten-year period ranged from three percent to over 19 percent, but actual expenditures in 1988 were actually less than in 1987. The chief of jail administration was well aware of the incremental pattern of the division's budget. What concerned him was his inability to apply professional jail management procedures to a facility that was overcrowded.

In 1985 a staff attorney from a nearby law school, with the assistance of law students, brought suit against Standard County for operating a jail that purportedly violated the plaintiffs' rights under the first, fourth, fifth, sixth, eighth, ninth and fourteenth amendments of the Constitution of the United States. The major part of the suit focused on jail overcrowding. While the legal arguments mirrored the general conditions corrections cases such as *Bell v. Wolfish* 441 U.S. 520 (1979) and *Rhodes v. Chapman* 452 U.S. 337 (1981), the immediate objective, according to the staff attorney, was to "get the inmates off the floor." The longer term objective was to force the

Figure 28.1   **Annual Total Admissions to County Jail**

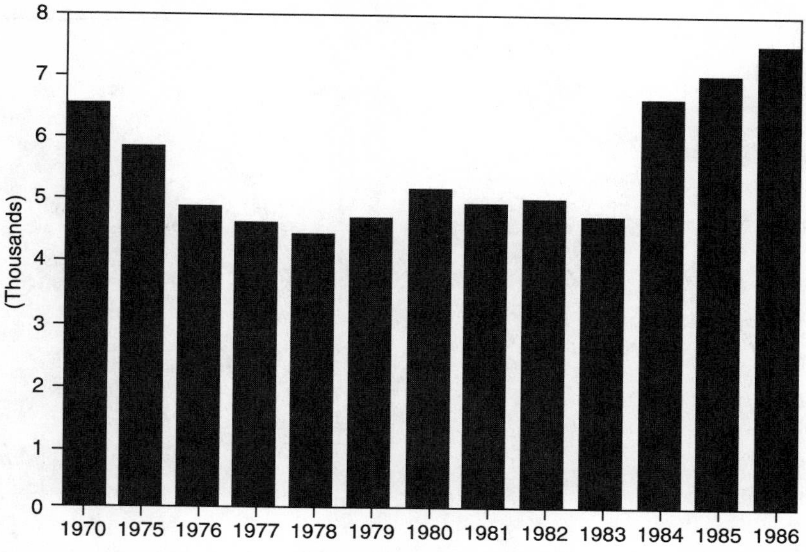

county to file a plan with the court detailing how the jail would be brought in line with constitutional safeguards.

There were clear differences of opinion among county personnel concerning the, litigation. The chief of jail administration welcomed the suit.[10] From his vantage point, he was in a "no-lose" situation. Since the jail was not a politically popular agency, he believed that it would take something like the overcrowding suit to force the county, especially a reluctant legislature, to develop and finance a viable option to the current untenable situation.

The budget director, interestingly, did not see the situation as primarily a budget issue.[11] In his words, it was a "social issue." While somewhat vague about what this meant, the budget director felt that the overcrowding issue was essentially part of a conservative drift toward law and order. This drift produced more inmates, pure and simple. While the budget director did not say that he welcomed the suit he observed that, since government operates on crises, the court would force action. He hoped that the judge would allow the county to develop a sensible solution to the overcrowding problem.

An assistant to the county executive took a somewhat different interpretation. Subtly critical of the elected sheriff, the assistant suggested that the overcrowding conditions were worsened by the non-county prisoners who were housed in the jail to generate revenues. In her view, the overcrowding suit might not have occured if the revenue strategy had not been pursued. She was also not persuaded that the current overcrowding was a chronic rather than a short-term phenomenon. Inmate projections and changing policy perspectives were, from her vantage point, most uncertain.[12]

Meanwhile, the litigation unfolded. In 1986 the state Department of Corrections removed all but ten state-ready prisoners. Although non-county inmates were no longer brought to the facility, the prisoner count at the jail on June 27, 1987 was 292, far above the rated capacity of 212. A court appointed master kept the judge informed about the county's progress in complying with the order to reduce overcrowding. The judge set an interim target of 248 and threatened to impose a fine of

Figure 28.2   **Jail Budget: Annual Percentage Increase Over Previous Actual**

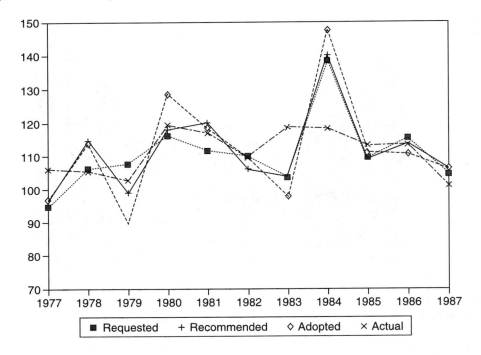

$5,000 per day for each prisoner above this mandated number. There was skepticism, however, about the seriousness of this threat since the judge did not provide an unequivocal deadline. Some county officials felt that the judge would not impose the fine if he could be satisfied that the county was making good faith efforts to rectify the problem.

In December 1987, the county and the plaintiffs were back in court. The county argued that an architectural study commissioned by the legislature and a $290,000 appropriation to convert the jail's gymnasium into 48 temporary cells were evidence of good faith efforts to resolve the overcrowding issue. The judge altered his threatened fines to a daily fine of between $1,000 and $10,000 a day for every prisoner above the rated capacity if the count was above the rated capacity for four consecutive days. The judge demanded an interim plan by March 15, 1988 and a permanent solution to the overcrowding problem by November 1, 1988. His reluctance to impose the fines may have been a combination of judicial restraint and an acknowledgement that the county was taking some steps to reduce overcrowding at the jail.

INTERPRETATIONS

The jail litigation case initially progressed according to the decree litigation model outlined earlier. The decision was triggered by the public interest law firm's suit. The conditions were ripe for a constitutional challenge since the average daily inmate count was well above the rated capacity. Moreover, since there was a proliferation of jail overcrowding cases around the country, the legal issues were routine. Yet, while liability was readily determined by the judge, fashioning a remedy has been a slow process. Why? The answer to this tells us a great deal about the impact of constitutional rights litigation on resource allocation in particular, and local public management in general.

The Crisis Technique

While the chief of the jail division agreed with the policy direction of the suit, it is by no means clear that all of the relevant parties did. Moreover, the fiscal climate was not conducive to significant capital spending given other projects. What budgetary tactic seemed appropriate? The suit illustrates Aaron Wildavsky's "crisis technique" where program advocates proclaim that a changed condition necessitates increased spending.[13] However, there is some difference of opinion about the effectiveness of the technique in the jail litigation case.

The budget director seemed undaunted by the suit. Recall that, while he thought that a "crisis" was often necessary to move government toward the resolution of a problem, he took the long view of the litigation. In other words, he saw the case as simply one piece of a larger cyclical pattern in criminal justice. While the litigation might influence some activity that otherwise might not have occurred, he believed that government officials needed to develop a more coherent criminal justice policy. This approach—stepping back from the immediate crisis and assessing the big picture—certainly does not stimulate quick action.

The county executive's assistant was not persuaded by the inmate population estimates, nor did she believe that the legislature would finance a major capital expansion to eliminate overcrowding. While not saying so directly, she seemed undaunted by the judicial threats and may have been willing to entertain a bit of judicial brinksmanship, testing the limits of the judge's patience with the county.

Interviews with key legislators suggest a difference of opinion regarding the value of the crisis technique. While the minority leader and the chairman of the public safety committee both felt that the chief of the jail division was acting appropriately by emphasizing the overcrowding problem and the need to address it even before the suit, the current majority leader of the legislature was not convinced that the problem is a long-term chronic one that requires major new capital expenditures.

Uncertainty

Even with a moderate amount of policy agreement among the major participants, there is a great deal of uncertainty. Some of the uncertainty comes from the information asymmetry between the agency head and the legislature. Scholars who take a public choice perspective on budgetary decision making would expect the manager to have an advantage in budgetary negotiations since the agency head has a monopoly of information.[14]

Consider estimates of jail capacity independent of the litigation. The jail administrator, when interviewed, suggested a rough compounding model of prisoner growth. He argued that the population would almost double in about eight years and claimed that this would occur despite the vigorous use of alternatives to incarceration. But he offered no data to substantiate his claim. A credible long-term forecast does not, in fact, exist.[15]

One prominent legislator suggested that the case for expansion was not adequately made. To compound the issue, estimates of the inmate population are sensitive to two major factors outside the control of county decisionmakers: intergovernmental factors, and sentencing patterns. Intergovernmental factors include both the capacity of the state prisons and state mandates. For example, current state procedure requires a minimum ninety-day incarceration for parole violators. Sentencing patterns reflect such things as conventional thinking on punishment, changing state laws, and prison capacity.

The Capital Spending Analysis

As a capital spending decision the jail litigation presents an interesting dilemma. The chief of jail Administration claims that the county should build a 200-cell expansion. His argument is based on the above claim of inmate growth and professional standards regarding proper inmate classification. He adds an interesting wrinkle to his argument. Essentially, he says that the expansion could be financed, at least in part, by revenues generated by housing non-county prisoners as in the pre-litigation period. This would include revenues from both the state and federal governments as well as prisoners from other local government jails. Of course, this scenario assumes that the inmate population will continue to grow throughout the state and, furthermore, that there will continue to be a shortage of cell space in other jurisdictions.

Delay

Legislators have a hedging orientation when it comes to a capital decision with little or no political benefits. Since the policy agreement with the intent of the suit is at best mixed, the interaction of the three variables—policy agreement, fiscal climate, and timing—predicts that political leaders will delay action to avoid a decision that has no obvious political advantages and clear budgetary costs. Funds spent on alleviating overcrowding in the jail are funds foregone for more politically desirable programs. Do the benefits of delay outweigh the costs?

To answer this question it is necessary to distinguish operating costs from capital costs. The operating costs of the jail continued to increase largely due to overtime pay for jail personnel necessitated by the growing jail population. The proposal to expand cell space through a capital project also involves a substantial increase in operating costs. The legislature would have to add new positions to the sheriff department; maintenance and utility costs would similarly increase. The jail administrator's proposal for offsetting some of the capital expansion costs with revenues from non-county prisoners housed in excess cell space is based on untested assumptions about state-wide prisoner populations and future decisions of other governments.

Alternatively, if an expansion is not undertaken or is slow in coming and the jail population continues to climb as estimated by the jail administrator, the operating costs will surely go up. In particular, the county will be forced to house prisoners in other jurisdictions. This cost is in addition to any penalties that may be imposed by the court.

A Game of Judicial "Chicken"

The game of judicial chicken revolves around the county's estimate of the probability that the judge will impose the fines. So far two court imposed deadlines have come and gone without the imposition of fines. Shouldn't this increase legislative budgetary foot-dragging? A positive answer assumes that the only objective is budgetary and the county, especially legislators, are inclined to analyze the options in narrow cost-benefit terms. Moreover, the judicial chicken image implies one-dimensional judicial negotiation: that is, the threat of fines is the only mechanism available to force compliance with the overcrowding decision. In general, as the time horizon between the trigger phase of the litigation and a potential remedy expands, the prospects for some policy agreement should erode. But, in this case, delay may not produce this expected outcome since the jail population shows no signs of decline.

Judicially Induced "Preference Revelation"

What do legislators really want to do in regard to the jail overcrowding problem? One legislator said that they will do the "right" thing. But the history of constitutional rights violations and the extensive and protracted remedial decrees that have been fashioned to implement judicial decisions show that it is extremely difficult to translate intentions into action.[16] In effect, the judge's difficult task is to extract from the defendant government a position that meets the legal requirements as established in the liability test and, at the same time, is also feasible from a political perspective.

Judges are not, of course, bound by defendant claims about implementation obstacles. For example, a jurisdiction's inability to finance improvements required to remedy unconstitutional conditions has been rejected as a defense.[17] Nevertheless, there is likely to be some political tolerance that is related to the impact of the scope of the decree on the jurisdiction.[18] In the jail overcrowding case there is some disagreement about the consequences of the litigation. One legislator offered the standard legislator's dilemma: the public wants a tough law-and-order position—keep them off the streets—but does not want to finance jail expansion.[19] The minority leader of the county legislature agreed. Absent the law suit, jail overcrowding was a low political priority since there are no major advocates to alleviate the problem. Moreover, the issue, in his view, has a political cost because the financial impact of corrective action will fall directly on the county tax rate.[20] Taking the high political road, the new chairman of the legislature said that legislators will not hide behind the judge if expansion was necessary. In his view the legislature will appropriate funds for cell expansion if that is the best way to resolve the overcrowding issue. On the other hand, he voiced the most skepticism over whether capital expansion was really needed. While he did not think that the judge's actions have been unfair, he had a cautious approach to meeting the requirements of the order. In his view, a modest expansion may alleviate over-crowding and thereby staisfy the judge. However, he also entertained the option of housing prisoners outside the county and reimbursing another jurisdiction when the maximum capacity was exceeded.[21]

Evolution of Cooperation or the Erosion of Discretion?

Did the suit make a difference? It is difficult to put this concept into operation. One way to do this is to ask whether policy and budgetary conditions have changed in the post-suit period. Consider, first, the daily jail inmate count. Between February 1985 and January 1986, the daily jail population exceeded the judge's limit of 248 prisoners 55 percent of the time, and there were no days where the daily population was below the rated capacity of 212. After the judge imposed the 248 limit early in 1986, however, it is clear that the daily jail population dropped considerably. Not only was the county within the rated capacity almost 40 percent of the year, the judge's maximum limit of 248 was only exceeded on 23 days in the first six-month period. Yet, by the next six-month period, the number of days in violation of the judge's maximum doubled to 52 and the population was only within the rated capacity for 6 days of the year. The data indicate that the population reduction had only been temporary and it was unlikely that the daily count population count would be within the 212 prisoner capacity. This increase in the average daily count suggests that the response to the litigation was, at best, partial.

Some additional spending could be tied directly to the suit. Additional personnel was added to the Sheriff Department, the jail study was commissioned by the legislature, and the jail's gymnasium was converted into forty-eight temporary cells. These expenditures would likely not have occurred without the law suit.

What were the perceptions of the interviewees? The budget director said that the suit brought the pressure always needed to move a sensitive issue, in his opinion. The chief of jail administration felt that no action on the overcrowding issue would have been taken without the litigation. All of the legislators interviewed similarly agreed that the suit was crucial in forcing action.

But can the null hypothesis be rejected? Could it be said that litigation forced decisions that would not have occurred in the absence of litigation? Perhaps in this case study the budget is little more than an incremental process. County officials, particularly the legislature, may decide to expand current jail capacity because of an assessment of need caused by overcrowding independent of the litigation.

The null hypothesis cannot be tested directly; nevertheless, there is evidence in support of the alternative hypothesis. First, the legislators interviewed claimed that they were well aware of the overcrowding situation before the litigation was initiated. Second, the chairman of the legislature claimed that the suit hastened legislative action by 12 to 24 months.

Obviously, the implication is that the legislature would have responded to the overcrowding problem without the suit. On the other hand, the Minority Leader believes that the threat of fines was necessary to raise the political salience of jail overcrowding. And the pressure of judicial timetables keeps the issue high on the political agenda. Surely from the vantage point of political process the case makes a difference. Whether the budget will look different from what it would be without the suit is a question that is not easily answered.

THE LARGER QUESTION

What is the impact of constitutional rights litigation on local government budgeting? Under certain circumstances the litigation may bolster the position of budgetary claimants. This is surely one of the consequences of the jail litigation case. The chief of jail administration was in an improved strategic position as a result of the suit since the jail was formerly a low political priority. Administrators will rarely openly admit that they welcome a suit against their agency. In some situations a suit may not be advantageous. A suit may force the earmarking of appropriations that is at odds with the administrator's preferences. For example, a judge may require a given staffing ratio when the administrator is negotiating capital, or non-personnel expenditures. Still, the case study shows that, under some conditions, litigation could enhance an administrator's negotiating posture.

At root, constitutional rights violation cases erode budgetary discretion, much in the way that a mandate may force a local government to do what it may not be inclined to do. Local officials may do the "right" thing. That is, they may take steps to alleviate jail overcrowding. The history of institutional litigation at the state level in corrections and mental retardation suggests otherwise. Voluntary compliance does not fit the facts of most institutional litigation cases; state agencies were compelled to redress unconstitutional conditions.

This leads us to a paradoxical conclusion. Rights-based budgeting drives out discretion since court decisions mortgage future budgetary increments. This is anathema to budgeteers who thrive on trade-offs and jealously guard any residue of flexibility that can be garnered in a process increasingly prone toward formula-based decisions.[22] Rights and allocation decisions do not easily co-exist.

Where is the paradox? The resolution of constitutional rights cases may lead to spending decisions that would not occur in the absence of litigation. When this happens budgetary discretion is circumscribed. Yet, it is precisely this erosion of discretion that may be necessary to provide the budgetary support for rights protection. It is in this sense that the courts have become silent partners in the budgetary process.

NOTES

1. The budgetary dimension of judicial decisions was first raised by George Hale. See his "The Federal Courts and the State Budgetary Process, *Administration and Society* 11 (Nov. 1979): 357–368. For an application to prisons see Linda Harriman and Jeffrey D. Straussman, "Do Judges Determine Budget Decisions? Federal Court Decisions in Prison Reform and State Spending for Corrections," *Public Administration Review* 43 (July/Aug. 1983): 343–351.

2. Cited in Anne Bolduc, "Jail Crowding," *The Annals* 478 (March 1985): 48.

3. Advisory Commission On Intergovernmental Relations, *Jails: Intergovernmental Dimensions Of A Local Problem* (Washington, D.C.: ACIR, May 1984), 28–29.

4. Todd R. Clear and Patricia M. Harris, "The Costs of Incarceration," *America's Correctional Crisis*. Stephen D. Gottredson and Sean McConville, eds. (New York: Greenwood Press, 1987), 40–41.

5. Ibid., 41.

6. Phillip J. Cooper, *Hard Judicial Choices* (New York: Oxford University Press, 1988), 16.

7. Ibid., 16–24.

8. For the "imperial judiciary" criticism see Nathan Glazer, "Towards an Imperial Judiciary?" *The Public Interest* 41 (Fall 1975): 104–123. Cooper's in-depth case studies show that federal district court judges are well aware of the problems of intervention in administration and do so reluctantly.

9. The following case study is based on events that occurred in a county government in the northeastern section of the United States. While the name of the jurisdiction has been changed, the case description reflects that chronology of events up to June 1988. Exactly how the judge's decision should be implemented is still a matter of political controversy and negotiation. In addition, while the usual caveats about the limitations of a case study methodology applies, we have no reason to believe that this case—and the political ramifications surrounding implementation—differs substantially from the large number of jail litigation cases where the substance is the alleged unconstitutional conditions in the facility.

10. Interview, 3 Nov. 1987.

11. Interview, 30 Nov. 1987. The budget director interviewed was the director during the period of jail overcrowding and the initiation of the litigation. Following an election for County Executive in November 1987 he was replaced, though he still holds a position as of this date in county government.

12. Interview, 30 Nov. 1987. This individual did not join the new administration.

13. Aaron Wildavsky, *The New Politics of the Budgetary Process* (Glenview, IL: Scott, Foresman and Company, 1988), 117.

14. The classic description of this situation is William A. Niskanen, Jr., *Bureaucracy and Representative Government* (Chicago: Aldine, 1971).

15. Forecasting prison population is a hazardous enterprise. See A. Blumstein, J. Cohen, and H. Miller, "Demographically Disaggregated Projections of Prison Populations," *Journal of Criminal Justice* 8 (1980): 1–25.

16. This is surely one conclusion that one could derive from Phillip Cooper's analysis of five cases where federal judges had to fashion remedial decrees. See Cooper, *Hard Judicial Choices,* 328–350.

17. See, for example, *Gates v. Collier,* 390 F. Supp 482 (1975); *Benjamin* v. *Malcolm, 495* F. Supp. 1363.

18. See Cooper, 336–344.

19. Interview, 13 Dec. 1987.

20. Interview, 4 Feb. 1988.

21. Interview, 4 Feb. 1988.

22. For an extended discussion of formula budgeting, see Eric Hanushek, "Formula Budgeting: The Economics and Analytics of Fiscal Policy Under Rules," *Journal of Policy Analysis and Management* 6 (Fall 1986): 3–19.

PART 6

PRIVATIZATION AND CONTRACTING

One of the long lasting effects of Proposition 13 in California and Proposition 2½ in Massachusetts was to usher in a period of revenue constraint, of elected officials' extreme reluctance to raise taxes and strong desire to lower them. Since this desire was not matched by citizens' desire to reduce the services they were getting from government, a gap began to grow, which was filled in part by privatization and contracting out. Similarly, part of the widely advertised effort to balance the federal budget during the 1990s and cut back the level of the federal workforce has put pressure on federal agencies to contract out—to save money, to replace the expertise lost by cutbacks, and to make the federal payroll look smaller.

Privatization means that a function that was performed by the public sector is given over or sold to the private sector, and the government no longer has anything to do with it. Contracting out means the government continues to be responsible for the function, which is still paid for through tax or fee revenue, but the service is actually provided by a private sector firm or a nonprofit agency.

Contracting out allows governments to continue to provide services while appearing to reduce in size and especially in the number of employees. For many governments contracts represent a way of taking advantage of private sector competition to keep costs down. If there is competition in the private sector, and if the process of contracting can take advantage of that competition, there may be savings to be had. Other reasons to contract out include improved services, where the private sector is able to pay staff better and provide more modern services as in the information technology area or water and sewer services.

Whether contracting works has been a topic earnestly debated, with financial and ideological stakes on each side. The research suggests that success is debatable, obtainable under certain conditions that do not always hold, and that promised successes often exceed realized gains. Still there has been learning over time. The federal government is shifting from a low bidder model to a more moderated package that includes quality and likelihood of good performance; that newer model may open the way for higher costs and more corruption in the award of bids, but it should eliminate the forced lowballing that results in bids lower than private companies can deliver the service for and the very common complaints of scope creep and cost increases after the initial years. Managing contracts takes skill and experience, and that skill and experience are accumulating in some places. In others, however, contracting occurs willy-nilly, to reduce the number of staff on board and make government look smaller, or to save money, in which case keeping an informed staff on board to oversee the contract may look too expensive.

Another problem with contracting is that it assumes that the private sector can do the work more cheaply, that competition will keep it lean. Sometimes, however, that means that the private sector hires cheaper, nonunionized staff, and experiences high turnover, with the consequence that there is no continuity and no learning, and contract performance deteriorates over time. Sometimes there is no competition in the private sector or the not-for-profit sector. In rural areas there may not be a variety of companies to compete to do the job, if there were some of them would be starving and ultimately die off until there was a match between the amount of work and the number or size of companies. In the nonprofit sector, there is no reason to have two organizations providing the same service, the goal is to cover the needs, one agency for each need. Moreover, in the nonprofit sector, economies are gained by cooperation rather than competition; the bidding process may induce or require competition that destroys the principles of cooperation that make such organizations efficient.

Regardless of whether contracting works and achieves its goals of service improvement or cost savings, contracts often diffuse responsibility and make accountability more difficult. Supporters of contracting often ignore this argument, but it remains an important one. It is often difficult to tell who is contracting for what service, and with what staff, whether the contract is or is not a good deal for the public, or even what the contract costs and what it provides. Costs of a contract over time, one measure by which to judge it, seldom or never make it into the budget document for the public or elected officials to read. While contractors are presumably to be held to performance standards by the terms of the contract, in fact, government officials who let in these contracts have reasons to make them appear to be successful. Failures are thus often tolerated and hidden, distorting the record.

The essays in this part deal with some of these issues. E.S. Savas, a longtime supporter of contracting, argues that in New York City, there is sufficient competition among the nonprofit social service agencies to allow for efficient contracting. Bruce Wallin describes the process of privatization in Massachusetts, mistakes made, and new processes invented.

CHAPTER 29

COMPETITION AND CHOICE IN
NEW YORK CITY SOCIAL SERVICES

E.S. SAVAS

INTRODUCTION

Local governments provide social welfare benefits in the United States through three main mechanisms: (1) directly, using their own personnel; (2) indirectly, through grants or contracts awarded to private nonprofit or for-profit organizations to supply services to government-designated, eligible individuals; and (3) indirectly, through vouchers that are given to eligible recipients, who can use them to purchase services from approved service suppliers.

These mechanisms differ significantly. Under direct government provision, as well as under grants and contracts, the producer of the service is subsidized, whereas with vouchers the consumers of the service are subsidized. Both contracts and grants on the one hand, and vouchers on the other, can introduce competition and choice. These ingredients—important for good performance—are lacking in direct, monopolistic government services, hence the move toward privatization of public services, where the principal benefits are achieved by competition (Savas 2000, 122–24).

In the 1970s, social services underwent a dramatic change as government awarded contracts and grants to the private, nonprofit sector to supply social services. Between 1971 and 1979, the fraction of state and local social services provided in this manner increased from 25 percent to 55 percent (Kettner and Martin 1994) because local governments could not mobilize internally fast enough to take advantage of the federal funding available for new social programs. By 1992, the fraction of U.S. local governments that relied entirely on their own in-house units for various programs was small, as illustrated in Table 29.1 (Miranda and Andersen 1994, 26–35). None of the responding local governments was operating its own homeless shelters, for example, while 54 percent contracted with private organizations for day care facilities and for homeless shelters.

The nonprofit world faces major environmental changes in the United States: devolution from the federal to state governments, welfare reform, tax reform, reinvented government, cuts in government budgets, managed health care, and the evolution of AIDS into a chronic illness, requiring relatively more outpatient social-support services and relatively less in-patient medical

From *Public Administration Review*, vol. 62, no. 1 (January/February 2002), 82–91. Copyright © 2002 by American Society for Public Administration. Reprinted with permission.

Table 29.1

Delivery Arrangements for Selected Social Services

Service	Percentage of local govern- ments relying entirely on in-house units	Percentage of local governments contracting with for-profit firms	Percentage of local governments contracting with nonprofit agencies
Day care facilities	6	54	35
Drug and alcohol treatment programs	7	20	34
Operation of homeless shelters	0	5	54

Source: Rowan Miranda and Karlyn Andersen, Alternative Service Delivery in Local Government, 1982–1992. *Municipal Year Book* (Washington, DC: International City Management Association, 1994), 26–35, tables 3/4 and 3/5.

Note: Governments can use both for-profit firms and nonprofit agencies; therefore, numbers in rows cannot be added together meaningfully.

care. Welfare reform alone is having a major impact, with renewed emphasis on job training, job placement, child care, and transportation. Nowhere do these changes have more impact than in New York City, which has some 19,500 nonprofit organizations, including about 5,650 active in social services and health care (Haycock 1992).

Government funding of nonprofits in New York City—by the federal, state, and city governments—has grown to significant proportions and even dominates some fields: Nonprofit agencies in health care receive 74 percent of their funds from government; in housing, 68 percent; and in social services, 66 percent (Haycock 1992). In 1998, New York City entered into 4,361 such contracts for $1.95 billion (Table 29.2); the vast majority of these were with nonprofit agencies, but the number with for-profit firms was rising. The average contract was for $447,000, an amount large enough, generally speaking, to affect the organization winning such an award.

RESEARCH QUESTIONS

This large-scale use of the private sector offers an opportunity to study the use of contracts for social services. The process of contracting for social services has been examined both conceptually and empirically, and, in particular, the issue of competition has been addressed. Kramer and Grossman (1987) identify major policy issues that arise in contracting for social services: Under what conditions should competition be encouraged? Should low bids always be accepted? Should nonprofit organizations be preferred over for-profits? Should government make special efforts to assist small nonprofit organizations so they can compete?

DeHoog (1984) asks the pertinent empirical question: "To what extent are [social] service environments characterized by competition?" In her limited study, she observes that few private agencies competed for contracts, which she attributes to several factors: (1) no tradition of competition, as agencies were created to serve unmet social needs, and, therefore, they became differentiated in their activities rather than rivals; (2) numerous entry barriers—no demand by government for new services unless more funds were available, requirements for matching private funds, and burden-some administrative procedures; (3) lack of formal solicitation procedures and evaluation criteria; (4) locational limitations—an agency with existing facilities had a geographic monopoly. As a result of limited competition, "decision makers retained previous services and contractors routinely, and only sought new alternatives when additional funds were allocated"

Table 29.2

Contracts Awarded by Selected New York City Agencies, 1998

Agency	Number of contracts	Value of contracts
Administration for Children's Services	1,165	$1,066,966,715
Department for the Aging	1,068	126,166,455
Department of Employment	474	67,576,580
Department of Homeless Services	503	252,927,848
Department of Social Services	1,151	436,413,022
Total	4,361	$1,950,050,620

Source: City of New York, Executive Budget, Fiscal Year 1998; actual year-end figures may differ significantly.

(69). Further, she notes that neither the private agencies nor the government agencies wanted competition, the latter because contracting is quick and easy when requests for proposals (RFPs), comprehensive mailing lists, and thorough consideration of alternatives are deemed unnecessary; when no agreement is needed on program priorities and proposal criteria; and when previous contractors submitted most of the proposals.

Kettl states that "[c]ompetition is by its very nature disruptive to social services. It imposes high transaction costs on both the buyer . . . and the seller. . . . The monopolistic behavior of government . . . has been replaced by monopolistic behavior [of] contractors" (1993, 173). deHoog (1990) recognizes the classic competition model might not apply under certain conditions: if the number of service suppliers is limited, if suppliers lack the organizational resources to cover transaction costs, or if future funding is uncertain. Therefore, she offers a continuum of contracting models, with competition at one end, negotiation in the middle, and cooperation at the other end. The competition model involves an arms-length relationship between government and the contractor, whereas in the cooperative model, the two are partners. In their survey of state officials who oversee social service contracting, Kettner and Martin (1994) note a growing tendency toward the partnership model and little effort to encourage competition. Only 63.6 percent of respondents actively solicit bids or proposals, only 51.5 percent advertise, and only 48.5 percent hold bidders' conferences.

Cigler (1990) notes the availability of suppliers as a significant problem in North Carolina. A study of competitive contracting for mental health care in Massachusetts finds a shortage of qualified bidders, circumvention of bidding requirements through waivers, and little real competition: The average RFP received only 1.7 responses (Schlesinger et al. 1986, 252). Moreover, the number of potential competitors declined over time because of industry consolidation and the desire of government administrators to stick with familiar contractors and to maintain continuity of care.

The empirical study reported here builds on this prior work and examines the extent to which the principal feature of privatization—namely, introducing competition and choice—is being realized through government contracts for social services. How much competition is there for government contracts for social services? Is the lack of competition noted by the above researchers universal? To what extent are contracts merely allocated to established providers rather than awarded through a competitive process? What are the details of the process? How are RFPs advertised and disseminated to nonprofits? To which organizations are they distributed? How many agencies respond? How are award decisions made? What is the duration of contracts? What is the renewal process, that is, is it competitive or more or less automatic, thereby assuring continuity of care, but perhaps at the expense of efficiency or effectiveness? In short, how much choice is in fact available to and exercised by governments when contracting for social services? While this study is limited to these quantitative and process questions and does not address the quality of the proposals or the contract services, it may prompt the next stage of inquiries into this important area.

These questions were studied in New York, where the city government has more than 4,000 contracts worth about $2 billion with social service providers. Although New York is unique, the results should be of broad interest and may apply to other large cities and counties. Three services with large budgets and large numbers of competitive contracts were examined: shelters for homeless adults, home care, and training programs for the unemployed.

Mayor Rudolph Giuliani made the relevant data available for the selected agencies and assured the cooperation of numerous officials, from agency heads and mayoral assistants to deputy commissioners and agency contracting officers. Among the documents examined were mailing lists of people and organizations who received RFPs, the RFPs themselves, registers showing who picked up the RFPs, lists of proposals submitted, proposals, contracts, contract award documents, and financial information.

SHELTERS FOR HOMELESS ADULTS

The Department of Homeless Services (DHS) provides emergency shelter and support services to homeless families and individuals. It also provides outreach services to people living in public places, determines eligibility for emergency housing services, assesses clients' service needs, and offers services to enable people to live independently. It works with other government agencies and private organizations to help homeless people identify and relocate to other long-term housing options. DHS shelters approximately 7,000 homeless adults (5,700 men and 1,300 women) each night and approximately 5,400 home-less families daily in temporary housing (City of New York 1997).

The peak number of homeless adults reached 10,000 in 1989, dropped to 6,000 in 1994, and has since edged up to 7,000. About 25,000 people use the single-adult shelters in the course of a year. The average stay in 1997 was about 100 days; about 40 percent stay less than a month and about 1,700 essentially live in the shelters year-round.

The department has been following an aggressive privatization program, getting out of the business of operating shelters directly (Holloway 1997, 1998). As of 1998, it had privatized 75 of 82 shelters for single, homeless adults, and one of the remaining seven currently operated directly by the department was in the process of being privatized (Wiviott 1999). The privatization of family shelters had started and six RFPs had been issued and were awaiting responses.

Analysis

The 11 RFPs issued between January 9, 1995, and November 18, 1997, and the resulting submissions and awards were studied. The RFPs were for single-adult shelters, family facilities, residential reception centers, and drop-in centers. Other extant proposals for outreach programs were not included in the analysis. Awards were made for six of the 11 RFPs issued in this period; the award process for the others had not yet been completed at the time of this analysis. Table 29.3 presents detailed information on these six RFPs, the responses, and the awards, whose combined cost was $100 million.

Examination of Table 29.3 shows several things:

Table 29.3

Contracting by the Department of Homeless Services

RFP number	Facilit type	Facility owner	Number of facilities	Number of letters sent out	Number of RFPs picked up	Facility/area	Number of proposals	Contract awarded to incumbent?	Contract duration (years)	Contract price (millions)
071–95H000078	Adult	City	1	1,600	50	Sumner	3	no	3	$9.846
		City	1			Kingsbridge	2	no	3	6.129
		City	1			Part Slope	3	no	3	5.498
		City	1			Park Avenue	2	no	3	6.588
		City	1			Fort Washington	1	no	3	9.774
		City	1			Jamaica	2	no	3	4.771
		City	1			Harlem 1	2	no	3	7.329
071–96S000025	Family	City	1	300	36	Jennie A, Clark	1	yes	3	4.236
		City	1			SENECA	1	yes	3	4.110
071–96S000032	Drop-in centers	Private	1	1,000	55	Grand Central	1	?	3	5.806
		City	1			Beaver	2	?	3	3.200
		Private	1			Citywide	1	?	3	.996
		Private	1			Peter's Place	1	?	3	4.195
		Private	1			25 Central Avenue (S.I.)	1	?	3	3.172
		Private	1			Olivieri	1	?	3	} 8.934
		Private	1			Open Door	1	?	3	}
071–97S000011	Drop-in center	City	1	200	30	Bond Street	3	yes	1	1.056
071–97S000013	Medical	?	1	40	3	Bronx Emergency Assistance Unit	2	yes	2	2.362
071–97S000018	Reception centers	City(1)	3	300	50	BRC Reception Center	} 6	yes	2	2.186
		Private (2)				VOA Reception Center	}	yes	2	2.099
Totals			21	3,440	224		36			$99.99

Source: Compiled from DHS records.
Note: The first RFP listed above, for adult shelters, represented privatization of previously DHS-operated facilities: therefore, there were no incumbents.

1. A major effort was made to inform potential bidders about the forthcoming contract award; 3,440 announcement letters were sent out for the six solicitations listed here, an average of 573 for each. The average is 680 if specialized requests for medical facilities are excluded, which went to only 40 potential bidders.

2. The announcement resulted in 224 organizations interested enough to go to DHS and pick up the RFP; that is, every 100 announcements led to 6.5 pickups, or one pickup for every 15.4 announcement letters sent out.

3. Thirty-six proposals were submitted, that is, one proposal for every 96 announcement letters sent out; one proposal was submitted for every 6.2 organizations interested enough to pick up the RFP.

4. The most competitive solicitation drew 15 final proposals for seven contracts, more than two per contract. Many more would-be bidders submitted their qualifications but failed to survive the initial screening. There were no incumbents, and therefore the competition for this RFP to operate adult shelters was wide open.

5. For 13 of the 20 awards, it was readily possible to determine whether incumbents or new entrants had won. Of these 13, seven had been operated directly by DHS and therefore had no incumbent contractors. Six had incumbents, and all six won. In two of these six cases, there were no other bids; in the other four cases, where there were competing proposals, seven bidders—in addition to the four winning incumbents—submitted proposals. None of them won.

Discussion

Most RFPs go through a one-step process, but this particular RFP for adult shelters (the first one listed in Table 29.3) was a two-step process in which the first step amounted to a qualifying round in which the basic credentials of many would-be bidders were examined. Those 15 organizations found qualified were invited to submit full proposals, which were then evaluated by a panel of four DHS staff members (from different units) in terms of experience (30 points out of 175), past performance (15 points), the proposed program (70 points), administration (15 points), budget and staffing (15 points), and community support (30 points). A minimum score had to be reached in each category, or the proposal was eliminated. Proposals with the highest overall score won.

Judging from the above analysis of the number of announcements, RFPs distributed, and proposals submitted, the processes were very competitive. Ultimately, however, the incumbents did very well, holding on to their contracts in all six cases in which they submitted bids, despite the brisk competition. This is not unusual in contracting. Typically the incumbent has acquired experience at that site and with that population of clients, and presumably it has performed adequately or it probably would have been disqualified or had its contract terminated.

This is a facility-based service, that is, one where the contractor operates a physical facility to which service recipients come. The incumbent already has an appropriate facility, and this gives it a great advantage in proposing to serve that same area again. A nonincumbent (a would-be new entrant) must show in its proposal that it has "site control," that is, an agreement with a property owner to use a particular space or facility, one that can be inspected by the award committee. The agreement is conditioned on being awarded the contract. Searching for suitable space for a facility and entering into an agreement for it is a disincentive to preparing and submitting a proposal.

One way to reduce this incumbent advantage might be for the city to own or otherwise control the space (another approach is discussed in the final section of the article.). For a city-controlled facility, the competition would be for a contract to provide the required services there. This effect is

Table 29.4

Proposals Submitted, by Facility Ownership

	Ownership	
	City	Other
Number of facilities	12	8
Number of proposals	24	10
Proposals per facility	2.0	1.25

Source: Table 29.3 and DHS records.

shown in Table 29.4. Twelve city-owned facilities were subjected to competition and 24 proposals were submitted for them. Only 10 proposals were submitted, however, for the eight areas that did not have city-owned facilities. These results support the hypothesis that new entrants are more likely to submit bids or proposals to operate city-owned facilities than privately owned facilities.

The typical contracts that were examined were for three years and could be renewed by mutual consent for no more than two additional three-year terms. The typical contract sets performance standards for outreach (recruiting homeless men), rules for residents, the allowed length of stay by any one resident, occupancy rates, case-management plans, and placement goals in terms of jobs and independent housing. DHS has significant approval authority over any changes and has the right to remove the director of a facility, who is the contractor's employee. DHS has the right to enter the premises and to monitor and evaluate the operation. The contractor is required to submit a variety of regular reports and minutes of advisory board meetings to DHS and to enter data directly into DHS's management information system. No evidence was obtained as to active or passive monitoring activities by DHS or the exercise of DHS supervisory rights.

Contracts and vouchers are two very different forms of privatization, but Thomas Main (1997) makes the valuable observation that contracting for shelter services creates a voucher-like system with desirable attributes: "Because clients have no right to a particular shelter, private shelters may require and enforce participation in their program as long as noncompliant clients are free to return to a general shelter. [This] gives clients a degree of choice that is not available in an all-city-run system. It also makes possible an exercise of authority that is less drastic than the impermissible denial of city shelters. Indeed, the provision of choice and the existence of a usable sanction go hand-in-hand. It is because clients make a voluntary choice to go to a certain program that the shelters can reasonably expect clients to adhere to their program" (174).

HOME CARE

The Department for the Aging (DFTA) promotes, administers, and coordinates the development and provision of services for older persons to help them maintain their independence and participate in their communities. It supports a broad range of services, both directly and through contracts with community-based organizations. It conducts an array of planning, advocacy, and management functions, including the administration of the city's 335 senior centers.

DFTA's home care program was studied. In 1997, the department provided 1.26 million hours of home care to 7,200 clients (City of New York 1997). Individuals are eligible for home care if they are at least 60 years old, at or above 100 (to 150) percent of poverty level, and are independent but functionally impaired. Two different kinds of home care are provided, housekeeping and

Table 29.5

Contracting for Home Care Services by the Department for the Aging

Program number	Community districts served	Number of proposals	Awarded to incumbent?	Price (thousands)
125 98 HC1 0160	Bronx 7–12	9	yes	$343
125 98 HC1 0163	Bronx 1–6	9	yes	901
125 98 HC1 02H2	Brooklyn 18	11	no	121
125 98 HC1 031N	Manhattan 2, 4, 5	10	yes	485
125 98 HC1 03H1	Manhattan 7	5	no	182
125 98 HC1 03H2	Manhattan 12	8	no	390
125 98 HC1 0389	Manhattan 6, 8	9	yes	538
125 98 HC1 0470	Brooklyn 11, 15; Queens 5, 6, 8–11, 13	12	yes	1,382
Totals		73		$4,342

Source: Compiled From DFTA records and interviews.

homemaker/personal care. The former consists of help in general cleaning, marketing, laundry, ironing, meal preparation, and errands. The latter consists of help in feeding, ambulation, bathing, toileting, personal grooming, dressing, and house keeping services. A case manager determines the level of care required by an eligible individual.

Home care is carried out by contracting with two complementary kinds of functional agents: Under DFTA guidelines, private, nonprofit agencies that serve as case managers control access into the system, receiving referrals from a broad spectrum of sources, determining eligibility, conducting assessments to determine the amount of home care a client requires, and prescribing the number of hours and type of service a client will receive. Private nonprofit and for-profit organizations, also under contract with DFTA, directly provide home care to individuals to whom they are assigned by the case manager; they provide services of the appropriate type for the number of hours per week as directed by the case manager.

Analysis

Contracts are awarded to serve particular community territories or multiple-district areas. Table 29.5 shows the results of a major solicitation for home care issued January 22, 1997, for service in eight areas from July 1, 1997 through June 30, 1998. Approximately 1,500 letters announcing the RFPs were sent out, 97 RFPs were picked up, and 73 proposals were submitted for the eight areas. In other words, every 15.5 letters resulted in one organization interested enough to pick up the RFP, and each RFP picked up resulted in 0.75 proposals. There were more than nine proposals per award. Five of the eight awards went to incumbents and three to nonincumbents.

Discussion

DFTA teams of three or more staff members evaluated the proposals. Scores were assigned by each team member and weighted by the following formula: program performance and experience, 45 percent; organization structure, administration, and fiscal history, 25 percent; staffing, personnel, and budgeting, 30 percent. Contracts were typically awarded for one year, with an option for two one-year renewals and a three-year renewal, for a total of six years.

Contracts typically did not specify performance standards or output measures, but instead specified many input and process standards such as employee qualifications, required record keeping, etc. Compliance is measured against these input and process standards. Hours of care produced in accordance with these standards serves as a workload measure or measure of immediate output. Given the nature of this work, it is not clear what more meaningful outputs (or outcomes) might be measured, as recovery with no further need for home care is relatively rare. Monitoring is essentially left in the hands of the case-management contractor, who assigns clients to the home care contractor. DFTA is beginning to rely on the state Department of Health monitoring of home care providers under licensing requirements; these exceed DFTA's standards for factors they have in common. Further research on performance standards in this area is warranted.

The evidence indicates the entire procurement was carried out well. The solicitation was announced widely and had the intended result: It attracted a lot of interest and yielded numerous competitive proposals—ranging in number from five to 12 per district. Therefore, DFTA was in the desirable position of being able to select the best proposal from a relatively large number of submissions. Of particular relevance is the fact that, unlike awards of contracts for homeless shelters, nonincumbents did very well, winning three of eight contracts. Unlike shelters, home care does not require the contractor to provide a physical facility for its clients. This would tend to increase the number of potential bidders, as they do not have to demonstrate that they occupy or can occupy specialized quarters in order to have their proposal considered. The result of this competition should have favorable long-term consequences for the service: An incumbent cannot become complacent and assume it has a natural advantage in winning new contracts whenever it applies.

According to DFTA officials, for-profit companies serve six of 30 catchment areas. One firm in particular is said to be performing very well, and its quality of care is at least as good as the nonprofits it succeeded. Moreover, it hired all the workers who had been working for the nonprofits and gave them training, which qualified them for certificates; the workers are often full-time employees, whereas they had been part-time employees in the nonprofits. The same company also does work for corporations, insurance companies, and certified home health care agencies (for lower levels of care). This creates career opportunities that workers lack in the nonprofits.

Can vouchers be used for home care ("consumer-directed care")? Some patients are fully capable of selecting and managing attendants, but most are not. One knowledgeable official estimates that no more than 30 percent of seniors could handle this responsibility, based on the incidence of Alzheimer's disease, percentage who are bedridden, etc. Moreover, extortion by family members (a form of elder abuse) is regrettably common. Extensive checks and balances would be needed. One approach would be to give the patient a check (not cash that family members could take) to give directly to a home attendant. More patients could be given more responsibility for their care, and they could share more of the costs. It may be, however, that the administrative effort to operate a voucher program and to protect it from fraud would outweigh the advantages.

EMPLOYMENT TRAINING

The Department of Employment (DOE)—in partnership with the Private Industry Council, its legislatively mandated oversight board—implements and oversees a workforce-development system of occupational assessment, skills training, educational remediation, and job placement for the city's unemployed and underemployed residents. This system helps to develop a qualified workforce for the city's businesses. Through a network of contracts with private firms and nonprofit service providers, the department serves approximately 64,000 youth and adults annually. It also works closely with the Human Resources Administration to provide employment-related services to public-assistance recipients (City of New York 1997).

Contracts

The DOE has been carrying out its mandate principally by contracting with private nonprofit and, increasingly, private for-profit organizations for different activities: (1) retraining under the Economic Dislocation and Worker Adjustment Assistance Act (EDWAA); (2) training under Title II of the Job Training Partnership Act (JTPA); (3) training under the Refugee/Entrant Targeted Assistance Program (RETAP); and (4) operating one-stop career centers. EDWAA is aimed at experienced workers who were displaced by plant closings and by the North American Free Trade Act, for example. JTPA provides skills training for disadvantaged adults, youths, and mature workers. RETAP offers training to recent immigrants and to refugees. One-stop career centers provide a wide variety of information and self-help resources for job seekers and employers, as well as intensive services such as assessment, workshops, classroom training, on-the-job training, counseling, and referral to skills training and literacy programs.

ANALYSIS

An analysis of three RFPs, one for each of the first three programs listed above, appears in Table 29.6. An examination of the table shows the following:

1. Unlike the facility-based awards for homeless shelters and senior centers, there was no limit on the number of contracts that would be awarded; there was a limit only on total funding under the RFP.
2. A major outreach program was carried out to attract bidders. A total of 4,700 announcement letters was sent out, an average of 1,567 for each RFP.
3. The announcements resulted in 1,014 potential bidders going to DOE and picking up the RFPs; that is, every 4.62 announcements resulted in a pickup. This suggests the mailing was well targeted.
4. There were 219 proposals submitted, an average of one proposal for every 21.46 announcement letters or one for every 4.63 RFPs picked up.
5. An average of 73 proposals were submitted per RFP. Inasmuch as 104 awards were made, the average number of proposals per award was 2.11, that is, more than two per award.
6. The concept of incumbency is not strictly applicable for these RFPs, as there was not a one-for-one replacement of existing programs. Moreover, the EDWAA program was new, and no one was providing exactly this kind of program. Whether proposers were operating under employment-training contracts with DOE at the time of these submissions and awards was not determined.

Discussion

Based on the data for announcements, RFP distributions, proposals, and awards, the processes for the three solicitations followed good procurement practices, with the result that effective competition was realized. Proposals were evaluated and scored by a three-person team according to the following formula: program plan, 55 percent; demonstrated effectiveness, 25 percent; cost

Table 29.6

Contracting for Employment Services by the Department of Employment

Program	Date RFP issued	Number of letters sent	Number of RFPs picked up	Number of proposals submitted	Number of awards	Number of proposals per award	Price (millions)
EDWAA	6/17/94	1,167	306	62	35	1.77	$25.177
JTPA Title II	10/24/94	2,133	487	140	63	2.22	64.419
RETAP	3/15/95	1,400	221	17	6	2.83	2.867
Total		4,700	1,014	219	104	2.11	$92.463

Source: Department of Employment records.

Table 29.7

Use of Vouchers and Conventional Retraining Contracts

	Vouchers	Retraining contracts	Voucher/contract ratio
Number of participants	1,942	1,772	1.10
Cost per participant	$3,445	$6,130	.56
Total program cost	$6,690,198	$10,862,290	.62
Placement rate upon completion (percent)	82	74	1.11
Average hourly wage at placement	$13.59	$11.18	1.22

effectiveness, 20 percent; organizational capacity, 0 percent to –20 percent (that is, organizational capacity to do the work was assumed, but failure to demonstrate it caused a loss of points). Contracts to train displaced workers were awarded for three years, with an option for DOE to renew for up to three more years.

The contract called for "input specifications," that is, the population to be served characterized by age, gender, education, race or ethnicity, and employment barrier. Detailed, quantitative output measures were prescribed in these solicitations, as this area lends itself to such measures, unlike home care and senior centers. Goals were stated for the number of participants in the training programs; the fraction of participants to be placed upon completion of the program (at least 70 percent); their average wage when placed (at least $9 per hour); and the fraction still employed 90 days after completing the program (at least 60 percent). Intermediate goals required competency testing after training. Training programs themselves were to reflect the advice of the private-sector employers on the contractor's advisory board.

Vouchers

Title 3 of the Joint Partnership Training Act encouraged the use of vouchers for dislocated workers in the late 1980s. EDWAA programs, described above, use vouchers as well as contracts. Under the principle of consumer choice, eligible workers are free to choose their own training provider or to register for one of the training programs offered by contractors selected by DOE through competitive bidding. The most popular types of training chosen by voucher recipients were computer-related (basic keyboard and computer work, programming, graphics, internet-related, desktop publishing), trades (commercial driving licenses, building maintenance), technical (network engineering, computer engineering) medical (nursing-related, medical billing, coding), and paralegal. Table 29.7 compares the use of vouchers and conventional retraining programs supplied by contractors in 1998 under EDWAA.

The results of training by vouchers seem to be superior to training by contract, in that costs are lower and placement rates and wages are higher. Such a conclusion is premature, however. The trainees were not identical in educational backgrounds, and they were not assigned randomly between voucher and contractor programs. Moreover, the allocation of the cost of Basic Readjustment Services and Worker Career Centers—which are included in the costs above—between voucher programs and contractor-provided training is complex and can be further refined. Closer study of the relative advantages of vouchers over contracts is needed to determine if even greater emphasis on vouchers is warranted and, if it is, to determine which segments of the trainee population should be encouraged to choose vouchers for their training.

DISCUSSION AND CONCLUSION

The proposal process in every case examined satisfied the requirements for effective contracting: clear specifications and timetable, ample advertising, convenient and free access to the RFP, scheduled site visit, pre-proposal conference, available list of pre-proposal conference attendees, an adequate interval between the date the RFP was issued and the date responses were due (to allow time to prepare proposals), a suitable interval between the date of award and the starting date of the contract (to permit smooth startup by the contractor), and a clearly stated procedure and formula for evaluating proposals (Savas 2000, 174–210).

Announcements of the RFPs were placed in the *City Record* and elsewhere, and mailings were sent to hundreds and sometimes thousands of interested parties, including current providers, other experienced service providers, community agencies, and local political leaders. The large number of responses indicates that distribution was widespread and effective. Those who wanted copies of the RFP picked them up at the agency and signed a register. (Names on the register are added to mailing lists for subsequent announcements.) Dissemination of bid information could be improved by the use of fax, email, and Web sites, where interested parties could get information easily and quickly and download copies of RFPs and draft contracts instead of picking them up. Organizations can submit more than one proposal in response to an RFP and can submit proposals for more than one facility or district for services that are facility-based or that must serve defined geographic areas. Most contracts have options in which the city department can renew the contracts for a limited number of additional terms if the stated performance criteria are satisfied.

A summary of the findings for the three services appears in Table 29.8. Overall, 328 proposals were submitted for the 132 awards, a ratio of 2.48 proposals per award. This is significantly higher than the 1.7 average reported by Schlesinger, Dorwart, and Pulice (1986) in Massachusetts. In the subjective judgment of the author, this is evidence that contracting for these social services in New York City is competitive, but others may not find these figures persuasive until other studies are conducted elsewhere and comparisons are made. Nevertheless, these findings suggest that one need not abandon the competition model altogether in favor of the negotiation model or the cooperation model at the other end of deHoog's useful continuum (1990). One should note, of course, that small communities may find it difficult to foster competition and may have to lean more heavily toward the other models.

There would be even greater competition if the facilities to be contracted out for site-based services were owned or leased by the city. This would weaken the power of de facto geographic monopolies (deHoog 1984). Appropriate sites may be in Housing Authority projects or other city-owned office buildings or housing. If possible, even greater use could be made of such facilities. This is not to suggest, however, that the city should retain otherwise unnecessary properties or buy property for facility-based contracted services, such as homeless shelters. The putative advantage of facility ownership must be balanced against the problems, inefficiencies, and other disadvantages associated with city ownership. A different approach might be to have the bid specifications require incumbents to rent their facilities to the winning bidder, at a fair price, if the incumbent fails to win the bid. For instance, the bid price could consist of two parts, the rent for the facility and the price of the service. The contract would be awarded based on the sum of the two prices, but the low bidder would have the choice of arranging for his own facility or renting the incumbent's facility at the rent bid by the incumbent.

Recent federal legislation, identified above, is leading to greater use of vouchers in job training and retraining programs that are aimed at experienced but displaced workers; this can be thought of

Table 29.8

Summary of Competitive Contracting

Service	Number of announcements sent	Number of RFPs picked up	Number of proposals submitted	Number of awards made	Pickups/ announcements sent	Proposals submitted/RFPs picked up	Proposals/ award
Shelters	3,440	224	36	20	0.06	0.16	1.8
Home care	1,500	97	73	8	0.06	0.77	9.13
Employment and training	4,700	1,014	219	104	0.22	0.22	2.11
Total	9,640	1,335	328	132	0.14	0.25	2.48

as an extension of the GI bill, under which the federal government paid for education. Greater use of vouchers—instead of contracts—is possible by those relatively few home care recipients who are disabled but otherwise able to choose their home care providers, gauge their performance, and exercise effective control. It may be, however, that the administrative effort to operate a voucher program and protect it from fraud would outweigh the advantages.

Community-based and other nonprofit organizations generally lack adequate working capital and are dependent on a steady stream of funding. From their point of view, contracts are vastly preferable to vouchers because they represent a predictable source of revenue, whereas they may find it difficult to survive if they had to compete to attract clients with vouchers. Thus, although vouchers may be good for service recipients, they are not necessarily good for service providers. It is easy to argue that the preferred program should emphasize client outcomes rather than agency interests.

Government funding of nonprofits through contracts may have some undesirable consequences. It can preclude innovative strategies and instead demand adherence to rigid guidelines and traditional approaches. It may mean that prevention of problems and early intervention to address problems will be slighted, "as governments usually fund and respond to seriously dysfunctional people, stepping in when problems become severe. We end up treating the unfortunate casualties too often, too late, and (at too high a price) in terms of both human suffering and tragedy and the financial burdens on society" (Dolan 1993, 1994).

Government funding has changed the very nature of nonprofits that receive much or most of their funds from government (Smith and Lipsky 1993). This "govemmentalization" of nonprofits has been deplored. ("Nonprofitization" is an apt term for this phenomenon of privatization through nonprofit organizations [Nathan et al. 1996]). This has substantially influenced the effectiveness and impact of private philanthropy such as foundation and corporate giving. It has been termed a "fatal embrace" because private nonprofit organizations with distinguished histories have effectively become government surrogates subject to coercive regulations that sap their initiative and thwart their efforts to find better ways to help the needy (Berger and Neuhaus 1996, 150).

By becoming agents—even appendages—of the state, many nonprofits are now heavily dependent on the state and increasingly are subject to many of the same problems that bedevil public agencies. They lose their independence as they scramble for government dollars. No longer are they "mediating institutions," serving as buffers between large, impersonal institutions and the individual (Berger and Neuhaus 1996, 157–64). Moreover, the practice of government funding has converted generous philanthropists into reluctant taxpayers (Savas 2000, 278).

Increasingly, for-profit firms are entering the social service field, providing services directly, such as child care and job training, and administering social programs under government contracts. Examples of the latter are determining eligibility for benefits, administering Welfare-to-Work programs, handling child welfare functions ranging from foster care to adoption to family services, and tracking down "deadbeat dads" to collect support payments.

As anecdotal evidence mounts—and if sound studies confirm—that for-profit firms can deliver high-quality services more cost effectively than nonprofits, more contracting can be expected. This outcome should come as no surprise, as for-profit firms generally provide quality goods and services at a lower cost than nonprofit governments (Savas 2000, 147–73). It is my observation that the social services profession generally bears an antimarket ethos and an antiprofit bias, together with a holier-than-thou attitude, which have blinded the nonprofit establishment to this development. This posture is strikingly similar to that of government officials 30 years ago who scoffed at the notion that for-profit private firms could undersell and outperform nonprofit government agencies. Now, of course, this is accepted as the rule rather than the exception (Goldsmith 1997; Norquist 1999; Osborne and Gaebler 1992,76–107).

Vouchers are emerging as the preferred privatization method for many social welfare services. They can be used for food, housing, education, health care, child care, home care, elder care, job training, and family services. They are growing in popularity for two reasons. Social services have been monopolistic, whereas vouchers introduce competition and user choice that dissolve monopolies and improve services (Reid 1972; Pruger and Miller 1973). Second, it is difficult to specify quality standards in social service contracts, but vouchers offer a solution because standards need not be articulated; voucher recipients simply choose the program they prefer from available suppliers—assuming there are several. For example, child care has been "voucherized" in two ways: with vouchers that permit parents to enroll their child in approved day care facilities, and with cash allowances that allow parents to hire a relative or friend to care for their child. Parents do not have to be professional educators, or even literate, to select the child care option they deem best for their children.

New York has moved from a system of social services provided by city agencies and employees to a system of contracts with the private sector. The process of competitive contracting appears to have been carried out well, on the whole, and has resulted in a satisfactory level of competition. I hope this subjective conclusion stimulates additional research into the nature and results of competition in social service contracting.

ACKNOWLEDGMENTS

The author gratefully acknowledges the support of the Achelis and Bodman Foundations, Joseph S. Dolan, executive director and secretary. I greatly appreciate the assistance and cooperation of many New York City officials, beginning with Mayor Rudolph W. Giuliani. Special thanks go to Deputy Mayor Anthony Coles. Thanks also to editor Larry D. Terry and the unknown reviewers of an earlier version of this article for their helpful comments.

REFERENCES

Berger, Peter L., and Richard John Neuhaus. 1996. *To Empower People: From State to Civil Society.* 2nd ed. Washington, DC: AEI Press.
Cigler, Beverly A. 1990. County Contracting: Reconciling the Accountability and Information Paradoxes. *Public Administration Quarterly* 14(3): 285–301.
City of New York. 1997. Mayor's Management Report.
deHoog, Ruth Hoogland. 1984. *Contracting Out for Human Services: Economic, Political, and Organizational Perspectives.* Albany, NY: State University of New York Press.
———. 1990. Competition, Negotiation, or Cooperation: Three Models for Service Contracting. *Administration and Society* 22(3): 317–40.
Dolan, Joe. 1993. Ominous Ramifications of Government Funds. *Chronicle of Philanthropy*, August 10, 44–45.
———. 1994. Non-Profit Groups Must Be Held Accountable, Too. *Chronicle of Philanthropy*, September 6, 42–43.
Goldsmith, Stephen. 1997. *The Twenty-first Century City: Resurrecting Urban America.* Washington, DC: Regnery Publishing.
Haycock, Nancy. 1992. *The Nonprofit Sector in New York City.* New York: Fund for the City of New York.
Holloway, Lynette. 1997. Shelters Improve Under Private Groups, Raising a New Worry. *New York Times*, November 12, B1.
———. 1998. New York City Plans to Take Diminished Role in Shelters. *New York Times*, June 21, B3.
Kettl, Donald F. 1993. *Sharing Power: Public Governance and Private Markets.* Washington, DC: Brookings Institution.
Kettner, Peter M., and Lawrence L. Martin. 1994. Purchase of Service at 20: Are We Using It Well? *Public Welfare* 52(3): 14–20.

Kramer, Ralph M., and Bart Grossman. 1987. Contracting for Social Services: Process Management and Resource Dependencies. *Social Service Review* 61(2): 32–55.

Main, Thomas J. 1997. Homeless Men in New York City: Toward Paternalism through Privatization. In *The New Paternalism: Supervisory Approaches to Poverty*, edited by Lawrence M. Mead, 161–81. Washington, DC: Brookings Institution.

Miranda, Rowan, and Karlyn Andersen. 1994. Alternative Service Delivery in Local Government, 1982–1992. In *Municipal Year Book*. Washington, DC: International City Management Association.

Nathan, Richard P., Elizabeth I. Davis, Mark J. McGarth, and William C. O'Heaney. 1996. *The Nonprofitization Movement as a Form of Devolution*. Albany, NY: Rockefeller Institute.

Norquist, John. 1999. *The Wealth of Cities: Revitalizing the Centers of American Life*. Washington, DC: Perseus Books.

Osborne, David, and Ted Gaebler. 1992. *Reinventing Government*. Reading, MA: Addison Wesley.

Pruger, Robert, and Leonard Miller. 1973. Competition and Public Social Services. *Public Welfare* 31(4): 16–25.

Reid, P. Nelson. 1972. Reforming the Social Service Monopoly. *Social Work* 17(6): 44–54.

Savas, E.S. 2000. *Privatization and Public Private Partnerships*. New York: Chatham House.

Schlesinger, Mark, Robert A. Dorwart, and Richard T. Pulice. 1986. Competitive Bidding and States' Purchase of Services. *Journal of Policy Analysis and Management* 5(2): 245–63.

Smith, Steven Rathgeb, and Michael Lipsky. 1993. *Nonprofits for Hire: The Welfare State in the Age of Contracting*. Cambridge, MA: Harvard University Press.

Wiviott, Susan. 1999. Telephone interview with the author, April 27.

CHAPTER 30

THE NEED FOR A PRIVATIZATION PROCESS
Lessons from Development and Implementation

BRUCE A. WALLIN

Privatization of government services, or the use of the private sector to attain public goals, has taken center stage in federal, state, and local government attempts to reform service delivery and lower cost (Gore, 1993; Gormley, 1991; Chi, 1993; Florestano, 1994; Cigler, 1990), Although much has been written about the advantages and disadvantages of privatization, the conditions which support it, and the service areas most readily privatized (Savas, 1987; Donohue, 1989), there has been remarkably little discussion in the literature of how the privatization decision process might best be structured, especially at the state level (Kettl, 1993a). That is, how should the rules for privatization be written? Who should be involved? How should proposals be initiated? What guidelines are needed? This article discusses such questions based on a case study of Governor William Weld's privatization efforts in Massachusetts.

Applied piecemeal in many states, privatization has not yet become an overarching theme for most states. While states differ in many ways, lessons can be learned from an analysis of the privatization politics and policy decisions of a state like Massachusetts, where privatization has been aggressively pursued by a Republican governor and equally aggressively opposed by a Democratically controlled legislature. Indeed privatization became one of the cornerstones of an administration that has increasingly attracted national attention, and yet, at the same time it remained a focal point of controversy within the Commonwealth. Although case studies have their limitations, they are clearly instructional in the early years of policy development and implementation (Pressman and Wildavsky, 1977). In their separate reviews of efforts at the state level, Florestano (1994), Kettl (1993a), and Chi (1993) have noted the need for more information on what states are doing with privatization, and how they are doing it.

Privatization must be done carefully. To overcome bureaucratic intransigence, union opposition, and partisan politics, proponents of privatization may feel that they have to aggressively promote their agenda. Privatization may then become a goal in itself, when it should be viewed as a means to more efficient and less costly provision of government services. Ideologically driven/overly promoted privatization crusades can, like most crusades, have innocent victims, with unintended consequences for those who deliver government services and for those who benefit from them.

From *Public Administration Review,* vol. 57, no. 1 (January/February 1997), 11–20. Copyright © 1997 by American Society for Public Administration. Reprinted with permission.

Opponents of privatization, on the other hand, may oppose its implementation for narrowly selfish personal or political reasons.

Privatization in the states is most often initiated in and implemented by the executive branch, with governors cited as the most active players in one survey (Chi, 1993, 24). Although the gubernatorial perspective can provide insight on alternative service delivery, the Massachusetts experience suggests that legislative involvement may be beneficial and may provide an important check on potentially overzealous privatization. Decisions that, in effect, weigh flexibility, efficiency, and cost savings in the provision of government services against expertise, stability, and control are important ones and are best made with input from both administrative and political perspectives.

The Massachusetts experience further suggests that, at the least, it is best to set up in advance of privatization a decision-making process that is well-specified, inclusive (especially including current government workers), and ideally has some independent check on the decisions, preferably by an office or organization with little to gain from the decision. Because of a favorable political climate, privatization policy in Massachusetts has moved in this direction, and the result is better policy.

THE POLITICS OF PRIVATIZATION IN MASSACHUSETTS

Privatization is not new to Massachusetts. Historically, there have been swings back and forth between public and private provision of services in the Commonwealth (Commonwealth, 1993d).

The first significant shift toward returning social services to the private sector came in the late 1960s and early 1970s. Fueled in part by Frederick Wiseman's film on state mental institutions, Massachusetts began to contract out certain human service programs, including mental health and youth services. The feeling was that large institutions had failed, that there was a need to get out from under civil service requirements in order to allow some program experimentation, and that putting people in community settings might work better (Dukakis, 1994). In addition, before he left office former governor Michael Dukakis had, for simple cost-cutting reasons, privatized certain transportation functions, including the cleaning of the Massachusetts Bay Transit Authority stations and grass cutting along highways.

THE EXECUTIVE'S INITIATIVE

The more recent privatization movement in Massachusetts provides a seemingly exponential leap, becoming the policy theme that best characterizes the Weld administration's approach to state government reform. Weld's victory in a predominantly Democratic state was a shock, producing the first Republican governor since 1974. Weld is fiscally conservative, a self-described "filthy supply-sider," and a social moderate/liberal bordering on libertarian. During the campaign, he espoused the traditional conservative position of "reducing big government," a theme more salient than usual in Massachusetts in the context of the Commonwealth's fiscal problems of 1988–89 (Wallin, 1995). Although Weld never explicitly promoted privatization during the campaign, one worker noted that the idea had been firmly implanted in his mind through readings and discussions with proponents. Privatization, Weld promised, would improve the quality of service while greatly lowering costs.

In addition to ringing true ideologically and offering the potential for efficiency gains, privatization made great political sense to Weld once he was in office. From an institutional perspective, it was a way to gain more control as chief executive over a bureaucracy which had grown under Democratic administrations. Further, it could be justified as part of the chief executive's duty to do what is in the best interest of all citizens of the state, not just the components represented in the legislature. From a partisan perspective, privatization fit the anti-big-government, anti-public-employee, and especially anti-public-employee-union position of most Republicans and increasingly the electorate. From an electoral (reelection) perspective, privatization could, in addition to satisfying the taxpayer, be used to punish those who had opposed the governor (in particular public employees and their unions), while allowing him to cast a wider, private-sector, campaign contribution net, gathering in those in the private sector who would benefit from increased state contracting.

The responsibility for spearheading the privatization initiative fell to the governor's most trusted aide and chief secretary, John Moffitt—the man who had turned around the gubernatorial campaign. The position of special research officer, created many years ago to perform background checks on potential gubernatorial appointments, was charged with researching privatization issues, One staff member explained that many of the initial privatization ideas came from conservative "think tanks," including the Pioneer Institute locally, and the Reason Foundation, Heritage Foundation, and Cato Institute nationally. On July 25, 1991, the Weld administration convened a "Privatization Summit" for all cabinet secretaries, with participants including academics and administrators from other states who had been involved with privatization.

Although some privatization initiatives were already underway in agencies, the secretary of administration and finance decentralized the targeting of programs for privatization by sending a memo to all cabinet secretaries and agency heads asking for new initiatives and offering criteria for their selection. Ideas were discussed at cabinet meetings. The first Weld administration privatizations began six months into the governor's first term.

The initial charge to the agencies calling for privatization initiatives offered only three simple criteria for selecting privatization projects: (1) the service involved must be one you can define distinctly in an RFP; (2) the privatized function must have measurable performance standards; and (3) there must be more than one vendor able to perform the service, or you lose the benefits of competition. The instructions were not very detailed, nor the criteria demanding. The requirement of more than one vendor, for example, is obviously not a very rigorous guarantee of competition.

The memo also listed a "number of conditions and criteria which might dictate *against* contracting out." These included:

- When other privatization strategies are deemed to be more effective.
- When services cannot be effectively measured as to cost, quality, process, and outcomes.
- When done in conjunction with services cuts.
- When privatization is explicitly forbidden by existing collective bargaining agreements, or when costs outweigh benefits.
- For so-called "core" functions of government, e.g., policy-making or enforcement functions.
- When public ends (i.e., equity, access, antidiscrimination) are ill-served by private provision.
- When services are not readily available from the private sector.
- Where legal barriers exist.

Of particular interest is the lack of specificity and the fear of initially tying privatization to service cuts, which might produce a political backlash.

In May of 1992, when Moffitt left the Weld administration for the private sector, the locus of privatization shifted to the executive office of administration and finance where a new position was created titled "director of privatization." A more detailed guide to privatization was drafted by

January 1993, and a final guide, including a "privatization checklist" for agencies, was published in November 1993 (discussed below).

By the November 1993 report, the Weld administration claimed to have saved Massachusetts taxpayers $273 million, about 2 percent of the annual budget, a number subject to much dispute and which aroused considerable debate (Massachusetts, 1993b). The completed privatizations (approximately 30) are too numerous to discuss separately. A few of the initiatives are worthy of mention.

The first initiative involved the closure of state hospitals and mental health facilities, with subsequent contracting out for patient care. Early in 1991, the governor appointed a commission on hospital consolidation, which reported that "the Commonwealth's inpatient facilities system, which was built to accommodate over 35,000 individuals at its peak, today cares for 6,200 clients" (Massachusetts, 1991, i). The commission recommended the closure of nine state hospitals and two other mental health facilities. Although there was strong protest, especially from patients and their families, and one long hunger strike by a patient that garnered media attention, eight hospitals and the two other facilities have been closed to date. These closures, with attributed savings of $143 million (from capital-avoidance costs), account for half the monetary success of all of the Weld privatization initiatives. (See Table 30.1 for a list of privatizations and cost savings as reported by the Weld administration.)

Overall, consolidation of the Health and Human Service facilities accounted for $203 million in savings when $60 million in operating costs are included. It is important to note that beside the potential for direct savings and better care, another goal was the maximization of federal reimbursements. For example, the commission report noted "although not reimbursable by Medicaid in a psychiatric institution . . . treatment for mental illness . . . is reimbursable when carried out in a general hospital" (Massachusetts, 1991, 36).

The privatization of prison health care appears to have been one of the most cost-effective privatizations of service delivery, although also not without controversy. In 1991, Massachusetts had the highest per-inmate cost for prison health care in the nation because of a reported lack of cost controls, weak central accountability, lax control of malpractice claims, and few standards for evaluation. After privatization in January 1992, the Weld administration claimed that by November 1993 costs went from $4,300 per inmate to $2,600, with half of the facilities receiving accreditation for the first time (Massachusetts, 1993a).

The single largest project involved the privatization of the entire maintenance function of a district office of the Massachusetts Highway Department. In September 1992, the state contracted with a private company for highway maintenance and drawbridge operation for the County of Essex. The administration and finance report (Massachusetts, 1993a; 24) noted that before privatization maintenance was spotty, the ratio of foremen to laborers was 1 to 2.15, and overtime costs were high. After privatization, savings were estimated to be $2 million in operating costs, $1 million in reallocated equipment, and $1.5 million in reallocated personnel.

The Weld administration has not been shy about publicizing its success. The executive summary of the administration and finance report on privatization claimed in addition to the tax savings a rigorous review and cost comparison analysis, increases in quantity, timeliness, and quality of services, public employee involvement, bipartisan support, a large number of bidders, and minimal job losses to state employees.

INTEREST GROUP OPPOSITION

The strongest interest group opposition to Governor Weld's privatization efforts naturally came from public employees and their unions. In particular, Council 93 of the American Federation

Table 30.1

Estimated Cost Savings from Privatization

Initiative	Start Date	Annual Savings[a] ($000)	Elapsed Months[b]	Savings to Date[a] ($000)
Administration & Finance				
Management of state transportation building	July 1992	1,000	14	1,166
Micrographics management services	August 1992	288	15	360
Procurement and delivery of pharmaceuticals	July 1992	3,000[c]	16	3,000
Fleet vehicle repair and maintenance—phase 1	July 1991	46	27	107
Fleet vehicle repair and maintenance—phase2	October 1993	150	1	13
Child support payment processing	September 1992	130	14	163
Collection of past due amounts	January 1993	200	11	200
Health and Human Services				
Hospital consolidation and community placements (DPH)	August 1991–March 1992	11,356	20	18,926
Hospital consolidation and community placements (DMH)	Ongoing	25,362	—	25,362
Hospital consolidation and community placements (DMR)	Ongoing	—	—	6,000
Hospital consolidation and closure, capital avoidance	August 1991–March 1992	—	—	143,000[d]
Managed mental health care and substance abuse services	April 1992	26,000	16	33,000
Accounts receivable collections for Medicaid (DPW)	Before January 1991	3,000	—	1,400
Institutional food services (DMR)	August 1993	5,600	3	1,400
Institutional food services (DPH)	August 1993	1,000	3	250
Institutional housekeeping services (DMR)	August 1993	4,000	3	1,000
Institutional housekeeping services (DPH)	August 1993	961	3	240
Institutional laundry services	October 1992	647	13	701
Institutional pharmaceutical services (EOHHS)	August 1993	800	3	200
Partnership clinics (DMH)	July 1991	6,500	28	15,167
Revenue collection (DSS)	July 1993	25,000	4	8,333
Public Safety				
Prison health care	January 1992	3,459	22	6,342
Prison food service	August 1992	313	15	391

Transportation & Construction

Highway maintenance, Essex County	September 1992	4,500[c]	14	4,783
Highway maintenance, Eastern Seaboard	November 1993	19,000[c]	0	0

Communities & Development

Utility conservation, public housing	—	5,000	0	0
Consumer Affairs	—			
Lemon law arbitration		310	—	—

Environmental Affairs

Skating rink management, phase 1	February 1992	237	21	415
		36[f]		72[f]
Skating rink management, phase 2	December 1992	712	11	652
		202[f]		202[f]
Skating rink management, phase 3	October 1993	119	1	10
		(44)[f]	(4)	
Zoos	August 1992	525	15	656
Total				273,507

Source: Massachusetts, 1993a.

[a] This represents the annual savings that the privatization, once fully implemented, is expected to realize. In some cases, savings to date exceed prorated annual savings because of better-than-expected performance or one-time gains.

[b] As of 1 November 1993.

[c] One-time savings.

[d] $143 million in deflected capital expense.

[e] Savings and value of additional services.

[f] Additional revenue/(expense).

of State, County and Municipal Employees (AFSCME) has consistently countered the alleged advantages of privatization.

Among AFSCME's charges is the argument that privatization's cost savings are inflated by omissions such as failing to include increased training costs and lower productivity from employee turnover. The union also emphasizes the decrease in government, accountability and control that occurs, including the potential bankruptcy of a private provider, and the tendency of privatized services to be controlled by a small number of companies, a condition that could lead to price collusion. In addition, the union has charged that privatization under Weld is another word for patronage, citing alleged favoritism in the awarding of contracts to politically connected individuals or firms. They placed particular emphasis on the fact that Weld's chief campaign fund raiser has been a private consultant for several firms doing business with the Commonwealth. The head of one union characterized privatization as "Republican patronage."

Some troubling testimony on the privatization process comes from Local 285 of the Service Employees International Union. For the Essex County highway maintenance privatization, the union representing the existing workers, had the low bid of $2.9 million compared to the winning bid of $3.7 million. The union's bid was denied because of what the Massachusetts Highway Department termed "missing items, certain unreasonably low cost estimates, and a failure to address the labor and equipment needs of other districts in the state" (Gow et al, 1953, 34–35). A study by students at the John F. Kennedy School of Government blamed the bid's failure on a lack of communication and understanding on the part of the union as to what was required and concluded that "the state's characterization of the proposal as 'unresponsive' seems a bit unfair." The study further concluded that the RFP process put the union "at a disadvantage versus private contractors." The union feels that the department failed to act in good faith and stacked the deck against them in future bidding by selling off or reallocating capital equipment, thus forcing any new bid to include the cost of acquiring new equipment. Their interpretation has been that the Weld administration wanted to guarantee the success of privatization by erecting barriers to future public employee union competitiveness. While union opposition to privatization may be motivated by the potential loss of jobs, or reduced wages and elimination of health care benefits, these charges are nonetheless disturbing.

Advocates for the mentally ill have also been vocal in their criticism, including the Alliance for the Mentally Ill of Massachusetts and the Partnership for Quality Care. In response to the state hospital closings, these groups note that stays in private hospitals generally cost twice as much as state-run facilities. They further express concern that patients have been moved from their local communities, where support systems exist, and that most private hospitals have in the past avoided accepting difficult-to-treat, long-term patients of the Department of Mental Health. Given this history, advocates worry about what options such patients will have if turned away from these facilities.

Finally, the Partnership for Quality Care notes that in mental health care, continuity of care is both extremely important and efficient (Kettl, 1993a). The history and relationship that have developed between a patient and doctor or counselor are not easily replaced. They further suggest that privatization's incentive to keep costs low drives down salaries, producing greater rates of staff turnover, further exacerbating the negative effects of discontinuity of care. Recent reports note a dramatic post-privatization increase in the number of suicides and deaths among those under the care of the Department of Mental Health (Bass, 1995).

Privatization produced an interesting split in the human service advocate community. Previous to privatization, social service providers and social service advocates were often joined in their opposition to many of the Republican governor's initiatives. Privatization, which can bring more business to the providers, has broken the coalition. Although it does not appear that this was a conscious strategy on the part of the Weld administration, its effect has been to weaken the opposition to privatization.

Finally, several inmates have unexpectedly died while under the care of the newly privatized prison health care services, although no interest group other than their own families has taken up their cause. Critics suggest that at least in one case, the desire to keep costs down prevented aggressive treatment (McNamara, 1992).

STATE LEGISLATIVE OPPOSITION AND REGULATION

Most of the powerful, countervailing action on privatization has come from the Democratic-controlled state legislature, specifically from the House Post-Audit and Oversight Committee (and its research bureau), and in a Senate-initiated privatization regulation bill carried by Senator Mark Pacheco.

The Post–Audit Committee has issued many reports on privatization in carrying out its role of legislative oversight. The most damning was its December 17, 1993, report, entitled "Privatization Savings: Where's the Beef?" (Massachusetts, 1993b). The report challenges the validity of $268 million of the $273 million in cost savings claimed by the Weld administration's privatization efforts. For example, it points out that, as noted above, the $143 million figure is derived from capital-avoidance costs resulting from closing state hospitals and mental health facilities. This number represents projected capital expenditure requirements that the Weld administration claims would have been necessary to meet federal certification requirements, but without independent verification. Further, the savings were presented to the media as "already saved," when they would have more accurately been spread over several years. Other Health and Human Services savings were disputed as being the result of a reduced census or reduced service.

The Audit Bureau also discloses that repeated visual and photographic inspections of the Essex Highway Maintenance project, the largest privatization project, do not support the claims of continued equivalent service at a savings of $1.9 million. It further charges that the administration would not provide information on the level of service before privatization took place, prohibiting adequate cost-service comparisons. This inability to compare and thus properly evaluate was worsened by a consolidation of Department of Public Works districts during the post-privatization period.

Overall, the bureau criticized the Weld administration privatization efforts for lack of planning, inappropriate oversight, deficient management, and shoddy accounting in terms of savings figures. It does suggest that in at least two cases privatization initiatives could have worked to the benefit of taxpayers if the proper drafting and management requirements had been built into the contracts.

The report further charges that no uniformity of records was provided by the administration under subpoena, and no uniform calculation process was followed to arrive at savings estimates. Costs that should be included do not appear, including the cost of employees who spent all or most of their time working on privatization, the costs of consultants hired to promote privatization, and the printing costs for promotional materials. Many of these findings are disturbing and raise questions about the legitimacy of both the Weld privatization process and its reporting. The administration produced no evidence to counter these charges.

While the Post–Audit Committee and its research bureau were doing their work, a bill regulating privatization was working its way through the Massachusetts Senate. In further proof that "all politics is local" (in addition to partisan and institutional), the chair of the Senate Administration Committee, Mark Pacheco, was first drawn to the privatization issue by attempts during both the Dukakis and Weld administrations to close several of the state schools and hospitals in his district.

While Pacheco was politically motivated by the loss of jobs of voters in his district, he had major policy concerns about the Weld privatization program, including:

- The transition of patients from state schools and hospitals to community settings, where lower levels of service would be available.
- The qualifications of the new care givers did not match those of state employees.
- The exclusion of the costs of unemployment, health insurance, and retraining programs for displaced state workers in the privatization decision.

Further, Pacheco also found flaws in the process, concluding that the Weld administration was exercising little or no oversight on privatization efforts and that the entire process was moving too quickly. Before there was any evaluation of one program, the next was begun. There apparently was little tracking of or concern for what happened to the clients of these facilities after they were closed; many were alleged to have ended up homeless. While there were treatment successes in many of the community residences, it seemed to Pacheco that the process was politically driven, part of an ideological and political campaign (Pacheco, 1995).

While a member of the house, Pacheco had introduced a bill to regulate privatization as early as June 1992. In March 1993, he carried S. 1257 to the Senate, an act to regulate privatization (an "anti-privatization bill," according to Weld) that merely required an in-house management study to determine the most efficient manner for delivering services before any decision to "privatize" a service could occur. S. 1514, the redrafted version, added what Weld tried to make a controversial element: that a service was to be privatized only if there was to be a documented saving of 10 percent with no decrease in the level of services. Although this provision was inserted to compensate for low bidders who might subsequently increase their costs once awarded the contract, and it has been the federal government's practice for decades, the Weld administration accused the legislature of stacking the deck against privatization. Pacheco felt that since Weld was claiming savings of 40 to 50 percent, the 10 percent threshold should not be difficult. The bill also required that health insurance be provided to employees of the contractor. Finally, it not surprisingly gave Pacheco's Committee on State Administration, along with the house and senate Ways and Means Committees, some discretionary power over privatization, requiring the secretary of administration and finance to submit a report justifying privatization *before* any contracts were let.

In late May 1993, a more detailed and more sophisticated bill, S. 1642, later to become S. 1664, was submitted by senate Ways and Means Committee members, with a companion bill introduced in the house. The controversial 10 percent savings requirement was dropped. The bill (as amended in conference) included the previous requirements of written statements on costs and quality of service measures and health care benefits. Major additions included:

- A five-year limit on any contract (a sunset law).
- Regulation of all contracts over $100,000.
- A guarantee for employees of contractors of the average private sector wage, or the state wage for similar services, whichever is lower.
- A requirement that employers offer positions to qualified state employees.
- A strong conflict-of-interest provision, prohibiting state employees involved in the contracting process from going to work for the vendor awarded the contract.
- Provisions for vendor compliance with affirmative action and equal opportunity laws.
- Oversight of the whole process by the state auditor.

The state auditor was in effect given a veto power over privatization. The state auditor in Massachusetts is an independently elected constitutional officer, charged with providing "the Governor, the Legislature, auditees, oversight agencies, and the general public . . . independent evaluation of the various agencies, activities, and programs operated by the Commonwealth" (Massachusetts, 1994a; 2). The position is currently held by a Democrat, a former member of the state legislature.

The final bill was passed by both houses of the legislature in November 1993, and, quite naturally, was vetoed by the governor, mostly for the power it gave to the state auditor. On December 16,1993, the veto was overridden.

THE GOVERNOR'S GUIDELINES REVISED

As the regulation of privatization bill was going through the legislative process, Weld's Office of Administration and Finance was developing a much more detailed set of guidelines for the privatization process, perhaps in an attempt to cut off the legislature's action, suggesting the value of a healthy clash of interests. The report, entitled *Privatization in Massachusetts: Getting Results,* was released in November 1993.

In a section entitled "Evaluating Privatization Initiatives," the report lists and discusses the ideal conditions for privatization, much expanded from the original Administration and Finance memo, and including:

1. Competitive marketplace—the desire for multiple potential providers and a warning to avoid creation of monopolies.
2. Potential for savings—decreased costs without passing costs on to service recipients through fees, and the special applicability of privatization to seasonal work.
3. Promise of enhanced quality or responsiveness—promotion of increased quality, consumer satisfaction, or responsiveness for the same cost.
4. Satisfactory assurance of government control and accountability—need to have services readily measurable in terms of quantity, quality, and desired performance, and government agency capacity to maintain oversight.
5. Minimal risk—including the likelihood of private failure, or reduction or stoppage of services if losses occur, and the consequences of such an occurrence.
6. No insurmountable legal, political, or practical barriers—desire to avoid strong opposition, loss of public trust, or conflict with federal and state law.
7. Minimal adverse employee impact—including avoidance of conflict with collective bargaining agreements and maintaining diversity of the work force (Massachusetts, 1993a; 4–6).

This is a strong and inclusive list of issues to be considered. Beside the many new issues raised, obvious examples of improvement over the initial privatization charge to agencies include the need for "multiple bidders" under a "competitive marketplace," and the category "potential for savings," which had surprisingly been missing from the original.

The Weld administration report also offers a parallel seven point guide to "mitigating imperfect conditions." Some of the strategies include:

1. To preserve and promote competition—permit in-house program managers and public employees to bid for the contract on a level playing field, contract with multiple vendors, and maintain an in-house capacity to perform the services.

2. To ensure that potential savings are realized and maximized—build cost controls and containments incentives into contracts.
3. To ensure quality and responsiveness—develop reliable measures of service quality, strengthen in-house monitoring capacity, and write contracts with periodic performance reporting.
4. To ensure accountability and control—write detailed contract specifications, and require record keeping and periodic reports.
5. To reduce risk—conduct pilot projects, phase in privatization slowly, and develop emergency contingency plans in the case of termination of service.
6. To overcome legal and political barriers—involve affected groups in the decision-making process, and sponsor remedial legislation.
7. To soften adverse impact on employees—enable public employees to have an equal opportunity to bid for the work, and develop a personnel redeployment plan, including a requirement that private firms interview displaced employees, and have the state provide job placement and retraining to affected employees (Massachusetts, 1993a; 6–8).

Of particular note is the emphasis in both strategies 1 and 7 on involving and assisting existing public employees in the bid process.

The issue of comparing costs between privatized and in-house provision is also treated in some detail. Particularly interesting issues include determining whether any retained costs result from the salaries of redeployed employees. The guidelines suggest that if they are placed in another already budgeted slot, then the savings are real, whereas if they are placed in a position that otherwise would be kept vacant, the budgetary savings are illusory. It is further suggested that start-up costs and capital investments be amortized over the life of the project, a fair perspective, and one traditionally followed in cost-benefit analysis (Massachusetts, 1993a; 8–10).

The report notes that to be realistic, cost comparisons should contain in-house conversion costs, including competitive procurement and contract development, as well as contract administration costs and contractor support (e.g., data processing, technical assistance, loaned facilities, equipment or staff). The failure to do this had been one of the criticisms made by both employee unions and the state legislature. Indirect costs of both the state agency and private vendor, such as employee payroll taxes and fringe benefits, are to be included in the comparison, while the report also warns of the potential for overlooking such private-sector costs as performance bonds, liability insurance, and legal fees (Massachusetts, 1993a; 10).

If cost estimates result in the likelihood that privatization is warranted, the Weld guidelines next mandate the determination of service specifications and performance standards. The guidelines call for them to be "clear and specific," focused on desired outcomes versus internal operations, quantifiable when possible, and realistic.

Finally, the report offers a privatization checklist to be followed by agencies, which the administration touts as capturing the "best demonstrated practice" of its early privatization initiatives (Massachusetts, 1993a; 3). Included are sections asking those developing privatization initiative questions regarding minority business participation, affirmative action, work force transition, quality assurance, public employee participation in bidding, conflict of interest provisions, cost comparison, and implementation.

In sum, the report offers a comprehensive model for the privatization decision process.

AN ASSESSMENT

The Weld administration approach to privatization offers useful information for other states. The use of a privatization summit with invitees including administrators of privatization efforts in other states is a good strategy for state officials embarking on any new policy. Promoting the decentralization of privatization initiatives in the executive branch allows for the initiation of ideas from those closer to service delivery, while a designated position of Director of Privatization (a practice followed in many other nations) in the agency that oversees the budget allows for internal oversight and a locus for the accumulation of general privatization expertise.

The discussion of issues in the administration's November 1993 report, "Getting Results," is comprehensive, with very important and detailed sections on the ideal conditions for privatization and a guide to mitigating imperfect conditions, including an emphasis on involving current public employees. The discussion of cost comparisons is similarly excellent. The privatization checklist presents agencies with a very practical roadmap to follow through the privatization process and its potential pitfalls.

Yet the Weld experience with privatization suggests a gap between the rhetoric of the recent guidelines and past reality, reinforcing the ongoing controversy, and producing some lessons of its own. The intent of many of the current guidelines was clearly violated in the previous privatizations, as documented by legislative reports. Public employees felt that they were not as involved as they should be, cost comparisons were not comprehensive, and performance data were not presented. Indeed, many of the fears of opponents of privatization in general, and those affected in Massachusetts, were realized. After the adoption of the legislative check, the Weld administration stepped back from its privatization campaign, seeking only to expand on existing privatizations or to implement ones under the $100,000 limit that would trigger the state auditor review. To some, this suggests that justification of the privatization initiatives was problematic.

The rush to privatize produced policy mistakes. The most costly in both fiscal and human terms has been the inability of the state to find homes for many of the mental health patients displaced because of the state hospital closings. While partially reimbursable by the federal government's Medicaid program, the cost to the state of maintaining many of these patients in private hospitals has been considerably over budget, while reinforcing a medical orientation that may detract from community support objectives. The state has been realizing only half of the predicted savings from Medicaid reimbursement, as there are problems qualifying the homeless, illegal immigrants, and those who recently moved to the state. The administration had projected savings of $9.82 million in fiscal 1994 by moving Division of Mental Health patients into private hospitals but in actuality had saved only $4.5 million by July of that year, with potentially lower quality care (Bass, 1994a). The Commonwealth also had to spend an extra $3.3 million over 1993–94 to place hundreds of acutely ill mental health patients in private hospitals—patients who would have been treated in state facilities at about one-half the cost prior to privatization (Bass, 1994b).

After privatization, injuries more than doubled between 1993 and 1994, from 77 to 175, and the number of patients who walked away from residential placements or mental hospitals rose from 366 to 542. A psychiatrist in the system for 25 years remarked, "I think these statistics show that the privatization of mental health services is a social catastrophe" (Bass, 1995). In retrospect, some executive branch officials admit that they moved too fast, without proper evaluation of alternative care providers.

Legitimacy concerns have been raised by instances of revolving door behavior (the individual who negotiated the prison health care privatization has gone to work for the provider), the extravagant expenses of some contractors, and campaign contributions from vendors. While not illegal, these actions cause concern for the taxpaying public, and potentially damage privatization's reputation.

Disturbing criticisms also relate to the manner in which privatization decisions were made and the inability to document claimed savings and equal or better service. The legislature's Audit Bureau findings that the administration did not follow uniform cost-calculation process, and, among other things, failed to include the costs of conducting privatization studies and promotion, are worrisome, as is the administration's failure to provide data even when subpoenaed. Even more disturbing (and instructive) are charges that whether intentional or not, actions were taken that stacked the deck in favor of privatization, including

1. The inflation of expected savings.
2. The failure in some cases to adequately measure service levels and costs before privatization, thus prohibiting accurate comparison.
3. The reduction in resources for the highway maintenance project in the period before privatization, lowering performance, and thus increasing the likelihood of service improvement after privatization.
4. The redrawing or consolidation of district lines for highway maintenance, further hindering accurate pre- and post-privatization performance and cost.
5. The failure to explain bidding rules equally to all parties, and rejection of union bids on judgment calls.
6. The selling off of state equipment to create high switching costs and thus increase the cost of future bids by state workers; and
7. The failure to include the costs of unemployment, health insurance, and/or retraining for displaced state workers (Gow *et al.,* 1993: Commonwealth of Massachusetts, 1993a; 1995; 1994a; 1993c; Pacheco, 1995).

While some of the individual privatizations have proved their worth, the process for determining and justifying them has not been a consistent one. The new Weld administration guidelines respond to some of these criticisms, but whether they would have been developed in the absence of legislative opposition is an open question.

The Pacheco law to regulate privatization in Massachusetts offers some important policy considerations, and its development reminds us of certain principles which can inform the privatization process. First is the benefit of an independent check on privatization decisions, at least those of any magnitude. Partisan or institutional incentives may lead to a rush to privatize (or misinformed opposition to it) with mistakes potentially made. Better policy is likely to result from decision making which includes several perspectives in a clear, delineated process, and is potentially best served by such an independent check by an office with little to gain politically by the ultimate decision. The removal of the state legislature in Massachusetts from the umpire role was probably a wise decision. The involvement of a third party such as the auditor in Massachusetts is likely to reduce suspicion among state workers and their unions about "stacked decks" and thus promote legitimacy and potentially cooperation. The conflict of interest regulation in the Pacheco law is also an important addition to privatization policy and needs an objective administrator.

Second, it is important to encourage and assist bidding by state workers; after all, if existing state workers can match or lower outside bids, transition costs are eliminated and the need for further privatizations may be lessened as other state employees reconsider the existing system and weigh their options. Privatization should promote competition, not involve political punishment. Indeed, in Massachusetts state workers have in several cases changed their work rules and lowered their cost to the state to avoid privatization, including a 25 percent cut by some transit workers (Palmer, 1993). As one Massachusetts chapter of AFSCME said, "If laws need to be changed, let's change them." One of the least studied effects of privatization is its motivational effect on current state workers.

Finally, it is important to treat privatization, as we should any new policy, as an experiment. Cost and performance must be carefully measured before privatization so that a proper evaluation of privatization's effects can be made. Like all governmental policies, privatization should be easily reversible. The independent check on the privatization decision by the state auditor may help prevent attempts to stack the deck in its favor, which obviously can contaminate results, while the sunset provision enacted by the Massachusetts legislature is important to guarantee that the evaluation occurs. Although proof of savings and performance may, as in many programs, be difficult, legitimacy and accountability argue that it be attempted. As Kettl has suggested, efficiency and lower cost must be balanced by effectiveness, retained in-house capacity, responsiveness, and trust in government (1993b, 17–20).

POLITICS AND PRIVATIZATION POLICY

It is sometimes hard to find an arena in which a meaningful clash of interests, filtered through the political system, allows a policy to be developed to its fullest potential. The privatization agenda of Governor William Weld of Massachusetts, resisted by a Democratic legislature traditionally kind to public employee unions, provides us one such arena. "Politics as usual" in this case produced better policy.

Privatization, like many policies, is not always good and not always bad. The proof is in the tasting, or in this case, implementation and evaluation. It can do good; and it can be misused and have harmful effects. Partisan, institutional, or ideological predispositions may result in its overuse, or may hinder its adoption. The politics-administration dichotomy is difficult to maintain.

As John Donohue warned, "Unless we are luckier or more careful than we are likely to be, political pressures will tend to retain for the public sector functions where privatization would make sense, and to privatize tasks that would be better left to government" (Donohue, 1989, 13). Several important concerns are raised by the Massachusetts case and remind us of the need for careful, not lucky decision-making.

The difficulty in determining or agreeing on cost savings means that the process for making decisions becomes very important. The less you can prove, the more input, negotiation, and bargaining you need. The tendency of a proponent or opponent to try to stack the deck likewise argues for a sound, well-defined, and inclusive process. The Weld administration's refusing the low bid of the public employees for highway maintenance and subsequent sale of equipment are examples of proponent stacking; the 10 percent savings provision that the legislature attempted can be viewed as opponent rigging. Some evidence of revolving-door behavior warns us of the bad old days of patronage and kickbacks. Massachusetts has fairly strong campaign finance laws to prevent legal kickbacks, but not all states do. The need to regulate is clear.

What is also clear is the advantage of having some independent or bipartisan oversight. The inherent difficulty in measuring performance in most government services and in documenting cost savings from a change of service provider is a strong argument for careful consideration of privatization initiatives. This is especially true when privatization becomes a crusade.

The difficult question for other states may be how to institutionalize skepticism and oversight that grew out of the political climate and divided government of Massachusetts, and where to place the "check." Many institutional actors were considered for the role of referee, including attorney general, state inspector general, and state auditor. In same states, a bipartisan or nonpartisan commission might work best. Some double security as to the rights of public employees, service providers, service recipients, and taxpayers is warranted, however. The mechanism may need to conform to the political culture and institutions of each state. But mechanism there should be. While becoming Kettl's "smart buyer" in the privatization process, state officials must not forget the principles of good government, which call for procedure, access, and accountability.

ACKNOWLEDGMENT

The author gratefully acknowledges the research assistance of Jesse Decker, Bill Cole, and David Danek.

REFERENCES

Bass, Alison, 1994a. "Medicaid Payments Lagging for Mass." *Boston Globe* (August 5), 24.
———, 1994b. "Mental Health Shift Costs State $3.3m." *Boston Globe* (December 20), 1.
———, 1995. "DMH Sees Increase in Deaths." *Boston Globe* (June 11), 1.
Butler. Stuart, 1991. "Privatization for Public Purposes." In William Gormley, ed., *Privatization and Its Alternatives*. Madison, WI: University of Wisconsin Press, pp. 17–24.
Chi, Keon, 1993. "Privatization in State Government; Options for the Future." *State Trends Forecasts.* 2 (2): 1–39.
Cigler, B.A., 1990. "County Contracting: Reconciling the Accountability and Information Paradoxes." *Public Administration Quarterly,* vol. 14, 285–301.
Donahue, John, 1989. *The Privatization Decision: Public Ends, Private Means.* New York: Basic Books.
Dukakis, Michael, 1994. Interview, August 19.
Florestano, Patricia S., 1994. "State Commissions on Privatization: Research, Recommendations, and Cautions." Paper presented at the annual conference of the American Society for Public Administration.
Gore, Al, 1993. *The Gore Commission Report on Reinventing Government.* New York: Times Books.
Gormley, William T., 1991. "The Privatization Controversy." In William T. Gormley, ed., *Privatization and Its Alternatives*. Madison, WI: University of Wisconsin Press, pp. 3–16.
Gow, David *et al.,* 1993. "Highway Maintenance Services in Essex County." Excerpted from *From Public to Private: The Massachusetts Experience 1991–1993,* Cambridge, MA: John F. Kennedy School of Government, April.
Kettl, Donald F., 1993a. "The Myths, Realities, and Challenges of Privatization." In Frank J. Thompson, ed., *Revitalizing State and Local Public Service.* San Francisco: Jossey-Bass, pp. 246–275.
———, 1993b. *Sharing Power: Public Governance and Private Markets.* Washington, DC: Brookings Institution.
Massachusetts Governor's Special Commission on Consolidation of Health and Human Services Institutional Facilities, 1991. "Actions for Quality Care: A Plan for the Consolidation of Stare Institutions and for the Provision of Appropriate Care Services." June,
Massachusetts House Committee on Post Audit and Oversight, 1993a., "Privatization Savings: Where's the Beef" December 17.
Massachusetts Executive Office for Administration and Finance. 1993b, "Privatization in Massachusetts: Getting Results." November 1.
Massachusetts Senate Committee on Ways and Means, "Does Privatization Sell the Public Short?" in S1994, June, 1993.
Massachusetts House Committee on Post Audit and Oversight, Subcommittee on Privatization, 1993c. "Privatization of Essex County Highway Maintenance: Private Profits at Taxpayers' Expense." June 9.
Massachusetts House Committee on Post Audit and Oversight, 1994a. "Interim Report Review of Essex County Privatization." May.
Massachusetts Office of the State Auditor, 1994b. "Semi-Annual Report." November.
Massachusetts Office of the State Auditor, 1995. "State Auditor's Report on the Privatization of the Maintenance of State Roads in Essex County, October 7, 1992 to October 6. 1993." July 19.
McNamara, Eileen, 1992. "Paying Dearly for Privatization." *Boston Globe* (June 14), 14.
Pacheco, Mark, 1995. Interview, April 11.
Palmer, Thomas C., Jr., 1993. "Privatization Results in Layoffs of 160 Highway Workers." *Boston Globe* (October 10), 23.
Pressman, Jeffrey and Aaron Wildavsky, 1977. *Implementation.* Berkeley, CA: University of California Press.
Savas, E.S., 1987. *Privatization: The Key to Better Government.* Chatham, NJ: Chatham House.
Starr, Paul, 1987. "The Limits of Privatization." In Steven Hanke, ed., *Prospects for Privatization.* New York: Academy of Political Science, pp. 124–137.
Wallin, Bruce A., 1995. "Massachusetts: Downsizing State Government." In Steven D. Gold, ed., *The Fiscal Crisis of the States: Lessons for the Future.* Washington, DC: Georgetown University Press, pp. 252–295.

PART 7

BUDGET NORMS AND ETHICS

Ethics and norms logically belong at the beginning of a book on budgeting, rather than the end, as they ought to underlie and precede the decisions that budget actors make. However, they often do not become visible until they are absent, norms and ethics are not constants, but anchors that bring back decision makers after they have strayed too far. To see them at all, one has to focus on the glaring instances of the failure of budget actors to adhere to them; to understand why such failures occur, one has to understand the context, the constraints, and the incredible difficulty of trying to prioritize within those constraints.

The norms and ethics of budgeting are not easy to see because they are taken for granted. Only when actors break the rules do they become visible. Thus, the accumulation of annual deficits puts focus on the norms that require budgetary balance; violation of the budget concepts at the federal level calls attention to their existence and definition; shifts from one voting rule to another focus on how the rights of legislative and political minorities are protected; changes in the budget during the year underscore the accountability created by passing the budget openly in public. Similarly, scandals in financial management such as occurred in Orange County, California, where risky investments brought a very rich county to the edge of bankruptcy, and failure to adhere to revenue earmarking make one think about norms of accountability. Many of the selections in this part talk about or take off from one of these violations, not because they are that common, but because they reveal the inner workings of budgeting, the norms, the circumstances of their failure, and the return to the norms and ethical standards. That return is not in any sense guaranteed, but the cost of continued departure from the norms is loss of public trust, and a kind of chaos, where definitions are so blurred no one, not even the budgeteers themselves, can tell what the true financial condition is and there are no standards to judge a good budget.

Carol Lewis describes one of the most fundamental of budgeting norms, that of budgetary balance. She discovered that in many cases balance is not a legal requirement, but a widely shared norm.

Thomas Cuny calls attention to the effort at the federal level to establish key concepts and definitions, and to keep those definitions intact from one year to the next so that changes in policy would be visible. He wanted time series data to all be based on the same assumptions, to increase accountability and transparency; politicians on the other hand often wanted to alter definitions to make the results look more favorable, in the process eroding the quality of information. This tension between information consistency and degradation occurs at all levels of government, not just the federal level.

Kevin Kearns discusses the Orange County investment debacle, with a focus on what accountability means, and how it can be achieved. While Kearns approaches the subject of accountability generally, Charles Spindler addresses the issue in the concrete, looking at earmarked taxation to see if it is spent in accordance with those earmarks. He leaves readers with the question of how citizens respond when they have been defrauded—states promising they will spend the money one way, and in fact spending it a different way.

Bill Dauster addresses the question of the rules that govern consideration of the budget in the Senate. The Senate has often been considered the more deliberate and thoughtful house of Congress, one in which discussion can be longer and deeper, in part because there are only 100 senators, and in part because of the rules which allow objections by minorities to hold up legislation. Any time decisions must be made more by consensus than by simple majority rule there is likely to be more discussion. Dauster wonders what the consequences are for democracy and for budgeting when rules shift the emphasis from consensus decision making to majority rule: He fears the tyranny of the majority. Dauster has argued elsewhere that there are rules that enable the legislative body to function, allowing minority parties some influence and facilitating shifts in party majorities, for example, that are threatened or torn down by partisans seeking short-term advantage. He thus alerts the reader to the tension between rules that enable the democratic process to function in budgeting and extremes of partisanship that erode those same rules for short-term gain.

CHAPTER 31

BUDGETARY BALANCE
The Norm, Concept, and Practice in Large U.S. Cities

CAROL W. LEWIS

THE NORM OF BALANCE

The idea of budgetary balance is crucial to contemporary municipal budgeting in the United States. A concise metaphor for good government and a symbol of fiscal integrity and prudence, budgetary balance is pressed into service as a simple, summary measure of overall capacity to govern. A recent article in *The CPA Journal* notes, "The requirement of a balanced budget for governments is widely acclaimed as a means of achieving fiscal prudence and economy" (Granof and Mayper, 1991, p. 28, italics omitted). An article published by Moody's Investors Service proclaims budgetary balance to be "the key urban challenge" for this decade (Kennedy, 1991; 1–7).

The focus and clarity inherent in a single dimension no doubt contribute to the concept's prescriptive appeal. Capturing its allure in his 19th-century novel *David Copperfield,* Charles Dickens displays its arithmetic elegance: "Annual income twenty pounds, annual expenditure nineteen nineteen six, result happiness. Annual income twenty pounds, annual expenditure twenty pounds ought and six, result misery."

In more sophisticated analyses, balance represents more than arithmetic equivalency. Aaron Wildavsky (1992) interprets the chronic federal imbalance as evidence of deep political disagreement. The political functions attributed to balance include consensus building and enforcement. As disciplinarian, balance is "the most important constraint on budgeting" (Rubin, 1993; 164). Its absence customarily is interpreted as signaling that political will or political concord is absent as well. For these reasons (and perhaps because so few generalizations hold across municipalities), the conventional descriptive accent in municipal budgeting falls on budgetary balance. Cope (1992; 1099) states, "Most local governments are required by their charters, state laws, or both, to balance their operating budgets." Similarly, Rubin (1993; 198) comments, "Cities, like states, are required to balance their budgets."[1]

Is budgetary balance in fact the ideal and empirical reality portrayed in the prescriptive and descriptive literature on municipal budgeting? The precise meaning and potential impact of budgetary balance vary so widely among jurisdictions that component details are more informative

From *Public Administration Review,* vol. 54, no. 6 (November/December 1994), 515–524. Copyright © 1994 by American Society for Public Administration. Reprinted with permission.

than the generalization. Given possible permutations, how is balance operationalized in different municipalities? What patterns can be discerned?

To answer these and related questions, database searches and a telephone survey were conducted in fall 1992. Additional telephone calls to finance directors, budget officers, academic experts, and/or other knowledgeable informants were made where discrepancies or ambiguities indicated clarification was needed. Empirical evidence for the 100 most populous U.S. cities confirms and informs the general proposition that municipal budgets must be balanced.

Formal Provisions

An efficient investigation logically begins with the most general applicable rules; here, they are state-imposed budget requirements. The results of the database search of state statutes and constitutions show that at least 20 states require balanced municipal budgets (Table 31.1).[2] The findings necessarily are ambiguous because of: regulatory or backdoor provisions unidentifiable through a search by key words or of statutes (such as in Massachusetts), ambiguity in the law or its application (e.g., Texas), variable treatment of different classes of municipalities (e.g., Connecticut), and the fact that home rule charters supersede state law in some instances (e.g., Virginia and Pennsylvania). Therefore, states not listed in Table 31.1 do not necessarily permit imbalance, and individual cities located in rostered states are not necessarily covered by the general state requirement. Nonetheless, the data in Table 31.1 establish that states prescribe municipal budgetary balance in many cases where the formal, obligatory standard cannot be said to be a norm of municipal budgeting *per se*.

To supplement and enrich the database search, a telephone survey of finance or budget officers or analysts in the 100 most populous cities in the United States was conducted in fall 1992. Although almost all respondents replied at once that budgetary balance is required, many initially could not pinpoint specifics (and some graciously offered to research the information for the survey). This behavior suggests that balance is an accepted norm even in the absence of known legal requirements. In some instances, moreover, reported data were erroneous or contradictory, although this did not seem at all to the point for some respondents. One veteran finance professional spelled out his view of political and professional reality by explaining that the formal requirement was trivial compared to his community's insistence on balance. These interview experiences bear out that balance is a potent norm in municipal budgeting.

The budgetary balance requirements reported for the 100 most populous U.S. cities are reported in Table 31.2. All of the largest 50 cities and 99 of the 100 leading cities reported a balance requirement of some sort. The legal basis was reported as state law (53 percent) and/or city charter (58 percent). The dominance of California and Texas among the largest cities in Table 31.2, coupled with their absence from Table 31.1, colors any state-by-state analysis. All regions of the country are represented, although New England and the Mid-Atlantic states have relatively few cities on the roster.

Precisely when balance comes into play is one of the more important rules of the game in municipal budgeting. Table 31.2 displays the information for each city. Balance may be required upon submission, when the budget is adopted, for operating results (when a formal year-end deficit in the general fund is prohibited), or in some combination thereof. Each stage spotlights a different institution as responsible for meeting the standard: for submission, it is the executive; for adoption, the legislative body; and for operations, the municipal administration. More than four-fifths of the largest cities report requiring balance upon submission and/or adoption.

Because the constraint is more forceful the later it comes in the process, it is significant that

Table 31.1

States Requiring Balanced Municipal Budgets[a]

By Statute	By Constitution
Alabama	Idaho
Connecticut	Virginia
Georgia	Wyoming
Kansas	
Kentucky	
Massachusetts[b]	
Mississippi	
Montana	
New Hampshire	
North Dakota	
Ohio	
Oklahoma	
Oregon	
Pennsylvania	
Rhode Island	
Utah	
Wisconsin	

a. Inclusion indicates that the state requirement applies to any or all classes of municipalities. For example, Connecticut's requirement applies only to municipalities with Boards of Finance. Special legislation for an individual city (e.g., New York City) does not trigger inclusion here.

b. A follow-up telephone survey was conducted in fall 1992. CA, TX, and OH, negative on the database search, together account for 19 (38 percent) of the 50 most populous cities in Table 31.2. According to the Office of the Attorney General in the respective state, OH constitutionally requires municipalities to balance their budgets; California has no statewide municipal requirement; and the response for TX is variable (and confirmed by the Houston respondent's volunteered observation reported in Table 31.2). According to the Division of Local Services of the Massachusetts Department of Revenue, all municipalities, including Boston, must balance their budgets to gain this department's certification of the tax rate and of compliance with the levy limit (Proposition 2½); this indirect approach does not show up on a database search.

Source: Search of Lexis database conducted fall 1992 by key words; budget with municipal; budget; fund w/10 balance, deficit; surplus; appropriate; and balance w/10 budget. Supplemented by telephone interviews in selected states in fall 1992.

more than one-third (34) of the most populous cities must balance operating results over the course of implementation. In effect, they are required to *rebudget* (Forrester and Mullins, 1992a, 1992b). For example, the city charter prohibits a year-end balance in San Francisco, where this provision offsets some credit risk (Table 31.2). "Projected and midyear [sic] budget imbalances have occurred three years in a row since the city depleted its general fund budgetary balance in fiscal 1991. Previous gaps were closed as the strict city charter dictates" and "[c]harter requirements mandate reserves and reinforce fiscal discipline by requiring [the] controller to withhold appropriations if revenues are insufficient" (Fitch Research, 1993b; 1, 3). Conspicuous by its premier population ranking, history of financial disarray, and restrictive balance requirement, New York City must rebalance quarterly to meet the provisions of the state's special legislation. The requirement to balance operating results annually is on the books in 44 percent (22) of the 50 most populous cities, compared with 24 percent (12) of the 50 next most populous cities.

The purpose here is to describe budgetary balance in the largest cities and identify patterns. Data in Table 31.3 bear out that population is not an explanatory variable (no balance requirement

Table 31.2

Reported Balanced Budget Requirements in the Most Populous U.S. Cities, 1992–1993

City[a]	Required	By State	By City Charter	Other	Stage Required Submitted	Adopted	Year End[c]	Population Ranking[b]
New York	yes	statute	yes		yes	yes	yes[c]	1
Los Angeles	yes		yes		yes	yes		2
Chicago	yes	statute	yes		yes	yes	yes	3
Houston	yes	(d)		(e)	yes	yes		4
Philadelphia	yes		yes		yes	yes		5
San Diego	yes		yes			yes		6
Detroit	yes	statute	yes		yes	yes		7
Dallas	yes	constitution			yes	yes	yes	8
Phoenix	yes	statute			yes		yes	9
San Antonio	yes		yes		yes	yes	yes	10
San Jose	yes	(f)	(f)		yes	yes	yes	11
Baltimore	yes			(g)	yes	yes		12
Indianapolis	yes	statute			yes	yes	yes	13
San Francisco	yes		yes		yes		yes	14
Jacksonville	yes	statute	yes		yes			15
Columbus, OH	yes	constitution			yes	yes	yes	16
Milwaukee	yes		yes		yes			17
Memphis	yes		yes		yes	yes		18
Washington, DC	yes			(h)	yes	yes		19
Boston	yes	statute			yes	yes	yes	20
Seattle	yes	statute			yes	yes		21
El Paso	yes	statute	yes			yes		22
Cleveland	yes	statute			yes	yes		23
New Orleans	yes		yes		yes			24
Nashville	yes		yes		yes	yes	yes	25
Denver	yes	statute	yes		yes	yes		26
Austin	yes				yes	yes		27
Fort Worth	yes		yes		yes	yes		28
Oklahoma City	yes				yes	yes	(i)	29

426

City							#
Portland	*yes*	*statute*	*yes*	*yes*	*yes*	*yes*	*30*
Kansas City, MO	yes		yes	yes	yes	yes	31
Long Beach	yes		yes	yes	yes	yes	32
Tucson	yes	statute	yes	yes	yes	yes	33
St. Louis	yes		yes	yes	yes		34
Charlotte	yes	statute		yes	yes		35
Atlanta	*yes*	*statute*	*yes*	*yes*	*yes*		*36*
Virginia Beach	*yes*	*constitution*		*yes*	*yes*		*37*
Albuquerque	yes	statute	yes	yes	yes	yes	38
Oakland	yes		yes	yes		yes	39
Pittsburgh	*yes*		*yes*	*yes*	*yes*		*40*
Sacramento	yes		yes	yes			41
Minneapolis	yes	statute	yes	yes	yes		42
Tulsa	yes	statute		yes	yes	yes	43
Honolulu	yes		yes	yes	yes		44
Cincinnati	*yes*	*statute*		*yes*	*yes*	*yes*	*45*
Miami	yes	statute	yes	yes	yes		46
Fresno	yes		yes	yes	yes		47
Omaha	yes		yes	yes		yes	48
Toledo	*yes*		*yes*	*yes*	*yes*		*49*
Buffalo	yes		yes	yes	yes	yes	50
Wichita	no		yes	yes			51
Santa Ana	yes	statute	yes	yes	yes		52
Mesa	yes	statute		yes	yes		53
Colorado Springs	yes	statute	yes	yes	yes		54
Tampa	yes	statute		yes	yes		55
Newark	yes	statute		yes		yes	56
St. Paul	yes		yes	yes	yes		57
Louisville	*yes*	*statute*	*yes*	*yes*	*yes*		*58*
Anaheim	yes		yes	yes	yes		59
Birmingham	*yes*		*yes*	*yes*	*yes*	*yes*	*59*
Arlington, TX	yes		(c)	yes	yes		60
Norfollk	*yes*	*constitution*	*yes*	*yes*	*yes*		*61*
Las Vegas	yes	statute	yes	yes	yes		62
Corpus Christi	yes		yes	yes	yes		63
							64

(continued)

Table 31.2 *(continued)*

City[a]	Required	By State	By City Charter	Other	Stage Required Submitted	Adopted	Year End[b]	Population Ranking
St. Petersburg	yes	statute			yes	yes		65
Rochester	yes	statute			yes	yes		66
Jersey City	yes		yes		yes	yes		67
Riverside	yes		yes		yes	yes		68
Anchorage	yes		yes		yes	yes	yes	69
Lexington-Fayette	yes	statute	yes		yes	yes		70
Akron	yes	*statute*	*yes*		yes	*yes*		71
Aurora	yes	statute	yes		yes	yes		72
Baton Rouge	yes	statute			yes	yes	yes	73
Stockton	yes		yes		yes	yes		74
Raleigh	yes	statute			yes			75
Richmond	yes	*const. stat*	*yes*		yes	*yes*	*yes*	76
Shreveport	yes		yes		yes	yes		77
Jackson	yes	*statute*				*yes*		78
Mobile	yes	*statute*				*yes*	*yes*	79
Des Moines	yes	statute			yes	yes		80
Lincoln	yes	statute			yes	yes	yes	81
Madison	yes	*statute*			yes	*yes*	*yes*	82
Grand Rapids	yes	(f)	(f)		yes	yes		83
Yonkers	yes	statute	yes		yes	yes		84
Hialeah	yes	statute			yes	yes	yes	85
Montgomery	yes	*statute*			yes	*yes*	*yes*	86
Lubbock	yes					yes		87
Greensboro	yes	statute	yes		yes	yes	yes	88
Dayton	yes		*yes*			*yes*		89
Huntington Beach	yes		yes		yes	yes		90
Garland	yes		yes		yes	yes		91
Glendale	yes		yes		yes	yes		92
Columbus, GA	yes	*statute*			yes	*yes*		93

Spokane	yes	statute			yes	94
Tacoma	yes	statute			yes	95
Little Rock	yes	statute			yes	96
Bakersfield	yes		yes	yes	yes	97
Freemont	yes		yes	yes	yes	98
Fort Wayne	yes	statute			yes	99
Arlington, VA	*yes*	*constitution*	*yes*	*yes*	*yes*	*100*
Total	99	53	58	84	86	35

Source: Telephone interviews conducted 1992–1993 with finance or budget officials or analysts in reported cities. Population ranking is from U.S. Department of Commerce, Bureau of the Census (1991).

a. Italics indicate that Table 31.1 shows state requires balanced budget from any or all classes of municipalities. Note that city charter may supersede state requirements as in, for example, Philadelphia, Pittsburgh, and Virginia Beach.

b. Formal year-end deficit is prohibited; operating results must balance, but reserves and/or other tactics may be used to achieve operating balance.

c. Must rebalance quarterly.

d. As noted in Table 31.1, state statute is subject to varying legal interpretations.

e. Independently elected city comptroller certifies availability of funds.

f. Response of *don't know*.

g. City ordinance.

h. Federal law.

i. May not overexpend appropriations without budget amendment during fiscal year.

Table 31.3

Patterns of Budgetary Balance in the Most Populous U.S. Cities

Population Quintile	Stage Required Submission	Adoption	Year End	Required at All Stages
Lowest 1st	18	15	9	7
2nd	17	16	8	6
3rd	17	17	5	3
4th	20	19	5	5
Highest 5th	12	19	7	3
Total	84	86	34	24

Source: Table 31.2.

correlates significantly with population) but serves solely as the basis for selecting financially and politically interesting cities to describe. Frequency declines as stringency increases, except for adoption. The obvious disjuncture between the third and fourth columns speaks to the relative permissiveness of the balance requirement in the most populous cities.

An across-the-board obligation obviously is the most confining, but it also may diffuse responsibility by widely distributing it. As a tool of mutual restraint affecting strategy and outcomes for *all* participants *at every step,* budgetary balance is required at each of the three stages in the process in almost one-quarter (24) of the 100 most populous cities (see Table 31.3). State law and/or charter provisions apply and (again perhaps because of two states' dominance) no pattern is apparent in the legal source of the comprehensive requirement. Cities in every region of the country operate under a comprehensive balance requirement: Northeast/Mid-Atlantic, two; Southeast, six; Southwest, six; Midwest, six; and the Pacific region running from California to Alaska, four (Table 31.2).

The Balance Model

The fundamental premise that balance describes the desirable relationship between revenues and expenditures is illustrated in simplified terms in Figure 31.1. This relationship is represented as configurations A and F in Figure 31.1. Referring to the Dickens quote, Webber and Wildavsky (1986, p. 594) define *the Micawber principle.* "it is not the level of income and outgo but their relationship that matters [and] is essential to budgeting." The schematic representation of budgetary balance in Figure 31.1 summarizes the cumulative impact of the annual ritual described by Philip Dearborn (Shiff, 1991a). "The process of budgeting is always a difficult one. All budgets start out initially out of balance. . . . The demands for spending always exceed the resources that are available, and this leads to . . . a conflict . . . throughout the budget process, and it leads to very difficult times in balancing budgets . . ." (pp. 6–7).

Figure 31.1 depicts how balance theoretically "forces discipline on budget actors" (Rubin, 1993; 164) by linking revenue and expenditure decisions. This push toward equivalence does not, however, prescribe which variable(s) to alter, or when. For all its power, balance does not dictate the levels of revenues and spending, but just that they be coupled. In this way, allowance is made for variability in revenue capacity, political and tax preferences, responsiveness, procedures, and other local characteristics.

The link is long term. "Fund balance does not refer to cash balance, nor is it the difference between revenues and expenditures. Rather, fund balance is the cumulative difference of all revenues and expenditures from the government's creation" (Allan, 1990; 1, note omitted). The presumed

Figure 31.1   **The Balance Model**

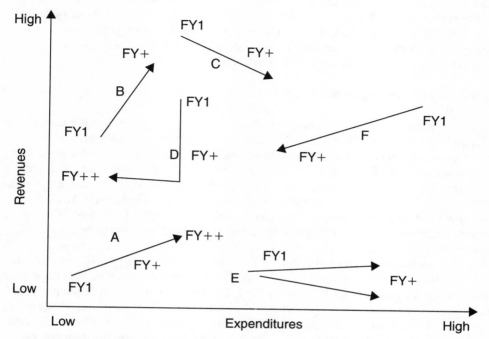

A and F = tendency towards equivalency.
B = overtaxing or building reserves.
C = revenue decline, spending increase.
D = revenue decline, stable spending; then spending cuts when reserves depleted.
E = potential insolvency.

dynamic underlying municipal budgeting is that a municipality tends over several fiscal periods to move closer toward a balanced relationship, rather than further from it.[3] As Dickens' quote implies, balance usually is revenue driven, but the predictive power presumably holds only over the longer term for a particular jurisdiction, and many permutations are possible in any single fiscal year. Sustained imbalance with excessive revenues logically and empirically stimulates tax cuts. Budgetary imbalance loading on the spending side predictably leads to insolvency in the long term. Configuration E in Figure 31.1 depicts two budgetary patterns heading in this unsustainable direction.

Budgetary balance is only one of many factors contributing to a jurisdiction's capacity and well-being, and says nothing about the quality of life in the community. Because any single measure of financial operations or condition necessarily includes and excludes selected factors and is intrinsically limited, it is useful to bear in mind George Bernard Shaw's (1904; 169) observation, "[T]he balance sheet of a city's welfare cannot be state in figures. Counters of a much more spiritual kind are needed, and some imagination and conscience to add them up, as well."[4]

Imbalance versus Insolvency

The recent literature on budgeting (Rubin, 1993), fiscal stress and distress (Cope, 1992; Mackey, 1993; MacManus *et al.,* 1989; Wolman, 1983, 1992), urban politics and political economy (Judd and Kantor, 1992; Kantor and David, 1992), and municipal debt (Sbragia, 1983, 1992) offers alternative perspectives on fiscal capacity, stress, and insolvency. Seeming contradictions arise from different definitions and purposes. In *Evaluating Financial Condition,* Groves (1980) use-fully distinguishes among four usages: *cash solvency* or short-term liquidity; *budgetary solvency* or fiscal-year balance, *long-run solvency* or balance; and *service-level solvency* that relates to meeting the community's service needs and/or demands.

Insolvency and the Bridgeport Bankruptcy Case

The Bridgeport bankruptcy case illustrates the limits of the concept of budgetary balance and how it differs from insolvency. When the mayor of Connecticut's largest city (140,000 population) filed for Chapter 9 protection in June 1991, Bridgeport became the largest general purpose unit of government ever to petition under the federal Bankruptcy Code (Lewis, 1994). Moreover, "the city became a national symbol of urban despair when the former mayor filed for bankruptcy" (Lomuscio, 1992).

Finding that the city was not insolvent at the time of the June filing, Judge Alan H. W. Shiff expe-ditiously dismissed the petition on August 1. (Appeals and cross-appeals to U.S. District Court were pulled and finalized in February 1992, and a stipulation of dismissal approved without prejudice.)

Insolvency is defined in 11 U.S.C. Section 101 (32) (C) for purposes of bankruptcy: "with reference to a municipality, financial condition such that the municipality is—(i) generally not paying its debts as they become due unless such debts are the subject of a bona fide dispute; or (ii) unable to pay its debts as they become due. . . ." The jurisdiction bears the burden of proof. The Advisory Commission on Intergovernmental Relations (1985, p. 39, hereafter ACIR) noted, "The principal unresolved question remains how to define insolvency for purposes of permit-ting the use of the federal bankruptcy code." The Bridgeport case resolved this core concern. A member of the city's legal team had remarked with evident foresight, "It would be an irony if the city of Bridgeport was [sic] unable to file bankruptcy because it was in too solid financial health" (Scheffey, 1991a; 14). Because of the relatively restrictive definition of insolvency used by the court, this is precisely what happened.

In his memorandum of decision, Bankruptcy Court Judge Shiff (1991b) unequivocally stated, "Bridgeport's insolvency should be judged by a cash flow, not a budget deficiency, analysis." He further determined, The [c]ity argues that since [sic] its expenditures will exceed its revenue, it has satisfied the burden of proving that it is insolvent. The [s]tate counters that if a prospective analysis is used, Bridgeport's solvency should be judged by a cash flow, not a budget deficiency, analysis. I agree with the [s]tate."

Proceeding from an altogether different perspective on insolvency, the city rejected the court's formulation. In its appeal (Bridgeport, 1991; 14–15), the city countered,

> The [c]ourt erroneously and without citing any legal precedent concluded that the ability of a municipality to "pay it's [sic] debts as they become due" can best and only be determined by a cash flow analysis. The [c]ity proposes that a cash flow analysis is only one, and not the most reliable, measure of a municipality's ability to "pay it's [sic] debts as they become due." . . . The court's cash flow standard is nowhere set forth in the Bankruptcy Act not in any prior decisions. . . . Rather, the case law disfavors adoption of such an exact standard, and instead requires an analysis of the particular facts and circumstances of an individual case to determine insolvency. . . . Under the [c]ourt-adopted cash flow analysis, Bridgeport indeed may have limited cash on hand at a time when its budget process mandates it reduce spending and/or raise taxes, two non-viable options.

The city's appeal further argued that, "Cash flow analysis is but one part of a fiscal examination, it is not *the* fiscal examination. The [c]ourt erred in focusing so narrowly. . . . The bottom line result of the cash flow analysis is that Bridgeport is in dire financial straits yet will be denied Chapter 9 relief at a time when it is fast approaching a time certain when it will no longer be 'able to pay its debts as they become due.'[1] Such a scenario could not have been contemplated or intended by Congress" (Bridgeport, 1991, p. 18).

Bridgeport's legal team (Bridgeport, 1991; 29) interpreted correctly but rejected the ruling. "If a municipality were to be limited by this [c]ourt's restrictively defined insolvency test in its access to the relief intended by Congress to be available through Chapter 9, then clearly Chapter 9 will have extremely limited application and utility." That the city was paying its creditors, covering the payroll, had cash on hand, and a substantial cash reserve (the latter restricted and extraneous to balancing the operating budget) was undisputed. The city's own finance and budget directors testified to these facts in court, and expert participants confirmed them in interviews with this author (Kirshbaum, 1992; Robinson, 1992; Savicsky, 1992). In fact, the city had promised in its initial petition to "guarantee the full payment of its debts with municipal bond holders and trade creditors." The argument concludes (Bridgeport, 1991; 29), "In a manner of speaking, the [c]ourt's ruling merely assures that Bridgeport will have money in its pockets when it dies."

Thomas Scheffey, in *The Connecticut Law Tribune* (1991b; 1), colorfully summarized the ruling as having "pegged Chapter 9 as little more than an oddball footnote in bankruptcy law, and not a powerful new tool to unsnarl the fiscal affairs of distressed cities. . . . The ruling sets out a one- to two-year test period in which a city must show more than that it's drowning in red ink. It must also be on the verge of exhausting all begged or borrowed cash, and about to start stiffing creditors, within that maximum 24-month period."

The inescapable lesson is that bankruptcy is an unavailing option for ameliorating fiscal stress defined as anything but insolvency and other issues are better addressed in other arenas. According to Bankruptcy Judge Shiff (1991b), broadening bankruptcy's scope is a congressional call: "The flaw in Bridgeport's argument is that the financial difficulties short of insolvency are not a basis for Chapter 9 relief. If such conditions are to be a criteria for municipal bankruptcy, Congress, not the courts, will have to make that change . . ." in the bankruptcy code.

Leaving "the perennial question" of budgetary balance to the political arena, Shiff (1991b; 7) observed, "The answer in the first instance must come from the political process, not the courts. If, however, a city is insolvent . . . [and eligible under law], Chapter 9 may be used. . . . but Chapter 9 is not available to a city simply because it is financially distressed."

Connecticut's Attorney General Richard Blumenthal (1991; 6) concurred. "The plain fact is that Chapter 9 does not provide a realistic solution for a major municipality in fiscal crisis. And the reason relates not only to specific provisions in Chapter 9—their defects or ambiguities—but more fundamentally to the nature of the financial difficulties faced by our major cities." Adding a political component, Blumenthal discerned, "A federal bankruptcy court clearly lacks—and constitutionally cannot be provided with—two ingredients essential to resolving the fiscal crises that plague our cities today: cash, and power." His conclusion is that "the bankruptcy process provides no real solution to a city facing long term, endemic problems. . . . As sympathetic as we must be to the problems and plight of our cities, bankruptcy isn't the solution."

Prospective Insolvency

The Bridgeport case also clarifies the question of projected insolvency raised by the second clause of the statutory definition. The judge opined, "The conclusion that Section 101 (32) (C) (ii) requires

a prospective analysis also comports with the purpose of Chapter 9 . . . Cities cannot go out of
business. Chapter 9 is intended to enable a financially distressed city to continue to provide its
residents with essential services such as police protection, fire protection, sewage and garbage
removal, and schools . . . while it works out a plan to adjust its debts and obligations."

A previous case involving the California school district of San Jose had raised the prospect
of impending inability to meet financial obligations (Winograd, 1985). Here the court found that
"the district was unable to meet its debts as they matured for the 1982–83 school year, was unable to balance its budget for the 1983–84 school year, and thus unable to meet its debts as they
matured in the 1983–84 school year," and was insolvent for Chapter 9 purposes (ACIR, 1985;
39). Allowing for prospective insolvency is evident in the judge's statement that "if you can pay
all your bills today, but everyone knows that you can't pay them tomorrow, then you would be
eligible." The ACIR (1985; 39) observed. "The anticipated fiscal 1984 budget imbalance in San
Jose that was used as a second basis for declaring insolvency also raises doubts about the definition of insolvency. At the time of filing, the school board still had over a year to make adjustments
in both the revenue and expenditures sides of the 1984 budget . . . [T]he claim of an unbalanced
budget for 1984 seems somewhat premature."

In contrast, the core of the Bridgeport decision states, "to be found insolvent a city must prove it
will be unable to pay its debts as they become due in its current fiscal year or, based on an adopted
budget, in its next fiscal year" (Shiff, 1991b).

Until this ruling, neither legislative history nor case law specified the duration of the standard—how far into the future the cash-flow standard reaches. The newly minted standard deliberately forecloses premature evaluation by narrowing the window to the current fiscal year *and
the next for which a budget has been adopted.* Accordingly, the judge determined, "A prediction
at the commencement of this case that Bridgeport will be unable to pay its debts as they become
due in the 1992–1993 fiscal year is unreliable. There are many reasons, not the least of which
is the uncertainty of its cash position during a fiscal year for which there is not even a proposed
budget." The new guideline establishes one fiscal year "as the 'target zone' in which a city must
convincingly show it will run out of gas" (Scheffey, 1991c; 1).

Although the Bridgeport case clarified the insolvency standard for bankruptcy purposes, the
court's ruling probably narrowed access to bankruptcy for the 86 of the 100 most populous cities
in the country reported in as legally required to *adopt* a balanced budget (Table 31.3). The second
clause of the insolvency test for eligibility is effectively nullified for these cities because they cannot show a duly adopted budget for the ensuing fiscal year as evidence of impending inability to
pay debts. Because it is difficult to imagine a court's entertaining admission of other than a legally
valid budget—and mandamus proceedings could overturn it—these cities effectively are limited
to the first or *current cash* definition of insolvency. The widespread requirement for adopting a
balanced budget means that the ruling retreated from the broad access the judge sought. In his
first memorandum on Bridgeport, Judge Shiff (1991a; 14–15, citations omitted) declared, "[I]n
general bankruptcy laws are to be liberally construed and ambiguities are to be resolved in favor
of the debtor, so that the debtor receives the full measure of relief afforded by Congress."

Balance in Bridgeport

Despite city leaders' unwillingness to shift to configuration F in Figure 31.1 and apparent preference for
using the federal court to sustain configuration E, Bridgeport is legally obligated to end the fiscal year
with a positive operating fund balance. Its experience illustrates the meaning of the stringent requirement
for year-end budgetary balance shared by 34 percent of the most populous cities (Table 31.3).

Chapter 6 of the city charter charges the legislative body with responsibility for adopting a balanced budget: "The common council shall have no power to make appropriations in excess of the revenues of the city for any year, and in no case shall the expenses of the city exceed its revenue for any year, except in cases and for purposes for which the bonds are so issued." With respect to taxation, the charter (Chapter 7, Section 95) dictates that "the common council shall, by resolution, set a mill rate for the ensuing fiscal year, which shall, together with other sources of revenues, generate sufficient funds to support the budget adopted by the common council." The mayor as chief executive is responsible for "causing the laws to be executed and enforced within the city" and "to recommend the adoption of all such measures connected with the policy, security, health, cleanliness, and ornament of the city, and the improvements of its government and finances as he shall deem expedient" (Section 24). In 1990, the State Supreme Court ruled that this latter provision "does make it clear that the mayor is charged with oversight responsibility for the city's finances" *(William Hennessey v. City of Bridgeport et al.* 213 Conn, 656).

It was the city's inability to finance its pyramiding operating deficit without state approval that closed off the public credit markers in June 1988 and thrust the city into crisis. The state responded with a special act (*An Act Authorizing the Issuance of Bonds by the Town and City of Bridgeport,* Special Act 88–80, as amended) that created the Bridgeport Financial Review Board to oversee the city's finances, permitted the city to bond its operating deficit, and guaranteed $35 million in city bonds. According to Donald Kirshbaum (1992), the former executive director of the state's financial oversight board for the city, the act requires a strict modified accrual basis of accounting precisely in order to keep the cash flowing; to forestall borrowing from oneself, even an internal service fund may not run a negative balance; revenues must be in cash, in the bank, and the city is not allowed to carry any receivables on the balance sheet.[5]

The city's evidentiary testimony during the bankruptcy proceedings and the subsequent appeal bemoaned the unusually stringent budgetary and accounting practices imposed by the state's special legislation. Using garbled argumentation, the appeal attacked the court's insolvency standard because the city is required to budget on the basis of generally accepted accounting principles (GAAP). "The accrual [accurately, cash] versus the GAP [sic] accounting places the [c]ity in a different position when analyzing its cash flow because unlike other municipalities in the state it does not have the ability to carry over any expenses to the following fiscal year. The cash flow analysis with these restrictions and distortions simply should not have been applied in the present situation" (Bridgeport, 1991; 10–11). Pointing to a state-imposed basis of accounting more restrictive than for other Connecticut municipalities, the city's leaders (Bridgeport, 1991; 16) self-servingly argued that "unlike the other municipalities, [Bridgeport] can only include actual or reasonably expected revenues" and the "accounting method distorts the viability of a cash flow analysis and exposes it as an unreliable measure of the [c]ity's true financial condition. It must be remembered that the [c]ity has a legal obligation to balance its budget within the present fiscal year."

THE DISCIPLINE OF BALANCE

While pleading for flexibility, city leaders were also making the somewhat perverse argument that they are foreclosed from using the expedients employed in other municipalities to formalistically comply with balance while actually evading it in a given fiscal year. Bridgeport simply must finance current services from current revenues.

Although the fact of balance itself might appear to outweigh the means of achieving it, the tactics actually employed inject policy content into budgetary balance. For example, Fitch (1993a; 2) ranks Cleveland's "[e]ffective budget measures resulting in a return to a positive year-end balance" as among this city's strengths. Such measures include "minimal wage increases for most employees, selective staff reductions, and health-care cost containment." From drawing down reserves or rainy day funds set aside for this very purpose to revenue *enhancements* (e.g., special assessment districts, user charges, service fees), and from *technical* reconciliations (e.g., adjusting the tax base) to David Stockman's notorious *magic asterisk,* anecdotal evidence points to more or less legitimate tactics suitable for the strategy of formalistic compliance with budgetary balance. These tactics are often stamped gimmicks—the stuff of smoke and mirrors—whereby they are painted as scheme or stratagem.

Short-Term Contrivances

Ironically, one purpose of balance is to accommodate the very flexibility these labels censure.[6] Investment rating services appear to value this flexibility in their assessments. According to Standard & Poor's (1993; 22), "The fund balance position is a measure of an [debt] issuer's financial flexibility to meet essential services during periods of limited liquidity. Standard & Poor's considers an adequate fund balance to be a credit strength." To the question about Moody's assessment of large fund balances, Moody's (1993: 9) responds, "Large fund balances often reflect sound financial management, but not always . . . the fund balance is a measure of financial position, but financial structure is important as well."

Addressing correcting imbalance, Moody's recommends (1993; 8), "although such decisions are best made by local representatives, an issuer should keep in mind that strategies can differ for short-term versus long-term objectives. . . . If an operating imbalance is expected to persist, then the response should achieve ongoing budget balance while also maintaining essential service provision and an adequate physical plant." Very much to the point, Moody's (1993; 8) notes, "The reason behind an operating deficit can be more important than the deficit itself."

A long-term perspective is useful. San Antonio, the nation's tenth most populous city, is shown in Table 31.2 as operating under a stringent balance requirement. Although its operations have been balanced through tax increases and discriminating spending cuts, Fitch (1992; 1, 5) identifies a risk: "Future operating surpluses may be harder to achieve given the significant measures taken to realize budgetary balance to date." Table 31.5 indicates that the General Accounting Office (GAO) (1993b) assesses San Antonio as among the "fiscally weakest" cities in its study.

The literature on budgeting conveniently inventories both prosaic and exceptional techniques short of outright tax increases, service cuts, or cost reductions (Kennedy, 1991; Rubin, 1993; 164–206; Webber and Wildavsky, 1986). Examples of such techniques include: use of reserves; one-shot revenues such as asset sales; shifting costs off the general fund, interfund transfers, and shifting costs to the capital budget; underfunding accrued liabilities such as pensions; delaying deliveries, payrolls, and payments to the next fiscal year, estimation manipulation or distortion; using plugs such as anticipated and even unidentified (and perhaps illusory) savings or revenues; and turning to off-budget entities, indiscernible credit arrangements, loan guarantees, and tax expenditures. Not surprisingly, some entrenched techniques sacrifice efficiency for economy; for example, manipulation of employee benefits may translate into future cost escalations.[7] A testament to ingenuity, this litany accommodates tactics designed for both short-term flexibility and formalistic compliance.

As the Bridgeport case suggests, certain tactics derive from the nature of fund accounting, whereby "it is possible to balance the revenues and expenditures of the general fund, to which political attention is paid and to which balanced budget requirements apply, by making discrete transfers among funds or by budgeting selected activities in funds other than the general fund"

Table 31.4

19 States Requiring Generally Accepted Accounting Principles for Municipal Financial Reporting

Colorado	Kentucky	Nebraska	Oregon
Connecticut	Louisiana	Nevada	Virginia
Illinois	Maine	North Carolina	Wisconsin
Iowa	Massachusetts	Ohio	Wyoming
Kansas	Minnesota	Oklahoma	

Source: Search of Lexis database conducted fall 1992 for generally accepted accounting principles, financial reporting, and by related key words.

(Granof and Mayper, 1991; 30). The basis of accounting may offer additional maneuverability. Whereas the data in Table 31.4 show that at least 19 states require generally accepted accounting principles for municipal financial *reporting,* municipal budgets "are generally on a cash or near-cash basis" (Granof and Mayper, 1991; 28).

Bridgeport's experience also suggests that estimation procedures are especially fruitful. Projecting a $16 million imbalance for the next fiscal year and a five-year projected deficit of $259 million (Bridgeport, 1991, p. 14), city leaders urged that insolvency be measured by long-term projections. The state alleged that the city's tale was "replete with distortions, inaccuracies, false assumptions and ignored options" (Connecticut, 1991; 35). Having allowed consideration of prospective balance, the bankruptcy judge "indirectly set a requirement for credible, complete budget predictions" (Scheffey, 1991c; 1). Adjusting estimates and projections is evidently common enough to have provoked legal remedies. For example, the independently elected city comptroller in Arlington, Texas, certifies the availability of funds (Table 31.2). The annotation accompanying Pennsylvania's statute (Section 2–302) specifies, "To prevent over-optimistic estimates by the body which must impose taxes . . . the [m]ayor's estimate of revenue yield is made binding upon the [c]ouncil. Until the budget is balanced, no money may be spent under the annual operating budget."

Current-Year Balance versus Formal Compliance

Authentic compliance with budgetary balance represents the triumph of technical competence and administrative capacity. Webber and Wildavsky (1986; 592) point out, "The subject of budget balance as a rough equivalence between revenue and expenditure in total could hardly have arisen in modern form before the last 125 years or so, because methods of accounting were too imprecise. . . . [N]ew budgetary devices dominate modern governmental spending . . . These new budget instruments either do not show up in the budget or, by much reducing the formal budget's size, serve to confuse the calculation of balances." They also ask (p. 592), "Nowadays, presumably, we know how far from this norm [of balance] we have wandered. Or do we?"

Recent research suggests some provocative answers. The declining frequency of current-year surpluses evident since 1988 (GAO, 1993b; Lamphere, 1990) is attributable to recession, fading or inadequate intergovernmental aid, and other factors, including idiosyncratic community features. In the Bridgeport case, the state (Connecticut, 1991; 41–42) cited the National League of Cities' finding that general expenditures exceeded revenues in 1991 for a majority of cities responding to its survey. Citing the same study, the GAO (1992; 56) finds, "Municipal and county [like many states'] fund balances have also been depleted. For example, 59 percent of cities expected to draw

Table 31.5

Current Budgetary Imbalance and Credit Ratings for Selected Cities, Fiscal Year 1990

	GO Bond Rating[b]	
Budget as Adopted[a]	Moody's	Standard and Poor's
Atlanta	Aa	AA
Baltimore	Al	A
Boston	A	A
Buffalo[d]	Baaal	BBB+
Cincinnati	Aa	AA+
Cleveland[d]	Baal	A–
Columbus	Aal	AA+
Dallas	Aaa	AAA
Denver	Aa	AA
Houston	Aa	AA
Indianapolis	Aaa	NR
Jacksonville	Al	AA
Kansas City	Aa	AA
Memphis[d]	Aa	AA
Milwaukee[d]	Aa	AA+
Minneapolis	Aaa	AAA
New Orleans[d]	Baa	A–
Philadelphia[d]	B	CCC
Pittsburgh	Baal	A
St. Louis	Baa	BBB
San Antonio[d]	Aa	AA
San Francisco	Aa	AA
Seattle	Aal	AA
	GO Bond Rating[b]	
Year-End Results[c]	Moody's	Standard and Poor's
Cincinnati	Aa	AA+
Columbus	Aal	AA+
Dallas	Aaa	AAA
Indianapolis	Aaa	NR
Phoenix	Aa	AA+
San Antonio[d]	Aa	AA
Seattle	AA1	AA

Source: Table 31.2; U.S. General Accounting Office (1993b; 112–113); budget data from Dearborn, Peterson, and Kirk (1992, Table 7); and bond ratings from "The Top 50 Cities, 5th Annual Financial Report" (1990; 12–13).

a. In these cities, the adopted budget must formally balance (Table 31.2) and current-year expenditures outstripped current-year revenues in the budget as adopted.

b. GO signifies general obligation bonds backed by the "full faith and credit" of the jurisdiction.

c. In these cities, year-end operations must balance (Table 31.2) and a current gap was offset using more or less legitimate devices.

d. Identified by the U.S. General Accounting office in 1993 as among the "fiscally weakest" quartile of cites.

down their fund balances in 1991. In addition, 39 percent of the nation's most populous counties and 34 percent of counties under 100,000 population experienced a budget shortfall in fiscal year 1991, thus reducing available local balances," (GAO's own study [1993b] confirmed declining year-end operating budget surpluses at all levels of government.)

In evidentiary hearings, the state's expert witness, Philip Dearborn, testified that, in the preceding two years, at least one-half of the 30 largest U.S. cities had unbalanced budgets in the sense that current revenues outstripped current expenditures and formal balance drew upon various contrivances. His and colleagues' subsequent analysis of financial reports for 28 of the 30 largest cities identifies a current-year imbalance for fiscal year 1990 in 25 cities (Dearborn, Peterson, and Kirk, 1992, Table 7). As shown in Table 31.5, 23 cities of the 25 are prohibited from formally adopting an unbalanced budget and 7 are prohibited from ending the year with an operating deficit. Corresponding credit ratings confirm the analytic inadequacy of using operating balance in a single fiscal year as the sole or even summary measure of financial performance or condition.

CONCLUSION

The evidence presented here confirms empirically the pivotal role of balance in municipal budgeting. Findings show that budgetary balance is, in fact, a common legal requirement and, perhaps more importantly, is articulated as an operative norm by participants in the budgetary process. Bridgeport's brief flirtation with bankruptcy cautions against overrating the power of balance as budgetary disciplinarian. Given the many devices for achieving formal compliance, balance need not and often does not translate into equivalency between current revenues and current expenditures.

Municipal budgeting cannot be reduced fruitfully to a single criterion, even one as widely accepted as budgetary balance. Bound by charter and statute, Bridgeport's city leaders unavailingly sought to bypass the strictest of balance requirements *via* federal bankruptcy court. Their contribution to municipal budgeting and "[t]he net gain for bankruptcy law . . . may be just that cities contemplating a bankruptcy know how to plan for it better" (Scheffey, 1991b; 1). Although the fiscal woes of many U.S. cities has heightened interest in bankruptcy (Cohen, 1991), the case demonstrates that while "persistent balance sheet deficits" are among the several financial warning signs (Standard & Poor's, 1989; 12), balance is most usefully distinguished from insolvency and that tactics underlying the balance and other factors warrant attention. Further undercutting the power of a concept whose attraction is related in no small measure to its simplicity, this conclusion calls to mind H. L. Mencken's observation, "For every human problem, there is a solution that is simple, neat, and wrong."

NOTES

The author acknowledges: Peter Arkins, graduate student in the Master of Public Affairs program, The University of Connecticut, for his exacting research assistance; the generous support of The University of Connecticut's Graduate Research Foundation; and, for reading and commenting upon the draft manuscript, David RePass and Morton J. Tenor, professors emeriti of the University of Connecticut, and Professor W. Bartley Hildreth.

1. The GAO (1993; 3) found that all but Vermont and Wyoming among the 50 states have balanced budget requirements. "In most states, the balanced budget mandates apply to enacted budgets or to the governors' proposed budgets. Few balanced budget requirements specifically mandate year-end balance."

2. The ACIR(1993;46) identified only eight states mandating by constitution or statute that city budgets be balanced.

3. This expectation is predicated upon the presumedly universal desire to reduce uncertainty and enhance stability. "Two important goals of local governments are the maintenance of a stable tax and revenue structure and the orderly provision of services to residents" (Allan, 1990; 2).

4. In this regard, only Kentucky, Pennsylvania, and Ohio of the 13 states with statutory provisions specify budgetary imbalance among the criteria triggering assistance to local governments with "severe, immediate fiscal problems" (Mackey, 1993; 3–6).

5. Section 11 of the act specifies that the financial plan under the aegis of the review board "shall provide for the (1) Elimination of all deficits in the general fund; (2) restoration to all funds and accounts, including capital funds and accounts, of any moneys from such funds and accounts that were used for purposes not within the purposes of such funds and accounts or borrowed from such funds or accounts"; (3) balancing of the operating funds in accordance with the provisions of this act."

6. According to the GAO (1993b; 10), "many jurisdictions had fewer year-end budget funds to carry forward to help finance the succeeding year's programs, suggesting a diminished flexibility, at least in the short-run, to increase the funding of current services or undertake major new spending initiatives."

7. "In addition to the hidden costs of benefits, Moody's is seeing salary increases that are partially funded with changes in actuarial pension earnings assumptions, an approach that requires fewer operating fund dollars today. Although this approach may be appropriate for cities with historically conservative assumptions, such changes require careful actuarial scrutiny, and funding levels must be revisited frequently to assure that the more aggressive earnings assumptions are, in fact, being achieved" (Kennedy, 1991; 3).

REFERENCES

Advisory Commission on Intergovernmental Relations, 1985. *Bankruptcies, Defaults, and Other Local Government Financial Emergencies.* Report A-99. Washington, DC: Advisory Commission on Intergovernmental Relations.
———, 1993. *State Laws Governing Local Government Structure and Administration.* Report M-186. Washington. DC: Advisory Commission on Intergovernmental Relations.
Allan, Ian J., 1990. "Unreserved Fund Balance and Local Government Finance." *Research Bulletin,* Washington, DC: Government Finance Research Center of the Government Finance Officers Association, November, pp. 1–8.
Blumenthal, Richard, 1991. "Remarks by Attorney General Richard Blumenthal before the 65th Annual Meeting of National Conference of Bankruptcy Judges." San Francisco, CA, October 31.
Bridgeport, City of, 1991. On Appeal from the Judgment of the Bankruptcy Court for the Judicial District of Connecticut, Brief of the Debtor, Appellant City of Bridgeport, filed with United States Bankruptcy Court, District of Connecticut, October 31.
Cohen, Jeffrey, 1991. "Declining Health of U.S. Cities Raises New Interest in Chapter 9." *National Law Journal,* August 5, p. 15.
Cope, Glenn H, 1992. "Walking the Fiscal Tightrope: Local Budgeting and Fiscal Stress." *International Journal of Public Administration,* vol. 5, pp. 1097–1120.
Connecticut, State of, Office of the Attorney General, 1991. Brief by the Appellee/Cross Appellant. Filed on appeal and cross-appeal from orders of the United States Bankruptcy Court for the District of Connecticut, November 15.
Dearborn, Philip M., George E. Peterson, and Richard H. Kirk, 1992. *City Finances in the 1990s.* Washington, DC: The Urban Institute, September draft, Table 7.
Fitch Research, 1992. *San Antonio, Texas.* New York: Fitch Investors Service, Inc., July 27.
———. 1993a. *Cleveland, Ohio.* New York: Fitch Investors Service, Inc. April 12.
———. 1993b. *San Francisco, California.* New York: Fitch Investors Service, Inc., April 21.
Forrester, John P. and Daniel R. Mullins, 1992a. *Rebudgeting in Larger U.S. Municipalities,* Baseline Data Report, vol. 23, no. 4. Washington, DC: International City/County Management Association.
———. 1992b. "Rebudgeting: The Serial Nature of Municipal Budgetary Processes." *Public Administration Review,* vol. 52 (September/October), pp. 467–473.
Granof, Michael H. and Alan Mayper, 1991. "Current State of Government Budgets." *The CPA Journal,* vol. 61, no. 7, pp. 28–32.
Groves, Sanford M., 1980. *Evaluating Financial Condition,* Handbook No. 1. Washington, DC: International City Management Association.
Judd, Dennis and Paul Kantor, 1992. "Introduction." In Dennis Judd and Paul Kantor, eds., *Enduring Tensions in Urban Politics.* New York: Macmillan, pp. 1–8.
Kantor, Paul and Stephen David, 1992. "The Political Economy of Change in Urban Budgetary Politics: A Framework for Analysis and a Case Study." In Dennis Judd and Paul Kantor, eds., *Enduring Tensions in Urban Politics.* New York: Macmillan, pp. 364–583. Originally published in 1983 in *British Journal of Political Science,* vol. 13, pp. 254–274.

Kennedy, Dina W., 1991. "Balancing the Budget: The Key Urban Challenge for the 1990s." *Moody's Municipal Issues*. [Moody's Investors Service] vol. 8, no. 1, pp. 1–7.

Kirshbaum, Donald, 1992. Treasurer's Office State of Connecticut Formerly executive director of Bridgeport Financial Review Board. Interviews with author, February 18, Hartford, and by telephone, May 12.

Lamphere, Amy, 1990. "Cities Seeing Red." *City & State,* vol. 19 (November), pp. 1, 35.

Lewis, Carol W., 1994. "Municipal Bankruptcy and the States: Authorization to File under Chapter 9." *Urban Affair Quarterly,* forthcoming.

Lomuscio, James, 1992. "Another View of Bridgeport's Problems." *New York Times* (March 1), p. CN3. An interview with Bridgeport Mayor Joseph P. Ganim.

Mackey, Scott R., 1993. *State Programs to Assist Distressed Local Governments.* Denver National Conference of State Legislatures.

MacManus, Susan A., Jessie M. Rattley, Patrick J. Ungaro, William R. Brown, Jr., Scott O'Dannell, Donald L. 'Pat' Shalmy, Norm Hickey, Denies Jubell, 1989. "A Decade of Decline: A Longitudinal Look at Big City and Big County Strategies to Cope with Declining Revenues." *International Journal of Public Administration,* vol. 12, pp. 749–796.

Moody's Investors Service, 1993. "Key Factors in Moody's Credit Analysis of Tax-Supported Debt." *Perspective on Municipal Issues.* Moody's Investors Service, Inc.

Robinson, Richard, 1992. Finance Director during bankruptcy filing and through Spring 1992 of Bridgeport, CT. Interview with author, February 11, Bridgeport, and by telephone, May 19.

Rubin, Irene. S., 1993. *The Politics of Public Budgeting.* 2nd ed. Chacham, NJ: Chatham House.

Savicsky, Linda, 1992. Director of Municipal Finance Services, Office of Policy and Management, State of Connecticut, and executive director of Bridgeport Financial Review Board. Personal and telephone interviews with author, February–September.

Sbragia, Alberta. M., 1992. "Politics, Local Government, and the Municipal Bond Market." In Dennis Judd and Paul Kantor, eds., *Enduring Tensions in Urban Politics.* New York: Macmillan, pp. 583–594.

———, 1983. *The Municipal Money Chase: The Politics of Municipal Finance.* Boulder: Westview Press.

Scheffey, Thomas, 1991a. "Bankruptcy Trial: State's Case Deflates." *The Connecticut Law Tribune* (July 29), pp. 1, 14–15.

———. 1991b. "Shiff: Bridgeport's Too Rich to Go Broke." *The Connecticut Law Tribune* (August 5), pp. 1, 16–17.

———, 1991c. "Postmortem on Bridgeport's Bankruptcy." *The Connecticut Law Tribune* (November 25), p. 1.

Shaw, George B., 1904. *The Common Sense of Municipal Trading.* Westminster: A. Constable & Co.

Shiff, Alan H. W., 1991a. 129 B.R. 339 (Bankr. D. Conn,). Bankruptcy court judge. Memorandum and Order on the Objection of the State of Connecticut to Chapter 9 Petition, July 22.

———. 1991b. 129 B.R. 339 (Bankr. D. Conn.). Memorandum and Second Order on the Objection of the State of Connecticut to Chapter 9 Petition. August 1.

Standard & Poor's, 1989. *SAP's Municipal Finance Criteria.* New York Standard & Poor's.

———. 1993. *Standard & Poor's Municipal Finance Criteria.* New York: Standard & Poor's.

U.S. Department of Commerce, Bureau of the Census, 1991. *Statistical Abstract of the United States,* 111th ed. Washington, DC: Government Printing Office.

U.S. General Accounting Office, 1992. *Intergovernmental Relations, Changing Patterns in State-Local Finances.* GAO/HRD-92–87FS. Washington, DC: GAO.

———, 1993a. *Balanced Budget Requirements, State Experiences and Implications for the Federal Government.* GAO/AFMD-93–58BR. Washington, DC: GAO.

———. 1993b. *State and Local Finances, Same Jurisdictions Confronted by Short- and Long-term Problems.* GAO/HRD094–1. Washington, DC: GAO.

Webber, C and Aaron Wildavsky, 1986. *A History of Taxation and Expenditure in the Western World.* New York: Simon and Schuster.

Wildavsky, Aaron, 1992. *The New Politics of the Budgetary Process,* 2nd ed. New York: HarperCollins.

Winograd, Barry, 1985. "San Jose Revisited: A Proposal for Negotiated Modification of Public Sector Bargaining Agreements Rejected Under Chapter 9 of the Bankruptcy Code." *Hastings L.J.,* vol. 37 (November), pp. 231–333.

Wolman, Harold, 1983. "Understanding Local Government Responses to Fiscal Pressure: A Cross-national Analysis." *Journal of Public Policy,* vol. 3, pp. 245–264.

———. 1992. "Urban Fiscal Stress." *Urban Affairs Quarterly,* vol. 27 (3), pp. 470–481.

CHAPTER 32

FEDERAL BUDGET CONCEPTS—
BRIGHT LINES OR BLACK HOLES?

THOMAS J. CUNY

Federal budget concepts constitute the articulated rationale or set of principles for the ways trans-actions are to be recorded in the federal budget. They are the budgetary equivalent of accounting standards.

Like accounting standards, budget concepts are tools. They must cover a multitude of different conditions, providing guidance for arraying a wide range of transactions in a rational manner that "hangs together" to convert what would otherwise be essentially random numbers into a coherent and intelligible structure.

However, not only must the data be arrayed in an intelligible fashion, but they must be closely related to the purpose of the array. Accounting standards, for example, are designed to provide information to owners, managers, and the public about the financial operations and conditions of firms or other economic entities. They tell owners, investors, managers, and others about the income, expenses, net worth, and other relevant financial data concerning the operations of the entity in question.

In a similar fashion, budget concepts are intended to guide the array of budgetary data in a fashion closely attuned to the nature and purposes of the budget.

Budget concepts are subject to abuse (i.e., efforts to create escape mechanisms and other forms of manipulation that undercut the rationale of the system). Just as one can read the business pages of major newspapers and see example after example of how corporations manipulate their public reporting (ostensibly within the range of guidance laid down by accounting standards), anyone who follows the permutations of the budgetary process can see analogous efforts to twist, torque, modify, redefine, or otherwise abuse budget concepts in order to arrive at recorded budgetary outcomes that are inconsistent with budgetary (or economic) reality.

This article explores some federal budget concepts, starting with the constitutional principles underlying the power of the purse and moving on to examine a range of elements that control the operation of the federal budget. To do this, we need to address two questions: "Why are federal budget concepts unique?" and "What is the nature of the federal budget?," and then to proceed to systematically analyze some (but far from all) of the key budget concepts and classification issues.

In the process, we will address various efforts—some successful, some unsuccessful—to undermine or evade these constraints. The reasons for evasions are multitudinous, but they generally come down to a single rationale—the belief by the proponents of evasions that their preferred policy outcomes are too important to allow them to be thwarted by having to go through the normal budgetary process and conform to the normal budgetary rules.

WHY ARE FEDERAL BUDGET CONCEPTS UNIQUE?

One must wonder if there is any reason for unique federal budget concepts. After all, there are fifty state and thousands of local governments in the United States—can't the federal government just follow their norms?

Part of the answer is that there is no unique set of norms for state and local governments—they exhibit a multitude of different patterns depending on historical accidents and local traditions. More importantly, as will become clear in the course of this article, the powers and responsibilities of the federal government exceed those of any state government by such a large margin that even if there was a norm for state governments, it would not necessarily be adequate for the federal government. We encounter the same condition with regard to federal accounting norms. For many years, the federal government sought to abide by general accounting standards for state and local governments, and the result was accounting reports that were largely unusable. The federal government established the Federal Accounting Standards Advisory Board to remedy that problem.[1]

WHAT IS THE NATURE OF THE FEDERAL BUDGET?

The Constitution, and the objectives of a free democratic society underlying the Constitution, are central to defining federal budget concepts. A useful starting point for exploring these concepts is a report issued a little over three decades ago, *The Report of the President's Commission on Budget Concepts.*[2] Page 2 of that report addressed the question of the "concept of the budget," and it listed the following points:

What is the budget of the United States? Fundamentally, it presents the essential ingredients of the financial plan of the Federal Government for the coming year. This plan has many aspects and must serve many purposes:

- *It sets forth the President's requests to Congress for new programs, appropriation of funds, and changes in revenue legislation;*
- *It proposes an allocation of resources to serve national objectives, between the private and the public sectors, and within the public sector;*
- *It embodies the fiscal policy of the Government for promoting high employment, price stability, healthy growth of the national economy, and equilibrium in the Nation's balance of payments;*
- *It provides the basis for executive and agency management of Federal Government programs; it gives the Treasury needed information for its management of cash resources and the public debt;*
- *It provides the public with information about the national economy essential for private business, labor, agriculture, and other groups, and for an informed assessment by citizens of governmental stewardship of the public's money and resources.*

Looking at this list from the perspective of three additional decades of experience, one can see that in some ways it is too narrow, in other ways it is too broad, but—in the main—it is centered on the right points. Examples include:

- The definition makes it sound as if "the budget" were simply a single document or collection of documents (and the data contained therein) issued by the president each January or February. In practice, as will be discussed below, "the budget" is as much a process as a document or set of documents.
- The definition makes it appear that the focus of "the budget" is concentrated almost entirely on one year—the forthcoming fiscal year. In practice, "the budget" includes information on past transactions, and over the past quarter century it has come to focus heavily on multi-year future issues.
- The definition gives greater credibility to the budget as an economic planning tool than has, in fact, proven to be the case. The *Report* was written at the heyday of Keynesian economics, when it was widely believed that the government could solve most of our macro-economic ills through fiscal policy. In retrospect, we have become a bit more humble with regard to what the government can accomplish.
- The definition (though not the full *Report*) focuses almost exclusively on the executive branch (i.e., the president and his subordinates). In constitutional theory and in practice, however, the legislative branch is central to the functioning of the budget.

Despite these caveats, this definition of the role of the budget is a good starting point for our analysis. Given that we have had an additional three decades of experience in using the budget, it would not be amiss to refine the issues based upon that experience.

THE FEDERAL BUDGET IS MUCH BROADER THAN A SINGLE DOCUMENT

The "federal budget" is not simply a document or set of documents that is issued by the president each January or February. Rather, it is the entire system (or process) of planning, proposing, authorizing, measuring, controlling, and reporting the conduct of federal fiscal activities.[3] The "actors" in this process include not only the president, the Congress, and the agencies, but the general public—the citizens, voters, and taxpayers who support and are served by the government.

Accordingly, "the federal budget" serves a minimum of five separate but closely related processes or activities:

1. In our Republic, the Constitution grants the "power of the purse" to a diffuse group of officials: the president and Congress *jointly* exercise this power, because the power of the purse must be exercised through the enactment and enforcement of law.

Central to the budget is that it is a decision making tool—the basic mechanism whereby the legal authorities decide which programs and activities to undertake, where, when, how, and with what amounts of resources to conduct these activities, and what tax and other revenue sources to tap to finance these programs.

In this sense, "the budget" is the totality of actions whereby the properly elected and appointed officials exercise the power to authorize and administer federal fiscal activities and related transactions (such as management of cash balances, borrowing, and debt repayment).

In turn, these officials are the people's representatives—they are accountable to the citizens and voters for their performance in office. This has important implications for budget classification and reporting: the budget is not simply a tool for public officials to use to carry out their jobs, but it is also a key tool for public officials to render an accounting to the people on their conduct in office.

2. The conduct of budgetary activities is not some random set of financial activities. For the budget to serve its multiple purposes, it must possess an *authorization and control process* that includes a *classification system* that: (a) is *comprehensive of all federal fiscal activities,* (b) is *meaningful for decision making,* and (c) *allows and requires that similar transactions be classified in a similar fashion.*

Thus, department X must classify transactions in a fashion similar to department Y so that all interested parties can understand what is going on, compare transactions across the board, and be assured that the transactions have been carried out both efficiently and consistent with the law.

3. An important element in the authorization and control process is that it *allows and, indeed, forces the president and Congress to make explicit choices and trade-offs.*

A basic consideration is the need to make sure that all of the legitimate participants in the budgetary process (which, in our Republic, include the taxpayers and voters) can understand the allocation decisions made by their agents (i.e., can see the size, composition, and timing of the flows of federal fiscal activities and can use this information to make rational judgments about how their agents—the president, Congress, and other officials—are conducting the public business).

4. In turn, the budget (taken in the broad sense as defined above) must provide adequate *control* of the conduct of federal fiscal activities.

In a constitutional sense, control means that the government follows the requirement that federal activities be conducted in accordance with law.

It is not up to the Internal Revenue Service to decide how much any particular individual is to pay as income taxes this year; the IRS and the taxpayer are hedged in by the legal requirements, so that each side should be able to compute a determinate sum that constitutes the taxpayer's income tax liability based upon the law of the land.

Similarly, the amount of money obligated and expended and the purposes for which it is obligated should be consistent with the legal authority of the executive, legislative, or judicial branch to enter into obligations. In order to ensure that the law is followed, the obligations and expenditures—and the performance of the services or the other factors that give rise to the obligations—should all occur under a system of measurement and classification that allows the parties to the transactions (which include the taxpayers and voters) to know what is going on. Among other things, both agency auditors and the General Accounting Office should be able to examine the books and determine whether the collections and spending are carried out in a manner consistent with the requirements of law.[4]

Control, of course, must ultimately be related back to the actions of Congress and the president. This means, for example, that the budget must score (record) the authority to undertake budgetary transactions front-end (not after the fact). Consider, for example, one of the issues we will discuss later in this article—the question of capital investment. In a budgetary control sense, recording the cost of capital investment on a depreciation basis is a "no brainer" because it is impossible to control that cost when the depreciation occurs. Thus, it is important for the budget to record and control the cost of capital investment at the point that the cost can be controlled—before and during the acquisition process, not after the acquisition has already occurred.

5. *Reporting* is also a key part of this process. The money that the federal government raises and spends comes from the public—in the main, from the citizens and voters of this country—and they have a right to know what the government is doing with *their money.* Congress and the president, similarly, have legal rights and obligations to see that the laws are faithfully executed, and they

can only perform their roles if the budget system provides adequate reporting of fiscal outcomes. Thus, proper reporting not only includes requiring that program administrators provide clear evidence that they have conducted the programs in a fashion consistent with the requirements of the law, but it includes the obligation that they provide information about the accomplishments of the program—what have we spent, and what have we received in return?

Proper reporting also includes providing the public with comprehensive, clear, and uniform reports about public finances, including information about the impact of these activities on the government's (and the Nation's) long-range fiscal position (or condition). The reporting should be able to answer questions such as the following: Have we run a deficit and increased the debt? Have we built up assets (physical or human capital) that will serve the public for years to come? Have we conducted the public's business in such a way as to "preserve domestic tranquillity, provide for the common defense, and promote the general welfare?"

Seen from this perspective, "the budget" is central to the financing of the government in a fashion that simultaneously meets the constitutional requirements and the specific requirements established by the proper legal authorities (the president, Congress, and other higher-level officials) in order to meet the needs of our country, and it is central to providing adequate reporting to the people on the way the government is using their money.

DOES THIS MEAN THAT ALL FEDERAL FINANCIAL FLOWS ARE BUDGETARY IN NATURE?

All federal financial flows (i.e., all money that comes within the control of federal government officials in their official capacities) belong within the broad system of classification, control, and reporting, but not all of them are of a nature that calls for them to be reported as budgetary transactions (i.e., receipts or outlays). "The budget" is centered on the use of the "power of the purse"—the allocation of public money or other resources to conduct government programs, and the collection of tax revenue or other income to finance such spending. However, there are numerous associated financial transactions that should not be treated in the same way as budgetary transactions.

(a) Borrowing and debt repayment are nonbudgetary in nature, because these transactions constitute the principal means of financing deficits or disposing of surpluses. To define borrowing or debt repayment as budgetary would mean to define away the meaning of the terms "surplus," "balanced budget," and "deficit."[5]

(b) Since the adoption of credit reform, the subsidy value of federal direct loans is counted in the budget at the time that the loans are made, while the nonsubsidized portions of federal direct loans are nonbudgetary. The nonsubsidized portion of the loans are the converse of borrowing or debt repayment—they leave the government in exactly the same fiscal position as it would have been if the government had not conducted the credit transactions (i.e., they simply change the form in which cash is being held).[6] Following the same logic, the subsidy value of loan guarantees is counted in the budget at the time the guarantees take effect, even though the associated cash payouts will occur at some future dates.[7]

This approach is consistent with the logic of the *Report of the President's Commission on Budget Concepts*. There was a long hiatus between the time that this report was issued and credit reform was put into place—because of both technical and political reasons—but credit reform is a move in the right direction (i.e., because it moves in the direction of recording the cost of resource allocation at the time that it occurs and can be controlled).

(c) Shifts of federal money between the Treasury and the Federal Reserve or conventional banks are also nonbudgetary in nature. These sorts of transactions simply change the form in which cash is being kept, hence, they are neither receipts nor spending. In turn, when payments to the government are deposited into the government's accounts at either the Federal Reserve or conventional banks, the collections constitute cash received by the government, and checks drawn on those accounts are counted as outlays.

(d) There is a range of other federal financial flows that are nonbudgetary in nature. These include, for example, deposit funds or suspense accounts. Funds of this nature include state income tax withholdings from federal employee pay that have not yet been transmitted to the state, and any money withheld from federal employee pay for investment in federal bonds but that has not yet been so invested.

Thus, a significant number of federal financial transactions are appropriately classified as being nonbudgetary (i.e., they do not flow through the receipts or outlays recorded in the budget) but still belong as part of the reporting related to the budget.[8] Indeed, that is exactly the purpose of the "means of financing" table in the budget documents and associated tables in Treasury reporting.

In sum, if the budgetary classification and reporting system is to meet the intent of the Constitution, it must be as clear, accurate, meaningful, comprehensive, and consistent as feasible under the circumstances.

WHAT IS THE NATURE OF THE POLITICAL PROCESS?

As can readily be seen, the budget process includes a multitude of different players—the president, each House of Congress and the various committees and members thereof, the heads of the various departments and agencies, their subordinates, the judiciary, and (not insignificantly) the citizens, residents, and voters who are the members of the political community known as the United States of America.

Given such a conglomerate of different persons involved in the process, "the budget" must satisfy a multitude of different perspectives, interests, and concerns.

- One does not expect the Secretary of Defense to worry overmuch about whether the budget is—or is not—in balance, but one expects him to be concerned with the adequacy of our national defense.
- In contrast, one does not expect the Secretary of Health and Human Services to worry overmuch about our national defense—that is someone else's job—but the Secretary of HHS must be concerned about the functioning of Medicare, Medicaid, and other activities under her jurisdiction.
- The same thing goes for the president, for the various members of Congress and, in general, for the general public. Each of us is differently placed from others; each of us has specialized concerns and sets of priorities that outweigh (for us) the priorities and concerns of others who are differently placed.

Since what we are concerned with is the conduct of federal fiscal activities, "the budget" (defined broadly) is the arena for settling these differences.

WHAT DO WE SEE HAPPENING?

A multitude of individuals and groups—whether elected or appointed officials, federal employees, private citizens, or whoever—are seeking to game the process. They are trying to give their pet programs a higher place on the pecking order than competing programs.

If one tries to obtain larger appropriations for program xx at the expense of program yy, this, of course, is the process—that is what the power of the purse is all about. "Gaming the process" is when one uses subterfuges, inappropriate mechanisms, or other ways to obtain more favorable treatment for one's preferred outcome. This distinction will become clearer as we proceed through this article.

I. BUDGETING FOR EARMARKED TAXES AND SPENDING

Of course, budget concepts allow for Congress and the president—through legislation—to provide certain programs with preferred funding status.[9] Whenever, by law, Congress and the president provide automatic mechanisms to finance programs (Social Security, for example) and thereby protect these programs from much of the give and take of the budget, this is perfectly consistent with federal budget concepts. In other cases, the law provides a presumption of financing priority (as in the case of most user charge funded programs) but, depending on the way the law is worded, that presumption may, or may not, actually translate into a preferred standing in the budget rationing process.[10]

Since giving preferred status is legitimate under federal budget concepts, what constitutes illegitimate "gaming"? It is any approach that allows the associated spending (or financing) in through the back door. There are standard ways to finance the budget, and as long as those standards are followed the debate is confined to issues such as whether the government should be undertaking the activity, when, in what magnitude, etc.—all questions that are relevant to the budget debate. It is when obscure provisions of law override the normal processes (such as provisions hidden in omnibus legislation, and such as provisions that essentially require the budgetary presentation to misstate the reality of what is occurring) that an approach is illegitimate (according to budget concepts). As we proceed through this article we will see examples of these sorts of actions.

It is important to recognize that giving programs such as Social Security special treatment does not mean that such programs thereby become nonbudgetary in nature—they are just as budgetary in nature as are income tax collections, spending for military personnel, grants to states, or the cost of operating the Federal Bureau of Investigation.

Aha, say proponents of earmarked funds (Social Security, the Highway Fund, or whatever), those are not the government's moneys—they have been collected under a solemn obligation to be held in trust and used for the purposes for which they were collected. We should not—indeed, we cannot—count such money as part of the budget. The budget concepts are misleading the public.

The budget concepts response is to say that most earmarked funds in the federal budget are, indeed, classified *by law* as being "trust funds." However, as explained in the annual budget documents, the term "trust funds" is used differently in federal budgetary parlance than the way it is commonly used in the private sector—they are trust funds in name, but not in fact.[11] (This mislabeling itself is illegitimate, but the practice is too far gone for anyone to reasonably hope that we might undergo a truth in budgeting campaign that would change it.)

Federal budget concepts focus on the nature of the transactions, and they say that if the money were the legal property of the beneficiary and held in trust by the government (i.e., in a fiduciary capacity, in which the trustee were not free to change the rules, but was required to administer the money according to the terms of the trust), such money would not belong in the budget. This is because the federal budget is the budget of the federal government—it should be confined to the fiscal activities of the government, and the administration of privately owned funds that are simply held in trust by the government do not constitute federal fiscal activities.

However, the nature of virtually every program that the budget records as being "trust funds" is that it is earmarked funds whose transactions occur under federal law.[12] The collections to finance these programs generally come into the Treasury under compulsion of law, they are held in whatever form the law prescribes, they go out whenever and to whomever the law prescribes, and the law can be changed to prescribe different outcomes, sometimes with retroactive effect. (Thus, the security of these programs is not based on a fiduciary relationship, but upon political promises. What the political process can give, it can take away.) Hence, regardless of the labels given to these programs, funds of this nature belong in the federal budget.

Given the special protected status of these funds, appropriate budget classification calls for reporting these transactions in a way that highlights their separation from other federal fiscal activities. However, it would be misleading to exclude these programs from the budget (as had been done for decades prior to the adoption of the unified budget) because to do so would drastically understate the totality of the resources that the federal government allocates through taxes and spending. It would also mislead with regard to the composition of federal taxes and spending and the impact of the budget on financing federal fiscal activities through borrowing or other means.

But what about Social Security (i.e., the Federal Old Age, Survivors, and Disability Insurance funds)? The law specifically requires them to be "off-budget." What business does the budgeting community have associating these programs into aggregate totals and focusing on those totals? Aren't you violating the law?

No. The budget documents (both those issued by the executive branch and those issued by the legislative branch) take full cognizance of the requirements of the law and they carefully label Social Security as being "off-budget." However, the budget documents also recognize the importance under the Constitution (and, for that matter, under common sense) of reporting the full size and scope of what the government is taxing and spending. In order to do that, the budget documents associate the on-budget and off-budget amounts into consolidated totals, and they focus heavily on the consolidated amounts.

In sum, to the extent possible, the budget focuses on fiscal reality, not legal fictions. In practice, legal fictions have controlled from time to time. Anyone who peruses past budget documents can find a number of cases—such as the Postal Service fund, the Rural Electrification fund, the Rural Telephone Bank, and the Federal Financing Bank (FFB)—that, for a time, were excluded from the budget by law or by executive determination and were not included in any aggregate totals.[13] However, eventually (1) budget practitioners came up with a way to overcome most of the damage caused by this approach (by creating budget plus off-budget aggregates and focusing on the broader totals); and (2) subsequent legislation repealed the off-budget status of most of these programs (but it moved Social Security to an off-budget status).[14]

II. BUDGETING FOR CAPITAL INVESTMENT

But, other critics ask, what about capital budgeting? It is all well and good to count the cost of capital in the budget, but the cost should be counted when the capital is a true cost (i.e., when it depreciates or is used up) rather than when the capital investment is made. After all, capital investment is simply a change in the form of assets—cash is exchanged for physical (or other) assets, leaving the government in the same fiscal condition as it was before the investment.

Not so, say the federal budget concepts. To adequately understand the reasons for the present usage, we need to consider several facets of the federal budget and several facets of federal capital investment.[15]

Aspects of the Budget

As should be clear from the preceding discussion, the budget serves a multitude of purposes. In order to accomplish its manifold objectives, an aspect—indeed, an overriding aspect, according to the *Report of the President's Commission on Budget Concepts* (and the preceding argument concerning the Constitution)—is that the budget should be comprehensive of the universe of federal fiscal activities. Any failure to be comprehensive contravenes the budget's ability to control federal receipts and spending (outlays) and to report adequately on the size, scope, and composition of federal receipts, spending, and the resultant surplus or deficit.

However, it should also be clear that budget concepts accommodate a great range of budget control differences. If Congress and the president decide that program X (say, federal grants for highway construction) should be excluded from most control mechanisms, that is perfectly compatible with federal budget concepts. What the concepts do not allow is spending such sums and not counting them at the time that the spending occurs and Congress and the president can control it.

To be more specific: presidents and Congresses routinely find themselves in a bind, because the sum of the spending that they would like to undertake exceeds the total amount of spending that they believe is desirable.[16] This is no different from most families, of course—most of us have "unmet needs" that we would like to meet, but we must make choices and live within our means, or suffer the consequences thereof. The same thing is true for the federal government—the demands for spending always greatly exceed the totals that we believe to be prudent.

The federal government has three choices: (1) increase income (in most cases, taxes), (2) hold spending for specific programs to amounts compatible to the acceptable total (i.e., ration spending), or (3) accept deficits that are incompatible with the amounts that the political leadership believes to be prudent. Some individuals and groups perceive what they think is a fourth choice: define the problem away by not counting some of the spending. The budget concepts reject the fourth as being unacceptable—it amounts to adopting the third option but trying to hide the results thereof.

Hence, federal budget concepts say nothing about how Congress and the president are to decide the total amounts or composition of taxes, other income sources, and spending—they simply say that you must count the money when it comes in and when it goes out—no cheating.

But, capital budget advocates assert, that is just the point—since money financing capital is investment, not spending (just as the unsubsidized value of loans is an exchange of monetary assets, not spending), we should count capital investment on an amortization or a depreciation basis, rather than charge it to the budget when we make the investment.

Again, federal budget concepts disagree. There is probably no case when depreciation, as such, makes sense for any form of budget.[17] However, for many economic entities—families, private businesses, and state and local governments—it frequently (but not always) makes sense to finance spending for major capital investments on an amortization basis (i.e., to budget based on the ability to borrow to finance the capital investment, and to pay the interest and principal connected with that borrowing as it comes due). However, the nature of the federal government (both its powers and the bulk of its investments) calls for counting the cost of such investments when the investments take place rather than for recording the costs in the budget on an amortization basis.

One has only to look at the budget historical tables document to see that over the past several decades the federal government has run massive annual and cumulative deficits (not only in absolute terms, but relative to our economic base—the GDP). No state could have run proportionately as large deficits. Not only do most states have constitutional restrictions on deficits and borrowing, but had any state emulated that policy, the market would have quickly rejected new bonds from that state as being too risky. That was not, and is not, what happens with the federal debt, because it is the strength of the whole economy that stands behind that debt.[18]

Powers. We have one national government, in contrast to fifty state governments, several thousand counties, and tens of thousands of cities, special districts, and other political jurisdictions. That one government is sovereign in a sense that no subordinate jurisdiction is sovereign. The voters, state constitutions, and the money markets all provide checks on state and local borrowing, and states commonly limit the ability of their subordinate jurisdictions to borrow. Thus, if a state or city gets out of line, there are all sorts of checks to constrain possible abuses.[19] However, for the national government, the old problem exists: "Who polices the policemen?"

Congress and the president together have a degree of power unmatched by any other institution (or any likely combination of institutions) in the country. As we have seen for Social Security, for example, all it takes is for the law to exclude an activity from the budget, and that item simply disappears from the reported budget totals.[20] There is no constitutional limitation on borrowing, no oversight authority capable of limiting borrowing (except for the very institutions—Congress and the president—that would do the borrowing) and, because federal debt essentially has no default risk, the credit markets exercise no constraint comparable to the constraints that they exercise over state and local borrowing.

Of course, all democratic governments are constrained by the power of the voters to "vote the bums out," but the higher the level of government, the further removed from popular control, and the greater the opportunities to obfuscate what the government is spending. That is, Washington is further removed from the public than are the state capitals, and the local governments are even closer to the people. Additionally, because of the size of the federal government and the complexity of its fiscal operations, it has a far wider range of opportunities to obfuscate than generally exists at lower levels of government, and it exercises control over far larger sums of money. As a result, it takes a much greater effort to ferret out cheating by the federal government—or to hold federal officials accountable—than is true for lower levels of government, and the total amounts of money subject to abuse are much larger.

Thus, if the lower level officials "mess up," the damage is inherently limited by the more limited scope of their powers. In contrast, serious errors by the federal government can have disastrous consequences for the entire nation.

Responsibilities. The responsibilities of state and local governments are much more restricted than those of the federal government. The federal responsibilities include, among others, (a) preserving domestic tranquillity, (b) providing for the common defense, (c) promoting the general welfare, and (d) the conduct of foreign affairs. True, to a significant degree state and local governments share in many of these responsibilities (except for national defense and the conduct of foreign affairs), but they are much more constrained in the degree to which they can commit their fiscal resources relative to the commitments of the federal government.

At the federal level these responsibilities are so open ended that they are breathtaking. Take a simple example:

As the United States emerged from the combination of twelve years of the Great Depression and four years of World War II, the nation worried that we might slip back into another depression. Additionally, the notion became popular in governmental circles that the adoption of Keynesian economics could prevent this from happening (or at least mitigate the damage and speed up recovery from such an eventuality). As a result, Congress and the president agreed upon enactment of the Employment Act of 1946—an act that committed the federal government to use its powers to promote maximum feasible employment (i.e., minimize unemployment). What would it take to achieve this objective? Nobody knew—yet legislation was enacted committing the federal government to doing just that. No state (nor any combination of states) felt it had similar powers—but the federal government passed that legislation, and has spent massive amounts of fiscal resources seeking to redeem those promises.

Alternatively, consider the size and scope of federal social insurance programs (Social Security, Medicare, unemployment insurance, and the like). It is true that states participate in some of these (such as unemployment insurance) and have a few independent programs (such as workers compensation), but the federal government commitment vastly outweighs the combined commitments of all state and local governments in this regard.

In sum, the powers and responsibilities of the federal government are such that capital budgeting norms for states (or private businesses or private individuals) are in a different league, and the rules concerning them should be evaluated accordingly. After all, to the extent that states, businesses, and individuals do not finance capital investment from current income, other net cash inflows, or accumulated balances, they must finance them from borrowing—the very thing that sets effective limits on everybody except the national government.

Nature of Federal Capital Investment

It is frequently argued that capital investment is *investment*—not spending—because the investor exchanges money or other financial assets for physical assets of equal value. While this argument is generally legitimate for private investments, it ignores the predominant nature of federal investments.

What forms of investment does the federal government make?

- In order to provide for the common defense, the federal government invests tens of billions of dollars a year in research and development of weapons systems, then it spends tens of billions more each year to purchase those weapons systems, and then tens of billions more to operate them. True, most of us believe that we need such R&D, procurement, and operations. However, such investments do not increase our economic base, nor are they disposable in any economically effective way.[21] (The only likely bidders for many of our "excess" weapons systems would be our potential enemies.)
- The federal government also invests tens of billions of dollars a year in the form of human capital (education, training, etc.), nondefense research and development, and grants to states, localities, and non-profit groups for physical and human capital. Clearly we hope that such investments increase our nation's well being, but do they constitute federal assets? If states, localities or private businesses were to make similar payments, would they count these as assets on their balance sheets?[22]
- In sum, only a small fraction, probably less than 5 percent, of what might expansively be called federal capital investment is for things that would reasonably count on balance sheets. The rest would be—and should be—written off as current expenses.

O.K.—that may be so, says the reluctant supporter of a federal capital budget. However, isn't there still a strong case for classifying that remaining fraction as capital investment that should be counted in the budget on an amortization basis (with the rate of amortization closely related to the rate of depreciation)?

All other things being equal, that might be so. However, all other things are not equal. One of the key differences between budgeting and accounting is that budgeting is forward looking, focusing on decisions and control, whereas accounting is retrospective, focusing on outcomes from past occurrences. If we do not record the cost of an "investment" at the time that it can be controlled, we then convert the budget from being a mechanism for controlling capital spending to being simply accounting for a sunk cost. For example, one can do little about reducing the cost of building a $25 billion space station once it is finished. The only time that one can control the cost is when one is authorizing and building the facility. Second, people make mistakes, and sometimes people spend money wastefully. When they do, they must live with the consequences. Similarly, businesses make mistakes and can spend money wastefully, and they must live with the consequences. In each case, there is a learning curve—if we err once, we will be likely to be more careful the next time around. Similarly, state and local governments make mistakes and sometimes spend money wastefully—it is up to the voters to cure that problem or live with it. But how about the federal government?

One of the facts of political life is that a dollar spent on behalf of current constituents is worth more to most sitting officeholders than a somewhat higher amount to be spent on future constituents (especially since current constituents are the only ones to vote in current elections). Hence, the term "pork barrel" is especially a matter of concern to the federal government. Pork barrel generally has the connotation of waste—but waste from whose perspective? If spending on something "wasteful" from the long-range perspective of the country helps a particular politician (or group of politicians) get reelected, the money is not wasted from their narrow perspective. By requiring that capital investment be recorded front-end, at least the budget requires Congress and the president to take the heat for the deficit impact of such "investments" at the time that they can be controlled. Delayed cost recognition, in turn, increases the ease with which pork barrel spending can be undertaken.

In sum, from an understanding of the nature of the federal government's powers, responsibilities, and the pressures that drive the political process, the President's Commission on Budget Concepts strongly supported the traditional practice of counting the cost of capital investment as budget outlays at the time that the investment is made (and can be controlled) rather than on a depreciation (or amortization) basis.[23]

The Ronald Reagan Building—an Example of a "Successful" Escape from Normal Budget Scoring of Capital Investment. (See *The Washington Post,* November 16 and 17, 1997, page A–1, for an analysis of this construction program, and November 23, 1997, page C–7, for Senator Moynihan's response.)

Background. In 1986 Terence Golden was appointed Administrator of the General Services Administration (GSA). According to the *Post,* Golden "was obsessed with what he considered government shortsightedness in paying $329 million in annual rent to house half of the federal workers in greater Washington."[24]

In turn, Kenneth Sparks, executive vice president of a civic and business group known as the Federal City Council, approached Golden with the idea of constructing a massive International Trade Center in Washington, D.C. (i.e., a federal office building that would combine office space for agencies concerned with international affairs, along with private groups with an international orientation).[25]

Golden signed on to the idea as a partial cure to his concern (by bypassing the normal budget process) and, in turn, he approached Senator Moynihan, then chairman of the Senate subcommittee overseeing public buildings, with this ostensible lease-purchase proposal.[26]

The basic idea was for the Federal Government to arrange for the construction of the building as the final link in the Federal Triangle, but to do so in ways that side stepped normal budget and management processes. A convoluted oversight system was created involving a newly created entity (the International Trade Center Commission), the Pennsylvania Avenue Development Corporation (an existing federal agency that had been created to oversee the development of the Federal Triangle), and the GSA.

In theory, this was to be a lease-purchase, in which private entrepreneurs put their own capital at risk, with the expectation that they would be able to find enough federal and non-federal tenants to make the building financially viable. In practice, this lease-purchase was a mirage—when one unscrambled the lines of responsibility, it turned out to be simply a direct federal construction program (and it came to be financed by borrowing from the FFB, since that was the most cost-effective source of financing under the circumstances).[27]

We will not discuss this building in great detail (it is well worthwhile reading the *Post* articles), but we observe:

Pro. As Senator Moynihan notes, the building is almost complete, and (a) it provides an impressive finishing touch to the Federal Triangle, and (b) the federal government ends up owning the building—it is not something that will be leased for a few decades and then remain in private ownership.[28]

Con. (1) The entire process from start to finish was a scam to get around budget concepts.

(2) Construction of the building was put on a "fast-track" schedule (probably at least in part out of fear that Congress might have second thoughts and repeal the authorizing legislation). As a result, construction began before design was complete, and design went forward before the managers had any idea who would occupy the space. In turn, this resulted in massive cost overruns when the leases were arranged, and the configuration had to be redesigned to meet the needs of the eventual tenants.

(3) The authorizing legislation created a complex oversight process that made it virtually impossible to pin anyone down as being responsible for cost overruns or other deficiencies, but that left the government financially responsible for virtually anything that went wrong.

(4) The government ended up with what is essentially a public monument (i.e., a significant amount of the cost of the building was to pay for monumental architecture features beyond any needed for office space) without Congress ever voting to create such a monument. (It is inappropriate for the government to create public monuments without specific approval of Congress.)

(5) The "international" justification for the original project was chimerical. In practice, the building will primarily house agencies conducting domestic programs. (This is perfectly appropriate, of course, but it undercuts the original rationale for the building and for some of its more elaborate monumental features.)

(6) The cost overruns were so great that the building is coming in at a price tag of more than double the original estimates. Because the building had sidetracked the normal budget review processes, as these cost overruns became apparent, the building never came back before Congress for further review to see if changes should be made.

(7) The building is being managed through the GSA's Federal Buildings Fund, and in order to pay the costs associated with this building, that fund is to be drained of financial resources that might have been used to finance other federal buildings. In turn, the agencies that are to rent space in this building will have to pay extremely high rental fees in order to compensate the Federal Buildings Fund for its costs.

Does This Mean That the Budget Must Have an Inherent Bias Against Federal Capital Investment?

It is important to recognize that bias is a two-way street—there is a political bias in favor of spending the "government's money" (*sic*—it is the people's money) on grandiose projects that politicians can boast about. This bias works strongest when the project is located in the state or district represented by the chief sponsor—it is harder to create political support for construction of public buildings in the nation's capital.

Thus, given the political proclivities for the members of Congress to want to brag about how much federal construction they have brought to their respective districts, there probably is a bias in favor of federal capital investment.

However, there does seem to be a considerable bias in the budget against direct federal capital investment (in lieu of leases) for housing the federal work force located in the national capital region, and particularly in the District of Columbia (a bias related to the lack of D.C. representation in Congress).

The bias occurs because of the political desire to make the budget appear as small as possible.[29] Suppose the government is considering leasing or purchasing an office building. If we buy the building (under traditional budgetary norms), we record the full cost of the purchase up front—when the building is purchased or built. In contrast, if someone else holds at least nominal title to the building, we can lease it and only record part of the lease cost up front.

A good example of this bias is the Department of Transportation headquarters. Presumably DOT will be with us forever—it is a cabinet department that conducts large-scale program activities that the federal government is likely to continue indefinitely.[30] Despite this condition, DOT continues to occupy a leased building for its headquarters, because the political leadership was unwilling to finance the purchase of a DOT headquarters building front-end.[31]

Federal budget concepts are silent on the issue of the amount of capital investments the federal government should make. (However, nothing in the budget concepts is intended to encourage cost ineffective approaches to capital investment. There are few, if any, cases where long-term leases or lease-purchases are as cost effective for the government as direct purchase, so, obviously, the failure of Congress and presidents to choose cost effective approaches is a scandal.)

There are ways that Congress and the president can compensate for putative biases against capital investment if we have the political will. Various possible approaches could be adopted within the context of budget scoring. One way, for example, would be to provide a "protected" category (similar to the protection given to mandatory spending) for the cost of constructing or acquiring a physical plant needed to house any agency that is (a) permanent in nature, but (b) occupying leased space. A different approach was the scorekeeping change that required counting the cost of long term leases "without substantial risk" on a purchase equivalent basis (that is, it counted front end the present value of future lease payments).[32] A third approach would be to decide—through the political process—on a set target for such spending, and to provide room within the budget resolution process for that amount of investment spending.[33]

Budget concepts are totally silent on the question of whether Congress and the president should create "protected" categories within federal spending in order to facilitate more capital spending. They simply insist that the spending be counted when it occurs—that we recognize that if we have increased spending in this category, we need to (a) have offsetting decreases in other categories, (b) increase revenue proportionately, or (c) live with a larger real (and recorded) deficit. The choice is for the president and Congress to make. What budget concepts seek to prevent is any rejection of the reality that $1 + 2 = 3$ (we cannot control both sides of the equation independently).

III. CLASSIFICATION CATEGORIES WITHIN THE BUDGET

All of the budgetary rules in the world do not do us a bit of good if we abrogate them through misclassifications. In this section we will address three major classification issues concerning items *within* the budget, while the following section will address classification (or misclassification) designed to escape budgetary scoring entirely.

Issue: Abuse of the Tax Refund Mechanism

When the Budget and Accounting Act of 1921 was enacted, the norm was to count tax refunds as spending.[34] Starting with the 1950 Budget, this was changed so that the budget began to record receipts on a net basis. That is, tax (and other) refunds are recorded as being offsets to (reductions in) budget receipts rather than being counted as spending. Page M–11 of the 1950 Budget included the following explanation:

> Note.—Payments of refunds of government receipts are now reported as deductions from total receipts; previously, they were reported as expenditures. Overpayments by the taxpayers are not true receipts of the government nor are they, when refunded, properly chargeable as operating costs of the government.

Also starting with the 1950 Budget, the authority to make internal revenue refunds became "permanent indefinite appropriations." That is, no further action by Congress was required; the IRS could and can make whatever refund payments are called for under terms of the law. The authority to make refunds of miscellaneous receipts and of Customs duties was also converted to permanent indefinite appropriations by the time of the 1951 Budget.[35]

The basic rationale for the changeover was simple: not all funds received by the government belong to the government. Those funds collected in excess of the taxes due are "not true receipts" since they belong to the payer; in turn, refunds of these overpayments are "not properly operating costs of the government'" since they never belonged to the government.

Obviously there is a critical difference between refunds of taxes and spending. The refunds simply return to the taxpayer money that the government collected in excess of the amount legally payable, whereas spending is the use of public funds to make payments. In turn, under the budget control process, receipts are in a separate category from the various spending categories.

The Tax Reduction Act of 1975 (P.L. 94–12) provided for "earned income tax credits" (the EITC). The conference report on the bill described this provision as: "a tax credit of 10 percent of earned income up to a maximum of $400. The amount of the credit is to be phased out from the maximum amount down to zero as earned income (or adjusted gross income, if greater) increases from $4,000 to $8,000."

In turn, the Act directed the payment of "refunds" of these earned income credits, even in cases where an individual's credit exceeds the tax liability otherwise due. In sum, if the person's income was low enough, he or she would receive a payment from the Treasury under the guise of a tax refund.

After a substantial internal debate, OMB concluded that any payments of true refunds were, indeed, refunds, but that any payments in excess of bona fide refunds constitute federal spending.[36] The associated spending was recorded this way in the 1977 and 1978 budgets. However, in the spring of 1977, the Secretary of the Treasury and the Director of OMB, at the behest of the Chairman of the Senate Finance Committee, agreed to reverse this treatment *for this case only* (i.e., this was not to be a precedent for any other similar ostensible refunds in excess of the amounts collected from the taxpayers), and this reversal of treatment appeared in the 1979 Budget.

The result, of course, was disastrous: if OMB/Treasury caved on one such provision, how could they be able to hold the line on other similar provisions? During the course of calendar year 1977 a plethora of similar provisions were proposed (though not enacted):[37]

- Two senators proposed legislation to provide "refundable tax credits" to corporations losing money or making profits too low to use all of their potential investment tax credits. The proposed legislation would also provide credits (payments) to nonprofit hospitals, universities, and other tax-exempt organizations. The senators would have labeled all of these payments "refunds."
- The Senate version of the Social Security amendments of 1977 included a proposal to provide tax credits for college and vocational school students and to provide cash payments, identified as "tax refunds," to families with tax liabilities too low to take advantage of the credits.
- Six "refundable tax credits" were included in the Senate version of the energy bill, again with "credits" in excess of liabilities and the implication that they, too, should be treated as offsets to receipts. Both the Senate and House Budget Committees explicitly rejected this accounting treatment.

After one rough year, the OMB and Treasury—with the strong support of the Budget Committees—reversed course and resumed counting the EITC payments in excess of tax liabilities as outlays rather than as refunds of receipts. (The EITC currently accounts for over $20 billion a year in outlays.)

Where Does This Leave Us? It turned out that the F.Y. 1997 budgetary caps for receipts were set aside because the receipts legislation called for net tax increases; as a result, anything included in the revenue legislation was outside of the caps. In turn, Congress decided to use this as an opening to *spend* money by authorizing the subsidy to Amtrak to occur through the tax refund mechanism rather than through appropriations (which came under a different section of the budget control process). The *Washington Post* article described the funding as follows: "The $2.3 billion is actually a convoluted tax break that was included in this year's major tax bill. Amtrak would be entitled to deduct its losses from taxes paid by freight railroads in the years before Amtrak was formed in 1971, up to $2.3 billion."[38]

Does it make sense to deduct losses in 1998 or subsequently in computing taxes paid prior to 1971? Is it legitimate to create putative "refunds" of taxes paid by railroads other than Amtrak to offset against Amtrak's losses? Clearly, this was not a normal "loss carryover"; it was nothing but spending money under the guise of tax collections—and spending money that had never even been paid by Amtrack.

The absurdity is apparent, but what is even worse is that the OMB and Treasury (with CBO concurrence) decided to ignore that nature of the transactions and the standard budgetary rules, and to classify this spending as tax refunds. Obviously, this opens the floodgates for a lot more spending disguised as refunds of receipts (a handy way to simultaneously increase taxes and spending without recording their magnitudes).

Issue: Abuse of the Functional Classification

The budget contains three standard ways of displaying the aggregate of federal outlays: by agency, by function and subfunction, and by composition category.[39]

For decades the budget has recognized that aggregations of spending by agency is of little use to the general public, because the agency structure is so idiosyncratic. As a result, starting in the 1940s the budget began to aggregate spending data by a standard set of categories known as the functional structure. This structure seeks to provide an overview of spending (outlays) by end purpose: national defense, international affairs, income security, health, etc. Traditionally the budget documents included two sets of discussions on the spending: the "budget message" (and associated materials) varied from budget to budget, focusing on whatever set of spending the administration wanted to focus on, while the "Part 5" presentation was based on the functional structure.

This was standard usage for decades, so that by the time the *Report of the President's Commission on Budget Concepts* was issued, it stated that "the Commission endorses the general approach which has been followed for many years in the President's budget of explaining the broad allocation of government resources in terms of a functional and subfunctional classification of budget expenditures cutting across agency lines."[40]

The functional structure follows a standard set of rules. It (a) covers the entire spending side of the budget—no double counting and no components left out; (b) it focuses on the "big money"—it is not concerned with minutiae, but with allowing budgetary users to follow the broad patterns of federal spending; (c) it is relatively stable over time—while changes in the structure are made from time to time to meet new needs, the basic structure has been retained indefinitely; in turn, when changes are made, the historical data are revised to reflect comparable definitions; and (d) it was the organizing principle for the primary discussion of trends and policy recommendations in the budget.

In sum, while the basic discussion associated with outlays by function always had some political spin, the data themselves were intended to provide the budget user with a coherent tabulation of spending (outlay) data that would allow the budget user to grasp the size, composition, and trends in federal spending.

The "composition of outlays" structure is a more recent development, and it focuses on spending by character. It provides a defense/nondefense split, and it provides data on payments to or for individuals (essentially, income transfers in cash or in kind), on grants to state and local governments, on net interest, and on other outlays. The composition structure was well adapted to producing data on a constant dollar basis, and that is one of its major uses.

In the main, neither of these structures is used for budget control (or to guide legislation)—their principal value is to the informed reader, the press, and the general public, providing them with overviews of the distribution of federal spending.[41]

However, again, the old rule of GIGO (garbage in, garbage out) holds: the value of these data are only as good as their integrity. So what do we see?

"Drug Control Chief Won't Let Pentagon Just Say No."[42] It turns out that the government is spending nearly a billion dollars a year of defense appropriations to fight the "war" against drugs, and these funds are being carried as part of the spending in the national defense function. Not only that, but the White House drug czar has authority to certify (or to refuse to certify) the defense budget based on how good a job the Pentagon does in requesting money (called "defense" spending) to fight the importation of drugs into the United States.

Clearly, this is a major abuse of the functional classification. It means that the budget is overstating what we are spending on national defense, and understating what we are spending on law enforcement and justice (one of the major nondefense functions) by very substantial amounts. (As the late Senator Everett Dirkson was wont to say, "a billion here and a billion there can add up to real money.")

Technically, the OMB (which has primary responsibility for maintaining the functional structure) can claim that this classification is consistent with the functional structure definitions, which defines subfunction 051 (Department of Defense, Military) as including "the entire agency."[43] However, such inclusion was done on the premise that no major "cheating" would occur. Given the proclivity of the political process to hide things, it was (and is) quite common for relatively small amounts of money that clearly have no relationship to national defense to be appropriated in the Defense Department budget; and given the focus of the functional structure on major trends and big money, it was agreed that creating a difference between the "Department of Defense, Military" spending in the agency structure and the functional structure for relatively small differences would be counterproductive. However, $800 million is not a relatively small difference—clearly the budget should be classifying this money in the law enforcement and justice function, rather than in the national defense function.[44]

Issue: Classification of Compulsory Collections as Offsetting (Rather Than Governmental) Receipts

One of the key classification distinctions governing the quantification of the budget is the distinction between governmental receipts and offsetting collections.[45] This distinction is similar to the distinction between refunds and outlays discussed above. Basically, the validity of the quantification of the budget (i.e., the magnitude of receipts and outlays, and the composition of their components) depends in large measure on classifying the components in the correct category.

The essential concept of budget receipts is the amount of revenue the government raises in its capacity *as government* (i.e., it is roughly what the average person thinks of when he or she refers to "taxes"). In turn, budget outlays are not the aggregate of gross spending. Instead, any collections by the government that arise from bona fide voluntary (or commercial) operations are offset against gross outlays to arrive at a net outlay figure.

In both cases, the effort is to measure the size of the government on a comparable basis, and to allow comparisons of relative magnitudes (such as the percentage of outlays that goes to national defense in comparison with the percentage that goes for law enforcement and justice, or total receipts in any particular year as a percentage of the economic base).

What happens is that the political process demands larger components and smaller totals—a physical (but not a statistical gimmickry) impossibility. One way that this can be accomplished within the context of budget concepts is to convert some activities from being compulsory to being voluntary. If people are forced to pay taxes to finance, say, highway construction, the budget concepts say that the taxes belong on the revenue side of the budget. If the government changes the financing mechanism so that highways are financed by tolls and users are free to pay the tolls in order to use the highways (or free to forego use of the highway in order to avoid the tolls), the toll income is offsetting collections.

Of course, almost any time one constructs such a line of demarcation, there will inevitably be close calls—transactions that have some characteristics related to each side of the line. In turn, someone must make a "call"—decide that, in the aggregate, the "governmental" characteristics are predominant (and, hence, the collections belong as budget receipts rather than offsetting collections) or else that the "voluntary" characteristics predominate (and, hence, the collections belong as offsetting rather than governmental).

The problem in the real world is that the pressures to understate the size and the relative magnitudes of the components of federal receipts and outlays leads to a consistent bias in favor of offsetting, so that over time the significance of this distinction (which, of course, is critical) becomes fuzzy.

One handy formula for determining this line of distinction is that if the federal government requires an activity (such as health and safety inspection, meat and poultry inspection, or immigration or passport permits) and then charges a "user fee" for the "service," the "fee" derives from the government's power *as government,* and the "fee" belongs as budget (not offsetting) receipts.

However, as one examines budget after budget (such as Tables 4–1 and 4–2 of the 1999 Budget *Analytical Perspectives* document) and then traces the classification of the fees, time after time one sees misclassifications of existing "fees" and, particularly, of proposed "fees" (i.e., where the proposal is to treat compulsory collections as offsetting receipts).

In most cases the magnitude of each individual "fee" is small relative to the budget, but the cumulative effect is to understate the size of both total federal receipts and outlays and of the components.

IV. EVASIONS OF BUDGETARY COVERAGE

This section covers one final (but very critical) form of budgetary evasion: disguising federal programs in such a way as to pretend that their costs do not belong in the budget, or simply classifying programs that are clearly budgetary in nature as being nonbudgetary.

Over the history of the federal budget, numerous devices have been used to allow the government to conduct activities that are budgetary in nature, but to exclude the transactions from the federal budget. In the decades prior to adoption of the unified budget, they included:

1. Defining "the budget" too narrowly (i.e., the "administrative budget"). This allowed creation of tax and spending programs (such as Social Security), entitling them "trust funds," and then excluding them from the budget on the grounds that trust funds did not belong in the administrative budget.
2. Creating "government corporations" (such as the TVA) and declaring them to be "self-financing" business enterprises that did not belong in the budget.
3. During the Great Depression, creating "emergency spending" programs that were excluded from the focus of the budget (i.e., have the budget focus on the "normal" spending that excluded these expenditures).
4. Using "creative" ways to borrow money and count it as income (i.e., offsets to spending).
5. Constructing military family housing financed from special borrowing authority, and recording the spending when the debt was amortized rather then when the housing was constructed.

The unified budget was an effort to end such creative budgeting, and to a considerable degree it did. However, it is far from successful in blocking all such "creative" forms of budgeting.

One mechanism used to circumvent the unified budget concept was to simply declare particular funds to be non-federal and, hence, nonbudgetary. Among the worst abuses in this regard was the creation of two government entities (the Financing Corporation and the Resolution Funding Corporation) and declare them to be "Government-Sponsored Enterprises."[46] Through this process the government spent billions of dollars to honor thrift institution failures without counting the spending in the budget when the payments occurred.

Another mechanism was to create the Federal Financing Bank to serve as a "frictionless conduit" to finance agency borrowing. Since borrowing and debt repayment are "means of financing" (rather than receipts or outlays), this allowed the supporters of the FFB to designate (by law) the FFB as being off-budget. In turn, agencies then used the FFB to finance a range of credit and non-credit activities and hide their costs outside of the budget.[47] (The FFB is now on-budget and, therefore, is now truly a frictionless mechanism to finance agency borrowing.)

A third mechanism was simply to exclude an account from the budget as a result of a political deal. A number of funds—primarily Agriculture Department credit activities plus the Postal Service fund—were moved off-budget for a period of time. These funds were all moved back on-budget, but the Postal Service was subsequently moved back off-budget.

However, efforts to have your cake and eat it have not ceased—they are alive and kicking. The greatest threat to the integrity of federal budget concepts that occurred in recent years was the effort of the Clinton Administration and other proponents of nationalized health care to design a program that involved having the government take over financing of virtually all medical care in the country, but to hide most of the financial flows outside of the federal budget.[48]

The central element of that plan was to use the power of the federal government to regulate commerce in such an intrusive manner that the government effectively would control the conduct of commerce, but to insist that since it was "regulatory" in nature, it did not belong in the budget. In order to understand this issue, we need to explore the nature of federal regulatory power and its relationship to budget concepts.

The Use of the Federal Power to Regulate Commerce

As a general rule, federal budget concepts treat the use of the regulatory process as being nonbudgetary. It is a political judgment whether we should have, or eliminate, this or that set of regulations, but the regulations, as such, are simply regulations. This approach stems from two factors.

Firstly, the Constitution grants the federal government the power to regulate interstate and foreign commerce (use of this power is commonly called federal mandates). Secondly, the federal budget is the budget of the federal government—through it we seek to record, measure, and control the fiscal activities of the federal government.

Thus, budget concepts have a "go, no go" approach: either an activity is federal fiscal activity (and, hence, comes within the purview of budget concepts) or it is not. Clearly, the conduct of commerce, as such, is not federal fiscal activity (except, of course, when the federal government itself is conducting the commercial activity, as in the case of TVA).

One broad set of federal mandates includes requirements designed to ensure the safety of the nation's food and water supply. These include requiring that providers of these goods or services meet certain standards of safety, purity, etc., as a condition of being allowed to provide their services to the public.

The budget treats the costs of these mandates—though they are frequently substantial—as not budgetary in nature (i.e., it considers them to be simply part of the cost of conducting the non-federal activity).[49] The issue in question is whether there are any cases in which the use of the federal government's power to mandate something through its use of the regulatory power is so intrusive that the activity in question belongs in the budget. In turn, if the answer is "yes," one of the related questions is how they should be reported in the budgetary classification and reporting system.

Thus the issue at stake is whether there are (or should be) any exceptions to this exclusion of the exercise of regulatory power from the budget.

Some people (generally supporters of the particular "regulatory" action) argue *"no"* to the basic question. They argue that by its very nature, regulation is nonbudgetary, and there are never circumstances under which the financial flows derived from a mandate are budgetary in nature.

The Federal budgeting community—including, but not limited to, OMB and CBO—has carefully examined the issue and decided to the contrary (a decision that is based largely on the sort of logic outlined above). They concluded that there is a point at which the exercise of "regulatory" power can become nothing but a cover for the conduct of budgetary activities, and the regulatory fig leaf should not be accepted as a means of hiding this reality.

Consider the consequences of adopting the alternative position. It would mean that we would have an open-ended mechanism for hiding the size, scope, and composition of the government's fiscal activities from the very mechanism and process—the budget—that was created to perform these services. (For example, it would not take too much thought for some clever lawyer, lobbyist, or staff person to design a "private" national defense security corporation that could take over most of the current operations of the Department of Defense and, therefore, "privatize" them and convert them into being "regulatory" rather than being "budgetary." Just think what we could do to reduce the size of the *recorded* tax burden, the *recorded* size of the budget, and the *recorded* deficit, borrowing, etc.)[50]

But wait a minute, says a supporter of these approaches! Just what sort of a mess are you getting us into? After all, the federal government has an impact on virtually every single financial transaction that takes place in our country (and many nonfinancial transactions as well). Does this mean that you want to include the entire economic base (the GNP, the GDP, or whatever) within the federal budget?

To ask the question is to answer it. Of course not—what we are trying to do is to distinguish between reality and legal fictions. Insofar as transactions are, in reality, private (or non-federal), we most certainly do not want to include them in the federal budget. However, if the reality of the activity is that it is budgetary in nature, we want to capture it within the budget universe.

But, supporters of the President's health program stated that counting this activity in the budget would kill *a desirable reform!! We must not let these pettifogging "bean counters" get in the way of doing good.*[51]

One line of argument holds that the cost of government regulations is simply part of the price of the right to conduct commerce. If, for example, the government requires coal mine operators to maintain certain environmental standards, isn't this society simply requiring that the operations cover the external, as well as the internal, cost of carrying on the activity?

A counter argument is that many of the costs of mandates are not related to external costs, but constitute a hidden cost of the government conducting social policy. Thus, for example, when the government requires that buildings include ramps, elevators, and other special facilities to make them accessible to the handicapped, this argument holds that these added costs are simply an effort for the government to provide services to a class of people, but to do so in a way that their costs are not reflected in the budget.

Beyond "cost," there is another way that regulations can affect business operations. The government (at the federal, state, and local levels) exercises a multitude of regulatory functions concerning what businesses can or cannot do, what prices they may charge, what services they must provide, whether they can build or locate in this specific area or that, minimum wages they are required to pay, insurance benefits they are required to provide, and a plethora of other regulations concerning their operations.

It is not an easy thing to determine whether, or to what extent, the cumulative result (both in terms of cost and in terms of freedom to conduct business operations) of federal mandates should be considered as forcing the entity to perform a service for the government (as the representative of the society), in contrast with when they are simply a matter of forcing the business to pay the full societal costs of operations.[52]

In practice, we have no way of measuring (with any reasonable degree of precision) the add-on costs of conforming to federal mandates. Thus, even if there were agreement that such costs belonged in the budget (and, obviously, such agreement does not exist), we do not have a way to capture the costs in the budget measurement base. (Efforts are being made to estimate such costs for a "regulatory budget," but the measurements lack precision.) Hence, to a great degree, the issue is moot—it simply is not practical, at this stage, to include the cost of most regulatory mandates in the budget.

The response from the budget concepts is that enactment of the proposal may, indeed, do good, but that if that action cannot stand the light of public scrutiny (i.e., if the only way to get the proposal enacted is to carefully craft the form in order to hide the substance) then we must suffer the consequences of giving up this "good" in order to have the "better"—constitutional government.

But we hear another claim: "Congress and the president have the constitutional right to enact laws, so if the law says that the program is regulatory (and, hence, nonbudgetary), the budget should conform to the law."

Clearly, there is a point at which the budget concepts technicians can be told to "shut up"—the boss has made the decision, and the subordinate will carry out his or her orders. (Indeed, that appears to be exactly what happened in OMB and other executive branch agencies when the president decided to pretend that a federal takeover of something like 6 percent of the GDP—his national health plan—could be disguised as a mandate and, therefore, be excluded from the federal budget.) Fortunately, CBO was not constrained in such a fashion—it classified the proposal according to its nature, Congress considered the program based on the merits of the case (including CBO's conclusion that the program was unworkable as designed), and decided not to enact the proposal.

However, there is an old saying that "the law is an ass." If Congress had chosen to ignore the CBO, treat the proposal as nonbudgetary, and enact the legislation, both OMB and CBO would have complied with the requirements of the law. The law would be out of place (i.e., legislating lies), but the budgetary communities in both the legislative and executive branches would have complied with the legal requirements.

Clearly, it is not the purpose of federal budget concepts and classifications to make it possible to expand the size and scope of federal budgetary activities, nor is it their purpose to deter expansion. Each proposal should be decided according to the relative merits (in the eyes of Congress, the president, and the public) of the proposal. But to do so, it is essential that the proposal be honestly classified according to its basic nature—not only to keep the president and Congress informed about what they are doing, but, perhaps even more importantly, to keep the public informed about what their government is doing with their money.

Given the Conclusion That the Financial Flows of Some "Regulatory" Programs Are Budgetary in Nature, How Can We Identify Them?

What we are dealing with are continuums of the regulatory process—at one end of such continuums, the activities are clearly nonbudgetary; at the other end they are clearly budgetary. A major part of the problem is to determine where the line should be drawn. In principle, this should be where the degree of federal intervention becomes so intrusive that the activity ceases to be effectively nonfederal, i.e., when it changes from simply being subject to federal regulation to being effectively controlled by the federal government. At that point the program tips from being nonbudgetary to budgetary in nature.

There are at least four types of continuums (or dimensions) where these conditions may arise:[53]

- One is the government using its regulatory power to set conditions for the operation of public utilities, including the assessment of compulsory charges on one group of economic actors in order to subsidize a different group of economic actors.

A good example of this is telecommunications. Clearly, the government can regulate telecommunications carriers by requiring that, as a condition of providing services to their area, they cover the entire service area on an even basis. (That is, the carriers are not allowed to simply "cream" the most lucrative sectors and leave the more expensive sectors without services.) The government says, in effect, that the telecommunications carrier is a public utility that must provide certain standard (or minimum) services throughout its service area as a condition of being allowed to operate. (Obviously, the question of whether the government *should* impose such conditions is a political/moral judgment, not a matter of budget concepts.)

However, the same powers can be carried so far that the cost of the "mandate" ceases to be regulatory. Thus, for example, if the government requires that firms operating in urban areas make payments (in cash or in kind) to underwrite the costs of other firms that are operating in rural areas (where the costs per customer may be significantly higher than the cost per customer in the urban areas), we do not have simply a regulatory situation. Rather, we have a hidden tax (in cash or in kind) that the government is levying on one set of economic entities in order to subsidize a different set of economic entities.

In the latter case, the budget should report the cash (or cash equivalent) flows as federal budget receipts and the payments to the beneficiaries of these subsidies as federal budget outlays.[54]

- A second type of a continuum can occur if the degree of governmental control effectively destroys the market.

An example where this could occur is medical care or insurance. The government, using its sovereign power, may require that any health insurer, as a condition of participating in interstate commerce (i.e., providing the health insurance), meet specified standards, such as being able to demonstrate solvency, accountability, and provision of services on a nondiscriminatory basis. All such regulations interfere with the "free market," but—as long as they leave the substance of a free market—they are simply regulatory.

However, there is some point at which the government's ostensible regulation effectively destroys the market and replaces it with a set of government controlled entities. That, indeed, was the centerpiece of the Clinton health plan. If and when that occurs (and, inherently, the line is fuzzy—at least in part because the sponsors of the legislation want to make it fuzzy in order to have the substance of federal programs with the appearance of private), the program belongs in the budget.

- A third type of such a continuum—and one that currently is a hot potato—is the idea of curtailing (i.e., reducing or phasing out) some forms of federal social insurance by creating what are ostensibly private savings plans that would curtail the need for the federal social insurance.

The basic argument is that if we can get individuals or families to increase their current savings adequately, by the time the need arises, they will have the financial resources to meet the need without any federal income transfer. This is theoretically sound, but how is the government to make the system work in practice?

Proposals are being advanced in which the government would compel individuals (frequently with a matching payment from their employers) to put aside funds from current income in order to have them available to meet future needs. There are various proposals, of course, and they have many different permutations, but the basic idea is that the government would substitute its judgment about how people should save for the future in place of letting the affected individuals make such decisions. The government effectively would take the person's money through forced saving and promise that he or she would get back control of the money (along with interest, dividends, and stock appreciation) at some future point in time (determined by the government). The economic decision would be made by the government, but ostensibly the transactions would be simply regulatory.

Clearly, at this point the logic says that the transactions would become budgetary, since they would involve the use of the government's sovereign power in order to take control of money away from the owners and use it for the purposes that are determined by the government. That, effectively, would be a tax—even if the money went back to the same people. (Additionally, the payment to them would not be a tax refund but spending, because the very nature of the transaction would be to shift control of the money for some time period from the individual to the government.)

The most commonly discussed way of conducting this sort of program would be to allow the individual a substantial amount of choice over what the government would do with his or her money—it might be invested in portfolios of stocks, into a mix of stocks and bonds, etc., depending on (a) the degree of market freedom the government decided to grant to the taxpayer and (b) the taxpayer's use of those options. According to such proposals, title to the money would vest in the individual (but the "owner" would not be able to tap it until the government gave its permission).

Assuming that the title to the assets were firm (i.e., the government could not reverse title without calling it a new tax) and assuming that the permission to withdraw were generic (i.e., that the government could not delay the control beyond predetermined stated conditions, such as age or death), the appropriate budgetary classification would be to record something close to simultaneous budget receipts and spending. The taxes should be recorded when the government collected the money, and the spending should be recorded when the government transferred title to the asset (which presumably would be at the time the money was invested). In sum, this would be a sort of backhanded transfer payment.[55]

Under this approach, the size of the budget would appropriately reflect the magnitude of these transactions, but the budget deficit/surplus would be virtually unaffected, since the receipts and outlays would be close to being simultaneous and equal transactions.

- A fourth type of such continuum could arise if the government hid the nature of its compulsion. It is perfectly possible to conceive of cases where the government might use incentives (i.e., the "carrot" rather than the stick) to achieve its objectives, but that it might do so in such a heavy-handed manner that the entire activity would become federalized.

Consider, for example, the possibility of the federal government agreeing to subsidize medical insurance. The subsidy payment would be budgetary in nature, whereas the actual medical insurance (including the beneficiary's insurance premiums to private carriers) would be nonbudgetary. However, the government could tie so many strings to participation in the subsidy, and it could make the cost of not participating so high, that it effectively forced participation, and it would transfer from the individual to the government effective control over how the payments and benefits were to work. In this case, not only the subsidy but the entire medical insurance program would belong on-budget.

As we can see, central to the *design* of such programs is an effort to have the money (or cash equivalents) pass hands from one party or set of parties to another without ever being captured in Treasury's reporting system. The money would not enter the cognizance of a recognized fiscal agent of the Treasury, so the Treasury has not developed a system of reporting transactions of this sort.

This is exactly what happened in the case of the United Mine Workers of America benefit funds, where the law levies a tax, spends the money, but simply has the money flow through a third party in an effort to escape budget scoring. (Fortunately, in this case, both OMB and CBO recognized the charade for what it is, and the budget records the transactions accordingly. See, for example, page 1144 of the Appendix to the 1999 Budget.)

In sum, earmarking, providing automatic financing, using funds for capital investment, or providing any sort of special arrangement (including designing the program so that the financial flows never go through the Treasury) do nothing to make the activities nonbudgetary. Regardless of the form the programs or activities take, if they are federal in nature, they are budgetary to the extent that they involve receipts and/or spending. The transactions should be classified and reported in accordance with law, but they should also be reported according to their nature in the central public forum—i.e., the budget—created for the president, Congress, and the citizens and voters to assess and control federal taxes and spending.

That Said, Are There any Special Operational Principles Needed to Address These Sorts of Issues?

At least three come to mind:

1. The political process is perfectly capable of designing a multitude of different ways to attempt to have the substance of being federal and the appearance of being nonbudgetary. The basic objective must always be kept in mind—the budget should seek to record the substance of what is occurring; it is important to avoid being misled by focusing exclusively on the form.
2. No matter where the boundary line is drawn, there will always be close calls—transactions that might go either way. Thus, one needs to start with a decision about who should make the close calls. For example, should OMB and CBO budget technicians throw their hands up in the air and say that the proponents and opponents of the program must battle it out to reach agreement and then instruct the technicians how to classify such proposals? Of course not. It is up to the budget technicians to use their best judgment, recognizing that they will not always be right, that they may be overruled, and that they will always be criticized by someone who does not like the way the decision went.

    Additionally, we must expect that wherever the boundary is drawn, proponents of new programs are almost certain to design their programs in such a way as to be very close to the border between budgetary and nonbudgetary. Central to the political process is the attempt to control—to have the government do "good"—but to avoid the political cost of recognizing such programs in the budget. Hence, we need to recognize that close calls are likely to multiply, not decrease, with time.[56]
3. Is there any operationally possible way for the budget scorekeepers to change the incentives to make these close calls less commonplace?

    Yes, by adopting a rebuttable presumption that if the legislation is designed in such a way as to straddle the border, the program should be classified as being budgetary unless there is compelling evidence to the contrary. (And, by definition, such evidence would not exist, or the program would not be hugging the borderline.) That way, program proponents would have a strong incentive to honestly admit the program was budgetary, and would design the program accordingly, or else they would have strong reasons to want the program to be regulatory in fact, as well as in name, and they would design the program accordingly.

    This approach would have another significant benefit. Near the beginning of this article we said that it is important that "both agency auditors and the General Accounting Office should be able to examine the books and determine whether the collections and spending are carried out consistent with the requirements of law." Clearly, when federal taxes and spending are hidden from view, it becomes very difficult for this sort of audit to occur. Thus, creating incentives to keep the programs legitimate also reduce the likelihood of fraud and abuse.

A supporting set of criteria for making some of these determinations comes from the actuarial literature, which lists three characteristics as having "fundamental importance" to determining whether a particular program is, indeed, government social insurance: (1) mandatory participation; (2) government operation (so that program termination is not an important consideration); and (3) the ability to change laws and regulations without the consent of the participants.[57]

Consider the case of individual health insurance mandates: participation would be compulsory, the entities that would be eligible to provide the insurance (and the salient characteristics of those entities and that insurance) would be determined by the federal government, and the federal government could change the conditions under which the insurance was provided (whereas the beneficiaries could change the conditions only to the extent that the federal government permitted).

Do these conclusions have any relevance for federal accounting norms, given that accounting is not directly related to the budget? Yes—the basic objectives should be the same, even though accounting standards differ from budget concepts. The accounting standards, like the budget concepts, should have the objectives of being comprehensive, clear, consistent, and intelligible.

Do any of these conclusions diverge from previous Congressional Budget Office positions? (We have already noted a problem that OMB had with the policy overruling these concepts in the case of the president's proposal to nationalize the health care system, and noted some other misclassifications that OMB has participated in.) Apparently they diverge on several borderlines.

1. *CBO's previous analyses have laid great stress in distinguishing between creation of new entities to carry out federal "mandates" versus the use of existing entities. That is, if a new entity were created, this would strongly incline CBO toward calling the action budgetary, whereas if an existing non-federal entity or entities (e.g., existing corporations) were used, it would incline against CBO calling the action budgetary.*

   The line of argument used in this article says that the "entity" question is irrelevant to the points at issue. In all of the cases considered above, the point is that someone—either an existing entity or a new entity (or set of entities)—performs a service *as an agent for the federal government.* No matter who is handling the money, no matter how the transactions are disguised, the point is that the program or activity is governmental, and *someone* is operating it as an agent of the federal government.

2. *CBO's previous analyses have relied very heavily on using the specific criteria listed in the* Report of the President's Commission on Budget Concepts *in order to determine whether an entity should be classified as private or federal.*

   The problem, of course, is that program designers can simply take the characteristics listed in that report and change some of the parameters of the program in order to have the entity possess the essence of being federal (or, at a minimum, of acting as an agent for the federal government) but not be characterized as being federal. CBO should always seek to conform as closely as possible to the substance by penetrating such fog banks. Thus, the criteria listed in that report should be the starting point in determining whether an entity is federal, but other factors should also be taken into account.

3. *CBO also seems to have made too much of the word "program" as used in the* Report of the President's Commission on Budget Concepts.

Again, the Commission was working in the atmosphere of the shenanigans used in 1967 and earlier. Thus, it used terminology that, in its day, seemed to be sufficient for the needs. Others immediately began crafting ways to have the essence of being federal activities while carefully skirting being entitled "programs." Going back to our basic principles, this article says that the CBO focus should *always* be on trying to capture the substance, and that if "clever" technicians (or politicians) come up with something that has the substance of being federal but with some new torque to give it the appearance of not being federal, the CBO should not placidly accept the disguise—it should always focus on substance over form. (I recognize that this is difficult to do in practice, but by laying this out as the basic objective, CBO should be able to do much to avoid internal confusion and, simultaneously, it should be in a better position to defend its decisions against criticism.)

4. *In at least one case* (i.e., *CBO's August 1994 memorandum on The Budgetary Treatment of an Individual Mandate to Buy Health Insurance), the CBO reached the conclusion that it (CBO) could not reach a conclusion. That is, it decided that it lacked "definitive guidance or precedents," and was not prepared to make a ruling in this specific case.*

I disagree with this conclusion. It seems to me that it is *central* to the nature of CBO (and its legal mandate) that it *must* reach conclusions (no matter how touchy) on issues such as this. Failure to do so (a) detracts from CBO's mandate to be a neutral scorekeeping entity, and (b) allows the borderline between budgetary and nonbudgetary to be manipulated endlessly by those who simply are "clever" enough to design programs that hug the border.

I suggest that rule 3 above would do much to alleviate this situation. I do not recall having seen the details of the particular proposal in question (the Chafee health insurance mandates in the 103rd Congress), but as a starting point I would contend that if the proposal did essentially what the Clinton Administration health plan sought to do (i.e., provide mandatory universal coverage), it should have been ruled to be budgetary.

5. *At times CBO has a tendency to be lax with regard to budgetary classifications, and, in particular, to bow to political pressures.*[58] Thus, for example, CBO did not object to the decision to classify the subsidy to Amtrak as being tax refunds, when the payments were clearly outlays. Similarly, CBO did not object to the classification of large-scale payments for drug interdiction as being national defense spending. CBO's laxity in these areas is dangerous, because once one accepts flagrant violations of budgetary logic, it becomes increasingly difficult to oppose other violations based upon the application of principles (since the principles are applied inconsistently).

RECAPITULATION

We have dealt with some—but far from all—of the basic challenges to the integrity of the concepts underlying the federal budget. Among the major sets of issues we have largely bypassed is the perennial argument over whether the budget should be on a cash or an accrual basis. We have done so largely because the space limits and the fact that efforts to promote this conversion have died down (at least for the moment). The principal promoters of that approach are accountants, and the Federal Accounting Standards Advisory Board has reached agreement that it would be inappropriate for accounting to try to convert the budget to an accrual basis.[59]

One may ask: "How important is it that the federal budget be based on a consistent set of principles along these sorts of lines?" A partial answer comes from reading our daily newspapers. For example, as this article was being written, the press was full of articles about the financial busts in East Asia—Japan, Thailand, South Korea, Indonesia, the Philippines and, possibly, communist China. Article after article tells us that one cannot trust the economic and financial data that the governments, banks, and other corporations of those countries have been supplying for years. Time and again the producers of these reports have juggled the books to make the record appear far better than the reality.[60]

It would be a shame if the United States were to abuse its budgetary practices for similar shortsighted reasons, and, in the process, end up with the International Monetary Fund hectoring us about the uselessness or worse of our federal budgetary data.

NOTES

The author wishes to acknowledge the tremendous contributions that Robert W. Kilpatrick of OMB made to this article and all previous articles that Mr. Cuny produced for publication in PB&F. The opinions stated in this article are those of the author and do not represent the official positions of either OMB or CBO.

1. See Thomas J. Cuny, "The Pending Revolution in Federal Accounting Standards," *Public Budgeting & Finance,* Vol. 15, No. 3 (Fall 1995).

2. *Report of the President's Commission on Budget Concepts* (Washington, D.C., U.S. Government Printing Office, 1967).

3. Indeed, in federal budgetary practice, the president's budget documents are essentially a device for aggregating budgetary data. Congress does not enact "the budget" in the same sense, for example, as the California legislature adopts the state budget. For over half of our nation's history the federal budget process existed without a presidential budget, and when the presidential budget was eventually developed, Congress chose to retain its old (decentralized) ways of authorizing taxes and spending, so that the president's budget never became the central tool for congressional budget authorizations and appropriations. Instead, as "the budget" wends its way through Congress, it occurs in the form of thirteen appropriations bills, numerous pieces of authorizing legislation (some of which provide permanent appropriations), and various pieces of revenue legislation. In recent practice, all three of these approaches might also be combined in a single "omnibus" reconciliation bill.

4. This is one of the reasons why it is so important that budget evasion techniques such as proposed under the Clinton health plan not be adopted. Under that plan, large portions of federal fiscal activity would have been hidden outside of the budget and never come under Treasury fiscal control. In turn, this would have greatly reduced the ability of the General Accounting Office to audit these activities.

5. The 1999 *Budget* (see, for example, page 10) shows projections for the years 1999 through 2008 in which it includes a placeholder entitled "Reserve Pending Social Security Reform" that is equal to the projected surpluses, and then shows zero surpluses or deficits for these years. This is clearly an expedient for trying to prevent tax reductions or other actions that would use up these projected surpluses. If these surpluses were to eventuate, the result would be to reduce the federal debt held by the public by essentially equal amounts, thereby contributing to national savings.

6. However, the legislation adopting credit reform was imperfect, so that, at best, the recorded budgetary transactions under this system only approximate the amounts that should be reported as outlays in the federal budget. See my article "Credit Reform Implementation" in the *International Encyclopedia of Public Policy and Administration* (Boulder, CO, Westview Press, 1998).

7. Another way of stating the rationale is to say that the budget is concerned with the allocation of resources, and credit reform allows the budget to compare the cost of the resources being allocated (i.e., the subsidy portion of the loan) with all other resources being allocated by the government. This is the focus of the analysis presented in the *Analytical Perspectives* budget document. (See the 1999 *Analytical Perspectives* document, chapters 21 and 24.)

8. For further discussion of these transactions, see chapter 13 of the 1999 *Budget Analytical Perspectives* document, especially Table 13–2, and the comparable Table S–15 (page 367) in the main budget volume.

9. That is, Congress and the president may have perfectly valid reasons for earmarking some income sources (such as Social Security receipts) to finance associated spending. Similarly, they may have perfectly legitimate reasons for segregating various spending programs into different budget control categories. Federal budget concepts are neutral with regard to these sorts of decisions. What they are not neutral about is decisions such as not to count certain federal income or spending as income or spending, or to count the money in ways that mislead.

10. Indeed, the big fight over the highway and airport and airways trust funds occurs because the spending is *not* automatic—Congress works its will by making the money available to spend, but then fights year after year over the question of the degree to which the spending should be constrained by the budget rationing process.

11. See, chapters 17 and 24 of the *Analytical Perspectives* and page 3 of the *Historical Tables* of the 1999 *Budget* documents.

12. There is at least one case in which bona fide trust funds are included in the budget. A significant part of the Indian Tribal funds administered by the Interior Department fit the definition of bona fide trust funds (and should be excluded from the budget). According to standard budget concepts, these funds do not belong within the budget, but they belong within the broader reporting covered by the Means of Financing, since they are administered by the federal government.

13. In all but one case the off-budget status was required by law. In 1972 the administration decided to exclude the Postal Service fund by executive action, asserting that this was consistent with the intent of the law. (This was a politically convenient fiction, since the Postal Service had been authorized to undergo a massive modernization using borrowed funds and, by excluding the Postal Service fund from the budget, the government could exclude the spending of the proceeds of this borrowing from the recorded budget outlays and deficits.)

14. Indeed, the timing of the legislation was such that it allowed the government to have a double count gimmick in recording of some of these transactions. From its origin until it was moved on-budget by law, the Federal Financing Bank was off-budget. The FFB made loans to, and purchased loan assets of, other Federal agencies and programs. While the FFB was off-budget, this practice allowed agencies to hide much of the cost of their credit programs outside of the budget. When the FFB was moved on-budget, it had a significant corpus of outstanding loan assets that the government could dispose of (through asset sales or loan repayments) and the proceeds were recorded as offsetting collections and, therefore, reduced recorded budget outlays and deficits.

15. Which, with minor exceptions, have been in place since the start of the Republic.

16. Thus, use of escape mechanisms may be purely a matter of window dressing—the willingness of Congress and the president to spend money, as long as they can disguise the cost thereof (i.e., as long as they can pretend that the spending does not add to current outlays and the current deficit). This creates the political appeal for various escape mechanisms—such as lease purchases—in which the budgetary decision to purchase is made front-end, but the cost is spread out to future periods. There are times when these mechanisms are used simply because they are the easiest ways that supporters can get the spending through the political maze. Thus, for example, when Senator Moynihan sponsored the legislation authorizing the International Trade Center, he was able to control the action through his committee and bypass the appropriations committee.

17. Depreciation is commonly used in accounting in order to measure costs and net worth, but it is little used for budgeting, even in the private sector.

18. The *Analytical Perspectives* portion of the annual Federal budget documents have additional discussions relevant to these issues. See, in particular, the discussion starting on page 153 of the 1999 document.

19. And even so, problems and abuses do occur—units of government sometimes get into financial binds as a result of imprudent financial management (as happened in the case of New York City).

20. However, under current budget practice, the budget and off-budget totals are added together to arrive at a consolidated total, and then focus in on that consolidated total.

21. A common argument for state and local borrowing is to spread the cost of the assets to the generations that use them. Since people frequently move in or out of the jurisdiction, the rationale says that each year the people who live in the jurisdiction that year (and benefit from the facilities) should pay their proportionate share of the cost. Private borrowing is commonly used to finance investments expected to provide returns to the borrower sufficient to pay interest, repay the principal, and provide additional profits.

22. Again, a common argument used in defense of borrowing is that the proceeds of the borrowing is used to finance the acquisition of assets of equivalent value, so the net worth of the borrower is unchanged.

23. The Commission specifically dealt with depreciation, rather than debt amortization, in its report. However, the arguments against the one are essentially the same as the arguments against the other.

24. This was, and is, a scandal. Successive presidents and Congresses have simply been unwilling to make enough room within the budget to build or purchase a supply of federal office space adequate to the requirements of the staffs that they authorized. As a result, the taxpayers were (and are) out large sums of money to finance much more costly leased space. The argument in this article centers on the means that proponents of this project used to bypass the budget process. I agree with Senator Moynihan and Mr. Golden that Congress

ought to have authorized and financed substantially more federal office buildings to house the authorized staff (though the decision to include monumental features in the building without specific approval of the Congress was also illegitimate).

25. This building was recently renamed in honor of former President Ronald Reagan. However, as one of Mr. Reagan's sons pointed out, this building embodies the antithesis of what Reagan stood for.

26. It can be argued any lease purchase arrangement is essentially a purchase—not a lease—from the start. However, while there seem to be bona fide reasons for some private interests to enter into lease purchase arrangements (those reasons might simply be for tax benefits, of course), there probably is never a case when it makes sense for the federal government to use this mechanism *except to escape budgetary controls.*

27. Hence, from the perspective of the government as a whole, the "lease" component disappeared—it was a straight purchase.

28. However, Sen. Moynihan is in error when he says that it is a "lease-to-own building, which in a quarter-century will be ours, and thereafter we will live rent free." (1) From start to finish it was and is a federally owned building—the putative lease is simply part of the disguise of the project. The entire financing was federal (primarily or entirely through the FFB). (2) It will never be rent free in terms of substance. Any building of that size will always have major repair, maintenance, and operating costs. As a point of comparison, for example, the Pentagon was completed in 1940, and is now undergoing a massive renovation and expansion that is scheduled to cost the government over $1 billion—substantially more (in nominal dollars) than the original cost of that building (see the *Washington Post,* December 17, 1997, page A–1).

29. This bias is reflected in the old saying that the budget is the only thing in the world that is larger on the inside than on the outside.

30. Obviously, I am making no judgment about what might or might not be "privatized" in the future.

31. The *Washington Post* had a recent article (Oct. 28, 1997, page C–1, *"To Some, a Gateway Could Become a Giveaway on the Anacostia")* indicating that someone is cooking up a scheme akin to the International Trade Center for constructing a DOT headquarters on an ostensible lease purchase basis. The article misses the whole point of the budget evasion, but it illustrates the basic elements of that process.

32. See OMB Circular A–11 (1997), Appendix A *(Scorekeeping Guidelines)* item 11, and Appendix B *(Scoring Lease-Purchases and Leases of Capital Assets).*

33. This is an approach that the GAO appears to favor. However, interestingly enough, the GAO would exclude Federal office buildings and associated equipment from its capital component, so that the GAO approach would be of no help in cases such as the shortage of federally owned office space in the national capital region. See GAO statement on *Budgeting for Capital* (GAO/T-AIMD-98–99).

34. This is the act that authorized the president to create an executive budget and to submit it annually to Congress, and this act established the Bureau of the Budget, the predecessor agency to the Office of Management and Budget.

35. See page 1383 of the 1950 *Budget* and page 1157 of the 1951 *Budget.*

36. The OMB staff view of the EITC (and any similar tax "refunds" in excess of the taxes collected) was expressed as follows in an OMB memo dated February 2, 1977: *"That portion of the earned income credit that reduces tax liabilities should be treated as tax refunds (negative receipts). These refunds differ in no significant respect from the other provisions of the tax code establishing rates exemptions. etc. in determining the basic total of taxes due. That part of any 'refund' that exceeds income tax liabilities otherwise due and therefore results in a payment of money from the Treasury beyond any income tax received from the taxpayer should be treated as budget outlays. These payments differ in no significant respect from other cash transfer payments by the Treasury. Indeed to do otherwise would open the door to a new form of backdoor financing by permitting outlays to be treated as negative receipts. For example, it would permit billions of dollars of welfare payments to be treated as offsets to receipts should a negative income tax plan be adopted."*

37. There is little consolation in the fact that they were not enacted because, if this loophole had remained in place over time, it would have been a virtual certainty that other programs of this nature would have been enacted.

38. November 8,1997, page D–1.

39. See section 4 of the annual *Historical Tables* document (of the 1999 Budget documents) for historical data on outlays by agency, section 3 for data on outlays by function and subfunction, and section 6 for data on outlays by composition category.

40. *Report of the President's Commission on Budget Concepts,* p. 17.

41. However, the functional structure plays a role in the congressional budget resolutions and from time to time the defense/nondefense split has played a role in the budget control process. Additionally, pages 149 to 256 of the 1999 Budget are devoted to a presentation on a functional basis.

42. Headline of a *Washington Post* story on November 24, 1997, page A–27.

43. Those definitions can be seen in the GAO publication, *A Glossary of Terms Used in the Federal Budget Process* (GAO/AFMD-2.1.1), January 1993, starting on page 102.

44. The issue is not a question of how much to spend on drug control interdiction or the degree to which the Defense Department should participate in this effort. The issue raised herein is strictly a question of the way the money should be reflected in the functional (and related composition of outlays) data bases.

45. See Thomas J. Cuny, "Offsetting Collections in the Federal Budget," *Public Budgeting & Finance*, Vol. 8, Number 3, Autumn 1988, and "Offsetting Collections," *International Encyclopedia of Public Policy and Administration*, (Boulder, CO, The Westview Press, 1998) for discussions of these concepts.

46. In theory, GSEs are private financial institutions that operate with federal sponsorship in order to achieve—through the private market—goals important to the government. The budget Appendix has a separate section disclosing the financial status of these entities.

47. For example, NASA financed a string of communications satellites through the FFB, and the Defense Department financed some ships through an ostensible "lease purchase" arrangement. Beyond that, the agencies that were engaged in credit activities routinely used the FFB as a way of hiding or obfuscating their losses (i.e., subsidies to borrowers). See Thomas J. Cuny, "Federal Credit Reform," *Public Budgeting & Finance*, Vol. 11, No. 2 (Summer 1991) for a discussion of the role of the FFB in this process.

48. The proposal itself was extremely complicated—the draft legislation was hundreds of pages long and was subject to various changes in order to accommodate critics. The CBO cost estimate on this proposal was succinct, discussed the basic issues, and concluded (a) that should the proposal be enacted, the financial flows belong on-budget and (b) that the design of the program was so complex that it could not work as designed. (While the CBO report did not say so, much of the complexity of the design flowed from the administration's efforts to nationalize the health care industry and to hide that nationalization from the budget.) The CBO document, *An Analysis of the Administration's Health Proposals*, is available through the Government Printing office (ISBN 0–16–043093–3).

49. In recent years, significant efforts have also gone into trying to estimate the cost of such regulations, and to facilitate a public process of making trade-offs between the cost and benefits of regulations.

50. How might this be done? By enacting legislation creating a defense corporation, requiring that "fees" paid to that corporation and spending by that corporation be excluded from the budget (on the grounds that the corporation was nonfederal), and then using the federal government's regulatory power (rather than its tax powers) to mandate that people pay such fees. Absurd? Take a look at the "United Mine Workers Benefit Funds"—that is exactly what occurred, and that is exactly why OMB and CBO agreed that this program belongs on budget, even though it is ostensibly regulatory in nature. Might this be done on a large scale? Yes! This is the essence of the Clinton health insurance plan (using a whole series of entities rather than a single one), and it would have nationalized around 6 percent of our GDP.

51. And, at this point the CBO and the OMB had to take different routes. The logic that CBO used in analyzing and classifying the president's health plan was the same as the logic that both OMB and CBO had used in analyzing and classifying the United Mine Workers Benefit funds. In the former case, the two agencies agreed. In the latter case, since it was the president himself who was proposing this gimmick, only CBO was free to call it according to its basic nature. (And, of course, CBO was under tremendous political pressure to fudge on the issue. I personally commend Bob Reischauer—then Director of CBO—for his integrity and strength of character in dealing with the matter.)

52. We are dealing with federal budget concepts. The question of whether state and/or local mandates become so intrusive that they should be budgetary is a legitimate issue, but it is outside the scope of this article.

53. A commentator stated that these are not necessarily four discrete types of continuums. However, the intent is to illustrate a range of potential issues in an easily understandable fashion, so I will not concern myself with trying to deal with this comment.

54. This is the case of the "Universal Service Fund" being administered by the Federal Communications Commission. A major defect of that fund (according to budget logic) is that it is the FCC, not Congress, that sets the "charges" (i.e., taxes) to finance the fund and determines how much money to spend and who is to receive the subsidies. This makes the legislation susceptible to judicial attack as being unconstitutional.

55. When CBO analyzed the Clinton health plan, it concluded that while the transactions would be budgetary in nature, the financial flows should be segregated separately from the rest of the budget. This makes sense, both because of the magnitudes of the flows and the uncertainty of the data. Similarly, if a plan along these lines should be enacted, the flows would be legitimately budgetary but should not be commingled with any other budgetary flows.

56. Indeed, one of the greatest threats to the integrity of federal budget concepts is that activities might be nationalized through such small steps that no individual step was deemed to trigger the crossover, but the cumulative result would achieve the same objective. This is possible in the case of medical care.

57. The third exposure draft of the Actuarial Standards Board, Proposed Actuarial Standard of Practice, *Social Insurance.*

58. Of course, the same is true of OMB—none of us is perfect.

59. That is, FASAB concluded that questions relating to budget concepts should be resolved based on the norms appropriate to the budget. If, or to the extent that, such concepts are the same as those derived from accounting standards, that is fine, but accounting logic should not drive budgetary quantification. This does not rule out the use of accruals either internal to the budget (as in the case of Federal employee retirement programs) or accruals which change the quantification of the budget totals (as in the case of credit reform). The critical point is that if such changes were to be made, they should be made based upon improving the budget *as a budget.* For a discussion of the case for requantifying some Federal insurance programs in a fashion similar to credit reform, see the GAO testimony *Budgeting for Federal Insurance Programs* (GAO/T-AIMD-98–147).

60. Example: "South Koreans Called to Account," the *Washington Post,* January 2, 1998, A–1. This article speaks of how, as part of the international financial rescue package, the Koreans must reform their "murky economic practices" and can no longer "cook the books," and it cites the "international language spoken by bookkeepers in the global economy" which is "the standard set by the U.S. CPA exam."

CHAPTER 33

ACCOUNTABILITY AND ENTREPRENEURIAL PUBLIC MANAGEMENT
The Case of the Orange County Investment Fund

KEVIN P. KEARNS

On December 6, 1994, the financial world was rocked by news that Orange County, California had declared bankruptcy. Its vast $20 billion investment pool, representing over 180 county and municipal agencies, had experienced $1.7 billion in unrealized losses due to the fund's heavy reliance on investments that fell in value as interest rates rose in 1994. Nervous creditors who had made loans to the fund to finance its aggressive investment strategies liquidated $11 billion in collateral on the loans. Then, with its leverage hopelessly constricted, the county fund filed for protection under Chapter 9 of the U.S. Bankruptcy Code, much like the way private firms seek protection under Chapter 11 of the Code. It was the largest municipal bankruptcy in the history of the federal code.

The news was especially shocking because the manager of the Orange County fund, county treasurer Robert Citron, had built a reputation as a successful public sector entrepreneur. Under Citron's direction, the Orange County fund had been hailed as an example of how an aggressive investment strategy could help diversify local government revenues, thereby reducing reliance on property taxes and other traditional revenue sources. Orange County's investment portfolio included a class of *derivative* securities, which fluctuated inversely with interest rates. The fund also used short-term leverage borrowing to purchase certain securities as well as *reverse repurchase arrangements* in which securities in the portfolio were used as collateral on the short-term loans. This approach has been embraced by several other California communities as well as by government agencies in several other states.[1]

The potential gains from such a strategy can be enormous, but the risks are proportional to the gains. For several years, Citron played the financial markets masterfully and his approach may have helped the Orange County jurisdictions hold their own when property values and tax revenues fell in recent years.[2] But Citron's strategy was based on one key assumption: that interest rates would continue to fall as they did in 1992 and 1993. His investment strategy backfired when rates began to climb.

The Orange County investors lost millions, Robert Citron lost his job, and the citizens lost

From *Public Budgeting and Finance,* vol. 15, no. 3 (Autumn 1995), 3–21. Copyright © 1995 by Public Financial Publications, Inc. Reprinted with permission.

confidence in their government. Ripple effects within the financial world and among state and local governments will likely be felt for a very long time.

It is *not* the intent of this article to analyze the fine details of the Orange County case in terms of the specific investment securities chosen by Robert Citron and his advisors or the decision processes they used to make these investments. Nor does the article discuss the specifics of the regulatory environment in which Citron and his financial advisors operated. The details of the Orange County debacle will unfold in the months (and perhaps years) ahead as investors, creditors, regulators, and the courts put together the pieces of the puzzle.

Instead, this article examines the broad facts and general context of the case from a conceptual and theoretical perspective of *public sector accountability.* Specifically, this article presents a conceptual framework that illuminates four different types of accountability environments facing public managers today. The framework is a heuristic tool that may be helpful in retrospective analysis of cases like the Orange County bankruptcy and many other accountability controversies in the public sector. The framework can also be used in a prospective way by public officials to help them diagnose their accountability environment and develop targeted strategies to enhance their role as stewards of the public trust.

THE "REINVENTION" OF PUBLIC SECTOR ACCOUNTABILITY

In some important respects, the Orange County case is a story of how prevailing standards of accountability, and the management systems that support those standards, can shift in response to the economic, political, and intellectual environment.[3]

In the field of public financial management, the prevailing standard of accountability historically has been rooted in *stewardship* of the public trust. Financial managers in the public sector generally are not risk-takers and certainly there are very few incentives—financial or political—to gamble with the investment of public funds. Consequently, the priorities of public financial managers traditionally have been: *first,* to protect the investment's principal, generally through relatively safe instruments such as government securities and certificates of deposit; *second,* to maintain liquidity, guaranteeing that cash is readily available to meet expenditure obligations; and, *third,* to derive a reasonable yield or return on investments within the limits imposed by the first two principles. Naturally, this conservative approach does not produce dramatic returns on investment, but in most cases it does ensure the safety and liquidity of public funds. Many states, in fact, have laws restricting public investments to conservative and relatively liquid instruments.

In Orange County and other California communities, the shift in the accountability environment began in 1978 when voters there approved Proposition 13, essentially capping property tax revenues on which local governments had come to rely as a predictable and steadily growing source of revenue. Public officials in California, and in several other "tax revolt" states, responded to this challenge with determination and, in some cases, with remarkable success by finding creative and entrepreneurial ways to diversify government revenues and by improving the efficiency and effectiveness of government services.

It was in this political and economic environment that California removed some of the legal and regulatory constraints on financial managers like Robert Citron, freeing them to be more entrepreneurial with public investments. In fact, Citron helped draft the California law that allowed county treasurers, with permission of their boards of supervisors, to use reverse repurchase agreements in which investment securities serve as collateral on loans for the purchase of additional securities.[4] Proposition 13 was designed to *limit* the discretionary authority of public officials to raise tax rates, and it certainly succeeded in doing that. Ironically, the environment created in part by Proposition

13 had the opposite effect in the domain of investment management by shifting the standard of accountability *away* from compliance with strict legal and regulatory constraints and *toward* greater reliance on professional discretion and entrepreneurship. Within this environment, an emerging generation of public sector entrepreneurs are attempting to manage government organizations "like a business" with aggressive strategies to diversify revenues, privatize operations, tailor services to customer needs, and generally enhance government responsiveness and flexibility.

This free-market, entrepreneurial paradigm of public management was given intellectual credibility with the publication of *Reinventing Government*.[5] The philosophy espoused by David Osborne and Ted Gaebler sent shock waves through bureaucratic and political circles. Their book was the first public administration text to become a best-seller, and their philosophy was given political legitimacy when it was endorsed by candidate Bill Clinton during the 1992 presidential campaign. More than just esoteric theory, *Reinventing Government* provided the blueprint for Vice President Al Gore's *National Performance Review,* which recommended actions, currently being implemented, to improve the effectiveness and efficiency of the federal government.[6] The post-Proposition 13 environment in California provided much of the inspiration for Osborne and Gaebler. Many of the case histories and illustrations used in their book are drawn from the experiences of local governments in California.

Briefly, Osborne and Gaebler believe that government organizations must be liberated from the strangle-hold of regulations, bureaucratic procedures, line-item budgets, and risk-averse organizational cultures if they are to be more entrepreneurial and customer-focused. They argue persuasively, and with many examples, that bureaucracy is the ultimate obstacle to improving government responsiveness and performance. Among their many recommendations are that management systems in government should be less rule-driven and more mission-focused. Public officials, they argue, should be given more discretion and authority to develop strategies to earn money rather than simply spend money. Essentially, they say that governments can and should adapt business management principles to the public sector context in order to more effectively meet the needs of citizens, taxpayers, and future generations.

Intellectually, these are very attractive and exciting themes. In practice, however, they require fundamental shifts in the accountability environment of government agencies at the federal, state, and local levels.[7] The bureaucratic structures and red tape, which Osborne and Gaebler denounce, do indeed inhibit the flexibility and entrepreneurship of government agencies. But the bureaucracy, with all of its well-documented shortcomings, is still the primary instrument of public sector accountability, and its ultimate purpose is to prevent abuse of power and to limit the autonomy and discretion of public officials. Historically, for better or worse, we have relied on these bureaucratic mechanisms—rules, regulations, operating procedures, chains of command, checks and balances—to constrain administrative discretion and to ensure proper stewardship of the public trust.[8] Eliminating this red tape, and the larger bureaucratic framework that produces it, will require the development of *new* instruments of accountability to replace the old.

Osborne and Gaebler claim that their management philosophy does not supplant the notion of accountability, but rather redefines it by freeing public officials to manage more strategically in response to rapidly changing conditions and emerging public needs. In effect, the Osborne and Gaebler philosophy calls for higher standards of accountability based on professionalism, expertise, delegation, and empowerment of citizens to play a larger and more meaningful role in public affairs.

Let there be no misunderstanding here. This article is *not* suggesting that the Orange County fiasco can be laid at the feet of Osborne and Gaebler or of anyone who follows their philosophy. But the Orange County case does present a classic example of the risks associated with any "reinvented" notion of accountability that is based on an entrepreneurial model of public management. A more constructive approach, employed in this article, is to try to learn something from the Orange County case by studying it within an expanded framework of accountability. This framework, unlike the narrow and confining bureaucratic framework, is capable of surfacing some plausible public management strategies that are both responsive to changing needs and accountable to the overriding notion of serving the public interest.

SOME DEFINITIONS OF ACCOUNTABILITY

The notion of accountability is perhaps *the* core philosophical concept in public management. Still, there remains considerable debate on its meaning. In its most narrow interpretation, accountability involves answering "to a higher authority—legal or organizational—for one's action in society at large or within one's organization."[9] This narrow definition of accountability draws a very clear distinction between two fundamental questions: 1) *To whom* is the organization (or individual worker) *accountable?* and 2) for *what* is the organization (or individual worker) *responsible?*

Strictly speaking, only the first question pertains to "accountability" per se. It deals primarily with mechanisms of supervision, oversight, and reporting to a higher authority in a formal chain of command. Formally, the second question has more to do with concepts like professional *responsibility* and *obligation,* which are distinct and are often treated as such in the scholarly literature.[10]

Others have eschewed the bureaucratic bias implied in these traditional definitions of accountability. A performance-based (versus compliance-based) notion of accountability says that it involves some standard with which to "hold individuals and organizations responsible for performance measured as objectively as possible."[11] Naturally, performance includes the exercise of professional judgement. Therefore, Rosen argues that accountability involves, among other things, the exercise of "lawful and sensible administrative discretion" and efforts to "enhance citizen confidence in . . . administrative institutions."[12] Then, of course, there is the on-going debate, beginning with the seminal exchange between Carl Friedrich[13] and Herman Finer,[14] on how to monitor professional discretion—whether accountability is best enforced by outside oversight or internal management controls. Finally, a strategic perspective on accountability is put forth by Romzek and Dubnick, who say that "accountability involves the means by which public agencies and their workers *manage* the diverse expectations generated within and outside the organization" (emphasis added).[15]

These broader perspectives on accountability introduce an element of strategic management whereby public officials attempt to anticipate shifting public expectations, interpret changing standards of accountability, and position their agencies for proactive as well as reactive responses. In the process, public managers are transformed from a role of passive compliance into one of active participation in framing the accountability standards by which they are judged.[16]

This article embraces the broader concept of accountability—one that is more messy than precise operational definitions but probably more consistent with the "popular" usage of the term. In this view, accountability includes much more than just the formal processes and channels for reporting to a higher authority. Rather, the term "accountability" generally is used to refer to a wide spectrum of public expectations and performance standards that are used to judge the performance, responsiveness, and even "morality" of government organizations. These expectations often include implicit performance criteria that are far more subjective and ill-structured than are formal mandates or explicit rules. And, in this broader conception of accountability, the range of people and institutions to whom government officials must "account" includes not only higher authorities in the institutional chain of command but also the general public, the news media, peer agencies, donors, and many other stakeholders.

As a member of the scholarly community, I have some misgivings about blurring formal distinctions between terms and concepts that have been so carefully defined and articulated by my colleagues. But, as a pragmatist, I sense that the broader conception of accountability is a fact of life in terms of how this topic is discussed in the real world of professional practice. Thus, with apologies to the purists, I will use the term "accountability" throughout this article to refer to the broader notions described above.

A CONCEPTUAL FRAMEWORK FOR ANALYZING ACCOUNTABILITY

Elsewhere, I have proposed a conceptual framework for identifying four different types of accountability and some important management issues associated with each.[17] The framework assumes that any system of accountability contains at least two dimensions: 1) a set of accountability standards—explicit or implicit—generated by the organization's strategic environment; and 2) a response—reactive or proactive—from inside the organization.

Even novice public officials quickly learn that they are accountable to at least two types of performance standards. First, they are accountable for *explicit* performance standards that are often codified in law, administrative regulations, or contractual obligations. These accountability standards represent the bureaucratic and regulatory environment that public officials confront on a daily basis. Second, they are accountable for *implicit* standards that involve generally accepted notions of appropriate administrative action, professional discretion, and organizational performance. These implicit standards are defined not so much by laws and regulations as by societal values, beliefs, professional norms, and assumptions. Any public official who has confronted the wrath of a citizen ("So *this* is how you are spending my hard-earned money!") is familiar with these implicit and subjective standards of accountability.

The second dimension of the framework assumes that public managers have several options with which to respond to accountability standards. First, they may respond with *tactical* (reactive) approaches when accountability standards are presented to them either in the form of explicit requirements or of implicit expectations. The tactical approach is essentially a stimulus-response, driven by intense pressure from the accountability environment to take some action. Second, they may take *strategic* (proactive) actions to anticipate new or emerging accountability standards and to position their organization within a dynamic accountability environment. The strategic approach requires foresight and a willingness to take corrective action before the organization is forced or pressured to do so.

Superimposing these two dimensions yields a matrix with four cells as illustrated in Figure 33.1.

Let us examine each cell of the matrix in greater detail and with illustrations from the Orange County case. Keep in mind that these four cells are conceptual representations of important segments of the accountability environment. In the real world, the boundaries between the cells may not be as clear and precise as those represented here. But this tool provides a point of departure for additional in-depth analysis and, perhaps, adaptation by decisionmakers to the unique context of their organization.

Compliance Accountability (Cell #1)

The upper left quadrant of the matrix denotes the most familiar, and most narrowly interpreted, form of accountability—*compliance* by a government organization with an explicit and publicly stated standard of performance or operational procedure. The accountability standards in this cell

Figure 33.1 **Four Types of Accountability**

		Accountability Standards	
		Explicit	**Implicit**
Internal Response System	Tactical (Reactive)	1) Compliance Accountability	2) Negotiated Accountability
	Strategic (Proactive)	4) Anticipatory (Advocacy) Accountability	3) Discretionary (Enterpreneurial) Accountability

Source: Adapted from Kevin P. Kearns, "The Strategic Management of Accountability in Nonprofit Organizations: An Analytical Framework," *Public Administration Revier 54* (March/April 1994) 188.

are often codified and enforced by an outside oversight organization and, therefore, carry the force of law. Alternatively, the standards might be embedded in the bureaucratic procedures, chains of command, hierarchies of authority, and checks and balances *within* the organization. While these internal bureaucratic mechanisms do not always carry the force of law, they are very explicit and vigorously enforced as part of the organization's management control system.

Whether the accountability standards are enforced externally or internally, compliance is viewed as essentially *reactive* in nature. That is, the organization (or the individual worker) awaits the formulation of precise and clearly articulated standards and then tries to follow the rules, subject to oversight and periodic audits, or evaluations. This type of accountability environment requires a clear hierarchy of authority that is recognized as legitimate by all actors. Also, compliance involves a relatively heavy reliance on the traditional notion of *bureaucracy* that, especially in government, has been a principal instrument for ensuring that the public trust is not abused.

While compliance is always reactive, it is rarely a *passive,* or knee-jerk, response. Indeed, truly effective compliance requires active participation from the people and organizations that are subject to these explicit standards of accountability. For example, they must design administrative and operational procedures in accordance with the laws and regulations. They must train employees and volunteers to work within those parameters. They must anticipate problems and barriers to overcome during implementation. They must allocate (and perhaps reallocate) sufficient resources to the effort. And, of course, they must monitor their own behavior and compile appropriate information in order to demonstrate (literally "account" for) their compliance. Still, all of these actions are essentially in response to the *stimulus* provided by the law, the regulation, or the bureaucratic standard of accountability that is imposed upon them.

This cell of the framework is used by many states and localities to regulate the investment practices of government jurisdictions, and it is the cell in which Orange County operated prior to the liberalization of California's public investment regulations. Also, it is the cell used by the Securities and Exchange Commission (SEC) to regulate the activities of financial advisors and brokers.

Negotiated Accountability (Cell #2)

The cell in the upper right corner of Figure 33.1 addresses several different accountability contexts. First, government organizations are often held accountable to emerging performance standards that are implicit—that is, standards that arise from shifting societal values and beliefs or from emerging political values and priorities that have not yet been codified in law, administrative regulations, or bureaucratic controls. In such cases, the accountability standards are only loosely defined (or completely undefined) and, therefore, open to debate.

A second circumstance in this cell, and one that also is quite familiar to public administrators, is the need to be accountable for performance standards that are, in fact, codified, but where the laws and regulations (or other contractual arrangements) are vaguely worded and, therefore, subject to interpretation and "translation" by public administrators charged with their implementation.

In both cases, the accountability standards are implicit and imprecise, leading to conflicting standards of performance and relatively high levels of uncertainty among all stakeholders. Even with their ambiguity, however, these accountability standards (or their advocates) are often powerful enough to capture the organization's immediate attention, providing a catalyst for tactical actions and relatively rapid response. Often this response involves some form of negotiation between the organization and its environment. The purpose of the negotiation is to clarify the ambiguous circumstances and to reach agreement on commonly understood standards of accountability.

Thus, this cell of the framework is labeled *negotiated accountability*. In some cases, the negotiations may take place with a particularly powerful (or interested) constituency—individuals or groups who have an unusually high stake in the outcome—such as citizen groups, advocacy organizations, and other coalitions of stakeholders. In other cases, the negotiations may involve a regulating body that enforces a vaguely worded law, regulation, or contract.

The concept of negotiated accountability could apply to several aspects and phases of the Orange County case. First, at the front-end (before the bankruptcy), there is the prospect that everyone associated with the Orange County investment pool—investors, creditors, the County Board of Supervisors, the SEC, and even citizens—would, in retrospect, have wanted to negotiate and reach agreement on: 1) a specified set of objectives for the investment pool, expressed in terms of acceptable levels of risk in relation to potential returns on investment; 2) a portfolio of investment instruments that would best meet the fund's objectives; and 3) how best to manage the portfolio to ensure internal oversight and accountability. Immediately following the crisis, there was speculation that some investors may not have been fully informed regarding the management of the portfolio and, in particular, the use of a single broker for the fund.[18] Also, there is the curious aspect that school districts in Orange County were mandated to participate in the fund, thereby removing any opportunity for them to negotiate.

Second, at the back-end (in the wake of the bankruptcy), there is the very real prospect that some form of negotiated accountability will be required to clarify the obligations of Orange County and the rights of investors under Chapter 9 of the U.S. Bankruptcy Code.[19] Some people believe that Chapter 9 inappropriately relieves the jurisdiction of its legitimate accountability to its creditors since, in theory, the governments involved still have at their disposal certain options to generate more revenue.[20] According to some legal experts, there is even a possibility that Merrill Lynch & Co., the sole broker for the Orange County investment pool, may be liable for some of the fund's losses, just as a bartender is liable for the consequences of serving an obviously intoxicated patron.[21] The legal concept of fiduciary responsibility can be murky and, of course, Merrill Lynch denies any liability. Still, ten years ago the firm negotiated a modest settlement arising from losses incurred by San Jose, California, which employed an investment strategy very similar to that of the Orange County fund. Other securities firms paid a total of $26 million in judgments and penalties arising from the San Jose crisis. Not surprisingly, Merrill Lynch's stock (which itself is a noteworthy instrument of "negotiated accountability") fell 3.4 percent following news of the Orange County bankruptcy.[22]

The concept of negotiated accountability is a very important domain of public management, but it has received relatively little attention in the literature. What are the implicit standards of accountability by which the organization is judged? Are there external stakeholders who are particularly interested in the enforcement of these standards? Are any of these accountability standards negotiable? Would it be in the organization's best interest to negotiate now or later? On what philosophical or legal grounds should the organization negotiate?

These questions may highlight several types of *threats* for the organization. As described above, this cell of the matrix often involves disagreements among stakeholders regarding accountability standards and measures, leading to *conflict* between the organization and its environment. Conflict, in turn, generally involves *risk* and uncertainty because the outcome of the dispute and its long-term effects cannot be fully controlled or easily predicted. Also, low-level conflicts can quickly and unpredictably *escalate* to major controversies, especially when one party or the other perceives that escalation will enhance their power and control of the situation.

However, decisionmakers may perceive several types of opportunities in this cell of the accountability environment. *Timing* is one factor that can offer opportunities. Zartman and Berman say that negotiations may be especially timely when some type of significant change has taken place in the environment that alters the relative power of stakeholders or their respective perceptions of the situation.[23] Negotiations may provide the opportunity to *clarify expectations* and performance standards, thereby reducing uncertainty and risk. In the process, there may be opportunities to *build trust* among participants, especially when negotiations take place in good faith and with mutual disclosure of information.

Discretionary (Entrepreneurial) Accountability (Cell #3)

The cell in the bottom right corner of Figure 33.1 portrays the context in which accountability standards and expectations are implicit. But, unlike the previous cell, these standards are not yet powerful enough to demand an immediate tactical response, such as negotiations with the external environment. In fact, in this cell there may be no identifiable parties with whom to negotiate. Instead, there is tremendous latitude for the exercise of professional judgement and discretionary authority by government officials on behalf of their constituents. This cell recognizes knowledge and expertise as the primary instruments of accountability rather than laws, bureaucratic hierarchies, or negotiated agreements on performance standards. As John Burke says, "Professional responsibility is grounded in the public's high regard for and recognition of knowledge and expertise, and it reflects the great value placed on specialization and professional skill in modern bureaucracies."[24]

This cell is labeled *discretionary (entrepreneurial) accountability* because there is very little meaningful oversight other than the self-defined and self-enforced norms and standards of professional practice. In the absence of meaningful threats or sanctions from the external environment, public officials must take personal and professional responsibility for anticipating and interpreting emerging standards of acceptable professional behavior and organizational performance, weighing long-term risks as well as short-term benefits. Consequently, there can be enormous pressures on public managers in this cell of the matrix. North Carolina's state treasurer, Harlan Boyles, said that, prior to the Orange County incident, he was under intense political pressure from local governments in his state to liberalize investment regulations and restrictions so that they too could begin reaping the high investment dividends enjoyed by communities in California, Texas, Ohio, and elsewhere. Boyles said that he received more than a dozen calls a month from brokers around the country hoping to sway his views. "It's a constant pressure. They'll call and say, 'Let us show you what we did in California.' Thankfully, our General Assembly has never been inclined to liberalize the investment laws."[25]

There is also pressure from peer organizations in this cell of the accountability matrix. David Bronner, director of Alabama's pension fund, said, "I remember a group outing two years ago with the Orange County people. They were very boastful about how well they were doing and how antiquated I was." Bonner also noted that, until recently, he had unilateral discretionary authority to make investments in whatever instruments he deemed appropriate, regardless of their risk.[26]

This is the cell in which Robert Citron was operating when he was managing the Orange County investment pool. In California's deregulated, post-Proposition 13 environment, Citron was given substantial discretionary authority. In his defense, Citron responded by achieving steady gains in the portfolio's value. Clearly, however, there are enormous risks, as well as potential benefits, associated with the notion of discretionary (entrepreneurial) accountability.

Significantly, this is the cell of the matrix that Osborne and Gaebler suggest be enhanced by, in effect, giving government officials *more* discretionary authority to respond to public needs as they arise. The dilemma, only partially addressed by Osborne and Gaebler, is how to reconcile an entrepreneurial spirit, which requires swift unilateral responses to emerging opportunities, with the fundamental principles of representative bureaucracy, which require time-consuming efforts to build consensus on long-term as well as short-term goals. Indeed, this is the dilemma that has drawn some of the sharpest critiques of the entrepreneurial paradigm in the literature. Bellone and Goerl foretold the Orange County debacle:

> When engaged in *non-mandated risk taking,* the responsibilities of the public administrator become even more a stewardship issue. High-risk investment schemes that have gone wrong and resulted in economic losses, failed arbitrage efforts in investing federal grant funds, and short-term borrowing to pay operating costs . . . are all examples of entrepreneurial risk-taking that ignored the prudent concern for the long-term public good. (emphasis added)[27]

However, the authors go on to suggest that the notions of entrepreneurship and democracy can be reconciled by providing more opportunities for meaningful citizen participation in the affairs of government. They state that a "strong theory of entrepreneurship requires a strong theory of citizenship."[28] This argument is also made by Osborne and Gaebler. But this optimistic view of citizen participation is not shared by everyone. For example, Terry responds that entrepreneurship requires dangerous concentrations of power and a commitment to fundamental change in the traditional notion of political authority and representative bureaucracy on which the profession of public administration is based. He concludes that "we should abandon the misconceived quest to reconcile public entrepreneurship with democracy," and that Bellone and Goerl's notion of civic-regarding entrepreneurship "seems to be a wolf in sheep's clothing."[29]

Coincidentally, there is evidence in the Orange County case that seems to confirm suspicions about the limited ability of citizens to provide a meaningful check on entrepreneurship, especially in a specialized domain like public investment strategies. Robert Citron was reelected to the treasurer's office in June 1994, only six months before the financial crisis. His opponent in the race was John Moorlach, a certified public accountant who based his campaign on Citron's risky investments and the vulnerability of the Orange County investment fund to fluctuating interest rates. Moorlach captured barely one-third of the vote and failed to generate any meaningful or lasting public dialogue on the Orange County investment strategy. Evidently, the voters were either: 1) unconcerned about Citron's management of the investment pool; 2) incapable of making informed judgements because of the complexity of the issues; or 3) distracted by another political issue, Proposition 187 (limiting the rights of illegal immigrants), which had more emotional appeal than did the intellectually challenging notions of reverse repurchase agreements, derivatives, and fluctuating interest rates. Even after the bankruptcy, citizen reactions seemed mixed. A local radio station sponsored "an hour of rage" after the financial crisis, allowing callers to vent their anger. The station received very few angry calls.

While most of us readily embrace the democratic notions of citizen participation and consultation, it is highly unlikely that "typical" citizens would be able to engage in informed and reasoned discourse on this issue. Still, this cell raises important strategic issues for public managers. What opportunities (if any) exist for citizen input on a given entrepreneurial venture? Can such opportunities be created or enhanced? In the absence of citizen input, is the organization prepared to defend its actions in terms of the public interest and in both long-term and short-term perspectives? To what extent are the organizational cultures and professional norms of public agencies compatible with this entrepreneurial paradigm? Are public administrators and elected officials professionally competent to play the entrepreneurial game?

There are many threats in this cell that can be attributed directly to the freedom that public and nonprofit organizations enjoy under these conditions. A major threat in this cell involves increased *exposure to risk.* When discretionary initiatives in this cell fail, the organization cannot hide behind the skirts of a formal regulatory framework by saying, "Well, yes, things did go dreadfully wrong, but we were only following the directives from above!" In effect, this segment of the accountability environment sometimes gives public officials enough rope to hang themselves.

Another type of threat in this cell relates to the *culture* of the organization. Within an unregulated environment, the organization can become inebriated with the seemingly endless possibilities to enhance or diversify revenues, to reallocate resources, to revise programs and procedures, to reach out to new clients, and so on. In the process, the organization can gradually "drift" from its traditional values and comparative advantages. Also, it can lose sight of its ultimate accountability to the public, even drifting from its legal mandate.

A related type of threat concerns the *core competencies* of the organization. Some government professionals are accustomed to working in a free-market competitive environment, but many are not. They are more comfortable (and more competent) in an environment structured by guidelines, rules, regulations, and other explicit parameters of accountability.

However, the relatively unregulated environment in Cell #3 provides the organization with opportunities for greater *flexibility* and *responsiveness* to changing needs. A related opportunity involves the prospect of seeking *input* and meaningful *participation* from clients, donors, and other stakeholders in designing accountability measures that are relevant to their needs and their perceptions of the public interest. This approach holds the prospect of building support and trust for the organization as well as generating creative ideas that would otherwise not be explored. Another type of opportunity involves the prospect of exercising *leadership* by serving as a *benchmark* of excellence for comparable organizations.

Finally, this environment provides organizations with the opportunity to invest in the *professional development* of staff and elected officials. As described above, this segment of the accountability environment requires new skills to fulfill professional obligations and responsibilities. It requires people who are self-starters and proactive in their efforts to serve the public trust. It requires creativity and innovation. It requires vision and leadership. But most of all, it requires competence.

Anticipatory (Advocacy) Accountability (Cell #4)

Finally, the bottom left cell of the matrix portrays situations in which government agencies face the prospect of explicit accountability standards imposed from the outside. The strategic choices are: 1) to position themselves for compliance with these standards; or 2) to actively participate in developing the new standards. For example, a legislative body or regulatory agency may be considering steps to tighten (or loosen) regulatory controls. In this cell, the decisionmakers seek to anticipate the formulation of these standards in order to position the organization for eventual compliance. Members of the organization may even attempt to play an advocacy role in shaping and defining the standards that they believe will eventually be imposed.

The notion of anticipatory (advocacy) accountability requires that public officials try to stay "ahead of the curve" by being prepared for likely changes in their accountability environment. It also places responsibility on public administrators to educate elected officials and other policy actors on emerging public needs and the risks and benefits associated with contemplated political actions. Thus, the notion of anticipatory accountability is consistent with the concept of "administrative advocacy,"[30] wherein public managers are not only responsible for implementing policy initiatives dictated from above, but also for advocating legislative or administrative initiatives to serve the public interest. This responsibility implies additional burdens of accountability. Summarizing Paul Appleby's normative model of administrative morality, Stephen Baily says, "Politics and hierarchy induce the public servant to search imaginatively for a *public-will-to-be*. In this search, the public servant is often a leader in the creation of a new public will, so he is in part accountable to what he in part creates."[31]

Most likely, in the wake of the Orange County problem, there will be renewed calls for a stricter regulatory environment governing investment of public funds. Naturally, state and local agencies will be well advised to closely monitor these developments as they unfold and, if appropriate, attempt to influence the outcome of these legislative debates.

Significantly, the Orange County case also illustrates the pitfalls of accountability from the standpoint of administrative advocacy. In 1979, Robert Citron, acting as head of the state association of county treasurers, was a prime architect and vocal promoter of legal and regulatory changes, which allowed the use of reverse repurchase arrangements with oversight and approval by local elected officials.[32] As such, Citron and other advocates bore responsibility (at the time they advocated the change) to: 1) relate it to a pressing need in the public interest; 2) build in meaningful oversight mechanisms to monitor impacts and to prevent abuse; and 3) educate legislators and, by extension, the general public regarding risks as well as benefits. Having successfully advocated the new legislation, they bore responsibility to follow the spirit as well as the letter of the law, as suggested by the notion of compliance accountability discussed above.

There are several threats that are unique to this segment of the accountability environment. First, there are *political risks* associated with any form of advocacy. The organization's direct involvement in the formal policy-making process can galvanize widespread debate and controversy, potentially focusing unwanted attention and scrutiny on the organization itself. Also, there is the risk of *alienating powerful constituencies* and jeopardizing the organization's traditional base of support. Finally, there are potential *legal threats,* especially for organizations that have strict limits on their political activity. For these organizations, it is wise to seek professional legal counsel before engaging in any political activity.

However, there are opportunities as well as threats in this accountability environment. There is the opportunity to build *networks* and *coalitions* of other stakeholders who share similar interests and objectives. These coalitions can have beneficial effects long after the political issue has been resolved. Also, there is the opportunity to exercise *leadership* and to focus *favorable attention* on the organization if its motives are widely perceived to advance the public interest. As in Cell #2 (negotiation), there are opportunities to *educate* relevant stakeholders and to *preempt* events that might lead to the imposition of inappropriate standards.

DISCUSSION

The matrix presented in Figure 33.1 illustrates four types of accountability that can be used to highlight, retrospectively, certain aspects of the Orange County situation. Also, embedded within each cell of the matrix are management issues and plausible strategies that public administrators might use to their advantage and, ultimately, to the public's advantage, as they apply strategic management approaches while fulfilling their obligations as stewards of the public trust.

Compliance Accountability

Public organizations—even those operating under an entrepreneurial paradigm—must occasionally conduct a compliance audit. At the most elementary level, this audit should attempt to document the organization's legal obligations as follows:

- A complete listing of oversight agencies to which the organization is generally accountable or that have jurisdiction over selected portions of the organization's mandate and mission,
- a compilation and analysis of the legal or regulatory standards of accountability to which the organization is bound by its mandate, charter, authorizing legislation, and contractual arrangements with other organizations;
- assessments of how well the organization has performed in meeting these standards;
- assessments of compliance with the "spirit" and the "letter" of the law; and
- demonstrated efforts to provide full disclosure of the organization's performance in both the "spirit" and the "letter" of the law.

These approaches, of course, address the most narrowly interpreted aspects of accountability—answering to a higher authority regarding performance and compliance with explicit mandates; they are also among the most important questions decisionmakers will ask when conducting an accountability audit.

Negotiated Accountability

Most of the literature on negotiation approaches the topic from an adversarial perspective—that any form of negotiation is, in effect, a zero sum game wherein the interests of one or more players are advanced at the expense of others. But when attempting to enhance accountability in public management, the adversarial approach to negotiation is unacceptable. Instead, the objective of negotiated accountability is to clarify and define the "public interest" and to reach agreement on what mechanisms and strategies best serve those interests. A cursory list of objectives would include:

- To clarify the multiple and, perhaps, conflicting interpretations of the "public interest" and "accountability" to those interests within the context of specific programmatic activities or proposals,
- to clarify which (if any) accountability issues in a specific programmatic domain are "negotiable" and to distinguish them from those that are "nonnegotiable;"
- to clarify the respective objectives and interests of various policy stakeholders and to separate these objectives and interests from specific proposals or programs to achieve them;
- to clarify and agree on reasonable standards of compliance or performance to which an organization or an individual should be held accountable;

- to reach agreement on reasonable measures, behaviors, processes, or outcomes with which to assess organizational or personal accountability;
- to reach agreement on whether there are uncontrollable factors and contingencies that may affect the accountability relationship in order to ensure, in advance, that actors are not held responsible for events beyond their control;
- to reach agreement on what resources and investments are needed to maintain given levels of accountability and the marginal costs and benefits of incrementally greater (or lesser) degrees of control; and ultimately,
- to build trust among the participants in the negotiation process.

Toward these objectives, the philosophy of "principled bargaining," advanced by Fisher and Ury,[33] seems appropriate. Naturally, considering the high financial and political stakes involved, it is very likely that any negotiations emerging from the Orange County case will be more "adversarial" than "principled."

Discretionary (Entrepreneurial) Accountability

Managers at all levels of government are feeling the same types of pressures, to a greater or lesser degree, as those experienced by Robert Citron. Taxpayers are quick to demand higher levels and improved quality of government services, but they are not inclined to provide additional resources. Moreover, the fiscal pressures on state and local governments are likely to increase with the new Republican leadership in Washington. These fiscal and political pressures, combined with the seemingly endless stream of "antibureaucracy" proposals—in the media, the scholarly literature, the popular literature, and in government—ensure that public managers will continue to use discretionary judgement and entrepreneurial approaches.

But there must be a democratic process—rooted in the political authority of elected officials—through which to decide when professional autonomy and discretion are warranted and when they are not, especially when " . . . professional practice is likely to conflict with the desires and interests of the public or its representatives."[34]

What principles should guide public managers to maintain accountability in a relatively unregulated environment?

- Above all, discretionary actions or entrepreneurial ventures must be consistent with the legal mandate and formal authority of the organization;
- such actions or ventures should be mission-focused, guided by an explicit and publicly slated set of goals, operating philosophies, and measures of success;
- all participants must take professional responsibility to obtain full information on the risks as well as the potential benefits;
- discretionary programs, especially entrepreneurial ventures, should have an internal (preferably formal) system of checks and balances to avoid concentrations of power and authority in the hands of one or of several people;
- less formally, participants should foster an organizational culture or "climate" wherein dissenting opinions among participants and stakeholders are not only tolerated but also encouraged and facilitated;
- discretionary initiatives, especially entrepreneurial ventures, should be informed by a formal process of scenario construction wherein the participants examine probabilities of various chains of events (however improbable) and consequences of those events, leading to "best case, worst case, and most likely case" scenarios;

- in the absence of meaningful citizen input, participants in discretionary ventures should engage in a "rehearsal of defenses"[35] by asking, "how and to whom would we defend our actions if called upon to do so?";
- in the absence of citizen input, there should be a mechanism for periodic disclosure of how well the initiative has performed in meeting its objectives;
- discretionary initiatives, especially entrepreneurial ventures, must have a contingency plan that allows the organization to withdraw or otherwise adjust its commitment if the public interest becomes threatened by unforeseen or uncontrollable events; and
- discretionary investments should be overseen by a review body, with prohibitions against single-bet, winner-take-all investment strategies.

Certainly, Robert Citron and his advisors made certain assumptions that interest rates would continue to drop. What we do not know is whether there were mechanisms or processes built into the management systems (or even the organizational culture) that allowed and facilitated the expression of counter-assumptions and alternative strategies for consideration.

The professional obligation to be fully informed and knowledgeable in any entrepreneurial venture was expressed by Charles Cox, finance director of Farmers Branch, Texas, when he said, "If I don't understand it, and I don't know how it works, I'm not going to invest in it."[36] A recent survey of members of the Government Finance Officers Association (GFOA) found that only 4 percent were knowledgeable about derivative securities, 20 percent said that they had limited knowledge, and 76 percent said that they had some or no knowledge.[37]

Anticipatory Accountability

Levine, Peters, and Thompson state that "accountability tends to serve democracy best when administrators anticipate the legitimate preferences of elected officials and adjust their behavior accordingly."[38] Certainly, there is no crystal ball issued to public managers when they take their office. Still, several principles should guide their efforts to remain accountable to the public trust when operating in this type of accountability environment:

- Develop and nurture organizational routines for continuously scanning changes in the accountability environment,
- use multiple methods to stay in touch with citizens, elected officials, and peers in order to continuously monitor emerging needs; and
- work with legislators in a bi-partisan or nonpartisan way to craft legislative proposals that are responsive to the public interest.

These steps will help ensure that public managers stay on top of emerging issues and position themselves and their organizations accordingly.

SUMMARY

This article has examined the cursory facts of the Orange County bankruptcy within a conceptual framework that recognizes four perspectives on accountability. Also, the article presents a set of management strategies to enhance public sector accountability within a shifting environment.

It would be the height of arrogance to suggest that these methods could have prevented an incident like the Orange County debacle. But they do provide a heuristic device that can be used by practitioners and scholars to assess the multiple dimensions of accountability and the management systems appropriate to each.

ACKNOWLEDGMENT

The author gratefully acknowledges the constructive comments of the anonymous reviewers as well as his colleague, Professor Iris Young, at the Graduate School of Public and International Affairs, University of Pittsburgh.

NOTES

1. Leslie Wayne, "The Search for Municipal Cowboys." *New York Times,* December 8,1994, p. c1.

2. Seth Mydans, "Shock and Confusion in Offices and Streets." *New York Times,* December 8, 1994, p. c16.

3. See also, Barbara Romzek and Melvin J. Dubnick, "Accountability in the Public Sector: Lessons from the Challenger Tragedy." *Public Administration Review* 47 (May/June 1987): 227–238.

4. Sallie Hofmeister, "A Strategy's Creator Also Drafted the Law." *New York Times,* December 8, 1994, p. c16.

5. David Osborne and Ted Gaebler. *Reinventing Government* (Reading: Addison-Wesley, 1992).

6. Vice President Al Gore. *Creating a Government That Works Better and Costs Less: Report of the National Performance Review* (Washington, D.C.: U.S. Government Printing Office, 1993).

7. See Larry D. Terry, "Why We Should Abandon the Misconceived Quest to Reconcile Public Entrepreneurship with Democracy." *Public Administration Review* 53 (July/August 1993): 393–395; see also, Ronald C. Moe, "The 'Reinventing Government' Exercise: Misinterpreting the Problem, Misjudging the Consequences." *Public Administration Review* 54 (March/April 1994): 111–122.

8. Charles T. Goodsell. *The Case for Bureaucracy: A Public Administration Polemic,* 3rd ed. (Chatham, N.J.: Chatham House, 1985).

9. Jay M. Shafritz. *The HarperCollins Dictionary of American Government and Politics* (New York: HarperCollins, 1992), 4.

10. Terry L. Cooper. *The Responsible Administrator* (San Francisco. Jossey-Bass Publishers, 1990), 59–62.

11. Samuel Paul, "Strengthening Public Sector Accountability: A Conceptual Framework" (Washington, D C.: World Bank Discussion Paper #136, 1991), 2.

12. Bernard Rosen. *Holding Government Bureaucracies Accountable,* 2d. ed. (New York: Preager, 1989), 4.

13. Carl J. Friedrich, "Public Policy and the Nature of Administrative Responsibility," in *Public Policy, 1940,* ed. Carl J. Friedrich (Cambridge Harvard University Press, 1940).

14. Herman Finer, "Administrative Responsibility in Democratic Government," *Public Administration Review* 1 (Summer 1941). 335–350.

15. Romzek and Dubnick, "Accountability in the Public Sector," 228.

16. For a full discussion of both the positive and negative aspects of professional discretion in setting accountability standards, see John Burke, *Bureaucratic Responsibility* (Baltimore. Johns Hopkins University Press, 1986).

17. Kevin P. Kearns, "The Strategic Management of Accountability in Nonprofit Organizations: An Analytical Framework," *Public Administration Review* 54 (March/April 1994) 185–192.

18. G. Bruce Knecht, "Merrill Lynch's Role as Broker to Fund May Expose It to Liability, Lawyers Say," *Wall Street Journal,* December 8, 1994, p. A9.

19. Tom Herman and Wade Lambert, "Filing Spotlights Murky Corner of Finance," *Wall Street Journal,* December 8, 1994, p. A9.; see also, Harrison Golden, "How Orange County Can Dig Out of Its Hole," *Wall Street Journal,* December 14, 1995, p. A12.

20. John E. Petersen, "It's Better Not to Belly-Up," *Governing* (February 1995): 56.

21. Knecht, "Merrill Lynch's Role," A9.

22. Ibid., A9.

23. I. William Zartman and Maureen R Berman. *The Practical Negotiator* (New Haven Yale University Press, 1982), 47–54.

24. Burke, *Bureaucratic Responsibility,* 25.

25. *Wall Street Journal,* "Public Finance Chiefs Are Often Very Boring: That's The Good News," December 8, 1994, p. C1.

26. Ibid., C1.

27. Carl J Bellone and George Frederick Goerl, "Reconciling Public Entrepreneurship and Democracy." *Public Administration Review* 52 (March/April 1992): 132.

28. Ibid. 133.

29. Terry, "Why We Should Abandon the Misconceived Quest," 394–395.

30. Shafritz, *The Dictionary of American Government,* 10.

31. Stephen K. Baily, "Ethics and the Public Service," in *Public Administration Concepts and Cases,* ed. Richard J. Stillman (Boston: Houghton Mifflin, 1984), 480.

32. Hofmeister, "A Strategy's Creator," C16.

33. Roger Fisher, William Ury, and Bruce Patton. *Getting to Yes: Negotiating Agreement Without Giving In,* 2d ed. (New York. Penguin, 1991).

34. Burke, *Bureaucratic Responsibility,* 148.

35. Terry Cooper. *The Responsible Administrator* (San Francisco: Jossey-Bass, 1990), 23.

36. *Wall Street Journal,* "Public Finance Chiefs," 1.

37. Ibid., 1.

38. Charles H. Levine, B. Guy Peters, and Frank J. Thompson. *Public Administration. Challenges, Choices, Consequences* (Glenview. Scott, Foresman/Little Brown, 1990), 190.

CHAPTER 34

THE LOTTERY AND EDUCATION
Robbing Peter to Pay Paul?

CHARLES J. SPINDLER

State gaming is one budget innovation that appears destined for near universal acceptance among the states. The number of states with lotteries and casino gambling continues to grow: thirty-six states have adopted the lottery since 1963, and there are ten states with casino gambling. The momentum for state gaming is strong. Since the reintroduction of lotteries in New Hampshire in 1964, only one state (North Dakota in both 1986 and 1988) has defeated lottery referenda.[1]

Despite the increasing popularity of the lottery and casinos among the states, state sponsored gaming remains controversial. This article examines one of the more contentious issues of state lotteries: the impact of lotteries on state funding for education. The fungibility of lottery revenues is an important issue with implications for governmental accountability.[2] Nine states earmark net lottery revenues solely for education. Seven states are included in this study (date of implementation shown in parentheses): New York (1967), New Hampshire (1967), Ohio (1974), Michigan (1982), California (1987), Montana (1987), and Florida (1988).[3] Does lottery revenue increase state funding for education in these states or merely substitute for general revenues that used to go for education?

This article begins with a brief discussion of research on the lottery. Next, the impact of the lottery on state expenditures for education is analyzed with a "comparative case-study" approach using time-series data.[4] There are two questions to be investigated. Are lottery revenues fungible? And, what is the net impact of the lottery on education spending? Do lotteries earmarked for education actually increase net education revenues, or does the lottery permit the state to rob Peter to pay Paul? Finally, some conclusions are drawn regarding the fungibility of lottery revenues and the continued importance of politics in budgetary decisions.

BACKGROUND

The public issues underlying state lotteries and other forms of gaming are complex. These issues include the politics of lotteries,[5] demand for lottery products and the predictors of demand,[6] the incidence of state lotteries,[7] state lottery sales,[8] the lottery as a revenue source,[9] earmarking and fungibility,[10] and the relationship between the lottery and crime[11] and the economy.[12]

From *Public Budgeting and Finance*, vol. 15, no. 3 (Autumn 1995), 54–62. Copyright © 1995 by Public Financial Publications, Inc. Reprinted with permission.

The lottery is frequently marketed to the public as a means of supporting worthwhile programs. Several states have pledged all net lottery revenues to education. That the lottery adds only a small percentage to total state revenues is not in question; however small, lottery revenues are new revenues.

Methodological Issues Underlying Lottery Research

To thoroughly consider the fungibility of lotteries, time-series analysis is necessary. While previous lottery studies have analyzed lottery time-series data, analysis tends to focus on trend or ordinary least squares (OLS) regression analysis. A general difficulty in using OLS analysis for time-series data is that it ignores problems often associated with the time series itself such as autocorrelation and heteroscedasticity. Simple trend analysis by itself is not a robust technique.

One of the earlier studies of the impact of the lottery on education expenditures uses simple trend analysis.[13] If lottery revenues are fungible, then the study hypothesized that the percent of total direct general expenditures accounted for by education would increase. The research suggested that, in only one state studied, lottery revenues were fungible. However, only simple trend analysis was used to describe changes in the ratio of education expenditures to general revenues. The study did not examine any statistical relationships. The conclusions, while suggestive, could be more strongly supported by a more robust methodology.

A study by Borg, Mason, and Shapiro also examined the impact of lotteries on funding levels and educational revenues.[14] Multivariate regression was used to analyze cross-sectional data for the periods 1974–75, 1979–80, and 1984–85. The possible problems of this research include multicollinearity between variables and collinearity in the time series. The authors suggest that "Tests on residuals did not show heteroskedasticity."[15] However, the use of single-year time periods or a pooled time series of three nonsequential years would not be expected to show heteroscedasticity. The use of three separate time periods eliminates the opportunity to analyze the underlying time-series model.

A plot of the error term in OLS regression will frequently show nonrandom variation. A Box-Jenkins (ARIMA) model of the time series can determine the correlation pattern for the error series. An ARIMA model can then be developed to control for the autocorrelation of the error terms.

MEASURING THE IMPACT OF THE LOTTERY

The impact of the lottery on education funding will be measured in two ways: first by examining the fungibility of lottery revenues, and second, through the cumulative effect of the lottery on education expenditures. The sum of each year's change in the time series over a five-year period will represent the net cumulative effect of the lottery. Thus, lottery revenues may be fungible and the net cumulative effect on education funding can be either positive, negative, or neutral.

The variables considered in the analysis include own-source general revenues, own-source education expenditures, the ratio of own-source education expenditures to own-source general revenues (the dependent variable), and the year the lottery was adopted. Federal and local intergovernmental revenues and education expenditures are deducted from total state general revenues and education expenditures to create each state, "own-source" variable.

The impact of federal education assistance on state matching programs was examined to determine the type of statistical controls necessary. Federal agencies with significant educational expenditures in 1993 include the Department of Education ($30.7 billion), the Department of Health and Human Services ($11.3 billion), the Department of Agriculture ($8.3 billion), the

Department of Defense ($4.0 billion), the Department of Labor ($3.9 billion), and the Department of Energy ($2.8 billion).[16]

Approximately $19 billion in nonfederal expenditures for education were generated by federal programs in 1993. The largest source of nonfederal matching funds was the Guaranteed Student Loans program ($18 billion). Other programs that generated nonfederal matching funds include Perkins loans ($24.9 million), State Student Incentive Grants ($599.6 million), Supplemental Educational Opportunity Grants ($184.6 million), and Work-study Aid ($190.5 million).[17] The impact of federal funding for education on state education expenditures is not very significant; most federal funding is directed at student loans. Therefore, the statistical control of including federal education expenditures as an independent variable in the analysis was not necessary. The impact of federal and local intergovernmental transfers on state education spending were controlled by subtracting these transfers from state general revenues and state expenditures for education.

Methodology

ARIMA time-series modeling is used to control for autocorrelation in the time series. ARIMA modeling is a variation of the basic regression model that utilizes time-series data.[18] The time-series data for each state is from 1961–1992.[19] To measure the impact of the lottery, the year of lottery implementation is introduced in each time-series model as a step function; for example, STEP89 would indicate that the lottery was in use in 1989 and for each year thereafter, and the dummy variable would be coded 1.[20]

The underlying ARIMA model is first identified by the autocorrelation function (ACF) and partial autocorrelation function (PACF) of the dependent variable. Once the model is identified, it is confirmed using a plot of the errors (residuals). The fit of the model to the data is determined by the residual analysis and the coefficient of the model, t-score, and significance of the t-score. Once the model is identified, then the impact of the lottery on the education spending ratio is analyzed. The model identification and the coefficients of impact are presented for each state in Table 34.1.

A first-order autoregressive process was identified for the dependent variable in each state. The ARIMA model for each of the time series is (1,0,0), except for Montana, which is (1,1,0). For Montana, the time series was differenced once to stabilize the series. The results of the model identification process indicate a good fit between the model and the time-series data as shown by the coefficient of the model, t-ratio, and significance of the t-ratio in Table 34.1. All models are significant at .001, except the model for Montana, which is significant at .003. Once the time-series data is modeled to correct for autocorrelation, the impact of the lottery on education expenditures can be examined.

The partial correlations between the predictor variable (the lottery) and the dependent variable were derived using a step function. As discussed, in years prior to implementation of the lottery, the step was coded 0, and for years following the lottery it was coded 1. The coefficients of the predictor variable are interpreted as measures of the effect of the lottery on the dependent variable. The sum of the coefficients represents the cumulative impact of the lottery on the education spending ratio. Caution should be exercised in interpreting the coefficients of the predictor variable in Table 34.1 beyond a reasonable period, perhaps five years.

The Fungibility of Lottery Revenues

The impact of the lottery on state education funding varies between states and over the years for each state. For all states in the study, lottery revenues appear fungible. In four states, the cumula-

Table 34.1

	New York			New Hampshire			Ohio		
	ARIMA model (1,0,0)			ARIMA model (1,0,0)			ARIMA model (1,0,0)		
	Coefficient of AR1 model 0.676	t-ratio 5.17	Significance of t 0.00001413	Coefficient of AR1 model 0.75	t-ratio 6.38	Significance of t 0.00000048	Coefficient of AR1 model 0.818	t-ratio 8.509	Significance of t 0.000000001
B				B			B		
AR1	0.99713876			0.98742565			0.99313875		
STEP67	−0.01844334			0.01731179					
STEP68	0.00717253			0.04233989					
STEP69	−0.01206178			0.02887165					
STEP70	−0.01945371			0.01075143					
STEP71	0.05484473			−0.11264935					
STEP72	−0.02438907			0.01270709					
STEP73	−0.06146730			0.03481666					
STEP74	0.00241635			0.04673339			0.01752374		
STEP75	−0.00591264			−0.05697894			0.01595540		
STEP76	0.00190022			−0.01886004			0.02289942		
STEP77	−0.02638254			−0.05043367			0.02745825		
STEP78	0.01824915			−0.04550387			−0.02524547		
STEP79	−0.00997224			0.04338933			0.02856291		
STEP80	−0.02103504			−0.00600818			0.02934073		
STEP81	0.01047726			0.03759483			−0.03694838		
STEP82	0.00760059			0.02578388			−0.06084161		
STEP83	−0.00559650			0.00899324			0.04716109		
STEP84	−0.02383219			−0.01991463			−0.04898894		
STEP85	−0.00581063			−0.10870528			0.00592769		
STEP86							0.01809075		
STEP87							0.01063031		
STEP88							−0.01489126		
STEP89							0.00683533		
STEP90							0.03307950		
STEP91							−0.00211940		
STEP92							−0.00086168		

493

(continued)

Table 34.1 *(continued)*

Michigan

ARIMA model (1,0,0)

Coefficient of AR1 model	Significance of t	t-ratio
0.684	5.307	0.00000976

	B
AR1	0.99550147
STEP82	-0.14050913
STEP83	0.09061480
STEP84	-0.04771961
STEP85	0.00856880
STEP86	0.02616234
STEP87	0.01352957
STEP88	0.03805697
STEP89	-0.02483946
STEP90	0.01221235

California

ARIMA model (1,0,0)

Coefficient of AR1 model	Significance of t	t-ratio
0.555	3.723	0.0008114

	B
AR1	0.99493029
STEP87	-0.00726384
STEP88	0.03289812
STEP89	-0.00739060
STEP90	-0.02613564
STEP91	-0.01379030
STEP92	0.00502766

Montana

ARIMA model (1,0,0)

Coefficient of AR1 model	Significance of t	t-ratio
-0.514	-3.213	0.00320393

	B
AR1	-0.42598480
STEP87	0.03007645
STEP88	-0.06709366
STEP89	0.07492797
STEP90	-0.06069347
STEP91	0.14021687
STEP92	-0.06240330

Florida

ARIMA model (1,0,0)

Coefficient of AR1 model	t-ratio	Significance of t
0.7278	5.89	0.00000185

	B
AR1	0.99771177
STEP88	-0.00886544
STEP89	-0.00888143
STEP90	0.00555846
STEP91	0.05028323
STEP92	-0.03914352

tive effect of the lottery is negative; the education spending ratio tends to decline once a lottery is introduced.

New York. Lottery revenues are fungible in New York, substituting general revenue expenditures for education. In the first year of the lottery (1967), the education spending ratio declined 1.8 percent. There is a small increase in 1968, followed by two years of decline. The years of decrease are generally larger than the years of increase. This pattern is repeated throughout the time series. However, the net cumulative impact of the lottery on the education spending ratio is positive (1.2 percent) for the first five years.

New Hampshire. Lottery revenues were not fungible during the early years following lottery implementation. However, the decline of education expenditures of approximately 11 percent in 1971 counteracts previous gains. This pattern of several annual increases is followed by an abrupt decrease throughout the time series. The net cumulative impact of the lottery on the education spending ratio is negative (−1.3 percent) for the first five years.

Ohio. The lottery is associated with four years of increased education expenditures, followed by a decrease in 1978 of 2.5 percent. The magnitude of the decrease is small in comparison to that of New Hampshire. The results of the analysis indicate that lottery revenues are not very fungible. The net cumulative impact of the lottery on the education spending ratio is positive (5.8 percent) for the first five years.

Michigan. Lottery revenues appear highly fungible in the first year; introduction of the lottery is associated with a 14 percent decline in the education spending ratio. There is a small increase in the second year followed by a small decrease in the third year. Over a five-year period, the gains do not offset the loss incurred the first year. The net cumulative impact of the lottery on the education spending ratio is negative (−6.28 percent) for the first five years.

California. The fungibility of lottery revenues is relatively slight in California. Interpretation of the coefficients is difficult because changes in the education spending ratio are small, and the time series for the lottery is short. Other factors may influence the dependent variable that are not captured in the model. With these caveats taken into consideration, the analysis suggests that the lottery has a slight negative effect on education expenditures. The net cumulative impact of the lottery on the education spending ratio is negative (−2.16 percent) for the first five years.

Montana. Lottery revenues appear highly fungible; an increase in education expenditures the first year alternates with a decrease the following year. This pattern is repeated in the time series. The net cumulative impact of the lottery on the education spending ratio is positive (11.7 percent) for the first five years.

Florida. Two years of decreases are followed by two years of increases. Lottery revenue is fungible, but the overall impact of the lottery on the education spending ratio appears neutral or slightly negative. The net cumulative impact of the lottery on the education spending ratio is slightly negative (−0.1 percent) for the first five years.

CONCLUSIONS

The impact of the lottery on state education expenditures varies between the states and over the years following adoption. In some states, the lottery produces a positive cumulative effect on education expenditures, while in other states the effect is negative.

In each of the seven states studied, lottery revenues were earmarked, but despite the earmarking, lottery revenues were fungible. For some states, the lottery did rob Peter to pay Paul.

The politics of the budgetary process may help explain revenue fungibility. Education policy has significant financial and political constraints.[21] Education expenditures constitute a large share of state spending, attracting significant political attention. Finally, education policy, and the lottery in particular, are policies which are highly visible to the public.

Despite the earmarking of net lottery revenues, there is no guarantee that state legislatures will not substitute lottery revenues for general education funding. It will be difficult to remedy this lack of accountability for several reasons. First, no state has committed to maintaining a constant ratio of education expenditures to general revenues following adoption of the lottery. Second, other state agencies will fight for access to new revenues, despite earmarking. Finally, the public is not given complete information regarding education spending. The lottery has wide public acceptance, and the political costs associated with the lottery are generally low, especially when revenues are dedicated to a popular program. The lottery remains an appealing revenue source to the states because it represents a new source of income.

While lottery revenues were determined to be fungible, this fungibility did not produce consistent results. Two patterns emerge from the analysis which suggest politics of the budgetary process at work. The first pattern is a steady increase in education revenues for the first few years of the lottery, followed by an abrupt decline. In New Hampshire and Ohio, four positive years are followed by one negative year. Budgetary politics may eventually force an equalization in revenues between state departments.

The second pattern is a constant incremental adjustment in the education budget each year. In New York, Michigan, California, Montana, and Florida there is constant fluctuation in education expenditures from year to year following adoption of the lottery.

The fungibility of lottery revenues and the incremental adjustments of state education expenditures are by-products of the politics of budgeting. The lottery can be sold as a means to increase funding for education, while lottery revenues substitute for general fund expenditures. In states where earmarked lottery revenues are used to offset state expenditures for education, the lottery is robbing Peter to pay Paul.

NOTES

1. John L Mikesell, "A Note on the Changing Incidence of State Lottery Finance," *Social Science Quarterly* 70 (June 1989) 513.
2. See John L. Mikesell and C. Kurt Zorn, "State Lotteries as Fiscal Savior or Fiscal Fraud: A Look at the Evidence." *Public Administration Review* 46 (July/Aug 1986) 311–320, for a discussion on fungibility.
3. Kentucky (1989) and Georgia (1993) also earmark net revenues for education, but the time-series data appear insufficient for analysis.
4. Susan A. MacManus, "The Missing Element, An Examination of Analytic Time Frames." *Urban Affairs Quarterly* 24 (September 1988): 39–45.
5. Charles J. Clotfelter and Philip J. Cook, *Selling Hope. State Lotteries in America.* (Cambridge, Mass.: Harvard University Press, 1989) 141–159.
6. Ibid., Charles J. Clotfelter and Philip J Cook, "On the Economics of State Lotteries," *The Journal of Economic Perspectives* 4 (Fall 1990): 105–119, John L. Mikesell, "A Note on the Changing Incidence of State Lottery Finance," *Social Science Quarterly* 70/2 (June 1989). 513–521.
7. Mary O. Borg and Paul M. Mason, "The Budgeting Incidence of a Lottery to Support Education," *National Tax Journal* 41 (March 1988). 75–86; Idem, "Earmarked Lottery Revenues: Positive Windfalls or Concealed Redistribution Mechanisms?" *Journal of Education Finance* 52 (April 1989): 75–85, Roger E. Brinner and Charles T Clotfelter, "An Economic Appraisal of State Lotteries," *National Tax Journal* 28 (1975). 395–404; Charles T. Clotfelter, "On the Regressivity of State-Operated 'Numbers' Games," *National Tax Journal* 28 (Dec. 1979). 543–48; Charles J. Clotfelter and Philip J. Cook, "Implicit Taxation in Lottery Finance," *National Tax Journal* 32 (Dec. 1987) 533–546; Idem, *Selling Hope: State Lotteries in America.* (Cambridge, Mass: Harvard University Press, 1989), Jerome F. Heavey, "The Incidence of State Lottery Taxes," *Public Finance Quarterly* 6 (Oct 1978). 415–26;

Michael H. Spiro, "On the Tax Incidence of the Pennsylvania Lottery" *National Tax Journal* 27 (March 1974) 57–62. For summaries of previous studies of the incidence of state lotteries, see Clotfelter and Cook, *Selling Hope. State Lotteries in America;* and John L. Mikesell, "A Note on the Changing Incidence of State Lottery Finance," 513–521.

8. Larry DeBoer, "Lottery Taxes May be Too High," *Journal of Policy Analysis and Management* 5 (Spring 1986) 594–596; Mikesell "A Note on the Changing Incidence of State Lottery Finance," Idem, "The Effect of Maturity and Competition on State Lottery Markets," *Journal of Policy Analysis and Management* 6 (Winter 1987) 251–253, John David Vasche, "Are Taxes on Lotteries Too High" *Journal of Policy Analysis and Management* 4 (Winter 1989) 269–271.

9. John L Mikesell and C. Kurt Zorn, "State Lotteries as Fiscal Savior or Fiscal Fraud: A Look at the Evidence" *Public Administration Review* 46 (July/Aug 1986): 311–320.

10. Borg and Mason, "Earmarked Lottery Revenues: Positive Windfalls or Concealed Redistribution Mechanisms?," Susan A. MacManus and Charles J. Spindler, "Florida's Lottery: How Long Education's Sacred Cow?" *Florida Policy Review* 4 (Winter 1989): 1–4, Mikesell and Zorn, "State Lotteries as Fiscal Savior or Fiscal Fraud: A Look at the Evidence."

11. John Mikesell and Maureen A. Pirog-Good, "State Lotteries and Crime The Regressive Revenue Producer is Linked with a Crime Rate Higher by 3 Percent," *American Journal of Economics and Sociology* 49 (January 1990) 7–19.

12. Mary O. Borg, Paul M. Mason, and Stephen L. Shapiro, *The Economic Consequences of State Lotteries* (New York: Praeger, 1991), Charles J. Clotfelter and Philip J. Cook, "On the Economics of State Lotteries," *The Journal of Economic Perspectives* 4 (Fall 1990) 105–119; John L. Mikesell, "State Lottery Sales and Economic Activity," *National Tax Journal* 47 (March 1994): 165–171. Mikesell and Pirog-Good, "State Lotteries and Crime: The Regressive Revenue Producer is Linked with a Crime Rate Higher by 3 Percent."

13. Mikesell and Zorn, "State Lotteries as Fiscal Savior or Fiscal Fraud: A Look at the Evidence."

14. Mary O. Borg, Paul M Mason, and Stephen L. Shapiro *The Economic Consequences of State Lotteries.* (New York: Praeger, 1991).

15. Ibid., p. 46.

16. U.S. Department of Education. *Digest of Education Statistics 1993.* U.S. Department of Education, Office of Educational Research and Improvement, National Center for Education Statistics (Washington, D.C.: U.S. Government Printing Office, 1993). 351.

17. Ibid., p. 363.

18. Charles W. Ostrom, Jr. *Time Series Analysis Regression Techniques,* 2d ed. Sage University Paper series on Quantitative Applications in the Social Sciences, series no. 07–009. (Newberry Park, CA. Sage, 1990).

19. U.S. Bureau of the Census. *State Government Finances.* Years vary; Series GF-61–3 through GF-92–3. (Washington, D.C.: U.S. Government Printing Office, 1961 through 1992).

20. David McDowall, Richard McCleary, Errol E. Meidinger, and Richard A. Hay, Jr. *Interrupted Time Series Analysis,* Sage University Paper series on Quantitative Applications in the Social Sciences, series no. 07–021 (Beverly Hills, CA: Sage, 1980).

21. For a discussion of the allocational policy arena including human resource policies and education, see Charles J. Spindler and John P. Forrester, "Economic Development Policy. Explaining Policy Preferences Among Competing Models," *Urban Affairs Quarterly* 29 (September 1993): 28–53.

CHAPTER 35

THE MONSTER THAT ATE THE UNITED STATES SENATE

BILL DAUSTER

Let's start with three stories from the real world:

STORY ONE[1]

Four-year-old Sarah Jean lives with her aunt Sherry in Phoenix. Because of her physical and cognitive problems, Sarah weighs 29 pounds, has trouble speaking, and is not toilet trained. Aunt Sherry earns $800 a month working part time as a private health aide, and uses federal aid under the Supplemental Security Income program, or SSI, to replace her lost income and buy diapers and food supplements to get Sarah to gain weight. Implementing the 1996 welfare law, the Social Security Administration terminated Sarah's SSI benefits and those of more than 135,000 low-income, disabled children because only children whose problems cause "marked and severe functional limitations" are now eligible for SSI. The new Social Security Commissioner Ken Apfel has taken steps to review and reverse large numbers of these terminations, but the welfare law continues to disrupt the lives of tens of thousands of families.

STORY TWO[2]

Seventy-five-year-old Henry Block works in Kansas City as the chairman of the board of H&R Block, the tax preparation company. In large part because of the 1997 tax law, H&R Block's stock has soared more than 50 percent this last year. Because of the 1997 law, the tax code has 290 new sections. Block plans to open 250 new offices for the coming tax season. Henry says: "Every time the government changes things, business does increase." He adds: "Every year a few more people throw up their hands and say, 'I can't prepare my own return any more.'"

STORY THREE[3]

Rose Naff works in Tallahassee as Director of Florida's Healthy Kids Corporation, a state-subsidized health insurance program for families with incomes just above those that qualify for Medicaid.[4]

Because of the 1997 balanced budget law, Rose is thinking about how Florida will spend its share of a $24 billion national fund to finance child health coverage. Florida has the third highest number of uninsured children, with a quarter of children eligible for Medicaid not enrolled. Many poorer South Floridians do not speak English well enough to understand what is available or fill out the forms. Rose is suggesting a toll-free number for people to call to learn how to enroll their kids.

I tell these three stories to bring to life a thing that is happening in the United States Congress, a thing that is illustrated by the three laws that affect Sarah, Henry, and Rose. I am not talking about the merits of the three laws—we can debate the good and bad things about each of them. The thing about which I want to talk to you today is the lawmaking *process* that led to these three laws. For, like them or loathe them, the welfare law, the tax law, and the balanced budget law were the only three laws enacted that had more than $5 billion in consequences in any fiscal year since the change in control of the Congress. Like them or loathe them, all three laws resulted from the budget reconciliation process. It is my argument to you today that the budget reconciliation process is becoming more and more central to the lawmaking process. It is my argument that the budget reconciliation process is the *monster* that ate the United States Senate.

Let us start at the beginning. As it says in the Good Book, "In the beginning . . . the [Senate] was without form, and void."[5] Perhaps the Living version captures the meaning better when it says: "[The Senate] was at first a shapeless, chaotic mass."[6]

That is to say that in its formative years, from 1806, when it repealed the rule allowing senators to move the previous question, through 1917, when it adopted rule XXII, the cloture rule, the Senate was a place where, in Woodrow Wilson's words in connection with the Armed Ship bill, "a little group of willful men, representing no opinion but their own, [could] render the great Government of the United States helpless and contemptible."[7] Even after the Senate adopted rule XXII, it still required a supermajority vote to bring debate to a close: two-thirds[8] until 1975 and 60 senators since then—except for changes to the Standing Rules of the Senate, where two-thirds are still required.[9]

The congressional budget process has changed all that. One might say that it has brought order out of the chaos. But one might also debate whether chaos might have been a better thing. My argument to you today is that the congressional budget process, like it or loathe it, has brought about the biggest change in legislative process since the adoption of the cloture rule.

The change came about in three steps. In step one, Congress enacted the Congressional Budget Act of 1974. In it, Congress created a fast-track vehicle, the concurrent resolution on the budget, with which to set fiscal policy. The budget resolution provides rules for *Congress;* the president does not sign the resolution. And the resolution paints with a broad brush; by convention it does not deal with amounts smaller than $100 million.

But the resolution gives every spending committee its allocation of spending for the year and gives Congress as a whole overall caps on spending and a floor on revenues.[10] These levels provide the basis for procedural objections, or "points of order," that enforce the Government's fiscal policy later in the year.

The change was that the Senate considers the budget resolution under rules that restrict debate and amendment. As a result, senators cannot wage a filibuster against it. A simple majority of senators voting will determine what amendments the Senate will adopt, and a simple majority can pass the resolution. The Congressional Budget Act thus expedited Congress's making of fiscal policy and enhanced the power of the majority party.

One can find discussions of the early years of the budget resolution in books by the University of Maryland's Allen Schick[11] and Emory's Dennis Ippolito.[12]

Participants in the federal budget process initially underestimated the power of the budget resolution. They failed completely, however, to foresee the power of a second fast-track procedure called "reconciliation." The Congressional Budget Act originally provided for two budget resolutions: the first would advise, and the second, passed closer to the start of the fiscal year, would bind. The Act provided that the second budget resolution could instruct committees of Congress to reconcile laws passed within their jurisdiction to the new budget priorities of the second budget resolution.

The reconciliation process did not turn out quite as modest as the drafters of the Congressional Budget Act had intended. Rather, it became a fast-track, coordinated deficit-reduction vehicle of immense power to direct committees to change spending or taxes. In years when the budget resolution contains reconciliation instructions, the authorizing committees instructed must report changes in law within their jurisdictions to change spending or taxes by at least the overall amount that the resolution instructed. The authorizing committees report their recommendations to the Budget Committee, which packages them together without substantive change and brings them to the floor as a reconciliation bill. As with the budget resolution, the Senate considers the reconciliation bill under fast-track procedures unusual for that body.

The reconciliation process thus combines legislative work products from disparate committees into one vehicle, a process also unusual in the Senate. Senators and representatives can then vote for the overall bill and the idea of deficit reduction, while avowing disagreement with particular parts of the larger compromise.

The major innovation in reconciliation came in 1981 under Budget Committee Chair Pete V. Domenici. In an effort to expedite President Reagan's first budget, under Office of Management and Budget Director David Stockman, the budget resolution included instructions for years beyond the first fiscal year covered by the resolution, extending the reach of the reconciliation vehicle to more permanent changes in law.

Since Congress used the process so powerfully in 1981 to implement President Reagan's economic program, reconciliation has become a regular feature of most budget resolutions. Since 1981, Congress has accomplished most significant deficit reduction through the reconciliation process. (Early scholarly review of this period of reconciliation can be found in Miller and Range's piece in the *Harvard Journal on Legislation*[13] and another book by Allen Schick.[14])

The power of reconciliation thus attracted much matter not strictly related to the budget-related purposes of the process. In response to such "extraneous" matter, in 1985 the Senate adopted the Byrd Rule, named after its sponsor, Democratic Leader Robert C. Byrd. At the pain of requiring a sixty-vote waiver, the Byrd Rule prohibited any of a number of provisions that fall into the Rule's complex provisions, including items that do not affect the deficit, items not within the jurisdiction of the reporting committee, and items whose budgetary components are "merely incidental" to their non-budgetary components. The Byrd Rule highlights the tension inherent in the reconciliation process between the desire to expedite deficit reduction widely shared among jurisdictions and the dangers of reconciliation's tight restrictions on debate and amendment.

Step three of the expansion of reconciliation came two years ago, as the new Republican Congress sought to move three reconciliation bills—on welfare, Medicare, and tax cuts. In a marked departure from past practice, the Republican budget devoted one of the three reconciliation bills—the one to cut taxes—solely to *worsening* the deficit.

On May 21, 1996, Democratic Leader Tom Daschle formally challenged the procedure. The parliamentarian gave it his blessing. In a series of exchanges with the presiding officer, Leader Daschle demonstrated that the new procedure has few limits. After Leader Daschle appealed the ruling, the Senate sustained the procedure on a straight party-line vote. From now on, the Senate will conduct much of its business at its hallmark deliberative pace only if the majority wants it that way.

After last year's precedent, the majority party can create as many reconciliation bills as it wants, and the majority can use them to increase spending or cut taxes, worsening the deficit. From now on, the majority can use the reconciliation process to move its entire legislative agenda through the Senate with simple majority votes and few distractions. The old Senate is dead.

Some may say, "Good riddance." After all, as a Democratic Member of Congress once said, "In the Senate, you can't go to the bathroom without sixty votes." If a simple majority can now pass important legislation in the Senate, perhaps a lot more will get done.

But the character of the Senate has been unmistakably altered. The deliberative rights of senators serve as a vital bulwark of individual rights. As Senator Kennedy warned in another debate that year: "This . . . is a vote about whether this body is going to be governed by a neutral set of rules that protect the rights of all members, and by extension, the rights of all Americans. If the rules of the Senate can be twisted and broken and overridden to achieve a momentary legislative goal we will have diminished the institution itself."

The budget reconciliation process is thus transforming the Senate into a much more majoritarian institution. What does this mean for the law? A number of things. For example, it creates an opportunity to revisit the longstanding debate over simple majority voting.

The threads of this debate on majority voting may lead on in a variety of different directions. Majority rule is a principle fundamental to the distinction of democracy. For example, one finds John Locke in his *Second Treatise* imagining that when people have entered into a public or civil society, they submit to whatever the legislature may decide by majority vote. And the weaknesses of the Articles of Confederation, with its supermajority voting among states, were foremost among the complaints of the founders at the Constitutional convention.

But that same generation, and many of the Founders, also expressed much of the classical liberal distrust of the tyranny of the majority. Madison, for example, said that "[i]n Republics, the great danger is, that the majority may not sufficiently respect the rights of the minority."[15] And I could produce similar quotes from Madison,[16] Thomas Jefferson,[17] John Adams,[18] and Edmund Jennings Randolph.[19] And the need for supermajorities is seen in the Constitution in the veto power, the ratification of treaties, the amendment process, and a number of other places. Similarly, bicameralism supported the classical liberal antipathy to legislation.

As the needs of society have grown, so also have grown calls for a more effective, more responsible government. But, as well, the classical liberal tradition is reflected in public choice theory. Applying game theory, Kenneth Arrow demonstrated that where choices are not bipolar, where, for example, three separate pluralities favor three distinct results, majority voting may yield a variety of possible results.[20] And depending on how choices are structured, majorities may cycle from one result to another.

In *The Calculus of Consent,* Buchanan and Tullock add a transactional analysis to this discussion.[21] What if legislators trade a vote for one thing for another, what if they engage in what public choice calls "strategic" voting, what legislators commonly call "logrolling"? Buchanan and Tullock argue that in a budgetary context, logrolling can very easily lead to a majority voting for more spending than any legislators in the majority actually want. They thus argue that the constitution needs rules that require supermajorities, what they call "reinforced majorities," as a break on the logical excesses of simple majority voting. Plainly, the new budget reconciliation process is a step in the opposite direction.

A number of institutional critics have faulted public choice analysis from a variety of perspectives. For example, Farber and Frickey argue in their book, *Law and Public Choice,* that political parties can help limit cycling.[22] Parties help to focus legislative choices into bipolar choices. Although party affiliation may not be what it used to be, it still controls many situations.

Then again, Moe and Wilson argue that public choice theory often gives short shrift to the role of the president.[23] The president has a focused backing and a single voice, and may thus dominate Congress. In such an environment, one might be looking for ways to enhance the power of the legislature, not diminish it. Presidents are capable of much undemocratic behavior. As J. William Fullbright once said, "The greatest single virtue of a strong legislature is not what it can do but what it can prevent."

These days, I must admit that I often find myself thinking with Mark Twain that "whenever you find yourself on the side of the majority, it's time for reform."

But one may be able to separate disagreement with what the government is doing from a belief that the government ought to be able to do something. Perhaps there is value in showing the voters what they are getting in a clear, understandable way. Or as H.L. Mencken said, "Democracy is the theory that the . . . people know what they want, and deserve to get it good and hard."[24]

NOTES

This article was originally delivered before the faculty of the Washington College of Law at American University, Washington, D.C., January 13, 1998.

1. Barbara Vobejda, "As Children Are Cut From Disability Rolls, New System Is Challenged," *Washington Post,* Dec. 17, 1997, at A14.

2. Tom Herman, "Growth Industry," *Wall Street Journal,* Dec. 31, 1997, at Al; Amity Shales, "The Market Value of the Tax Code," *Wall Street Journal,* Dec. 31, 1997, at A11.

3. "Get Children Signed Up," *Palm Beach Post,* Jan. 5, 1998, at 16A.

4. *<http://www.healthykids.org/>*

5. Genesis 1:1–2 (King James Version) *<http://ccel.wheaton.edu/bible/kjv/Genesis/1.html>*.

6. Ibid, (Living Bible).

7. Statement of Mar. 4, 1917, *<http://www.elibrary.compuserve.com/qotd/10087/fetch/philk_01.htm>*.

8. See S. Res. 5, 63 *CONG. REC.* 19–45 (Mar. 8, 1917).

9. See S. Res. 4,131 *CONG. REC.* 21, 433–34 (June 25, 1975).

10. Of the 16 standing Senate committees (see Standing Rules of the Senate Rule XXV(1)), 15 have spending jurisdiction, and only the Committee on the Budget itself does not. In addition to the standing committees, the Committee on Indian Affairs has spending jurisdiction.

11. Allen Schick, *Congress and Money* (1980).

12. Dennis S. Ippolito, *Congressional Spending* (1981).

13. James A. Miller & James D. Range, "Reconciling an Irreconcilable Budget: The New Politics of the Budget Process," 20 *Harvard Journal on Legislation,* 4 (1983).

14. Allen Schick, *Reconciliation and the Congressional Budget Process* (1981).

15. James Madison, speech to the Virginia constitutional convention, Richmond, Virginia, Dec. 2, 1829.

16. "There is no maxim, in my opinion, which is more liable to be misapplied, and which, therefore, more needs elucidation, than the current one, that the interest of the majority is the political standard of right and wrong." James Madison, letter to James Monroe, Oct. 5, 1786, "On a candid examination of history, we shall find the turbulence, violence, and abuse of power, by the majority, trampling on the rights of the minority, have produced factions and commotions which, in republics, have, more frequently than any other cause, produced despotism." James Madison, speech to the Virginia Convention on the adoption of the U.S. Constitution, June 5, 1788.

17. "Though the will of the majority is in all cases to prevail, that will, to be rightful, must be reasonable. . . . The Minority possess their equal rights, which equal laws must protect, and to violate which would be oppression." Thomas Jefferson, first inaugural address, Mar. 4, 1801.

18. "That the desires of the majority of the people are often for injustice and inhumanity against the minority, is demonstrated by every page of the history of the whole world." John Adams. *A Defence of the Constitution of the Government of the United States,* 1787–88.

19. "Our chief danger arises from the democratic parts of our constitutions." Edmund Jennings Randolph, attributed remark in debate at Constitutional Convention, May 29, 1787.

20. Kenneth Arrow, *Social Choice and Individual Values* (2d ed. 1963).

21. James M. Buchanan & Gordon Tullock, *The Calculus of Consent* (1962).

22. Daniel A. Farber &. Philip P. Frickey, *Law and Public Choice* 56 (1991).

23. Terry Moe & Scott Wilson, "Presidents and the Politics of Structure," 57 *Law & Contemp.* Probs. 1 (Spring 1994).

24. H.L. Mencken, "Sententiae" *A Book of Burlesques,* 1920.

INDEX

Boldface page references indicate figures and tables.

ABOUT THE EDITOR

Irene S. Rubin received her PhD in Sociology from the University of Chicago in 1977. She taught at the University of Maryland College Park from 1979 to 1981, and at Northern Illinois University in DeKalb, Illinois, from 1981 to 2004, when she retired from teaching. She has spent her professional career studying the fiscal problems of federal, state, and local governments. Among her books are *Running in the Red: The Political Dynamics of Urban Fiscal Stress; Class Tax and Power: Municipal Budgeting in the United States; Balancing the Federal Budget: Eating the Seed Corn or Trimming the Herds;* and *The Politics of Public Budgeting.*